Readings in International Relations

Elizabeth Bloodgood

Julian Schofield

Axel Hülsemeyer

Concordia University

Kendall Hunt
publishing company

Cover image © Shuttertstock

Kendall Hunt
p u b l i s h i n g   c o m p a n y

www.kendallhunt.com
Send all inquiries to:
4050 Westmark Drive
Dubuque, IA 52004-1840

Printed in the United States of America
10   9   8   7   6   5   4   3

Contents

iv   Contents

Contents

INTRODUCTION

Our goal with this reader is to give students an introduction to International Relations theory sufficient to provide a perspective on the approaches and concepts necessary to continue their study at the intermediate level. The included readings highlight major theoretical issues within the discipline. Topics are subdivided into five parts: (1) theoretical approaches to International Relations; (2) international institutions and cooperation; (3) use of force and statecraft; (4) international political economy, and (5) non-state actors in international relations. Each section begins with an introduction that provides a preliminary guide to understanding the key concepts necessary for the interpretation of individual readings.

We chose this particular collection of readings with some very important teaching principles in mind. Regardless of the ultimate academic objectives of our students, our goal is to prepare them to be professionals by mastering key concepts, which are often complicated to apply. We have consequently chosen readings that examine the keystone concepts a scholar in International Relations would most frequently encounter. Most of the included readings are written by influential scholars and will not initially be easily understood by the political science initiate. It is our experience that there is no substitute for reading directly from the original works. Exposure to scholarly writing is the most effective way of learning the terminology and scientific style of writing typical of political science. The readings are demanding, and they will have to be read carefully and perhaps more than once. This does not mean that political science writing is itself is incomprehensible. The best political science writing is simple and direct. Yet, the complexity of the issues addressed by political science often requires sophisticated approaches and concepts that may not be either intuitive or fully grasped on the first reading.

THE ORIGINS OF INTERNATIONAL RELATIONS

What we mean by the study of International Relations is the understanding, explanation, and testing of theories of large-scale political behavior in the world. Why do wars
happen? When do depressions occur? What happens to global trade when the influence
of great powers goes into decline? The study of international relations has historically
been the preserve of professional court bureaucrats since antiquity. The Sumerians
(3200-1950 BCE), the Mohenjo-Daro and Harrappa Culture (2500-1800 BCE), and
the countries of the Warring States Period in China (403-221 BCE) all possessed
some degree of professional diplomats and full-time advisors in international treaty-
making, trade, and war. Tribes, monarchies, empires, and states since then have all
had to execute the functions of war, alliance-making, and trade, with varying degrees
of success and self-reflection. Given the narrowness of the literate elites of these premodern states, the importance of concealment in negotiations, and the often fatal consequences of the failure of diplomacy, there was little room for academic scholarship
to reflect on these activities. One notable exception is the Arthasastra (Manual of
Politics) by Kautilya, a chief minister of Chandragupta, conqueror of much of India
(321-297 BCE). Although not a scholarly treatise, but rather a how-to manual for
an emerging prince, it elaborates on an embryonic form of balance of power theory
whose elements have found their way into modern thought.[1]

Publicly open debate, stimulated by far-reaching commerce and constant local
and regional warfare, prompted Greek writers to reflect on the nature of large-scale
events, particularly major conflicts. Herodotus (484-425 BCE), author of the *Histories*,
sought to explain the Greco-Persian Wars (500-479 BCE) by focusing on the ethical
behavior of leaders to determine whether outcomes were favorable or disastrous for
themselves and their followers.[2] The Herodotan practice of predicting outcomes based
on whether the leaders were seemingly decadent or behaving in accordance with the
prevailing social norms is an approach that persists to this day. Medieval papal encyc-
licals proscribed some uses of violence through a Christian code of *jus bellum* (just
war) in Europe. Islamic International Relations cannot be understood without reference to Islamic theology, which prescribes action. The Western tradition of political
science has its origins in the Greek historian Thucydides (460-396 BCE), author of
the *Peloponnesian War*, which was a history and study of the fighting between democratic Athens and despotic Sparta (431-404 BCE). Thucydides explained events in the
world as the result of the natural outcomes of the actions of people and states, not the
result of divine intervention or deviation from ethical norms. It is this people-centered

---

[1]L.N. Rangarajan (trans), *Kautilya, The Arthasastra* (New York: Penguin, 1992).
[2]Herodotus, *The History of the Persian Wars* (Chicago: Henry Regnery, 1949).

understanding of how politics happens that set him apart from his predecessors and established Thucydides as the first scholar in our study of International Relations. This does not mean scholars of political science must be atheists, but that in the study of International Relations, we look for political causes elsewhere.

The discipline of International Relations that we study is primarily a Western practice, with a Renaissance European background informed by Byzantine and Arabic translations of Greek and Roman texts. Through the Arabs the tradition was informed further by Kautilya, and the Roman Flavius Vegetius Renatus, author of *De Re Militari*, who coined the infamous saying, "Si Vis Pacem Para Bellum" (If you want peace, prepare for war).[3] Writing within this backdrop, Niccolo Machiavelli (1469-1527), author of *The Prince* (1513), provided pragmatic (and controversial) advice on the rule by leaders of city states in Northern Italy of the early sixteenth century. The Western tradition, however, is currently being exposed to an array of alternate approaches and explanations of international behavior made possible by globalization. Students must therefore be conscious of the primordial Western bias in international relations theory.

Contemporary political science emerged in the nineteenth century where advances in the physical sciences promoted a mechanistic understanding of nature known as *behaviorism*. There followed a gradual borrowing of the scientific method from chemistry and engineering into the social sciences, especially in the fields of sociology and economics. The early political science research was being conducted in the areas of public administration and domestic institutions, both of which were dominated by legalistic approaches. The First World War stimulated the development of International Relations as a discipline by raising questions about the desirability and inevitability of war. Seventeen million deaths, the collapse of the Austrian, German, Ottoman, and Russian empires, and the near bankruptcy of England and France were important shocks. However, the defining step was the massification of foreign policy caused by the spread of the universal male franchise, which made politics and diplomacy accessible to democratic population and to scholars.[4]

Realism and liberalism, the two primordial theoretical approaches (elaborated in Part I), have their origins in the inter-war period leading up to the Second World War. Realism was an abstracted articulation of the activity of power politics or *realpolitik* as understood by practioners of diplomacy. Liberalism was an approach that drew on the medieval legalistic tradition and optimistic scientific approach to improving human nature, and sought to address the problem of violence in the wake of the

[3]Steven Lattimore (trans), *Thucydides, The Peloponnesian War* (Indianapolis: Hackett, 1998).
[4]Stanley Hoffman, "An American Social Science: International Relations," *Daedalus* 106 (Summer 1977), 41-59.

problem of the First World War. This approach tended to be idealistic in the sense that it was prescriptive (how the world *ought to* be) rather than descriptive (how the world actually *is*). Other traditions were legalistic. They sought to transpose the domestic practice of law onto the international stage by simply making war illegal, or by organizing international institutions to help states avoid wars by regulating away weapons and certain policies.   The defeat of Germany, Japan, and Italy in the Second World War had transformed the isolationist United States into a global power and leader of the Western alliance. Lacking substantial experience as a colonial power with global reach, the U.S. State Department and military were not well informed about politics in different regions of the world. The U.S. use of military power to defeat the Axis powers in the Second World War, and its subsequent role as a major protagonist in the Cold War, underlined the importance of International Relations and stimulated an aggressive investment in producing American political scientists who could populate various key institutions of government. Since the 1950s, the study of International Relations has shifted from area studies focused on specific states and institutions to more scientific, incorporating formal and quantitative methods of research.

INTERNATIONAL RELATIONS AS A SCIENCE

International Relations, as a sub-discipline of political science, follows scientific principles in its execution. Governments provide funds for political science teaching and research in order to produce skilled individuals able to examine challenges that policymakers are concerned about in world politics. These problems include war, the rise and fall of great powers, depressions, the durability of international institutions, terrorism, foreign aid, environmental cooperation, regional political integration, neocolonialism and inequality, arms control, responses to environmental challenges, international terrorism, as well as many others. It is the task of International Relations to apply the scientific method to understand these issues sufficiently to be able to describe, explain, and predict them within a logical framework.

International Relations is a different type of science from the physical sciences. The physical sciences propose tight *deterministic* processes between variables. By deterministic we mean that cause-and-effect relationships are highly predictable (even if statistically). Water, for example, changes physical states at predictable intervals. There are stochastic or probabilistic processes in the physical sciences, especially as one examines events at the subatomic level. In contrast, the social sciences are entirely *probabilistic*. Gabriel Almond compared the approach of the physical sciences to the study of clocks, and the social sciences to the study of clouds. Clouds are substantive objects but predicting their precise shape at any given time is nearly impossible, despite their constant mass. The number of variables at play, such as cloud density, wind currents, and temperature, create all sorts of possible variations in the shape of the cloud.[5] Social processes are similar in their complexity to clouds. As social scientists, when we try to determine what the effect will be of a global deflationary depression on the likelihood of interstate relations, we are dealing with a process at least as complex as a cloud, and also politically important for policymakers. Competitive increases in tariffs in the 1930s fed the rise of fascist governments that eventually produced the Second World War. The challenges in attaining precision that social scientists are often accused of by physical scientists are unavoidable given the complexity of the subject. No laboratory scientific method would provide any better explanation or prediction of how deflation can affect interstate relations that can lead to world war.

It is through the application of the scientific method that International Relations as a discipline attempts to describe, explain, and predict phenomena in world politics. International Relations relies on the scientific method for its usefulness in providing answers to specific questions. However, the scientific method itself is often a target of criticism, and even among its supporters there are keen debates over different aspects of what constitutes scientific. The scientific method seeks first to establish the epistemological problem of "how do we know what we know?" If we are to use our research to provide advice to decision makers, then how do we establish the degree of confidence we can have in the conclusions we produce?[6]

In order to determine this, we need to become familiar with some basic scientific concepts; the definition of five terms is crucial for our purposes: (1) law, (2) theory, (3) hypothesis, (4) variable, and (5) indicator. First, a *law* denotes a repeatedly observed relationship between two or more causes and effects. Consider the effects of the law of gravity. In this case, the physical law is *deterministic* ("if *A*, then always *B*"). By contrast, nearly all laws in the social sciences are *probabilistic* ("if *A*, then sometimes *B* with probability *X*"). It is important to note the following aspects here: (a) "repeatedly" means that *up to this point in time* there is no evidence that would contradict the law; (b) it follows that one can *never* "prove" a law, since we do not know if at some future point new scientific methods prompt us to establish findings that are contrary to the law in question, or whether the law is simply the result of a pattern of impermanent repetition; and (c) laws are descriptive, in that they tell us *that* a relationship between two or more phenomena holds—at least so far.

[5]Gabriel Almond and Stephen Genco, "Clouds, Clocks, and the Study of Politics," *World Politics* (July 1977), 489-522.

[6]Stephen Van Evera, *Guide to Methods for Students of Political Science* (Ithaca, NY: Cornell University Press, 1997); Gary King, Robert O. Keohane, and Sidney Verba, *Designing Social Inquiry: Scientific Inference in Qualitative Research* (Princeton, NJ: Princeton University Press, 1994).

Second, what we do not know is *how* the given relationship occurs; this then is the purpose of a "good" *theory*. It takes the descriptive nature of a law (probabilistic in the social sciences) as its starting point and attempts to *explain* the repeatedly observed relationship by examining its variables. We will elaborate on the five parts of a theory farther below. Third, we need to determine whether a given theory holds true, or the degree to which this is the case. To accomplish this, one or more generalizable *hypotheses* must be derived from a theory that prescribe anticipated behavior, or predictions we can test. *If* the theory were correct, *then* we would expect to observe certain relationships in nature; a hypothesis is a statement predicting a cause-effect relationship. For example, we can hypothesize that deflationary pressures will lead to unemployment that could provoke extremist domestic groups to seize political power and put into effect their political agenda. By a generalizable hypothesis we mean a hypothesis that applies to as broad a category of cases as possible, within the scope condition of the cases that fit the phenomena we are trying to explain. As social scientists we want to uncover fundamental relationships that help us explain as broad a class of events as possible, rather than a single event, or a small sample of events. A good hypothesis is that the Second World War was caused by the Great Depression. A better hypothesis is that all periods of depression produce global wars. The hypotheses may be false, but the second seeks to achieve the broadest scope.

There are two ideal types of causes that almost never occur in the social sciences but are worth conceptualizing: *necessary* and *sufficient* causes. A necessary cause is a cause that must be active for the outcome to occur. However, the complexity of nature causes the social sciences to produce at best probabilistic predictions of outcomes, so there are rarely necessary causes in nature except trivial ones. Thus while one could propose that a necessary cause of war is a depression, we would notice that there was no depression prior to the First World War but that war occurred anyway. Trivial necessary conditions, such as the need for oxygen to have a war, do not explain variance and are therefore not useful for advancing science. Sufficient causes are causes, which if they are present, produce the predicted outcome. However, sufficient causes are also rare in the social sciences. If one were to propose that all states affected by depression would embark on war, we would need to explain why Turkey and Sweden avoided entry into the Second World War despite being affected by the Depression. Sufficient causes are usually formalized through an *if/then* statement, such as *if* depression, *then* war.

This being said, it is important to highlight that hypotheses are not simply about making predictions. Hypotheses do not, for instance, simply predict that depressions produce wars. Given the purpose of a theory, hypotheses must also contain explanations of events. *Why* or *how* depressions produce wars must be explained. The explanation is often as important as the prediction because the explanation provides the processes and mechanisms through which decision makers make policies to stop subsequent wars, and thereby helps the scholars and decision makers identify the variables at play.

Fourth, a hypothesis is built through the use of *variables*. In order to explore the cause-effect relationship, we need an *independent* and a *dependent* variable; the former causes the latter to vary. As the name suggests, variables vary, i.e. they can have different values like the "degree of democracy" in a given country or the "share of the vote" for a specific political party in an election, and these values can be measured o a range. If the independent variable varied but the dependent variable did *not* vary, our hypothesis would be wrong; we say it would be "falsified," because one variable did not correlate with the other. For example, if we take the above hypothesis that all periods of depression (the independent variable) produce global wars (the dependent variable) then variation on the former (depression vs. non-depression) must be related to variation on the latter (war vs. peace). Whenever there is depression, we must expect the outbreak of war; conversely, in times of an economic boom, there would be no war. If we are in a severe depression but global war does not break out, then we have movement on the range in the independent variable but *none* in the dependent variable. Therefore, the hypothesis is falsified because the variables are unrelated.

When independent and dependent variables interact to cause variance, they produce relationships, which are called *correlations*. *Correlation* between two variables is not necessarily *causation*. In the former case, two events occur at the same time by coincidence; neither one is responsible for the other, and they may be caused by a common prior cause. In the latter instance, we can establish which one is the independent and which one the dependent variable. For example, the Second World War seemed to follow from the Great Depression in time, and so we can assume that the Great Depression caused the Second World War. However, if we look closer in our research we see that the effect of the reparation payments instituted against Germany at the end of the First World War may provide a better explanation. The economic disruption of the reparation payments could have been responsible for the Depression in Weimar Germany. Simultaneously, the humiliation of the reparations led many Germans to support extreme fascist regimes. In this formulation, the Depression did not cause the Second World War. Rather, both the Depression and the Second World War were the result of the policy of reparation payments, a prior common cause. Reparation payments we term a *confounding* variable. It is labeled as such because it confounds the relationship between the independent and dependent variable in our original model. There is thus a *spurious* relationship between our independent and dependent variable, meaning that the relationship was proposed but did not occur in nature. To check against confounding variables we must always be on the search for antecedent causes that explain the variance in the independent and dependent variable. We must *never* conflate correlation with causation.

It is possible to build on the explanation to include a web of variables, so that instead of a single independent and dependent variable, you can have a chain of variables in which the intervening causes are termed *intervening* variables. For example, an intervening variable between depression and war could be the presence of a strongly militarized generation in the affected states. In states such as Japan where there was a strong military, the depression produced an expansionist military ideology that led to war. In the United States, where there was a weak army tradition, the depression created poverty, but not military expansionism.

All hypotheses emerge from the interplay of *deduction* and *induction*, although theories should be deduced because only prior theory can help identify what facts to look for in nature. Deduction is the logical extraction of conclusions from postulates. For example, if we conclude that all states prefer to be rich rather than poor, then we can deduce that a state that goes to war does so in expectation of acquiring more resources to become rich. The criterion for a good deduction is whether the argument is logically consistent. Induction, the opposite of deduction, is empirical reasoning, or the drawing of conclusions from observed behavior in nature. By "empirical" we mean knowledge obtained through research on nature. If we wanted to know why Benito Mussolini led Italy to invade France in 1940, then we would proceed to Italy and examine the facts. Induction uses external consistency criteria (from nature) for validation. As researchers we use both. We use deduction when we have difficulty observing nature, perhaps because of access restrictions or the loss of data since the event. Since interviewing Mussolini would be difficult, we can formulate general hypotheses about the foreign policy behavior of fascist state leaders in general. We use induction when we are not sufficiently confident about the underlying causal logic of the phenomenon we are observing. For example, if we are confused by Francesco Franco's regime in Spain, we would travel there to uncover why the Depression did not lead Spain to participate in the Second World War.

Fifth, in order to actually measure variation on the variables, that is, to assign a range of values like "high/medium/low" to them, we need to choose *indicators* to ultimately relate a theory to reality; this is termed *operationalization*. Physical scientists rely on hard indicators such as mass, density, and temperature. Economists make use of currency amounts, and domestic political scientists may look at votes. Scholars of International Relations are left with the difficult task of quantifying intangible concepts such as power, security, military strength, the national interest, and national confidence. In our recurrent example, we can draw on the skills of economists to define a depression, perhaps through an indicator that measures the average deflation across states. If it falls below a certain range, which is our indicator, we can declare that the independent variable of the status of international economic health is in the depression category. Defining war may be more difficult. Do states have to invade each other for there to be a war event? Defining fascist governments may be even more difficult. Were Hungary or Romania fascist states, or simply authoritarian? This is often the most complicated part of developing a theory because it requires making the link between your theory and measures of the real world.

SCIENTIFIC APPLICATION

How are theories used in academic work (whether books, journal articles, or term papers)? We can identify, again, five major elements to theoretical scholarship. The first is the *research question* or *puzzle*. For example, a national leader may inquire of a social scientist what causes war. The social scientist would then proceed to propose a hypothesis to explain an answer. A puzzle is a counterintuitive or conclusion that seems to contradict the conventional wisdom. For example, if we can conclude that no state would willingly begin a war that would make them worse off than if they had not begun it, then why the Italians joined Germany in the Second World War leaves us with a contradiction that challenges conventional wisdom. Puzzles and theories that oppose conventional wisdom tend to be the most interesting because of their broader implications for our confidence in what we think we know.

The second element is the formulation of a set of generalizable hypotheses whereby, as mentioned above, a broader scope is principally preferable over a narrow explanatory range. In addition, hypotheses must be phrased clearly and explicitly. The third element of a theory is the identification of the variables, and then their *operationalization*. The universe is nearly infinitely complex. As humans, however, we have finite, and actually limited, cognitive ability. Most of us cannot even begin to grasp all of the variables that play a role in our ability to read this text. What is sufficient for us is to focus on the important factors that determine outcomes. Did I remember to bring my book? Do I have enough light? Is my radio off? Am I comfortable in my chair? What we have done here is artificially simplified the infinite complexity of the universe into a manageable model with just a few variables. In most cases, satisfying these causes will produce the effect of making it possible that we will be able to read this book. Thus, we create deliberately, artificial abstractions of reality because we want to be cognitively economical. These we call *models*, which are merely representations of reality. We must never forget, however, that these models are representations of reality, not reality itself.

The goal in creating a model is to explain as much variance, or change in values, in the dependent variable. A good model is one that explains a great deal of change between categories in the dependent variable, as the independent variable changes in value. It is important to avoid the use of *constants*. For example, explaining the incidences of depression, war, or trade by looking at human nature should produce no result since the independent variable does not vary. Human nature is fixed and unchanging and cannot therefore produce change.

The fourth element of a theory is the *testing of the hypotheses*. It is important that theories can never be tested, only their hypotheses. There are many different ways to conduct tests, but all of them have the same goal of determining whether the hypotheses produce the predicted outcome. We identify two basic test procedures. The first is the large-*n* (i.e., many case) statistical test in which all the variables are run against each other to see if there is a correlation between the independent and dependent variables. Normally a computer program will tell you whether there is a relationship and how strong it is. The problem with quantitative tests is that they need to generalize common indicators across all cases, which tends to make the output difficult to understand. The second type of test is the case study; they mainly are employed *comparatively*, meaning between a small number of cases, or across time in a single case. Under very specific circumstances, a *single* case study can be justified. Cases have the advantage of permitting considerable richness of detail to be considered in the test.

Finally, the fifth element is linked to the first, in which the scholar or the policymaker outlined the problem to be studied. Ultimately it is important that the researcher translate their findings and report them back to the policymaker in a policy-usable fashion. Political science was designed to provide solutions to major problems.

INTERPRETING THE READINGS

For each of the readings you do, impose the five elements of the theory. What is the hypothesis of the author? What are the dependent and independent variables in the model? How are the variables indicated? To what do the concepts the author discusses refer to in nature? Are there alternative explanations that provide a more convincing explanation and prediction than those of the author? How can a given hypothesis be tested? What are the policy implications of the theory? Recall that political science is meant to be written in a clear style, so that if an author you are reading has written a text that evades this type of classification, it is probably also suffering from major theoretical shortcomings.

Part I

THEORETICAL APPROACHES TO INTERNATIONAL RELATIONS

INTRODUCTION

International Relations is divided into two principal theoretical approaches, realism and liberalism, that correspond to basic assumptions about how the international system works. Usually major theories in the discipline rely on the assumptions of one or the other approach. In Part I we highlight these approaches and their key concepts.

Realism, while related to the venerable tradition of *realpolitik*, has its scientific origins in the inter-war period. E.H. Carr, author of *The Twenty Years Crisis* (1939), criticized the idealist paradigm that had been dominant since World War I and called for a more realistic theory to explain the rise of world militarism in the 1930s. Classical realism as articulated by Carr and Hans Morgenthau, in his *Politics Among Nations* (1948), argue that in world politics, states are the main actors and behave rationally, that state interest is defined in terms of power, and that the only morality in state actions is prudence. As mentioned in the introduction to this reader, both Carr and Morgenthau have based their approaches to explaining international relations on the basis of the idea of power discussed in a small section of Thucydides' book, the *History of the Peloponnesian War,* focusing on a discussion between the Athenians and the Melians.

Kenneth N. Waltz, author of *Theory of International Politics* (1979), sought to articulate a new or neorealist elaboration of international politics grounded on microeconomic theory. In an earlier publication in 1959, *Man, the State and War* (1959), he argued that the cause of war lay not in the nature of humanity or in the types of governments of states, but rather in the international system.[1] He thus proposed that any system could be characterized by three factors. First, the principle of organization of the international system was one characterized by anarchy rather than by hierarchy. By anarchy he was pointing not to the lack of patterns in relations between states, but in the absence

---

[1]Kenneth N. Waltz, *Man, the State and War* (New York: Columbia University Press, 1959).

of any world government. Therefore states behave according to the principle of self-help to survive. Second, there was no functional differentiation of units in an international system, as each state had to satisfy all of its own needs. Third, it is the distribution of capabilities within that system that explains outcomes, such as war. The reading on "The Anarchic Structure of World Politics" by Kenneth N. Waltz is drawn from this work.

Classical realism argues that outcomes are the result of human nature and the practice of states seeking power in anarchy. The importance of state power was emphasized by the work of Thomas Hobbes in his *Leviathan*. Neorealism argues that it is the anarchy of the international system that causes states to feel insecure, which drives international politics. The implications of neorealism are that cooperation is difficult because states are afraid of being exploited by other states. Therefore, the struggle for survival is a zero-sum game, in which states are sensitive to relative power rankings. The distribution of relative gains in any interaction is important because if one state accumulates too much power, it may use it to threaten the security of another state. The reading by Joseph M. Grieco on "Anarchy and the Limits of Cooperation" explores this. Since only states matter, international organizations either do not matter or are merely the reflection of the underlying distribution of power between states. Realism is also the theoretical basis for balance of power theories, as discussed by Stephen M. Walt in "Alliances: Balancing and Bandwagoning." While the majority of this section concerns theories of international relations, selected pieces suggest how theories can and have been applied to the practice of international politics. George F. Kennan's iconic "Sources of Soviet Conduct" warns that applications of power must be fine-grained and applied carefully to the policy at hand.

Recently, a new strain of realism, neoclassical realism, has sought to reconcile neorealism's focus on the international system and scientific theory with classical realism's emphasis on domestic politics and leadership. In particular, neoclassical realists agree that states respond to changes in the distribution of power in the international system and the threats and opportunities they create. Nonetheless, they argue that, in Gideon Rose's terms, states are an "imperfect transmission belt" for systemic pressures.[2] Depending on domestic political arrangements, including state-society relationships, societal cleavages, the nature of decision-making institutions, and the character of individual leaders, different states will have varying abilities to respond as the international system requires. As a result, states will occasionally behave inconsistently with systemic preferences, for example, the British and French failure to balance against Hitler in the 1930s,[3] or construct unique national responses to systemic challenges. Therefore,

[2]Gideon Rose, "Neoclassical Realism and Theories of Foreign Policy," *World Politics* 51 (1998), pp. 144–172.

[3]Randall Schweller, "Unanswered Threats: A Neoclassical Realist Theory of Underbalancing," *International Security* 29 (2004), pp. 159–201.

to understand both state behavior and international outcomes, we need to examine both challenges at the international level and the specific domestic contexts of states.

Liberalism is the oldest approach in International Relations and tends to be linked to nineteenth-century considerations of the role trade could have in enhancing the peaceful relations between states. Its different streams have argued that states governed by their own citizens tend to be more peaceful, that trade promotes peace, and that institutional methods of governance in the world can promote peace. The circumstances under which this can be the case are elaborated in the reading by Robert O. Keohane and Joseph S. Nye entitled "Complex Interdependence and the Role of Force." The first strand of liberalism, commercial liberalism, can be seen in readings by Richard Rosencrance and Robert Gilpin in Part IV. The second strand of liberalism, neoliberal institutionalism, appears in readings by Kenneth Oye and Ernst Haas in Part II. The third strand of liberalism is called democratic peace theory and dates back to Kant's focus on perpetual peace among states with republican forms of government. According to the more modern variant, wars almost never occur *between* democracies because of structural and normative restraints, that is, because their *domestic* form of resolving disagreements is peaceful, democracies also exhibit this behavior vis-à-vis each other. Democracies are no less war prone than non-democracies, however, but target their wars against non-democracies. Michael W. Doyle discusses this in "Liberalism and World Politics." The Fourteen Points Address to the U.S. Congress by President Woodrow Wilson offers a practical illustration of all three variants of liberal ideas.

Realism and liberalism differ in the domains of their theories. Realist theories focus mostly on wars and great power politics, but cannot explain outcomes concerning economic institutions, regional integration, or even alliance durability. The assumptions of liberalism are far more conducive to explaining variance in economic relations and the persistence of international institutions, but provide poor explanations when the actors hold relative gains assumptions, even in the absence of a security threat.

In this vein, so-called neoliberal institutionalism is a response to neorealism. It accepts many of the systemic assumptions of neorealism, but disagrees about their implications. Neoliberalism assumes that anarchy can be mitigated by institutions that facilitate cooperation and that international institutions can be independent actors. Its major assumption is that states are rational egoists and measure *absolute* rather than *relative* gains.

Proponents of constructivism, or critical theory, argue that both realism and liberalism have fundamentally misrepresented the nature of anarchy, power, and international relations. According to constructivists, it is necessary to examine the interactions between different actors in a particular time and place in order to understand how these actors see each other (their identities) and thus what they expect and want from one another. Identities and interests as well as power are constructed, and reconstructed, and thus change over time and between sets of countries or non-state actors. A greater range of actors is capable of using a greater variety of tools, including ideas, norms, and knowledge, for power, seen as social as well as material, to achieve their different interests. Alexander Wendt explores how intersubjective identity formation between states can produce very different outcomes in international relations depending upon how anarchy is constructed. Martha Finnemore and Kathryn Sikkink examine the creation, dissemination, and effects of norms on international relations in "International Norms Dynamics and Political Change." J. Ann Tickner goes even further to reconceptualize international relations as a gendered realm, reexamining the masculine norms and forms of power supporting realism and realist policy prescriptions. By questioning how our understanding and conduct of international politics might change if these norms were challenged, Tickner asserts that women in international relations might foster cooperation by imbuing foreign policy with a more balanced mix of masculine and feminine values.

THE MELIAN DIALOGUE[1]

M.I. Finchley

1. Next summer Alcibiades sailed to Argos with twenty ships and seized 300. Argive citizens who were still suspected of being pro-Spartan. These were put by the Athenians into the nearby islands under Athenian control.

The Athenians also made an expedition against the island of Melos. They had thirty of their own ships, six from Chios, and two from Lesbos; 1,200 hoplites, 300 archers, and twenty mounted archers, all from Athens; and about 1,500 hoplites from the allies and the islanders.

The Melians are a colony from Sparta. They had refused to join the Athenian empire like the other islanders, and at first had remained neutral without helping either side; but afterwards, when the Athenians had brought force to bear on them by laying waste their land, they had become open enemies of Athens.

Now the generals Cleomedes, the son of Lycomedes, and Tisias, the son of Tisimachus, encamped with the above force in Melian territory and, before doing any harm to the land, first of all sent representatives to negotiate. The Melians did not

From "The Melian Dialogue" from *The History of The Peloponnesian War* by Thucydides, translated by Rex Warner, with an introduction and notes by M.I. Finley (Penguin Classics 1954, Revised edition 1972), pp. 400–407. Translation copyright © 1954 by Rex Warner. Introduction and Appendices copyright © 1972 by M.I. Finley. Reproduced by permission of Penguin Books Ltd.

[1]See Appendix 3

invite these representatives to speak before the people, but asked them to make the statement for which they had come in front of the governing body and the few. The Athenian representatives then spoke as follows:

2. 'So we are not to speak before the people, no doubt in case the mass of the people should hear once and for all and without interruption an argument from us which is both persuasive and incontrovertible, and should so be led astray. This, we realize, is your motive in bringing us here to speak before the few. Now suppose that you who sit here should make assurance doubly sure. Suppose that you, too, should refrain from dealing with every point in detail in a set speech, and should instead interrupt us whenever we say something controversial and deal with that before going on to the next point? Tell us first whether you approve of this suggestion of ours.'

3. The Council of the Melians replied as follows:

'No one can object to each of us putting forward our own views in a calm atmosphere. That is perfectly reasonable. What is scarcely consistent with such a proposal is the present threat, indeed the certainty, of your making war on us. We see that you have come prepared to judge the argument yourselves, and that the likely end of it all will be either war, if we prove that we are in the right, and so refuse to surrender, or else slavery.'

4. *Athenians:* If you are going to spend the time in enumerating your suspicions about the future, or if you have met here for any other reason except to look the facts in the face and on the basis of these facts to consider how you can save your city from destruction, there is no point in our going on with this discussion. If, however, you will do as we suggest, then we will speak on.

5. *Melians:* It is natural and understandable that people who are placed as we are should have recourse to all kinds of arguments and different points of view. However, you are right in saying that we are met together here to discuss the safety of our country and, if you will have it so, the discussion shall proceed on the lines that you have laid down.

6. *Athenians:* Then we on our side will use no fine phrases saying, for example, that we have a right to our empire because we defeated the Persians, or that we have come against you now because of the injuries you have done us—a great mass of words that nobody would believe. And we ask you on your side not to imagine that you will influence us by saying that you, though a colony of Sparta, have not joined Sparta in the war, or that you have never done us any harm. Instead we recommend that you should try to get what it is possible for you to get, taking into consideration what we both really do think; since you know as well as we do that, when these matters are discussed by practical people, the standard of justice depends on the equality of power to compel and that in fact the strong do what they have the power to do and the weak accept what they have to accept.

7. *Melians:* Then in our view (since you force us to leave justice out of account and to confine ourselves to self-interest)—in our view it is at any rate useful that you

should not destroy a principle that is to the general good of all men—namely, that in the case of all who fall into danger there should be such a thing as fair play and just dealing, and that such people should be allowed to use and to profit by arguments that fall short of a mathematical accuracy. And this is a principle which affects you as much as anybody, since your own fall would be visited by the most terrible vengeance and would be an example to the world.

8. *Athenians:* As for us, even assuming that our empire does come to an end, we are not despondent about what would happen next. One is not so much frightened of being conquered by a power which rules over others, as Sparta does (not that we are concerned with Sparta now), as of what would happen if a ruling power is attacked and defeated by its own subjects. So far as this point is concerned, you can leave it to us to face the risks involved. What we shall do now is to show you that it is for the good of our own empire that we are here and that it is for the preservation of your city that we shall say what we are going to say. We do not want any trouble in bringing you into our empire, and we want you to be spared for the good both of yourselves and of ourselves.

9. *Melians:* And how could it be just as good for us to be the slaves as for you to be the masters?

10. *Athenians:* You, by giving in, would save yourselves from disaster; we, by not destroying you, would be able to profit from you.

11. *Melians:* So you would not agree to our being neutral, friends instead of enemies, but allies of neither side?

12. *Athenians:* No, because it is not so much your hostility that injures us; it is rather the case that, if we were on friendly terms with you, our subjects would regard that as a sign of weakness in us, whereas your hatred is evidence of our power.

13. *Melians:* Is that your subjects' idea of fair play—that no distinction should be made between people who are quite unconnected with you and people who are mostly your own colonists or else rebels whom you have conquered?

14. *Athenians:* So far as right and wrong are concerned they think that there is no difference between the two, that those who still preserve their independence do so because they are strong, and that if we fail to attack them it is because we are afraid. So that by conquering you we shall increase not only the size but the security of our empire. We rule the sea and you are islanders, and weaker islanders too than the others; it is therefore particularly important that you should not escape.

15. *Melians:* But do you think there is no security for you in what we suggest? For here again, since you will not let us mention justice, but tell us to give in to your interests, we, too, must tell you what our interests are and, if yours and ours happen to coincide, we must try to persuade you of the fact. Is it not certain that you will make enemies of all states who are at present neutral, when they see what is happening here and naturally conclude that in course of time you will attack them too? Does not this

mean that you are strengthening the enemies you have already and are forcing others to become your enemies even against their intentions and their inclinations?

16. *Athenians:* As a matter of fact we are not so much frightened of states on the continent. They have their liberty, and this means that it will be a long time before they begin to take precautions against us. We are more concerned about islanders like yourselves, who are still unsubdued, or subjects who have already become embittered by the constraint which our empire imposes on them. These are the people who are most likely to act in a reckless manner and to bring themselves and us, too, into the most obvious danger.

17. *Melians:* Then surely, if such hazards are taken by you to keep your empire and by your subjects to escape from it, we who are still free would show ourselves great cowards and weaklings if we failed to face everything that comes rather than submit to slavery.

18. *Athenians:* No, not if you are sensible. This is no fair fight, with honour on one side and shame on the other. It is rather a question of saving your lives and not resisting those who are far too strong for you.

19. *Melians:* Yet we know that in war fortune sometimes makes the odds more level than could be expected from the difference in numbers of the two sides. And if we surrender, then all our hope is lost at once, whereas, so long as we remain in action, there is still a hope that we may yet stand upright.

20. *Athenians:* Hope, that comforter in danger! If one already has solid advantages to fall back upon, one can indulge in hope. It may do harm, but will not destroy one. But hope is by nature an expensive commodity, and those who are risking their all on one cast find out what it means only when they are already ruined; it never fails them in the period when such a knowledge would enable them to take precautions. Do not let this happen to you, you who are weak and whose fate depends on a single movement of the scale. And do not be like those people who, as so commonly happens, miss the chance of saving themselves in a human and practical way, and, when every clear and distinct hope has left them in their adversity, turn to what is blind and vague, to prophecies and oracles and such things which by encouraging hope lead men to ruin.

21. *Melians:* It is difficult, and you may be sure that we know it, for us to oppose your power and fortune, unless the terms be equal. Nevertheless we trust that the gods will give us fortune as good as yours, because we are standing for what is right against what is wrong; and as for what we lack in power, we trust that it will be made up for by our alliance with the Spartans, who are bound, if for no other reason, then for honour's sake, and because we are their kinsmen, to come to our help. Our confidence, therefore, is not so entirely irrational as you think.

22. *Athenians:* So far as the favour of the gods is concerned, we think we have as much right to that as you have. Our aims and our actions are perfectly consistent with

the beliefs men hold about the gods and with the principles which govern their own conduct. Our opinion of the gods and our knowledge of men lead us to conclude that it is a general and necessary law of nature to rule whatever one can. This is not a law that we made ourselves, nor were we the first to act upon it when it was made. We found it already in existence, and we shall leave it to exist for ever among those who come after us. We are merely acting in accordance with it, and we know that you or anybody else with the same power as ours would be acting in precisely the same way. And therefore, so far as the gods are concerned, we see no good reason why we should fear to be at a disadvantage. But with regard to your views about Sparta and your confidence that she, out of a sense of honour, will come to your aid, we must say that we congratulate you on your simplicity but do not envy you your folly. In matters that concern themselves or their own constitution the Spartans are quite remarkably good; as for their relations with others, that is a long story, but it can be expressed shortly and clearly by saying that of all people we know the Spartans are most conspicuous for believing that what they like doing is honourable and what suits their interests is just. And this kind of attitude is not going to be of much help to you in your absurd quest for safety at the moment.

23. *Melians:* But this is the very point where we can feel most sure. Their own self-interest will make them refuse to betray their own colonists, the Melians, for that would mean losing the confidence of their friends among the Hellenes and doing good to their enemies.

24. *Athenians:* You seem to forget that if one follows one's self-interest one wants to be safe, whereas the path of justice and honour involves one in danger. And, where danger is concerned, the Spartans are not, as a rule, very venturesome.

25. *Melians:* But we think that they would even endanger themselves for our sake and count the risk more worth taking than in the case of others, because we are so close to the Peloponnese that they could operate more easily, and because they can depend on us more than on others, since we are of the same race and share the same feelings.

26. *Athenians:* Goodwill shown by the party that is asking for help does not mean security for the prospective ally. What is looked for is a positive preponderance of power in action. And the Spartans pay attention to this point even more than others do. Certainly they distrust their own native resources so much that when they attack a neighbour they bring a great army of allies with them. It is hardly likely therefore that, while we are in control of the sea, they will cross over to an island.

27. *Melians:* But they still might send others. The Cretan sea is a wide one, and it is harder for those who control it to intercept others than for those who want to slip through to do so safely. And even if they were to fail in this, they would turn against your own land and against those of your allies left unvisited by Brasidas. So, instead of troubling about a country which has nothing to do with you, you will find trouble nearer home, among your allies, and in your own country.

28. *Athenians:* It is a possibility, something that has in fact happened before. It may happen in your case, but you are well aware that the Athenians have never yet relinquished a single siege operation through fear of others. But we are somewhat shocked to find that, though you announced your intention of discussing how you could preserve yourselves, in all this talk you have said absolutely nothing which could justify a man in thinking that he could be preserved. Your chief points are concerned with what you hope may happen in the future, while your actual resources are too scanty to give you a chance of survival against the forces that are opposed to you at this moment. You will therefore be showing ar extraordinary lack of common sense if, after you have asked us to retire from this meeting, you still fail to reach a conclusion wiser than anything you have mentioned so far. Do not be led astray by a false sense of honour—a thing which often brings men to ruin when they are faced with an obvious danger that somehow affects their pride. For in many cases men have still been able to see the dangers ahead of them, but this thing called dishonour, this word, by its own force of seduction, has drawn them into a state where they have surrendered to an idea, while in fact they have fallen voluntarily into irrevocable disaster, in dishonour that is all the more dishonourable because it has come to them from their own folly rather than their misfortune. You, if you take the right view, will be careful to avoid this. You will see that there is nothing disgraceful in giving way to the greatest city in Hellas when she is offering you such reasonable terms—alliance on a tribute-paying basis and liberty to enjoy your own property. And, when you are allowed to choose between war and safety, you will not be so insensitively arrogant as to make the wrong choice. This is the safe rule—to stand up to one's equals, to behave with deference towards one's superiors, and to treat one's inferiors with moderation. Think it over again, then, when we have withdrawn from the meeting, and let this be a point that constantly recurs to your minds—that you are discussing the fate of your country, that you have only one country, and that its future for good or ill depends on this one single decision which you are going to make.

29. The Athenians then withdrew from the discussion. The Melians, left to themselves, reached a conclusion which was much the same as they had indicated in their previous replies. Their answer was as follows:

'Our decision, Athenians, is just the same as it was at first. We are not prepared to give up in a short moment the liberty which our city has enjoyed from its foundation for 700 years. We put our trust in the fortune that the gods will send and which has saved us up to now, and in the help of men—that is, of the Spartans; and so we shall try to save ourselves. But we invite you to allow us to be friends of yours and enemies to neither side, to make a treaty which shall be agreeable to both you and us, and so to leave our country.'

30. The Melians made this reply, and the Athenians, just as they were breaking off the discussion, said:

'Well, at any rate, judging from this decision of yours, you seem to us quite unique in your ability to consider the future as something more certain than what is before your eyes, and to see uncertainties as realities, simply because you would like them to be so. As you have staked most on and trusted most in Spartans, luck, and hopes, so in all these you will find yourselves most completely deluded.'

31. The Athenian representatives then went back to the army, and the Athenian generals, finding that the Melians would not submit, immediately commenced hostilities and built a wall completely round the city of Melos, dividing the work out among the various states. Later they left behind a garrison of some of their own and some allied troops to blockade the place by land and sea, and with the greater part of their army returned home. The force left behind stayed on and continued with the siege.

OF THE NATURAL CONDITION OF MANKIND AS CONCERNING THEIR FELICITY AND MISERY

Thomas Hobbes

1. Nature hath made men so equal in the faculties of body and mind, as that, though there be found one man sometimes manifestly stronger in body or of quicker mind than another; yet when all is reckoned together, the difference between man and man is not so considerable as that one man can thereupon claim to himself any benefit to which another may not pretend as well as he. For as to the strength of body, the weakest has strength enough to kill the strongest, either by secret machination or by confederacy with others that are in the same danger with himself.

2. And as to the faculties of the mind, setting aside the arts grounded upon words, and especially that skill of proceeding upon general and infallible rules, called science, which very few have and but in few things, as being not a native faculty born with us, nor attained, as prudence, while we look after somewhat else, I find yet a greater equality amongst men than that of strength. For prudence is but experience, which

Thomas Hobbes. *Leviathan* edited by A.P. Martinich. Peterborough, Ont.: Broadview Press, 2002, pp. 92–97.

equal time equally bestows on all men in those things they equally apply themselves unto. That which may perhaps make such equality incredible is but a vain conceit of one's own wisdom, which almost all men think they have in a greater degree than the vulgar, that is, than all men but themselves and a few others, whom by fame or for concurring with themselves, they approve. For such is the nature of men that howsoever they may acknowledge many others to be more witty or more eloquent or more learned, they will hardly believe there be many so wise as themselves; for they see their own wit at hand and other men's at a distance. But this proveth rather that men are in that point equal, than unequal. For there is not ordinarily a greater sign of the equal distribution of anything than that every man is contented with his share.

3. From this equality of ability ariseth equality of hope in the attaining of our ends. And therefore if any two men desire the same thing, which nevertheless they cannot both enjoy, they become enemies; and in the way to their end (which is principally their own conservation, and sometimes their delectation only) endeavour to destroy or subdue one another. And from hence it comes to pass that where an invader hath no more to fear than another man's single power, if one plant, sow, build, or posses a convenient seat, others may probably be expected to come prepared with forces united to dispossess and deprive him, not only of the fruit of his labour, but also of his life or liberty. And the invader again is in the like danger of another.

4. And from this diffidence of one another, there is no way for any man to secure himself so reasonable as anticipation, that is, by force or wiles, to master the persons of all men he can so long till he see no other power great enough to endanger him; and this is no more than his own conservation requireth, and is generally allowed. Also, because there be some that, taking pleasure in contemplating their own power in the acts of conquest, which they pursue farther than their security requires, if others, that otherwise would be glad to be at ease within modest bounds, should not by invasion increase their power, they would not be able, long time, by standing only on their defence, to subsist. And by consequence, such augmentation of dominion over men being necessary to a man's conservation, it ought to be allowed him.

5. Again, men have no pleasure (but on the contrary a great deal of grief) in keeping company where there is no power able to overawe them all. For every man looketh that his companion should value him at the same rate he sets upon himself, and upon all signs of contempt or undervaluing naturally endeavours, as far as he dares (which amongst them that have no common power to keep them in quiet is far enough to make them destroy each other), to extort a greater value from his contemners, by damage; and from others, by the example.

6. So that in the nature of man, we find three principal causes of quarrel. First, competition; secondly, diffidence; thirdly, glory.

7. The first maketh men invade for gain; the second, for safety; and the third, for reputation. The first use violence to make themselves masters of other men's

persons, wives, children, and cattle; the second, to defend them; the third, for trifles, as a word, a smile, a different opinion, and any other sign of undervalue, either direct in their persons or by reflection in their kindred, their friends, their nation, their profession, or their name.

8. Hereby it is manifest that during the time men live without a common power to keep them all in awe, they are in that condition which is called war; and such a war as is of every man against every man. For WAR consisteth not in battle only, or the act of fighting, but in a tract of time, wherein the will to contend by battle is sufficiently known; and therefore the notion of *time* is to be considered in the nature of war, as it is in the nature of weather. For as the nature of foul weather lieth not in a shower or two of rain, but in an inclination thereto of many days together, so the nature of war consisteth not in actual fighting, but in the known disposition thereto during all the time there is no assurance to the contrary. All other time is PEACE.

9. Whatsoever therefore is consequent to a time of war, where every man is enemy to every man, the same consequent to the time wherein men live without other security than what their own strength and their own invention shall furnish them withal. In such condition there is no place for industry, because the fruit thereof is uncertain; and consequently no culture of the earth; no navigation, nor use of the commodities that may be imported by sea; no commodious building; no instruments of moving and removing such things as require much force; no knowledge of the face of the earth; no account of time; no arts; no letters; no society; and which is worst of all, continual fear, and danger of violent death; and the life of man, solitary, poor, nasty, brutish, and short.

10. It may seem strange to some man that has not well weighed these things that nature should thus dissociate and render men apt to invade and destroy one another; and he may therefore, not trusting to this inference, made from the passions, desire perhaps to have the same confirmed by experience. Let him therefore consider with himself; when taking a journey, he arms himself and seeks to go well accompanied; when going to sleep, he locks his doors; when even in his house he locks his chests; and this when he knows there be laws and public officers, armed to revenge all injuries shall be done him; what opinion he has of his fellow subjects, when he rides armed; of his fellow citizens, when he locks his doors; and of his children, and servants, when he locks his chests. Does he not there as much accuse mankind by his actions as I do by my words? But neither of us accuse man's nature in it. The desires and other passions of man are in themselves no sin. No more are the actions that proceed from those passions till they know a law that forbids them; which, till laws be made, they cannot know; nor can any law be made till they have agreed upon the person that shall make it.

11. It may peradventure be thought there was never such a time nor condition of war as this; and I believe it was never generally so, over all the world; but there are many places where they live so now. For the savage people in many places of America, except the government of small families, the concord whereof dependeth

on natural lust, have no government at all, and live at this day in that brutish manner, as I said before. Howsoever, it may be perceived what manner of life there would be, where there were no common power to fear, by the manner of life which men that have formerly lived under a peaceful government use to degenerate into a civil war.

12. But though there had never been any time wherein particular men were in a condition of war one against another; yet in all times kings and persons of sovereign authority, because of their independency, are in continual jealousies, and in the state and posture of gladiators, having their weapons pointing and their eyes fixed on one another, that is, their forts, garrisons, and guns upon the frontiers of their kingdoms, and continual spies upon their neighbours, which is a posture of war. But because they uphold thereby the industry of their subjects, there does not follow from it that misery which accompanies the liberty of particular men.

13. To this war of every man against every man, this also is consequent; that nothing can be unjust. The notions of right and wrong, justice and injustice, have there no place. Where there is no common power, there is no law; where no law, no injustice. Force and fraud are in war the two cardinal virtues. Justice and injustice are none of the faculties neither of the body nor mind. If they were, they might be in a man that were alone in the world, as well as his senses and passions. They are qualities that relate to men in society, not in solitude. It is consequent also to the same condition that there be no propriety, no dominion, no *mine* and *thine* distinct; but only that to be every man's that he can get, and for so long as he can keep it. And thus much for the ill condition which man by mere nature is actually placed in; though with a possibility to come out of it, consisting partly in the passions, partly in his reason.

14. The passions that incline men to peace are fear of death, desire of such things as are necessary to commodious living, and a hope by their industry to obtain them. And reason suggesteth convenient articles of peace upon which men may be drawn to agreement. These articles are they which otherwise are called the laws of nature.

SIX PRINCIPLES OF
POLITICAL REALISM

HANS J. MORGANTHAL

1. Political realism believes that politics, like society in general, is governed by objective laws that have their roots in human nature. In order to improve society it is first necessary to understand the laws by which society lives. The operation of these laws being impervious to our preferences, men will challenge them only at the risk of failure.

Realism, believing as it does in the objectivity of the laws of politics, must also believe in the possibility of developing a rational theory that reflects, however imperfectly and one-sidedly, these objective laws. It believes also, then, in the possibility of distinguishing in politics between truth and opinion—between what is true objectively and rationally, supported by evidence and illuminated by reason, and what is only a subjective judgment, divorced from the facts as they are and informed by prejudice and wishful thinking.

From "Six Principles of Political Realism" from *Politics Among Nations*, 5th Edition, by Hans J. Morgenthau, copyright © 1972 by Alfred A. Knopf, a division of Random House, Inc. Used by permission of Alfred A. Knopf, a division of Random House, Inc.

Human nature, in which the laws of politics have their roots, has not changed since the classical philosophies of China, India, and Greece endeavored to discover these laws. Hence, novelty is not necessarily a virtue in political theory, nor is old age a defect. The fact that a theory of politics, if there be such a theory, has never been heard of before tends to create a presumption against, rather than in favor of, its soundness. Conversely, the fact that a theory of politics was developed hundreds or even thousands of years ago—as was the theory of the balance of power—does not create a presumption that it must be outmoded and obsolete. A theory of politics must be subjected to the dual test of reason and experience. To dismiss such a theory because it had its flowering in centuries past is to present not a rational argument but a modernistic prejudice that takes for granted the superiority of the present over the past. To dispose of the revival of such a theory as a "fashion" or "fad" is tantamount to assuming that in matters political we can have opinions but no truths.

For realism, theory consists in ascertaining facts and giving them meaning through reason. It assumes that the character of a foreign policy can be ascertained only through the examination of the political acts performed and of the foreseeable consequences of these acts. Thus we can find out what statesmen have actually done, and from the foreseeable consequences of their acts we can surmise what their objectives might have been.

Yet examination of the facts is not enough. To give meaning to the factual raw material of foreign policy, we must approach political reality with a kind of rational outline, a map that suggests to us the possible meanings of foreign policy. In other words, we put ourselves in the position of a statesman who must meet a certain problem of foreign policy under certain circumstances, and we ask ourselves what the rational alternatives are from which a statesman may choose who must meet this problem under these circumstances (presuming always that he acts in a rational manner), and which of these rational alternatives this particular statesman, acting under these circumstances, is likely to choose. It is the testing of this rational hypothesis against the actual facts and their consequences that gives meaning to the facts of international politics and makes a theory of politics possible.

2. The main signpost that helps political realism to find its way through the landscape of international politics is the concept of interest defined in terms of power. This concept provides the link between reason trying to understand international politics and the facts to be understood. It sets politics as an autonomous sphere of action and understanding apart from other spheres, such as economics (understood in terms of interest defined as wealth), ethics, aesthetics, or religion. Without such a concept a theory of politics, international or domestic, would be altogether impossible, for without it we could not distinguish between political and nonpolitical facts, nor could we bring at least a measure of systematic order to the political sphere.

We assume that statesmen think and act in terms of interest defined as power, and the evidence of history bears that assumption out. That assumption allows us to retrace and anticipate, as it were, the steps a statesman—past, present, or future—has taken or will take on the political scene. We look over his shoulder when he writes his dispatches; we listen in on his conversation with other statesmen; we read and anticipate his very thoughts. Thinking in terms of interest defined as power, we think as he does, and as disinterested observers we understand his thoughts and actions perhaps better than he, the actor on the political scene, does himself.

The concept of interest defined as power imposes intellectual discipline upon the observer, infuses rational order into the subject matter of politics, and thus makes the theoretical understanding of politics possible. On the side of the actor, it provides for rational discipline in action and creates that astounding continuity in foreign policy which makes American, British, or Russian foreign policy appear as an intelligible, rational continuum, by and large consistent within itself, regardless of the different motives, preferences, and intellectual and moral qualities of successive statesmen. A realist theory of international politics, then, will guard against two popular fallacies: the concern with motives and the concern with ideological preferences.

To search for the clue to foreign policy exclusively in the motives of statesmen is both futile and deceptive. It is futile because motives are the most illusive of psychological data, distorted as they are, frequently beyond recognition, by the interests and emotions of actor and observer alike. Do we really know what our own motives are? And what do we know of the motives of others?...

A realist theory of international politics will also avoid the other popular fallacy of equating the foreign policies of a statesman with his philosophic or political sympathies, and of deducing the former from the latter. Statesmen, especially under contemporary conditions, may well make a habit of presenting their foreign policies in terms of their philosophic and political sympathies in order to gain popular support for them. Yet they will distinguish with Lincoln between their *"official* duty," which is to think and act in terms of the national interest, and their *"personal* wish," which is to see their own moral values and political principles realized throughout the world.

It stands to reason that not all foreign policies have always followed so rational, objective, and unemotional a course. The contingent elements of personality, prejudice, and subjective preference, and of all the weaknesses of intellect and will which flesh is heir to, are bound to deflect foreign policies from their rational course. Especially where foreign policy is conducted under the conditions of democratic control, the need to marshal popular emotions to the support of foreign policy cannot fail to impair the rationality of foreign policy itself. Yet a theory of foreign policy which aims at rationality must for the time being, as it were, abstract from these irrational elements and seek to paint a picture of foreign policy which presents the rational essence to be found in experience, without the contingent deviations from rationality which are also found in experience....

The difference between international politics as it actually is and a rational theory derived from it is like the difference between a photograph and a painted portrait. The photograph shows everything that can be seen by the naked eye; the painted portrait does not show everything that can be seen by the naked eye, but it shows, or at least seeks to show, one thing that the naked eye cannot see: the human essence of the person portrayed.

Political realism contains not only a theoretical but also a normative element. It knows that political reality is replete with contingencies and systemic irrationalities and points to the typical influences they exert upon foreign policy. Yet it shares with all social theory the need, for the sake of theoretical understanding, to stress the rational elements of political reality; for it is these rational elements that make reality intelligible for theory. Political realism presents the theoretical construct of a rational foreign policy which experience can never completely achieve.

At the same time political realism considers a rational foreign policy to be good foreign policy; for only a rational foreign policy minimizes risks and maximizes benefits and, hence, complies both with the moral precept of prudence and the political requirement of success. Political realism wants the photographic picture of the political world to resemble as much as possible its painted portrait. Aware of the inevitable gap between good—that is, rational—foreign policy and foreign policy as it actually is, political realism maintains not only that theory must focus upon the rational elements of political reality, but also that foreign policy ought to be rational in view of its own moral and practical purposes.

Hence, it is no argument against the theory here presented that actual foreign policy does not or cannot live up to it. That argument misunderstands the intention of this book, which is to present not an indiscriminate description of political reality, but a rational theory of international politics. Far from being invalidated by the fact that, for instance, a perfect balance of power policy will scarcely be found in reality, it assumes that reality, being deficient in this respect, must be understood and evaluated as an approximation to an ideal system of balance of power.

3. Realism assumes that its key concept of interest defined as power is an objective category which is universally valid, but it does not endow that concept with a meaning that is fixed once and for all. The idea of interest is indeed of the essence of politics and is unaffected by the circumstances of time and place. Thucydides statement, born of the experiences of ancient Greece, that "identity of interests is the surest of bonds whether between states or individuals" was taken up in the nineteenth century by Lord Salisbury's remark that "the only bond of union that endures" among nations is "the absence of all clashing interests." It was erected into a general principle of government by George Washington:

> A small knowledge of human nature will convince us, that, with far the greatest
> part of mankind, interest is the governing principle; and that almost every man is
> more or less, under its influence. Motives of public virtue may for a time, or in par-
> ticular instances, actuate men to the observance of a conduct purely disinterested;
> but they are not of themselves sufficient to produce persevering conformity to the
> refined dictates and obligations of social duty. Few men are capable of making a
> continual sacrifice of all views of private interest, or advantage, to the common

good. It is vain to exclaim against the depravity of human nature on this account; the fact is so, the experience of every age and nation has proved it and we must in a great measure, change the constitution of man, before we can make it otherwise. No institution, not built on the presumptive truth of these maxims can succeed.[1]

It was echoed and enlarged upon in our century by Max Weber's observation:

> Interests (material and ideal), not ideas, dominate directly the actions of men. Yet the "images of the world" created by these ideas have very often served as switches determining the tracks on which the dynamism of interests kept actions moving.[2]

Yet the kind of interest determining political action in a particular period of history depends upon the political and cultural context within which foreign policy is formulated. The goals that might be pursued by nations in their foreign policy can run the whole gamut of objectives any nation has ever pursued or might possibly pursue.

The same observations apply to the concept of power. Its content and the manner of its use are determined by the political and cultural environment. Power may comprise anything that establishes and maintains the control of man over man. Thus power covers all social relationships which serve that end, from physical violence to the most subtle psychological ties by which one mind controls another. Power covers the domination of man by man, both when it is disciplined by moral ends and controlled by constitutional safeguards, as in Western democracies, and when it is that untamed and barbaric force which finds its laws in nothing but its own strength and its sole justification in its aggrandizement.

Political realism does not assume that the contemporary conditions under which foreign policy operates, with their extreme instability and the ever present threat of large-scale violence, cannot be changed. The balance of power, for instance, is indeed a perennial element of all pluralistic societies, as the authors of *The Federalist* papers well knew; yet it is capable of operating, as it does in the United States, under the conditions of relative stability and peaceful conflict. If the factors that have given rise to these conditions can be duplicated on the international scene, similar conditions of stability and peace will then prevail there, as they have over long stretches of history among certain nations.

What is true of the general character of international relations is also true of the nation state as the ultimate point of reference of contemporary foreign policy. While the realist indeed believes that interest is the perennial standard by which political

[1]*The Writings of George Washington*, edited by John C. Fitzpatrick (Washington: United States Printing Office, 1931–44), Vol. X, p. 363.

[2]Marianne Weber, *Max Weber* (Tuebingen: J. C. B. Mohr, 1926), pp. 347–8. See also Max Weber, Gesammelte Aufsätze zur Religionssociology (Tuebingen: J. C. B. Mohr, 1920), p. 252.

action must be judged and directed, the contemporary connection between interest and the nation state is a product of history, and its therefore bound to disappear in the course of history. Nothing in the realist position militates against the assumption that the present division of the political world into nation states will be replaced by larger units of a quite different character, more in keeping with the technical potentialities and the moral requirements of the contemporary world.

The realist parts company with other schools of thought before the all-important question of how the comtemporary world is to be transformed. The realist is persuaded that this transformation can be achieved only through the workmanlike manipulation of the perennial forces that have shaped the past as they will the future. The realist cannot be persuaded that we can bring about that transformation by confronting a political reality that has its own laws with an abstract ideal that refuses to take those laws into account.

4. Political realism is aware of the moral significance of political action. It is also aware of the ineluctable tension between the moral command and the requirements of successful political action. And it is unwilling to gloss over and obliterate that tension and thus to obfuscate both the moral and the political issue by making it appear as though the stark facts of politics were morally more satisfying than they actually are, and the moral law less exacting than it actually is.

Realism maintains that universal moral principles cannot be applied to the actions of states in their abstract universal formulation, but that they must be filtered through the concrete circumstances of time and place. The individual may say for himself: "Fiat *justitia, pereat mundus* (Let justice be done, even if the world perish)," but the state has no right to say so in the name of those who are in its care. Both individual and state must judge political action by universal moral principles, such as that of liberty. Yet while the individual has a moral right to sacrifice himself in defense of such a moral principle, the state has no right to let its moral disapprobation of the infringement of liberty get in the way of successful political action, itself inspired by the moral principle of national survival. There can be no political morality without prudence; that is without consideration of the political consequences of seemingly moral action. Realism, then, considers prudence—the weighing of the consequences of alternative political actions—to be supreme virtue in politics. Ethics in the abstract judges action by its conformity with the moral law; political ethics judges action by its political consequences. Classical and medieval philosophy knew this, and so did Lincoln when he said.

> I do the very best I know how, the very best I can, and I mean to keep doing so until the end. If the end brings me out all right, what is said against me won't amount to anything. If the end brings me out wrong, ten angels swearing I was right would make no difference.

5. Political realism refuses to identify the moral aspirations of a particular nation with the moral laws that govern the universe. As it distinguishes between truth and opinion, so it distinguishes between truth and idolatry. All nations are tempted—and few have been able to resist the temptation for long—to clothe their own particular aspirations and actions in the moral purposes of the universe. To know that nations are subject to the moral law is one thing, while to pretend to know with certainty what is good and evil in the relations among nations is quite another. There is a world of difference between the belief that all nations stand under the judgment of God, inscrutable to the human mind, and the blasphemous conviction that God is always on one's side and that what one wills oneself cannot fail to be willed by God also.

The lighthearted equation between a particular nationalism and the counsels of Providence is morally indefensible, for it is that very sin of pride against which the Greek tragedians and the Biblical prophets have warned rulers and ruled. That equation is also politically pernicious, for it is liable to engender the distortion in judgment which, in the blindness of crusading frenzy, destroys nations and civilization—in the name of moral principle, ideal, or God himself.

On the other hand, it is exactly the concept of interest defined in terms of power that saves us from both that moral excess and that political folly. For if we look at all nations, our own included, as political entities pursuing their respective interests defined in terms of power, we are able to do justice to all of them. And we are able to do justice to all of them in a dual sense: We are able to judge other nations as we judge our own and, having judged them in this fashion, we are then capable of pursuing policies that respect the interests of other nations, while protecting and promoting those of our own. Moderation in policy cannot fail to reflect the moderation of moral judgment.

6. The difference, then, between political realism and other schools of thought is real, and it is profound. However much the theory of political realism may have been misunderstood and misinterpreted, there is no gainsaying its distinctive intellectual and moral attitude to matters political.

Intellectually, the political realist maintains the autonomy of the political sphere, as the economist, the lawyer, the moralist maintain theirs. He thinks in terms of interest defined as power, as the economist thinks in terms of interest as wealth; the lawyer, of the conformity of action with legal rules; the moralist, of the conformity of action with moral principles. The economist asks: "How does this policy affect the wealth of society, or a segment of it?" The lawyer asks: "Is this policy in accord with the rules of law?" The moralist asks: "Is this policy in accord with moral principles?" And the political realist asks: "How does this policy affect the power of the nation?" (Or of the federal government, of Congress, of the party, of agriculture, as the case may be.)

The political realist is not unaware of the existence and relevance of standards of thought other than political ones. As political realist, he cannot but subordinate these other standards to those of politics. And he parts company with other schools when they impose standards of thought appropriate to other spheres upon the political sphere.[3] . . .

This realist defense of the autonomy of the political sphere against its subversion by other modes of thought does not imply disregard for the existence and importance of these other modes of thought. It rather implies that each should be assigned its proper sphere and function. Political realism is based upon a pluralistic conception of human nature. Real man is a composite of "economic man," "political man," "moral man," "religious man," etc. A man who was nothing but "political man" would be a beast, for he would be completely lacking in moral restraints. A man who was nothing but "moral man" would be a fool, for he would be completely lacking in prudence. A man who was nothing but "religious man" would be a saint, for he would be completely lacking in worldly desires.

Recognizing that these different facets of human nature exist, political realism also recognizes that in order to understand one of them one has to deal with it on its own terms. That is to say, if I want to understand "religious man," I must for the time being abstract from the other aspects of human nature and deal with its religious aspect as if it were the only one. Furthermore, I must apply to the religious sphere the standards of thought appropriate to it, always remaining aware of the existence of other standards and their actual influence upon the religious qualities of man. What is true of this facet of human nature is true of all the others. No modern economist, for instance, would conceive of his science and its relations to other sciences of man in any other way. It is exactly through such a process of emancipation from other standards of thought, and the development of one appropriate to its subject matter, that economics has developed as an autonomous theory of the economic activities of man. To contribute to a similar development in the field of politics is indeed the purpose of political realism.

It is in the nature of things that a theory of politics which is based upon such principles will not meet with unanimous approval—nor does, for that matter, such a foreign policy. For theory and policy alike run counter to two trends in our culture which are not able to reconcile themselves to the assumptions and results of a rational, objective theory of politics. One of these trends disparages the role of power in society

---

[3]See the other examples discussed in Hans J. Morgenthau, "Another 'Great Debate': The National Interest of the United States," *The American Political Science Review*, Vol. XLVI (December 1952), pp. 979 ff. See also Hans J. Morgenthau, *Politics in the 20th Century*, Vol. I, *The Decline of Democratic Politics* (Chicago: University of Chicago Press, 1962), pp. 79 ff; and abridged edition (Chicago: University of Chicago Press, 1971), pp. 204 ff.

on grounds that stem from the experience and philosophy of the nineteenth century; we shall address ourselves to this tendency later in greater detail.[4] The other trend, opposed to the realist theory and practice of politics, stems from the very relationship that exists, and must exist, between the human mind and the political sphere. For reasons that we shall discuss later[5] the human mind in its day-by-day operations cannot bear to look the truth of politics straight in the face. It must disguise, distort, belittle, and embellish the truth—the more so, the more the individual is actively involved in the processes of politics, and particularly in those of international politics. For only by deceiving himself about the nature of politics and the role he plays on the political scene is man able to live contentedly as a political animal with himself and his fellow men.

Thus it is inevitable that a theory which tries to understand international politics as it actually is and as it ought to be in view of its intrinsic nature, rather than as people would like to see it, must overcome a psychological resistance that most other branches of learning need not face. A book devoted to the theoretical understanding of international politics therefore requires a special explanation and justification.

[4]See pages 33 ff.
[5]See pages 89 ff.

THE INTERNATIONAL SYSTEM AND BALANCES OF POWER

KENNETH WALTZ

I

A system is composed of a structure and of interacting units. The structure is the system-wide component that makes it possible to think of the system as a whole. The problem, unsolved by the systems theorists considered in Chapter 3, is to contrive a definition of structure free of the attributes and the interactions of units. Definitions of structure must leave aside, or abstract from, the characteristics of units, their behavior, and their interactions. Why must those obviously important matters be omitted? They must be omitted so that we can distinquish between variables at the level of the units and variables at the level of the system. The problem is to develop theoretically useful concepts to replace the vague and varying systemic notions that are customarily employed—notions such as environment, situation, context, and milieu. Structure is a useful concept if it gives clear and fixed meaning to such vague and varying terms.

We know what we have to omit from any definition of structure if the definition is to be useful theoretically. Abstracting from the attributes of units means leaving aside questions about the kinds of political leaders, social and economic institutions, and ideological commitments states may have. Abstracting from relations means leaving aside questions about the cultural, economic, political, and military interactions of states. To say what is to be left out does not indicate what is to be put in. The negative point is important nevertheless because the instruction to omit attributes is often violated and the instruction to omit interactions almost always goes unobserved. But if attributes and interactions are omitted, what is left? The question is answered by considering the double meaning of the term "relation." As S. F. Nadel points out, ordinary language obscures a distinction that is important in theory. "Relation" is used to mean both the interaction of units and the positions they occupy via-à-vis each other (1957, pp. 8–11). To define a structure requires ignoring how units relate with one another (how they interact) and concentrating on how they stand in relation to one another (how they are arranged or positioned). Interactions, as I have insisted, take place at the level of the units. How units stand in relation to one another, the way they are arranged or positioned, is not a property of the units. The arrangement of units is a property of the system.

By leaving aside the personality of actors, their behavior, and their interactions, one arrives at a purely positional picture of society. Three propositions follow from this. First, structures may endure while personality, behavior, and interactions vary widely. Structure is sharply distinguished from actions and interactions. Second, a structural definition applies to realms of widely different substance so long as the arrangement of parts is similar (cf. Nadel, pp. 104–109). Third, because this is so, theories developed for one realm may with some modification be applicable to other realms as well.

A structure is defined by the arrangement of its parts. Only changes of arrangement are structural changes. A system is composed of a structure and of interacting parts. Both the structure and the parts are concepts, related to, but not identical with, real agents and agencies. Structure is not something we see. The anthropologist Meyer Fortes put this well. "When we describe structure," he said, "we are in the realm of grammar and syntax, not of the spoken word. We discern structure in the 'concrete reality' of social events only by virtue of having first established structure by abstraction from 'concrete reality'" (Fortes 1949, p. 56). Since structure is an abstraction, it cannot be defined by enumerating material characteristics of the system. It must instead be defined by the arrangement of the system's parts and by the principle of that arrangement.

This is an uncommon way to think of political systems, although structural notions are familiar enough to anthropologists, to economists, and even to political scientists who deal not with political systems in general but with such of their parts as political parties and bureaucracies. In defining structures, anthropologists do not ask about the habits and the values of the chiefs and the Indians; economists do not ask about the organization and the efficiency of particular firms and the exchanges among them; and political scientists do not ask about the personalities and the interests of the individuals occupying various offices. They leave aside the qualities, the motives, and the interactions of the actors, not because those matters are uninteresting or unimportant, but because they want to know how the qualities, the motives, and the interactions of tribal units are affected by tribal structure, how decisions of firms are influenced by their market, and how people's behavior is molded by the offices they hold.

II

The concept of structure is based on the fact that units differently juxtaposed and combined behave differently and in interacting produce different outcomes. I first want to show how internal political structure can be defined. In a book on international-political theory, domestic political structure has to be examined in order to draw a distinction between expectations about behavior and outcomes in the internal and external realms. Moreover, considering domestic political structure now will make the elusive international-political structure easier to catch later on.

Structure defines the arrangement, or the ordering, of the parts of a system. Structure is not a collection of political institutions but rather the arrangement of them. How is the arrangement defined? The constitution of a state describes some parts of the arrangement, but political structures as they develop are not identical with formal constitutions. In defining structures, the first question to answer is this: What is the principle by which the parts are arranged?

Domestic politics is hierarchically ordered. The units—institutions and agencies—stand vis-à-vis each other in relations of super- and subordination. The ordering principle of a system gives the first, and basic, bit of information about how the parts of a realm are related to each other. In a polity the hierarchy of offices is by no means completely articulated, nor are all ambiguities about relations of super- and subordination removed. Nevertheless, political actors are formally differentiated according to the degrees of their authority, and their distinct functions are specified. By "specified" I do not mean that the law of the land fully describes the duties that different agencies perform, but only that broad agreement prevails on the tasks that various parts of a government are to undertake and on the extent of the power they legitimately wield. Thus Congress supplies the military forces; the President commands them. Congress makes the laws; the executive branch enforces them; agencies administer laws; judges interpret them. Such specification of roles and differentiation of functions is found in any state, the more fully so as the state is more highly developed. The specification of functions of formally differentiated parts gives the second bit of structural information. This second part of the definition adds some content to the structure, but only enough to say more fully how the units stand in relation to one another. The roles and the functions of the British Prime Minister and Parliament, for example, differ from those of the American President and Congress. When offices are juxtaposed and functions are combined in different ways, different behaviors and outcomes result, as I shall shortly show.

The placement of units in relation to one another is not fully defined by a system's ordering principle and by the formal differentiation of its parts. The standing of the units also changes with changes in their relative capabilities. In the performance of their functions, agencies may gain capabilities or lose them. The relation of Prime Minister to Parliament and of President to Congress depends on, and varies with, their relative capabilities. The third part of the definition of structure acknowledges that even while specified functions remain unchanged, units come to stand in different relation to each other through changes in relative capability.

A domestic political structure is thus defined, first, according to the principle by which it is ordered, second, by specification of the functions of formally differentiated units; and third, by the distribution of capabilities across those units. Structure is a highly abstract notion, but the definition of structure does not abstract from everything. To do so would be to leave everything aside and to include nothing at all. The three-part definition of structure includes only what is required to show how the units of the system are positioned or arranged. Everything else is omitted. Concern for tradition and culture, analysis of the character and personality of political actors, consideration of the conflictive and accommodative processes of politics, description of the making and execution of policy—all such matters are left aside. Their omission does not imply their unimportance. They are omitted because we want to figure out the expected effects of structure on process and of process on structure. That can be done only if structure and process are distinctly defined. . . .

III

I defined domestic political structures first by the principle according to which they are organized or ordered, second by the differentiation of units and the specification of their functions, and third by the distribution of capabilities across units. Let us see how the three terms of the definition apply to international politics.

1. Ordering Principles

Structural questions are questions about the arrangement of the parts of a system. The parts of domestic political systems stand in relations of super- and subordination. Some are entitled to command; others are required to obey. Domestic systems are centralized and hierarchic. The parts of international-political systems stand in relations of coordination. Formally, each is the equal of all the others. None is entitled to command; none is required to obey. International systems are decentralized and anarchic. The ordering principles of the two structures are distinctly different, indeed, contrary to each other. Domestic political structures have governmental institutions and offices as their concrete counterparts. International politics, in contrast, has been called "politics in the absence of government" (Fox 1959, p. 35). International organizations do exist, and in ever-growing numbers. Supranational agents able to act effectively, however, either themselves acquire some of the attributes and capabilities of states, as did the medieval papacy in the era of Innocent III, or they soon reveal their inability to act in important ways except with the support, or at least the acquiescence, of the principal states concerned with the matters at hand. Whatever elements of authority emerge internationally are barely once removed from the capability that provides the foundation for the appearance of those elements. Authority quickly reduces to a particular expression of capability. In the absence of agents with system-wide authority, formal relations of super- and subordination fail to develop.

The first term of a structural definition states the principle by which the system is ordered. Structure is an organizational concept. The prominent characteristic of international politics, however, seems to be the lack of order and of organization. How can one think of international politics as being any kind of an order at all? The anarchy of politics internationally is often referred to. If structure is an organizational concept, the terms "structure" and "anarchy" seem to be in contradiction. If international politics is "politics in the absence of government," what are we in the presence of? In looking for international structure, one is brought face to face with the invisible, an uncomfortable position to be in.

The problem is this: how to conceive of an order without an orderer and of organizational effects where formal organization is lacking. Because these are difficult questions, I shall answer them through analogy with microeconomic theory. Reasoning by analogy is helpful where one can move from a domain for which theory is well developed to one where it is not. Reasoning by analogy is permissible where different domains are structurally similar.

Classical economic theory, developed by Adam Smith and his followers, is microtheory. Political scientists tend to think that microtheory is theory about small-scale matters, a usage that ill accords with its established meaning. The term "micro" in economic theory indicates the way in which the theory is constructed rather than the scope of the matters it pertains to. Microeconomic theory describes how an order is spontaneously formed from the self-interested acts and interactions of individual units—in this case, persons and firms. The theory then turns upon the two central concepts of the economic units and of the market. Economic units and economic markets are concepts, not descriptive realities or concrete entities. This must be emphasized since from the early eighteenth century to the present, from the sociologist Auguste Comte to the psychologist George Katona, economic theory has been faulted because its assumptions fail to correspond with realities (Martineau 1853, II, 51–53; Katona 1953). Unrealistically, economic theorists conceive of an economy operating in isolation from its society and polity. Unrealistically, economists assume that the economic world is the whole of the world. Unrealistically, economists think of the acting unit, the famous "economic man," as a single-minded profit maximizer. They single out one aspect of man and leave aside the wondrous variety of human life. As any moderately sensible economist knows, "economic man" does not exist. Anyone who asks businessmen how they make their decisions will find that the assumption that men are economic maximizers grossly distorts their characters. The assumption that men behave as economic men, which is known to be false as a descriptive statement, turns out to be useful in the construction of theory.

Markets are the second major concept invented by microeconomic theorists. Two general questions must be asked about markets: How are they formed? How do they work? The answer to the first question is this: The market of a decentralized economy is individualist in origin, spontaneously generated, and unintended. The market arises out of the activities of separate units—persons and firms—whose aims and efforts are directed not toward creating an order but rather toward fulfilling their own internally defined interests by whatever means they can muster. The individual unit acts for itself. From the coaction of like units emerges a structure that affects and constrains all of them. Once formed, a market becomes a force in itself, and a force that the constitutive units acting singly or in small numbers cannot control. Instead, in lesser or greater degree as market conditions vary, the creators become the creatures of the market that their activity gave rise to. Adam Smith's great achievement was to show how self-interested, greed-driven actions may produce good social outcomes if only political and social conditions permit free competition. If a laissez-faire economy is harmonious, it is so because the intentions of actors do *not* correspond with the outcomes their actions produce. What intervenes between the actors and the objects of their action in order to thwart their purposes? To account for the unexpectedly favorable outcomes of selfish acts, the concept of a market is brought into play. Each unit seeks its own good; the result of a number of units simultaneously doing so transcends the motives and the aims of the separate units. Each would like to work less hard and price his product higher. Taken together, all have to work harder and price their products lower. Each firm seeks to increase its profit; the result of many firms doing so drives the profit rate downward. Each man seeks his own end, and, in doing so, produces a result that was no part of his intention. Out of the mean ambition of its members, the greater good of society is produced.

The market is a cause interposed between the economic actors and the results they produce. It conditions their calculations, their behaviors, and their interactions. It is not an agent in the sense of *A* being the agent that produces outcome c. Rather it is a structural cause. A market constrains the units that comprise it from taking certain actions and disposes them toward taking others. The market, created by self-directed interacting economic units, selects behaviors according to their consequences (cf. Chapter 4, part III). The market rewards some with high profits and assigns others to bankruptcy. Since a market is not an institution or an agent in any concrete or palpable sense, such statements become impressive only if they can be reliably inferred from a theory as part of a set of more elaborate expectations. They can be. Microeconomic theory explains how an economy operates and why certain effects are to be expected. It generates numerous "if-then" statements that can more or less easily be checked. Consider, for example, the following simple but important propositions. If the money demand for a commodity rises, then so will its price. If price rises, then so will profits. If profits rise, then capital will be attracted and production will increase. If production increases, then price will fall to the level that returns profits to the producers of the commodity at the prevailing rate. This sequence of statements could be extended and refined, but to do so would not serve my purpose. I want to point out that although the stated expectations are now commonplace, they could not be arrived at by economists working in a pre-theoretic era. All of the statements are, of course, made at an appropriate level of generality. They require an "other things being equal" stipulation. They apply, as do statements inferred from any theory, only to the extent that the conditions contemplated by the theory obtain. They are idealizations, and so they are never fully borne out in practice. Many things—social customs, political interventions—will in fact interfere with the theoretically predicted outcomes. Though interferences have to be allowed for, it is nevertheless extraordinarily useful to know what to expect in general.

International-political systems, like economic markets, are formed by the coaction of self-regarding units. International structures are defined in terms of the primary political units of an era, be they city states, empires, or nations. Structures emerge from the coexistence of states. No state intends to participate in the formation of a structure by which it and others will be constrained. International-political systems, like economic markets, are individualist in origin, spontaneously generated, and unintended. In both systems, structures are formed by the coaction of their units. Whether those units live, prosper, or die depends on their own efforts. Both systems are formed and maintained on a principle of self-help that applies to the units. To say that the two realms are structurally similar is not to proclaim their identity. Economically, the self-help principle applies within governmentally contrived limits. Market economies are hedged about in ways that channel energies constructively. One may think of pure food-and-drug standards, antitrust laws, securities and exchange regulations, laws against shooting a competitor, and rules forbidding false claims in advertising. International politics is more nearly a realm in which anything goes. International politics is structurally similar to a market economy insofar as the self-help principle is allowed to operate in the latter.

In a microtheory, whether of international politics or of economics, the motivation of the actors is assumed rather than realistically described. I assume that states seek to ensure their survival. The assumption is a radical simplification made for the sake of constructing a theory. The question to ask of the assumption, as ever, is not whether it is true but whether it is the most sensible and useful one that can be made. Whether it is a useful assumption depends on whether a theory based on the assumption can be contrived, a theory from which important consequences not otherwise obvious can be inferred. Whether it is a sensible assumption can be directly discussed.

Beyond the survival motive, the aims of states may be endlessly varied; they may range from the ambition to conquer the world to the desire merely to be left alone. Survival is a prerequisite to achieving any goals that states may have, other than the goal of promoting their own disappearance as political entities. The survival motive is taken as the ground of action in a world where the security of states is not assured, rather than as a realistic description of the impulse that lies behind every act of state. The assumption allows for the fact that no state always acts exclusively to ensure its survival. It allows for the fact that some states may persistently seek goals that they value more highly than survival; they may, for example, prefer amalgamation with other states to their own survival in form. It allows for the fact that in pursuit of its security no state will act with perfect knowledge and wisdom—if indeed we could know what those terms might mean. Some systems have high requirements for their functioning. Traffic will not flow if most, but not all, people drive on the proper side of the road. If necessary, strong measures have to be taken to ensure that everyone does so. Other systems have medium requirements. Elevators in skyscrapers are planned so that they can handle the passenger load if most people take express elevators for the longer runs and locals only for the shorter ones. But if some people choose locals for long runs because the speed of the express makes them dizzy, the system will not break down. To keep it going, most, but not all, people have to act as expected. Some systems, market economies and international politics among them, make still lower demands. Traffic systems are designed on the knowledge that the system's requirements will be enforced. Elevators are planned with extra capacity to allow for human vagaries. Competitive economic and international-political systems work differently. Out of the interactions of their parts they develop structures that reward or punish behavior that conforms more or less nearly to what is required of one who wishes to succeed in the system. Recall my description of the constraints of the British parliamentary system. Why should a would-be Prime Minister not strike out on a bold course of his own? Why not behave in ways markedly different from those of typical British political leaders? Anyone can, of course, and some who aspire to become Prime Ministers do so. They rarely come to the top. Except in deepest crisis, the system selects others to hold the highest office.

One may behave as one likes to. Patterns of behavior nevertheless emerge, and they derive from the structural constraints of the system.

Actors may perceive the structure that constrains them and understand how it serves to reward some kinds of behavior and to penalize others. But then again they either may not see it or, seeing it, may for any of many reasons fail to conform their actions to the patterns that are most often rewarded and least often punished. To say, that "the structure selects" means simply that those who conform to accepted and successful practices more often rise to the top and are likelier to stay there. The game one has to win is defined by the structure that determines the kind of player who is likely to prosper.

Where selection according to behavior occurs, no enforced standard of behavior is required for the system to operate, although either system may work better if some standards are enforced or accepted. Internationally, the environment of states' action, or the structure of their system, is set by the fact that some states prefer survival over other ends obtainable in the short run and act with relative efficiency to achieve that end. States may alter their behavior because of the structure they form through interaction with other states. But in what ways and why? To answer these questions we must complete the definition of international structure.

2. The Character of the Units

The second term in the definition of domestic political structure specifies the functions performed by differentiated units. Hierarchy entails relations of super- and subordination among a system's parts, and that implies their differentiation. In defining domestic political structure the second term, like the first and third, is needed because each term points to a possible source of structural variation. The states that are the units of international-political systems are not formally differentiated by the functions they perform. Anarchy entails relations of coordination among a system's units, and that implies their sameness. The second term is not needed in defining international-political structure, because so long as anarchy endures, states remain like units. International structures vary only through a change of organizing principle or, failing that, through variations in the capabilities of units. Nevertheless I shall discuss these like units here, because it is by their interactions that international-political structures are generated.

Two questions arise: Why should states be taken as the units of the system? Given a wide variety of states, how can one call them "like units"? Questioning the choice of states as the primary units of international-political systems became popular in the 1960s and '70s as it was at the turn of the century. Once one understands what is logically involved, the issue is easily resolved. Those who question the state-centric view do so for two main reasons. First, states are not the only actors of importance on the international scene. Second, states are declining in importance, and other actors are gaining, or so it is said. Neither reason is cogent, as the following discussion shows.

States are not and never have been the only international actors. But then structures are defined not by all of the actors that flourish within them but by the major ones. In defining a system's structure one chooses one or some of the infinitely many objects comprising the system and defines its structure in terms of them. For international-political systems, as for any system, one must first decide which units to take as being the parts of the system. Here the economic analogy will help again. The structure of a market is defined by the number of firms competing. If many roughly equal firms contend, a condition of perfect competition is approximated. If a few firms dominate the market, competition is said to be oligopolistic even though many smaller firms may also be in the field. But we are told that definitions of this sort cannot be applied to international politics because of the interpenetration of states, because of their inability to control the environment of their action, and because rising multinational corporations and other nonstate actors are difficult to regulate and may rival some states in influence. The importance of nonstate actors and the extent of transnational activities are obvious. The conclusion that the state-centric conception of international politics is made obsolete by them does not follow. That economists and economically minded political scientists have thought that it does is ironic. The irony lies in the fact that all of the reasons given for scrapping the state-centric concept can be restated more strongly and applied to firms. Firms competing with numerous others have no hope of controlling their market, and oligopolistic firms constantly struggle with imperfect success to do so. Firms interpenetrate, merge, and buy each other up at a merry pace. Moreover, firms are constantly threatened and regulated by, shall we say, "nonfirm" actors. Some governments encourage concentration; others work to prevent it. The market structure of parts of an economy may move from a wider to a narrower competition or may move in the opposite direction, but whatever the extent and the frequency of change, market structures, generated by the interaction of firms, are defined in terms of them.

Just as economists define markets in terms of firms, so I define international-political structures in terms of states. If Charles P. Kindleberger were right in saying that "the nation-state is just about through as an economic unit" (1969, p. 207), then the structure of international politics would have to be redefined. That would be necessary because economic capabilities cannot be separated from the other capabilities of states. The distinction frequently drawn between matters of high and low politics is misplaced. States use economic means for military and political ends; and military and political means for the achievement of economic interests.

An amended version of Kindleberger's statement may hold: Some states may be nearly washed up as economic entities, and others not. That poses no problem for international-political theory since international politics is mostly about inequalities anyway. So long as the major states are the major actors, the structure of international politics is defined in terms of them. That theoretical statement is of course borne out in practice. States set the scene in which they, along with nonstate actors, stage their dramas or carry on their humdrum affairs. Though they may choose to interfere little in the affairs of nonstate actors for long periods of time, states nevertheless set the terms of the intercourse, whether by passively permitting informal rules to develop or by actively intervening to change rules that no longer suit them. When the crunch comes, states remake the rules by which other actors operate. Indeed, one may be struck by the ability of weak states to impede the operation of strong international corporations and by the attention the latter pay to the wishes of the former.

It is important to consider the nature of transnational movements, the extent of their penetration, and the conditions that make it harder or easier for states to control them (see Chapter 7). But the adequate study of these matters, like others, requires finding or developing an adequate approach to the study of international politics. Two points should be made about latter-day transnational studies. First, students of transnational phenomena have developed no distinct theory of their subject matter or of international politics in general. They have drawn on existing theories, whether economic or political. Second, that they have developed no distinct theory is quite proper, for a theory that denies the central role of states will be needed only if nonstate actors develop to the point of rivaling or surpassing the great powers, not just a few of the minor ones. They show no sign of doing that.

The study of transnational movements deals with important factual questions, which theories can help one to cope with. But the help will not be gained if it is thought that nonstate actors call the state-centric view of the world into question. To say that major states maintain their central importance is not to say that other actors of some importance do not exist. The "state-centric" phrase suggests something about the system's structure. Transnational movements are among the processes that go on within it. That the state-centric view is so often questioned merely reflects the difficulty political scientists have in keeping the distinction between structures and processes clearly and constantly in mind.

States are the units whose interactions form the structure of international-political systems. They will long remain so. The death rate among states is remarkably low. Few states die; many firms do. Who is likely to be around 100 years from now—the United States, the Soviet Union, France, Egypt, Thailand, and Uganda? Or Ford, IBM, Shell, Unilever, and Massey-Ferguson? I would bet on the states, perhaps even on Uganda. But what does it mean to refer to the 150-odd states of today's world, which certainly form a motley collection, as being "like units"? Many students of international politics are bothered by the description. To call states "like units" is to say that each state is like all other states in being an autonomous political unit. It is another way of saying that states are sovereign. But sovereignty is also a bothersome concept. Many believe, as the anthropologist M. G. Smith has said, that "in a system of sovereign states no state is sovereign."* The error lies in identifying the sovereignty of states with their ability to do as they wish. To say that states are sovereign is not to say that they can do as they please, that they are free of others' influence, that they are able to get what they want. Sovereign states may be hardpressed all around, constrained to act in ways they would like to avoid, and able to do hardly anything just as they would like to. The sovereignty of states has never entailed their insulation from the effects of other states' actions. To be sovereign and to be dependent are not contradictory conditions. Sovereign states have seldom led free and easy lives. What then is sovereignty? To say that a state is sovereign means that it decides for itself how it will cope with its internal and external problems, including whether or not to seek assistance from others and in doing so to limit its freedom by making commitments to them. States develop their own strategies, chart their own courses, make their own decisions about how to meet whatever needs they experience and whatever desires they develop. It is no more contradictory to say that sovereign states are always constrained and often tightly so than it is to say that free individuals often make decisions under the heavy pressure of events.

Each state, like every other state, is a sovereign political entity. And yet the differences across states, from Costa Rica to the Soviet Union, from Gambia to the United States, are immense. States are alike, and they are also different. So are corporations, apples, universities, and people. Whenever we put two or more objects in the same category, we are saying that they are alike not in all respects but in some. No two objects in this world are identical, yet they can often be usefully compared and combined. "You can't add apples and oranges" is an old saying that seems to be especially popular among salesmen who do not want you to compare their wares with others. But we all know that the trick of adding dissimilar objects is to express the result in terms of a category that comprises them. Three apples plus four oranges equals seven pieces of fruit. The only interesting question is whether the category that classifies objects according to their common qualities is useful. One can add up a large number of widely varied objects and say that one has eight million things, but seldom need one do that.

States vary widely in size, wealth, power, and form. And yet variations in these and in other respects are variations among like units. In what way are they like units? How can they be placed in a single category? States are alike in the tasks that they face, though not in their abilities to perform them. The differences are of capability,

---

*Smith should know better. Translated into terms that he has himself so effectively used, to say that states are sovereign is to say that they are segments of a plural society (1966, p. 122; cf. 1956).

not of function. States perform or try to perform tasks, most of which are common to all of them; the ends they aspire to are similar. Each state duplicates the activities of other states at least to a considerable extent. Each state has its agencies for making, executing, and interpreting laws and regulations, for raising revenues, and for defending itself. Each state supplies out of its own resources and by its own means most of the food, clothing, housing, transportation, and amenities consumed and used by its citizens. All states, except the smallest ones, do much more of their business at home than abroad. One has to be impressed with the functional similarity of states and, now more than ever before, with the similar lines their development follows. From the rich to the poor states, from the old to the new ones, nearly all of them take a larger hand in matters of economic regulation, of education, health, and housing, of culture and the arts, and so on almost endlessly. The increase of the activities of states is a strong and strikingly uniform international trend. The functions of states are similar, and distinctions among them arise principally from their varied capabilities. National politics consists of differentiated units performing specified functions. International politics consists of like units duplicating one another's activities.

3. The Distribution of Capabilities

The parts of a hierarchic system are related to one another in ways that are determined both by their functional differentiation and by the extent of their capabilities. The units of an anarchic system are functionally undifferentiated. The units of such an order are then distinguished primarily by their greater or lesser capabilities for performing similar tasks. This states formally what students of international politics have long noticed. The great powers of an era have always been marked off from others by practitioners and theorists alike. Students of national government make such distinctions as that between parliamentary and presidential systems; governmental systems differ in form. Students of international politics make distinctions between international-political systems only according to the number of their great powers. The structure of a system changes with changes in the distribution of capabilities across the system's units. And changes in structure change expectations about how the units of the system will behave and about the outcomes their interactions will produce. Domestically, the differentiated parts of a system may perform similar tasks. We know from observing the American government that executives sometimes legislate and legislatures sometimes execute. Internationally, like units sometimes perform different tasks. Why they do so, and how the likelihood of their doing so varies with their capabilities, are matters treated at length in the last three chapters. Meanwhile, two problems should be considered.

    The first problem is this: Capability tells us something about units. Defining structure partly in terms of the distribution of capabilities seems to violate my instruction to keep unit attributes out of structural definitions. As I remarked earlier, structure is a highly but not entirely abstract concept. The maximum of abstraction allows a minimum of content, and that minimum is what is needed to enable one to say how the units stand in relation to one another. States are differently placed by their power. And yet one may wonder why only *capability* is included in the third part of the definition, and not such characteristics as ideology, form of government, peacefulness, bellicosity, or whatever. The answer is this: Power is estimated by comparing the capabilities of a number of units. Although capabilities are attributes of units, the distribution of capabilities across units is not. The distribution of capabilities is not a unit attribute, but rather a system-wide concept. Again, the parallel with market theory is exact. Both firms and states are like units. Through all of their variations in form, firms share certain qualities: They are self-regarding units that, within governmentally imposed limits, decide for themselves how to cope with their environment and just how to work for their ends. Variation of structure is introduced, not through differences in the character and function of units, but only through distinctions made among them according to their capabilities.

The second problem is this: Though relations defined in terms of interactions must be excluded from structural definitions, relations defined in terms of groupings of states do seem to tell us something about how states are placed in the system. Why not specify how states stand in relation to one another by considering the alliances they form? Would doing so not be comparable to defining national political structures partly in terms of how presidents and prime ministers are related to other political agents? It would not be. Nationally as internationally, structural definitions deal with the relation of agents and agencies in terms of the organization of realms and not in terms of the accommodations and conflicts that may occur within them or the groupings that may now and then form. Parts of a government may draw together or pull apart, may oppose each other or cooperate in greater or lesser degree. These are the relations that form and dissolve within a system rather than structural alterations that mark a change from one system to another. This is made clear by an example that runs nicely parallel to the case of alliances. Distinguishing systems of political parties according to their number is common. A multiparty system changes if, say, eight parties become two, but not if two groupings of the eight form merely for the occasion of fighting an election. By the same logic, an international-political system in which three or more great powers have split into two alliances remains a multipolar system—structurally distinct from a bipolar system, a system in which no third power is able to challenge the top two. In defining market structure, information about the particular quality of firms is not called for, nor is information about their interactions, short of the point at which the formal merger of firms significantly reduces their number. In the definition of market structure, firms are not identified and their interactions are not described. To take the qualities of firms and the nature of their interactions as being parts of market structure would be to say that whether a sector of an economy is oligopolistic or not depends on how the firms are organized internally and how they deal with one another, rather than simply on how many major firms coexist. Market structure is defined by counting firms; international-political structure, by counting states. In the counting, distinctions are made only according to capabilities.

In defining international-political structures we take states with whatever traditions, habits, objectives, desires, and forms of government they may have. We do not ask whether states are revolutionary or legitimate, authoritarian or democratic, ideological or pragmatic. We abstract from every attribute of states except their capabilities. Nor in thinking about structure do we ask about the relations of states—their feelings of friendship and hostility, their diplomatic exchanges, the alliances they form, and the extent of the contacts and exchanges among them. We ask what range of expectations arises merely from looking at the type of order that prevails among them and at the distribution of capabilities within that order. We abstract from any particular qualities of states and from all of their concrete connections. What emerges is a positional picture, a general description of the ordered overall arrangement of a society written in terms of the placement of units rather than in terms of their qualities. . . .

ANARCHIC ORDERS AND BALANCES OF POWER

I

1. Violence at Home and Abroad

The state among states, it is often said, conducts its affairs in the brooding shadow of violence. Because some states may at any time use force, all states must be prepared to do so—or live at the mercy of their militarily more vigorous neighbors. Among states, the state of nature is a state of war. This is meant not in the sense that war constantly occurs but in the sense that, with each state deciding for itself whether or not to use force, war may at any time break out. Whether in the family, the community, or the world at large, contact without at least occasional conflict is inconceivable; and the hope that in the absence of an agent to manage or to manipulate conflicting parties the use of force will always be avoided cannot be realistically entertained. Among men as among states, anarchy, or the absence of government, is associated with the occurrence of violence.

The threat of violence and the recurrent use of force are said to distinguish international from national affairs. But in the history of the world surely most rulers have had to bear in mind that their subjects might use force to resist or overthrow them. If the absence of government is associated with the threat of violence, so also is its presence. A haphazard list of national tragedies illustrates the point all too well. The most destructive wars of the hundred years following the defeat of Napoleon took place not among states but *within* them. Estimates of deaths in China's Taiping Rebellion, which began in 1851 and lasted 13 years, range as high as 20 million. In the American Civil War some 600 thousand people lost their lives. In more recent history, forced collectivization and Stalin's purges eliminated five million Russians, and Hitler exterminated six million Jews. In some Latin American countries, coups d'états and rebellions have been normal features of national life. Between 1948 and 1957, for example, 200 thousand Colombians were killed in civil strife. In the middle 1970s most inhabitants of Idi Amin's Uganda must have felt their lives becoming nasty, brutish, and short, quite as in Thomas Hobbes's state of nature. If such cases constitute aberrations, they are uncomfortably common ones. We easily lose sight of the fact that struggles to achieve and maintain power, to establish order, and to contrive a kind of justice within states, may be bloodier than wars among them.

If anarchy is identified with chaos, destruction, and death, then the distinction between anarchy and government does not tell us much. Which is more precarious: the life of a state among states, or of a government in relation to its subjects? The answer varies with time and place. Among some states at some times, the actual or expected occurrence of violence is low. Within some states at some times, the actual or expected occurrence of violence is high. The use of force, or the constant fear of its use, are not sufficient grounds for distinguishing international from domestic affairs. If the possible and the actual use of force mark both national and international orders, then no durable distinction between the two realms can be drawn in terms of the use or the nonuse of force. No human order is proof against violence.

To discover qualitative differences between internal and external affairs one must look for a criterion other than the occurrence of violence. The distinction between international and national realms of politics is not found in the use or the nonuse of force but in their different structures. But if the dangers of being violently attacked are greater, say, in taking an evening stroll through downtown Detroit than they are in picnicking along the French and German border, what practical difference does the difference of structure make? Nationally as internationally, contact generates conflict and at times issues in violence. The difference between national and international politics lies not in the use of force but in the different modes of organization for doing something about it. A government, ruling by some standard of legitimacy, arrogates to itself the right to use force—that is, to apply a variety of sanctions to control the use of force by its subjects. If some use private force, others may appeal to the government. A government has no monopoly on the use of force, as is all too evident. An effective government, however, has a monopoly on the *legitimate* use of force, and legitimate here means that public agents are organized to prevent and to counter the private use of force. Citizens need not prepare to defend themselves. Public agencies do that. A national system is not one of self-help. The international system is.

2. Interdependence and Integration

The political significance of interdependence varies depending on whether a realm is organized, with relations of authority specified and established, or remains formally unorganized. Insofar as a realm is formally organized, its units are free to specialize, to pursue their own interests without concern for developing the means of maintaining their identity and preserving their security in the presence of others. They are free to specialize because they have no reason to fear the increased interdependence that goes with specialization. If those who specialize most benefit most, then competition in specialization ensues. Goods are manufactured, grain is produced, law and order are maintained, commerce is conducted, and financial services are provided by people who ever more narrowly specialize. In simple economic terms, the cobbler depends on the tailor for his pants and the tailor on the cobbler for his shoes, and each would be ill-clad without the services of the other. In simple political terms, Kansas depends on Washington for protection and regulation and Washington depends on Kansas for beef and wheat. In saying that in such situations interdependence is close, one need not maintain that the one part could not learn to live without the other. One need only say that the cost of breaking the interdependent relation would be high. Persons and institutions depend heavily on one another because of the different tasks they perform and the different goods they produce and exchange. The parts of a polity bind themselves together by their differences (cf. Durkheim 1893, p. 212).

Differences between national and international structures are reflected in the ways the units of each system define their ends and develop the means for reaching them. In anarchic realms, like units coact. In hierarchic realms, unlike units interact. In an anarchic realm, the units are functionally similar and tend to remain so. Like units work to maintain a measure of independence and may even strive for autarchy. In a hierarchic realm, the units are differentiated, and they tend to increase the extent of their specialization. Differentiated units become closely interdependent, the more closely so as their specialization proceeds. Because of the difference of structure, interdependence within and interdependence among nations are two distinct concepts. So as to follow the logicians' admonition to keep a single meaning for a given term throughout one's discourse, I shall use "integration" to describe the condition within nations and "interdependence" to describe the condition among them.

Although states are like units functionally, they differ vastly in their capabilities. Out of such differences something of a division of labor develops (see Chapter 9). The division of labor across nations, however, is slight in comparison with the highly articulated division of labor within them. Integration draws the parts of a nation closely together. Interdependence among nations leaves them loosely connected. Although the integration of nations is often talked about, it seldom takes place. Nations could mutually enrich themselves by further dividing not just the labor that goes into the production of goods but also some of the other tasks they perform, such as political management and military defense. Why does their integration not take place? The structure of international politics limits the cooperation of states in two ways.

In a self-help system each of the units spends a portion of its effort, not in forwarding its own good, but in providing the means of protecting itself against others. Specialization in a system of divided labor works to everyone's advantage, though not equally so. Inequality in the expected distribution of the increased product works strongly against extension of the division of labor internationally. When faced with the possibility of cooperating for mutual gain, states that feel insecure must ask how the gain will be divided. They are compelled to ask not "Will both of us gain?" but "Who will gain more?" If an expected gain is to be divided, say, in the ratio of two to one, one state may use its disproportionate gain to implement a policy intended to damage or destroy the other. Even the prospect of large absolute gains for both parties does not elicit their cooperation so long as each fears how the other will use its increased capabilities. Notice that the impediments to collaboration may not lie in the character and the immediate intention of either party. Instead, the condition of insecurity—at the least, the uncertainty of each about the other's future intentions and actions—works against their cooperation.

In any self-help system, units worry about their survival, and the worry conditions their behavior. Oligopolistic markets limit the cooperation of firms in much the way that international-political structures limit the cooperation of states. Within rules laid down by governments, whether firms survive and prosper depends on their own efforts. Firms need not protect themselves physically against assaults from other firms. They are free to concentrate on their economic interests. As economic entities, however, they live in a self-help world. All want to increase profits. If they run undue risks in the effort to do so, they must expect to suffer the consequences. As William Fellner says, it is "impossible to maximize joint gains without the collusive handling of all relevant variables." And this can be accomplished only by "complete disarmament of the firms in relation to each other." But firms cannot sensibly disarm even to increase their profits. This statement qualifies, rather than contradicts, the assumption that firms aim at maximum profits. To maximize profits tomorrow as well as today, firms first have to survive. Pooling all resources implies, again as Fellner puts it, "discounting the future possibilities of all participating firms" (1949, p. 35). But the future cannot be discounted. The relative strength of firms changes over time in ways that cannot be foreseen. Firms are constrained to strike a compromise between maximizing their profits and minimizing the danger of their own demise. Each of two firms may be better off if one of them accepts compensation from the other in return for withdrawing from some part of the market. But a firm that accepts smaller markets in exchange for larger profits will be gravely disadvantaged if, for example, a price war should break out as part of a renewed struggle for markets. If possible, one must resist accepting smaller markets in return for larger profits (pp. 132, 217–18). "It is," Fellner insists, "not advisable to disarm in relation to one's rivals" (p. 199). Why not? Because "the potentiality of renewed warfare always exists" (p. 177). Fellner's reasoning is much like the reasoning that led Lenin to believe that capitalist countries would never be able to cooperate for their mutual enrichment in one vast imperialist enterprise. Like nations, oligopolistic firms must be more concerned with relative strength than with absolute advantage.

A state worries about a division of possible gains that may favor others more than itself. That is the first way in which the structure of international politics limits the cooperation of states. A state also worries lest it become dependent on others through cooperative endeavors and exchanges of goods and services. That is the second way in which the structure of international politics limits the cooperation of states. The more a state specializes, the more it relies on others to supply the materials and goods that it is not producing. The larger a state's imports and exports, the more it depends on others. The world's well-being would be increased if an ever more elaborate division of labor were developed, but states would thereby place themselves in situations of ever closer interdependence. Some states may not resist that. For small and ill-endowed states the costs of doing so are excessively high. But states that can resist becoming ever more enmeshed with others ordinarily do so in either or both of two ways. States that are heavily dependent, or closely interdependent, worry about securing that which they depend on. The high interdependence of states means that the states in question experience, or are subject to, the common vulnerability that high interdependence entails. Like other organizations, states seek to control what they depend on or to lessen the extent of their dependency. This simple thought explains quite a bit of the behavior of states: their imperial thrusts to widen the scope of their control and their autarchic strivings toward greater self-sufficiency.

Structures encourage certain behaviors and penalize those who do not respond to the encouragement. Nationally, many lament the extreme development of the division of labor, a development that results in the allocation of ever narrower tasks to individuals. And yet specialization proceeds, and its extent is a measure of the development of societies. In a formally organized realm a premium is put on each unit's being able to specialize in order to increase its value to others in a system of divided labor. The domestic imperative is "specialize"! Internationally, many lament the resources states spend unproductively for their own defense and the opportunities they miss to enhance the welfare of their people through cooperation with other states. And yet the ways of states change little. In an unorganized realm each unit's incentive is to put itself in a position to be able to take care of itself since no one else can be counted on to do so. The international imperative is "take care of yourself"! Some leaders of nations may understand that the well-being of all of them would increase through their participation in a fuller division of labor. But to act on the idea would be to act on a domestic imperative, an imperative that does not run internationally. What one might want to do in the absence of structural constraints is different from what one is encouraged to do in their presence. States do not willingly place themselves in situations of increased dependence. In a self-help system, considerations of security subordinate economic gain to political interest. . . .

ALLIANCES: BALANCING AND BANDWAGONING

STEPHEN WALT

When confronted by a significant external threat, states may either balance or bandwagon. *Balancing* is defined as allying with others against the prevailing threat; *bandwagoning* refers to alignment with the source of danger. Thus two distinct hypotheses about how states will select their alliance partners can be identified on the basis of whether the states ally against or with the principal external threat.[1]

These two hypotheses depict very different worlds. If balancing is more common than bandwagoning then states are more secure, because aggressors will face combined opposition. But if bandwagoning is the dominant tendency, then security is scarce, because successful aggressors will attract additional allies, enhancing their power while reducing that of their opponents.

---

[1]My use of the terms *balancing* and *bandwagoning* follows that of Kenneth Waltz (who credits it to Stephen Van Evera) in his *Theory of International Politics* (Reading, Mass., 1979). Arnold Wolfers uses a similar terminology in his essay "The Balance of Power in Theory and Practice," in *Discord and Collaboration: Essays on International Politics* (Baltimore, Md., 1962), pp. 122–24.

Both scholars and statesmen have repeatedly embraced one or the other of these hypotheses, but they have generally failed either to frame their beliefs carefully or to evaluate their accuracy. Accordingly, I present each hypothesis in its simplest form and then consider several variations. I then consider which type of behavior—balancing or bandwagoning—is more common and suggest when each response is likely to occur.

Balancing Behavior

The belief that states form alliances in order to prevent stronger powers from dominating them lies at the heart of traditional balance of power theory.[2] According to this view, states join alliances to protect themselves from states or coalitions whose superior resources could pose a threat. States choose to balance for two main reasons.

First, they place their survival at risk if they fail to curb a potential hegemon before it becomes too strong. To ally with the dominant power means placing one's trust in its continued benevolence. The safer strategy is to join with those who cannot readily dominate their allies, in order to avoid being dominated by those who can.[3] As Winston Churchill explained Britain's traditional alliance policy: "For four hundred years the foreign policy of England has been to oppose the strongest, most aggressive, most dominating power on the Continent. . . . [I]t would have been easy . . . and tempting to join with the stronger and share the fruits of his conquest. However, we always took the harder course, joined with the less strong powers, . . . and thus defeated the Continental military tyrant whoever he was."[4] More recently, Henry Kissinger advocated a rapprochement with China, because he believed that in a triangular relationship it was better to align with the weaker side.[5]

---

[2]For analyses of the classical writings on the balance of power, see Edward V. Gulick, *Europe's Classical Balance of Power* (New York, 1955), pt. 1: F. H. Hinsley, *Power and the Pursuit of Peace: Theory and Practice in the History of Relations between States* (Cambridge, England, 1963), pt. I; Inis L. Claude, *Power and International Relations* (New York, 1962), chaps. 2 and 3; Robert E. Osgood and Robert W. Tucker, *Force, Order, and Justice* (Baltimore, Md., 1967), pp. 96–104 and passim; and Martin Wight, "The Balance of Power," in *Diplomatic Investigations*, ed. Martin Wight and Herbert Butterfield (London, 1966). Modern versions of the theory can be found in Waltz, *Theory of International Politics*, chap. 6; Kaplan, *System and Process in International Politics*; and Morgenthau, *Politics among Nations*, pt. 4.

[3]As Vattel wrote several centuries ago: "The surest means of preserving this balance of power would be to bring it about that no State should be much superior to the others. . . . [But] this idea could not be realized without injustice and violence. . . . It is simpler, . . . and more just to have recourse to the method . . . of forming alliances in order to make a stand against a very powerful sovereign and prevent him from dominating." Quoted in Gulick, *Europe's Classical Balance of Power*, p. 60.

[4]Winston S. Churchill, *The Second World War*, vol. 1: *The Gathering Storm* (Boston, 1948), pp. 207–8.

[5]Kissinger, *White House Years*, p. 178.

Second, joining the weaker side increases the new member's influence within the alliance, because the weaker side has greater need for assistance. Allying with the stronger side, by contrast, gives the new member little influence (because it adds relatively less to the coalition) and leaves it vulnerable to the whims of its partners. Joining the weaker side should be the preferred choice.[6]

Bandwagoning Behavior

The belief that states will balance is unsurprising, given the many familiar examples of states joining together to resist a threatening state or coalition.[7] Yet, despite the powerful evidence that history provides in support of the balancing hypothesis, the belief that the opposite response is more likely is widespread. According to one scholar: "In international politics, nothing succeeds like success. Momentum accrues to the gainer and accelerates his movement. The appearance of irreversibility in his gains enfeebles one side and stimulates the other all the more. The bandwagon collects those on the sidelines."[8]

The bandwagoning hypothesis is especially popular with statesmen seeking to justify overseas involvements or increased military budgets. For example, German admiral Alfred von Tirpitz's famous risk theory rested on this type of logic. By building a great battle fleet, Tirpitz argued, Germany could force England into neutrality or alliance with her by posing a threat to England's vital maritime supremacy.[9]

Bandwagoning beliefs have also been a recurring theme throughout the Cold War. Soviet efforts to intimidate both Norway and Turkey into not joining NATO reveal the Soviet conviction that states will accommodate readily to threats, although these

---

[6]In the words of Kenneth Waltz: "Secondary states, if they are free to choose, flock to the weaker side; for it is the stronger side that threatens them. On the weaker side they are both more appreciated and safer, provided, of course, that the coalition they form achieves enough defensive or deterrent strength to dissuade adversaries from attacking." See *Theory of International Politics*, pp. 126–27.

[7]This theme is developed in Ludwig Dehio, *The Precarious Balance* (New York, 1965): Hinsley, *Power and the Pursuit of Peace*; and Gulick, *Europe's Classical Balance of Power*.

[8]W. Scott Thompson, "The Communist International System," *Orbis*, 20, no. 4 (1977).

[9]See William L. Langer, *The Diplomacy of Imperialism* (New York, 1953), pp. 434–35; and Craig, *Germany 1866–1945*, pp. 303–14. This view was not confined to military circles in Germany. In February 1914, Secretary of State Jagow predicted that Britain would remain neutral in the event of a continental war, expressing the widespread view that drove German policy prior to World War l. As he told the German ambassador in London: "We have not built our fleet in vain, and . . . people in England will seriously ask themselves whether it will be just that simple and without danger to play the role of France's guardian angel against us." Quoted in Imanuel Geiss, *July 1914* (New York, 1967), pp. 24–25.

moves merely encouraged Norway and Turkey to align more closely with the West.[10] Soviet officials made a similar error in believing that the growth of Soviet military power in the 1960s and 1970s would lead to a permanent shift in the correlation of forces against the West. Instead, it contributed to a Sino-American rapprochement in the 1970s and the largest peacetime increase in U.S. military power in the 1980s.[11]

American officials have been equally fond of bandwagoning notions. According to NSC-68, the classified study that helped justify a major U.S. military buildup in the 1950s: "In the absence of an affirmative decision [to increase U.S. military capabilities] . . . our friends will become more than a liability to us, they will become a positive increment to Soviet power."[12] President John F. Kennedy once claimed that "if the United States were to falter, the whole world . . . would inevitably begin to move toward the Communist bloc."[13] And though Henry Kissinger often argued that the United States should form balancing alliances to contain the Soviet Union, he apparently believed that U.S. allies were likely to bandwagon. As he put it, "If leaders around the world . . . assume that the U.S. lacked either the forces or the will . . . they will accommodate themselves to what they will regard as the dominant trend."[14] Ronald Reagan's claim, "If we cannot defend ourselves [in Central America] . . . then we cannot expect to prevail elsewhere. . . . [O]ur credibility will collapse and our alliances will crumble," reveals the same logic in a familiar role—that of justifying overseas intervention.[15]

These assertions contain a common theme: states are attracted to strength. The more powerful the state and the more clearly this power is demonstrated, the more likely others are to ally with it. By contrast, a decline in a state's relative position will lead its allies to opt for neutrality at best or to defect to the other side at worst. The

[10]For the effects of the Soviet pressure on Turkey, see George Lenczowski, *The Middle East in World Affairs*, 4th ed. (Ithaca, 1980), pp. 134–38; and Bruce R. Kuniholm, *The Origins of the Cold War in the Near East* (Princeton, N.J., 1980), pp. 355–78. For the Norwegian response to Soviet pressure, see Herbert Feis, *From Trust to Terror: The Onset of the Cold War, 1945–50* (New York, 1970), p. 381; and Geir Lundestad, *America, Scandinavia, and the Cold War: 1945–1949* (New York, 1980), pp. 308–9.

[11]See Dimitri K. Simes, "Soviet Policy toward the United States," in Nye, *The Making of America's Soviet Policy*, pp. 307–8.

[12]NSC–68 ("United States Objectives and Programs for National Security"), reprinted in Gaddis and Etzold, *Containment*, p. 404. Similar passages can be found on pp. 389, 424, and 434.

[13]Quoted in Seyom Brown, *The Faces of Power: Constancy and Change in United States Foreign Policy from Truman to Johnson* (New York, 1968), p. 217.

[14]Quoted in U.S. House Committee on Foreign Affairs, *The Soviet Union and the Third World: Watershed in Great Power Policy?* 97th Cong., 1st sess., 1977, pp. 157–58.

[15]*New York Times*, April 28, 1983, p. A12. In the same speech, Reagan also said: "If Central America were to fall, what would the consequences be for our position in Asia and Europe and for alliances such as NATO? . . . Which ally, which friend would trust us then?"

belief that states are prone to bandwagoning implies that most alliances are extremely fragile.

What is the logic behind this hypothesis? Two distinct motives can be identified. First, bandwagoning may be a form of appeasement. By aligning with an ascendant state or coalition, the bandwagoner may hope to avoid an attack by diverting it elsewhere.

Second, a state may align with the dominant side in wartime in order to share the spoils of victory. Mussolini's declaration of war on France in 1940 and Russia's entry into the war against Japan in 1945 illustrate this type of bandwagoning, as do Italian and Rumanian alliance choices in World War I.[16] By joining the side that they believed would triumph, each hoped to make territorial gains at the end of the fighting.

Stalin's decision to align with Hitler in 1939 illustrates both motives nicely. The Nazi-Soviet Non-Aggression Treaty led to the dismemberment of Poland and may have deflected Hitler's ambitions westward temporarily. Stalin was thus able to gain both time and territory by bandwagoning with Germany.[17] In general, however, these two motives for bandwagoning are quite different. In the first, bandwagoning is chosen for defensive reasons, as a means of preserving one's independence in the face of a potential threat. In the second, a bandwagoning state chooses the leading side for offensive reasons, in order to share the fruits of victory. In either case, however, such behavior stands in sharp contrast to the predictions of the balancing hypothesis.

Different Sources of Threat

Balancing and bandwagoning are usually framed solely in terms of capabilities. Balancing is alignment with the weaker side, bandwagoning with the stronger.[18] This conception should be revised, however, to account for the other factors that statesmen consider when deciding with whom to ally. Although power is an important part of the equation, it is not the only one. It is more accurate to say that states tend to ally with or against the foreign power that poses the greatest threat. For example, states may balance by allying with other strong states if a weaker power is more dangerous

[16]See Denis Mack Smith, *Mussolini* (New York, 1982), pp. 234–35, 246–50; Adam Ulam, *Expansion and Coexistence: Soviet Foreign Policy, 1917–1973* (New York, 1974), pp. 394–98; and A. J. P. Taylor, *The First World War* (New York, 1980), pp. 88–90, 153.

[17]See Ulam, *Expansion and Coexistence*, pp. 276–77; Isaac Deutscher, *Stalin: A Political Biography* (London, 1966), pp. 437–43; and Jouchim Fest, *Hitler* (New York, 1974), pp. 583–84, 592–93.

[18]The preeminent example of balance of power theory based exclusively on the distribution of capabilities is Waltz, *Theory of International Politics*, chap. 6. For examples of theorists who argue that other factors can be important, see Gulick, *Europe's Classical Balance of Power*, pp. 25, 45–47, 60–62.

for other reasons. Thus the coalitions that defeated Germany in World War I and World War II were vastly superior in total resources, but they came together when it became clear that the aggressive aims of the Wilhelmines and Nazis posed the greater danger.[19] Because balancing and bandwagoning are more accurately viewed as a response to threats, it is important to consider other factors that will affect the level of threat that states may pose: aggregate power, geographic proximity, offensive power, and aggressive intentions. . . .

The Implications of Balancing and Bandwagoning

The two general hypotheses of balancing and bandwagoning paint starkly contrasting pictures of international politics. Resolving the question of which hypothesis is more accurate is especially important, because each implies very different policy prescriptions. What sort of world does each depict, and what policies are implied?

If balancing is the dominant tendency, then threatening states will provoke others to align against them. Because those who seek to dominate others will attract widespread opposition, status quo states can take a relatively sanguine view of threats. Credibility is less important in a balancing world, because one's allies will resist threatening states out of their own self-interest, not because they expect others to do it for them. Thus the fear of allies defecting will decline. Moreover, if balancing is the norm and if statesmen understand this tendency, aggression will be discouraged because those who contemplate it will anticipate resistance.

In a balancing world, policies that convey restraint and benevolence are best. Strong states may be valued as allies because they have much to offer their partners, but they must take particular care to avoid appearing aggressive. Foreign and defense policies that minimize the threat one poses to others make the most sense in such a world.

A bandwagoning world, by contrast, is much more competitive. If states tend to ally with those who seem most dangerous, then great powers will be rewarded if they

---

[19]In World War I, the alliance of Great Britain, France, and Russia controlled 27.9 percent of world industrial production, while Germany and Austria together controlled only 19.2 percent. With Russia out of the war but with the United States joining Britain and France, the percentage opposing the Dual Alliance reached 51.7 percent, an advantage of more than 2 to 1. In World War II, the defense expenditures of the United States, Great Britain, and Russia exceeded those of Germany by roughly 4.5 to 1. Even allowing for Germany's control of Europe and the burdens of the war against Japan, the Grand Alliance possessed an enormous advantage in overall capabilities. Thus the formation of the two most important alliances in the twentieth century cannot be explained by focusing on power alone. For these and other statistics on the relative power in the two wars, see Paul M. Kennedy, "The First World War and the International Power System," *International Security*, 9, no. 1 (1984); and *The Rise and Fall of British Naval Mastery* (London, 1983), pp. 309–15.

appear both strong and potentially aggressive. International rivalries will be more intense, because a single defeat may signal the decline of one side and the ascendancy of the other. This situation is especially alarming in a bandwagoning world, because additional defections and a further decline in position are to be expected. Moreover, if statesmen believe that bandwagoning is wide-spread, they will be more inclined to use force. This tendency is true for both aggressors and status quo powers. The former will use force because they will assume that others will be unlikely to balance against them and because they can attract more allies through belligerence or brinkmanship. The latter will follow suit because they will fear the gains their opponents will make by appearing powerful and resolute.[20]

Finally, misperceiving the relative propensity to balance or bandwagon is dangerous, because the policies that are appropriate for one situation will backfire in the other. If statesmen follow the balancing prescription in a bandwagoning world, their moderate responses and relaxed view of threats will encourage their allies to defect, leaving them isolated against an overwhelming coalition. Conversely, following the bandwagoning prescription in a world of balancers (employing power and threats frequently) will lead others to oppose you more and more vigorously.[21]

These concerns are not merely theoretical. In the 1930s, France failed to recognize that her allies in the Little Entente were prone to bandwagon, a tendency that French military and diplomatic policies reinforced.[22] As noted earlier, Soviet attempts to intimidate Turkey and Norway after World War II reveal the opposite error; they merely provoked a greater U.S. commitment to these regions and cemented their entry into NATO. Likewise, the self-encircling bellicosity of Wilhelmine Germany and

[20]It is worth noting that Napoleon and Hitler underestimated the costs of aggression by assuming that their potential enemies would bandwagon. After Munich, for example, Hitler dismissed the possibility of opposition by claiming that British and French statesmen were "little worms." Napoleon apparently believed that England could not "reasonably make war on us unaided" and assumed that the Peace of Amiens guaranteed that England had abandoned its opposition to France. On these points, see Fest, *Hitler*, pp. 594–95; Liska, *Nations in Alliance*, p. 45; and Geoffrey Bruun, *Europe and the French Imperium: 1799–1814* (New York, 1938), p. 118. Because Hitler and Napoleon believed in a bandwagoning world, they were excessively eager to go to war.

[21]This situation is analogous to Robert Jervis's distinction between the deterrence model and the spiral model. The former calls for opposition to a suspected aggressor, the latter for appeasement. Balancing and bandwagoning are the alliance equivalents of deterring and appeasing. See Robert Jervis, *Perception and Misperception in International Politics* (Princeton, N.J., 1976), chap. 3.

[22]The French attempt to contain Germany after World War I was undermined both by the Locarno Treaty (which guaranteed the French border with Germany but failed to provide similar guarantees for France's allies) and by the French adoption of a defensive military doctrine; which made it impossible for France to come to the aid of its allies. See Telford Taylor, *Munich: The Price of Peace* (New York, 1980), pp. 111–12; and Richard D. Challener, *The French Theory of the Nation in Arms* (New York, 1955). pp. 264–65.

Imperial Japan reflected the assumption, prevalent in both states, that bandwagoning was the dominant tendency in international affairs.

When Do States Balance? When Do They Bandwagon?

These examples highlight the importance of identifying whether states are more likely to balance or bandwagon and which sources of threat have the greatest impact on the decision. An answer to the questions of when states balance and when they bandwagon is deferred to chapter 5, but several observations can be made here. In general, we should expect balancing behavior to be much more common than bandwagoning, and we should expect bandwagoning to occur only under certain identifiable conditions.

Although many statesmen fear that potential allies will align with the strongest side, this fear receives little support from most of international history. For example, every attempt to achieve hegemony in Europe since the Thirty Years War has been thwarted by a defensive coalition formed precisely for the purpose of defeating the potential hegemon.[23] Other examples are equally telling.[24] Although isolated cases of bandwagoning do occur, the great powers have shown a remarkable tendency to ignore other temptations and follow the balancing prescription when necessary.

This tendency should not surprise us. Balancing should be preferred for the simple reason that no statesman can be completely sure of what another will do. Bandwagoning is dangerous because it increases the resources available to a threatening power and requires placing trust in its continued forbearance. Because perceptions are unreliable and intentions can change, it is safer to balance against potential threats than to rely on the hope that a state will remain benevolently disposed.

But if balancing is to be expected, bandwagoning remains a possibility. Several factors may affect the relative propensity for states to select this course.

---

[23]See Dehio, *The Precarious Balance*; Georg Schwarzenberger, *Power Politics* (London, 1941); Hinsley, *Power and the Pursuit of Peace*; and Jack S. Levy, "Theories of General War," unpublished manuscript, 1984. An extensively revised version of this paper can be found in *World Politics*, 37, no. 3 (1985).

[24]Prominent recent examples include (1) the enhanced cooperation among the ASEAN states following the U.S. withdrawal from Vietnam and the Vietnamese conquest of Cambodia; (2) the rapprochement between the Unites States and Communist China in the 1970s (and the renewed rivalry between China and Vietnam); (3) the alignment of the Front-Line States against South Africa throughout the 1970s; (4) the formation of a Gulf Cooperation Council in the Persian Gulf following the Iranian revolution. On the South African and Persian Gulf examples, see Mahnaz Z. Ispahani, "Alone Together: Regional Security Arrangements in Southern Africa and the Arabia Gulf," *International Security*, 8, no. 4 (1984). Whatever one thinks of the efficacy of these arrangements, the tendency they illustrate is striking.

Strong versus Weak States

In general, the weaker the state, the more likely it is to bandwagon rather than balance. This situation occurs because weak states add little to the strength of a defensive coalition but incur the wrath of the more threatening states nonetheless. Because weak states can do little to affect the outcome (and may suffer grievously in the process), they must choose the winning side. Only when their decision can affect the outcome is it rational for them to join the weaker alliance.[25] By contrast, strong states can turn a losing coalition into a winning one. And because their decision may mean the difference between victory and defeat, they are likely to be amply rewarded for their contribution.

Weak states are also likely to be especially sensitive to proximate power. Where great powers have both global interests and global capabilities, weak states will be concerned primarily with events in their immediate vicinity. Moreover, weak states can be expected to balance when threatened by states with roughly equal capabilities but they will be tempted to bandwagon when threatened by a great power. Obviously, when the great power is capable of rapid and effective action (i.e., when its offensive capabilities are especially strong), this temptation will be even greater.

The Availability of Allies

States will also be tempted to bandwagon when allies are simply unavailable. This statement is not simply tautological, because states may balance by mobilizing their own resources instead of relying on allied support. They are more likely to do so, however, when they are confident that allied assistance will be available. Thus a further prerequisite for balancing behavior is an effective system of diplomatic communication. The ability to communicate enables potential allies to recognize their shared interests and coordinate their responses.[26] If weak states see no possibility of outside assistance, however, they may be forced to accommodate the most imminent

---

[25]See Rothstein, *Alliances and Small Powers*, p. 11. This problem is one of collective goods. The weakest states cannot provide for their own security, so they bandwagon with the strongest while hoping others will defend them anyway.

[26]One reason for Rome's durable hegemony in the ancient world may have been the fact that her various opponents found it difficult to coordinate effective opposition against her. See Edward N. Luttwak, *The Grand Strategy of the Roman Empire* (Baltimore, Md., 1976), pp. 192, 199–200. By contrast, when a workable diplomatic system was established during the Renaissance, prospects for European hegemony declined drastically. On this point, see Gutick, *Europe's Classical Balance of Power*, p. 16; Hedley Bull, *The Anarchicul Society* (New York, 1977), p. 106 and chap. 7; Garrett Mattingly, *Renaissance Diplomacy* (Boston, 1971), chaps. 13–16; and Harold Nicolson, *Diplomacy* (London, 1963), chap. 1.

threat. Thus the first Shah of Iran saw the British withdrawal from Kandahar in 1881 as a signal to bandwagon with Russia. As he told the British representative, all he had received from Great Britain was "good advice and honeyed words—nothing else."[27] Finland's policy of partial alignment with the Soviet Union suggests the same lesson. When Finland joined forces with Nazi Germany during World War II, it alienated the potential allies (the United States and Great Britain) that might otherwise have helped protect it from Soviet pressure after the war.[28]

Of course, excessive confidence in allied support will encourage weak states to free-ride, relying on the efforts of others to provide security. Free-riding is the optimal policy for a weak state, because its efforts will contribute little in any case. Among the great powers, the belief that allies are readily available encourages buck-passing; states that are threatened strive to pass to others the burdens of standing up to the aggressor. Neither response is a form of bandwagoning, but both suggest that effective balancing behavior is more likely to occur when members of an alliance are not convinced that their partners are unconditionally loyal.[29]

Taken together, these factors help explain the formation of spheres of influence surrounding the great powers. Although strong neighbors of strong states are likely to balance, small and weak neighbors of the great powers may be more inclined to bandwagon. Because they will be the first victims of expansion, because they lack the capabilities to stand alone, and because a defensive alliance may operate too slowly to do them much good, accommodating a threatening great power may be tempting.[30]

[27]Quoted in C. J. Lowe, *The Reluctant Imperialists* (New York, 1967), p. 85.

[28]See Fred Singleton, "The Myth of Finlandisation," *International Affairs*, 57, no. 2 (1981), especially pp. 276–78. Singleton points out that the Western allies approved the 1944 armistice between Finland and the Soviet Union (which established Soviet predominance there) in 1947.

[29]For discussions on the problems of buck-passing, see Posen, *Sources of Military Doctrine*, pp. 63–64 and passim. See also Glenn Snyder's discussion of abandonment in his "Security Dilemma in Alliance Politics," pp. 466–68; and the discussion of the free-rider problem in Olson and Zeckhauser, "Economic Theory of Alliances."

[30]King Leopold of Belgium justified Belgium's policy of neutrality after World War I by saying, "An alliance, even if purely defensive, does not lead to the goal [of security] for no matter how prompt the help of an ally might be, it would not come until after the invader's attack which will be overwhelming." Quoted in Rothstein, *Alliances and Small Powers*, pp. 111–12. Urho Kekkonen of Finland argued for accommodation with the Soviet Union in much the same way: "It cannot be in Finland's interests to be the ally of some great power, constantly on guard in its peripheral position on the Russian border and the first to be overrun by the enemy, and devoid of political importance to lend any significance to its word when decisions over war and peace are being taken." See Urho Kekkonen, *A President's View* (London, 1982), pp. 42–43 and passim.

Peace and War

Finally, the context in which alliance choices are made will affect decisions to balance or bandwagon. States are more likely to balance in peacetime or in the early stages of a war, as they seek to deter or defeat the powers posing the greatest threat. But once the outcome appears certain, some will be tempted to defect from the losing side at an opportune moment. Thus both Rumania and Bulgaria allied with Nazi Germany initially and then abandoned Germany for the Allies, as the tides of war ebbed and flowed across Europe in World War II.[31]

The restoration of peace, however, restores the incentive to balance. As many observers have noted, victorious coalitions are likely to disintegrate with the conclusion of peace. Prominent examples include Austria and Prussia after their war with Denmark in 1864, Britain and France after World War I, the Soviet Union and the United States after World War II, and China and Vietnam after the U.S. withdrawal from Vietnam. This recurring pattern provides further support for the proposition that balancing is the dominant tendency in international politics and that bandwagoning is the opportunistic exception.[32] . . .

---

[31]For an analysis of Balkan diplomacy during World War II, see "Hungary, Rumania and Bulgaria, 1941–1944," in *Survey of International Affairs, 1939–46: Hitler's Europe*, ed. Arnold Toynbee and Veronica Toynbee (London, 1954), pp. 604–31.

[32]The role of different sources of threat also explains why coalitions possessing over-whelming power may stay together even after their enemies are clearly doomed (but not yet defeated). For example, focusing on aggregate power alone would have led us to expect the Grand Alliance to have disintegrated long before the end of the war (i.e., once the Axis was clearly overmatched). The fact that German and Japanese intentions appeared so malign helps explain why the Allies preserved their alliance long enough to obtain the unconditional surrender of both countries.

ANARCHY AND THE LIMITS OF COOPERATION

Joseph M. Grieco

The major challenger to realism has been what I shall call liberal institutionalism. . . .

The new liberal institutionalists basically argue that even if the realists are correct in believing that anarchy constrains the willingness of states to cooperate, states nevertheless can work together and can do so especially with the assistance of international institutions.

This point is crucial for students of international relations. If neoliberal institutionalists are correct, then they have dealt realism a major blow while providing the intellectual justification for treating their own approach, and the tradition from which it emerges, as the most effective for understanding world politics.

This essay's principal argument is that, in fact, neoliberal institutionalism misconstrues the realist analysis of international anarchy and therefore it misunderstands the realist analysis of the impact of anarchy on the preferences and actions of states.

Joseph M. Grieco, "Anarchy and the Limits of Cooperation: A Realist Critique of the Newest Liberal Institutionalism", *International Organization*, 42:3 (Summer, 1988), pp. 485-507. © 1988 by the World Peace Foundation and the Massachusetts Institute of Technology. Reprinted by permission of The MIT Press.

Indeed, the new liberal institutionalism fails to address a major constraint on the willingness of states to cooperate which is generated by international anarchy and which is identified by realism. As a result, the new theory's optimism about international cooperation is likely to be proven wrong.

Neoliberalism's claims about cooperation are based on its belief that states are atomistic actors. It argues that states seek to maximize their individual *absolute* gains and are indifferent to the gains achieved by others. Cheating, the new theory suggests, is the greatest impediment to cooperation among rationally egoistic states, but international institutions, the new theory also suggests, can help states overcome this barrier to joint action. Realists understand that states seek absolute gains and worry about compliance. However, realists find that states are *positional*, not atomistic, in character, and therefore realists argue that, in addition to concerns about cheating, states in cooperative arrangements also worry that their partners might gain more from cooperation than they do. For realists, a state will focus both on its absolute and relative gains from cooperation, and a state that is satisfied with a partner's compliance in a joint arrangement might nevertheless exit from it because the partner is achieving relatively greater gains. Realism, then, finds that there are at least two major barriers to international cooperation: state concerns about cheating and state concerns about relative achievements of gains. Neoliberal institutionalism pays attention exclusively to the former, and is unable to identify, analyze, or account for the latter.

Realism's identification of the relative gains problem for cooperation is based on its insight that states in anarchy fear for their survival as independent actors. According to realists, states worry that today's friend may be tomorrow's enemy in war, and fear that achievements of joint gains that advantage a friend in the present might produce a more dangerous *potential* foe in the future. As a result, states must give serious attention to the gains of partners. Neoliberals fail to consider the threat of war arising from international anarchy, and this allows them to ignore the matter of relative gains and to assume that states only desire absolute gains. Yet, in doing so, they fail to identify a major source of state inhibitions about international cooperation. . . .

2. THE NEW LIBERAL INSTITUTIONALISM

In contrast to earlier presentations of liberal institutionalism, the newest liberalism accepts realist arguments that states are the major actors in world affairs and are unitary–rational agents. It also claims to accept realism's emphasis on anarchy to explain state motives and actions. . . .

Yet neoliberals argue that realism is wrong to discount the possibilities for international cooperation and the capacities of international institutions. . . .

To develop this argument, neoliberals first observe that states in anarchy often face mixed interests and, in particular, situations which can be depicted by Prisoner's Dilemma.[1] In the game, each state prefers mutual cooperation to mutual noncooperation (CC>DD), but also successful cheating to mutual cooperation (DC>CC) and mutual defection to victimization by another's cheating (DD>CD); overall, then, DC>CC>DD>CD. In these circumstances, and in the absence of a centralized authority or some other countervailing force to bind states to their promises, each defects regardless of what it expects the other to do.

However, neoliberals stress that countervailing forces often do exist—forces that cause states to keep their promises and thus to resolve the Prisoner's Dilemma. They argue that states may pursue a strategy of tit-for-tat and cooperate on a conditional basis—that is, each adheres to its promises so long as partners do so. They also suggest that conditional cooperation is more likely to occur in Prisoner's Dilemma if the game is highly iterated, since states that interact repeatedly in either a mutually beneficial or harmful manner are likely to find that mutual cooperation is their best long-term strategy. Finally, conditional cooperation is more attractive to states if the costs of verifying one another's compliance, and of sanctioning cheaters, are low compared to the benefits of joint action. Thus, conditional cooperation among states may evolve in the face of international anarchy and mixed interests through strategies of reciprocity, extended time horizons, and reduced verification and sanctioning costs.

Neoliberals find that one way states manage verification and sanctioning problems is to restrict the number of partners in a cooperative arrangement.[2] However, neoliberals place much greater emphasis on a second factor—international institutions. In particular, neoliberals argue that institutions reduce verification costs, create iterativeness, and make it easier to punish cheaters. As Keohane suggests, "in general, regimes make it more sensible to cooperate by lowering the likelihood of being double-crossed."[3] Similarly, Keohane and Axelrod assert that "international regimes do not substitute for reciprocity; rather, they reinforce and institutionalize it. Regimes incorporating the norm of reciprocity delegitimize defection and thereby make it more costly."[4] In addition, finding that "coordination conventions" are often an element of conditional

---

[1]On the importance of Prisoner's Dilemma in neoliberal theory, see Axelrod, *Evolution of Cooperation*, p. 7; Keohane, *After Hegemony*, pp. 66–69; Axelrod and Keohane, "Achieving Cooperation," p. 231; Lipson, "International Cooperation," p. 2; and Stein, "Coordination and Collaboration," pp. 120–24.

[2]See Keohane, *After Hegemony*, p. 77; Axelrod and Keohane, "Achieving Cooperation," pp. 234–38. For a demonstration, see Lipson, "Bankers' Dilemmas."

[3]Keohane, *After Hegemony*, p. 97.

[4]Axelrod and Keohane, "Achieving Cooperation," p. 250.

cooperation in Prisoner's Dilemma, Charles Lipson suggests that "in international relations, such conventions, which are typically grounded in ongoing reciprocal exchange, range from international law to regime rules."[5] Finally, Arthur Stein argues that, just as societies "create" states to resolve collective action problems among individuals, so too "regimes in the international arena are also created to deal with the collective suboptimality that can emerge from individual [state] behavior."[6] Hegemonic power may be necessary to establish coooperation among states, neoliberals argue, but it may endure after hegemony with the aid of institutions. As Keohane concludes, "When we think about cooperation after hegemony, we need to think about institutions."[7]

3. REALISM AND THE FAILURE OF THE NEW LIBERAL INSTITUTIONALISM

The new liberals assert that they can accept key realist views about states and anarchy and still sustain classic liberal arguments about institutions and international cooperation. Yet, in fact, realist and neoliberal perspectives on states and anarchy differ profoundly, and the former provides a more complete understanding of the problem of cooperation than the latter.

Neoliberals assume that states have only one goal in mixed-interest interactions: to achieve the greatest possible individual gain. For example, Axelrod suggests that the key issue in selecting a "best strategy" in Prisoner's Dilemma—offered by neoliberals as a powerful model of the problem of state cooperation in the face of anarchy and mixed interests—is to determine "what strategy will yield a player the highest possible score."[8] Similarly, Lipson observes that cheating is attractive in a single play of Prisoner's Dilemma because each player believes that defecting "can maximize his own reward," and, in turning to iterated plays, Lipson retains the assumption that players seek to maximize individual payoffs over the long run.[9] Indeed, reliance upon conventional Prisoner's Dilemma to depict international relationships and upon iteration to solve the dilemma unambiguously requires neoliberalism to adhere to an

---

[5]Lipson, "International Cooperation," p. 6.

[6]Stein, "Coordination and Collaboration," p. 123.

[7]Keohane, *After Hegemony*, p. 246.

[8]Axelrod, *Evolution of Cooperation*, pp. 6, 14. Stein acknowledges that he employs an absolute-gains assumption and that the latter "is very much a liberal, not mercantilist, view of self-interest; it suggests that actors focus on their own returns and compare different outcomes with an eye to maximizing their own gains." See Stein, "Coordination and Collaboration," p. 134. It is difficult to see how Stein can employ a "liberal" assumption of state interest and assert that his theory of regimes, as noted earlier in note 34, is based on the "classic [realist?] characterization" of international politics.

[9]Lipson, "International Cooperation," pp. 2, 5.

individualistic payoff maximization assumption, for a player responds to an iterated conventional Prisoner's Dilemma with conditional cooperation *solely out of a desire to maximize its individual long-term total payoffs. . . .*

Driven by an interest in survival, states are acutely sensitive to any erosion of their relative capabilities, which are the ultimate basis for their security and independence in an anarchical, self-help international context. Thus, realists find that the major goal of states in any relationship is not to attain the highest possible individual gain or payoff. Instead, *the fundamental goal of states in any relationship is to prevent others from achieving advances in their relative capabilities.* For example, E. H. Carr suggested that "the most serious wars are fought in order to make one's own country militarily stronger or, *more often*, to prevent another from becoming militarily stronger."[10] Along the same lines, Gilpin finds that the international system "stimulates, and may compel, a state to increase its power; at the least, it necessitates that the prudent state prevent relative increases in the power of competitor states."[11] Indeed, states may even forgo increases in their absolute capabilities if doing so prevents others from achieving even greater gains. This is because, as Waltz suggests, "the first concern of states is not to maximize power but to maintain their position in the system."[12]

States seek to prevent increases in others' relative capabilities. As a result, states always assess their performance in any relationship in terms of the performance of others.[13] Thus, I suggest that states are positional, not atomistic, in character. Most significantly, *state positionality may constrain the willingness of states to cooperate.* States fear that their partners will achieve relatively greater gains; that, as a result, the partners will surge ahead of them in relative capabilities; and, finally, that their increasingly powerful partners in the present could become all the more formidable foes at some point in the future.[14]

---

[10]Carr, *Twenty-Years Crisis*, p. 111, emphasis added.

[11]Gilpin, *War and Change*, pp. 87–88.

[12]Waltz, *Theory of International Politics*, p. 126; see also Waltz, "Reflections," p. 334.

[13]On the tendency of states to compare performance levels, see Oran Young, "International Regimes: Toward a New Theory of Institutions," *World Politics* 39 (October 1986), p. 118. Young suggests that realists assume that states are "status maximizers" and attribute to states the tendency to compare performance levels because each seeks "to attain the highest possible rank in the hierarchy of members of the international community." The present writer offers a different understanding of realism: while realism acknowledges that *some* states may be positional in the sense noted by Young, its fundamental insight is that *all* states are positional and compare performance levels because they fear that *others* may attain a higher ranking in an issue-area.

[14]As Waltz suggests, "When faced with the possibility of cooperating for mutual gains, states that feel insecure must ask how the gain will be divided. They are compelled to ask not "Will both of us gain?" but "Who will gain more?" If an expected gain is to be divided, say, in the ratio of two to one, one state may use its disproportionate gain to implement a policy intended to damage or destroy the other." See Waltz, *Theory of International Politics*, p. 105.

State positionality, then, engenders a "relative gains problem" for cooperation. That is, a state will decline to join, will leave, or will sharply limit its commitment to a cooperative arrangement if it believes that partners are achieving, or are likely to achieve, relatively greater gains. It will eschew cooperation even though participation in the arrangement was providing it, or would have provided it, with large absolute gains. Moreover, a state concerned about relative gains may decline to cooperate even if it is confident that partners will keep their commitments to a joint arrangement. Indeed, if a state believed that a proposed arrangement would provide all parties absolute gains, but would also generate gains favoring partners, then greater certainty that partners would adhere to the terms of the arrangement would only accentuate its relative gains concerns. Thus, a state worried about relative gains might respond to greater certainty that partners would keep their promises with a lower, rather than a higher, willingness to cooperate. . . .

THE SOURCES OF SOVIET CONDUCT

George F. Kennan (X)

The political personality of Soviet power as we know it today is the product of ideology and circumstances: ideology inherited by the present Soviet leaders from the movement in which they had their political origin, and circumstances of the power which they now have exercised for nearly three decades in Russia. There can be few tasks of psychological analysis more difficult than to try to trace the interaction of these two forces and the relative rôle of each in the determination of official Soviet conduct. Yet the attempt must be made if that conduct is to be understood and effectively countered.

It is difficult to summarize the set of ideological concepts with which the Soviet leaders came into power. Marxian ideology, in its Russian-Communist projection, has always been in process of subtle evolution. The materials on which it bases itself are extensive and complex. But the outstanding features of Communist thought as it existed in 1916 may perhaps be summarized as follows: (a) that the central factor in the life of man, the factor which determines the character of public life and the "physiognomy of society," is the system by which material goods are produced and exchanged; (b) that the capitalist system of production is a nefarious one which inevitably leads to the exploitation of the working class by the capital-owning class and is incapable of developing adequately the economic resources of society or of distributing fairly the material goods produced by human labor; (c) that capitalism contains the seeds of its own destruction and must, in view of the inability of the capital-owning class to adjust itself to economic change, result eventually and inescapably in a revolutionary transfer of power to the working class; and (d) that imperialism, the final phase of capitalism, leads directly to war and revolution.

The rest may be outlined in Lenin's own words: "Unevenness of economic and political development is the inflexible law of capitalism. It follows from this that the victory of Socialism may come originally in a few capitalist countries or even in a single capitalist country. The victorious proletariat of that country, having expropriated the capitalists and having organized Socialist production at home, would rise against the remaining capitalist world, drawing to itself in the process the oppressed classes of other countries."[1] It must be noted that there was no assumption that capitalism would perish without proletarian revolution. A final push was needed from a revolutionary proletariat movement in order to tip over the tottering structure. But it was regarded as inevitable that sooner or later that push be given. . . .

The circumstances of the immediate post-revolution period—the existence in Russia of civil war and foreign intervention, together with the obvious fact that the Communists represented only a tiny minority of the Russian people—made the establishment of dictatorial power a necessity. The experiment with "war Communism" and the abrupt attempt to eliminate private production and trade had unfortunate economic consequences and caused further bitterness against the new revolutionary régime. While the temporary relaxation of the effort to communize Russia, represented by the New Economic Policy, alleviated some of this economic distress and thereby served its purpose, it also made it evident that the "capitalistic sector of society" was still prepared to profit at once from any relaxation of governmental pressure, and would, if permitted to continue to exist, always constitute a powerful opposing element to the Soviet régime and a serious rival for influence in the country. Somewhat the same situation prevailed with respect to the individual peasant who, in his own small way, was also a private producer.

Lenin, had he lived, might have proved a great enough man to reconcile these conflicting forces to the ultimate benefit of Russian society, though this is questionable. But be that as it may, Stalin, and those whom he led in the struggle for succession

---

[1]"Concerning the Slogans of the United States of Europe," August 1915. Official Soviet edition of Lenin's works.

to Lenin's position of leadership, were not the men to tolerate rival political forces in the sphere of power which they coveted. Their sense of insecurity was too great. Their particular brand of fanaticism, unmodified by any of the Anglo-Saxon traditions of compromise, was too fierce and too jealous to envisage any permanent sharing of power. From the Russian-Asiatic world out of which they had emerged they carried with them a skepticism as to the possibilities of permanent and peaceful coexistence of rival forces. Easily persuaded of their own doctrinaire "rightness," they insisted on the submission or destruction of all competing power. Outside of the Communist Party, Russian society was to have no rigidity. There were to be no forms of collective human activity or association which would not be dominated by the Party. No other force in Russian society was to be permitted to achieve vitality or integrity. Only the Party was to have structure. All else was to be an amorphous mass. . . .

Now the outstanding circumstance concerning the Soviet régime is that down to the present day this process of political consolidation has never been completed and the men in the Kremlin have continued to be predominantly absorbed with the struggle to secure and make absolute the power which they seized in November 1917. They have endeavored to secure it primarily against forces at home, within Soviet society itself. But they have also endeavored to secure it against the outside world. For ideology, as we have seen, taught them that the outside world was hostile and that it was their duty eventually to overthrow the political forces beyond their borders. The powerful hands of Russian history and tradition reached up to sustain them in this feeling. Finally, their own aggressive intransigence with respect to the outside world began to find its own reaction; and they were soon forced, to use another Gibbonesque phrase, "to chastise the contumacy" which they themselves had provoked. It is an undeniable privilege of every man to prove himself right in the thesis that the world is his enemy; for if he reiterates it frequently enough and makes it the background of his conduct he is bound eventually to be right.

Now it lies in the nature of the mental world of the Soviet leaders, as well as in the character of their ideology, that no opposition to them can be officially recognized as having any merit or justification whatsoever. Such opposition can flow, in theory, only from the hostile and incorrigible forces of dying capitalism. As long as remnants of capitalism were officially recognized as existing in Russia, it was possible to place on them, as an internal element, part of the blame for the maintenance of a dictatorial form of society. But as these remnants were liquidated, little by little, this justification fell away; and when it was indicated officially that they had been finally destroyed, it disappeared altogether. And this fact created one of the most basic of the compulsions which came to act upon the Soviet régime: since capitalism no longer existed in Russia and since it could not be admitted that there could be serious or widespread opposition to the Kremlin springing spontaneously from the liberated masses under its authority, it became necessary to justify the retention of the dictatorship by stressing the menace of capitalism abroad.

This began at an early date. In 1924 Stalin specifically defended the retention of the "organs of suppression," meaning, among others, the army and the secret police, on the ground that "as long as there is a capitalist encirclement there will be danger of intervention with all the consequences that flow from that danger." In accordance with that theory, and from that time on, all internal opposition forces in Russia have consistently been portrayed as the agents of foreign forces of reaction antagonistic to Soviet power.

By the same token, tremendous emphasis has been placed on the original Communist thesis of a basic antagonism between the capitalist and Socialist worlds. It is clear, from many indications, that this emphasis is not founded in reality. The real facts concerning it have been confused by the existence abroad of genuine resentment provoked by Soviet philosophy and tactics and occasionally by the existence of great centers of military power, notably the Nazi régime in Germany and the Japanese Government of the late 1930's, which did indeed have aggressive designs against the Soviet Union. But there is ample evidence that the stress laid in Moscow on the menace confronting Soviet society from the world outside its borders is founded not in the realities of foreign antagonism but in the necessity of explaining away the maintenance of dictatorial authority at home.

Now the maintenance of this pattern of Soviet power, namely, the pursuit of unlimited authority domestically, accompanied by the cultivation of the semi-myth of implacable foreign hostility, has gone far to shape the actual machinery of Soviet power as we know it today. Internal organs of administration which did not serve this purpose withered on the vine. Organs which did serve this purpose became vastly swollen. The security of Soviet power came to rest on the iron discipline of the Party, on the severity and ubiquity of the secret police, and on the uncompromising economic monopolism of the state. The "organs of suppression," in which the Soviet leaders had sought security from rival forces, became in large measure the masters of those whom they were designed to serve. Today the major part of the structure of Soviet power is committed to the perfection of the dictatorship and to the maintenance of the concept of Russia as in a state of siege, with the enemy lowering beyond the walls. And the millions of human beings who form that part of the structure of power must defend at all costs this concept of Russia's position, for without it they are themselves superfluous.

As things stand today, the rulers can no longer dream of parting with these organs of suppression. The quest for absolute power, pursued now for nearly three decades with a ruthlessness unparalleled (in scope at least) in modern times, has again produced internally, as it did externally, its own reaction. The excesses of the police apparatus have fanned the potential opposition to the régime into something far greater and more dangerous than it could have been before those excesses began.

But least of all can the rulers dispense with the fiction by which the maintenance of dictatorial power has been defended. For this fiction has been canonized in Soviet philosophy by the excesses already committed in its name; and it is now anchored in the Soviet structure of thought by bonds far greater than those of mere ideology.

II

So much for the historical background. What does it spell in terms of the political personality of Soviet power as we know it today?

Of the original ideology, nothing has been officially junked. Belief is maintained in the basic badness of capitalism, in the inevitability of its destruction, in the obligation of the proletariat to assist in that destruction and to take power into its own hands. But stress has come to be laid primarily on those concepts which relate most specifically to the Soviet régime itself: to its position as the sole truly Socialist régime in a dark and misguided world, and to the relationships of power within it.

The first of these concepts is that of the innate antagonism between capitalism and Socialism. We have seen how deeply that concept has become imbedded in foundations of Soviet power. It has profound implications for Russia's conduct as a member of international society. It means that there can never be on Moscow's side any sincere assumption of a community of aims between the Soviet Union and powers which are regarded as capitalist. It must invariably be assumed in Moscow that the aims of the capitalist world are antagonistic to the Soviet régime, and therefore to the interests of the peoples it controls. If the Soviet Government occasionally sets its signature to documents which would indicate the contrary, this is to be regarded as a tactical manœuvre permissible in dealing with the enemy (who is without honor) and should be taken in the spirit of *caveat emptor*. Basically, the antagonism remains. It is postulated. And from it flow many of the phenomena which we find disturbing in the Kremlin's conduct of foreign policy: the secretiveness, the lack of frankness, the duplicity, the wary suspiciousness, and the basic unfriendliness of purpose. These phenomena are there to stay, for the foreseeable future. There can be variations of degree and of emphasis. When there is something the Russians want from us, one or the other of these features of their policy may be thrust temporarily into the background; and when that happens there will always be Americans who will leap forward with gleeful announcements that "the Russians have changed," and some who will even try to take credit for having brought about such "changes." But we should not be misled by tactical manœuvres. These characteristics of Soviet policy, like the postulate from which they flow, are basic to the internal nature of Soviet power, and will be with us, whether in the foreground or the background, until the internal nature of Soviet power is changed.

This means that we are going to continue for a long time to find the Russians difficult to deal with. It does not mean that they should be considered as embarked upon a do-or-die program to overthrow our society by a given date. The theory of the inevitability of the eventual fall of capitalism has the fortunate connotation that there is no hurry about it. The forces of progress can take their time in preparing the final *coup de grâce*. Meanwhile, what is vital is that the "Socialist fatherland"—that oasis of power which has been already won for Socialism in the person of the Soviet Union—should be cherished and defended by all good Communists at home and abroad, its fortunes promoted, its enemies badgered and confounded. The promotion of premature, "adventuristic" revolutionary projects abroad which might embarrass Soviet power in any way would be an inexcusable, even a counter-revolutionary act. The cause of Socialism is the support and promotion of Soviet power, as defined in Moscow. . . .

. . . we have seen that the Kremlin is under no ideological compulsion to accomplish its purposes in a hurry. Like the Church, it is dealing in ideological concepts which are of long-term validity, and it can afford to be patient. It has no right to risk the existing achievements of the revolution for the sake of vain baubles of the future. The very teachings of Lenin himself require great caution and flexibility in the pursuit of Communist purposes. Again, these precepts are fortified by the lessons of Russian history: of centuries of obscure battles between nomadic forces over the stretches of a vast unfortified plain. Here caution, circumspection, flexibility and deception are the valuable qualities; and their value finds natural appreciation in the Russian or the oriental mind. Thus the Kremlin has no compunction about retreating in the face of superior force. And being under the compulsion of no timetable, it does not get panicky under the necessity for such retreat. Its political action is a fluid stream which moves constantly, wherever it is permitted to move, toward a given goal. Its main concern is to make sure that it has filled every nook and cranny available to it in the basin of world power. But if it finds unassailable barriers in its path, it accepts these philosophically and accommodates itself to them. The main thing is that there should always be pressure, unceasing constant pressure, toward the desired goal. There is no trace of any feeling in Soviet psychology that that goal must be reached at any given time.

These considerations make Soviet diplomacy at once easier and more difficult to deal with than the diplomacy of individual aggressive leaders like Napoleon and Hitler. On the one hand it is more sensitive to contrary force, more ready to yield on individual sectors of the diplomatic front when that force is felt to be too strong, and thus more rational in the logic and rhetoric of power. On the other hand it cannot be easily defeated or discouraged by a single victory on the part of its opponents. And the patient persistence by which it is animated means that it can be effectively countered not by sporadic acts which represent the momentary whims of democratic opinion but only by intelligent long-range policies on the part of Russia's adversaries—policies no less steady in their purpose, and no less variegated and resourceful in their application, than those of the Soviet Union itself.

In these circumstances it is clear that the main element of any United States policy toward the Soviet Union must be that of a long-term, patient but firm and vigilant containment of Russian expansive tendencies. It is important to note, however, that such a policy has nothing to do with outward histrionics: with threats or blustering or superfluous gestures of outward "toughness." While the Kremlin is basically flexible in its reaction to political realities, it is by no means unamenable to considerations of prestige. Like almost any other government, it can be placed by tactless and threatening gestures in a position where it cannot afford to yield even though this might be dictated by its sense of realism. The Russian leaders are keen judges of human psychology, and as such they are highly conscious that loss of temper and of self-control is never a source of strength in political affairs. They are quick to exploit such evidences of weakness. For these reasons, it is a *since qua non* of successful dealing with Russia that the foreign government in question should remain at all times cool and collected and that its demands on Russian policy should be put forward in such a manner as to leave the way open for a compliance not too detrimental to Russian prestige.

III

In the light of the above, it will be clearly seen that the Soviet pressure against the free institutions of the western world is something that can be contained by the adroit and vigilant application of counter-force at a series of constantly shifting geographical and political points, corresponding to the shifts and manœuvres of Soviet policy, but which cannot be charmed or talked out of existence. The Russians look forward to a duel of infinite duration, and they see that already they have scored great successes. It must be borne in mind that there was a time when the Communist Party represented far more of a minority in the sphere of Russian national life than Soviet power today represents in the world community.

But if ideology convinces the rulers of Russia that truth is on their side and that they can therefore afford to wait, those of us on whom that ideology has no claim are free to examine objectively the validity of that premise. The Soviet thesis not only implies complete lack of control by the west over its own economic destiny, it likewise assumes Russian unity, discipline and patience over an infinite period. Let us bring this apocalyptic vision down to earth, and suppose that the western world finds the strength and resourcefulness to contain Soviet power over a period of ten to fifteen years. What does that spell for Russia itself?

The Soviet leaders, taking advantage of the contributions of modern technique to the arts of despotism, have solved the question of obedience within the confines of their power. Few challenge their authority; and even those who do are unable to make that challenge valid as against the organs of suppression of the state.

The Kremlin has also proved able to accomplish its purpose of building up in Russia, regardless of the interests of the inhabitants, an industrial foundation of heavy metallurgy, which is, to be sure, not yet complete but which is nevertheless continuing to grow and is approaching those of the other major industrial countries. All of this, however, both the maintenance of internal political security and the building of heavy industry, has been carried out at a terrible cost in human life and in human hopes and energies. It has necessitated the use of forced labor on a scale unprecedented in modern times under conditions of peace. It has involved the neglect or abuse of other phases of Soviet economic life, particularly agriculture, consumers' goods production, housing and transportation. . . .

In addition to this, we have the fact that Soviet economic development, while it can list certain formidable achievements, has been precariously spotty and uneven. Russian Communists who speak of the "uneven development of capitalism" should blush at the contemplation of their own national economy. Here certain branches of economic life, such as the metallurgical and machine industries, have been pushed out of all proportion to other sectors of economy. Here is a nation striving to become in a short period one of the great industrial nations of the world while it still has no highway network worthy of the name and only a relatively primitive network of railways. Much has been done to increase efficiency of labor and to teach primitive peasants something about the operation of machines. But maintenance is still a crying deficiency of all Soviet economy. Construction is hasty and poor in quality. Depreciation must be enormous. And in vast sectors of economic life it has not yet been possible to instill into labor anything like that general culture of production and technical self-respect which characterizes the skilled worker of the west.

It is difficult to see how these deficiencies can be corrected at an early date by a tired and dispirited population working largely under the shadow of fear and compulsion. And as long as they are not overcome, Russia will remain economically a vulnerable, and in a certain sense an impotent, nation, capable of exporting its enthusiasms and of radiating the strange charm of its primitive political vitality but unable to back up those articles of export by the real evidences of material power and prosperity.

Meanwhile, a great uncertainty hangs over the political life of the Soviet Union. That is the uncertainty involved in the transfer of power from one individual or group of individuals to others.

This is, of course, outstandingly the problem of the personal position of Stalin. We must remember that his succession to Lenin's pinnacle of preëminence in the Communist movement was the only such transfer of individual authority which the Soviet Union has experienced. That transfer took 12 years to consolidate. It cost the lives of millions of people and shook the state to its foundations. The attendant tremors were felt all through the international revolutionary movement, to the disadvantage of the Kremlin itself.

It is always possible that another transfer of preëminent power may take place quietly and inconspicuously, with no repercussions anywhere. But again, it is possible that the questions involved may unleash, to use some of Lenin's words, one of those "incredibly swift transitions" from "delicate deceit" to "wild violence" which characterize Russian history, and may shake Soviet power to its foundations.

But this is not only a question of Stalin himself. There has been, since 1938, a dangerous congealment of political life in the higher circles of Soviet power. The All-Union Congress of Soviets, in theory the supreme body of the Party, is supposed to meet not less often than once in three years. It will soon be eight full years since its last meeting. During this period membership in the Party has numerically doubled. Party mortality during the war was enormous; and today well over half of the Party members are persons who have entered since the last Party congress was held. Meanwhile, the same small group of men has carried on at the top through an amazing series of national vicissitudes. Surely there is some reason why the experiences of the war brought basic political changes to every one of the great governments of the west. Surely the causes of that phenomenon are basic enough to be present somewhere in the obscurity of Soviet political life, as well. And yet no recognition has been given to these causes in Russia.

It must be surmised from this that even within so highly disciplined an organization as the Communist Party there must be a growing divergence in age, outlook and interest between the great mass of Party members, only so recently recruited into the movement, and the little self-perpetuating clique of men at the top, whom most of these Party members have never met, with whom they have never conversed, and with whom they can have no political intimacy.

Who can say whether, in these circumstances, the eventual rejuvenation of the higher spheres of authority (which can only be a matter of time) can take place smoothly and peacefully, or whether rivals in the quest for higher power will not eventually reach down into these politically immature and inexperienced masses in order to find support for their respective claims? If this were ever to happen, strange consequences could flow for the Communist Party: for the membership at large has been exercised only in the practices of iron discipline and obedience and not in the arts of compromise and accommodation. And if disunity were ever to seize and paralyze the Party, the chaos and weakness of Russian society would be revealed in forms beyond description. For we have seen that Soviet power is only a crust concealing an amorphous mass of human beings among whom no independent organizational structure is tolerated. In Russia there is not even such a thing as local government. The present generation of Russians have never known spontaneity of collective action. If, consequently, anything were ever to occur to disrupt the unity and efficacy of the Party as a political instrument, Soviet Russia might be changed overnight from one of the strongest to one of the weakest and most pitiable of national societies.

Thus the future of Soviet power may not be by any means as secure as Russian capacity for self-delusion would make it appear to the men in the Kremlin. That they can keep power themselves, they have demonstrated. That they can quietly and easily turn it over to others remains to be proved. Meanwhile, the hardships of their rule and the vicissitudes of international life have taken a heavy toll of the strength and hopes of the great people on whom their power rests. It is curious to note that the ideological power of Soviet authority is strongest today in areas beyond the frontiers of Russia, beyond the reach of its police power. This phenomenon brings to mind a comparison used by Thomas Mann in his great novel "Buddenbrooks." Observing that human institutions often show the greatest outward brilliance at a moment when inner decay is in reality farthest advanced, he compared the Buddenbrook family, in the days of its greatest glamour, to one of those stars whose light shines most brightly on this world when in reality it has long since ceased to exist. And who can say with assurance that the strong light still cast by the Kremlin on the dissatisfied peoples of the western world is not the powerful afterglow of a constellation which is in actuality on the wane? This cannot be proved. And it cannot be disproved. But the possibility remains (and in the opinion of this writer it is a strong one) that Soviet power, like the capitalist world of its conception, bears within it the seeds of its own decay, and that the sprouting of these seeds is well advanced.

IV

It is clear that the United States cannot expect in the foreseeable future to enjoy political intimacy with the Soviet régime. It must continue to regard the Soviet Union as a rival, not a partner, in the political arena. It must continue to expect that Soviet policies will reflect no abstract love of peace and stability, no real faith in the possibility of a permanent happy coexistence of the Socialist and capitalist worlds, but rather a cautious, persistent pressure toward the disruption and weakening of all rival influence and rival power.

Balanced against this are the facts that Russia, as opposed to the western world in general, is still by far the weaker party, that Soviet policy is highly flexible, and that

Soviet society may well contain deficiencies which will eventually weaken its own total potential. This would of itself warrant the United States entering with reasonable confidence upon a policy of firm containment, designed to confront the Russians with unalterable counter-force at every point where they show signs of encroaching upon the interests of a peaceful and stable world.

But in actuality the possibilities for American policy are by no means limited to holding the line and hoping for the best. It is entirely possible for the United States to influence by its actions the internal developments, both within Russia and throughout the international Communist movement, by which Russian policy is largely determined. This is not only a question of the modest measure of informational activity which this government can conduct in the Soviet Union and elsewhere, although that, too, is important. It is rather a question of the degree to which the United States can create among the peoples of the world generally the impression of a country which knows what it wants, which is coping successfully with the problems of its internal life and with the responsibilities of a World Power, and which has a spiritual vitality capable of holding its own among the major ideological currents of the time. To the extent that such an impression can be created and maintained, the aims of Russian Communism must appear sterile and quixotic, the hopes and enthusiasm of Moscow's supporters must wane, and added strain must be imposed on the Kremlin's foreign policies. For the palsied decrepitude of the capitalist world is the keystone of Communist philosophy. Even the failure of the United States to experience the early economic depression which the ravens of the Red Square have been predicting with such complacent confidence since hostilities ceased would have deep and important repercussions throughout the Communist world.

By the same token, exhibitions of indecision, disunity and internal disintegration within this country have an exhilarating effect on the whole Communist movement. At each evidence of these tendencies, a thrill of hope and excitement goes through the Communist world; a new jauntiness can be noted in the Moscow tread; new groups of foreign supporters climb on to what they can only view as the band wagon of international politics; and Russian pressure increases all along the line in international affairs.

It would be an exaggeration to say that American behavior unassisted and alone could exercise a power of life and death over the Communist movement and bring about the early fall of Soviet power in Russia. But the United States has it in its power to increase enormously the strains under which Soviet policy must operate, to force upon the Kremlin a far greater degree of moderation and circumspection than it has had to observe in recent years, and in this way to promote tendencies which must eventually find their outlet in either the break-up or the gradual mellowing of Soviet power.

CONTAINING THE DEFINITIVE ARTICLES FOR PERPETUAL PEACE AMONG STATES

Immanuel Kant

The state of peace among men living side by side is not the natural state (*status naturalis*); the natural state is one of war. This does not always mean open hostilities, but at least an unceasing threat of war. A state of peace, therefore, must be *established*, for in order to be secured against hostility it is not sufficient that hostilities simply be not committed; and, unless this security is pledged to each by his neighbor (a thing that can occur only in a civil state), each may treat his neighbor, from whom he demands this security, as an enemy.

FIRST DEFINITIVE ARTICLE FOR PERPETUAL PEACE

"The Civil Constitution of Every State Should Be Republican"

The only constitution which derives from the idea of the original compact, and on which all juridical legislation of the people must be based, is the republican. This constitution is established, firstly, by principles of the freedom of the members of a society (as men); secondly, by principles of dependence of all upon a single common legislation (as subjects); and, thirdly, by the law of their equality (as citizens). The republican constitution, therefore, is, with respect to law, the one which is the original basis of every form of civil constitution. The only question now is: Is it also the one which can lead to perpetual peace?

The republican constitution, besides the purity of its origin (having sprung from the pure source of the concept of law), also gives a favorable prospect for the desired consequence, i.e., perpetual peace. The reason is this: if the consent of the citizens is required in order to decide that war should be declared (and in this constitution it cannot but be the case), nothing is more natural than that they would be very cautious in commencing such a poor game, decreeing for themselves all the calamities of war. Among the latter would be: having to fight, having to pay the costs of war from their own resources, having painfully to repair the devastation war leaves behind, and, to fill up the measure of evils, load themselves with a heavy national debt that would embitter peace itself and that can never be liquidated on account of constant wars in the future. But, on the other hand, in a constitution which is not republican, and under which the subjects are not citizens, a declaration of war is the easiest thing in the world to decide upon, because war does not require of the ruler, who is the proprietor and not a member of the state, the least sacrifice of the pleasures of his table, the chase, his country houses, his court functions, and the like. He may, therefore, resolve on war as on a pleasure party for the most trivial reasons, and with perfect indifference leave the justification which decency requires to the diplomatic corps who are ever ready to provide it.

SECOND DEFINITIVE ARTICLE FOR A PERPETUAL PEACE

"The Law of Nations Shall be Founded on a Federation of Free States"

Peoples, as states, like individuals, may be judged to injure one another merely by their coexistence in the state of nature (i.e., while independent of external laws). Each of them may and should for the sake of its own security demand that the others enter with it into a constitution similar to the civil constitution, for under such a constitution each can be secure in his right. This would be a league of nations, but it would not have to be a state consisting of nations. That would be contradictory, since a state implies the relation of a superior (legislating) to an inferior (obeying), i.e., the people, and many nations in one state would then constitute only one nation. This contradicts the presupposition, for here we have to weigh the rights of nations against each other so far as they are distinct states and not amalgamated into one.

When we see the attachment of savages to their lawless freedom, preferring ceaseless combat to subjection to a lawful constraint which they might establish, and thus preferring senseless freedom to rational freedom, we regard it with deep contempt as barbarity, rudeness, and a brutish degradation of humanity. Accordingly, one would think that civilized people (each united in a state) would hasten all the more to escape, the sooner the better, from such a depraved condition. But, instead, each state places its majesty (for it is absurd to speak of the majesty of the people) in being subject to no external juridical restraint, and the splendor of its sovereign consists in the fact that many thousands stand at his command to sacrifice themselves for something that does not concern them and without his needing to place himself in the least danger[1]. The chief difference between European and American savages lies in the fact that many tribes of the latter have been eaten by their enemies, while the former know how to make better use of their conquered enemies than to dine off them; they know better how to use them to increase the number of their subjects and thus the quantity of instruments for even more extensive wars.

When we consider the perverseness of human nature which is nakedly revealed in the uncontrolled relations between nations (this perverseness being veiled in the state of civil law by the constraint exercised by government), we may well be astonished that the word "law" has not yet been banished from war politics as pedantic, and that no state has yet been bold enough to advocate this point of view. Up to the present, Hugo Grotius, Pufendorf, Vattel,[2] and many other irritating comforters have been cited in justification of war, though their code, philosophically or diplomatically formulated, has not and cannot have the least legal force, because states as such do not stand under a common external power. There is no instance on record that a state has ever been moved to desist from its purpose because of arguments backed up by the testimony of such great men. But the homage which each state pays (at, least in words) to the concept of law proves that there is slumbering in man an even greater moral disposition to become master of the evil principle in himself (which he cannot disclaim) and to hope for the same from others. Otherwise the word "law" would never be pronounced by states which wish to war upon one another; it would be used only ironically, as a Gallic prince interpreted it when he said, "It is the prerogative which nature has given the stronger that the weaker should obey him."

States do not plead their cause before a tribunal; war alone is their way of bringing suit. But by war and its favorable issue in victory, right is not decided, and though by a treaty of peace this particular war is brought to an end, the state of war, of always

---

[1] A Bulgarian prince gave the following answer to the Greek emperor who good-naturedly suggested that they settle their difference by a duel: "A smith who has tongs won't pluck the glowing iron from the fire with his bare hands."

[2] [Hugo Grotius (1583–1645), Samuel von Pufendorf (1632–1694), and Emer de Vattel (1714–1767) developed systems of international law which recognized the legitimacy of some wars. See Grotius, *De jure bellis ac pacis* (1625), Pufendorf, *De jure naturae et gentium* (1672), Vattel, *Le Droit des gens* (1758).]

finding a new pretext to hostilities, is not terminated. Nor can this be declared wrong, considering the fact that in this state each is the judge of his own case. Notwithstanding, the obligation which men in a lawless condition have under the natural law, and which requires them to abandon the state of nature, does not quite apply to states under the law of nations, for as states they already have an internal juridical constitution and have thus outgrown compulsion from others to submit to a more extended lawful constitution according to their ideas of right. This is true in spite of the fact that reason, from its throne of supreme moral legislating authority, absolutely condemns war as a legal recourse and makes a state of peace a direct duty, even though peace cannot be established or secured except by a compact among nations.

For these reasons there must be a league of a particular kind, which can be called a league of peace (*foedus pacificum*), and which would be distinguished from a treaty of peace (*pactum pacis*) by the fact that the latter terminates only one war, while the former seeks to make an end of all wars forever. This league does not tend to any dominion over the power of the state but only to the maintenance and security of the freedom of the state itself and of other states in league with it, without there being any need for them to submit to civil laws and their compulsion, as men in a state of nature must submit.

The practicability (objective reality) of this idea of federation, which should gradually spread to all states and thus lead to perpetual peace, can be proved. For if fortune directs that a powerful and enlightened people can make itself a republic, which by its nature must be inclined to perpetual peace, this gives a fulcrum to the federation with other states so that they may adhere to it and thus secure freedom under the idea of the law of nations. By more and more such associations, the federation may be gradually extended.

We may readily conceive that a people should say, "There ought to be no war among us, for we want to make ourselves into a state; that is, we want to establish a supreme legislative, executive, and judiciary power which will reconcile our differences peaceably." But when this state says, "There ought to be no war between myself and other states, even though I acknowledge no supreme legislative power by which our rights are mutually guaranteed," it is not at all clear on what I can base my confidence in my own rights unless it is the free federation, the surrogate of the civil social order, which reason necessarily associates with the concept of the law of nations—assuming that something is really meant by the latter.

The concept of a law of nations as a right to make war does not really mean anything, because it is then a law of deciding what is right by unilateral maxims through force and not by universally valid public laws which restrict the freedom of each one. The only conceivable meaning of such a law of nations might be that it serves men right who are so inclined that they should destroy each other and thus find perpetual peace in the vast grave that swallows both the atrocities and their perpetrators. For states in their relation to each other, there cannot be any reasonable way out of the lawless condition which entails only war except that they, like individual men, should give up their savage (lawless) freedom, adjust themselves to the constraints of public law, and thus establish a continuously growing state consisting of various nations (*civitas gentium*), which will ultimately include all the nations of the world. But under the idea of the law of nations they do not wish this, and reject in practice what is correct in theory. If all is not to be lost, there can be, then, in place of the positive idea of a world republic, only the negative surrogate of an alliance which averts war, endures, spreads, and holds back the stream of those hostile passions which fear the law, though such an alliance is in constant peril of their breaking loose again.[3] *Furor impius intus . . . . fremit horridus ore cruento* (Virgil)[4].

[3] It would not ill become a people that has just terminated a war to decree, besides a day of thanksgiving, a day of fasting in order to ask heaven, in the name of the state, for forgiveness for the great iniquity which the human race still goes on to perpetuate in refusing to submit to a lawful constitution in their relation to other peoples, preferring, from pride in their independence, to make use of the barbarous means of war even though they are not able to attain what is sought, namely, the rights of a single state. The thanksgiving for victory won during the war, the hymns which are sung to the God of Hosts (in good Israelitic manner), stand in equally sharp contrast to the moral idea of the Father of Men. For they not only show a sad enough indifference to the way in which nations seek their rights, but in addition express a joy in having annihilated a multitude of men or their happiness.

[4] ["Within, impious Rage, sitting on savage arms, his hands fast bound behind with a hundred brazen knots, shall roar in the ghastliness of blood-stained lips" (*Aeneid* I, 294–96, trans H. Rushton Fairclough, "Loeb Classical Library" edn.).]

FOURTEEN POINTS ADDRESS

Woodrow Wilson

. . .

It will be our wish and purpose that the processes of peace, when they are begun, shall be absolutely open and that they shall involve and permit henceforth no secret understandings of any kind. The day of conquest and aggrandizement is gone by; so is also the day of secret covenants entered into in the interest of particular governments and likely at some unlooked-for moment to upset the peace of the world. It is this happy fact, now clear to the view of every public man whose thoughts do not still linger in an age that is dead and gone, which makes it possible for every nation whose purposes are consistent with justice and the peace of the world to avow nor or at any other time the objects it has in view.

We entered this war because violations of right had occurred which touched us to the quick and made the life of our own people impossible unless they were corrected and the world secure once for all against their recurrence. What we demand in this war, therefore, is nothing peculiar to ourselves. It is that the world be made fit and safe to live in; and particularly that it be made safe for every peace-loving nation which, like our own, wishes to live its own life, determine its own institutions, be assured of justice and fair dealing by the other peoples of the world as against force and selfish aggression. All the peoples of the world are in effect partners in this interest, and for

President Woodrow Wilson, Speech to a Joint Session of Congress, January 8, 1918.

our own part we see very clearly that unless justice be done to others it will not be done to us. The program of the world's peace, therefore, is our program; and that program, the only possible program, as we see it, is this:

I. Open covenants of peace, openly arrived at, after which there shall be no private international understandings of any kind but diplomacy shall proceed always frankly and in the public view.

II. Absolute freedom of navigation upon the seas, outside territorial waters, alike in peace and in war, except as the seas may be closed in whole or in part by international action for the enforcement of international covenants.

III. The removal, so far as possible, of all economic barriers and the establishment of an equality of trade conditions among all the nations consenting to the peace and associating themselves for its maintenance.

IV. Adequate guarantees given and taken that national armaments will be reduced to the lowest point consistent with domestic safety.

V. A free, open-minded, and absolutely impartial adjustment of all colonial claims, based upon a strict observance of the principle that in determining all such questions of sovereignty the interests of the populations concerned must have equal weight with the equitable claims of the government whose title is to be determined.

VI. The evacuation of all Russian territory and such a settlement of all questions affecting Russia as will secure the best and freest cooperation of the other nations of the world in obtaining for her an unhampered and unembarrassed opportunity for the independent determination of her own political development and national policy and assure her of a sincere welcome into the society of free nations under institutions of her own choosing; and, more than a welcome, assistance also of every kind that she may need and may herself desire. The treatment accorded Russia by her sister nations in the months to come will be the acid test of their good will, of their comprehension of her needs as distinguished from their own interests, and of their intelligent and unselfish sympathy.

VII. Belgium, the whole world will agree, must be evacuated and restored, without any attempt to limit the sovereignty which she enjoys in common with all other free nations. No other single act will serve as this will serve to restore confidence among the nations in the laws which they have themselves set and determined for the government of their relations with one another. Without this healing act the whole structure and validity of international law is forever impaired.

VIII. All French territory should be freed and the invaded portions restored, and the wrong done to France by Prussia in 1871 in the matter of Alsace-Lorraine, which has unsettled the peace of the world for nearly fifty years, should be righted, in order that peace may once more be made secure in the interest of all.

IX. A readjustment of the frontiers of Italy should be effected along clearly recognizable lines of nationality.

X. The peoples of Austria-Hungary, whose place among the nations we wish to see safeguarded and assured, should be accorded the freest opportunity to autonomous development.

XI. Rumania, Serbia, and Montenegro should be evacuated; occupied territories restored; Serbia accorded free and secure access to the sea; and the relations of the several Balkan states to one another determined by friendly counsel along historically established lines of allegiance and nationality; and international guarantees of the political and economic independence and territorial integrity of the several Balkan states should be entered into.

XII. The Turkish portion of the present Ottoman Empire should be assured a secure sovereignty, but the other nationalities which are now under Turkish rule should be assured an undoubted security of life and an absolutely unmolested opportunity of autonomous development, and the Dardanelles should be permanently opened as a free passage to the ships and commerce of all nations under international guarantees.

XIII. An independent Polish state should be erected which should include the territories inhabited by indisputably Polish populations, which should be assured a free and secure access to the sea, and whose political and economic independence and territorial integrity should be guaranteed by international covenant.

XIV. A general association of nations must be formed under specific covenants for the purpose of affording mutual guarantees of political independence and territorial integrity to great and small states alike.

COMPLEX INTERDEPENDENCE

ROBERT KEOHANE AND JOSEPH NYE

One's assumptions about world politics profoundly affect what one sees and how one constructs theories to explain events. We believe that the assumptions of political realists, whose theories dominated the postwar period, are often an inadequate basis for analyzing the politics of interdependence. The realist assumptions about world politics can be seen as defining an extreme set of conditions or *ideal type*. One could also imagine very different conditions. In this chapter, we shall construct another ideal type, the opposite of realism. We call it *complex interdependence*. After establishing the differences between realism and complex interdependence, we shall argue that complex interdependence sometimes comes closer to reality than does realism. When it does, traditional explanations of change in international regimes become questionable and the search for new explanatory models becomes more urgent.

Excerpts pp. 20–31 from "Realism and Complex Interdependence," from *Power and Interdependence* by Robert O. Keohane and Joseph S. Nye. Copyright © 2001 by Robert O. Keohane and Joseph S. Nye. Reprinted by permission of Addison-Wesley Educational Publishers, Inc.

For political realists, international politics, like all other politics, is a struggle for power but, unlike domestic politics, a struggle dominated by organized violence. In the words of the most influential postwar textbook, "All history shows that nations active in international politics are continuously preparing for, actively involved in, or recovering from organized violence in the form of war." Three assumptions are integral to the realist vision. First, states as coherent units are the dominant actors in world politics. This is a double assumption: states are predominant; and they act as coherent units. Second, realists assume that force is a usable and effective instrument of policy. Other instruments may also be employed, but using or threatening force is the most effective means of wielding power. Third, partly because of their second assumption, realists assume a hierarchy of issues in world politics, headed by questions of military security: the "high politics" of military security dominates the "low politics" of economic and social affairs.

These realist assumptions define an ideal type of world politics. They allow us to imagine a world in which politics is continually characterized by active or potential conflict among states, with the use of force possible at any time. Each state attempts to defend its territory and interests from real or perceived threats. Political integration among states is slight and lasts only as long as it serves the national interests of the most powerful states. Transnational actors either do not exist or are politically unimportant. Only the adept exercise of force or the threat of force permits states to survive, and only while statesmen succeed in adjusting their interests, as in a well-functioning balance of power, is the system stable.

Each of the realist assumptions can be challenged. If we challenge them all simultaneously, we can imagine a world in which actors other than states participate directly in world politics, in which a clear hierarchy of issues does not exist, and in which force is an ineffective instrument of policy. Under these conditions—which we call the characteristics of complex interdependence—one would expect world politics to be very different than under realist conditions.

We will explore these differences in the next section of this chapter. We do not argue, however, that complex interdependence faithfully reflects world political reality. Quite the contrary: both it and the realist portrait are ideal types. Most situations will fall somewhere between these two extremes. Sometimes, realist assumptions will be accurate, or largely accurate, but frequently complex interdependence will provide a better portrayal of reality. Before one decides what explanatory model to apply to a situation or problem, one will need to understand the degree to which realist or complex interdependence assumptions correspond to the situation.

THE CHARACTERISTICS OF COMPLEX INTERDEPENDENCE

Complex Interdependence has Three Main Characteristics:

1. *Multiple channels* connect societies, including: informal ties between governmental elites as well as formal foreign office arrangements; informal ties among nongovernmental elites (face-to-face and through telecommunications); and transnational organizations (such as multinational banks or corporations). These channels can be summarized as interstate, transgovernmental, and transnational relations. *Interstate* relations are the normal channels assumed by realists. *Transgovernmental* applies when we relax the realist assumption that states act coherently as units; *transnational* applies when we relax the assumption that states are the only units.
2. The agenda of interstate relationships consists of multiple issues that are not arranged in a clear or consistent hierarchy. This *absence of hierarchy among issues* means, among other things, that military security does not consistently dominate the agenda. Many issues arise from what used to be considered domestic policy, and the distinction between domestic and foreign issues becomes blurred. These issues are considered in several government departments (not just foreign offices), and at several levels. Inadequate policy coordination on these issues involves significant costs. Different issues generate different coalitions, both within governments and across them, and involve different degrees of conflict. Politics does not stop at the waters' edge.
3. Military force is not used by governments toward other governments within the region, or on the issues, when complex interdependence prevails. It may, however, be important in these governments' relations with governments outside that region, or on other issues. Military force could, for instance, be irrelevant to resolving disagreements on economic issues among members of an alliance, yet at the same time be very important for that alliance's political and military relations with a rival bloc. For the former relationships this condition of complex interdependence would be met; for the latter, it would not.

Traditional theories of international politics implicitly or explicitly deny the accuracy of these three assumptions. Traditionalists are therefore tempted also to deny the relevance of criticisms based on the complex interdependence ideal type. We believe, however, that our three conditions are fairly well approximated on some global issues of economic and ecological interdependence and that they come close to characterizing the entire relationship between some countries. One of our purposes here is to prove that contention. In subsequent chapters we shall examine complex interdependence in oceans policy and monetary policy and in the relationships of the United States to Canada and Australia. In this chapter, however, we shall try to convince you to take these criticisms of traditional assumptions seriously.

Multiple Channels

A visit to any major airport is a dramatic way to confirm the existence of multiple channels of contact among advanced industrial countries; there is a voluminous literature to prove it. Bureaucrats from different countries deal directly with one another at meetings and on the telephone as well as in writing. Similarly, non-governmental elites frequently get together in the normal course of business, in organizations such as the Trilateral Commission, and in conferences sponsored by private foundations.

In addition, multinational firms and banks affect both domestic and interstate relations. The limits on private firms, or the closeness of ties between government and business, vary considerably from one society to another; but the participation of large and dynamic organizations, not controlled entirely by governments, has become a normal part of foreign as well as domestic relations.

These actors are important not only because of their activities in pursuit of their own interests, but also because they act as transmission belts, making government policies in various countries more sensitive to one another. As the scope of governments' domestic activities has broadened, and as corporations, banks, and (to a lesser extent) trade unions have made decisions that transcend national boundaries, the domestic policies of different countries impinge on one another more and more. Transnational communications reinforce these effects. Thus, foreign economic policies touch more domestic economic activity than in the past, blurring the lines between domestic and foreign policy and increasing the number of issues relevant to foreign policy. Parallel developments in issues of environmental regulation and control over technology reinforce this trend.

Absence of Hierarchy Among Issues

Foreign affairs agendas—that is, sets of issues relevant to foreign policy with which governments are concerned—have become larger and more diverse. No longer can all issues be subordinated to military security. As Secretary of State Kissinger described the situation in 1975:

> progress in dealing with the traditional agenda is no longer enough. A new and unprecedented kind of issue has emerged. The problems of energy, resources,

environment, population, the uses of space and the seas now rank with questions of military security, ideology and territorial rivalry which have traditionally made up the diplomatic agenda.

Kissinger's list, which could be expanded, illustrates how governments' policies, even those previously considered merely domestic, impinge on one another. The extensive consultative arrangements developed by the OECD, as well as the GATT, IMF, and the European Community, indicate how characteristic the overlap of domestic and foreign policy is among developed pluralist countries. The organization within nine major departments of the United States government (Agriculture; Commerce; Defense; Health, Education and Welfare; Interior; Justice; Labor; State; and Treasury) and many other agencies reflects their extensive international commitments. The multiple, overlapping issues that result make a nightmare of governmental organizations.

When there are multiple issues on the agenda, many of which threaten the interests of domestic groups but do not clearly threaten the nation as a whole, the problems of formulating a coherent and consistent foreign policy increase. In 1975 energy was a foreign policy problem, but specific remedies, such as a tax on gasoline and automobiles, involved domestic legislation opposed by auto workers and companies alike. As one commentator observed, "virtually every time Congress has set a national policy that changed the way people live . . . the action came after a consensus had developed, bit by bit, over the years, that a problem existed and that there was one best way to solve it." Opportunities for delay, for special protection, for inconsistency and incoherence abound when international politics requires aligning the domestic policies of pluralist democratic countries.

Minor Role of Military Force

Political scientists have traditionally emphasized the role of military force in international politics. As we saw in the first chapter, force dominates other means of power: *if* there are no constraints on one's choice of instruments (a hypothetical situation that has only been approximated in the two world wars), the state with superior military force will prevail. If the security dilemma for all states were extremely acute, military force, supported by economic and other resources, would clearly be the dominant source of power. Survival is the primary goal of all states, and in the worst situations, force is ultimately necessary to guarantee survival. Thus military force is always a central component of national power.

Yet particularly among industrialized, pluralist countries, the perceived margin of safety has widened: fears of attack in general have declined, and fears of attacks *by one another* are virtually nonexistent. France has abandoned the *tous azimuts* (defense in all directions) strategy that President de Gaulle advocated (it was not taken entirely seriously even at the time). Canada's last war plans for fighting the United States were abandoned half a century ago. Britain and Germany no longer feel threatened by each other. Intense relationships of mutual influence exist between these countries, but in most of them force is irrelevant or unimportant as an instrument of policy.

Moreover, force is often not an appropriate way of achieving other goals (such as economic and ecological welfare) that are becoming more important. It is not impossible to imagine dramatic conflict or revolutionary change in which the use or threat of military force over an economic issue or among advanced industrial countries might become plausible. Then realist assumptions would again be a reliable guide to events. But in most situations, the effects of military force are both costly and uncertain. . . .

THE POLITICAL PROCESSES OF COMPLEX INTERDEPENDENCE

The three main characteristics of complex interdependence give rise to distinctive political processes, which translate power resources into power as control of outcomes. As we argued earlier, something is usually lost or added in the translation. Under conditions of complex interdependence the translation will be different than under realist conditions, and our predictions about outcomes will need to be adjusted accordingly.

In the realist world, military security will be the dominant goal of states. It will even affect issues that are not directly involved with military power or territorial defense. Nonmilitary problems will not only be subordinated to military ones; they will be studied for their politico-military implications. Balance of payments issues, for instance, will be considered at least as much in the light of their implications for world power generally as for their purely financial ramifications. McGeorge Bundy conformed to realist expectations when he argued in 1964 that devaluation of the dollar should be seriously considered if necessary to fight the war in Vietnam. To some extent, so did former Treasury Secretary Henry Fowler when he contended in 1971 that the United States needed a trade surplus of $4 billion to $6 billion in order to lead in Western defense.

In a world of complex interdependence, however, one expects some officials, particularly at lower levels, to emphasize the *variety* of state goals that must be pursued. In the absence of a clear hierarchy of issues, goals will vary by issue, and may not be closely related. Each bureaucracy will pursue its own concerns; and although several agencies may reach compromises on issues that affect them all, they will find that a consistent pattern of policy is difficult to maintain. Moreover, transnational actors will introduce different goals into various groups of issues.

Linkage Strategies

Goals will therefore vary by issue area under complex interdependence, but so will the distribution of power and the typical political processes. Traditional analysis focuses on *the* international system, and leads us to anticipate similar political processes on a variety of issues. Militarily and economically strong states will dominate a variety of organizations and a variety of issues, by linking their own policies on some issues to other states' policies on other issues. By using their overall dominance to prevail on their weak issues, the strongest states will, in the traditional model, ensure a congruence between the overall structure of military and economic power and the pattern of outcomes on any one issue area. Thus world politics can be treated as a seamless web.

Under complex interdependence, such congruence is less likely to occur. As military force is devalued, militarily strong states will find it more difficult to use their overall dominance to control outcomes on issues in which they are weak. And since the distribution of power resources in trade, shipping, or oil, for example, may be quite different, patterns of outcomes and distinctive political processes are likely to vary from one set of issues to another. If force were readily applicable, and military security were the highest foreign policy goal, these variations in the issue structures of power would not matter very much. The linkages drawn from them to military issues would ensure consistent dominance by the overall strongest states. But when military force is largely immobilized, strong states will find that linkage is less effective. They may still attempt such links, but in the absence of a hierarchy of issues, their success will be problematic.

Dominant states may try to secure much the same result by using overall economic power to affect results on other issues. If only economic objectives are at stake, they may succeed: money, after all, is fungible. But economic objectives have political implications, and economic linkage by the strong is limited by domestic, transnational, and transgovernmental actors who resist having their interests traded off. Furthermore, the international actors may be different on different issues, and the international organizations in which negotiations take place are often quite separate. Thus it is difficult, for example, to imagine a military or economically strong state linking concessions on monetary policy to reciprocal concessions in oceans policy. On the other hand, poor weak states are not similarly inhibited from linking unrelated issues, partly because their domestic interests are less complex. Linkage of unrelated issues is often a means of extracting concessions or side payments from rich and powerful states. And unlike powerful states whose instrument for linkage (military force) is often too costly to use, the linkage instrument used by poor, weak states—international organization—is available and inexpensive.

Thus as the utility of force declines, and as issues become more equal in importance, the distribution of power within each issue will become more important. If linkages become less effective on the whole, outcomes of political bargaining will increasingly vary by issue area.

The differentiation among issue areas in complex interdependence means that linkages among issues will become more problematic and will tend to reduce rather than reinforce international hierarchy. Linkage strategies, and defense against them, will pose critical strategic choices for states. Should issues be considered separately or as a package? If linkages are to be drawn, which issues should be linked, and on which of the linked issues should concessions be made? How far can one push a linkage before it becomes counterproductive? For instance, should one seek formal agreements or informal, but less politically sensitive, understandings? The fact that world politics under complex interdependence is not a seamless web leads us to expect that efforts to stitch seams together advantageously, as reflected in linkage strategies, will, very often, determine the shape of the fabric.

The negligible role of force leads us to expect states to rely more on other instruments in order to wield power. For the reasons we have already discussed, less vulnerable states will try to use asymmetrical interdependence in particular groups of issues as a source of power; they will also try to use international organizations and transnational actors and flows. States will approach economic interdependence in terms of power as well as its effects on citizens' welfare, although welfare considerations will limit their attempts to maximize power. Most economic and ecological interdependence involves the possibility of joint gains, or joint losses. Mutual awareness of potential gains and losses and the danger of worsening each actor's position through overly rigorous struggles over the distribution of the gains can limit the use of asymmetrical interdependence.

Agenda Setting

Our second assumption of complex interdependence, the lack of clear hierarchy among multiple issues, leads us to expect that the politics of agenda formation and control will become more important. Traditional analyses lead statesmen to focus on politico-military issues and to pay little attention to the broader politics of agenda formation. Statesmen assume that the agenda will be set by shifts in the balance of power, actual or anticipated, and by perceived threats to the security of states. Other issues will only be very important when they seem to affect security and military power. In these cases, agendas will be influenced strongly by considerations of the overall balance of power.

Yet, today, some nonmilitary issues are emphasized in interstate relations at one time, whereas others of seemingly equal importance are neglected or quietly handled at a technical level. International monetary politics, problems of commodity terms of trade, oil, food, and multinational corporations have all been important during the last decade; but not all have been high on interstate agendas throughout that period.

Traditional analysts of international politics have paid little attention to agenda formation: to how issues come to receive sustained attention by high officials. The traditional orientation toward military and security affairs implies that the crucial problems of foreign policy are imposed on states by the actions or threats of other states. These are high politics as opposed to the low politics of economic affairs. Yet, as the complexity of actors and issues in world politics increases, the utility of force declines and the line between domestic policy and foreign policy becomes blurred: as the conditions of complex interdependence are more closely approximated, the politics of agenda formation becomes more subtle and differentiated.

Under complex interdependence we can expect the agendas to be affected by the international and domestic problems created by economic growth and increasing sensitivity interdependence that we described in the last chapter. Discontented domestic groups will politicize issues and force more issues once considered domestic onto the interstate agenda. Shifts in the distribution of power resources within sets of issues will also affect agendas. During the early 1970s the increased power of oil-producing governments over the transnational corporations and the consumer countries dramatically altered the policy agenda. Moreover, agendas for one group of issues may change as a result of linkages from other groups in which power resources are changing; for example, the broader agenda of North-South trade issues changed after the OPEC price rises and the oil embargo of 1973–74. Even if capabilities among states do not change, agendas may be affected by shifts in the importance of transnational actors. The publicity surrounding multinational corporations in the early 1970s, coupled with their rapid growth over the past twenty years, put the regulation of such corporations higher on both the United Nations agenda and national agendas.

Politicization—agitation and controversy over an issue that tend to raise it to the top of the agenda—can have many sources, as we have seen. Governments whose strength is increasing may politicize issues, by linking them to other issues. An international regime that is becoming ineffective or is not serving important issues may cause increasing politicization, as dissatisfied governments press for change. Politicization, however, can also come from below. Domestic groups may become upset enough to raise a dormant issue, or to interfere with interstate bargaining at high levels. In 1974 the American Secretary of State's tacit linkage of a Soviet-American trade pact with progress in detente was upset by the success of domestic American groups working with Congress to link a trade agreement with Soviet policies on emigration.

The technical characteristics and institutional setting in which issues are raised will strongly affect politicization patterns. In the United States, congressional attention is an effective instrument of politicization. Generally, we expect transnational economic organizations and transgovernmental networks of bureaucrats to seek to avoid politicization. Domestically based groups (such as trade unions) and domestically oriented bureaucracies will tend to use politicization (particularly congressional attention) against their transnationally mobile competitors. At the international level, we expect states and actors to "shop among forums" and struggle to get issues raised in international organizations that will maximize their advantage by broadening or narrowing the agenda.

Transnational and Transgovernmental Relations

Our third condition of complex interdependence, multiple channels of contact among societies, further blurs the distinction between domestic and international politics. The availability of partners in political coalitions is not necessarily limited by national boundaries as traditional analysis assumes. The nearer a situation is to complex interdependence, the more we expect the outcomes of political bargaining to be affected by transnational relations. Multinational corporations may be significant both as independent actors and as instruments manipulated by governments. The attitudes and policy stands of domestic groups are likely to be affected by communications, organized or not, between them and their counterparts abroad.

Thus the existence of multiple channels of contact leads us to expect limits, beyond those normally found in domestic politics, on the ability of statesmen to calculate the manipulation of interdependence or follow a consistent strategy of linkage. Statesmen must consider differential as well as aggregate effects of interdependence strategies and their likely implications for politicization and agenda control. Transactions among societies—economic and social transactions more than security ones—affect groups differently. Opportunities and costs from increased transnational ties may be greater for certain groups—for instance, American workers in the textile or shoe industries—than for others. Some organizations or groups may interact directly with actors in other societies or with other governments to increase their benefits from a network of interaction. Some actors may therefore be less vulnerable as well as less sensitive to changes elsewhere in the network than are others, and this will affect patterns of political action.

The multiple channels of contact found in complex interdependence are not limited to nongovernmental actors. Contacts between governmental bureaucracies charged with similar tasks may not only alter their perspectives but lead to transgovernmental coalitions on particular policy questions. To improve their chances of success, government agencies attempt to bring actors from other governments into their own decision-making processes as allies. Agencies of powerful states such as the United States have used such coalitions to penetrate weaker governments in such countries as Turkey and Chile. They have also been used to help agencies of other governments penetrate the United States bureaucracy. As we shall see in Chapter 7, transgovernmental politics frequently characterizes Canadian-American relations, often to the advantage of Canadian interests.

The existence of transgovernmental policy networks leads to a different interpretation of one of the standard propositions about international politics—that states act in their own interest. Under complex interdependence, this conventional wisdom begs two important questions: which self and which interest? A government agency may pursue its own interests under the guise of the national interest; and recurrent interactions can change official perceptions of their interests. As a careful study of the politics of United States trade policy has documented, concentrating only on pressures of various interests for decisions leads to an overly mechanistic view of a continuous process and neglects the important role of communications in slowly changing perceptions of self-interest.

The ambiguity of the national interest raises serious problems for the top political leaders of governments. As bureaucracies contact each other directly across national borders (without going through foreign offices), centralized control becomes more difficult. There is less assurance that the state will be united when dealing with foreign governments or that its components will interpret national interests similarly when negotiating with foreigners. The state may prove to be multifaceted, even schizophrenic. National interests will be defined differently on different issues, at different times, and by different governmental units. States that are better placed to maintain their coherence (because of a centralized political tradition such as France's) will be better able to manipulate uneven interdependence than fragmented states that at first glance seem to have more resources in an issue area.

Role of International Organizations

Finally, the existence of multiple channels leads one to predict a different and significant role for international organizations in world politics. Realists in the tradition of Hans J. Morgenthau have portrayed a world in which states, acting from self-interest, struggle for "power and peace." Security issues are dominant; war threatens. In such a world, one may assume that international institutions will have a minor role, limited by the rare congruence of such interests. International organizations are then clearly peripheral to world politics. But in a world of multiple issues imperfectly linked, in which coalitions are formed transnationally and transgovernmentally, the potential role of international institutions in political bargaining is greatly increased.

In particular, they help set the international agenda, and act as catalysts for coalition-formation and as arenas for political initiatives and linkage by weak states.

Governments must organize themselves to cope with the flow of business generated by international organizations. By defining the salient issues, and deciding which issues can be grouped together, organizations may help to determine governmental priorities and the nature of interdepartmental committees and other arrangements within governments. The 1972 Stockholm Environment Conference strengthened the position of environmental agencies in various governments. The 1974 World Food Conference focused the attention of important parts of the United States government on prevention of food shortages. The September 1975 United Nations special session on proposals for a New International Economic Order generated an intragovernmental debate about policies toward the Third World in general. The International Monetary Fund and the General Agreement on Tariffs and Trade have focused governmental activity on money and trade instead of on private direct investment, which has no comparable international organization.

By bringing officials together, international organizations help to activate potential coalitions in world politics. It is quite obvious that international organizations have been very important in bringing together representatives of less developed countries, most of which do not maintain embassies in one another's capitals. Third World strategies of solidarity among poor countries have been developed in and for a series of international conferences, mostly under the auspices of the United Nations. International organizations also allow agencies of governments, which might not otherwise come into contact, to turn potential or tacit coalitions into explicit transgovernmental coalitions characterized by direct communications. In some cases, international secretariats deliberately promote this process by forming coalitions with groups of governments, or with units of governments, as well as with nongovernmental organizations having similar interests.

International organizations are frequently congenial institutions for weak states. The one-state-one-vote norm of the United Nations system favors coalitions of the small and powerless. Secretariats are often responsive to Third World demands. Furthermore, the substantive norms of most international organizations, as they have developed over the years, stress social and economic equity as well as the equality of states. Past resolutions expressing Third World positions, sometimes agreed to with reservations by industrialized countries, are used to legitimize other demands. These agreements are rarely binding, but up to a point the norms of the institution make opposition look more harshly self-interested and less defensible.

International organizations also allow small and weak states to pursue linkage strategies. In the discussions on a New International Economic Order, Third World states insisted on linking oil price and availability to other questions on which they had traditionally been unable to achieve their objectives. . . .

LIBERALISM AND WORLD POLITICS

Michael Doyle

Despite the contradictions of liberal pacifism and liberal imperialism, I find, with Kant and other liberal republicans, that liberalism does leave a coherent legacy on foreign affairs. Liberal states are different. They are indeed peaceful, yet they are also prone to make war, as the U.S. and our "freedom fighters" are now doing, not so covertly, against Nicaragua. Liberal states have created a separate peace, as Kant argued they would, and have also discovered liberal reasons for aggression, as he feared they might. I conclude by arguing that the differences among liberal pacifism, liberal imperialism, and Kant's liberal internationalism are not arbitrary but rooted in differing conceptions of the citizen and the state.

From "Liberalism and World Politics" by Michael W. Doyle from *The American Political Science Review*, Vol. 80, No. 4, Dec. 1986, 1151–1169. © 1986 American Political Science Association. Reprinted with the permission of Cambridge University Press.

LIBERAL PACIFISM

There is no canonical description of liberalism. What we tend to call *liberal* resembles a family portrait of principles and institutions, recognizable by certain characteristics—for example, individual freedom, political participation, private property, and equality of opportunity—that most liberal states share, although none has perfected them all. Joseph Schumpeter clearly fits within this family when he considers the international effects of capitalism and democracy.

Schumpeter's "Sociology of Imperialisms," published in 1919, made a coherent and sustained argument concerning the pacifying (in the sense of nonaggressive) effects of liberal institutions and principles (Schumpeter, 1955; see also Doyle, 1986, pp. 155–59). Unlike some of the earlier liberal theorists who focused on a single feature such as trade (Montesquieu, 1949, vol. 1, bk. 20, chap. 1) or failed to examine critically the arguments they were advancing, Schumpeter saw the interaction of capitalism and democracy as the foundation of liberal pacifism, and he tested his arguments in a sociology of historical imperialisms.

He defines *imperialism* as "an objectless disposition on the part of a state to unlimited forcible expansion" (Schumpeter, 1955, p. 6). Excluding imperialisms that were mere "catchwords" and those that were "object-ful" (e.g., defensive imperialism), he traces the roots of objectless imperialism to three sources, each an atavism. Modern imperialism, according to Schumpeter, resulted from the combined impact of a "war machine," warlike instincts, and export monopolism.

Once necessary, the war machine later developed a life of its own and took control of a state's foreign policy: "Created by the wars that required it, the machine now created the wars it required" (Schumpeter, 1955, p. 25). Thus, Schumpeter tells us that the army of ancient Egypt, created to drive the Hyksos out of Egypt, took over the state and pursued militaristic imperialism. Like the later armies of the courts of absolutist Europe, it fought wars for the sake of glory and booty, for the sake of warriors and monarchs—wars *gratia* warriors.

A warlike disposition, elsewhere called "instinctual elements of bloody primitivism," is the natural ideology of a war machine. It also exists independently; the Persians, says Schumpeter (1955, pp. 25–32), were a warrior nation from the outset.

Under modern capitalism, export monopolists, the third source of modern imperialism, push for imperialist expansion as a way to expand their closed markets. The absolute monarchies were the last clear-cut imperialisms. Nineteenth-century imperialisms merely represent the vestiges of the imperialisms created by Louis XIV and Catherine the Great. Thus, the export monopolists are an atavism of the absolute monarchies, for they depend completely on the tariffs imposed by the monarchs and their militaristic successors for revenue (Schumpeter, 1955, p. 82–83). Without tariffs, monopolies would be eliminated by foreign competition.

Modern (nineteenth century) imperialism, therefore, rests on an atavistic war machine, militaristic attitudes left over from the days of monarchical wars, and export monopolism, which is nothing more than the economic residue of monarchical finance. In the modern era, imperialists gratify their private interests. From the national perspective, their imperialistic wars are objectless.

Schumpeter's theme now emerges. Capitalism and democracy are forces for peace. Indeed, they are antithetical to imperialism. For Schumpeter, the further development of capitalism and democracy means that imperialism will inevitably disappear. He maintains that capitalism produces an unwarlike disposition; its populace is "democratized, individualized, rationalized" (Schumpeter, 1955, p. 68). The people's energies are daily absorbed in production. The disciplines of industry and the market train people in "economic rationalism"; the instability of industrial life necessitates calculation. Capitalism also "individualizes"; "subjective opportunities" replace the "immutable factors" of traditional, hierarchical society. Rational individuals demand democratic governance.

Democratic capitalism leads to peace. As evidence, Schumpeter claims that throughout the capitalist world an opposition has arisen to "war, expansion, cabinet diplomacy"; that contemporary capitalism is associated with peace parties; and that the industrial worker of capitalism is "vigorously anti-imperialist." In addition, he points out that the capitalist world has developed means of preventing war, such as the Hague Court and that the least feudal, most capitalist society—the United States—has demonstrated the least imperialistic tendencies (Schumpeter, 1955, pp. 95–96). An example of the lack of imperialistic tendencies in the U.S., Schumpeter thought, was our leaving over half of Mexico unconquered in the war of 1846–48.

Schumpeter's explanation for liberal pacifism is quite simple: Only war profiteers and military aristocrats gain from wars. No democracy would pursue a minority interest and tolerate the high costs of imperialism. When free trade prevails, "no class" gains from forcible expansion because

> foreign raw materials and food stuffs are as accessible to each nation as though they were in its own territory. Where the cultural backwardness of a region makes normal economic intercourse dependent on colonization it does not matter, assuming free trade, which of the "civilized" nations undertakes the task of colonization. (Schumpeter, 1955, pp. 75–76)

Schumpeter's arguments are difficult to evaluate. In partial tests of quasi-Schumpeterian propositions, Michael Haas (1974, pp. 464–65) discovered a cluster that associates democracy, development, and sustained modernization with peaceful conditions. However, M. Small and J. D. Singer (1976) have discovered that there is no clearly negative correlation between democracy and war in the period 1816–1965—the period that would be central to Schumpeter's argument (see also Wilkenfeld, 1968, Wright, 1942, p. 841).

Later in his career, in *Capitalism, Socialism, and Democracy*, Schumpeter, (1950, pp. 127–28) acknowledged that "almost purely bourgeois common-wealths were often aggressive when it seemed to pay—like the Athenian or the Venetian commonwealths." Yet he stuck to his pacifistic guns, restating the view that capitalist democracy "steadily tells . . . against the use of military force and for peaceful arrangements, even when the balance of pecuniary advantage is clearly on the side of war which, under modern circumstances, is not in general very likely" (Schumpeter, 1950, p. 128). A recent study by R. J. Rummel (1983) of "libertarianism" and international violence is the closest test Schumpeterian pacifism has received. "Free" states (those enjoying political and economic freedom) were shown to have considerably less conflict at or above the level of economic sanctions than "nonfree" states. The free states, the partly free states (including the democratic socialist countries such as Sweden), and the nonfree states accounted for 24%, 26%, and 61%, respectively, of the international violence during the period examined.

These effects are impressive but not conclusive for the Schumpeterian thesis. The data are limited, in this test, to the period 1976 to 1980. It includes, for example, the Russo-Afghan War, the Vietnamese invasion of Cambodia, China's invasion of Vietnam, and Tanzania's invasion of Uganda but just misses the U.S., quasi-covert intervention in Angola (1975) and our not so covert war against Nicaragua (1981–). More importantly, it excludes the cold war period, with its numerous interventions, and the long history of colonial wars (the Boer War, the Spanish-American War, the Mexican Intervention, etc.) that marked the history of liberal, including democratic capitalist, states (Doyle, 1983b; Chan, 1984; Weede, 1984).

The discrepancy between the warlike history of liberal states and Schumpeter's pacifistic expectations highlights three extreme assumptions. First, his "materialistic monism" leaves little room for noneconomic objectives, whether espoused by states or individuals. Neither glory, nor prestige, nor ideological justification, nor the pure power of ruling shapes policy. These nonmaterial goals leave little room for positive-sum gains, such as the comparative advantages of trade. Second, and relatedly, the same is true for his states. The political life of individuals seems to have been homogenized at the same time as the individuals were "rationalized, individualized, and democratized." Citizens—capitalists and workers, rural and urban—seek material welfare. Schumpeter seems to presume that ruling makes no difference. He also presumes that no one is prepared to take those measures (such as stirring up foreign quarrels to preserve a domestic ruling coalition) that enhance one's political power, despite deterimental effects on mass welfare. Third, like domestic politics, world politics are homogenized. Materially monistic and democratically capitalist, all states evolve toward free trade and liberty together. Countries differently constituted seem to disappear from Schumpeter's analysis. "Civilized" nations govern "culturally backward" *regions*. These assumptions are not shared by Machiavelli's theory of liberalism.

LIBERAL IMPERIALISM

Machiavelli argues, not only that republics are not pacifistic, but that they are the best form of state for imperial expansion. Establishing a republic fit for imperial expansion is, moreover, the best way to guarantee the survival of a state.

Machiavelli's republic is a classical mixed republic. It is not a democracy—which he thought would quickly degenerate into a tyranny—but is characterized by social equality, popular liberty, and political participation (Machiavelli, 1950, bk. 1, chap. 2, p. 112; see also Huliung, 1983, chap. 2; Mansfield, 1970; Pocock, 1975, pp. 198–99; Skinner, 1981, chap. 3). The consuls serve as "kings," the senate as an aristocracy managing the state, and the people in the assembly as the source of strength.

Liberty results from "disunion"—the competition and necessity for compromise required by the division of powers among senate, consuls, and tribunes (the last representing the common people). Liberty also results from the popular veto. The powerful few threaten the rest with tyranny, Machiavelli says, because they seek to dominate. The mass demands not to be dominated, and their veto thus preserves the liberties of the state (Machiavelli, 1950, bk. 1, chap. 5, p. 122). However, since the people and the rulers have different social characters, the people need to be "managed" by the few to avoid having their recklessness overturn or their fecklessness undermine the ability of the state to expand (Machiavelli, 1950, bk. 1, chap. 53, pp. 249–50). Thus the senate and the consuls plan expansion, consult oracles, and employ religion to manage the resources that the energy of the people supplies.

Strength, and then imperial expansion, results from the way liberty encourages increased population and property, which grow when the citizens know their lives and goods are secure from arbitrary seizure. Free citizens equip large armies and provide soldiers who fight for public glory and the common good because these are, in fact, their own (Machiavelli, 1950, bk. 2, chap. 2, pp. 287–90). If you seek the honor of having your state expand, Machiavelli advises, you should organize it as a free and popular republic like Rome, rather than as an aristocratic republic like Sparta or Venice. Expansion thus calls for a free republic.

"Necessity"—political survival—calls for expansion. If a stable aristocratic republic is forced by foreign conflict "to extend her territory, in such a case we shall see her foundations give way and herself quickly brought to ruin"; if, on the other hand, domestic security prevails, "the continued tranquility would enervate her, or provoke internal disensions, which together, or either of them seperately, will apt to prove her ruin" (Machiavelli, 1950, bk. 1, chap. 6, p. 129). Machiavelli therefore believes it is necessary to take the constitution of Rome, rather than that of Sparta or Venice, as our model.

Hence, this belief leads to liberal imperialism. We are lovers of glory, Machiavelli announces. We seek to rule or, at least, to avoid being oppressed. In either case, we want more for ourselves and our states than just material welfare (materialistic monism). Because other states with similar aims thereby threaten us, we prepare ourselves for expansion. Because our fellow citizens threaten us if we do not allow them either to satisfy their ambition or to release their political energies through imperial expansion, we expand.

There is considerable historical evidence for liberal imperialism. Machiavelli's (Polybius's) Rome and Thucydides' Athens both were imperial republics in the Machiavellian sense (Thucydides, 1954, bk. 6). The historical record of numerous U.S. interventions in the postwar period supports Machiavelli's argument (Aron, 1973, chaps. 3–4; Barnet, 1968, chap. 11), but the current record of liberal pacifism, weak as it is, calls some of his insights into question. To the extent that the modern populace actually controls (and thus unbalances) the mixed republic, its diffidence may outweigh elite ("senatorial") aggressiveness.

We can conclude either that (1) liberal pacifism has at least taken over with the further development of capitalist democracy, as Schumpeter predicted it would or that (2) the mixed record of liberalism—pacifism and imperialism—indicates that some liberal states are Schumpeterian democracies while others are Machiavellian republics. Before we accept either conclusion, however, we must consider a third apparent regularity of modern world politics.

LIBERAL INTERNATIONALISM

Modern liberalism carries with it two legacies. They do not affect liberal states separately, according to whether they are pacifistic or imperialistic, but simultaneously.

The first of these legacies is the pacification of foreign relations among liberal states. During the nineteenth century, the United States and Great Britain engaged in nearly continual strife; however, after the Reform Act of 1832 defined actual representation as the formal source of the sovereignty of the British parliament, Britain and the United States negotiated their disputes. They negotiated despite, for example, British grievances during the Civil War against the North's blockade of the South, with which Britain had close economic ties. Despite severe Anglo-French colonial rivalry, liberal France and liberal Britain formed an entente against illiberal Germany before World War I. And from 1914 to 1915, Italy, the liberal member of the Triple Alliance with Germany and Austria, chose not to fulfill its obligations under that treaty to support its allies. Instead, Italy joined in an alliance with Britain and France, which prevented it from having to fight other liberal states and then declared war on Germany and Austria. Despite generations of Anglo-American tension and Britain's wartime restrictions on American trade with Germany, the United States leaned toward Britain and France from 1914 to 1917 before entering World War I on their side.

Beginning in the eighteenth century and slowly growing since then, a zone of peace, which Kant called the "pacific federation" or "pacific union," has begun to be established among liberal societies. More than 40 liberal states currently make up the union. Most are in Europe and North America, but they can be found on every continent . . .

Here the predictions of liberal pacifists (and President Reagan) are borne out: liberal states do exercise peaceful restraint, and a separate peace exists among them. This separate peace provides a solid foundation for the United States' crucial alliances with the liberal powers, e.g., the North Atlantic Treaty Organization and our Japanese alliance. This foundation appears to be impervious to the quarrels with our allies that be-deviled the Carter and Reagan administrations. It also offers the promise of a continuing peace among liberal states, and as the number of liberal states increases, it announces the possibility of global peace this side of the grave or world conquest.

Of course, the probability of the outbreak of war in any given year between any two given states is low. The occurrence of a war between any two adjacent states, considered over a long period of time, would be more probable. The apparent absence of war between liberal states, whether adjacent or not, for almost 200 years thus may have significance. Similar claims cannot be made for feudal, fascist, communist, authoritarian, or totalitarian forms of rule (Doyle, 1983a, pp. 222), nor for pluralistic or merely similar societies. More significant perhaps is that when states are forced to decide on which side of an impending world war they will fight, liberal states all wind up on the same side despite the complexity of the paths that take them there. These characteristics do not prove that the peace among liberals is statistically significant nor that liberalism is the sole valid explanation for the peace. They do suggest that we consider the possibility that liberals have indeed established a separate peace—but only among themselves. . . .

A further cosmopolitan source of liberal peace is the international market's removal of difficult decisions of production and distribution from the direct sphere of state policy. A foreign state thus does not appear directly responsible for these outcomes, and states can stand aside from, and to some degree above, these contentious market rivalries and be ready to step in to resolve crises. The interdependence of commerce and the international contacts of state officials help create crosscutting transnational ties that serve as lobbies for mutual accommodation. According to modern liberal scholars, international financiers and transnational and transgovernmental organizations create interests in favor of accommodation. Moreover, their variety has ensured that no single conflict sours an entire relationship by setting off a spiral of reciprocated retaliation (Brzezinski and Huntington, 1963, chap. 9; Keohane and Nye, 1977, chap. 7; Neustadt, 1970; Polanyi, 1944, chaps. 1–2). Conversely, a sense of suspicion, such as that characterizing relations between liberal and nonliberal governments, can lead to restrictions on the range of contacts between societies, and this can increase the prospect that a single conflict will determine an entire relationship. . . .

In their relations with nonliberal states, however, liberal states have not escaped from the insecurity caused by anarchy in the world political system considered as a whole. Moreover, the very constitutional restraint, international respect for individual rights, and shared commercial interests that establish grounds for peace among liberal states establish grounds for additional conflict in relations between liberal and non-liberal societies.

ANARCHY IS WHAT STATES MAKE OF IT

ALEXANDER WENDT

The debate between realists and liberals has reemerged as an axis of contention in international relations theory. Revolving in the past around competing theories of human nature, the debate is more concerned today with the extent to which state action is influenced by "structure" (anarchy and the distribution of power) versus "process" (interaction and learning) and institutions. Does the absence of centralized political authority force states to play competitive power politics? Can international regimes overcome this logic, and under what conditions? What in anarchy is given and immutable, and what is amenable to change? . . .

Alexander Wendt, "Anarchy is What States Make of It: The Social Construction of Power Politics", *International Organization*, 46:2 (Spring, 1992), pp. 391–425. © 1992 by the World Peace Foundation and the Massachusetts Institute of Technology. Reprinted by permission of The MIT Press.

ANARCHY AND POWER POLITICS

Classical realists such as Thomas Hobbes, Reinhold Niebuhr, and Hans Morgenthau attributed egoism and power politics primarily to human nature, whereas structural realists or neorealists emphasize anarchy. The difference stems in part from different interpretations of anarchy's causal powers. Kenneth Waltz's work is important for both. In *Man, the State, and War*, he defines anarchy as a condition of possibility for or "permissive" cause of war, arguing that "wars occur because there is nothing to prevent them."[1] It is the human nature or domestic politics of predator states, however, that provide the initial impetus or "efficient" cause of conflict which forces other states to respond in kind.[2] Waltz is not entirely consistent about this, since he slips without justification from the permissive causal claim that in anarchy war is always possible to the active causal claim that "war may at any moment occur."[3] But despite Waltz's concluding call for third-image theory, the efficient causes that initialize anarchic systems are from the first and second images. This is reversed in Waltz's *Theory of International Politics*, in which first- and second-image theories are spurned as "reductionist," and the logic of anarchy seems by itself to constitute self-help and power politics as necessary features of world politics.[4] . . .

Anarchy, Self-Help, and Intersubjective Knowledge

Waltz defines political structure on three dimensions: ordering principles (in this case, anarchy), principles of differentiation (which here drop out), and the distribution of capabilities.[5] By itself, this definition predicts little about state behavior. It does not predict whether two states will be friends or foes, will recognize each other's sovereignty, will have dynastic ties, will be revisionist or status quo powers, and so on. These factors, which are fundamentally intersubjective, affect states' security interests and thus the character of their interaction under anarchy. In an important revision of Waltz's theory, Stephen Walt implies as much when he argues that the "balance of threats," rather than the balance of power, determines state action, threats being socially constructed.[6] Put more generally, without assumptions about the structure of identities

[1]Kenneth Waltz, *Man, the State, and War* (New York: Columbia University Press, 1959), p. 232.

[2]Ibid., pp. 169–70.

[3]Ibid., p. 232. This point is made by Hidemi Suganami in "Bringing Order to the Causes of War Debates," *Millennium* 19 (Spring 1990), p. 34, fn. 11.

[4]Kenneth Waltz, *Theory of International Politics* (Boston: Addison-Wesley, 1979).

[5]Waltz, *Theory of International Politics*, pp. 79–101.

[6]Stephen Walt, *The Origins of Alliances* (Ithaca, N.Y.: Cornell University Press, 1987).

and interests in the system, Waltz's definition of structure cannot predict the content or dynamics of anarchy. Self-help is one such intersubjective structure and, as such, does the decisive explanatory work in the theory. The question is whether self-help is a logical or contingent feature of anarchy. In this section, I develop the concept of a "structure of identity and interest" and show that no particular one follows logically from anarchy.

A fundamental principle of constructivist social theory is that people act toward objects, including other actors, on the basis of the meanings that the objects have for them. States act differently toward enemies than they do toward friends because enemies are threatening and friends are not. Anarchy and the distribution of power are insufficient to tell us which is which. U.S. military power has a different significance for Canada than for Cuba, despite their similar "structural" positions, just as British missiles have a different significance for the United States than do Soviet missiles. The distribution of power may always affect states' calculations, but how it does so depends on the intersubjective understandings and expectations, on the "distribution of knowledge," that constitute their conceptions of self and other.[7] If society "forgets" what a university is, the powers and practices of professor and student cease to exist; if the United States and Soviet Union decide that they are no longer enemies, "the cold war is over." It is collective meanings that constitute the structures which organize our actions.

Actors acquire identities—relatively stable, role-specific understandings and expectations about self—by participating in such collective meanings. Identities are inherently relational: "Identity, with its appropriate attachments of psychological reality, is always identity within a specific, socially constructed world," Peter Berger argues.[8] Each person has many identities linked to institutional roles, such as brother, son, teacher, and citizen. Similarly, a state may have multiple identities as "sovereign," "leader of the free world," "imperial power," and so on. The commitment to and the salience of particular identities vary, but each identity is an inherently social definition of the actor grounded in the theories which actors collectively hold about themselves and one another and which constitute the structure of the social world.

Identities are the basis of interests. Actors do not have a "portfolio" of interests that they carry around independent of social context; instead, they define their interests in

---

[7]The phrase "distribution of knowledge" is Barry Barnes's, as discussed in his work *The Nature of Power* (Cambridge: Polity Press, 1988); see also Peter Berger and Thomas Luckmann, *The Social Construction of Reality* (New York: Anchor Books, 1966). The concern of recent international relations scholarship on "epistemic communities" with the cause-and-effect understandings of the world held by scientists, experts, and policymakers is an important aspect of the role of knowledge in world politics; see Peter Haas, "Do Regimes Matter? Epistemic Communities and Mediterranean Pollution Control," *International Organization* 43 (Summer 1989), pp. 377–404; and Ernst Haas, *When Knowledge Is Power*. My constructivist approach would merely add to this an equal emphasis on how such knowledge also *constitutes* the structures and subjects of social life.

[8]Berger, "Identity as a Problem in the Sociology of Knowledge," p. 111.

the process of defining situations. As Nelson Foote puts it: "Motivation . . . refer[s] to the degree to which a human being, as a participant in the ongoing social process in which he necessarily finds himself, defines a problematic situation as calling for the performance of a particular act, with more or less anticipated consummations and consequences, and thereby his organism releases the energy appropriate to performing it."[9] Sometimes situations are unprecedented in our experience, and in these cases we have to construct their meaning, and thus our interests, by analogy or invent them de novo. More often they have routine qualities in which we assign meanings on the basis of institutionally defined roles. When we say that professors have an "interest" in teaching, research, or going on leave, we are saying that to function in the role identity of "professor," they have to define certain situations as calling for certain actions. This does not mean that they will necessarily do so (expectations and competence do not equal performance), but if they do not, they will not get tenure. The absence or failure of roles makes defining situations and interests more difficult, and identity confusion may result. This seems to be happening today in the United States and the former Soviet Union: without the cold war's mutual attributions of threat and hostility to define their identities, these states seem unsure of what their "interests" should be.

An institution is a relatively stable set or "structure" of identities and interests. Such structures are often codified in formal rules and norms, but these have motivational force only in virtue of actors' socialization to and participation in collective knowledge. Institutions are fundamentally cognitive entities that do not exist apart from actors' ideas about how the world works. This does not mean that institutions are not real or objective, that they are "nothing but" beliefs. As collective knowledge, they are experienced as having an existence "over and above the individuals who happen to embody them at the moment."[10] In this way, institutions come to confront individuals as more or less coercive social facts, but they are still a function of what actors collectively "know." Identities and such collective cognitions do not exist apart from each other; they are "mutually constitutive."[11] On this view, institutionalization

[9]Nelson Foote, "Identification as the Basis for a Theory of Motivation," *American Sociological Review* 16 (February 1951), p. 15. Such strongly sociological conceptions of interest have been criticized, with some justice, for being "oversocialized"; see Dennis Wrong, "The Oversocialized Conception of Man in Modern Sociology," *American Sociological Review* 26 (April 1961), pp. 183–93. For useful correctives, which focus on the activation of presocial but nondetermining human needs within social contexts, see Turner, *A Theory of Social Interaction*, pp. 23–69; and Viktor Gecas, "The Self-Concept as a Basis for a Theory of Motivation," in Judith Howard and Peter Callero, eds., *The Self-Society Dynamic* (Cambridge: Cambridge University Press, 1991), pp. 171–87.

[10]Berger and Luckmann, *The Social Construction of Reality*, p. 58.

[11]See Giddens, *Central Problems in Social Theory;* and Alexander Wendt and Raymond Duvall, "Institutions and International Order," in Ernst-Otto Czempiel and James Rosenau, eds., *Global Changes and Theoretical Challenges* (Lexington, Mass.: Lexington Books, 1989), pp. 51–74.

is a process of internalizing new identities and interests, not something occurring outside them and affecting only behavior; socialization is a cognitive process, not just a behavioral one. Conceived in this way, institutions may be cooperative or conflictual, a point sometimes lost in scholarship on international regimes, which tends to equate institutions with cooperation. There are important differences between conflictual and cooperative institutions to be sure, but all relatively stable self-other relations—even those of "enemies"— are defined intersubjectively.

Self-help is an institution, one of various structures of identity and interest that may exist under anarchy. Processes of identity-formation under anarchy are concerned first and foremost with preservation or "security" of the self. Concepts of security therefore differ in the extent to which and the manner in which the self is identified cognitively with the other, and, I want to suggest, it is upon this cognitive variation that the meaning of anarchy and the distribution of power depends. Let me illustrate with a standard continuum of security systems.

At one end is the "competitive" security system, in which states identify negatively with each other's security so that ego's gain is seen as alter's loss. Negative identification under anarchy constitutes systems of "realist" power politics: risk-averse actors that infer intentions from capabilities and worry about relative gains and losses. At the limit—in the Hobbesian war of all against all—collective action is nearly impossible in such a system because each actor must constantly fear being stabbed in the back.

In the middle is the "individualistic" security system, in which states are indifferent to the relationship between their own and others' security. This constitutes "neoliberal" systems: states are still self-regarding about their security but are concerned primarily with absolute gains rather than relative gains. One's position in the distribution of power is less important, and collective action is more possible (though still subject to free riding because states continue to be "egoists").

Competitive and individualistic systems are both "self-help" forms of anarchy in the sense that states do not positively identify the security of self with that of others but instead treat security as the individual responsibility of each. Given the lack of a positive cognitive identification on the basis of which to build security regimes, power politics within such systems will necessarily consist of efforts to manipulate others to satisfy self-regarding interests.

This contrasts with the "cooperative" security system, in which states identify positively with one another so that the security of each is perceived as the responsibility of all. This is not self-help in any interesting sense, since the "self" in terms of which interests are defined is the community; national interests are international interests. In practice, of course, the extent to which states' identification with the community varies, from the limited form found in "concerts" to the full-blown form seen in "collective security" arrangements.[12] Depending on how well developed the collective self is, it will produce security practices that are in varying degrees altruistic or prosocial. This makes collective action less dependent on the presence of active threats and less prone to free riding. Moreover, it restructures efforts to advance one's objectives, or "power politics," in terms of shared norms rather than relative power.

This has an important implication for the way in which we conceive of states in the state of nature before their first encounter with each other. Because states do not have conceptions of self and other, and thus security interests, apart from or prior to interaction, we assume too much about the state of nature if we concur with Waltz that, in virtue of anarchy, "international political systems, like economic markets, are formed by the coaction of self-regarding units."[13] We also assume too much if we argue that, in virtue of anarchy, states in the state of nature necessarily face a "stag hunt" or "security dilemma."[14] These claims presuppose a history of interaction in which actors have acquired "selfish" identities and interests; before interaction (and still in abstraction from first- and second-image factors) they would have no experience upon which to base such definitions of self and other. To assume otherwise is to attribute to states in the state of nature qualities that they can only possess in society.[15] Self-help is an institution, not a constitutive feature of anarchy.

What, then, *is* a constitutive feature of the state of nature before interaction? Two things are left if we strip away those properties of the self which presuppose

[12]On the spectrum of cooperative security arrangements, see Charles Kupchan and Clifford Kupchan, "Concerts, Collective Security, and the Future of Europe," *International Security* 16 (Summer 1991), pp. 114–61; and Richard Smoke, "A Theory of Mutual Security," in Richard Smoke and Andrei Kortunov, eds., *Mutual Security* (New York: St. Martin's Press, 1991), pp. 59–111. These may be usefully set alongside Christopher Jencks' "Varieties of Altruism," in Jane Mansbridge, ed., *Beyond Self-Interest* (Chicago: University of Chicago Press, 1990), pp. 53–67.

[13]Waltz, *Theory of International Politics*, p. 91.

[14]See Waltz, *Man, the State, and War;* and Robert Jervis, "Cooperation Under the Security Dilemma," *World Politics* 30 (January 1978), pp. 167–214.

[15]My argument here parallels Rousseau's critique of Hobbes. For an excellent critique of realist appropriations of Rousseau, see Michael Williams, "Rousseau, Realism, and Realpolitik," *Millennium* 18 (Summer 1989), pp. 188–204. Williams argues that far from being a fundamental starting point in the state of nature, for Rousseau the stag hunt represented a stage in man's fall. On p. 190, Williams cites Rousseau's description of man prior to leaving the state of nature: "Man only knows himself; he does not see his own well-being to be identified with or contrary to that of anyone else; he neither hates anything nor loves anything; but limited to no more than physical instinct, he is no one, he is an animal." For another critique of Hobbes on the state of nature that parallels my constructivist reading of anarchy, see Charles Landesman, "Reflections on Hobbes: Anarchy and Human Nature," in Peter Caws, ed., *The Causes of Quarrel* (Boston: Beacon, 1989), pp. 139–48.

interaction with others. The first is the material substrate of agency, including its intrinsic capabilities. For human beings, this is the body; for states, it is an organizational apparatus of governance. In effect, I am suggesting for rhetorical purposes that the raw material out of which members of the state system are constituted is created by domestic society before states enter the constitutive process of international society, although this process implies neither stable territoriality nor sovereignty, which are internationally negotiated terms of individuality (as discussed further below). The second is a desire to preserve this material substrate, to survive. This does not entail "self-regardingness," however, since actors do not have a self prior to interaction with an other; how they view the meaning and requirements of this survival therefore depends on the processes by which conceptions of self evolve.

This may all seem very arcane, but there is an important issue at stake: are the foreign policy identities and interests of states exogenous or endogenous to the state system? The former is the answer of an individualistic or undersocialized systemic theory for which rationalism is appropriate; the latter is the answer of a fully socialized systemic theory. Waltz seems to offer the latter and proposes two mechanisms, competition and socialization, by which structure conditions state action.[16] The content of his argument about this conditioning, however, presupposes a self-help system that is not itself a constitutive feature of anarchy. As James Morrow points out, Waltz's two mechanisms condition behavior, not identity and interest.[17] This explains how Waltz can be accused of both "individualism" and "structuralism."[18] He is the former with respect to systemic constitutions of identity and interest, the latter with respect to systemic determinations of behavior.

---

[16]Waltz, *Theory of International Politics,* pp. 74–77.

[17]See James Morrow, "Social Choice and System Structure in World Politics," *World Politics* 41 (October 1988), p. 89.

[18]Regarding individualism, see Richard Ashley, "The Poverty of Neorealism," *International Organization* 38 (Spring 1984), pp. 225–86; Wendt, "The Agent-Structure Problem in International Relations Theory"; and David Dessler, "What's at Stake in the Agent-Structure Debate?" *International Organization* 43 (Summer 1989), pp. 441–74. Regarding structuralism, see R. B. J. Walker, "Realism, Change, and International Political Theory," *International Studies Quarterly* 31 (March 1987), pp. 65–86; and Martin Hollis and Steven Smith, *Explaining and Understanding International Relations* (Oxford: Clarendon Press, 1989). The behavioralism evident in neorealist theory also explains how neorealists can reconcile their structuralism with the individualism of rational choice theory. On the behavioral-structural character of the latter, see Spiro Latsis, "Situational Determinism in Economics," *British Journal for the Philosophy of Science* 23 (August 1972), pp. 207–45.

Anarchy and the Social Construction of Power Politics

If self-help is not a constitutive feature of anarchy, it must emerge causally from processes in which anarchy plays only a permissive role.[19] This reflects a second principle of constructivism: that the meanings in terms of which action is organized arise out of interaction.[20] . . .

Consider two actors—ego and alter—encountering each other for the first time. Each wants to survive and has certain material capabilities, but neither actor has biological or domestic imperatives for power, glory, or conquest (still bracketed), and there is no history of security or insecurity between the two. What should they do? Realists would probably argue that each should act on the basis of worst-case assumptions about the other's intentions, justifying such an attitude as prudent in view of the possibility of death from making a mistake. Such a possibility always exists, even in civil society; however, society would be impossible if people made decisions purely on the basis of worst-case possibilities. Instead, most decisions are and should be made on the basis of probabilities, and these are produced by interaction, by what actors *do*.

In the beginning is ego's gesture, which may consist, for example, of an advance, a retreat, a brandishing of arms, a laying down of arms, or an attack. For ego, this gesture represents the basis on which it is prepared to respond to alter. This basis is unknown to alter, however, and so it must make an inference or "attribution" about ego's intentions and, in particular, given that this is anarchy, about whether ego is a threat. The content of this inference will largely depend on two considerations. The first is the gesture's and ego's physical qualities, which are in part contrived by ego and which include the direction of movement, noise, numbers, and immediate consequences of the gesture. The second consideration concerns what alter would intend by such qualities were it to make such a gesture itself. Alter may make an attributional "error" in its inference about ego's intent, but there is also no reason for it to assume a priori—before the gesture—that ego is threatening, since it is only through a process of signaling and interpreting that the costs and probabilities of being wrong can be determined. Social threats are constructed, not natural.

Consider an example. Would we assume, a priori, that we were about to be attacked if we are ever contacted by members of an alien civilization? I think not. We would be highly alert, of course, but whether we placed our military forces on alert or launched

---

[19]The importance of the distinction between constitutive and causal explanations is not sufficiently appreciated in constructivist discourse. See Wendt, "The Agent-Structure Problem in International Relations Theory," pp. 362–65; Wendt, "The States System and Global Militarization," pp. 110–13; and Wendt, "Bridging the Theory/Meta-Theory Gap in International Relations," *Review of International Studies* 17 (October 1991), p. 390.

[20]See Blumer, "The Methodological Position of Symbolic Interactionism," pp. 2–4.

an attack would depend on how we interpreted the import of their first gesture for our security—if only to avoid making an immediate enemy out of what may be a dangerous adversary. The possibility of error, in other words, does not force us to act on the assumption that the aliens are threatening: action depends on the probabilities we assign, and these are in key part a function of what the aliens do; prior to their gesture, we have no systemic basis for assigning probabilities. . . .

This process of signaling, interpreting, and responding completes a "social act" and begins the process of creating intersubjective meanings. It advances the same way. The first social act creates expectations on both sides about each other's future behavior: potentially mistaken and certainly tentative, but expectations nonetheless. Based on this tentative knowledge, ego makes a new gesture, again signifying the basis on which it will respond to alter, and again alter responds, adding to the pool of knowledge each has about the other, and so on over time. The mechanism here is reinforcement; interaction rewards actors for holding certain ideas about each other and discourages them from holding others. If repeated long enough, these "reciprocal typifications" will create relatively stable concepts of self and other regarding the issue at stake in the interaction.[21]

It is through reciprocal interaction, in other words, that we create and instantiate the relatively enduring social structures in terms of which we define our identities and interests. . . .

Competitive systems of interaction are prone to security "dilemmas," in which the efforts of actors to enhance their security unilaterally threatens the security of the others, perpetuating distrust and alienation. The forms of identity and interest that constitute such dilemmas, however, are themselves ongoing effects of, not exogenous to, the interaction; identities are produced in and through "situated activity."[22] We do not *begin* our relationship with the aliens in a security dilemma; security dilemmas are not given by anarchy or nature. Of course, once institutionalized such a dilemma may be hard to change (I return to this below), but the point remains: identities and interests are constituted by collective meanings that are always in process. As Sheldon Stryker emphasizes, "The social process is one of constructing and reconstructing self and social relationships."[23] If states find themselves in a self-help system, this is because their practices made it that way. Changing the practices will change the intersubjective knowledge that constitutes the system.

[21]On "reciprocal typifications," see Berger and Luckmann, *The Social Construction of Reality*, pp. 54–58.

[22]See C. Norman Alexander and Mary Glenn Wiley, "Situated Activity and Identity Formation," in Morris Rosenberg and Ralph Turner, eds., *Social Psychology: Sociological Perspectives* (New York: Basic Books, 1981), pp. 269–89.

[23]Sheldon Stryker, "The Vitalization of Symbolic Interactionism," *Social Psychology Quarterly* 50 (March 1987), p. 93.

Predator States and Anarchy as Permissive Cause

The mirror theory of identity-formation is a crude account of how the process of creating identities and interests might work, but it does not tell us why a system of states—such as, arguably, our own—would have ended up with self-regarding and not collective identities. In this section, I examine an efficient cause, predation, which, in conjunction with anarchy as a permissive cause, may generate a self-help system. In so doing, however, I show the key role that the structure of identities and interests plays in mediating anarchy's explanatory role.

The predator argument is straightforward and compelling. For whatever reasons—biology, domestic politics, or systemic victimization—some states may become predisposed toward aggression. The aggressive behavior of these predators or "bad apples" forces other states to engage in competitive power politics, to meet fire with fire, since failure to do so may degrade or destroy them. One predator will best a hundred pacifists because anarchy provides no guarantees. This argument is powerful in part because it is so weak: rather than making the strong assumption that all states are inherently power-seeking (a purely reductionist theory of power politics), it assumes that just one is power-seeking and that the others have to follow suit because anarchy permits the one to exploit them.

In making this argument, it is important to reiterate that the possibility of predation does not in itself force states to anticipate it a priori with competitive power politics of their own. The possibility of predation does not mean that "war may at any moment occur"; it may in fact be extremely unlikely. Once a predator emerges, however, it may condition identity- and interest-formation in the following manner. . . .

The timing of the emergence of predation relative to the history of identity-formation in the community is therefore crucial to anarchy's explanatory role as a permissive cause. Predation will always lead victims to defend themselves, but whether defense will be collective or not depends on the history of interaction within the potential collective as much as on the ambitions of the predator. Will the disappearance of the Soviet threat renew old insecurities among the members of the North Atlantic Treaty Organization? Perhaps, but not if they have reasons independent of that threat for identifying their security with one another. Identities and interests are relationship-specific, not intrinsic attributes of a "portfolio"; states may be competitive in some relationships and solidary in others. "Mature" anarchies are less likely than "immature" ones to be reduced by predation to a Hobbesian condition, and maturity, which is a proxy for structures of identity and interest, is a function of process.[24]

[24]On the "maturity" of anarchies, see Barry Buzan, *People, States, and Fear* (Chapel Hill: University of North Carolina Press, 1983).

The source of predation also matters. If it stems from unit-level causes that are immune to systemic impacts (causes such as human nature or domestic politics taken in isolation), then it functions in a manner analogous to a "genetic trait" in the constructed world of the-state system. Even if successful, this trait does not select for other predators in an evolutionary sense so much as it teaches other states to respond in kind, but since traits cannot be unlearned, the other states will continue competitive behavior until the predator is either destroyed or transformed from within. However, in the more likely event that predation stems at least in part from prior systemic interaction—perhaps as a result of being victimized in the past (one thinks here of Nazi Germany or the Soviet Union)—then it is more a response to a learned identity and, as such, might be transformed by future social interaction in the form of appeasement, reassurances that security needs will be met, systemic effects on domestic politics, and so on. In this case, in other words, there is more hope that process can transform a bad apple into a good one. . . .

This raises anew the question of exactly how much and what kind of role human nature and domestic politics play in world politics. The greater and more destructive this role, the more significant predation will be, and the less amenable anarchy will be to formation of collective identities. Classical realists, of course, assumed that human nature was possessed by an inherent lust for power or glory. My argument suggests that assumptions such as this were made for a reason: an unchanging Hobbesian man provides the powerful efficient cause necessary for a relentless pessimism about world politics that anarchic structure alone, or even structure plus intermittent predation, cannot supply. . . .

Assuming for now that systemic theories of identity-formation in world politics are worth pursuing, let me conclude by suggesting that the realist-rationalist alliance "reifies" self-help in the sense of treating it as something separate from the practices by which it is produced and sustained. Peter Berger and Thomas Luckmann define reification as follows: "[It] is the apprehension of the products of human activity *as if* they were something else than human products—such as facts of nature, results of cosmic laws, or manifestations of divine will. Reification implies that man is capable of forgetting his own authorship of the human world, and further, that the dialectic between man, the producer, and his products is lost to consciousness. The reified world is . . . experienced by man as a strange facticity, an *opus alienum* over which he has no control rather than as the *opus proprium* of his own productive activity."[25] By denying or bracketing states' collective authorship of their identities and interests, in other words, the realist-rationalist alliance denies or brackets the

[25]See Berger and Luckmann, *The Social Construction of Reality*, p. 89. See also Douglas Maynard and Thomas Wilson, "On the Reification of Social Structure," in Scott McNall and Gary Howe, eds., *Current Perspectives in Social Theory*, vol. 1 (Greenwich, Conn.: JAI Press, 1980), pp. 287–322.

fact that competitive power politics help create the very "problem of order" they are supposed to solve—that realism is a self-fulfilling prophecy. Far from being exogenously given, the intersubjective knowledge that constitutes competitive identities and interests is constructed every day by processes of "social will formation."[26] It is what states have made of themselves. . . .

[26]See Richard Ashley, "Social Will and International Anarchy," in Hayward Alker and Richard Ashley, eds., *After Realism*, work in progress, Massachusetts Institute of Technology, Cambridge, and Arizona State University, Tempe, 1992.

INTERNATIONAL NORM DYNAMICS AND POLITICAL CHANGE

MARTHA FINNEMORE AND KATHRYN SIKKINK

DEFINITIONS

There is general agreement on the definition of a norm as a standard of appropriate behavior for actors with a given identity,[1] but a number of related conceptual issues still cause confusion and debate. First, whereas constructivists in political science talk a language of norms, sociologists talk a language of "institutions" to refer to these same behavioral rules. Thus, elsewhere in this issue March and Olsen define "institution" as "a relatively stable collection of practices and rules defining appropriate behavior for specific groups of actors in specific situations."[2] One difference between "norm" and "institution" (in the sociological sense) is aggregation: the norm

Martha Finnemore and Kathryn Sikkink, "Norms and International Relations Theory", *International Organization*, 52:4 (Autumn 1998), pp. 887–917. © 1998 by the IO Foundation and the Massachusetts Institute of Technology. Reprinted by permission of The MIT Press.

[1]See Katzenstein 1996b, 5; Finnemore 1996a, 22; and Klotz 1995b.
[2]March and Olsen, this issue.

definition isolates single standards of behavior, whereas institutions emphasize the way in which behavioral rules are structured together and interrelate (a "collection of practices and rules"). The danger in using the norm language is that it can obscure distinct and interrelated elements of social institutions if not used carefully. For example, political scientists tend to slip into discussions of "sovereignty" or "slavery" as if they were norms, when in fact they are (or were) collections of norms and the mix of rules and practices that structure these institutions has varied significantly over time.[3] Used carefully, however, norm language can help to steer scholars toward looking inside social institutions and considering the components of social institutions as well as the way these elements are renegotiated into new arrangements over time to create new patterns of politics.[4]

Scholars across disciplines have recognized different types or categories of norms. The most common distinction is between regulative norms, which order and constrain behavior, and constitutive norms, which create new actors, interests, or categories of action.[5] Some scholars have also discussed a category of norms called evaluative or prescriptive norms, but these have received much less attention and, indeed, are often explicitly omitted from analysis.[6] This lack of attention is puzzling, since it is precisely the prescriptive (or evaluative) quality of "oughtness" that sets norms apart from other kinds of rules. Because norms involve standards of "appropriate" or "proper" behavior, both the intersubjective and the evaluative dimensions are inescapable when discussing norms. We only know what is appropriate by reference to the judgments of a community or a society. We recognize norm-breaking behavior because it generates disapproval or stigma and norm conforming behavior either because it produces praise, or, in the case of a highly internalized norm, because it is so taken for granted that it provokes no reaction whatsoever.[7] Thus, James Fearon argues that social norms take the generic form "Good people do (or do not do) X in situations A, B, C . . ." because "we typically do not consider a rule of conduct to be a social norm unless a shared moral assessment is attached to its observance or non-observance."[8]

One logical corollary to the prescriptive quality of norms is that, by definition, there are no bad norms from the vantage point of those who promote the norm. Norms most of us would consider "bad"—norms about racial superiority, divine right, imperialism—were once powerful because some groups believed in the appropriateness

---

[3]Krasner 1984, 1988, 1993; Thomson 1994; Strang 1991; Ruggie 1993; and Spruyt 1994.

[4]For an excellent discussion of these issues, see Jepperson 1991.

[5]Ruggie, this issue; Searle 1995; Katzenstein 1996b; and Wendt forthcoming.

[6]Gelpi 1997. See, for example, the treatment in Katzenstein 1996b, 5, fn12.

[7]For a particularly good discussion of the way in which conventions produce judgments of social "oughtness" and morality, see Sugden 1989. See also Elster 1989a,c; and Sunstein 1997.

[8]Fearon 1997, 25, fn18.

(that is, the "goodness") of the norm, and others either accepted it as obvious or inevitable or had no choice but to accept it. Slaveholders and many non-slaveholders believed that slavery was appropriate behavior; without that belief, the institution of slavery would not have been possible. . . .

EVOLUTION AND INFLUENCE OF NORMS

In this section we advance some propositions about (1) the origins or emergence of international norms, (2) the processes through which norms influence state and non-state behavior, and (3) which norms will matter and under what conditions. We illustrate the arguments with material drawn from two major issue areas: women's rights, especially suffrage, and laws of war. International norms about women's rights often came into direct competition with strongly held domestic norms, and, typically, there was no self-evident state "interest" in the promotion of such norms. Although topics related to gender and women have been absent from the pages of *International Organization*,[9] the suffrage campaign led to the formal political participation of half of the world's population and therefore seems worthy of study. Laws of war allow us to discuss the impact of norms where we might least expect it—the traditional security field, where such norms limit state discretion in an area perceived as essential to national sovereignty and security.

The Norm "Life Cycle"

Norm influence may be understood as a three-stage process. The first two stages are divided by a threshold or "tipping" point, at which a critical mass of relevant state actors adopt the norm. This pattern of norm influence has been found independently in work on social norms in U.S. legal theory, quantitative research by sociology's institutionalists or "world polity" theorists, and various scholars of norms in IR.[10] The pattern is important for researchers to understand because different social processes and logics of action may be involved at different stages in a norm's "life cycle."

---

[9]In its first fifty years *International Organization* has published only one article on any issue related to gender or women, Craig Murphy's review essay on gender and international relations; Murphy 1996. We suggest that there may have been a well-internalized norm (with a taken-for-granted quality) that research on gender and women did not constitute an appropriate topic for international relations scholarship. Note that as with any well-internalized norm, this does not imply that the editors self-consciously rejected articles on gender-related topics. To the contrary, we know a strong norm is in effect when it does not occur to authors to write on the topic or submit articles because it is not generally understood as an appropriate topic.

[10]See Sunstein 1997; Meyer and Hannan 1979; Bergesen 1980; Thomas et al. 1987; and Finnemore 1993.

Thus, theoretical debates about the degree to which norm-based behavior is driven by choice or habit, specification issues about the costs of norm-violation or benefits from norm adherence, and related research issues often turn out to hinge on the stage of the norm's evolution one examines. Change at each stage, we argue, is characterized by different actors, motives, and mechanisms of influence.

The characteristic mechanism of the first stage, norm emergence, is persuasion by norm entrepreneurs. Norm entrepreneurs attempt to convince a critical mass of states (norm leaders) to embrace new norms. The second stage is characterized more by a dynamic of imitation as the norm leaders attempt to socialize other states to become norm followers. The exact motivation for this second stage where the norm "cascades" through the rest of the population (in this case, of states) may vary, but we argue that a combination of pressure for conformity, desire to enhance international legitimation, and the desire of state leaders to enhance their self-esteem facilitate norm cascades. At the far end of the norm cascade, norm internalization occurs; norms acquire a taken-for-granted quality and are no longer a matter of broad public debate. For example, few people today discuss whether women should be allowed to vote, whether slavery is useful, or whether medical personnel should be granted immunity during war. Completion of the "life cycle" is not an inevitable process. Many emergent norms fail to reach a tipping point, and later we offer arguments about which norms are more likely to succeed. Internalized or cascading norms may eventually become the prevailing standard of appropriateness against which new norms emerge and compete for support.

Research on women's suffrage globally provides support for the idea of the life cycle of norms and the notion of a "tipping point" or threshold of normative change. Although many domestic suffrage organizations were active in the nineteenth century, it was not until 1904, when women's rights advocates founded the International Women's Suffrage Association (IWSA), that an international campaign for suffrage was launched. In fact, rather than a single international campaign for women's suffrage, there were three or four overlapping campaigns with different degrees of coordination.[11] A quantitative analysis of the cross-national acquisition of suffrage rights reveals a different dynamic at work for early and late adopters of women's suffrage.[12] Prior to a threshold point in 1930, no country had adopted women's suffrage without strong pressure from domestic suffrage organizations. Between 1890 and 1930, Western countries with strong national women's movements were most likely to grant female suffrage. Although some original norm entrepreneurs came from the United States and the United Kingdom, this was not a case of "hegemonic socialization,"

[11]See Dubois 1994; and Berkovitch 1995.
[12] Ramirez, Soysal, and Shanahan 1997.

since the first states to grant women the right to vote (New Zealand, Australia, Finland) were not hegemons, and the United States and the United Kingdom lagged ten to twenty years behind. After 1930, international and transnational influences become far more important than domestic pressures for norm adoption, and countries adopted women's suffrage even though they faced no domestic pressures to do so. For women's suffrage, the first stage of norm emergence lasted over eighty years: it took from the Seneca Falls Conference in 1848 until 1930 for twenty states to adopt women's suffrage. In the twenty years that followed the tipping point, however, some forty-eight countries adopted women's suffrage norms.[13]

Stage 1: Origins or Emergence of Norms

Although little theoretical work has focused exclusively on the process of "norm building," the accounts of norm origins in most studies stress human agency, indeterminacy, chance occurrences, and favorable events, using process tracing or genealogy as a method.[14] Generalizing from these accounts, two elements seem common in the successful creation of most new norms: norm entrepreneurs and organizational platforms from which entrepreneurs act.

Norm Entrepreneurs.   Norms do not appear out of thin air; they are actively built by agents having strong notions about appropriate or desirable behavior in their community. Prevailing norms that medical personnel and those wounded in war be treated as neutrals and noncombatants are clearly traceable to the efforts of one man, a Genevese Swiss banker named Henry Dunant. Dunant had a transformative personal experience at the battle of Solferino in 1859 and helped found an organization to promote this cause (what became the International Committee of the Red Cross) through an international treaty (the first Geneva Convention). The international campaign for women's suffrage was similarly indebted to the initial leadership of such norm entrepreneurs as Elizabeth Cady Stanton and Susan B. Anthony in the United States and Millicent Garrett Fawcett and Emmeline Pankhurst in England. Both of these cases are consistent with the description Ethan Nadelmann gives of "transnational moral entrepreneurs" who engage in "moral proselytism."[15] Legal theorist Lessig uses the term "meaning managers" or "meaning architects" to describe the same kind of agency in the process of creating norms and larger contexts of social meaning.[16]

[13]Ibid.
[14]See Kowert and Legro 1996; and Price 1995.
[15]Nadelmann 1990.
[16]Lessig 1995.

Norm entrepreneurs are critical for norm emergence because they call attention to issues or even "create" issues by using language that names, interprets, and dramatizes them. Social movement theorists refer to this reinterpretation or renaming process as "framing."[17] The construction of cognitive frames is an essential component of norm entrepreneurs' political strategies, since, when they are successful, the new frames resonate with broader public understandings and are adopted as new ways of talking about and understanding issues. In constructing their frames, norm entrepreneurs face firmly embedded alternative norms and frames that create alternative perceptions of both appropriateness and interest. In the case of the Red Cross, Dunant and his colleagues had to persuade military commanders not to treat valuable medical personnel and resources they captured as spoils of war, to be treated as they saw fit. In the case of women's suffrage and later women's rights, norm entrepreneurs encountered alternative norms about women's interests and the appropriate role for women. In other words, new norms never enter a normative vacuum but instead emerge in a highly contested normative space where they must compete with other norms and perceptions of interest.

This normative contestation has important implications for our understandings of the ways in which a "logic of appropriateness" relates to norms.[18] Efforts to promote a new norm take place within the standards of "appropriateness" defined by prior norms. To challenge existing logics of appropriateness, activists may need to be explicitly "inappropriate." Suffragettes chained themselves to fences, went on hunger strikes, broke windows of government buildings, and refused to pay taxes as ways of protesting their exclusion from political participation. Deliberately inappropriate acts (such as organized civil disobedience), especially those entailing social ostracism or legal punishment, can be powerful tools for norm entrepreneurs seeking to send a message and frame an issue. Thus, at this emergent stage of a norm's life cycle, invoking a logic of appropriateness to explain behavior is complicated by the fact that standards of appropriateness are precisely what is being contested.

Given the costs of inappropriate action and many of the persuasive tools they use, one has to wonder what could possibly motivate norm entrepreneurs (see Table 1). Obviously the answer varies with the norm and the entrepreneur, but for many of the social norms of interest to political scientists, it is very difficult to explain the motivations of norm entrepreneurs without reference to empathy, altruism, and ideational commitment. Empathy exists when actors have the capacity for participating in another's feelings or ideas. Such empathy may lead to empathetic interdependence,

---

[17]David Snow has called this strategic activity *frame alignment*—"by rendering events or occurrences meaningful, frames function to organize experience and guide action, whether individual or collective." Snow et al. 1986, 464.

[18]March and Olsen 1989, and this issue.

TABLE 1. Stages of norms

	Stage 1 *Norm emergence*	Stage 2 *Norm cascade*	Stage 3 *Internalization*
Actors	Norm entrepreneurs with organizational platforms	States, international organizations, networks	Law, professions, bureaucracy
Motives	Altruism, empathy, ideational, commitment	Legitimacy, reputation, esteem	Conformity
Dominant mechanisms	Persuasion	Socialization, institutionalization, demonstration	Habit, institutionalization

where actors "are interested in the welfare of others for its own sake, even if this has no effect on their own material well-being or security."[19] Altruism exists when actors actually take "action designed to benefit another even at the risk of significant harm to the actor's own well-being."[20] Kristen Monroe argues that the essence or "heart" of altruism is a "shared perception of common humanity. . . . a very simple but deeply felt recognition that we all share certain characteristics and are entitled to certain rights, merely by virtue of our common humanity."[21] Ideational commitment is the main motivation when entrepreneurs promote norms or ideas because they believe in the ideals and values embodied in the norms, even though the pursuit of the norms may have no effect on their well-being.

Of course, many norm entrepreneurs do not so much act against their interests as they act in accordance with a redefined understanding of their interests. Suffragists, for example, were working on behalf of a coherent conception of women's political interests, but it was not an understanding initially shared by the great majority of women in the world. Women had to be persuaded that it was indeed in their interests to pursue suffrage. Similarly, the Red Cross had to persuade military leaders that protecting the wounded was compatible with their war aims.

Organizational Platforms. All norm promoters at the international level need some kind of organizational platform from and through which they promote their norms.

---

[19]See Keohane 1984, chap. 7; Keohane 1990a; and Mansbridge 1990.
[20]Monroe 1996. See also Oliner and Oliner 1988.
[21]Monroe 1996, 206.

Sometimes these platforms are constructed specifically for the purpose of promoting the norm, as are many nongovernmental organizations (NGOs) (such as Greenpeace, the Red Cross, and Transafrica) and the larger transnational advocacy networks of which these NGOs become a part (such as those promoting human rights, environmental norms, and a ban on land mines or those that opposed apartheid in South Africa).[22] Often, however, entrepreneurs work from standing international organizations that have purposes and agendas other than simply promoting one specific norm. Those other agendas may shape the content of norms promoted by the organization significantly.[23] The structure of the World Bank has been amply documented to effect the kinds of development norms promulgated from that institution; its organizational structure, the professions from which it recruits, and its relationship with member states and private finance all filter the kinds of norms emerging from it.[24] The UN, similarly, has distinctive structural features that influence the kinds of norms it promulgates about such matters as decolonization, sovereignty, and humanitarian relief.[25] The tripartite structure of the International Labor Organization, which includes labor and business as well as states, strongly influences the kinds of norms it promotes and the ways it promotes them.[26]

One prominent feature of modern organizations and an important source of influence for international organizations in particular is their use of expertise and information to change the behavior of other actors. Expertise, in turn, usually resides in professionals, and a number of empirical studies document the ways that professional training of bureaucrats in these organizations helps or blocks the promotion of new norms within standing organizations. Peter Haas's study of the cleanup of the Mediterranean shows how ecologists were successful in promoting their norms over others' in part because they were able to persuade governments to create new agencies to deal with the cleanup and to staff those posts with like-minded ecologists. Studies of the World Bank similarly document a strong role for professional training in filtering the norms that the bank promotes. In this case, the inability to quantify many costs and benefits associated with antipoverty and basic human needs norms created resistance among the many economists staffing the bank, because projects promoting these norms could not be justified on the basis of "good economics."[27]

Whatever their platform, norm entrepreneurs and the organizations they inhabit usually need to secure the support of state actors to endorse their norms and make

[22]See Sikkink 1993a; Keck and Sikkink 1998; Klotz 1995a,b; and Price 1997.
[23]See Strang and Chang 1993; Finnemore 1996a; Adler 1992; and Ikenberry and Kupchan 1990.
[24]See Ascher 1983; Miller-Adams 1997; Wade 1996b; and Finnemore 1996a.
[25]See Barnett 1995, 1997; McNeely 1995; and Weiss and Pasic 1997.
[26]Strang and Chang 1993.
[27]See Ascher 1983; Miller-Adams 1997; and Finnemore 1996a.

norm socialization a part of their agenda, and different organizational platforms provide different kinds of tools for entrepreneurs to do this.[28] International organizations like the UN and the World Bank, though not tailored to norm promotion, may have the advantage of resources and leverage over weak or developing states they seek to convert to their normative convictions. Networks of NGOs and intergovernmental organizations (IGOs) dealing with powerful states, however, are rarely able to "coerce" agreement to a norm—they must persuade. They must take what is seen as natural or appropriate and convert it into something perceived as wrong or inappropriate. This process is not necessarily or entirely in the realm of reason, though facts and information may be marshaled to support claims. Affect, empathy, and principled or moral beliefs may also be deeply involved, since the ultimate goal is not to challenge the "truth" of something, but to challenge whether it is good, appropriate, and deserving of praise.[29] In these cases, what the organizational network provides is information and access to important audiences for that information, especially media and decision makers.

In most cases, for an emergent norm to reach a threshold and move toward the second stage, it must become institutionalized in specific sets of international rules and organizations.[30] Since 1948, emergent norms have increasingly become institutionalized in international law, in the rules of multilateral organizations, and in bilateral foreign policies. Such institutionalization contributes strongly to the possibility for a norm cascade both by clarifying what, exactly, the norm is and what constitutes violation (often a matter of some disagreement among actors) and by spelling out specific procedures by which norm leaders coordinate disapproval and sanctions for norm breaking. Institutionalization of norms about biological and chemical weapons, for example, has been essential to coordinating the near universal sanctions on Iraq following the Gulf War and has enabled states to coordinate an invasive inspections regime aimed at securing compliance with those norms. Institutionalization is not a necessary condition for a norm cascade, however, and institutionalization may follow, rather than precede, the initiation of a norm cascade. Women's suffrage was not institutionalized in international rules or organizations prior to the beginning of the norm cascade. The first intergovernmental agency created to deal with women's issues was a regional organization, the Inter-American Commission of Women (CIM), established in 1928. Although scholars locate the tipping point on women's

---

[28]Paul Wapner points out that there are exceptions to the centrality of the state in these processes in environmental politics where activists lobby polluting corporations directly to bring about change (for example, the campaign against McDonald's clamshell containers for its sandwiches). Wapner 1996.

[29]Fearon 1997.

[30]See Goldstein and Keohane 1993b; and Katzenstein 1996b.

suffrage around 1930, the norm cascaded in similar ways both in Latin America (where it was institutionalized) and in other places around the world where women's rights were not similarly institutionalized.

Tipping or Threshold Points.   After norm entrepreneurs have persuaded a critical mass of states to become norm leaders and adopt new norms, we can say the norm reaches a threshold or tipping point. Although scholars have provided convincing quantitative empirical support for the idea of a norm tipping point and norm cascades, they have not yet provided a theoretical account for why norm tipping occurs, nor criteria for specifying a priori where, when, and how we would expect it. We propose two tentative hypotheses about what constitutes a "critical mass" and when and where to expect norm tipping. First, although it is not possible to predict exactly how many states must accept a norm to "tip" the process, because states are not equal when it comes to normative weight, empirical studies suggest that norm tipping rarely occurs before one-third of the total states in the system adopt the norm.[31] In the case of women's suffrage, Francisco Ramirez, Yasemin Soysal, and Suzanne Shanahan place the threshold point in 1930, when twenty states (or approximately one-third of the total states in the system at that time) had accepted women's suffrage.[32] In case of land mines, by May 1997 the number of states supporting the ban on anti-personnel land mines reached 60, or approximately one-third of the total states in the system. After that point, a norm cascade occurred, and 124 states ratified the Ottawa land mine treaty in December 1997. . . .

Stage 2: Norm Cascades

Up to the tipping point, little normative change occurs without significant domestic movements supporting such change. After the tipping point has been reached, however, a different dynamic begins. More countries begin to adopt new norms more rapidly even without domestic pressure for such change. Empirical studies suggest that, at this point, often an international or regional demonstration effect or "contagion" occurs in which international and transnational norm influences become more important than domestic politics for effecting norm change.[33] Contagion, however, is too passive a metaphor; we argue that the primary mechanism for promoting norm cascades is an active process of international socialization intended to induce norm breakers to

---

[31]International law has had to wrestle with this problem repeatedly, since many modern international norms are embodied in treaties. Treaties implicitly recognize this concept of critical mass by specifying that a particular number of countries must ratify for the treaty to enter into force. Where treaties exist, the entry into force of the treaty may be a useful proxy for the critical mass necessary to say that a norm exists.

[32]Ramirez, Soysal, and Shanahan 1997.

[33]See Ramirez, Soysal, and Shanahan 1997; and Whitehead 1996.

become norm followers.[34] Kenneth Waltz suggested some of the ways socialization in occurs: emulation (of heroes), praise (for behavior that conforms to group norms), and ridicule (for deviation).[35] In the context of international politics, socialization involves diplomatic praise or censure, either bilateral or multilateral, which is reinforced by material sanctions and incentives. States, however, are not the only agents of social-ization. Networks of norm entrepreneurs and international organizations also act as agents of socialization by pressuring targeted actors to adopt new policies and laws and to ratify treaties and by monitoring compliance with international standards. The International Committee of the Red Cross (ICRC) certainly did not disappear with the signing of the first Geneva Convention. Instead, the ICRC became its chief socializing agent, helping states to teach the new rules of war to their soldiers, collecting informa-tion about violations, and publicizing them to pressure violators to conform.

Socialization is thus the dominant mechanism of a norm cascade—the mechanism through which norm leaders persuade others to adhere—but what makes socialization work? What are the motives that induce states opposed to the norm to adhere and adhere quickly? We argue that states comply with norms in stage 2 for reasons that relate to their identities as members of an international society. Recognition that state identity fundamentally shapes state behavior, and that state identity is, in turn, shaped by the cultural-institutional context within which states act, has been an important contribution of recent norms research.[36] James Fearon similarly argues that one's identity is as a member of a particular social category, and part of the definition of that category is that all members follow certain norms.[37] What happens at the tipping point is that enough states and enough critical states endorse the new norm to redefine appropriate behavior for the identity called "state" or some relevant subset of states (such as a "liberal" state or a European state).

To the degree that states and state elites fashion a political self or identity in rela-tion to the international community, the concept of socialization suggests that the cumulative effect of many countries in a region adopting new norms "may be analo-gous to 'peer pressure' among countries."[38] Three possible motivations for responding to such "peer pressure" are legitimation, conformity, and esteem.

Scholars have long understood that legitimation is important for states and have recognized the role of international sources of legitimation in shaping state behavior.

[34]Socialization involves the "induction of new members . . . into the ways of behavior that are pre-ferred in a society." Barnes, Carter, and Skidmore 1980, 35. Socialization can thus be seen as a mechanism through which new states are induced to change their behavior by adopting those norms preferred by an international society of states. See also Risse, Ropp, and Sikkink, forthcoming.

[35]Waltz 1979, 75–76.

[36]Katzenstein 1996b.

[37]Fearon 1997.

[38]Ramirez, Soysal, and Shanahan 1997.

Claude, for example, described international organizations as "custodians of the seals of international approval and disapproval," and emphasized their crucial role in establishing and assuring adherence to international norms.[39] Certainly there are costs that come with being labeled a "rogue state" in international interactions, since this entails loss of reputation, trust, and credibility, the presence of which have been amply documented to contribute to Pareto-improving effects from interstate interaction. We argue, though, that states also care about international legitimation because it has become an essential contributor to perceptions of domestic legitimacy held by a state's own citizens. Domestic legitimacy is the belief that existing political institutions are better than other alternatives and therefore deserve obedience.[40] Increasingly, citizens make judgments about whether their government is better than alternatives by looking at those alternatives (in the international and regional arena) and by seeing what other people and countries say about their country. Domestic legitimation is obviously important because it promotes compliance with government rules and laws; ruling by force alone is almost impossible. Thus, international legitimation is important insofar as it reflects back on a government's domestic basis of legitimation and consent and thus ultimately on its ability to stay in power. This dynamic was part of the explanation for regime transitions in South Africa, Latin America, and southern Europe.[41]

Conformity and esteem similarly involve evaluative relationships between states and their state "peers." Conformity involves what Robert Axelrod refers to as "social proof"—states comply with norms to demonstrate that they have adapted to the social environment—that they "belong." "By conforming to the actions of those around us, we fulfill a psychological need to be part of a group."[42] Esteem is related to both conformity and legitimacy, but it goes deeper, since it suggests that leaders of states sometimes follow norms because they want others to think well of them, and they want to think well of themselves.[43] Social norms are sustained, in part, by "feelings of embarrassment, anxiety, guilt, and shame that a person suffers at the prospect of violating them."[44] Fearon has argued that identity is based on those aspects of the self in which an individual has special pride or from which an individual gains self-esteem.[45] Thus, the desire to gain or defend one's pride or esteem can explain norm following. In this sense, states care about following norms associated with liberalism because

---

[39]Claude 1966. For more contemporary arguments that international organizations continue to play this role, see Barnett 1997, 1995; and Barnett and Finnemore 1997.

[40]Linz 1978.

[41]See Klotz 1995a,b; and Whitehead 1996.

[42]Axelrod 1986, 1105.

[43]Fearon 1997.

[44]Elster 1989c.

[45]Fearon 1997, 23.

being "liberal states" is part of their identity in the sense of something they take pride in or from which they gain self-esteem. . . .

Stage 3: Internalization

At the extreme of a norm cascade, norms may become so widely accepted that they are internalized by actors and achieve a "taken-for-granted" quality that makes conformance with the norm almost automatic. For this reason, internalized norms can be both extremely powerful (because behavior according to the norm is not questioned) and hard to discern (because actors do not seriously consider or discuss whether to conform). Precisely because they are not controversial, however, these norms are often not the centerpiece of political debate and for that reason tend to be ignored by political scientists. Institutionalists in sociology, however, have made many of these most internalized norms the centerpiece of their research program and have done us the service of problematizing and "denaturalizing" many of the most prominent Western norms that we take for granted—such as those about market exchange, sovereignty, and individualism. Instead of trying to explain variation in state behavior, these scholars are puzzled by the degree of similarity or "isomorphism" among states and societies and how those similarities have increased in recent years. Their explanations for these similarities point to past norm cascades leading to states taking up new responsibilities or endowing individuals with new rights as a matter of course.[46]

Professions often serve as powerful and pervasive agents working to internalize norms among their members. Professional training does more than simply transfer technical knowledge; it actively socializes people to value certain things above others. Doctors are trained to value life above all else. Soldiers are trained to sacrifice life for certain strategic goals. Economists, ecologists, and lawyers all carry different normative biases systematically instilled by their professional training. As state bureaucracies and international organizations have become more and more professionalized over the twentieth century, we should expect to see policy increasingly reflecting the normative biases of the professions that staff decision-making agencies.[47] A number of empirical studies have already documented a role for highly internalized norms held by professionals determining policy. In addition to the role of economists at the World Bank mentioned earlier, Anne-Marie Burley's work shows a crucial role for legal professional norms in creating the post—World War II political order, and her work with Walter Mattli shows their importance in the European Union.[48]

[46]See Bergesen 1980; Thomas et al. 1987; Scott and Meyer 1994; McNeely 1995; Meyer et al. 1997; and Finnemore 1996b.

[47]See Haas 1989; Ascher 1983; Adler 1992; Miller-Adams 1997; Finnemore 1995; and Barnett and Finnemore 1997.

[48]See Burley 1993; and Burley and Mattli 1993. These empirical findings are consistent with theoretical arguments made by DiMaggio and Powell 1983.

Another powerful and related mechanism contributing to the consolidation and universalization of norms after a norm cascade may be iterated behavior and habit. Political scientists have understood the power of these mechanisms for years but have not connected them theoretically to norms and social construction debates. The core of the neofunctionalist argument about integration in Europe, after all, was that frequent interactions among people involving joint work on technical tasks would ultimately create predictability, stability, and habits of trust. As trust became habitual, it would become internalized and internalized trust would, in turn, change affect among the participants. Changed affect meant changed identity and changed norms as empathy and identification with others shifted. Thus, the engine of integration was indirect and evolutionary. Diplomatic tools such as confidence-building measures and track 2 diplomacy may follow a similar logic. Generalized, this argument suggests that routes to normative change may be similarly indirect and evolutionary: procedural changes that create new political processes can lead to gradual and inadvertent normative, ideational, and political convergence.[49] . . .

[49]See also Rosenau 1986.

FEMINIST PERSPECTIVES ON NATIONAL SECURITY

J. ANN TICKNER

It is difficult to find definitions by women of national security. While it is not necessarily the case that women have not had ideas on this subject, they are not readily accessible in the literature of international relations. When women speak or write about national security, they are often dismissed as being naive or unrealistic. An example of this is the women in the United States and Europe who spoke out in the early years of the century for a more secure world order. Addressing the International Congress of Women at the Hague during World War I, Jane Addams spoke of the need for a new internationalism to replace the self-destructive nationalism that contributed so centrally to the outbreak and mass destruction of that war. Resolutions adopted at the close of the congress questioned the assumption that women, and civilians more generally, could be protected during modern war. The conference concluded that assuring security through military means was no longer possible owing to the indiscriminate nature of modern warfare, and it called for disarmament as a more appropriate course for ensuring future security.

At the Women's International Peace Conference in Hali-fax, Canada, in 1985, a meeting of women from all over the world, participants defined security in various ways depending on the most immediate threats to their survival; security meant safe working conditions and freedom from the threat of war or unemployment or the economic squeeze of foreign debt. Discussions of the meaning of security revealed divisions between Western middle-class women's concerns with nuclear war, concerns that were similar to those of Jane Addams and her colleagues, and Third World women who defined insecurity more broadly in terms of the structural violence associated with imperialism, militarism, racism, and sexism. Yet all agreed that security meant nothing if it was built on others' insecurity.

The final document of the World Conference to Review and Appraise the Achievements of the United Nations Decade for Women, held in Nairobi in 1985, offered a similarly multidimensional definition of security. The introductory chapter of the document defined peace as "not only the absence of war, violence and hostilities at the national and international levels but also the enjoyment of economic and social justice." All these definitions of security take issue with realists' assumptions that security is zero-sum and must therefore be built on the insecurity of others.

Jane Addams's vision of national security, which deemphasizes its military dimension and was dismissed at the time as impractical, is quite compatible with the new thinking on common security I have just described. Like women at the Halifax and Nairobi conferences, contemporary new thinkers also include the elimination of structural violence in their definition of security. Feminist peace researcher Elise Boulding tells us that women peace researchers were among the pioneers in this contemporary redefinition of security, although, like Jane Addams at the beginning of the century, their work did not receive the attention it deserved. It is often the case that new ideas in any discipline do not receive widespread attention unless they are adopted by significant numbers of men, in which case women's work tends to become invisible through co-optation. Boulding claims that the one area in which women are not in danger of co-optation is their analysis of patriarchy and the linkage of war to violence against women. Like most other feminists, Boulding believes that these issues must also be included in any comprehensive definition of security.

Given these various definitions of security offered by women, it is evident that feminist perspectives on security would grow out of quite different assumptions about the individual, the state, and the international system. Using feminist literature from various disciplines and approaches I shall now suggest what some of these perspectives might look like.

REEXAMINING THE ANARCHY/ORDER DISTINCTION

The pervasiveness of internal conflict within states in the latter part of the twentieth century and the threats that militarized states pose to their own populations have called into question the realist assumption about the anarchy/order distinction. Critics of realism have also questioned the unitary actor assumption that renders the domestic affairs of states unproblematic when talking about their international behavior. Claiming that militarism, sexism, and racism are inter-connected, most feminists would agree that the behavior of individuals and the domestic policies of states cannot be separated from states' behavior in the international system. Feminists call attention to the particular vulnerabilities of women within states, vulnerabilities that grow out of hierarchical gender relations that are also interrelated with international politics. Calling into question the notion of the "protected," the National Organization for Women in their "Resolution on Women in Combat" of September 16, 1990, estimated that 80–90 percent of casualties due to conflict since World War II have been civilians, the majority of whom have been women and children. In militarized societies women are particularly vulnerable to rape, and evidence suggests that domestic violence is higher in military families or in families that include men with prior military service. Even though most public violence is committed by men against other men, it is more often women who feel threatened in public places. Jill Radford suggests that when women feel it is unsafe to go out alone, their equal access to job opportunities is limited. Studies also show that violence against women increases during hard economic times; when states prioritize military spending or find themselves in debt, shrinking resources are often accompanied by violence against women.

Feminist theories draw our attention to another anarchy/order distinction—the boundary between a public domestic space protected, at least theoretically, by the rule of law and the private space of the family where, in many cases, no such legal protection exists. In most states domestic violence is not considered a concern of the state, and even when it is, law enforcement officials are often unwilling to get involved. Domestic assaults on women, often seen as "victim precipitated," are not taken as seriously as criminal assaults. Maria Mies argues that the modernization process in the Third World, besides sharpening class conflict, has led to an increase in violence against women in the home as traditional social values are broken down. While poor women probably suffer the most from family violence, a growing women's movement in India points to an increase in violence against educated middle-class women also, the most extreme form of which is dowry murder when young brides are found dead in suspicious circumstances. Eager to marry off their daughters, families make promises for dowries that exceed their means and that they are subsequently unable to pay. In 1982 there were 332 cases of "accidental burning" of women in New Delhi; many more cases of "dowry deaths" go unreported.

Recent studies of family violence in the United States and Western Europe have brought to light similar problems. When the family is violence-prone, it is frequently beyond the reach of the law; citing a 1978 report of the California Commission on the Status of Women, Pauline Gee documents that in 1978 one-quarter of the murders in the United States occurred within the family, one-half of these being husband-wife killings. Much of this family violence takes place outside the sanction of the legal system; it has been estimated that only 2 percent of men who beat their wives or female living partners are ever prosecuted.

Maria Mies argues that this line, which demarcates public and private, separates state-regulated violence, the rule of right for which there are legally sanctioned punishments, and male violence, the rule of might for which, in many societies, no such legal sanctions exist. The rule of might and the rule of right are descriptions that have also been used in international relations discourse to distinguish the international and domestic spheres. By drawing our attention to the frequently forgotten realm of family violence that is often beyond the reach of the law, these feminists point to the interrelationship of violence and oppression across all levels of analysis. Feminist perspectives on security would assume that violence, whether it be in the international, national, or family realm, is interconnected. Family violence must be seen in the context of wider power relations; it occurs within a gendered society in which male power dominates at all levels. If men are traditionally seen as protectors, an important aspect of this role is protecting women against certain men. Any feminist definition of security must therefore include the elimination of all types of violence, including violence produced by gender relations of domination and subordination. The achievement of this comprehensive vision of security requires a rethinking of the way in which citizenship has traditionally been defined, as well as alternative models for describing the behavior of states in the international system.

CITIZENSHIP REDEFINED

Building on the notion of hegemonic masculinity, the notion of the citizen-warrior depends on a devalued femininity for its construction. In international relations, this devalued femininity is bound up with myths about women as victims in need of protection; the protector/protected myth contributes to the legitimation of a militarized version of citizenship that results in unequal gender relations that can precipitate violence against women. Certain feminists have called for the construction of an enriched version of citizenship that would depend less on military values and more on an equal recognition of women's contributions to society. Such a notion of citizenship cannot come about, however, until myths that perpetuate views of women as victims rather than agents are eliminated.

One such myth is the association of women with peace, an association that has been invalidated through considerable evidence of women's support for men's wars in many societies. In spite of a gender gap, a plurality of women generally support war and national security policies; Bernice Carroll suggests that the association of women and peace is one that has been imposed on women by their disarmed condition. In the West, this association grew out of the Victorian ideology of women's moral superiority and the glorification of motherhood. This ideal was expressed by feminist Charlotte Perkins Gilman whose book *Herland* was first serialized in *The Forerunner* in 1915. Gilman glorified women as caring and nurturing mothers whose private sphere skills could benefit the world at large. Most turn-of-the-century feminists shared Gilman's ideas. But if the implication of this view was that women were disqualified from participating in the corrupt world of political and economic power by virtue of their moral superiority, the result could only be the perpetuation of male dominance. Many contemporary feminists see dangers in the continuation of these essentializing myths that can only result in the perpetuation of women's subordination and reinforce dualisms that serve to make men more powerful. The association of femininity with peace lends support to an idealized masculinity that depends on constructing women as passive victims in need of protection. It also contributes to the claim that women are naive in matters relating to international politics. An enriched, less militarized notion of citizenship cannot be built on such a weak foundation.

While women have often been willing to support men's wars, many women are ambivalent about fighting in them, often preferring to leave that task to men. Feminists have also been divided on this issue; some argue, on the grounds of equality, that women must be given equal access to the military, while others suggest that women must resist the draft in order to promote a politics of peace. In arguing for women's equal access to the military, Judith Stiehm proposes that a society composed of citizens equally likely to experience violence and be responsible for its exercise would be stronger and more desirable. Stiehm claims that if everyone, women and men alike, were protectors, less justification for immoral acts would be found; with less emphasis on the manliness of war, new questions about its morality could be raised. She suggests that women's enhanced role in the military could lead to a new concept of citizen-defender rather than warrior-patriot.

Just as the notion of a soldier as a wife and mother changes our image of soldiering, citizen-defenders change our image of war. Citizen-defenders are quite compatible with what Stephen Nathanson, in his redefinition of the meaning of patriotism, calls a moderate patriot. Rather than the traditional view of patriotism built on aggression and war, Nathanson suggests thinking of patriotism as support for one's own nation while not inflicting harm on others. Such patriotism could be consistent with a defensive strategy in war if everyone were to comply.

Discarding the association between women and pacifism allows us to think of women as activists for the kind of change needed to achieve the multidimensional security I have already discussed. Even if not all women are pacifists, peace is an issue that women can support in their various roles as mothers, war victims, and preservers of states' and the world's good health. Women at Greenham Common demonstrating against the installation off cruise missiles in Britain in 1981 came to see themselves as strong, brave, and creative—experiences frequently confined to men. The Madres de la Plaza de Mayo, demonstrating during the 1980s in support of those who had disappeared in Argentina during the military dictatorship, experienced similar empowerment. Sara Ruddick suggests conscripting women in the interests of peace; Ruddick claims that while caring for children is not "natural" for women, it has been a womanly practice in most societies and one that she believes is an important resource for peace politics. Ruddick defines maternal thinking as focused on the preservation of life and the growth of children. Maternal practice requires the peaceful settlement of disputes; since she feels that it is a mode of thinking to be found in men as well as women, it is one that could be useful for a politics of peace were it to be validated in the public realm.

In spite of many women's support for men's wars, a consistent gender gap in voting on defense-related issues in many countries suggests that women are less supportive of policies that rest on the use of direct violence. Before the outbreak of the Persian Gulf war in 1990, women in the United States were overwhelmingly against the use of force and, for the first time, women alone turned the public opinion polls against opting for war. During the 1980s, when the Reagan administration was increasing defense budgets, women were less likely to support defense at the expense of social programs, a pattern that, in the United States, holds true for women's behavior more generally.

Explanations for this gender gap, which in the United States appears to be increasing as time goes on, range from suggestions that women have not been socialized into the practice of violence to claims that women are increasingly voting their own interests. While holding down jobs, millions of women also care for children, the aged, and the sick—activities that usually take place outside the economy. When more resources go to the military, additional burdens are placed on such women as public sector resources for social services shrink. While certain women are able, through access to the military, to give service to their country, many more are serving in these traditional care-giving roles. A feminist challenge to the traditional definition of patriotism should therefore question the meaning of service to one's country. In contrast to a citizenship that rests on the assumption that it is more glorious to die than to live for one's state, Wendy Brown suggests that a more constructive view of citizenship could center on the courage to sustain life. In similar terms, Jean Elshtain asserts the need to move toward a politics that shifts the focus of political loyalty and identity from sacrifice to responsibility. Only when women's contributions to society are seen as equal to men's can these reconstructed visions of citizenship come about.

FEMINIST PERSPECTIVES ON STATES' SECURITY-SEEKING BEHAVIOR

Realists have offered us an instrumental version of states' security-seeking behavior, which, I have argued, depends on a partial representation of human behavior associated with a stereotypical hegemonic masculinity. Feminist redefinitions of citizenship allow us to envisage a less militarized version of states' identities, and feminist theories can also propose alternative models for states' international security-seeking behavior, extrapolated from a more comprehensive view of human behavior.

Realists use state-of-nature stories as metaphors to describe the insecurity of states in an anarchical international system. I shall suggest an alternative story, which could equally be applied to the behavior of individuals in the state of nature. Although frequently unreported in standard historical accounts, it is a true story, not a myth, about a state of nature in early nineteenth-century America. Among those present in the first winter encampment of the 1804–1806 Lewis and Clark expedition into the Northwest territories was Sacajawea, a member of the Shoshone tribe. Sacajawea had joined the expedition as the wife of a French interpreter; her presence was proving invaluable to the security of the expedition's members, whose task it was to explore uncharted territory and establish contact with the native inhabitants to inform them of claims to these territories by the United States. Although unanticipated by its leaders, the presence of a woman served to assure the native inhabitants that the expedition was peaceful since the Native Americans assumed that war parties would not include women: the expedition was therefore safer because it was not armed.

This story demonstrates that the introduction of women can change the way humans are assumed to behave in the state of nature. Just as Sacajawea's presence changed the Native American's expectations about the behavior of intruders into their territory, the introduction of women into our state-of-nature myths could change the way we think about the behavior of states in the international system. The use of the Hobbesian analogy in international relations theory is based on a partial view of human nature that is stereotypically masculine; a more inclusive perspective would see human nature as both conflictual and cooperative, containing elements of social reproduction and interdependence as well as domination and separation. Generalizing from this more comprehensive view of human nature, a feminist perspective would assume that the potential for international community also exists and that an atomistic, conflictual view of the international system is only a partial representation of reality. Liberal individualism, the instrumental rationality of the marketplace, and the defector's self-help approach in Rousseau's stag hunt are all, in analogous ways, based on a partial masculine model of human behavior.

These characterizations of human behavior, with their atomistic view of human society, do not assume the need for interdependence and cooperation. Yet states frequently exhibit aspects of cooperative behavior when they engage in diplomatic negotiations. As Cynthia Enloe states, diplomacy runs smoothly when there is trust and confidence between officials representing governments with conflicting interests. She suggests that many agreements are negotiated informally in the residences of ambassadors where the presence of diplomatic wives creates an atmosphere in which trust can best be cultivated. As Enloe concludes, women, often in positions that are unremunerated or undervalued, remain vital to creating and maintaining trust between men in a hostile world.

Given the interdependent nature of contemporary security threats, new thinking on security has already assumed that autonomy and self-help, as models for state behavior in the international system, must be rethought and redefined. Many feminists would agree with this, but given their assumption that interdependence is as much a human characteristic as autonomy, they would question whether autonomy is even desirable. Autonomy is associated with masculinity just as femininity is associated with interdependence: in her discussion of the birth of modern science in the seventeenth century, Evelyn Keller links the rise of what she terms a masculine science with a striving for objectivity, autonomy, and control. Perhaps not coincidentally, the seventeenth century also witnessed the rise of the modern state system. Since this period, autonomy and separation, importantly associated with the meaning of sovereignty, have determined our conception of the national interest. Betty Reardon argues that this association of autonomy with the national interest tends to blind us to the realities of interdependence in the present world situation. Feminist perspectives would thus assume that striving for attachment is also part of human nature, which, while it has been suppressed by both modern scientific thinking and the practices of the Western state system, can be reclaimed and revalued in the future.

Evelyn Keller argues for a form of knowledge that she calls "dynamic objectivity . . . that grants to the world around us its independent integrity, but does so in a way that remains cognizant of, indeed relies on, our connectivity with that world." Keller's view of dynamic objectivity contains parallels with what Sandra Harding calls an African world-view. Harding tells us that the Western liberal notion of instrumentally rational economic man, similar to the notion of rational political man upon which realism has based its theoretical investigations, does not make sense in the African worldview where the individual is seen as part of the social order and as acting within that order rather than upon it. Harding believes that this view of human behavior has much in common with a feminist perspective; such a view of human behavior could help us to begin to think from a more global perspective that appreciates cultural diversity but at the same time recognizes a growing interdependence that makes anachronistic the exclusionary thinking fostered by the state system.

Besides a reconsideration of autonomy, feminist theories also offer us a different definition of power that could be useful for thinking about the achievement of the type of positive-sum security that the women at The Hague and in Halifax and Nairobi described as desirable. Hannah Arendt, frequently cited by feminists writing about power, defines power as the human ability to act in concert or action that is taken with others who share similar concerns. This definition of power is similar to that of psychologist David Mc-Clelland's portrayal of female power which he describes as shared rather than assertive. Jane Jaquette argues that, since women have had less access to the instruments of coercion (the way power is usually used in international relations), women have more often used persuasion as a way of gaining power through coalition building. These writers are conceptualizing power as mutual enablement rather than domination. While not denying that the way power is frequently used in international relations comes closer to a coercive mode, thinking about power in these terms is helpful for devising the cooperative solutions necessary for solving the security threats identified in the Halifax women's definitions of security.

These different views of human behavior as models for the international behavior of states point us in the direction of an appreciation of the "other" as a subject whose views are as legitimate as our own, a way of thinking that has been sadly lacking as states go about providing for their own security. Using feminist perspectives that are based on the experiences and behavior of women, I have constructed some models of human behavior that avoid hierarchical dichotomization and that value ambiguity and difference; these alternative models could stand us in good stead as we seek to construct a less gendered vision of global security.

Feminist perspectives on national security take us beyond realism's statist representations. They allow us to see that the realist view of national security is constructed out of a masculinized discourse that, while it is only a partial view of reality, is taken as universal. Women's definitions of security are multilevel and multidimensional. Women have defined security as the absence of violence whether it be military, economic, or sexual. Not until the hierarchical social relations, including gender relations, that have been hidden by realism's frequently depersonalized discourse are brought to light can we begin to construct a language of national security that speaks out of the multiple experiences of both women and men. As I have argued, feminist theory sees all these types of violence as interrelated. I shall turn next to the economic dimension of this multidimensional perspective on security.

Part II

INTERNATIONAL INSTITUTIONS AND COOPERATION

INTRODUCTION

Explaining the existence or absence of cooperation between states is a major issue in International Relations. Liberals examine the ways states might cooperate to solve common problems or obtain common goals, including organizing themselves in international institutions. Realists tend to doubt the durability of interstate cooperation beyond a pressing security need.[1] This is why states form and abandon alliances. Constructivists expect cooperation between states to emerge from shared values, norms, or ideas, while conflicting identities and misunderstandings might undermine organizations. In this section, we explore the problem of cooperation, the conditions under which cooperation may occur, game-theoretic solutions to the problem, and constructivist explanations for international institutions.

The neoliberal and neorealist disagreement on the feasibility of cooperation is the principal point of contention between the two approaches. Neoliberals argue that international organizations provide a number of solutions to collective action problems, allowing states to cooperate. According to the collective action problem, the ease of free riding on the public good provided by the organization prevents states from contributing sufficiently. The larger the number of participants, the worse the problem becomes. Sanctioning a defecting state is made difficult by the tendency of states to want to buck-pass the responsibility and costs of enforcing an agreement.[2] Neoliberals argue that unsanctioned free-riding could ultimately lead to the collapse of the agreement or organization, unless states institute means to reliably catch and punish cheating. Neorealists counter that neoliberals miss the point—international cooperation is problematic for states because of fundamental relative gains concerns,

[1] David A. Baldwin, ed., *Neorealism and Neoliberalism: The Contemporary Debate* (New York: Columbia University Press, 1993).
[2] Mancur Olson, *The Logic of Collective Action* (Cambridge: Harvard University Press, 1965).

not problems with compliance. Neorealists argue cooperation is made nearly impossible by the fear of exploitation by a state defecting from an agreement, as well as the collective action problem, as Joseph M. Grieco argues in "Anarchy and the Limits of Cooperation" in Part I.

The study of cooperation draws heavily on rational choice theory. Rational choice theories use the simplified assumption that behavior and political outcomes can be modeled as choices by actors with fixed preferences seeking to maximize these preferences based on expected payoffs. Strategic interaction—when the actions of each party depend not only its own preferences but also expectations about others' preferences which in turn depend upon expectations of their preferences, and the knowledge that each players' choice will affect the outcomes for all—characterizes both rational choice thinking and the international system. Rational choice approaches contend that we can generate important insights about international politics, even if foreign policy decisions aren't always rational, if we model them *as if* they were rational. In particular, they assume (1) that states act as unitary rational actors and make decisions based on their objective national interest, (2) that the national interest can be calculated in a complete and consistent fashion, and (3) that leaders can calculate how to maximize utility.[3] Leaders do not always get what they want or intend, however. Individually rational choices often lead to collectively irrational outcomes, and rational choice models help us to understand why. In "The Tragedy of the Commons," Garrett Hardin elaborates a recurring cooperation failure. Even under circumstances of complete information, there are instances in which completely rational actors will make choices that will ultimately result in sub-optimal outcomes. In particular, when the costs of exploiting a resource are borne unevenly, there are incentives to cheat that result in the (avoidable) destruction of a common resource.

Rational choice theorists often draw on game-theoretical models to clarify strategic interaction and explain possible but unexpected outcomes. The simplest of such models presents problems of cooperation on a 2×2 matrix, where two states have the options only to cooperate (C) or defect (D). The Prisoners' Dilemma is the most common game of this sort and is used to illustrate the potential for even rational actors acting rationally to achieve both collectively and individually suboptimal outcomes due to a payoff structure (DD>CD and DC>CC) that makes it preferable for states to defect in an anarchical international system regardless of the other actor's choices. Nonetheless, if the game is iterated (if it is repeated many times among the same actors, who are aware that they will play subsequent rounds), cooperation becomes possible, as states can aim for higher payoffs in subsequent rounds by linking behavior in later rounds to the choices made in earlier rounds. Such iteration can occur in

---

[3]David A. Lake and Robert Powell, eds., *Strategic Choice and International Relations* (Princeton: Princeton University Press, 1999).

international politics through issue linkage, cooperating in small incremental steps, or working within international institutions, which facilitate repeated interaction between member-states. Kenneth A. Oye argues in the "The Conditions for Cooperation in World Politics" that cooperation in international organizations is possible even in anarchy as long as the benefits to states are high enough, states intend to interact in the future, and there aren't too many players.

But material interests and incentives may not be enough to sustain cooperation in the long term, particularly when conditions in the international system are uncertain or likely to change.[4] While the benefit of cooperation exceeds the costs of cooperation, states have an interest in working together, but they may not know the best means to solve their common problems or obtain their goals. Technical cooperation and problem solving may draw states more deeply into political cooperation and lead to the elaboration of international regimes, as Ernst B. Haas argues in "Functionalism." International regimes, as "principles, norms, rules, and decision-making procedures around which actor expectations converge in a given issue-area,"[5] help to deepen cooperation and fill in the blanks in formal agreements, allowing the regime to adjust to emerging issues. International regime theories argue that regimes help to reduce transaction costs, increase the predictability of international politics, monitor and punish defection, and provide information and a forum for the resolution of disputes. States have also worked to elaborate international law as standards that states should hold, with mixed results. Realists assert that international law and organizations are likely to have little independent influence on state behavior, as they reflect underlying power structures rather than changing state behavior. Liberals counter that international institutions and laws can change the incentives and information of states and thus change a state's strategy to obtain its goals. Constructivists go even further to argue that international institutions, including norms as well as formal international organizations, can change the very definition of states' goals and identity. Gareth Evans and Mohamed Sahnoun examine the potential of international law to change interests and norms to stop genocide in "The Responsibility to Protect."

International organizations (IOs) are the common institutional embodiment of international cooperation. According to Keohane and Nye, as well as other work by Keohane, IOs facilitate bargaining via issue-linkage so that everyone gains, increase states' confidence that each state will uphold its side of the bargain, and help to

---

[4]Robert Keohane, "The Demand for International Regimes," *International Organization* 36 (1982); George W. Downs and David M. Rocke, *Optimal Imperfection?* (Princeton: Princeton University Press, 1995).

[5]Stephen D. Krasner, "Structural Causes and Regime Consequences: Regimes as Intervening Variables," in Stephen D. Krasner, ed. *International Regimes* (Ithaca: Cornell University Press, 1983), p. 1.

monitor agreements and punish cheating. The United Nations (UN) as one of the oldest, largest, and richest international organizations receives a preponderance of attention. The UN stands out because states have entrusted it with the task of maintaining international peace and security and given one of its bodies, the Security Council, particular powers to help it do so. Erik Voeten, in "The Political Origins of the UN Security Council's Ability to Legitimize the Use of Force," examines why this is the case and what the Security Council has done to help preserve international peace and security over the last 65 years.

RATIONAL CHOICE THEORIES OF COOPERATION

EXPLAINING COOPERATION UNDER ANARCHY

KENNETH A. OYE

I. INTRODUCTION

Nations dwell in perpetual anarchy, for no central authority imposes limits on the pursuit of sovereign interests. This common condition gives rise to diverse outcomes. Relations among states are marked by war and concert, arms races and arms control, trade wars and tariff truces, financial panics and rescues, competitive devaluation and monetary stabilization. At times, the absence of centralized international authority precludes attainment of common goals. Because as states, they cannot cede ultimate control over their conduct to an supranational sovereign, they cannot guarantee that they will adhere to their promises. The possibility of a breach of promise can impede cooperation even when cooperation would leave all better off. Yet, at other times, states do realize common goals through cooperation under anarchy. Despite the absence of any ultimate international authority, governments often bind themselves to mutually advantageous courses of action. And, though no international sovereign stands ready

From "Explaining Cooperation under Anarchy: Hypotheses and Strategies" by Kenneth A. Oye from *World Politics*, Vol. 38, No. 1, October 1985, pp. 1–24. © 1985 by Trustees of Princeton University. Reprinted by permission of Cambridge University Press.

to enforce the terms of agreement, states can realize common interests through tacit cooperation, formal bilateral and multilateral negotiation, and the creation of international regimes. The question is: If international relations can approximate both a Hobbesian state of nature and a Lockean civil society, why does cooperation emerge in some cases and not in others?

The contributors to this symposium address both explanatory and prescriptive aspects of this perennial question. *First, what circumstances favor the emergence of cooperation under anarchy?* Given the lack of a central authority to guarantee adherence to agreements, what features of situations encourage or permit states to bind themselves to mutually beneficial courses of action? What features of situations preclude cooperation? *Second, what strategies can states adopt to foster the emergence of cooperation by altering the circumstances they confront?* Governments need not necessarily accept circumstances as given. To what extent are situational impediments to cooperation subject to willful modification? Through what higher order strategies can states create the preconditions for cooperation?

The problem of explaining and promoting international cooperation encompasses many of the principal questions in the disciplines of political economy and security studies. However, divergent terminological conventions and substantive applications have impeded the comparison of answers. In the essays presented here, a unified analytic framework, derived from elementary game theory and microeconomics, has been superimposed on cases in international security and economic affairs. This use of the austere abstractions of game theory and microeconomics offers several advantages. First, superficial differences often obscure the parallelism of questions, explanations, and prescriptions in the two fields. By reducing concepts to fundamentals, the use of elements of game theory and microeconomics permits ready identification of parallels. Second, intrinsic differences between the politics of war and the politics of wealth and welfare may give rise to divergent explanations and prescriptions. A unified analytic framework facilitates explicit recognition of differences in the extent and causes of, and prospects for, cooperation in security and economic affairs. Finally, uneven intellectual development may give rise to divergent explanations and prescriptions. A unified analytic framework fosters transference of useful concepts between the fields.

In this introductory essay, I submit that three circumstantial dimensions serve both as proximate explanations of cooperation and as targets of longer-term strategies to promote cooperation. Each of the three major sections of this piece defines a dimension, explains how that dimension accounts for the incidence of cooperation and conflict in the absence of centralized authority, and examines associated strategies for enhancing the prospects for cooperation.

II. PAYOFF STRUCTURE: MUTUAL AND CONFLICTING PREFERENCES

The structure of payoffs in a given round of play—the benefits of mutual cooperation (CC) relative to mutual defection (DD) and the benefits of unilateral defection (DC) relative to unrequited cooperation (CD)—is fundamental to the analysis of cooperation. The argument proceeds in three stages. First, how does payoff structure affect the significance of cooperation? More narrowly, when is cooperation, defined in terms of conscious policy coordination, necessary to the realization of mutual interests? Second, how does payoff structure affect the likelihood and robustness of cooperation? Third, through what strategies can states increase the long-term prospects for cooperation by altering payoff structures?

A. Payoff Structure and Cooperation

How does payoff structure determine the significance of cooperation? More narrowly, when is *cooperation*, defined in terms of conscious policy coordination, *necessary* to the realization of *mutual benefits*? For a *mutual benefit* to exist, actors must prefer mutual cooperation (CC) to mutual defection (DD). For coordination to be *necessary* to the realization of the mutual benefit, actors must prefer unilateral defection (DC) to unrequited cooperation (CD). These preference orderings are consistent with the familiar games of Prisoners' Dilemma, Stag Hunt, and Chicken. Indeed, these games have attracted a disproportionate share of scholarly attention precisely because cooperation is desirable but not automatic. In these cases, the capacity of states to cooperate under anarchy, to bind themselves to mutually beneficial courses of action without resort to any ultimate central authority, is vital to the realization of a common good.

In the class of games—including Prisoners' Dilemma, Stag Hunt, and Chicken—where cooperation is necessary to the realization of mutual benefits, how does payoff structure affect the likelihood and robustness of cooperation in these situations? Cooperation will be less likely in Prisoners' Dilemma than in Stag Hunt or Chicken. To understand why, consider each of these games in conjunction with the illustrative stories from which they derive their names.

Prisoners' Dilemma Two prisoners are suspected of a major crime. The authorities possess evidence to secure conviction on only a minor charge. If neither prisoner squeals, both will draw a light sentence on the minor charge (CC). If one prisoner squeals and the other stonewalls, the rat will go free (DC) and the sucker will draw a very heavy sentence (CD). If both squeal, both will draw a moderate sentence (DD). Each prisoner's preference ordering is: DC > CC > DD > CD. If the prisoners expect to "play" only one time, each prisoner will be better off squealing than stonewalling, no matter what his partner chooses to do (DC > CC and DD > CD). The temptation of the rat payoff and fear of the sucker payoff will drive single-play Prisoners' Dilemmas toward mutual defection. Unfortunately, if both prisoners act on this reasoning, they will draw a moderate sentence on the major charge, while cooperation could have led to a light sentence on the minor charge (CC > DD). In single-play Prisoners' Dilemmas, individually rational actions produce a collectively suboptimal outcome.

Stag Hunt   A group of hunters surround a stag. If all cooperate to trap the stag, all will eat well (CC). If one person defects to chase a passing rabbit, the stag will escape. The defector will eat lightly (DC) and none of the others will eat at all (CD). If all chase rabbits, all will have some chance of catching a rabbit and eating lightly (DD). Each hunter's preference ordering is: CC > DC > DD > CD. The mutual interest in plentiful venison (CC) relative to all other outcomes militates strongly against defection. However, because a rabbit in the hand (DC) is better than a stag in the bush (CD), cooperation will be assured only if each hunter believes that all hunters will cooperate. In single-play Stag Hunt, the temptation to defect to protect against the defection of others is balanced by the strong universal preference for stag over rabbit.

Chicken   Two drivers race down the center of a road from opposite directions. If one swerves and the other does not, then the first will suffer the stigma of being known as a chicken (CD) while the second will enjoy being known as a hero (DC). If neither swerves, both will suffer grievously in the ensuing collision (DD). If both swerve, damage to the reputation of each will be limited (CC). Each driver's preference ordering is: DC > CC > CD > DD. If each believes that the other will swerve, then each will be tempted to defect by continuing down the center of the road. Better to be a live hero than a live chicken. If both succumb to this temptation, however, defection will result in collision. The fear that the other driver may not swerve decreases the appeal of continuing down the center of the road. In single-play Chicken, the temptations of unilateral defection are balanced by fear of mutual defection.

In games that are not repeated, only ordinally defined preferences matter. Under single-play conditions, interval-level payoffs in ordinally defined categories of games cannot (in theory) affect the likelihood of cooperation. In the illustrations above, discussions of dominant strategies do not hinge on the magnitude of differences among the payoffs. Yet the magnitude of differences between CC and DD and between DC and CD can be large or small, if not precisely measurable, and can increase or decrease. Changes in the magnitude of differences in the value placed on outcomes can influence the prospects for cooperation through two paths.

First, changes in the value attached to outcomes can transform situations from one ordinally defined class of game into another. For example, in "Cooperation under the Security Dilemma" Robert Jervis described how difficult Prisoners' Dilemmas may evolve into less challenging Stag Hunts if the gains from mutual cooperation

(CC) increase relative to the gains from exploitation (DC). He related the structure of payoffs to traditional concepts of offensive and defensive dominance, and offensive and defensive dominance to technological and doctrinal shifts. Ernst Haas, Mary Pat Williams, and Don Babai have emphasized the importance of cognitive congruence as a determinant of technological cooperation. The diffusion of common conceptions of the nature and effects of technology enhanced perceived gains from cooperation and diminished perceived gains from defection, and may have transformed some Prisoners' Dilemmas into Harmony.[1]

Second, under iterated conditions, the magnitude of differences among payoffs *within* a given class of games can be an important determinant of cooperation. The more substantial the gains from mutual cooperation (CC-DD) and the less substantial the gains from unilateral defection (DC-CD), the greater the likelihood of cooperation. In iterated situations, the magnitude of the difference between CC and DD and between DC and CD in present and future rounds of play affects the likelihood of cooperation in the present. This point is developed at length in the section on the shadow of the future.

B. Strategies to Alter Payoff Structure

If payoff structure affects the likelihood of cooperation, to what extent can states alter situations by modifying payoff structures, and thereby increase the long-term likelihood of cooperation? Many of the tangible and intangible determinants of payoff structure, discussed at the outset of this section, are subject to willful modification through unilateral, bilateral, and multilateral strategies. In "Cooperation under the Security Dilemma," Robert Jervis has offered specific suggestions for altering payoff structures through unilateral strategies. Procurement policy can affect the prospects for cooperation. If one superpower favors procurement of defensive over offensive weapons, it can reduce its own gains from exploitation through surprise attack (DC) and reduce its adversary's fear of exploitation (CD). Members of alliances have often resorted to the device of deploying troops on troubled frontiers to increase the likelihood of cooperation. A state's use of troops as hostages is designed to diminish the payoff from its own defection—to reduce its gains from exploitation (DC)—and thereby render defensive defection by its partner less likely. Publicizing an agreement diminishes payoffs associated with defection from the agreement, and thereby lessens gains from exploitation. These observations in international relations are paralleled by recent developments in microeconomics. Oliver Williamson has identified unilateral

---

[1]Haas, Williams, and Babai, *Scientists and World Order: The Uses of Technical Knowledge in International Organizations* (Berkeley: University of California Press, 1977).

and bilateral techniques used by firms to facilitate interfirm cooperation by diminishing gains from exploitation. He distinguishes between specific and nonspecific costs associated with adherence to agreements. Specific costs, such as specialized training, machine tools, and construction, cannot be recovered in the event of the breakdown of an agreement. When parties to an agreement incur high specific costs, repudiation of commitments will entail substantial losses. Firms can thus reduce their gains from exploitation through the technique of acquiring dedicated assets that serve as hostages to continuing cooperation. Nonspecific assets, such as general-purpose trucks and airplanes, are salvageable if agreements break down; firms can reduce their fear of being exploited by maximizing the use of nonspecific assets, but such assets cannot diminish gains from exploitation by serving as hostages.[2] Unilateral strategies can improve the prospects of cooperation by reducing both the costs of being exploited (CD) and the gains from exploitation (DC). The new literature on interfirm cooperation indirectly raises an old question on the costs of unilateral strategies to promote cooperation in international relations.

In many instances, unilateral actions that limit one's gains from exploitation may have the effect of increasing one's vulnerability to exploitation by others. For example, a state could limit gains from defection from liberal international economic norms by permitting the expansion of sectors of comparative advantage and by permitting liquidation of inefficient sectors. Because a specialized economy is a hostage to international economic cooperation, this strategy would unquestionably increase the credibility of the nation's commitment to liberalism. It also has the effect, however, of increasing the nation's vulnerability to protection by others. In the troops-as-hostage example, the government that stations troops may promote cooperation by diminishing an ally's fear of abandonment, but in so doing it raises its own fears of exploitation by the ally. In an example from the neoconservative nuclear literature, Paul Nitze, Colin Gray, William Van Cleave, and others assume that missiles will be fired against missiles rather than against industries or cities, and conclude that a shift from counterforce toward countervalue weapons may purchase a reduction in gains from exploitation at the expense of heightened vulnerability to exploitation.[3] Cognitive, domestic, and international structural factors affect payoff structure directly, and also influence perceptions of the benefits and limits of unilateral strategies to alter payoffs.

Unilateral strategies do not exhaust the range of options that states may use to alter payoff structures. Bilateral strategies—most significantly strategies of issue

---

[2]Williamson (fn.5).

[3]See Paul Nitze, "Assuring Strategic Stability in an Era of Detente," *Foreign Affairs* 54 (January 1976), 207-32, for the seminal article in this tradition. Nitze's recommendations hinge on acceptance of the precepts of what has come to be known as nuclear utilization theory. Jervis's recommendations depend on acceptance of the precepts of mutual assured destruction (fn. 5).

linkage—can be used to alter payoff structures by combining dissimilar games. Because resort to issue linkage generally assumes iteration, analysis of how issue linkage can be used to alter payoffs is presented in the section on the shadow of the future. Furthermore, bilateral "instructional" strategies can aim at altering another country's understanding of cause-and-effect relationships, and result in altered perceptions of interest. For example, American negotiators in SALT I sought to instruct their Soviet counterparts on the logic of mutual assured destruction.[4]

Multilateral strategies, centering on the formation of international regimes, can be used to alter payoff structures in two ways. First, norms generated by regimes may be internalized by states, and thereby alter payoff structure. Second, information generated by regimes may alter states' understanding of their interests. As Ernst Haas argues, new regimes may gather and distribute information that can highlight cause-and-effect relationships not previously understood. Changing perceptions of means-ends hierarchies can, in turn, result in changing perceptions of interest.[5]

III. THE SHADOW OF THE FUTURE: SINGLE-PLAY AND ITERATED GAMES

The distinction between cases in which similar transactions among parties are unlikely to be repeated and cases in which the expectation of future interaction can influence decisions in the present is fundamental to the emergence of cooperation among egotists. As the previous section suggests, states confronting strategic situations that resemble single-play Prisoners' Dilemma and, to a lesser extent, single-play Stag Hunt and Chicken, are constantly tempted by immediate gains from unilateral defection, and fearful of immediate losses from unrequited cooperation. How does continuing interaction affect prospects for cooperation? The argument proceeds in four stages. First, why do iterated conditions improve the prospects for cooperation in Prisoners' Dilemma and Stag Hunt while diminishing the prospects for cooperation in Chicken? Second, how do strategies of reciprocity improve the prospects for cooperation under iterated conditions? Third, why does the effectiveness of reciprocity hinge on conditions of play—the ability of actors to distinguish reliably between cooperation and defection by others and to respond in kind? Fourth, through what strategies can states improve conditions of play and lengthen the shadow of the future?[6]

Before turning to these questions, consider the attributes of iterated situations. First, states must expect to continue dealing with each other. This condition is, in

---

[4]See John Newhouse, *Cold Dawn: The Story of SALT I* (New York: Holt, Rinehart & Winston, 1973).
[5]See Haas, "Words Can Hun You; Or Who Said What to Whom About Regimes," in Krasner (fn. 5).
[6]This section is derived largely from axelrod (fn. 7), and Telsor (fn. 6).

practice, not particularly restrictive. With the possible exception of global thermonuclear war, international politics is characterized by the expectaton of future interaction. Second, payoff structures must not change substantially over time. In other
words, each round of play should not alter the structure of the game in the future.
This condition is, in practice, quite restrictive. For example, states considering surprise attack when offense is dominant are in a situation that has many of the characteristics of a single-play game: attack alters options and payoffs in future rounds of
interaction.

Third, the size of the discount rate applied to the future affects the iterativeness of
games. If a government places little value on future payoffs, its situation has many of
the characteristics of a single-play game. If it places a high value on future payoffs,
its situation may have many of the characteristics of an iterated game. For example,
political leaders in their final term are likely to discount the future more substantially than political leaders running for, or certain of, reelection.

A. The Shadow of the Future and Cooperation

How does the shadow of the future affect the likelihood of cooperation? Under single-play conditions without a sovereign, adherence to agreements is often irrational.
Consider the single-play Prisoners' Dilemma. Each prisoner is better off squealing,
whether or not his partner decides to squeal. In the absence of continuing interaction,
defection would emerge as the dominant strategy. Because the prisoners can neither
turn to a central authority for enforcement of an agreement to cooperate nor rely on the
anticipation of retaliation to deter present defection, cooperation will be unlikely under
single-play conditions. If the prisoners expect to be placed in similar situations in the
future, the prospects for cooperation improve. Experimental evidence suggests that
under iterated Prisoners' Dilemma the incidence of cooperation rises substantially.[7]
Even in the absence of centralized authority, tacit agreements to cooperate through
mutual stonewalling are frequently reached and maintained. Under iterated Prisoners'
Dilemma, a potential defector compares the immediate gain from squealing with the
possible sacrifice of future gains that may result from squealing. In single-play Stag
Hunt, each hunter is tempted to defect in order to defend himself against the possibility of defection by others. A reputation for reliability, for resisting temptation, reduces
the likelihood of defection. If the hunters are a permanent group, and expect to hunt
together again, the immediate gains from unilateral defection relative to unrequited
cooperation must be balanced against the cost of diminished cooperation in the future.

---

[7]See Anatol Rapoport and Albert Chammah, *Prisoner's Dilemma* (Ann Arbor: University of
    Michigan Press, 1965), and subsequent essays in *Journal of Conflict Resolution*.

In both Prisoners' Dilemma and Stag Hunt, defection in the present *decreases* the likelihood of cooperation in the future. In both, therefore, iteration improves the prospects for cooperation. In Chicken, iteration may decrease the prospects for cooperation. Under single-play conditions, the temptation of unilateral defection is balanced by the fear of the collision that follows from mutual defection. How does iteration affect this balance? If the game is repeated indefinitely, then each driver may refrain from swerving in the present to coerce the other driver into swerving in the future. Each driver may seek to acquire a reputation for not swerving to cause the other driver to swerve. In iterated Chicken, one driver's defection in the present may decrease the likelihood of the other driver's defection in the future.[8]

B. Strategies of Reciprocity and Conditions of Play

It is at this juncture that strategy enters the explanation. Although the expectation of continuing interaction has varying effects on the likelihood of cooperation in the illustrations above, an iterated environment permits resort to strategies of reciprocity that may improve the prospects of cooperation in Chicken as well as in Prisoners' Dilemma and Stag Hunt. Robert Axelrod argues that strategies of reciprocity have the effect of promoting cooperation by establishing a direct connection between an actor's present behavior and anticipated future benefits. Tit-for-Tat, or conditional cooperation, can increase the likelihood of joint cooperation by shaping the future consequences of present cooperation or defection.

In iterated Prisoners' Dilemma and Stag Hunt, reciprocity underscores the future consequences of present cooperation and defection. The argument presented above—that iteration enhances the prospects for cooperation in these games—rests on the assumption that defection in the present will decrease the likelihood of cooperation in the future. Adoption of an implicit or explicit strategy of matching stonewalling with stonewalling, squealing with squealing, rabbit chasing with rabbit chasing, and cooperative hunting with cooperative hunting validates the assumption. In iterated Chicken, a strategy of reciprocity can offset the perverse effects of reputational considerations on the prospects for cooperation. Recall that in iterated Chicken, each driver may refrain from swerving in the present to coerce the other driver into swerving in the future. Adoption of an implicit or explicit strategy of Tit-for-Tat in iterated games of Chicken alters the future stream of benefits associated with present defection. If a strategy of reciprocity is credible, then the mutual losses associated with future collisions can encourage present swerving. In all three games, a promise to respond to present cooperation with future cooperation

---

[8]On iterated Chicken, see Snyder and Diesing (fn. 4), 43–44.

and a threat to respond to present defection with future defection can improve the prospects for cooperation.

The effectiveness of strategies of reciprocity hinges on conditions of play—the ability of actors to distinguish reliably between cooperation and defection by others and to respond in kind. In the illustrations provided above, the meaning of "defect" and "cooperate" is unambiguous. Dichotomous choices—between squeal and stone-wall, chase the rabbit or capture the stag, continue down the road or swerve—limit the likelihood of misperception. Further, the actions of all are transparent. Given the definitions of the situations, prisoners, hunters, and drivers can reliably detect defection and cooperation by other actors. Finally, the definition of the actors eliminates the possibility of control problems. Unitary prisoners, hunters, and drivers do not suffer from factional, organizational, or bureaucratic dysfunctions that might hinder implementation of strategies of reciprocity.

In international relations, conditions of play can limit the effectiveness of reciprocity. The definition of cooperation and defection may be ambiguous. For example, the Soviet Union and the United States hold to markedly different definitions of "defection" from the terms of détente as presented in the Basic Principles Agreement;[9] the European Community and the United States differ over whether domestic sectoral policies comprise indirect export subsidies. Further, actions may not be transparent. For example, governments may not be able to detect one another's violations of arms control agreements or indirect export subsidies. If defection cannot be reliably detected, the effect of present cooperation on possible future reprisals will erode. Together, ambiguous definitions and a lack of transparency can limit the ability of states to recognize cooperation and defection by others.

C. Strategies to Improve Recognition and Lengthen the Shadow of the Future

To what extent can governments promote cooperation by creating favorable conditions of play and by lengthening the shadow of the future? The literature on international regimes offers several techniques for creating favorable conditions of play. Explicit codification of norms can limit definitional ambiguity. The very act of clarifying standards of conduct, of defining cooperative and uncooperative behavior, can permit more effective resort to strategies of reciprocity. Further, provisions for surveillance—for example, mechanisms for verification in arms control agreements or for sharing information on the nature and effects of domestic sectoral policies—can

[9]See Alexander L. George, *Managing U.S.-Soviet Rivalry: Problems of Crisis Prevention* (Boulder, CO: Westview, 1983).

increase transparency. In practice, the goal of enhancing recognition capabilities is often central to negotiations under anarchy.

The game-theoretic and institutional microeconomic literatures offer several approaches to increasing the iterative character of situations. Thomas Schelling and Robert Axelrod suggest tactics of decomposition over time to lengthen the shadow of the future.[10] For example, the temptation to defect in a deal promising thirty billion dollars for a billion barrels of oil may be reduced if the deal is sliced up into a series of payments and deliveries. Cooperation in arms reduction or in territorial disengagement may be difficult if the reduction or disengagement must be achieved in one jump. If a reduction or disengagement can be sliced up into increments, the problem of cooperation may be rendered more tractable. Finally, strategies of issue linkage can be used to alter payoff structures and to interject elements of iterativeness into single-play situations. Relations among states are rarely limited to one single-play issue of overriding importance. When nations confront a single-play game on one issue, present defection may be deterred by threats of retaliation on other iterated issues. In international monetary affairs, for instance, a government fearing one-time reserve losses if another state devalues its currency may link devaluation to an iterated trade game. By establishing a direct connection between present behavior in a single-play game and future benefits in an iterated game, tacit or explicit cross-issue linkage can lengthen the shadow of the future.[11]

IV. NUMBER OF PLAYERS: TWO-PERSON AND N-PERSON GAMES

Up to now, I have discussed the effects of payoff structure and the shadow of the future on the prospects of cooperation in terms of two-person situations. What happens to the prospects for cooperation as the number of significant actors rises? In this section, I explain why the prospects for cooperation diminish as the number of players increases; examine the function of international regimes as a response to the problems created by large numbers; and offer strategies to improve the prospects for cooperation by altering situations to diminish the number of significant players.

The numbers problem is central to many areas of the social sciences. Mancur Olson's theory of collective action focuses on N-person versions of Prisoners'

[10]Schelling (fn. 2), 43–46, and Axelrod (fn. 7), 126–32.

[11]For analyses of issue linkage, see Robert D. Tollison and Thomas D. Willett, "An Economic Theory of Mutually Advantageous Issue Linkages in International Negotiations," *International Organization* 33 (Autumn 1979) 425–49; Oye (fn. 12), chap. 3, "Bargaining: The Logic of Contingent Action"; and Axelrod and Keohane in the concluding essay of this symposium.

Dilemma. The optimism of our earlier discussions of cooperation under iterated Prisoners' Dilemma gives way to the pessimism of analyses of cooperation in the provision of public goods. Applications of Olsonian theory to problems ranging from cartelization to the provision of public goods in alliances underscore the significance of "free-riding" as an impediment to cooperation.[12] In international relations, the numbers problem has been central to two debates. The longstanding controversy over the stability of bipolar versus multipolar systems reduces to a debate over the impact of the number of significant actors on international conflict.[13] A more recent controversy, between proponents of the theory of hegemonic stability and advocates of international regimes, reduces to a debate over the effects of large numbers on the robustness of cooperation.[14]

A. Number of Players and Cooperation

How do numbers affect the likelihood of cooperation? There are at least three important channels of influence.[15] First, cooperation requires recognition of opportunities for the advancement of mutual interests, as well as policy coordination once these opportunities have been identified. As the number of players increases, transactions and information costs rise. In simple terms, the complexity of N-person situations militates against identification and realization of common interests. Avoiding nuclear war during the Cuban missile crisis called for cooperation by the Soviet Union and the United States. The transaction and information costs in this particularly harrowing crisis, though substantial, did not preclude cooperation. By contrast, the problem of identifying significant actors, defining interests, and negotiating agreements that embodied mutual interests in the N-actor case of 1914 was far more difficult. These secondary costs associated

---

[12]See Mancur Olson, Jr., *The Logic of Collective Action: Public Goods and the Theory of Groups* (Cambridge: Harvard University Press, 1965), and Mancur Olson and Richard Zeckhauser, "An Economic Theory of Alliances," *Review of Economics and Statistics* 48 (August 1966), 266–79. For a recent elegant summary and extension of the large literature on dilemmas of collective action, see Russell Hardin, *Collective Action* (Baltimore: Johns Hopkins University Press, 1982).

[13]See Kenneth N. Waltz, "The Stability of a Bipolar World," *Daedalus* 93 (Summer 1964), and Richard N. Rosecrance, "Bipolarity, Multipolarity, and the Future," *Journal of Conflict Resolution* (September 1966), 314–27.

[14]On hegemony, see Robert Gilpin, *U.S. Power and the Multinational Corporation* (New York: Basic Books, 1975), 258–59. On duopoly, see Timothy McKeown, "Hegemonic Stability Theory and 19th-Century Tariff Levels in Europe," *International Organization* 37 (Winter 1983), 73–91. On regimes and cooperation, see Keohane (fn. II), and Krasner (fn. 5). On two-person games and N-person public-goods problems, see Charles Kindleberger, "Dominance and Leadership in the International Economy: Exploitation, Public Goods, and Free Rides," *International Studies Quarterly* 25 (June 1981), 242–54.

[15]See Keohane (fn. II), chap. 6, for extensions of these points.

with attaining cooperative outcomes in N-actor cases erode the difference between CC and DD. More significantly, the intrinsic difficulty of anticipating the behavior of other players and of weighing the value of the future goes up with the number of players. The complexity of solving N-person games, even in the purely deductive sense, has stunted the development of formal work on the problem. This complexity is even greater in real situations, and operates against multilateral cooperation.

Second, as the number of players increases, the likelihood of autonomous defection and of recognition and control problems increases. Cooperative behavior rests on calculations of expected utility—merging discount rates, payoff structures, and anticipated behavior of other players. Discount rates and approaches to calculation are likely to vary across actors, and the prospects for mutual cooperation may decline as the number of players and the probable heterogeneity of actors increases. The chances of including a state that discounts the future heavily, that is too weak (domestically) to detect, react, or implement a strategy of reciprocity, that cannot distinguish reliably between cooperation and defection by other states, or that departs from even minimal standards of rationality increase with the number of states in a game. For example, many pessimistic analyses of the consequences of nuclear proliferation focus on how breakdowns of deterrence may become more likely as the number of countries with nuclear weapons increases.[16]

Third, as the number of players increases, the feasibility of sanctioning defectors diminishes. Strategies of reciprocity become more difficult to implement without triggering a collapse of cooperation. In two-person games, Tit-for-Tat works well because the costs of defection are focused on only one other party. If defection imposes costs on all parties in an N-person game, however, the power of strategies of reciprocity is undermined. The infeasibility of sanctioning defectors creates the possibility of free-riding. What happens if we increase the number of actors in the iterated Prisoners' Dilemma from 2 to 20? Confession by any one of them could lead to the conviction of all on the major charge; therefore, the threat to retaliate against defection in the present with defection in the future will impose costs on all prisoners, and could lead to wholesale defection in subsequent rounds. For example, under the 1914 system of alliances, retaliation against one member of the alliance was the equivalent of retaliation against all. In N-person games, a strategy of conditional defection can have the effect of spreading, rather than containing, defection.

B. Strategies of Institutionalization and Decomposition

Given a large number of players, what strategies can states use to increase the likelihood of cooperation? Regime creation can increase the likelihood of cooperation

---

[16]See Lewis A. Dunn, *Controlling the Bomb* (New Haven: Yale University Press, 1982).

in N-person games.[17] First, conventions provide rules of thumb that can diminish transaction and information costs. Second, collective enforcement mechanisms both decrease the likelihood of autonomous defection and permit selective punishment of violators of norms. These two functions of international regimes directly address problems created by large numbers of players. For example, Japan and the members of NATO profess a mutual interest in limiting flows of militarily useful goods and technology to the Soviet Union. Obviously, all suppliers of militarily useful goods and technology must cooperate to deny the Soviet Union access to such items. Although governments differ in their assessment of the military value of some goods and technologies, there is consensus on a rather lengthy list of prohibited items. By facilitating agreement on the prohibited list, the Coordinating Committee of the Consultative Group of NATO (CoCom) provides a relatively clear definition of what exports would constitute defection. By defining the scope of defection, the CoCom list forestalls the necessity of retaliation against nations that ship technology or goods that do not fall within the consensual definition of defection.[18] Generally, cooperation is a prerequisite of regime creation. The creation of rules of thumb and mechanisms of collective enforcement and the maintenance and administration of regimes can demand an extraordinary degree of cooperation. This problem may limit the range of situations susceptible to modification through regimist strategies.

What strategies can reduce the number of significant players in a game and thereby render cooperation more likely? When governments are unable to cooperate on a global scale, they often turn to discriminatory strategies to encourage bilateral or regional cooperation. Tactics of decomposition across actors can, at times, improve the prospects for cooperation. Both the possibilities and the limits of strategies to reduce the number of players are evident in the discussions that follow. First, reductions in the number of actors can usually only be purchased at the expense of the magnitude of gains from cooperation. The benefits of regional openness are smaller than the gains from global openness. A bilateral clearing arrangement is less economically efficient than a multilateral clearing arrangement. Strategies to reduce the number of players in a game generally diminish the gains from cooperation

---

[17]In addition to providing a partial solution to the problems of large numbers, regimes may affect the order and intensity of actor preferences as norms are internalized, and may heighten the iterativeness of situations as interaction becomes more frequent.

[18]For a full analysis of intra-alliance cooperation on East-West trade, see Michael Mastanduno, "Strategies of Economic Containment: U.S. Trade Relations with the Soviet Union," *World Politics* 37 (July 1985), 503–31, and Beverly Crawford and Stephanie Lenway, "Decision Modes and International Regime Change: Western Collaboration on East-West Trade, *World Politics* 37 (April 1985), 375–402.

while they increase the likelihood and robustness of cooperation.[19] Second, strategies to reduce the number of players generally impose substantial costs on third parties. These externalities may motivate third parties to undermine the limited area of cooperation or may serve as an impetus for a third party to enlarge the zone of cooperation. In the 1930s, for example, wholesale resort to discriminatory trading policies facilitated creation of exclusive zones of commercial openness. When confronted by a shrinking market share, Great Britain adopted a less liberal and more discriminatory commercial policy in order to secure preferential access to its empire and to undermine preferential agreements between other countries. As the American market share diminished, the United States adopted a more liberal and more discriminatory commercial policy to increase its access to export markets. It is not possible, however, to reduce the number of players in all situations. For example, compare the example of limited commercial openness with the example of a limited strategic embargo. To reduce the number of actors in a trade war, market access can simply be offered to only one country and withheld from others. By contrast, defection by only one supplier can permit the target of a strategic embargo to obtain a critical technology. These problems may limit the range of situations susceptible to modification through strategies that reduce the number of players in games.

[19]For a pure libertarian argument on private exchange as an alternative to public management, see Conybeare (fn. 12).

THE TRAGEDY OF THE COMMONS

Garrett Hardin

. . . We can make little progress in working toward optimum poulation size until we explicitly exorcize the spirit of Adam Smith in the field of practical demography. In economic affairs, *The Wealth of Nations* (1776) popularized the "invisible hand," the idea that an individual who "intends only his own gain," is, as it were, "led by an invisible hand to promote . . . the public interest". Adam Smith did not assert that this was invariably true, and perhaps neither did any of his followers. But he contributed to a dominant tendency of thought that has ever since interfered with positive action based on rational analysis, namely, the tendency to assume that decisions reached individually will, in fact, be the best decisions for an entire society. If this assumption is correct it justifies the continuance of our present policy of laissez-faire in reproduction. If it is correct we can assume that men will control their individual fecundity so as to produce the optimum population. If the assumption is

Excerpt from Garrett Hardin, "The Tragedy of the Commons," *Science*, 162:1243–1267 (1968). AAAS. Reprinted by permission of American Association for the Advancement of Science.

not correct, we need to reexamine our individual freedoms to see which ones are defensible.

TRAGEDY OF FREEDOM IN A COMMONS

The rebuttal to the invisible hand in population control is to be found in a scenario first sketched in a little-known pamphlet in 1833 by a mathematical amateur named William Forster Lloyd (1794–1852). We may well call it "the tragedy of the commons," using the word "tragedy" as the philosopher Whitehead used it: "The essence of dramatic tragedy is not unhappiness. It resides in the solemnity of the remorseless working of things." He then goes on to say, "This inevitableness of destiny can only be illustrated in terms of human life by incidents which in fact involve unhappiness. For it is only by them that the futility of escape can be made evident in the drama."

The tragedy of the commons develops in this way. Picture a pasture open to all. It is to be expected that each herdsman will try to keep as many cattle as possible on the commons. Such an arrangement may work reasonably satisfactorily for centuries because tribal wars, poaching, and disease keep the numbers of both man and beast well below the carrying capacity of the land. Finally, however, comes the day of reckoning, that is, the day when the long-desired goal of social stability becomes a reality. At this point, the inherent logic of the commons remorselessly generates tragedy.

As a rational being, each herdsman seeks to maximize his gain. Explicitly or implicitly, more or less consciously, he asks, "What is the utility *to me* of adding one more animal to my herd?" This utility has one negative and one positive component.

1. The positive component is a function of the increment of one animal. Since the herdsman receives all the proceeds from the sale of the additional animal, the positive utility is nearly $+1$.
2. The negative component is a function of the additional overgrazing created by one more animal. Since, however, the effects of overgrazing are shared by all the herdsmen, the negative utility for any particular decision-making herdsman is only a fraction of -1.

Adding together the component partial utilities, the rational herdsman concludes that the only sensible course for him to pursue is to add another animal to his herd. And another; and another. . . . But this is the conclusion reached by each and every rational herdsman sharing a commons. Therein is the tragedy. Each man is locked into a system that compels him to increase his herd without limit—in a world that is limited. Ruin is the destination toward which all men rush, each pursuing his own best interest in a society that believes in the freedom of the commons. Freedom in a commons brings ruin to all. . . .

POLLUTION

In a reverse way, the tragedy of the commons reappears in problems of pollution. Here it is not a question of taking something out of the commons, but of putting something in—sewage, or chemical, radioactive, and heat wastes into water; noxious and dangerous fumes into the air; and distracting and unpleasant advertising signs into the line of sight. The calculations of utility are much the same as before. The rational man finds that his share of the cost of the wastes he discharges into the commons is less than the cost of purifying his wastes before releasing them. Since this is true for everyone, we are locked into a system of "fouling our own nest," so long as we behave only as independent, rational, free-enterprisers.

The tragedy of the commons as a food basket is averted by private property, or something formally like it. But the air and waters surrounding us cannot readily be fenced, and so the tragedy of the commons as a cesspool must be prevented by different means, by coercive laws or taxing devices that make it cheaper for the polluter to treat his pollutants than to discharge them untreated. We have not progressed as far with the solution of this problem as we have with the first. Indeed, our particular concept of private property, which deters us from exhausting the positive resources of the earth, favors pollution. The owner of a factory on the bank of a stream—whose property extends to the middle of the stream—often has difficulty seeing why it is not his natural right to muddy the waters flowing past his door. The law, always behind the times, requires elaborate stitching and fitting to adapt it to this newly perceived aspect of the commons. . . .

HOW TO LEGISLATE TEMPERANCE?

Analysis of the pollution problem as a function of population density uncovers a not generally recognized principle of morality, namely: *the morality of an act is a function of the state of the system at the time it is performed.* Using the commons as a cesspool does not harm the general public under frontier conditions, because there is no public; the same behavior in a metropolis is unbearable. A hundred and fifty years ago a plainsman could kill an American bison, cut out only the tongue for his dinner, and discard the rest of the animal. He was not in any important sense being wasteful. Today, with only a few thousand bison left, we would be appalled at such behavior. . . .

That morality is system-sensitive escaped the attention of most codifiers of ethics in the past. "Thou shalt not . . ." is the form of traditional ethical directives which make no allowance for particular circumstances. The laws of our society follow the pattern of ancient ethics, and therefore are poorly suited to governing a complex, crowded, changeable world. Our epicyclic solution is to augment statutory law with administrative law. Since it is practically impossible to spell out all the conditions under which it is safe to burn trash in the back yard or to run an automobile without smog-control, by law we delegate the details to bureaus. The result is administrative law, which is rightly feared for an ancient reason—*Quis custodiet ipsos custodes?*— "Who shall watch the watchers themselves?" John Adams said that we must have "a government of laws and not men." Bureau administrators, trying to evaluate the morality of acts in the total system, are singularly liable to corruption, producing a government by men, not laws.

Prohibition is easy to legislate (through not necessarily to enforce); but how do we legislate temperance? Experience indicates that it can be accomplished best through the mediation of administrative law. We limit possibilities unnecessarily if we suppose that the sentiment of *Quis custodiet* denies us the use of administrative law. We should rather retain the phrase as a perpetual reminder of fearful dangers we cannot avoid. The great challenge facing us now is to invent the corrective feedbacks that are needed to keep custodians honest. We must find ways to legitimate the needed authority of both the custodians and the corrective feedbacks.

FREEDOM TO BREED IS INTOLERABLE

The tragedy of the commons is involved in population problems in another way. In a world governed solely by the principle of "dog eat dog"—if indeed there ever was such a world—how many children a family had would not be a matter of public concern. Parents who bred too exuberantly would leave fewer descendants, not more, because they would be unable to care adequately for their children. David Lack and others have found that such a negative feedback demonstrably controls the fecundity of birds. But men are not birds, and have not acted like them for millenniums, at least.

If each human family were dependent only on its own resources; *if* the children of improvident parents starved to death; *if*, thus, overbreeding brought its own "punishment" to the germ line—*then* there would be no public interest in controlling the breeding of families. But our society is deeply committed to the welfare state, and hence is confronted with another aspect of the tragedy of the commons.

In a welfare state, how shall we deal with the family, the religion, the race, or the class (or indeed any distinguishable and cohesive group) that adopts overbreeding as a policy to secure its own aggrandizement? To couple the concept of freedom to breed with the belief that everyone born has an equal right to the commons is to lock the world into a tragic course of action. . . .

CONSCIENCE IS SELF-ELIMINATING

It is a mistake to think that we can control the breeding of mankind in the long run by an appeal to conscience. Charles Galton Darwin made this point when he spoke on the centennial of the publication of his grandfather's great book. The argument is straightforward and Darwinian.

People vary. Confronted with appeals to limit breeding, some people will undoubtedly respond to the plea more than others. Those who have more children will produce a larger fraction of the next generation than those with more susceptible consciences. The difference will be accentuated, generation by generation.

In C. G. Darwin's words: "It may well be that it would take hundreds of generations for the progenitive instinct to develop in this way, but if it should do so, nature would have taken her revenge, and the variety *Homo contracipiens* would become extinct and would be replaced by the variety *Homo progenitivus*". . . .

MUTUAL COERCION MUTUALLY AGREED UPON

The social arrangements that produce responsibility are arrangements that create coercion, of some sort. Consider bank-robbing. The man who takes money from a bank acts as if the bank were a commons. How do we prevent such action? Certainly not by trying to control his behavior solely by a verbal appeal to his sense of responsibility. Rather than rely on propaganda we follow Frankel's lead and insist that a bank is not a commons; we seek the definite social arrangements that will keep it from becoming a commons. That we thereby infringe on the freedom of would-be robbers we neither deny nor regret.

The morality of bank-robbing is particularly easy to understand because we accept complete prohibition of this activity. We are willing to say "Thou shalt not rob banks," without providing for exceptions. But temperance also can be created by coercion. Taxing is a good coercive device. To keep downtown shoppers temperate in their use of parking space we introduce parking meters for short periods, and traffic fines for longer ones. We need not actually forbid a citizen to park as long as he wants to; we need merely make it increasingly expensive for him to do so. Not prohibition, but carefully biased options are what we offer him. A Madison Avenue man might call this persuasion; I prefer the greater candor of the word coercion. . . .

RECOGNITION OF NECESSITY

Perhaps the simplest summary of this analysis of man's population problems is this: the commons, if justifiable at all, is justifiable only under conditions of low-population density. As the human population has increased, the commons has had to be abandoned in one aspect after another.

First we abandoned the commons in food gathering, enclosing farm land and restricting pastures and hunting and fishing areas. These restrictions are still not complete throughout the world.

Somewhat later we saw that the commons as a place for waste disposal would also have to be abandoned. Restrictions on the disposal of domestic sewage are widely accepted in the Western world; we are still struggling to close the commons to pollution by automobiles, factories, insecticide sprayers, fertilizing operations, and atomic energy installations. . . .

Every new enclosure of the commons involves the infringement of somebody's personal liberty. Infringements made in the distant past are accepted because no contemporary complains of a loss. It is the newly proposed infringements that we vigorously oppose; cries of "rights" and "freedom" fill the air. But what does "freedom" mean? When men mutually agreed to pass laws against robbing, mankind became more free, not less so. Individuals locked into the logic of the commons are free only to bring on universal ruin; once they see the necessity of mutual coercion, they become free to pursue other goals. I believe it was Hegel who said, "Freedom is the recognition of necessity."

The most important aspect of necessity that we must now recognize, is the necessity of abandoning the commons in breeding. No technical solution can rescue us from the misery of overpopulation. Freedom to breed will bring ruin to all. At the moment, to avoid hard decisions many of us are tempted to propagandize for conscience and responsible parenthood. The temptation must be resisted, because an appeal to independently acting consciences selects for the disappearance of all conscience in the long run, and an increase in anxiety in the short.

The only way we can preserve and nurture other and more precious freedoms is by relinquishing the freedom to breed, and that very soon. "Freedom is the recognition of necessity"—and it is the role of education to reveal to all the necessity of abandoning the freedom to breed. Only so, can we put an end to this aspect of the tragedy of the commons.

FUNCTIONALISM

ERNST B. HAAS

. . . Functionalists, in the specific sense of the term, are interested in identifying those aspects of human needs and desires that exist and clamor for attention outside the realm of the political. They believe in the possibility of specifying technical and "non-controversial" aspects of governmental conduct, and of weaving an ever-spreading web of international institutional relationships on the basis of meeting such needs. They would concentrate on commonly experienced needs initially, expecting the circle of the non-controversial to expand at the expense of the political, as practical cooperation became coterminous with the totality of interstate relations. At that point a true world community will have arisen.

The philosophical reasoning underlying this program does not at the moment concern us. What matters is the notion of function: it is, according to the explicit intent of the Functionalist writers, equivalent in meaning to "organizational task." The function of the Food and Agriculture Organization is to increase agricultural productivity and the world food supply; the function of the Universal Postal Union is to speed the world's mail; the function of the International Labor Organization is to raise and equalize the living standards of workers throughout the world. Apparently, there are no half-hidden relationships to systems and models, no intended or unintended consequences: function means task. Functionalism, then, becomes both an analytical tool for criticizing the deplorable present and an ideological prescription for ushering in a better future. The question next arises: Is it possible to reformulate the sociologist's notion of functionalism, to strip it of its ambiguities, so that a purified version can then be applied to the study of international institutions?

Certain awkward questions had best be faced at the outset. Does not the Functionalist notion of function also carry the connotation of cognitively perceived need on the part of the actor, leading to the creation of an organizational task designed to meet the need? If so, cannot the implementation of the task carry with it consequences not planned or intended by the actor, which may then somehow transform both the organization and the actor's initial perceptions? The task may be carried out to fulfill the initial need, but once implemented, it may create an entirely new situation, setting up novel relationships affecting the total context in which action takes place. In that event, has the notion of function not been linked again, however involuntarily, to a system of some kind? . . .

Whether we wish it or not, such an orientation involves us in political theory, the theory of analyzing *and* prescribing for the international society. This prescriptive intent is central to Functionalist theory: the Functionalists claim to possess a theoretical apparatus capable of analyzing existing society and of pinpointing the causes of its undesirable aspects; they claim, further, to know the way in which a normatively superior state of affairs can be created. Such, however, is not my theoretical intent. To quote Nadel once more, I am interested in functional theory as "a body of propositions (still interconnected) which serve to *map out* the problem area and thus prepare the ground for its empirical investigation by appropriate methods. More precisely, the propositions serve to classify phenomena, to analyze them into relevant units or indicate their interconnections, and to define 'rules of procedure' and 'schemes of interpretation.' 'Theory' here equals conceptual scheme or logical framework." Thus armed, let us leave the semantic aspect and address ourselves to the reconciliation of Functionalism and functionalism.

INTERNATIONAL FUNCTIONALISM AS REFORMIST IDEOLOGY

Functionalism has no single prophet, no scriptures, and no dogma. As an ideology seeking to reform the form and substance of international life it has had a variety of spokesmen since the 1870's. But far from constituting a coherent body of militants, these people are united only by a vague and shifting syndrome of common attitudes and propositions: in fact, it is of the essence of Functionalism to avoid rigidity and dogma. Those qualifying to be called Functionalist have been considered to include Paul S. Reinsch, Leonard Woolf, G. D. H. Cole, H. R. G. Greaves, Pitman Potter, Edgar Saveney, and a host of lesser-known writers preparing blueprints for the brave new world that was to arise at the end of World War II. The chief exponent of Functionalism, however, is undoubtedly David Mitrany; yet it should be borne in mind that no one work of his contains the Functionalist gospel, but that the component parts are to be found scattered in books, articles, and speeches. Nor do all Functionalists agree on all points or maintain consistency in their emphases over a generation of writing. Aspects of the Functionalist argument singled out by me as crucial have not necessarily been so treated by all Functionalist writers. Yet when I was convinced that a proposition was implicit in the Functionalist case, even though not necessarily given prominence by an author, I have felt free to incorporate it in the mainstream of the argument. . . .

Guild Socialism and Pluralism furnished the criteria for diagnosing the human condition. Man is by nature good, rational, and devoted to the common weal; when society is organized so as to bring out man's tendency to mobilize his energies for the general welfare, the forces of peace and harmony rule. This happy state of affairs is approximated whenever a maximum of authority is exercised by technicians and administrators dedicated to the common weal, working in close conjunction with the voluntary professional groups that form part of any modern industrial society. But, cautions Mitrany, "In all societies there are both harmonies and disharmonies. It is largely within our choice which we pick out and further. . . . We must begin anew, therefore, with a clear sense that the nations can be bound together into a world community only if we link them up by what unites, not by what divides."

Disharmonies and conflict prevail in a society in which authority is exercised by politicians rather than technicians, by parliaments rather than voluntary groups.* Power, instead of the common good, then determines policy, and irrational behavior follows. Like Saint-Simon and Lenin, the Functionalist would hold that the human condition will improve only when "the government of men" is replaced by "the administration of things"; but whereas the Liberal will assume merely a quantitative distinction between politics and administration and recognize their mutual dependencies, the Functionalist will insist on a rigorous qualitative difference. Politics is identified with the pursuit of power and with residual infantile behavior traits, and technical management with a

---

*The distinction between "politicians" (concerned with doctrine and ideology) and "technicians" or "experts" (concerned with doing practical tasks) is implicit or explicit in most Functional writing. Mitrany, however, prefers to distinguish between *a priori* ideology and an *a priori* setting of social purpose, with the second the more desirable.

mature mind and a healthy society. Preaching the administration and construction of the common good is itself part of the therapy for a disharmonious society. This is all the more urgent because technological and industrial progress makes the attainment of the general welfare an immediately realizable goal. A healthy society would control the forces of progress for the benefit of mankind; a power-oriented society would let the opportunity escape. When men's loyalties are penned up within the territorial confines of the exclusivist nation-state, there is little hope of working for the general welfare. However, these loyalties, once freed from the shackles of national insecurity and allowed to identify with humanity at large, will achieve the true common good.

This diagnosis brings into focus the distorting role of the modern state with respect to the possibilities of human fulfillment. Here again the Guild Socialist heritage of the Functionalist approach is manifest. Pre-industrial and pre-national primary occupational groups were the true focuses for human happiness because they afforded a sense of participation in the solution of practical problems. The rise of the territorially bounded, omni-competent national state changed all that. Group spontaneity was lost, the tendency of man to identify with his occupational colleague elsewhere was choked off, the search for national security became the focus of life in the state. Even the administration of general welfare measures, such as social security legislation, took place within the depersonalized context of the state structure. The unnatural state took the place of natural society, a fact that was merely codified by the rules of nineteenth-century international law. According to Mitrany, "Our social activities are cut off arbitrarily at the limit of the state and, if at all, are allowed to be linked to the same activities across the border only by means of uncertain and cramping political ligatures."

Lack of fulfillment, of course, is closely linked to the element of human and group creativity. For the Functionalist a cooperative national effort aiming only at the negative goal of security is uncreative. So is the minimal program of assuring law and order. True creativity must be tied to the positive goals identified with the modern service state, "an instrument of life and not merely an order." The definition of new rights flowing from an expanding welfare concept is a creative task still possible to the state, provided it once again makes available to voluntary groups channels of creative participation. Hence the recurrence of the terms "work" and "working" in the Functionalist vocabulary. Creative work aims at a general good that normally tends to be obscured by centralization, power-drives, and uncreative preoccupation with force and national military security.

As long as the state remains unreformed with respect to human fulfillment internally, its international role will hardly be more reassuring. While the Functionalist is interested in peace, of course, he stresses the elements of creativity and work, of replacing the negatively political in international affairs with the positively functional:

The task that is facing us is how to build up the reality of a common interest in peace. . . . *Not a peace that would keep the nations quietly apart, but a peace that* *would bring them actively together; not the old static and strategic view of peace, but a social view of it. . . .* We must put our faith not in a protected but in a working peace; it would indeed be nothing more nor less than the idea and aspiration of social security taken in its widest range.*

This passage from Mitrany bears rereading: it contains the essence of the Functionalist diagnosis of the negative existing order and the germ for its positive successor. The peace of statesmen, of collective security, of disarmament negotiations, of conferences of parliamentarians, of sweeping constitutional attempts at federation, all this is uncreative. It is so much power instead of creative work. The reintroduction of man, united in natural occupational groupings that ignore territorial boundaries, functioning through voluntary associations dedicated to welfare measures on which there is general agreement, this is the creative solution. The practical implication, naturally enough, is that working peace-making efforts should address themselves first and foremost to economic and social reform: to the joint management of scarce resources, unemployment, commodity price fluctuations, labor standards, and public health. This would have the result not only of correcting the faults of existing society, but of removing economic causes of war and international insecurity.

But at this point Functionalist thought must be sharply distinguished from simple internationalism of the "one world" variety. The Functionalists' emphasis on social and economic primacy in the elements of a future international order is combined with a recognition that group loyalty and national attachments are more real than vague international good will. If domestic harmony can be mobilized by engaging the common aspirations of men with respect to tasks that unite them—welfare rather than order—then the same would be true internationally. By tackling global conflict head-on, a direct political approach rather than an indirect welfare one, existing nationalisms are merely triggered into explosive action; in seeking solutions through political international gestures and institutions, man's remoteness from modern life is exacerbated.

International conflict is best tamed by entrusting the work of increasing human welfare to experts, technical specialists, and their professional associations. Being interested in tasks rather than power, they can be expected to achieve agreement where statesmen will fail. They will be unconcerned with "rightful" authorities and jurisdictions; rightful ends, proper functions to be performed, are their concern. Further, conflict is simply sidestepped if the territorial principle of representation is abandoned. Tasks will be entrusted to agencies possessing functional jurisdiction, i.e. concerning themselves with a specific welfare task; they will be staffed by specialists free

*Mitrany, *A Working Peace System*, p. 51 (italics mine).

from territorial referents. A supreme political authority would be as impossible as it is unnecessary. An ever-widening mesh of task-oriented welfare agencies would come to pre-empt the work now done by some governments, leading eventually to the creation of a universal welfare orientation. Since men in many nations already share certain welfare aims, this process could be set in motion without involving political sources of friction, thus sidestepping the still blazing national loyalties. "National problems would then appear, and would be treated, as what they are, the local segments of general problems." . . .

The reform of the state and of interstate relations in the direction of human welfare can bring with it a new type of world only if the Functionalist is able to indicate *how* the new world will supersede the old: if he has an explicit or implicit theory of change. To this problem we must now turn—not an easy subject for investigation, since on this vital theoretical (rather than ideological) issue the Functionalist theses are somewhat vague.

Put in the starkest and most abstract terms, the theory of change seems to be a purely systemic one. If the nations take full advantage of what, initially, are merely converging technical interests, eventually these interests will become fused. "In the end," wrote one early Functionalist, "the nations would find themselves federated, after a fashion, by the very force of things." This choice of words suggests an automatic process of change once the initial carving out of converging task contexts has taken place. Further, there is a dialectical quality to the automaticity. Since the Functionalist admits that national loyalties are too powerful to be overcome merely by appealing to the symbols of One World, he also stresses that world government cannot come into existence until the sentiment of world community has come to flourish. Such a feeling, however, can evolve only gradually on the basis of joint tasks of equal interest to all. Thus, the thesis of national exclusiveness can be outflanked by the antithesis of creative work dedicated to welfare, yielding the eventual synthesis of world community. To cap off this conception it must be stressed that the Functionalist not only assumes an automatic and dialectical process of change, but puts his faith into action rather than advance planning of necessary steps, action as creative endeavor and as an index of the degree to which the dialectic "force of things" has gotten the better of the status quo: "Promissory Covenants and Charters may remain a headstone to unfulfilled good intentions, but the functional way is action itself, and therefore an inescapable test of where we stand and how far we are willing to go in building up a new international society."

In other contexts, however, a more human notion of change emerges in the Functionalist literature, resulting in a doctrine of attitudinal reorientation on the basis of "learning." A necessary presupposition is the distinction between "technical" and "political" modes of thought. Change can be introduced by maximizing the responsibility of the expert and the manager: he is committed to performing his task for the benefit of all; conversely, he is indifferent to representing specific (power-infused?) interests. Functional agencies, suggests Mitrany, might be based on "equality in nonrepresentation."* The differentiation seems to be the Rousseauan one between the General Will and the Will of All: the manager stands for the General Will, whereas the politician represents merely the Will of All, i.e. the interests of his constituents, which are by definition selfish and therefore not necessarily geared to transforming the system. The General Will is strengthened by isolating an ever larger slice (Mitrany often refers to "layers of action and of peace") of technical matters, which will be administered so as to extend the range of the technical still further.

Yet the problem remains: Do people "learn" to think in non-national terms merely because of a pattern of technical cooperation? This is indeed the central issue in the Functionalist theory of change. At first, it seems to be only the experts and managers who learn. They become habituated to consulting with their opposite numbers from other nations about technical problems, and eventually they come to see all problems from the perspective of mankind as a whole. Thus the answer to maximizing the learning process lies in extending the range of participation in practical problem-solving. In the end, others besides experts, managers, and civil servants will participate and undergo the same process, particularly by way of greatly increased work and responsibility on the part of international voluntary groups. Learning becomes a species of group therapy.

The practical Functionalist program is implied in its theoretical position. Instead of attacking nationalism and sovereignty frontally, the Functionalist aims at solving these problems by simply ignoring them and relying on systemic forces and a learning process for eventually transcending, rather than defeating, the old order. An increasing number of institutions of global scope dedicated to social service, administered for the benefit of all, manned by technical experts, and supported by the voluntary participation of non-political groups would do the job. The result would be first a world community of sentiment, followed by a world government, something Mitrany once called "federalism by installments." The necessary loyalties of sentiment would develop naturally as people's expectations gradually came to be focused on these new social welfare agencies rather than on the present nations. Existing international bodies consisting of like-minded professional and occupational groups provide logical building blocks for the new structure of society. We cannot improve on Engle's summary of the Functional program: "These three features—a reliance predominantly upon functional units, an expectation of an eventual system of government made up primarily of interlocking functional units, and the assumption that in functional cooperation certain dynamic behavioral mechanisms of an 'institution-building' and a

*As quoted in Engle, p. 85.

'consensus-building' nature are at work—constitute, then, the ideal type of the functionalist theory at the international level."

FUNCTIONALIST IDEOLOGY AND HISTORY

In principle, any of the myriad "technical" activities of international organizations provide the case study material for investigating the validity of the Functionalist ideology. For the reformulation of this ideology to which we proceed in the next chapter, many of these cases did in fact furnish the historical basis. Here our purpose is more modest. Without attempting a critique of the ideology, we shall review the growth of "functional" preoccupations in two specific cases, seeking to highlight, first, the rival roles of experts and diplomats, and, second, the distinction between power-infused and welfare-dominated aspirations. A superficial view of these cases may well suggest that the Functional perspective is remarkably accurate, and the ideology firmly grounded in historical experience; a second view, however, shows that extensive reformulation is needed.

Our first case deals with the growth of international measures for the control of contagious diseases, beginning with the pioneering health conferences of the nineteenth century and ending with establishment of the World Health Organization. What were the chief issues? All European governments seemed agreed that the Moslem pilgrim traffic was responsible for the recurrent plague and cholera epidemics that threatened the world, but here agreement ended. The medical profession was divided into two major schools of thought: those who held that these diseases were spread by contagion, and those who felt that they originated in unsanitary atmospheric, housing, sewerage, and food conditions. The profession was further divided in its evaluation of the effectiveness of quarantine, with the environmentalists generally arguing that the isolation of patients and infected vessels was of no avail. Finally, there was dispute on where cholera, in particular, originated. Most medical people were convinced that it was in Bengal, but British physicians tended to deny this. Let us note two salient features: the experts were sharply divided on the technical issues involved, and the respective technical positions that they embraced corresponded strikingly with the political positions espoused by their governments. All the major maritime nations, notably Britain, defended the environmentalist position, ridiculed quarantine, and continually stressed the hardships that international quarantine regulations would impose on commerce and shipping! Britain refused to initiate quarantine measures to isolate Mecca-bound pilgrims in the Egyptian facilities over which she assumed control after 1881. Turkey denied that environmental conditions in territories under her sway contributed to disease conditions. Persia denied the efficacy of quarantines. The British medical profession even opposed the creation of an expert commission to study the diffusion of epidemics.

Between 1850 and 1903 no less than nine international conferences were convened to arrive at common measures to deal with these diseases. They were attended by national delegations composed either entirely of medical men or of medical men assisted by lay delegates. Although the lay delegates made constant efforts to persuade the medical men to compromise the rival views of contagionists and environmentalists, progress was very slow. Some headway was made after several severe outbreaks of cholera and plague during the half-century, but until the 1890's the conventions for quarantines, ship inspections, bills of health, and expert studies were so poorly ratified and implemented by the participating states that even so "non-controversial" a field as public health showed all the marks of major political conflict. Apparently it was the severe epidemics of 1893 and 1897 that eventually brought success. By joining the two rival medical views, the major maritime powers were able to come to terms: they agreed to reinstitute quarantines, disinfect ships, impose standardized inspection of vessels, and notify all other governments when cases of plague were discovered. Turkey and Persia, despite their objection to these measures as infringing the rights of Moslems, were compelled to ratify. The edifice was completed in 1907 with the creation of the International Office of Public Health, which was entrusted with the task of conducting scientific studies, carrying out epidemiological intelligence, and suggesting to member states new control devices as the older ones proved inadequate. However, the jurisdiction of the Office was limited to the five major contagious diseases.

The record is far from "proving" whether extended contacts among medical experts were the factor that caused eventual success. It certainly took a long time for the pure welfare component of the health activities to be recognized. But it seems clear that the interest of all in common action and rules was directly influenced by the dangers posed by given epidemics. Once the breakthrough had been scored, so to speak, international health efforts were not only sustained but intensified. The League of Nations created a new health organization staffed entirely by uninstructed experts, which carried out the same activities as the International Office for diseases not covered by the Office, as well as initiating the first international technical assistance operations by training national public health officials and encouraging them to keep in touch with each other. From then on the deliberate, expert-dominated standardization of national public health regulations proceeded quite smoothly. Goodman, for one, attributes this new measure of agreement to constantly growing medical knowledge. As inoculations and uniformly administered health certificates took the place of cruder inspections and quarantines, the commercial and political sting was taken out of the "function." But does this demonstrate the growing non-controversiality of health? Since the original issue was, in effect, side-stepped, no clear answer can be given. Still, it should be noted that as the epidemics grew more perilous, objections to international regulations previously drafted or recommended at the many conferences died down; in a sense, then, the opinions of experts were implemented as a common sense of danger and need gripped governments and the medical profession alike.

It seems incontestable, however, that since the advent of the World Health Organization in 1948, the consolidation of power in the expert has been as complete as the separation of welfare from politics. And the scope of WHO operations has expanded accordingly. Even though medical supplies are not distributed, they are supplied for demonstration purposes. Instead of merely conducting epidemiological intelligence, WHO seeks to eradicate diseases. Far from merely standardizing public health procedures, WHO assumes responsibility for inoculations in emergencies. Further, "action to meet emergencies is giving place to programmes, planned in advance, for a period of years; projects to bring about a particular advance are giving place to educational work from which general advance may come; and emergency action to control communicable diseases is giving place to investigation of their fundamental causes, and to work for the eradication of some." WHO possesses some legislative power in the very area in which the conferences of the nineteenth century could find so little agreement. The major initial decisions of the Organization were made by well-known national public health officials, selected for their competence and not for their national allegiance. And in subsequent activities rigorous professionalism ruled, a consistent desire to limit participation to qualified (if nationally appointed) physicians, nurses, therapists, and public health administrators. The program of the Organization was consciously geared to strengthening the competence and autonomy of national and local professional bodies, which were conceived in so strict a medical context that no thought of "political" involvement could occur to anyone.

Or could it? Compared with the pre-1945 scope of responsibilities of international health organizations, the program and powers of WHO point clearly to that inevitable expansion of function that Mitrany predicts on the basis of minimizing power and maximizing welfare. But did power shrink at the expense of advancing welfare? It could well be argued that the very professionalism of the experts who rule WHO defeats further inroads on the realm of power and politics. True, American physicians, despite their fixation on free enterprise, have so far refrained from attacking WHO and have joined in the general professional support of its work. But they have done so because WHO undertook to stay away from the field of "socialized medicine," thus giving the World Medical Association a target in the ILO's social security program instead. WHO's efforts to relate health development programs to such politically infused (but welfare-dominated) activities as rural sanitation and control of water resources have been less successful. And suggestions that population control relates to world health have been met by threats of withdrawal on the part of Belgium, Ireland, and several Latin American countries. Perhaps WHO's very success is due to a professionalism that resists the temptation to push back the boundary of power and politics. . . .

All this is based essentially on a utilitarian calculus: man will seek his rational advantage in maximizing his physical welfare by cooperating with other men when necessary. The Functionalists, however, differ from the Utilitarians by stressing the necessity of service rather than the benefits of competition. Advantage is maximized by pooling efforts, by joining in common creative tasks, by stressing what unites men, groups, and nations. This, in turn, implies a theory of conflict at variance with the Utilitarians'. Social conflict is not considered natural and inevitable by the Functionalists if and when there is an abundance of economic resources; only scarcity begets conflict. If intergroup and international conflict prevails even in the presence of material abundance, the reason must be found in some "devil" who perversely sidetracks man from the natural. H. G. Wells discovered this devil to inhabit the diplomatic services and the foreign offices of the Powers; Mitrany, more circumspectly, found it in the frustrations and anxieties of modern man compelled to live in the uncreative nation-state, which conditions him to confuse genuine national differences with nationalistic prejudices and the fears they produce. Service rather than social conflict, then, is the natural condition of man.

Like the modern group therapist, the Functionalist rejects the notion that group conflict is inevitable. Conflicts can be creatively transcended without self-conscious sacrifice. Politics need not be envisaged as the crude clash of interests, each rationally conceived and defended, but may yield to problem-solving. Interests need not be "reconciled" if they can be "integrated" at a higher level of perception by engaging the actor in a "working" effort. This conception opens up possibilities of international integration that are nowhere spelled out in detail by the Functionalists. But it is vital to note that the future structure of international relations would be qualitatively different from the old, precisely because a new moral component—integration rather than conflict—would be its central pillar. To this theme we will return later.

The Functionalist's critique of other theories of international order consists of disputing the validity of a series of propositions fundamental to the so-called Realist school of thought. He hopes to arrive at a totally different conception of world order simply by challenging these assumptions, and since his critique hinges on *separating* notions held to be one by Realists, I shall approach it as a series of "separability" propositions.

We find four propositions. (1) The Functionalist separates power from welfare. Both are thought of as representing types of human and state aims; great insistence is placed upon the distinction, and a great many programmatic points follow from it.

(2) The Functionalist further separates various governmental tasks into discrete elements, even if only temporarily. But he insists on completely separating military-defense (power-oriented) task from economic-abundance (welfare-oriented) tasks, in addition to isolating various kinds of welfare tasks. However, through the learning process he predicates, the Functionalist eventually gathers these tasks together again

into one, at which point all governmental activities are coterminous with the achievement of welfare. An important corollary of the separation of functional spheres is the notion of transferability of lessons. Integrative lessons learned in one functional context will later be applied by the actor in new contexts until the dichotomy between functional contexts is overcome. Unlimited learning and transferability are apparently assumed.

(3) A still finer separation occurs in the crucial distinction between the political and the technical, the work of the politician and that of the expert. Again a series of practical consequences follow from this distinction, leading to the conquest, at the hand of the welfare-oriented expert, of the political by the economic. Closely related is the distinction between the wholesome work of the voluntary group and the suspect activities of the government. This brings up the question of whether an expert can contribute to international integration by serving a government rather than a private group, a point on which Functionalist writing is silent.*

(4) A final, but equally crucial, separation occurs between the loyalties imputed to the political actor. Functionalists, along with many social scientists, hold that any one person can entertain a variety of loyalties to a number of focuses, whether hierarchically arranged or not; but unlike many others, they also assume that loyalties are created by functions, and that the transfer of functions can produce shifts in loyalty. A plurality of loyalties in any one nation is produced by the variety of functions carried out by various focuses for the person in question. The Functionalist, on the basis of this separation, hopes to transfer loyalties to international focuses carrying out functions. In doing so he seems to deny any existing hierarchical supremacy of nationalism, even though in other contexts he seems to deplore this supremacy.

Functionalists, as I emphasized before, do not think in explicitly functional-systemic terms. Existing needs give rise to appropriate tasks which, by virtue of the theoretical propositions outlined, are expected to give rise to a new and more wholesome international configuration of relationships. The end product of the process is a world federation emerging from an indefinite number of task-oriented agencies that overlie the sovereign state and detach man's loyalty from it. The redirection of loyalties is crucial here because it is expected to yield a *community* of sentiments and loyalties, which, in turn, is conceived as a psychological prerequisite for political federation. Functionalists, then, work with a terminal concept of immanent community much as Marxists use the notion of the classless society. What are the properties of the community concept?

Mitrany defines political community as the sum of the functions carried out by its members. At other times he speaks of it as the commitment to the common good of the members, the common good being the realization of welfare for all. This formulation leaves in doubt whether the "members" are individuals, voluntary groups, or functional agencies, and begs the question of the nature of the functions involved, for Mitrany surely cannot mean all the functions, including waging war, that at present are within the scope of political communities. Finally, the notion of the common good cannot be readily accepted unless one also grants as valid the nature of the learning process and the transferability concept advanced by Functionalists. Otherwise the common good can be no more than the sum of individual group wills. Despite the emotional language used, however, the essentially mechanistic nature of the community stands revealed. It is immanent in man's present condition because of the universality of needs and tasks; the fulfillment of these needs leads naturally to its emergence.

Have we not, in effect, now squared the circle? Is not an immanent community a system in disguise? Are not needs and tasks "functions" in terms of their contribution to the development of the system? The fact that the Functionalists have not faced this apparent theoretical convergence does not mean we should be equally negligent. Suggestive as the convergence may be, it cannot be explored and restated until we have examined Functionalist theory critically.

A CRITIQUE OF FUNCTIONALISM

We can easily summarize the criticism leveled at Functionalism by writers in the Realist tradition: they merely assert the primacy of the political and take for granted the presumed hard outer shell of the sovereign nation-state. Further, they minimize the chances of penetrating or softening the elephantine epidermis. More to the point is the criticism made by Claude, Sewell, and Engle, none of whom is *a priori* committed to the Realist approach. Yet they reject the theoretical assumptions of Functionalism in no uncertain terms simply by denying the adequacy of the separability propositions to sum up the potentialities of human development. Engle arrives at this conclusion on the basis of a study of the European Coal and Steel Community; Claude bases himself on the activities of the specialized agencies of the United Nations; and Sewell's analysis is centered on the International Bank for Reconstruction and Development. Their indictment runs as follows.

Power and welfare are far from separable. Indeed, commitment to welfare activities arises only within the confines of purely political decisions, which are made largely on the basis of power considerations. Specific functional contexts cannot be separated from general concerns. Overall economic decisions must be made before any one functional sector can be expected to show the kind of integrative evolution that the Functionalist describes. Lessons learned in one functional context cannot be expected to be readily transferred to new contexts; success in one functional sphere does not set up a corresponding motion in other spheres: on the contrary, it may fail to develop and be forgotten. The distinction between the political and the technical, between the politician and the expert, simply does not hold because issues were made technical by a prior political decision. Hence voluntary groups are most unlikely to have the salutary effect on international relations that the Functionalist predicts. Most important, both Claude and Engle deny that loyalties develop from the satisfaction of needs, can be separated and rearranged so as to ignore the nation.* "There is room for doubt that functionalists have found the key which infallibly opens the doors that keep human loyalties piled up in sovereign warehouses, thereby permitting those loyalties to spill out into the receptacles of internationalism."

Certainly Functionalism provides no infallible key. But I submit that even if the separability propositions, which are the heart of Functionalist theory, are not accepted in full, there remains considerable hope that they may be revised and refined so as to get us beyond the blind alley of Realist analysis. Anyone who uses the distinction between *kratos* and *ethos* as an analytical device will raise the same objections to Functionalist theory as the Realists do. Even the Functionalists, since they accept the dichotomy as fundamental in their distinction between power and welfare, are in a weak position. Conceding the "reality" of both orientations in international life, they must themselves put up with an unsatisfactory Manichean struggle, and hope for the best. The genuine Realist can then come back and agree to the epic struggle, and confidently predict the victory of *kratos*. Or, better, he can argue, as does Kenneth W. Thompson, that "men seem obstinately to reject the view that state behavior at some point is not a fit subject for moral judgment. One sign that this principle is accepted as relevant is the apparent compulsion of political actors to justify their needs in moral terms. Hypocrisy is the tribute vice pays to virtue." Thompson goes on to point out that expediency and morality move dialectically in international politics, so that a position taken by a government purely for reasons of expediency but extolling some moral principle may come to bind that government in some future situation merely because, by repetition, the principle has been accepted by other governments in the meantime. "On some points at least the practical and moral march hand in hand."

The paradox is now complete: by granting the existence of a power orientation, the Functionalist approaches the Realist; by modifying the absolute victory of power, some Realists join hands with the Functionalists. Those, like Claude and Engle, who deny the first separability proposition are then forced to a subordination of Functionalism to Realism without really investigating the empirical scope of the remaining notions of separation. And the bulk of Functionalist theory goes unexamined.

It is precisely the merit of Functionalism that it broke away from the clichés of Realist political theory. Its fault lies in not having broken radically enough. The separability propositions point the way toward a rapprochement between international relations theory and the rest of the social sciences, specifically political sociology and the empirical study of politics—though they do not point clearly enough in their present form. Our first task, then, must be a refinement of these propositions in the light of social science theory and contemporary empirical studies. . . .

THE POLITICAL ORIGINS OF
THE UN SECURITY COUNCIL'S
ABILITY TO LEGITIMIZE
THE USE OF FORCE

Erik Voeten

In a 1966 article, Claude observed that the function of collective legitimization in global politics is increasingly conferred on international organizations (IOs), and that the United Nations (UN) has become the primary custodian of this legitimacy. Claude argued that "the world organization has come to be regarded, and used, as a dispenser of politically significant approval and disapproval of the claims, policies, and actions of states."[1] This assertion is even more relevant now than it was in 1966. States, including the United States, have shown the willingness to incur significant cost in terms of time, policy compromise, and side-payments simply to obtain the stamp of approval from the UN Security Council (SC) for military actions. To be sure, if the

---

[1]Claude 1966, 367.

attempt to achieve a SC compromise proved unsuccessful, the United States has not shied away from using other means to pursue its ends. Nevertheless, the failure to acquire SC approval is generally perceived as costly, giving SC decisions considerable clout in international politics.

Given its lack of enforcement capabilities, the SC's leverage resides almost entirely in the perceived legitimacy its decisions grant to forceful actions.[2] Governments across the globe appear more willing to cooperate voluntarily once the SC has conferred its blessing on a use of force. Why has the SC become the most impressive source of international legitimacy for the use of military force? That it would be so is far from obvious. Claude, for instance, thought of the UN General Assembly (GA) as the ultimate conferrer of legitimacy.[3] Franck argued in his influential 1990 treatise on legitimacy that if one were interested in identifying rules in the international system with a strong compliance pull, the provisions in the UN Charter that grant the SC military enforcement powers (Chapter VII) should be set aside.[4] Since then, these provisions have been invoked with great regularity to legitimize uses of force.

The development is also puzzling from a theoretical perspective. Most theorists seek the origins of modern institutional legitimacy in legal or moral principles. However, the SC has been inconsistent at best in applying legal principles; its decision-making procedures are not inclusive, transparent, or based on egalitarian principles; its decisions are frequently clouded by the threat of outside action; and the morality of its (non-) actions is widely debated. Hence, it is unlikely that the institution has the ability to appear depoliticized, an argument that motivates most constructivist accounts of institutional legitimacy in the international arena.[5]

On the other hand, scholars who study the strategic aspects of international politics have largely dismissed the UN from their analyses.[6] This article provides a firmer base for the role of the SC in strategic interactions. I argue that when governments and citizens look for an authority to legitimize the use of force, they generally do not seek an independent judgment on the appropriateness of an intervention; rather, they want political reassurance about the consequences of proposed military adventures. The rationale is based on an analysis of the strategic dilemmas that impede cooperation in a unipolar world. In the absence of credible limits to power, fears of exploitation stifle cooperation. Because no single state can credibly check the superpower, enforcing limits on the superpower's behavior involves overcoming a complex coordination dilemma. A cooperative equilibrium that implies self-enforcing limits to

[2]See Barnett 1997; Caron 1993; and Hurd 1999 and 2002.
[3]Claude 1966, 373.
[4]Franck 1990, 42.
[5]See especially Barnett and Finnemore 1999.
[6]Hoffmann 1998, 179.

the exercise of power exists but is unlikely to emerge spontaneously given that governments have conflicting perceptions about what constitute legitimate actions and fundamental transgressions by the superpower. The SC provides a focal solution that has the characteristics of an elite pact: an agreement among a select set of actors that seeks to neutralize threats to stability by institutionalizing nonmajoritarian mechanisms for conflict resolution. The elite pact's authority depends on the operation of a social norm in which SC approval provides a green light for states to cooperate, whereas its absence triggers a coordinated response that imposes costs on violators. The observance of this norm allows for more cooperation and restraint than can be achieved in the absence of coordination on the SC as the proper institutional device. Hence the extent to which the SC confers legitimacy on uses of force depends not on the perceived normative qualities of the institution, but on the extent to which actors in international politics believe that norm compliance produces favorable outcomes.

The attractiveness of the elite pact account resides partly in its ability to explain the emergence of a limited degree of governance in the international system without assuming the existence of a collective global identity that generates an ideological consensus over appropriate forms of global governance. There is little evidence that such a consensus exists. Thus accounts that require only a limited set of a priori common values appear more plausible. Furthermore, the elite pact model better fits the SC's institutional design than alternative accounts and provides a plausible explanation for the sudden surge in authority following the Gulf War. Finally, the model stresses that elite pacts need to be self-enforcing. This opens a more promising avenue for analyzing norm stability than the constructivist assumption that norms are internalized.

The article proceeds with a broad overview of temporal fluctuations in the extent to which states have historically put weight on SC decisions. The next section explains why SC authority stems from its ability to legitimize uses of force and provides an operational definition. While there is a large literature that asserts that SC decisions confer legitimacy on uses of force, explanations for this phenomenon are rarely made explicit. One of the contributions of this article is to more precisely identify the various plausible roles of the SC in the international system. After discussing the four most common (though often implicit) explanations, the elite pact argument is introduced more elaborately. The conclusion discusses the implications for theories of international legitimacy and the future of SC legitimacy.

THE SECURITY COUNCIL AND ITS AUTHORITY OVER USES OF FORCE

When states sign the UN Charter, they pledge not to use or threaten force "against the territorial integrity or political independence of any state, or in any manner inconsistent with the Purposes of the United Nations."[7] The Charter delegates significant authority to the SC to decide whether particular uses of force meet these purposes. This delegation is necessitated by the incompleteness of any contract that seeks to regulate the use of force but falls short of forbidding it outright. The Charter provides some guidance by explicitly specifying two general circumstances in which force may be exercised.

First, Article 51 of the Charter affirms the inherent right of states to use force in individual or collective self-defense against armed attacks. In principle, states are not obliged to obtain the approval of the SC for invoking this right.[8] . . .

Second, Chapter VII of the Charter defines a more active role for the SC in the management of international security. This chapter lays out a set of procedures through which the SC can authorize uses of force in response to the "existence of any threat to the peace, breach of the peace, or act of aggression."[9] . . .

Although the UN's effectiveness and decisiveness were often limited, the UN was actively involved in the management of many international conflicts in the first twenty-five years of its existence. Decisions by the UN's political organs carried some weight, even to realists such as Hans Morgenthau, who argued that the United States should be willing to compromise to "to keep the United Nations in existence and make it an effective instrument of international government."[10] Between the late-1960s and 1989, however, neither the GA nor the SC exercised much influence over when or whether states resorted to force, a development characterized by Haas as evidence for "regime decay."[11] . . .

The successful cooperation between states in the first Persian Gulf War abruptly turned the SC into the natural first stop for coalition building.[12] It is important to appreciate the magnitude of the sudden the shift in SC activity immediately after operation Desert Storm. Between 1977 and the start of the Gulf War, the SC had adopted only two resolutions under Chapter VII.[13] Between 1990 and 1998, the Council approved 145 Chapter VII resolutions.[14] The number of UN commanded missions that used force beyond traditional peacekeeping principles went from one (Congo) before 1990 to five thereafter.[15] The number of missions where the authority to exercise force

---

[7] UN Charter, Article 2(4).

[8] See Schachter 1989; and Franck 2001. Under the Charter, states do have an obligation to notify the SC.

[9] UN Charter, Article 39.

[10] Morgenthau 1954, 11.

[11] Haas 1983.

[12] Baker 1995, 278.

[13] See SC Resolution 502, 3 April 1982; SC Resolution 598, 20 July 1987; and Bailey and Daws 1998, 272.

[14] Bailey and Daws 1998, 271.

[15] Jakobsen 2002.

was delegated to interested parties went from one (Korea) to twelve.[16] Since 1990, the SC has authorized uses of force by coalitions of able and willing states in Europe (for example, the former Yugoslavia), Africa (for example, Sierra Leone, Somalia, the Great Lakes Region), Latin America (for example, Haiti), Oceania (for example, East-Timor), and Asia (For example, Afghanistan).

This spurt in activity does not simply reflect a newfound harmony in the preferences of the five veto powers. China and Russia frequently abstained from SC votes and often accompanied their abstentions with statements of discontent.[17] Reaching agreement often involved difficult compromises that had a noticeable impact on the implementation of operations, as exemplified most prolifically by the Bosnia case.[18] On several occasions, the United States made significant side-payments to obtain SC blessing for operations it could easily, and de facto did, execute alone or with a few allies. For instance, in exchange for consent for the U.S. intervention in Haiti, China and Russia obtained sizeable concessions, including a favorable World Bank loan and U.S. support for peacekeeping in Georgia.[19] Thus, attaining SC approval for a use of force is no easy task. . . .

The observation that, since the Persian Gulf War, it has become costly to circumvent the authority of the SC is not completely undermined by the two main cases where this authority has been ignored: the Kosovo intervention and the 2003 Iraq intervention. The absence of SC authorization for the Kosovo intervention was generally (and explicitly) perceived as unfortunate by the U.S. administration and even more so by its allies in the North Atlantic Treaty Organization (NATO).[20] NATO motivated its actions by referring to previous SC resolutions and obtained SC authorization for the peacekeeping mission and transitional authority that were set up in the immediate aftermath of the military campaign. Similarly, the United States went to considerable length to persuade the SC to authorize the Iraq intervention, argued repeatedly that it was implementing past SC resolutions, and returned to the SC in the immediate aftermath of the intervention.[21] Moreover, the absence of SC authorization is often used domestically in the argument that the lack of allies makes the war unnecessarily expensive. That NATO and the United States eventually went ahead without SC authorization does demonstrate, however, that the SC may raise the costs of unilateral action but cannot prevent it altogether.[22] As former U.S. Secretary of

---

[16]Ibid.
[17]Voeten 2001.
[18]See Christopher 1998.
[19]Malone 1998.
[20]Daalder and O'Hanlon 2000, 218–19.
[21]See also Frederking 2003.
[22]See also Hurd 2003, 205.

Defense William Cohen said about SC authorization for the Kosovo intervention: "It's desirable, not imperative."[23]

LEGITIMACY

The previous section illustrates that since the Persian Gulf War, the main states in world politics have behaved "as if" it is costly to circumvent the authority of the SC when deciding on uses of force. How can one explain this observation given that the SC lacks independent capabilities to enforce its decisions? Several commonplace explanations for IO authority apply poorly to the SC. There are few, if any, institutional mechanisms that allow states to create credible long-term commitments to the institution, making it an unlikely candidate for locking in policies, along the lines suggested by Ikenberry.[24] The tasks that the SC performs are not routine and do not require high levels of specific expertise or knowledge. Thus, delegation of decision-making authority to the SC does not result in similar gains from specialization that plausibly explain why states are willing to delegate authority to IOs such as the World Bank[25] and the International Monetary Fund (IMF).[26]

In the absence of obvious alternative sources, the origins of the SC authority are usually assumed to lie in the legitimacy it confers on forceful actions.[27] Actions that are perceived as legitimate are obeyed voluntarily rather than challenged. Hence, obtaining legitimacy for proposed interventions is valuable. This clearly implies that legitimacy resides entirely in the subjective beliefs of actors.[28] This contrasts with the conception that legitimacy properly signifies an evaluation on normative grounds, usually derived from democratic theory. In this view, if an institution fails to meet a set of specified standards it is illegitimate, regardless of how individual actors perceive the institution. While it is important to evaluate how democratic principles ought to be extended to a global arena,[29] such a normative approach is unlikely to generate much insight into the question why SC decisions confer the legitimacy they do.

I define legitimacy perceptions as the beliefs of actors that the convention or social norm that the SC authorizes and forbids discretionary uses of force by states against

---

[23]See *New York Times*, 12 June 1998, A1.

[24]Ikenberry 2001. Accordingly, Ikenberry focuses on NATO and GATT/WTO.

[25]Nielson and Tierney 2003.

[26]Martin 2003.

[27]See Caron 1993; and Hurd 1999.

[28]Weber 1978.

[29]For example, Held 1995.

states should be upheld. Discretionary uses of force are those that do not involve direct and undisputed self-defense against an attack. Thus the authority of the SC resides in the beliefs of actors that violating this social norm is costly, undesirable, or inappropriate. This focus on perceptions and on the social aspect of legitimacy is consistent with constructivist approaches.[30] It also fits rationalist accounts of self-enforcing conventions and social norms.[31]

The primary actors are governments, who decide on uses of force and are the members of the UN. However, because governments, especially democratically elected ones, rely on the support of citizens, the perceptions of individuals also matter in an indirect way. In addition, it may well be that actors in the state with the intent to use force, most often the United States in our examples, and actors in other states may have different motivations for insisting on SC authorization.[32]

EXPLANATIONS

Why do state actors believe that a failure to achieve SC authorization is undesirable? What sustains these beliefs? To find convincing answers to these questions one needs to appreciate not only why states demand some form of multilateralism, but also the reasons that would lead actors to rely on the SC rather than alternatives, such as the GA, regional institutions (for example, NATO), or multilateral coalitions that are not embedded in formal IOs. Thus, pointing to a general inclination toward multilateralism does not form a satisfactory explanation of the empirical pattern.[33] Besides institutional form, a persuasive account must provide useful insights about the sources for temporal variation in the authority of the SC, including its sudden surge following the Gulf War. Moreover, it should give a plausible explanation for how these beliefs can be sustained given the behavior of the SC.

Most theoretical accounts argue that the legitimacy of international institutions resides in their ability to appear depoliticized by faithfully applying a set of rules, procedures, and norms that are deemed desirable by the international community.[34] I discuss three variants of this general argument that each stresses a different role for institutions: consistently applying legal rules, facilitating deliberation, and increasing accountability and fairness. Alternatively, the origins of the SC's

---

[30]See especially Hurd 1999.
[31]See Lewis 1969; and Young 1993.
[32]See also Thompson 2004.
[33]See Ruggie 1993.
[34]Barnett and Finnemore 1999, 708.

legitimacy may lie in beliefs that granting the SC the authority to legitimize force generally lead to more desirable outcomes. The public goods explanation discussed below fits this mold, as does the elite pact account.

Legal Consistency

Much legal scholarship assumes that the SC derives its ability to legitimize and delegitimize the use of force from its capacity to form judgments about the extent to which proposed actions fit a legal framework that defines a system of collective security. Although the SC is explicitly a political institution rather than a court, there is a body of customary and written international law that provides a basis for determinations about the legality of self-defense actions and other uses of force.[35] The indiscriminatory nature of legal norms potentially makes legal uses of force more acceptable to governments and citizens than actions that do not meet legal standards. To maintain its standing as a legitimate conferrer of legal judgments, an institution must thus strive for consistency in its rulings and motivate deviations from past practice with (developing) legal principles. This standard has usefully been applied to other bodies, such as dispute resolution mechanisms in trade organizations[36] and the European Court of Justice (ECJ).[37] That legal consistency is the institutional behavior that reinforces legitimacy beliefs also motivates concerns by legal scholars that the SC squanders its legitimacy when it behaves in ways that are inconsistent with general principles of international law.[38] . . .

There is, however, no empirical evidence that legal consistency has been a driving force behind SC decisions. During the Cold War, the judgments by UN bodies on the legality of self-defense actions were widely perceived as politically motivated and not persuasive on the issue of lawfulness.[39] The SC has not developed a consistent doctrine on this matter since the end of the Cold War. The most noteworthy decision is the previously noted Resolution 1373, which affirms the right of the United States to act forcefully in its self-defense against terrorist activities. The extensive scope of the resolution has led some to question its legal foundations. As Farer puts it: "At this point, there is simply no cosmopolitan body of respectable legal opinion that could be invoked to support so broad a conception of self-defense."[40]

[35]See Murphy 1997 for an overview.
[36]Kelemen 2001.
[37]Burley and Mattli 1993.
[38]See Alvarez 1995; Farer 2002; Glennon 2001; and Kirgis 1995.
[39]Schachter 1989.
[40]Farer 2002, 359.

Forum for Deliberation

A second set of scholars claim that while legal arguments are not decisive in the SC, law plays a broader role in the process of justificatory discourse.[41] This view relies on the notion that governments generally feel compelled to justify their actions on something other than self-interest. This may be so because governments seek to acquire the support of other governments, domestic political actors, or public opinion. Or, it may be that governments have internalized standards for appropriate behavior that are embedded in international legal norms. The importance of law in persuasion resides in its ability to put limits on the set of arguments that can acceptably be invoked.[42] Moreover, professional experts (international lawyers) help distinguish good arguments from poor ones in the evaluation of truth claims. Of course, the extent to which legal specialists can perform this function depends on the presence of a relatively coherent body of international law that regulates uses of force. . . .

The above view provides a promising account for why states frequently appeal to legal arguments, precedents, and collective security rules, even if final decisions often violate those rules. However, this view does not provide a plausible explanation for the role of the SC in this discursive process. It is widely recognized that the SC falls far short of Habermasian conditions for effective communicative action.[43] There is only a shallow set of common values, participants are unequal, and the SC relies extensively on unrecorded and informal consultations between subsets of the permanent members.[44] U.S. Secretary of State Colin Powell's public exposition of evidence for the case against Iraq was highly unusual and of questionable efficacy as a persuasive effort.[45] More frequently, the most visible efforts at persuasion occur outside of the institutional context of the SC. SC debates are usually recitations by representatives of statements prepared by their state departments. Strategic incentives further impede deliberation. There are clear and obvious incentives for states to misrepresent their positions, as the stakes are clear and the relevant actors few. In short, it is hard to see how the institutional setting of the SC contributes to the process of justificatory discourse and why, if deliberation were so important, institutional reforms have not been undertaken or alternative venues such as the GA have not grown more relevant.

[41]See Johnstone 2003; and Sandholtz and Stone Sweet 2004.
[42]Johnstone 2003.
[43]See Johnstone 2003; and Risse 2000.
[44]See Bailey and Daws 1998; Woods 1999; and Wood 1996.
[45]Colin Powell, "Remarks to the United Nations Security Council," New York City, 5 February 2003.

Appropriate Procedures

An institution's decisions may be seen as legitimate because the institution's decision-making process corresponds to practice deemed desirable by members of the community. Beliefs about the appropriateness of a decision-making process constitute an important source of authority for domestic political institutions, particularly in democracies. Citizens may attach inherent value to procedures that conform to principles widely shared in a society. As a consequence, decisions of an institution may be perceived as legitimate even if these produce outcomes deemed undesirable.[46] In a similar vein, accountability, procedural fairness, and broad participation are often seen as inherent elements of the legitimacy of IOs.[47] This assumption underlies the common argument that the main threat to SC legitimacy is that the institution is dominated by a few countries and that its procedures are opaque and unfair.[48] The assertion is that the SC's decisions would carry greater legitimacy if its procedures more closely matched liberal norms, which allegedly have become increasingly important in international society.[49]

The many attempts to reform the SC indicate that the legitimacy of the SC may be enhanced from the perspective of some if its decision-making procedures more closely corresponded to liberal principles. But one cannot plausibly explain the legitimacy the SC does confer on uses of force from the assumption that governments and citizens demand appropriate process. As outlined earlier, SC practice sets a low standard if measured against any reasonable set of liberal principles. One may object that a use of force authorized by the SC more closely approximates standards of appropriate procedure than unilateral actions. But if demands for appropriate procedure were strong, one would surely expect a greater use of more inclusive IOs, such as a return to the "uniting for peace" procedure popular in the 1950s and 1960s, perhaps under a weighted voting system. Instead, the GA has grown increasingly irrelevant for legitimizing uses of force. Alternatively, one might have expected reforms that increase transparency and accountability, which have been moderately successful in international financial institutions. Some argue that accountability has worsened in the 1990s, as the GA can no longer hold the SC accountable through the budget by qualified majority rule,[50] and because of the increasingly common practice of delegating the authority to use force to states and regional organizations.[51] . . .

[46]Gibson 1989.
[47]For example, see Keohane and Nye 2001; and Woods 1999.
[48]See especially Caron 1993.
[49]See the discussion in Barnett 1997.
[50]Woods 1999.
[51]Blokker 2000.

Finally and most fundamentally, there is no set of common values that generate consensus about what constitutes appropriate global governance. Disagreements have become especially apparent in debates about voting rules and membership questions, but they have also surfaced in virtually any other area where meaningful reforms have been proposed.[52] Even liberal democracies generally disagree on if and how liberal principles ought to be extended to global governance.[53] Explanations that emphasize strong common values are less likely to be successful for a diverse global organization than for an institution with more homogenous membership.

Global Public Goods

An alternative view is that the SC helps solve collective action problems that arise in the production of global public goods.[54] Successful peacekeeping operations reduce suffering and save lives. Globalization and the end of the Cold War may have increased demands for international actions that produce such effects.[55] In addition, UN-authorized interventions may provide a measure of stability and security that benefits virtually all nations. For example, the first Gulf War reinforced the norm that state borders not be changed forcibly and secured the stability of the global oil supply.[56] These benefits accrue to all status quo powers and are not easily excludable.

Models of public good provision predict that poor nations will be able to free ride off the contributions of wealthier nations and that the public good will be underprovided because contributors do not take into account the spillover benefits that their support confers to others. The SC may help alleviate underprovision and free riding in three ways. First, the fixed burden-sharing mechanism for peacekeeping operations provides an institutional solution that helps reduce risks of bargaining failures and lessens transaction costs.[57] Second, the delegation of decision-making authority to a small number of states may facilitate compromise on the amount of public good that ought to be produced.[58] Third, the SC helps states pool resources.[59] The existence of selective incentives induces some states to incur more than their required share of the peacekeeping burden. For example, Kuwait paid two-thirds of the bill for

[52]Luck 2003.

[53]See Schmitz and Sikkink 2002, 521; and Slaughter 1995.

[54]For analyses along these lines see Khanna, Sandler, and Shimizu 1998; Bobrow and Boyer 1997; and Shimizu and Sandler 2002.

[55]Jakobsen 2002.

[56]Bennett, Lepgold, and Unger 1994.

[57]This system was put in place in 1973 by General Assembly Resolution 310.

[58]Martin 1992, 773.

[59]Abbott and Snidal 1998.

the UN Iraq-Kuwait Observation Mission through voluntary contributions. Australia proved willing to shoulder a disproportionate share of the peacekeeping burden in East-Timor. States are more likely to make such contributions when these add to the efforts of others in a predictable manner.

The absence of enforcement mechanisms implies that the survival of this cooperative solution depends on a social norm. This norm first and foremost requires states to pay their share of the burden. The more states believe that this norm is followed, the fewer incentives they have to free ride in any particular case. In individual instances, states must be willing to shoulder a larger share of the burden than they would with a voluntary mechanism, because they believe that the benefits from upholding the social norm (greater public good production in the long run) exceed the short-term benefits of shirking. Hence, interventions authorized by the SC could be perceived as more legitimate in the sense that they signal a longer-term commitment to global public good production.

Although this argument is plausible theoretically, it fails to account for some noticeable empirical patterns. First, the belief among rational actors that the SC plays this role should and probably has weakened considerably since the early 1990s. The much-publicized failures in Somalia, Rwanda, and Bosnia should have reduced beliefs that the SC is the appropriate mechanism for coordination that helps solve problems of public good production. . . .

Second, the public goods rationale does not explain why states value SC authorization even when they do not use its fixed burden-sharing mechanism. . . .

Third, the decision-making procedures grant veto power to states that contribute little to UN operations and exclude some of the most significant contributors. Japan and Germany are the second and third largest contributors but have no permanent seat at the table. . . .

THE SECURITY COUNCIL AS AN ELITE PACT

An alternative perspective is that the SC is an institutional manifestation of a central coalition of great powers.[60] This view does not proclaim that the SC enforces a broad system of collective security, but rather that it may serve as a useful mechanism that facilitates cooperative efforts in an anarchic world characterized by the security dilemma.[61] Concerts were historically designed to deal with situations of multipolarity that followed the defeat of hegemony. However, similar incentives for cooperation

[60]Rosecrance 1992.

[61]Jervis 1985. Other realists believe that concerts were mostly epiphenomenal. See Downs and Iida 1994.

exist in a unipolar world characterized by interdependence. There are substantial potential gains from cooperation between the superpower and other states on economic issues such as trade and financial stability. Moreover, many governments face common security threats such as terrorism and states with the capacity and intention to challenge status quo boundaries or produce nuclear weapons. The main impediment to cooperation under the security dilemma is fear of exploitation.[62] Such fears are also relevant in a unipolar world where the superpower can use its preponderant capabilities to extract concessions, set the terms for cooperation, and act against the interests of individual states without being checked by a single credible power.

In such asymmetrical situations, credible limits to the use of force potentially benefit both the superpower and the rest of the world.[63] In the absence of credible guarantees, one observes suboptimal levels of cooperation as states pay a risk premium, captured for instance by increased military expenditure or other actions targeted at limiting the superpower's relative primacy. Institutions, such as NATO, help increase the credibility of security guarantees by raising the cost of reneging from a commitment. However, the absence of an outside threat and strong collective identity make such arrangements much more difficult to achieve at the global level.

Game-theoretic analyses that treat institutions as self-enforcing equilibria suggest an alternative route by which institutions help achieve better outcomes: they aid in solving the coordination dilemma among those actors that fear exploitation. Potential individual challenges are unlikely to deter a superpower from engaging in transgressions. However, the prospect of a coordinated challenge may well persuade the superpower to follow restraint. For this to succeed, states would have to agree on a mechanism that credibly triggers a coordinated response. For example, Greif, Milgrom, and Weingast argue that merchant guilds during the late medieval period provided a credible threat of costly boycotts if trade centers violated merchants' property rights.[64] Without these guilds, trade centers were unable to credibly commit to not exploit individual merchants and consequentially, merchants traded less than desired by the trade centers. As such, cooperation with the guilds became self-enforcing: it was in the self-interest of all actors to abide by the cooperative norm and defend against violations of the norm. Therefore, breaches of the norm came to be seen as illegitimate actions. . . .

To domestic publics this convention performs a signaling function. Citizens are generally unprepared to make accurate inferences about the likely consequences of forceful actions. If the convention operates as specified above, SC agreement provides the public with a shortcut on the likely consequences of foreign adventures. SC authorization indicates that no costly challenges will result from the action. The absence

[62]Jervis 1985, 69.

[63]Ikenberry 2001.

[64]Greif, Milgrom, and Weingast 1994.

of SC authorization on the other hand, signals the possibility of costly challenges and reduced cooperation. A U.S. public that generally wants the United States to be involved internationally but is fearful of overextension[65] may value such a signaling function. To foreign publics, SC approval signals that a particular use of force does not constitute an abuse of power that should lead to a coordinated, costly response.[66] Clearly this conception of the SC poses fewer informational demands on general publics than alternatives. Moreover, it does not rely on the assumption that citizens share common values about the normative qualities of global governance. All citizens need to understand is that SC authorization implies some measure of consent and cooperation, whereas the absence of authorization signals potential challenges. The symbolic (focal point) aspect of SC approval allows for analogies to past experiences in a way that cooperative efforts through ad hoc coalitions do not.

More generally, the elite pact account does not depend on the existence of a broad set of common values that generates a consensus about what global governance should look like. For a cooperative equilibrium to survive, it is not necessary that each actor believe that the norm that sustains the equilibrium is morally appropriate, as long as most nonbelievers assume that other actors would react to violations. This is consistent with Weber's view on why a social order is binding on an individual level.[67] It helps explain the observation that governments insist on SC authorizations of uses of force even if they challenge the normative qualities of the institution. As observed earlier, powerful states such as Germany, Japan, and India, as well as many developing countries, regularly criticize the SC for its composition and decision-making procedures. Yet, they also insist on SC authorization of uses of force and in some cases even adjust their domestic laws to make cooperation conditional on SC.

The elite pact account has several other interesting implications that put it at odds with the alternative accounts. The remainder of this section discusses three of these: the mode of transformation, institutional design, and the self-enforcing character of the pact.

Mode of Transformation

The alternative explanations either do not give a clear prediction of how a shift in the authority of the SC takes place or (implicitly) assume that change occurs in response to gradual normative shifts toward greater reliance on liberal values or globalization.[68] The elite pact model predicts that if a shift toward a more cooperative equilibrium

---

[65]Holsti 2004.
[66]For a similar argument, see Thompson 2004.
[67]Weber 1978.
[68]See Barnett 1997; and Jakobsen 2002.

occurs, it will be in response to a discrete event. Elite pacts cannot be formed at just any time. In the most natural uncoordinated equilibrium, groups of actors exploit others and have no direct incentive to stop this practice. Elite pacts are therefore imposed following galvanizing events that disturb the beliefs on which a preceding equilibrium rested.[69] The conclusion of major wars is particularly likely to upset previously held beliefs and payoff structures.[70]

This is compatible with the empirical record. Concerts were imposed following the defeat of a hegemon in a major war; a characterization that also fits the formation of the SC in the immediate aftermath of World War II.[71] Nevertheless, the pact was not self-enforcing and had little bearing on whatever stability there was during most of the Cold War.[72] The end of the Cold War created uncertainty in the perceptions of states about new equilibrium behavior. In such a situation it is highly likely that the manner by which a cooperative resolution to the first major international conflict was reached greatly influenced beliefs among policymakers, politicians and citizens about the future resolution of conflicts, and hence that adherence to the norm that the SC authorizes force helps enforce a stable (but limited) form of governance. . . .

Institutional Design

. . . Rather, I maintain that given that the SC functioned as it did at a time of great uncertainty about equilibrium behavior, it is plausible that it impressed beliefs on state actors that a cooperative equilibrium could be played with the SC as a focal solution. Nevertheless, the institutional design of the SC did make it a more viable candidate for such a role than alternative institutions.

First, elite pacts eschew majoritarian decision making and commonly grant influential actors the power to veto decisions.[73] This is understandable because the goal of elite pacts is stability, not proper procedure. Stability is threatened if those with the power to disturb it are overruled in the decision process. Thus the GA would be a poor coordination device and indeed has been largely irrelevant in security affairs throughout the 1990s.

Second, the process by which compromises in elite cartels are achieved is generally secretive rather than transparent. Public deliberation manifests heterogeneity and

---

[69]Weingast 1997. See also Rustow 1970.

[70]This logic is also apparent in Ikenberry 2001, who also stresses the importance of creating credible limits to the exercise of power through institutions. However, the logic that grants the SC authority is different here than in Ikenberry.

[71]See Claude 1964; and Jervis 1985.

[72]It is beyond the scope of this paper to speculate on the reasons. A potential answer is that its purpose, to restrain a weak defeated state (Germany), was rapidly resolved.

[73]Andeweg 2000.

commits actors to take stands from which it is costly to recede. For the most part, the public record of SC meetings is uninformative about true motivations actors have as most compromises are achieved in unrecorded negotiations. Extensive public debate is uncommon and counterproductive, as commented on in the section on deliberation.

Third, elite cartels usually embrace principles of subsidiarity or segmental authority.[74] Delegating discretion to influential actors within their own domain helps preserve satisfaction with the status quo. It has become the modal option for the SC to de facto delegate the authority to use force to regional organizations (for example, NATO, Economic Community of West African States) or regional powers (for example, United States, Australia). This creates serious problems of accountability and has questionable legal foundations in the Charter.[75] It fits, however, within the purpose of an elite pact. . . .

Norm Stability

Constructivists have criticized rationalist approaches for being ontologically inclined to revisionism and therefore unable to adequately explain the persistence of norms, since self-interested actors do not value the norms themselves, just the benefits directly accruing from them.[76] Instead, constructivists typically assume that actors internalize social norms. The concept of internalization is borrowed from the developmental and social psychology literature, where it is used to characterize the process by which humans absorb norms and values present in their social environment to develop standards for appropriate behavior. Once these standards are internalized, actors do not reevaluate adherence to them when choosing between alternative courses of action. There are both good theoretical and empirical reasons to suspect that internalization is not a prominent source of norm stability in the case under investigation. Theoretically, it is not at all obvious how the internalization concept extends to state actors, especially when these are making decisions regarding behavior than can hardly be described as habitual: the use of military force. Empirically, there are examples aplenty where state actors consciously and explicitly evaluated the trade-off between the legitimacy benefits of the SC and the costs of compromise necessary to obtain those benefits.[77] This suggests a different thought process than internalization would.

That internalization is unlikely does imply that norm stability is a concern. In the elite pact model, a stable norm reflects a self-enforcing equilibrium. This indeed requires that governments must find that their expected utility of abiding by the norm exceeds their utility from acting otherwise. Whether the norm is self-enforcing

[74]Ibid.
[75]Blokker 2000.
[76]See Hurd 1999, 387; and Wendt 1999.
[77]For example, Voeten 2001.

depends at least partly on the behavior of the institution itself. If the SC conforms to the expectations of actors regarding its function, the legitimacy beliefs on which its authority is based are reinforced. If, however, the SC defies those expectations, these beliefs are undermined. If the behavior of the SC reinforces the social norm, more actors in more situations perceive it to be in their interest to adhere to it. If the behavior of the SC undermines the social norm, fewer actors in fewer situations support it. This self-undermining process can reach a critical level at which the equilibrium is no longer self-enforcing and institutional change should follow.[78] This point is consistent with the common assumption that regimes weaken when actual practice is inconsistent with the rules and norms that constitute the regime.[79]

Behavior associated with the SC reinforces the social norm if it contributes to keeping U.S. power in check while avoiding costly challenges and maintaining beneficial forms of global cooperation. It undermines the social norm if it either fails to provide an adequate check on U.S. power or leads to costly challenges. In observing a SC authorization for the use of force, one should not observe meaningful challenges to the United States by other states. If important states would retaliate even after the United States obtains SC authorization, the United States may be less inclined to follow the social norm in future instances. In addition, the decision to authorize force cannot merely be a rubber stamp. If those states that are delegated the responsibilities to constrain U.S. power give too much leeway, SC decisions lose their utility to other states. This implies that to maintain the equilibrium it will sometimes be necessary for permanent members to defend the interests of important states not represented in the Council.[80] If they would fail to do so, the social norm would be of little use to these states and they might challenge it.

Besides the Persian Gulf War, other reinforcing examples include the Haitian and Somalian invasions, and the various resolutions on Bosnia. These cases may not have been resolved in a manner that is satisfactory from a moral, legal, or efficiency standpoint, but they did not result in an overextension of U.S. power or in costly challenges against its power, despite disagreements between states over the proper courses of action. . . .

CONCLUSIONS

The ability of the SC to successfully restrain the United States is at the heart of its aptitude to play a legitimizing role in international politics. In this conception, a

[78]Grief and Laitin 2004. Legitimacy beliefs can be understood as "quasi-parameters." These are parameters that can gradually be altered by the implications of the institution, but a marginal change will not necessarily cause behavior associated with the institution to change.

[79]Krasner 1982.

[80]On the practice of informal consultations, see Hurd 1997.

legitimate exercise of power abides by certain accepted limits. SC authorization signals the observance of these limits, which are defined not by legal, moral, or efficiency standards, but by an undemocratic political process that seeks to achieve compromise among elite actors. It is important to understand that although the role of the SC depends entirely on the configuration of state interests, this fact does not make the institution epiphenomenal. There are many potential equilibria and convergence on a particular (semicooperative) equilibrium has important implications. This is true even if the restraint on the exercise of power is limited to raising the cost of unilateralism. . . .

THE RESPONSIBILITY
TO PROTECT

GARETH EVANS AND MOHAMED SAHNOUN

REVISITING HUMANITARIAN INTERVENTION

The international community in the last decade repeatedly made a mess of handling the many demands that were made for "humanitarian intervention": coercive action against a state to protect people within its borders from suffering grave harm. There were no agreed rules for handling cases such as Somalia, Bosnia, Rwanda, and Kosovo at the start of the 1990s, and there remain none today. Disagreement continues about whether there is a right of intervention, how and when it should be exercised, and under whose authority.

Since September 11, 2001, policy attention has been captured by a different set of problems: the response to global terrorism and the case for "hot preemption" against countries believed to be irresponsibly acquiring weapons of mass destruction. These issues, however, are conceptually and practically distinct. There are indeed common questions, especially concerning the precautionary principles that should apply to any military

"The Responsibility to Protect" by Gareth Evans and Mohamed Sahnoun. Reprinted by permission of *Foreign Affairs*, Vol. 81, No. 6, November/December 2002. Copyright © 2002 by the Council on Foreign Relations, Inc. www.ForeignAffairs.com.

action anywhere. But what is involved in the debates about intervention in Afghanistan, Iraq, and elsewhere is the scope and limits of countries' rights to act in self-defense—not their right, or obligation, to intervene elsewhere to protect peoples other than their own.

Meanwhile, the debate about intervention for human protection purposes has not gone away. And it will not go away so long as human nature remains as fallible as it is and internal conflict and state failures stay as prevalent as they are. The debate was certainly a lively one throughout the 1990s. Controversy may have been muted in the case of the interventions, by varying casts of actors, in Liberia in 1990, northern Iraq in 1991, Haiti in 1994, Sierra Leone in 1997, and (not strictly coercively) East Timor in 1999. But in Somalia in 1993, Rwanda in 1994, and Bosnia in 1995, the UN action taken (if taken at all) was widely perceived as too little too late, misconceived, poorly resourced, poorly executed, or all of the above. During NATO's 1999 intervention in Kosovo, Security Council members were sharply divided; the legal justification for action without UN authority was asserted but largely unargued; and great misgivings surrounded the means by which the allies waged the war.

It is only a matter of time before reports emerge again from somewhere of massacres, mass starvation, rape, and ethnic cleansing. And then the question will arise again in the Security Council, in political capitals, and in the media: What do we do? This time around the international community must have the answers.[1] Few things have done more harm to its shared ideal that people are all equal in worth and dignity than the inability of the community of states to prevent these horrors. In this new century, there must be no more Rwandas.

Secretary-General Kofi Annan, deeply troubled by the inconsistency of the international response, has repeatedly challenged the General Assembly to find a way through these dilemmas. But in the debates that followed his calls, he was rewarded for the most part by cantankerous exchanges in which fervent supporters of intervention on human rights grounds, opposed by anxious defenders of state sovereignty, dug themselves deeper and deeper into opposing trenches.

If the international community is to respond to this challenge, the whole debate must be turned on its head. The issue must be reframed not as an argument about the "right to intervene" but about the "responsibility to protect." And it has to be accepted that although this responsibility is owed by all sovereign states to their own citizens in the first instance, it must be picked up by the international community if that first-tier responsibility is abdicated, or if it cannot be exercised.

---

[1]In September 2000, the government of Canada established the ICISS. Our colleagues were Gisele Cote-Harper, Lee Hamilton, Michael Ignatieff, Vladimir Lukin, Klaus Naumann, Cyril Ramaphosa, Fidel Ramos, Cornelio Sommaruga, Eduardo Stein, and Ramesh Thakur. We met as a commission in Africa, Asia, Europe, and North America and consulted comprehensively in Latin America, the Middle East, Russia, and China. This article is a distillation of the report.

Sovereignty as Responsibility

Using this alternative language will help shake up the policy debate, getting governments in particular to think afresh about what the real issues are. Changing the terminology from "intervention" to "protection" gets away from the language of "humanitarian intervention." The latter term has always deeply concerned humanitarian relief organizations, which have hated the association of "humanitarian" with military activity. Beyond that, talking about the "responsibility to protect" rather than the "right to intervene" has three other big advantages. First, it implies evaluating the issues from the point of view of those needing support, rather than those who may be considering intervention. The searchlight is back where it should always be: on the duty to protect communities from mass killing, women from systematic rape, and children from starvation. Second, this formulation implies that the primary responsibility rests with the state concerned. Only if that state is unable or unwilling to fulfill its responsibility to protect, or is itself the perpetrator, should the international community take the responsibility to act in its place. Third, the "responsibility to protect" is an umbrella concept, embracing not just the "responsibility to react" but the "responsibility to prevent" and the "responsibility to rebuild" as well. Both of these dimensions have been much neglected in the traditional humanitarian-intervention debate. Bringing them back to center stage should help make the concept of reaction itself more palatable.

At the heart of this conceptual approach is a shift in thinking about the essence of sovereignty, from control to responsibility. In the classic Westphalian system of international relations, the defining characteristic of sovereignty has always been the state's capacity to make authoritative decisions regarding the people and resources within its territory. The principle of sovereign equality of states is enshrined in Article 2, Section 1, of the UN Charter, and the corresponding norm of nonintervention is enshrined in Article 2, Section 7: a sovereign state is empowered by international law to exercise exclusive and total jurisdiction within its territorial borders, and other states have the corresponding duty not to intervene in its internal affairs. But working against this standard has been the increasing impact in recent decades of human rights norms, bringing a shift from a culture of sovereign impunity to one of national and international accountability. The increasing influence of the concept of human security has also played a role: what matters is not just state security but the protection of individuals against threats to life, livelihood, or dignity that can come from within or without. In short, a large and growing gap has been developing between international behavior as articulated in the state-centered UN Charter, which was signed in 1946, and evolving state practice since then, which now emphasizes the limits of sovereignty.

Indeed, even the strongest supporters of state sovereignty will admit today that no state holds unlimited power to do what it wants to its own people. It is now commonly acknowledged that sovereignty implies a dual responsibility: externally, to respect the sovereignty of other states, and internally, to respect the dignity and basic rights of all the people within the state. In international human rights covenants, in UN practice, and in state practice itself, sovereignty is now understood as embracing this dual responsibility. Sovereignty as responsibility has become the minimum content of good international citizenship. Although this new principle cannot be said to be customary international law yet, it is sufficiently accepted in practice to be regarded as a de facto emerging norm: the responsibility to protect.

Military Intervention: Setting the Bar

The responsibility to protect implies a duty to react to situations in which there is compelling need for human protection. If preventive measures fail to resolve or contain such a situation, and when the state in question is unable or unwilling to step in, then intervention by other states may be required. Coercive measures then may include political, economic, or judicial steps. In extreme cases—but only extreme cases—they may also include military action. But what is an extreme case? Where should we draw the line in determining when military intervention is defensible? What other conditions or restraints, if any, should apply in determining whether and how that intervention should proceed? And, most difficult of all, who should have the ultimate authority to determine whether an intrusion into a sovereign state, involving the use of deadly force on a potentially massive scale, should actually go ahead? These questions have generated an enormous literature and much competing terminology, but on the core issues there is a great deal of common ground, most of it derived from "just war" theory. To justify military intervention, six principles have to be satisfied: the "just cause" threshold, four precautionary principles, and the requirement of "right authority."

Operation Just Cause

As for the "just cause" threshold, our starting point is that military intervention for human protection purposes is an extraordinary measure. For it to be warranted, civilians must be faced with the threat of serious and irreparable harm in one of just two exceptional ways. The first is large-scale loss of life, actual or anticipated, with genocidal intent or not, which is the product of deliberate state action, state neglect, inability to act, or state failure. The second is large-scale "ethnic cleansing," actual or anticipated, whether carried out by killing, forced expulsion, acts of terror, or rape.

   Why does the bar for just cause need to be set so high? There is the conceptual reason that military intervention must be very exceptional. There is also a practical political rationale: if intervention is to happen when it is most necessary, it cannot be called on too often. In the two situations identified as legitimate triggers, we do not quantify what is "large scale" but make clear our belief that military action can be legitimate as an anticipatory measure in response to clear evidence of likely large-scale killing or ethnic cleansing. Without this possibility, the international community would be placed in the morally untenable position of being required to wait until genocide begins before being able to take action to stop it. The threshold criteria articulated here not only cover the deliberate perpetration of horrors such as in the cases of Bosnia, Rwanda, and Kosovo. They can also apply to situations of state collapse and the resultant exposure of the population to mass starvation or civil war, as in Somalia. Also potentially covered would be overwhelming natural or environmental catastrophes, in which the state concerned is either unwilling or unable to help and significant loss of life is occurring or threatened. What are not covered by our "just cause" threshold criteria are human rights violations falling short of outright killing or ethnic cleansing (such as systematic racial discrimination or political oppression), the overthrow of democratically elected governments, and the rescue by a state of its own nationals on foreign territory. Although deserving of external action—including in appropriate cases political, economic, or military sanctions—these are not instances that would seem to justify military action for human protection purposes.

Precautionary Principles

Of the precautionary principles needed to justify intervention, the first is "right intention." The primary purpose of the intervention, whatever other motives intervening states may have, must be to halt or avert human suffering. There are a number of ways of helping ensure that this criterion is satisfied. One is to have military intervention always take place on a collective or multilateral basis. Another is to look at the extent to which the intervention is actually supported by the people for whose benefit the intervention is intended. Yet another is to look to what extent the opinion of other countries in the region has been taken into account and is supportive. Complete disinterestedness may be an ideal, but it is not likely always to be a reality: mixed motives, in international relations as everywhere else, are a fact of life. Moreover, the budgetary cost and risk to personnel involved in any military action may make it imperative for the intervening state to be able to claim some degree of self-interest in the intervention, however altruistic its primary motive.

The second precautionary principle is "last resort": military intervention can be justified only when every nonmilitary option for the prevention or peaceful resolution of the crisis has been explored, with reasonable grounds for believing lesser measures would not have succeeded. The responsibility to react with military coercion can be justified only when the responsibility to prevent has been fully discharged. This guideline does not necessarily mean that every such option must literally have been tried and failed; often there is simply not enough time for that process to work itself out. But it does mean that there must be reasonable grounds for believing that, given the circumstances, other measures would not have succeeded.

The third principle is "proportional means": the scale, duration, and intensity of the planned military intervention should be the minimum necessary to secure the defined objective of protecting people. The scale of action taken must be commensurate with its stated purpose and with the magnitude of the original provocation. The effect on the political system of the country targeted should be limited to what is strictly necessary to accomplish the intervention's purpose. Although the precise practical implications of these strictures are always open to argument, the principles involved are clear enough.

Finally, there is the principle of "reasonable prospects": there must be a reasonable chance of success in halting or averting the suffering that has justified the intervention; the consequences of action should not be worse than the consequences of inaction. Military action must not risk triggering a greater conflagration. Applying this precautionary principle would, on purely utilitarian grounds, likely preclude military action against any one of the five permanent members of the Security Council, even with all other conditions for intervention having been met. Otherwise, it is difficult to imagine a major conflict being avoided or success in the original objective being achieved. The same is true for other major powers that are not permanent members of the Security Council. This raises the familiar question of double standards, to which there is only one answer: The reality that interventions may not be plausibly mounted in every justifiable case is no reason for them not to be mounted in any case.

Whose Authority?

The most difficult and controversial principle to apply is that of "right authority." When it comes to authorizing military intervention for human protection purposes, the argument is compelling that the United Nations, and in particular its Security Council, should be the first port of call. The difficult question—starkly raised by the Kosovo war—is whether it should be the last.

The issue of principle here is unarguable. The UN is unquestionably the principal institution for building, consolidating, and using the authority of the international community. It was set up to be the linch-pin of order and stability, the framework within which members of the international system negotiate agreements on the rules of behavior and the legal norms of proper conduct to preserve the society of states. The authority of the UN is underpinned not by coercive power but by its role as the applicator of legitimacy. The concept of legitimacy acts as the connecting link between the exercise of authority and the recourse to power. Attempts to enforce authority can be made only by the legitimate agents of that authority. Nations regard collective intervention blessed by the UN as legitimate because a representative international body duly authorized it, whereas unilateral intervention is seen as illegitimate because it is self-interested. Those who challenge or evade the authority of the un run the risk of eroding its authority in general and undermining the principle of a world order based on international law and universal norms.

The task is not to find alternatives to the Security Council as a source of authority, but to make the council work better than it has. Security Council authorization should, in all cases, be sought prior to any military intervention being carried out. Those advocates calling for an intervention should formally request such authorization, ask the council to raise the matter on its own initiative, or demand that the secretary-general raise it under Article 99 of the un Charter. The Security Council should deal promptly with any request for authority to intervene where there are allegations of large-scale loss of life or ethnic cleansing. It should, in this context, also seek adequate verification of facts or conditions on the ground that might support a military intervention. And the council's five permanent members should agree to not exercise their veto power (in matters where their vital state interests are not involved) to block resolutions authorizing military intervention for human protection purposes for which there is otherwise majority support. We know of at least one that will so agree.

If the Security Council is unable or unwilling to act in a case crying out for intervention, two institutional solutions are available. One is for the General Assembly to consider the matter in an emergency special session under the "Uniting for Peace" procedure, used in the cases of Korea in 1950, Egypt in 1956, and Congo in 1960. Had it been used, that approach could well have delivered a speedy majority recommendation for action in the Rwanda and Kosovo cases. The other is action within an area of jurisdiction by regional or subregional organizations under Chapter VIII of the un Charter, subject to their seeking subsequent authorization from the Security Council; that is what happened with the West African interventions in Liberia in the early 1990s and in Sierra Leone in 1997. But interventions by ad hoc coalitions (or individual states) acting without the approval of the Security Council, the General Assembly, or a regional or subregional grouping do not find wide international favor. As a matter of political reality, then, it would simply be impossible to build consensus around any set of proposals for military intervention that acknowledged the validity of any intervention not authorized by the Security Council or General Assembly.

There are many reasons to be dissatisfied with the role that the Security Council usually plays: its generally uneven performance, its unrepresentative membership, and its inherent institutional double standards with the permanent-five veto power. But there is no better or more appropriate body than the Security Council to deal with military intervention issues for human protection purposes. The political reality—quite apart from the force of the argument in principle—is that if international consensus is ever to be reached about how military intervention should happen, the Security Council will clearly have to be at the heart of that consensus.

But what if the Security Council fails to discharge its own responsibility to protect in a conscience-shocking situation crying out for action, as was the case with Kosovo? A real question arises as to which of two evils is the worse: the damage to international order if the Security Council is bypassed, or the damage to that order if human beings are slaughtered while the Security Council stands by. The answer to this dilemma is twofold, and these messages have to be delivered loud and clear. First, if the Security Council does fail to discharge its responsibility in such a case, then concerned individual states simply may not rule out other means to address the gravity and urgency of the situation. It follows that there will be a risk that such interventions, without the discipline and constraints of UN authorization, will not be conducted for the right reasons or with the right commitment to the necessary precautionary principles. Second, if the council does fail to act and a military intervention by an ad hoc coalition or individual state follows and respects all the necessary threshold and precautionary criteria—and if that intervention succeeds and is seen by the world to have succeeded—this outcome may have enduringly serious consequences for the stature of the UN itself. This is essentially what happened with the NATO intervention in Kosovo. The UN cannot afford to drop the ball too many times on that scale.

The Problem of Political Will

As important as it is to reach consensus on the principles that should govern intervention for human protection purposes, unless the political will is mustered to act when necessary, the debate will be largely academic. As events during the 1990s too often demonstrated, even a decision by the Security Council to authorize international action in humanitarian cases has been no guarantee that any action would be taken, or taken effectively. The most compelling task now is to work to ensure that when the call for action goes out to the community of states, it will be answered.

Part of the problem is that there are few countries in the global community who have the assets most in demand in implementing intervention mandates. There are real constraints on how much spare capacity exists to take on additional burdens. United Nations peacekeeping peaked in 1993 at 78,000 personnel; today, if NATO and other multinational force operations (e.g., in Afghanistan) are included along with UN missions, the number of soldiers in international peace operations has grown by about 45 percent, to 113,000. Even states willing in principle to look at new foreign military commitments need to make choices about how to use limited and strained military capabilities.

If the right choices are to be made in the right situations, there is no alternative but to generate the necessary political will in the relevant constituencies. Too often more time is spent lamenting the absence of political will than on analyzing its ingredients and how to mobilize them. The key to mobilizing international support for intervention is to mobilize domestic support, or at least to neutralize domestic opposition. It is usually helpful to press three buttons in particular.

Moral appeals inspire and legitimize in almost any political environment: political leaders often underestimate the sheer sense of decency and compassion that prevails among their electorates. Financial arguments also have their place: preventive strategies are likely to be far cheaper than responding after the event through military action, humanitarian relief assistance, postconflict reconstruction, or all three. If coercive action is required, however, earlier is always cheaper than later. National interest appeals are the most comfortable and effective of all and can be made at many different levels. Avoiding the disintegration of a neighbor, given the refugee outflows and general regional security destabilization associated with it, can be a compelling motive in many contexts. National economic interests often can be equally well served by keeping resource supply lines, trade routes, and markets undisrupted. And whatever may have been the case in the past, nowadays peace is generally regarded as much better for business than is war.

For those domestic constituencies who may actually demand that their governments not be moved by altruistic "right intention," the best short answer may be that these days good international citizenship is a matter of national self-interest. With the world as interdependent as it now is, and with crises as capable as they now are of generating major problems elsewhere (such as terrorism, refugee outflows, health pandemics, narcotics trafficking, and organized crime), it is in every country's interest to help resolve such problems, quite apart from the humanitarian imperative.

It is the responsibility of the whole international community to ensure that when the next case of threatened mass killing or ethnic cleansing invariably comes along, the mistakes of the 1990s will not be repeated. A good place to start would be agreement by the Security Council, at least informally, to systematically apply the principles set out here to any such case. So too would be a declaratory UN General Assembly resolution giving weight to those principles and to the whole idea of the "responsibility to protect" as an emerging international norm. There is a developing consensus around the idea that sovereignty must be qualified by the responsibility to protect. But until there is general acceptance of the practical commitments this involves, more tragedies such as Rwanda will be all too likely.

Part III

FORCE AND WAR

INTRODUCTION

States differ in their international clout; the means at their disposal to influence their position are called *statecraft*. There are some aspects that a state cannot alter, like population size or geographical location, while others, especially wealth and military power, are more readily employed. "Power" as a key resource in statecraft can take one of two forms: the traditional version is *relational* power, which is defined as the ability of actor A to get actor B to do something that B would otherwise not do; Realism concentrates on this form. Liberals tend to focus a bit more on *structural* power, which is the ability to determine the rules of the game, for instance, in the World Trade Organization. The assumption is that large states tend to influence the writing of the rules in a manner that favors their policy agenda.[1] It is assumed in statecraft that power is a scarce resource in the international system and that states need it for their security. In either case, power is a concept measured vis-à-vis other actors, rather than as the property of a given state.

In this context, three primary questions arise for the study of statecraft: first, in which ways can power be deployed, that is, what functions may it serve? Second, is it possible, and if so to what degree, to take a power resource used in one scope and apply it to another? For example, can the military power of one state play a role in convincing another state that economic relations should be improved, or would it be completely irrelevant? Third, and this makes the interconnection with *war* particularly pertinent, in which forms can *diplomacy*, a key feature of statecraft, be drawn on in a violent sense? Thomas C. Schelling explains the use of force both to achieve military objectives, as well as to inflict pain in "The Diplomacy of Violence." Robert Pape examines the logic of political violence in the practice of suicide terrorism. But

---

[1] Susan Strange, *States and Markets* (London: Pinter, 1988)

as Robert Baldwin explains, the use of power and force has economic underpinnings that must be understood to practice effective statecraft.

In Western states, where most of political science has developed, *war* has been viewed as a calamity, and therefore something to be explained in order to be avoided. War is defined as an armed contest between two independent political units by means of organized military force, usually fought for political ends or for glory.

When we speak about *causes* of war, we usually refer to three types: (1) causes of war as an activity related to our human nature, which is assumed to produce some constant frequency of war; (2) the cause of a specific war; and (3) causes of war and *peace* that explain variance across time. War is statistically rare given the total possible opportunities for war between all states in the international system. Measured this way, states have spent the vast majority of their histories in peace. Furthermore, there is never a single cause for either war or peace. Surprisingly, there is also no evidence for the existence of accidental wars. Rather, war can be analogized as a calculated risk involved in coercive bargaining. When people drive to the store to buy bread, they risk an accident to obtain the bread even where they do not intend to have an accident.

There are two broad conceptions of the causes of war. Some argue that war is typically unintended, the result of a miscalculation by a state's decision-maker. World War I is raised as the archetypal example of an unintended war in the sense that all of the major participants were worse off because of the war than if it had never happened. The German, Russian, Austro-Hungarian, and Ottoman Empires all collapsed, and the British and the French were nearly bankrupted. With hindsight, all of those major actors would likely have avoided taking the same steps that led to war. They were lured to war through the so-called *security dilemma*, in which mutual insecurity is generated through the difficulty of distinguishing between preparations for defense and for offense; this ultimately makes war appear inevitable. Typically, the policy recommendations for this position are to avoid unnecessary arms races and provide facilities to encourage negotiations and concessions. Robert Jervis elaborates on the security dilemma in the reading entitled "Offense, Defense, and the Security Dilemma."

Others argue that war is the result of aggressors initiating wars when opportunities become available. The role of Germany and Japan in World War II is frequently cited as an example of an aggressor war. It is argued that there existed no concession that could have deterred Germany or Japan because their goals were nearly unlimited. This perspective usually labels the more peaceful state as the status quo power, because it has a preference for the preservation of the current system. The challenger or revisionist state seeks to overturn the system and is constantly seeking windows of opportunity through which to challenge the status quo state. Since even small states have unlimited ambitions, every state has the potential to be an aggressor. The policy recommendation from this perspective would be for strong deterrence, involving a rapid increase in military armaments to send a clear signal to potential aggressors.

Kenneth N. Waltz investigates this line of reasoning in the reading "Peace, Stability, and Nuclear Weapons."

The problem is that the policy recommendations for one conception of world politics can produce counter productive results in the other conception. In a world of aggressors, restraint in arming oneself, and the granting of concessions, undermines deterrence and encourages the aggressor to behave even more boldly. In a world of the security dilemma, in which there are states afraid for their security but none are aggressors, a stiff deterrence policy is likely to lead to provocation and to a tragically unintended outcome. The key therefore lies in being able to distinguish between preparations for war from preparations for defense, which depends in large part on the possibility to tell apart offensive and defensive weapons.

The end of the Cold War has shifted the locus of security competition from between the superpowers to more localized concerns such as inter-ethnic and identity based conflict between civilizations. Neither set of causes is straightforward or easily tested. In "The Clash of Civilizations," Samuel Huntington argues that future wars will occur along the boundary lines between the world's eight primary civilizations. Chaim Kaufmann, in "Possible and Impossible Solutions to Ethnic Civil War," discusses the outcomes of ethnic conflict, which is particularly acute in the developing world.

THE DIPLOMACY OF VIOLENCE

Thomas C. Schelling

The usual distinction between diplomacy and force is not merely in the instruments, words or bullets, but in the relation between adversaries—in the interplay of motives and the role of communication, understandings, compromise, and restraint. Diplomacy is bargaining; it seeks outcomes that, though not ideal for either party, are better for both than some of the alternatives. In diplomacy each party somewhat controls what the other wants, and can get more by compromise, exchange, or collaboration than by taking things in his own hands and ignoring the other's wishes. The bargaining can be polite or rude, entail threats as well as offers, assume a status quo or ignore all rights and privileges, and assume mistrust rather than trust. But whether polite or impolite, constructive or aggressive, respectful or vicious, whether it occurs among friends or antagonists and whether or not there is a basis for trust and goodwill, there must be some common interest, if only in the avoidance of mutual damage, and an awareness of the need to make the other party prefer an outcome acceptable to oneself.

With enough military force a country may not need to bargain. Some things a country wants it can take, and some things it has it can keep, by sheer strength, skill and ingenuity. It can do this *forcibly*, accommodating only to opposing strength, skill, and ingenuity and without trying to appeal to an enemy's wishes. Forcibly a country can repel and expel, penetrate and occupy, seize, exterminate, disarm and disable, confine, deny access, and directly frustrate intrusion or attack. It can, that is, if it has enough strength. "Enough" depends on how much an opponent has.

There is something else, though, that force can do. It is less military, less heroic, less impersonal, and less unilateral; it is uglier, and has received less attention in Western military strategy. In addition to seizing and holding, disarming and confining, penetrating and obstructing, and all that, military force can be used *to hurt*. In addition to taking and protecting things of value it can *destroy* value. In addition to weakening an enemy militarily it can cause an enemy plain suffering.

Pain and shock, loss and grief, privation and horror are always in some degree, sometimes in terrible degree, among the results of warfare; but in traditional military science they are incidental, they are not the object. If violence can be done incidentally, though, it can also be done purposely. The power to hurt can be counted among the most impressive attributes of military force.

Hurting, unlike forcible seizure or self-defense, is not unconcerned with the interest of others. It is measured in the suffering it can cause and the victims' motivation to avoid it. Forcible action will work against weeds or floods as well as against armies, but suffering requires a victim that can feel pain or has something to lose. To inflict suffering gains nothing and saves nothing directly; it can only make people behave to avoid it. The only purpose, unless sport or revenge, must be to influence somebody's behavior, to coerce his decision or choice. To be coercive, violence has to be anticipated. And it has to be avoidable by accommodation. The power to hurt is bargaining power. To exploit it is diplomacy—vicious diplomacy, but diplomacy.

THE CONTRAST OF BRUTE FORCE WITH COERCION

There is a difference between taking what you want and making someone give it to you, between fending off assault and making someone afraid to assault you, between holding what people are trying to take and making them afraid to take it, between losing what someone can forcibly take and giving it up to avoid risk or damage. It is the difference between defense and deterrence, between brute force and intimidation, between conquest and blackmail, between action and threats. It is the difference between the unilateral, "undiplomatic" recourse to strength, and coercive diplomacy based on the power to hurt.

The contrasts are several. The purely "military" or "undiplomatic" recourse to forcible action is concerned with enemy strength, not enemy interests; the coercive use of the power to hurt, though, is the very exploitation of enemy wants and fears. And brute strength is usually measured relative to enemy strength, the one directly opposing the other, while the power to hurt is typically not reduced by the enemy's power to hurt in return. Opposing strengths may cancel each other, pain and grief do not. The willingness to hurt, the credibility of a threat, and the ability to exploit the power to hurt will indeed depend on how much the adversary can hurt in return; but there is little or nothing about an adversary's pain or grief that directly reduces one's own. Two sides cannot both overcome each other with superior strength; they may both be able to hurt each other. With strength they can dispute objects of value; with sheer violence they can destroy them.

And brute force succeeds when it is used, whereas the power to hurt is most successful when held in reserve. It is the *threat* of damage, or of more damage to come, that can make someone yield or comply. It is *latent* violence that can influence someone's choice—violence that can still be withheld or inflicted, or that a victim believes can be withheld or inflicted. The threat of pain tries to structure someone's motives, while brute force tries to overcome his strength. Unhappily, the power to hurt is often communicated by some performance of it. Whether it is sheer terroristic violence to induce an irrational response, or cool premeditated violence to persuade somebody that you mean it and may do it again, it is not the pain and damage itself but its influence on somebody's behavior that matters. It is the expectation of *more* violence that gets the wanted behavior, if the power to hurt can get it at all.

To exploit a capacity for hurting and inflicting damage one needs to know what an adversary treasures and what scares him and one needs the adversary to understand what behavior of his will cause the violence to be inflicted and what will cause it to be withheld. The victim has to know what is wanted, and he may have to be assured of what is not wanted. The pain and suffering have to appear *contingent* on his behavior; it is not alone the threat that is effective—the threat of pain or loss if he fails to comply—but the corresponding assurance, possibly an implicit one, that he can avoid the pain or loss if he does comply. The prospect of certain death may stun him, but it gives him no choice.

Coercion by threat of damage also requires that our interests and our opponent's not be absolutely opposed. If his pain were our greatest delight and our satisfaction his greatest woe, we would just proceed to hurt and to frustrate each other. It is when his pain gives us little or no satisfaction compared with what he can do for us, and the action or inaction that satisfies us costs him less than the pain we can cause, that there is room for coercion. Coercion requires finding a bargain, arranging for him to be better off doing what we want—worse off not doing what we want—when he takes the threatened penalty into account. . . .

This difference between coercion and brute force is as often in the intent as in the instrument. To hunt down Comanches and to exterminate them was brute force; to raid their villages to make them behave was coercive diplomacy, based on the power to hurt. The pain and loss to the Indians might have looked much the same one way as the other; the difference was one of purpose and effect. If Indians were killed because they were in the way, or somebody wanted their land, or the authorities despaired of making them behave and could not confine them and decided to exterminate them, that was pure unilateral force. If *some* Indians were killed to make *other* Indians behave, that was coercive violence—or intended to be, whether or not it was effective. The Germans at Verdun perceived themselves to be chewing up hundreds of thousands of French soldiers in a gruesome "meatgrinder." If the purpose was to eliminate a military obstacle—the French infantryman, viewed as a military "asset" rather than as a warm human being—the offensive at Verdun was a unilateral exercise of military force. If instead the object was to make the loss of young men—not of impersonal "effectives," but of sons, husbands, fathers, and the pride of French manhood—so anguishing as to be unendurable, to make surrender a welcome relief and to spoil the foretaste of an Allied victory, then it was an exercise in coercion, in applied violence, intended to offer relief upon accommodation. And of course, since any use of force tends to be brutal, thoughtless, vengeful, or plain obstinate, the motives themselves can be mixed and confused. The fact that heroism and brutality can be either coercive diplomacy or a contest in pure strength does not promise that the distinction will be made, and the strategies enlightened by the distinction, every time some vicious enterprise gets launched. . . .

War appears to be, or threatens to be, not so much a contest of strength as one of endurance, nerve, obstinacy, and pain. It appears to be, and threatens to be, not so much a contest of military strength as a bargaining process—dirty, extortionate, and often quite reluctant bargaining on one side or both—nevertheless a bargaining process.

The difference cannot quite be expressed as one between the *use* of force and the *threat* of force. The actions involved in forcible accomplishment, on the one hand, and in fulfilling a threat, on the other, can be quite different. Sometimes the most effective direct action inflicts enough cost or pain on the enemy to serve as a threat, sometimes not. The United States threatens the Soviet Union with virtual destruction of its society in the event of a surprise attack on the United States; a hundred million deaths are awesome as pure damage, but they are useless in stopping the Soviet attack—especially if the threat is to do it all afterward anyway. So it is worth while to keep the concepts distinct—to distinguish forcible action from the threat of pain—recognizing that some actions serve as both a means of forcible accomplishment and a means of inflicting pure damage, some do not. Hostages tend to entail almost pure pain and damage, as do all forms of reprisal after the fact. Some modes of self-defense may exact so little in blood or treasure as to entail negligible violence; and some forcible actions entail so much violence that their threat can be effective by itself.

The power to hurt, though it can usually accomplish nothing directly, is potentially more versatile than a straightforward capacity for forcible accomplishment.

By force alone we cannot even lead a horse to water—we have to drag him—much less make him drink. Any affirmative action, any collaboration, almost anything but physical exclusion, expulsion, or extermination, requires that an opponent or a victim *do* something, even if only to stop or get out. The threat of pain and damage may make him want to do it, and anything he can do is potentially susceptible to inducement. Brute force can only accomplish what requires no collaboration. The principle is illustrated by a technique of unarmed combat: one can disable a man by various stunning, fracturing, or killing blows, but to take him to jail one has to exploit the man's own efforts. "Come-along" holds are those that threaten pain or disablement, giving relief as long as the victim complies, giving him the option of using his own legs to get to jail. . . .

The fact that violence—pure pain and damage—can be used or threatened to coerce and to deter, to intimidate and to blackmail, to demoralize and to paralyze, in a conscious process of dirty bargaining, does not by any means imply that violence is not often wanton and meaningless or, even when purposive, in danger of getting out of hand. Ancient wars were often quite "total" for the loser, the men being put to death, the women sold as slaves, the boys castrated, the cattle slaughtered, and the buildings leveled, for the sake of revenge, justice, personal gain, or merely custom. If an enemy bombs a city, by design or by carelessness, we usually bomb his if we can. In the excitement and fatigue of warfare, revenge is one of the few satisfactions that can be savored; and justice can often be construed to demand the enemy's punishment, even if it is delivered with more enthusiasm than justice requires. When Jerusalem fell to the Crusaders in 1099 the ensuing slaughter was one of the bloodiest in military chronicles. "The men of the West literally waded in gore, their march to the church of the Holy Sepulcher being gruesomely likened to 'treading out the wine press' . . . ," reports Montross (p. 138), who observes that these excesses usually came at the climax of the capture of a fortified post or city. "For long the assailants have endured more punishment than they were able to inflict; then once the walls are breached, pent up emotions find an outlet in murder, rape and plunder, which discipline is powerless to prevent." The same occurred when Tyre fell to Alexander after a painful siege, and the phenomenon was not unknown on Pacific islands in the Second World War. Pure violence, like fire, can be harnessed to a purpose; that does not mean that behind every holocaust is a shrewd intention successfully fulfilled.

But if the occurrence of violence does not always bespeak a shrewd purpose, the absence of pain and destruction is no sign that violence was idle. Violence is most purposive and most successful when it is threatened and not used. Successful threats are those that do not have to be carried out. By European standards, Denmark was virtually unharmed in the Second World War; it was violence that made the Danes submit. Withheld violence—successfully threatened violence—can look clean, even merciful. . . .

THE STRATEGIC ROLE OF PAIN AND DAMAGE

Pure violence, nonmilitary violence, appears most conspicuously in relations between unequal countries, where there is no substantial military challenge and the outcome of military engagement is not in question. Hitler could make his threats contemptuously and brutally against Austria; he could make them, if he wished, in a more refined way against Denmark. It is noteworthy that it was Hitler, not his generals, who used this kind of language; proud military establishments do not like to think of themselves as extortionists. Their favorite job is to deliver victory, to dispose of opposing military force and to leave most of the civilian violence to politics and diplomacy. But if there is no room for doubt how a contest in strength will come out, it may be possible to bypass the military stage altogether and to proceed at once to the coercive bargaining.

A typical confrontation of unequal forces occurs at the *end* of a war, between victor and vanquished. Where Austria was vulnerable before a shot was fired, France was vulnerable after its military shield had collapsed in 1940. Surrender negotiations are the place where the threat of civil violence can come to the fore. Surrender negotiations are often so one-sided, or the potential violence so unmistakable, that bargaining succeeds and the violence remains in reserve. But the fact that most of the actual damage was done during the military stage of the war, prior to victory and defeat, does not mean that violence was idle in the aftermath, only that it was latent and the threat of it successful.

Indeed, victory is often but a prerequisite to the exploitation of the power to hurt. When Xenophon was fighting in Asia Minor under Persian leadership, it took military strength to disperse enemy soldiers and occupy their lands; but land was not what the victor wanted, nor was victory for its own sake.

> Next day the Persian leader burned the villages to the ground, not leaving a single house standing, so as to strike terror into the other tribes to show them what would happen if they did not give in. . . . He sent some of the prisoners into the hills and told them to say that if the inhabitants did not come down and settle in their houses to submit to him, he would burn up their villages too and destroy their crops, and they would die of hunger.[1]

Military victory was but the *price of admission*. The payoff depended upon the successful threat of violence.

---

[1]Xenophon, *The Persian Expedition*, Rex Warner, transl. (Baltimore, Penguin Books, 1949), p. 272. "The 'rational' goal of the threat of violence," says H.L. Nieburg, "is an accommodation of interests, not the provocation of actual violence. Similarly the 'rational' goal of actual violence is demonstration of the will and capability of action, establishing a measure of the credibility of future threats, not the exhaustion of that capability in unlimited conflict." "Uses of Violence," *Journal of Conflict Resolution, 7* (1963), 44.

Like the Persian leader, the Russians crushed Budapest in 1956 and cowed Poland and other neighboring countries. There was a lag of ten years between military victory and this show of violence, but the principle was the one explained by Xenophon. Military victory is often the prelude to violence, not the end of it, and the fact that successful violence is usually held in reserve should not deceive us about the role it plays.

What about pure violence during war itself, the infliction of pain and suffering as a military technique? Is the threat of pain involved only in the political use of victory, or is it a decisive technique of war itself?

Evidently between unequal powers it has been part of warfare. Colonial conquest has often been a matter of "punitive expeditions" rather than genuine military engagements. If the tribesmen escape into the bush you can burn their villages without them until they assent to receive what, in strikingly modern language, used to be known as the Queen's "protection." British air power was used punitively against Arabian tribesmen in the 1920s and 30s to coerce them into submission.[2]

If enemy forces are not strong enough to oppose, or are unwilling to engage, there is no need to achieve victory as a prerequisite to getting on with a display of coercive violence. When Caesar was pacifying the tribes of Gaul he sometimes had to fight his way through their armed men in order to subdue them with a display of punitive violence, but sometimes he was virtually unopposed and could proceed straight to the punitive display. To his legions there was more valor in fighting their way to the seat of power; but, as governor of Gaul, Caesar could view enemy troops only as an obstacle to his political control, and that control was usually based on the power to inflict pain, grief, and privation. In fact, he preferred to keep several hundred hostages from the unreliable tribes, so that his threat of violence did not even depend on an expedition into the countryside.

Pure hurting, as a military tactic, appeared in some of the military actions against the plains Indians. In 1868, during the war with the Cheyennes, General Sheridan decided that his best hope was to attack the Indians in their winter camps. His reasoning was that the Indians could maraud as they pleased during the seasons when their ponies could subsist on grass, and in winter hide away in remote places. "To disabuse their minds from the idea that they were secure from punishment, and to strike at a

<hr>

[2]A perceptive, thoughtful account of this tactic, and one that emphasizes its "diplomatic" character, is in the lecture of Air Chief Marshal Lord Portal, "Air Force Cooperation in Policing the Empire." "The law-breaking tribe must be given an alternative to being bombed and . . . be told in the clearest possible terms what that alternative is." And, "It would be the greatest mistake to believe that a victory which spares the lives and feelings of the losers need be any less permanent or salutary than one which inflicts heavy losses on the fighting men and results in a 'peace' dictated on a stricken field." *Journal of the Royal United Services Institution* (London, May 1937), pp. 343–58.

period when they were helpless to move their stock and villages, a winter campaign was projected against the large bands hiding away in the Indian territory."[3]

These were not military engagements; they were punitive attacks on people. They were an effort to subdue by the use of violence, without a futile attempt to draw the enemy's military forces into decisive battle. They were "massive retaliation" on a diminutive scale, with local effects not unlike those of Hiroshima. The Indians themselves totally lacked organization and discipline, and typically could not afford enough ammunition for target practice and were no military match for the cavalry; their own rudimentary strategy was at best one of harassment and reprisal. Half a century of Indian fighting in the West left us a legacy of cavalry tactics; but it is hard to find a serious treatise on American strategy against the Indians or Indian strategy against the whites. The twentieth is not the first century in which "retaliation" has been part of our strategy, but it is the first in which we have systematically recognized it. . . .

Making it "terrible beyond endurance" is what we associate with Algeria and Palestine, the crushing of Budapest and the tribal warfare in Central Africa. But in the great wars of the last hundred years it was usually military victory, not the hurting of the people, that was decisive; General Sherman's attempt to make war hell for the Southern people did not come to epitomize military strategy for the century to follow. To seek out and to destroy the enemy's military force, to achieve a crushing victory over enemy armies, was still the avowed purpose and the central aim of American strategy in both world wars. Military action was seen as an *alternative* to bargaining, not a *process* of bargaining.

The reason is not that civilized countries are so averse to hurting people that they prefer "purely military" wars. (Nor were all of the participants in these wars entirely civilized.) The reason is apparently that the technology and geography of warfare, at least for a war between anything like equal powers during the century ending in World War II, kept coercive violence from being decisive before military victory was achieved. Blockade indeed was aimed at the whole enemy nation, not concentrated on its military forces; the German civilians who died of influenza in the First World War were victims of violence directed at the whole country. It has never been quite clear whether blockade—of the South in the Civil War or of the Central Powers in both world wars, or submarine warfare against Britain—was expected to make war unendurable for the people or just to weaken the enemy forces by denying economic support. Both arguments were made, but there was no need to be clear about the purpose as long as either purpose was regarded as legitimate and either might be served. "Strategic bombing" of enemy homelands was also occasionally rationalized in terms of the pain and privation it could inflict on people and the civil damage it could do to the nation, as an effort to display either to the population or to the enemy leadership

[3]Paul I. Wellman, *Death on the Prairie* (New York, Macmillan, 1934), p. 82.

that surrender was better than persistence in view of the damage that could be done. It was also rationalized in more "military" terms, as a way of selectively denying war material to the troops or as a way of generally weakening the economy on which the military effort rested.[4]

But as terrorism—as violence intended to coerce the enemy rather than to weaken him militarily—blockade and strategic bombing by themselves were not quite up to the job in either world war in Europe. (They might have been sufficient in the war with Japan after straightforward military action had brought American aircraft into range.) Airplanes could not quite make punitive, coercive violence decisive in Europe, at least on a tolerable time schedule, and preclude the need to defeat or to destroy enemy forces as long as they had nothing but conventional explosives and incendiaries to carry. Hitler's V-1 buzz bomb and his V-2 rocket are fairly pure cases of weapons whose purpose was to intimidate, to hurt Britain itself rather than Allied military forces. What the V-2 needed was a punitive payload worth carrying, and the Germans did not have it. Some of the expectations in the 1920s and the 1930s that another major war would be one of pure civilian violence, of shock and terror from the skies, were not borne out by the available technology. The threat of punitive violence kept occupied countries quiescent; but the wars were won in Europe on the basis of brute strength and skill and not by intimidation, not by the threat of civilian violence but by the application of military force. Military victory was still the price of admission. Latent violence against people was reserved for the politics of surrender and occupation.

The great exception was the two atomic bombs on Japanese cities. These were weapons of terror and shock. They hurt, and promised more hurt, and that was their purpose. The few "small" weapons we had were undoubtedly of some direct military value, but their enormous advantage was in pure violence. In a military sense the United States could gain a little by destruction of two Japanese industrial cities; in a civilian sense, the Japanese could lose much. The bomb that hit Hiroshima was a threat aimed at all of Japan. The political target of the bomb was not the dead of Hiroshima or the factories they worked in, but the survivors in Tokyo. The two bombs were in the tradition of Sheridan against the Comanches and Sherman in Georgia. Whether in the end those two bombs saved lives or wasted them, Japanese lives or American lives; whether punitive coercive violence is uglier than straightforward military force or more civilized; whether terror is more or less humane than military destruction; we can at least perceive that the bombs on Hiroshima and Nagasaki represented violence

---

[4]For a reexamination of strategic-bombing theory before and during World War II, in the light of nuclear-age concepts, see George H. Quester, *Deterrence before Hiroshima* (New York, John Wiley and Sons, 1966). See also the first four chapters of Bernard Brodie, *Strategy in the Missile Age* (Princeton, Princeton University Press, 1959), pp. 3–146.

against the country itself and not mainly an attack on Japan's material strength. The effect of the bombs, and their purpose, were not mainly the military destruction they accomplished but the pain and the shock and the promise of more.

THE NUCLEAR CONTRIBUTION TO TERROR AND VIOLENCE

Man has, it is said, for the first time in history enough military power to eliminate his species from the earth, weapons against which there is no conceivable defense. War has become, it is said, so destructive and terrible that it ceases to be an instrument of national power. "For the first time in human history," says Max Lerner in a book whose title, *The Age of Overkill*, conveys the point, "men have bottled up a power . . . which they have thus far not dared to use."[5] And Soviet military authorities, whose party dislikes having to accommodate an entire theory of history to a single technological event, have had to reexamine a set of principles that had been given the embarrassing name of "permanently operating factors" in warfare. Indeed, our era is epitomized by words like "the first time in human history," and by the abdication of what was "permanent."

For dramatic impact these statements are splendid. Some of them display a tendency, not at all necessary, to belittle the catastrophe of earlier wars. They may exaggerate the historical novelty of deterrence and the balance of terror.[6] More important, they do not help to identify just what is new about war when so much destructive energy can be packed in warheads at a price that permits advanced countries to have them in large numbers. Nuclear warheads are incomparably more devastating than anything packaged before. What does that imply about war?

It is not true that for the first time in history man has the capability to destroy a large fraction, even the major part, of the human race. Japan was defenseless by

[5]New York, Simon and Schuster, 1962, p. 47.

[6]Winston Churchill is often credited with the term, "balance of terror," and the following quotation succinctly expresses the familiar notion of nuclear mutual deterrence. This, though, is from a speech in Commons in November 1934. "The fact remains that when all is said and done as regards defensive methods, pending some new discovery the only direct measure of defense upon a great scale is the certainty of being able to inflict simultaneously upon the enemy as great damage as he can inflict upon ourselves. Do not let us undervalue the efficacy of this procedure. It may well prove in practice—I admit I cannot prove it in theory—capable of giving complete immunity. If two Powers show themselves equally capable of inflicting damage upon each other by some particular process of war, so that neither gains an advantage from its adoption and both suffer the most hideous reciprocal injuries, it is not only possible but it seems probable that neither will employ that means." A fascinating reexamination of concepts like deterrence, preemptive attack, counterforce and countercity warfare, retaliation, reprisal, and limited war, in the strategic literature of the air age from the turn of the century to the close of World War II, is in Quester's book, cited above.

August 1945. With a combination of bombing and blockade, eventually invasion, and if necessary the deliberate spread of disease, the United States could probably have exterminated the population of the Japanese islands without nuclear weapons. It would have been a gruesome, expensive, and mortifying campaign; it would have taken time and demanded persistence. But we had the economic and technical capacity to do it; and, together with the Russians or without them, we could have done the same in many populous parts of the world. Against defenseless people there is not much that nuclear weapons can do that cannot be done with an ice pick. And it would not have strained our Gross National Product to do it with ice picks.

It is a grisly thing to talk about. We did not do it and it is not imaginable that we would have done it. We had no reason; if we had had a reason, we would not have the persistence of purpose, once the fury of war had been dissipated in victory and we had taken on the task of executioner. If we and our enemies might do such a thing to each other now, and to others as well, it is not because nuclear weapons have for the first time made it feasible.

Nuclear weapons can do it quickly. That makes a difference. When the Crusaders breached the walls of Jerusalem they sacked the city while the mood was on them. They burned things that they might, with time to reflect, have carried away instead and raped women that, with time to think about it, they might have married instead. To compress a catastrophic war within the span of time that a man can stay awake drastically changes the politics of war, the process of decision, the possibility of central control and restraint, the motivations of people in charge, and the capacity to think and reflect while war is in progress. It *is* imaginable that we might destroy 200,000,000 Russians in a war of the present, though not 80,000,000 Japanese in a war of the past. It is not only imaginable, it is imagined. It is imaginable because it could be done "in a moment, in the twinkling of an eye, at the last trumpet."

This may be why there is so little discussion of how an all-out war might be brought to a close. People do not expect it to be "brought" to a close, but just to come to an end when everything has been spent. It is also why the idea of "limited war" has become so explicit in recent years. Earlier wars, like World Wars I and II or the Franco-Prussian War, were limited by *termination*, by an ending that occurred before the period of greatest potential violence, by negotiation that brought the *threat* of pain and privation to bear but often precluded the massive *exercise* of civilian violence. With nuclear weapons available, the restraint of violence cannot await the outcome of a contest of military strength; restraint, to occur at all, must occur during war itself.

This is a difference between nuclear weapons and bayonets. It is not in the number of people they can eventually kill but in the speed with which it can be done, in the centralization of decision, in the divorce of the war from political processes, and in computerized programs that threaten to take the war out of human hands once it begins.

That nuclear weapons make it *possible* to compress the fury of global war into a few hours does not mean that they make it *inevitable*. We have still to ask whether that is the way a major nuclear war would be fought, or ought to be fought. Nevertheless, that the whole war might go off like one big string of fire-crackers makes a critical difference between our conception of nuclear war and the world wars we have experienced. . . .

There is another difference. In the past it has usually been the victors who could do what they pleased to the enemy. War has often been "total war" for the loser. With deadly monotony the Persians, Greeks, or Romans "put to death all men of military age, and sold the women and children into slavery," leaving the defeated territory nothing but its name until new settlers arrived sometime later. But the defeated could not do the same to their victors. The boys could be castrated and sold only after the war had been won, and only on the side that lost it. The power to hurt could be brought to bear only after military strength had achieved victory. The same sequence characterized the great wars of this century; for reasons of technology and geography, military force has usually had to penetrate, to exhaust, or to collapse opposing military force—to achieve military victory—before it could be brought to bear on the enemy nation itself. The Allies in World War I could not inflict coercive pain and suffering directly on the Germans in a decisive way until they could defeat the German army; and the Germans could not coerce the French people with bayonets unless they first beat the Allied troops that stood in their way. With two-dimensional warfare, there is a tendency for troops to confront each other, shielding their own lands while attempting to press into each other's. Small penetrations could not do major damage to the people; large penetrations were so destructive of military organization that they usually ended the military phase of the war.

Nuclear weapons make it possible to do monstrous violence to the enemy without first achieving victory. With nuclear weapons and today's means of delivery, one expects to penetrate an enemy homeland without first collapsing his military force. What nuclear weapons have done, or appear to do, is to promote this kind of warfare to first place. Nuclear weapons threaten to make war less military, and are responsible for the lowered status of "military victory" at the present time. *Victory is no longer a prerequisite for hurting the enemy.* And it is no assurance against being terribly hurt. One need not wait until he has won the war before inflicting "unendurable" damages on his enemy. One need not wait until he has lost the war. There was a time when the assurance of victory—false or genuine assurance—could make national leaders not just willing but sometimes enthusiastic about war. Not now.

Not only *can* nuclear weapons hurt the enemy before the war has been won, and perhaps hurt decisively enough to make the military engagement academic, but it is widely assumed that in a major war that is *all* they can do. Major war is often discussed as though it would be only a contest in national destruction. If this is indeed the case—if the destruction of cities and their populations has become, with nuclear weapons, the primary object in an all-out war—the sequence of war has been reversed. Instead of destroying enemy forces as a prelude to imposing one's will on the enemy nation, one would have to destroy the nation as a means or a prelude to destroying the enemy forces. If one cannot disable enemy forces without virtually destroying the country, the victor does not even have the option of sparing the conquered nation. He has already destroyed it. Even with blockade and strategic bombing it could be supposed that a country would be defeated before it was destroyed, or would elect surrender before annihilation had gone far. In the Civil War it could be hoped that the South would become too weak to fight before it became too weak to survive. For "all-out" war, nuclear weapons threaten to reverse this sequence.

So nuclear weapons do make a difference, marking an epoch in warfare. The difference is not just in the amount of destruction that can be accomplished but in the role of destruction and in the decision process. Nuclear weapons can change the speed of events, the control of events, the sequence of events, the relation of victor to vanquished, and the relation of homeland to fighting front. Deterrence rests today on the threat of pain and extinction, not just on the threat of military defeat. We may argue about the wisdom of announcing "unconditional surrender" as an aim in the last major war, but seem to expect "unconditional destruction" as a matter of course in another one.

Something like the same destruction always *could* be done. With nuclear weapons there is an expectation that it *would* be done. It is not "overkill" that is new; the American army surely had enough 30 caliber bullets to kill everybody in the world in 1945, or if it did not it could have bought them without any strain. What is new is plain "kill"—the idea that major war might be just a contest in the killing of countries, or not even a contest but just two parallel exercises in devastation.

That is the difference nuclear weapons make. At least they *may* make that difference. They also may not. If the weapons themselves are vulnerable to attack, or the machines that carry them, a successful surprise might eliminate the opponent's means of retribution. That an enormous explosion can be packaged in a single bomb does not by itself guarantee that the victor will receive deadly punishment. Two gunfighters facing each other in a Western town had an unquestioned capacity to kill one another; that did not guarantee that both would die in a gunfight—only the slower of the two. Less deadly weapons, permitting an injured one to shoot back before he died, might have been more conducive to a restraining balance of terror, or of caution. The very efficiency of nuclear weapons could make them ideal for starting war, if they can suddenly eliminate the enemy's capability to shoot back.

And there is a contrary possibility: that nuclear weapons are not vulnerable to attack and prove not to be terribly effective against each other, posing no need to shoot them quickly for fear they will be destroyed before they are launched, and with no task available but the systematic destruction of the enemy country and no necessary reason to do it fast rather than slowly. Imagine that nuclear destruction *had* to go slowly—that the bombs could be dropped only one per day. The prospect would look very different, something like the most terroristic guerilla warfare on a massive scale. It happens that nuclear war does not have to go slowly; but it may also not have to go speedily. The mere existence of nuclear weapons does not itself determine that everything must go off in a blinding flash, any more than that it must go slowly. Nuclear weapons do not simplify things quite that much. . . .

FROM BATTLEFIELD WARFARE TO THE DIPLOMACY OF VIOLENCE

Almost one hundred years before Secretary McNamara's speech, the Declaration of St. Petersburg (the first of the great modern conferences to cope with the evils of warfare) in 1868 asserted, "The only legitimate object which states should endeavor to accomplish during war is to weaken the military forces of the enemy." And in a letter to the League of Nations in 1920, the President of the International Committee of the Red Cross wrote; "The Committee considers it very desirable that war should resume its former character, that is to say, that it should be a struggle between armies and not between populations. The civilian population must, as far as possible, remain outside the struggle and its consequences."[7] His language is remarkably similar to Secretary McNamara's.

The International Committee was fated for disappointment, like everyone who labored in the late nineteenth century to devise rules that would make war more humane. When the Red Cross was founded in 1863, it was concerned about the disregard for noncombatants by those who made war; but in the Second World War noncombatants were deliberately chosen as targets by both Axis and Allied forces, not decisively but nevertheless deliberately. The trend has been the reverse of what the International Committee hoped for.

In the present era noncombatants appear to be not only deliberate targets but primary targets, or at least were so taken for granted until about the time of Secretary McNamara's speech. In fact, noncombatants appeared to be primary targets at both ends of the scale of warfare; thermonuclear war threatened to be a contest in the destruction of cities and populations; and, at the other end of the scale, insurgency is almost entirely terroristic. We live in an era of dirty war.

[7]International Committee of the Red Cross, *Draft Rules for the Limitation of the Dangers Incurred by the Civilian Population in Time of War* (2d ed. Geneva, 1958), pp. 144, 151.

Why is this so? Is war properly a military affair among combatants, and is it a depravity peculiar to the twentieth century that we cannot keep it within decent bounds? Or is war inherently dirty, and was the Red Cross nostalgic for an artificial civilization in which war had become encrusted with etiquette—a situation to be welcomed but not expected?

To answer this question it is useful to distinguish three stages in the involvement of noncombatants—of plain people and their possessions—in the fury of war. These stages are worth distinguishing; but their sequence is merely descriptive of Western Europe during the past three hundred years, not a historical generalization. The first stage is that in which the people may get hurt by inconsiderate combatants. This is the status that people had during the period of "civilized warfare" that the International Committee had in mind.

From about 1648 to the Napoleonic era, war in much of Western Europe was something superimposed on society. It was a contest engaged in by monarchies for stakes that were measured in territories and, occasionally, money or dynastic claims. The troops were mostly mercenaries and the motivation for war was confined to the aristocratic elite. Monarchs fought for bits of territory, but the residents of disputed terrain were more concerned with protecting their crops and their daughters from marauding troops than with whom they owed allegiance to. They were, as Quincy Wright remarked in his classic *Study of War*, little concerned that the territory in which they lived had a new sovereign. Furthermore, as far as the King of Prussia and the Emperor of Austria were concerned, the loyalty and enthusiasm of the Bohemian farmer were not decisive considerations. It is an exaggeration to refer to European war during this period as a sport of kings, but not a gross exaggeration. And the military logistics of those days confined military operations to a scale that did not require the enthusiasm of a multitude.

Hurting people was not a decisive instrument of warfare. Hurting people or destroying property only reduced the value of the things that were being fought over, to the disadvantage of both sides. Furthermore, the monarchs who conducted wars often did not want to discredit the social institutions they shared with their enemies. Bypassing an enemy monarch and taking the war straight to his people would have had revolutionary implications. Destroying the opposing monarchy was often not in the interest of either side; opposing sovereigns had much more in common with each other than with their own subjects, and to discredit the claims of a monarchy might have produced a disastrous backlash. It is not surprising—or, if it is surprising, not altogether astonishing—that on the European continent in that particular era war was fairly well confined to military activity.

One could still, in those days and in that part of the world, be concerned for the rights of noncombatants and hope to devise rules that both sides in the war might observe. The rules might well be observed because both sides had something to gain from preserving social order and not destroying the enemy. Rules might be a nuisance, but if they restricted both sides the disadvantages might cancel out.

This was changed during the Napoleonic wars. In Napoleon's France, people cared about the outcome. The nation was mobilized. The war was a national effort, not just an activity of the elite. It was both political and military genius on the part of Napoleon and his ministers that an entire nation could be mobilized for war. Propaganda became a tool of warfare, and war became vulgarized.

Many writers deplored this popularization of war, this involvement of the democratic masses. In fact, the horrors we attribute to thermonuclear war were already foreseen by many commentators, some before the First World War and more after it; but the new "weapon" to which these terrors were ascribed was people, millions of people, passionately engaged in national wars, spending themselves in a quest for total victory and desperate to avoid total defeat. Today we are impressed that a small number of highly trained pilots can carry enough energy to blast and burn tens of millions of people and the buildings they live in; two or three generations ago there was concern that tens of millions of people using bayonets and barbed wire, machine guns and shrapnel, could create the same kind of destruction and disorder.

That was the second stage in the relation of people to war, the second in Europe since the middle of the seventeenth century. In the first stage people had been neutral but their welfare might be disregarded; in the second stage people were involved because it was *their* war. Some fought, some produced materials of war, some produced food, and some took care of children; but they were all part of a war-making nation. When Hitler attacked Poland in 1939, the Poles had reason to care about the outcome. When Churchill said the British would fight on the beaches, he spoke for the British and not for a mercenary army. The war was about something that mattered. If people would rather fight a dirty war than lose a clean one, the war will be between nations and not just between governments. If people have an influence on whether the war is continued or on the terms of a truce, making the war hurt people serves a purpose. It is a dirty purpose, but war itself is often about something dirty. The Poles and the Norwegians, the Russians and the British, had reason to believe that if they lost the war the consequences would be dirty. This is so evident in modern civil wars—civil wars that involve popular feelings—that we expect them to be bloody and violent. To hope that they would be fought cleanly with no violence to people would be a little like hoping for a clean race riot.

There is another way to put it that helps to bring out the sequence of events. If a modern war were a clean one, the violence would not be ruled out but merely saved for the postwar period. Once the army has been defeated in the clean war, the victorious enemy can be as brutally coercive as he wishes. A clean war would determine which side gets to use its power to hurt coercively after victory, and it is likely to be worth some violence to avoid being the loser.

"Surrender" is the process following military hostilities in which the power to hurt is brought to bear. If surrender negotiations are successful and not followed by overt violence, it is because the capacity to inflict pain and damage was successfully used in the bargaining process. On the losing side, prospective pain and damage were averted by concessions; on the winning side, the capacity for inflicting further harm was traded for concessions. The same is true in a successful kidnapping. It only reminds us that the purpose of pure pain and damage is extortion; it is *latent* violence that can be used to advantage. A well-behaved occupied country is not one in which violence plays no part; it may be one in which latent violence is used so skillfully that it need not be spent in punishment.

This brings us to the third stage in the relation of civilian violence to warfare. If the pain and damage can be inflicted during war itself, they need not wait for the surrender negotiation that succeeds a military decision. If one can coerce people and their governments while war is going on, one does not need to wait until he has achieved victory or risk losing that coercive power by spending it all in a losing war. General Sherman's march through Georgia might have made as much sense, possibly more, had the North been losing the war, just as the German buzz bombs and V-2 rockets can be thought of as coercive instruments to get the war stopped before suffering military defeat.

In the present era, since at least the major East–West powers are capable of massive civilian violence during war itself beyond anything available during the Second World War, the occasion for restraint does not await the achievement of military victory or truce. The principal restraint during the Second World War was a temporal boundary, the date of surrender. In the present era we find the violence dramatically restrained during war itself. The Korean War was furiously "all-out" in the fighting, not only on the peninsular battlefield but in the resources used by both sides. It was "all-out," though, only within some dramatic restraints: no nuclear weapons, no Russians, no Chinese territory, no Japanese territory, no bombing of ships at sea or even airfields on the United Nations side of the line. It was a contest in military strength circumscribed by the threat of unprecedented civilian violence. Korea may or may not be a good model for speculation on limited war in the age of nuclear violence, but it was dramatic evidence that the capacity for violence can be consciously restrained even under the provocation of a war that measures its military dead in tens of thousands and that fully preoccupies two of the largest countries in the world.

A consequence of this third stage is that "victory" inadequately expresses what a nation wants from its military forces. Mostly it wants, in these times, the influence that resides in latent force. It wants the bargaining power that comes from its capacity to hurt, not just the direct consequence of successful military action. Even total victory over an enemy provides at best an opportunity for unopposed violence against the enemy population. How to use that opportunity in the national interest, or in some wider interest, can be just as important as the achievement of victory itself; but traditional military science does not tell us how to use that capacity for inflicting pain. And if a nation, victor or potential loser, is going to use its capacity for pure violence to influence the enemy, there may be no need to await the achievement of total victory.

Actually, this third stage can be analyzed into two quite different variants. In one, sheer pain and damage are primary instruments of coercive warfare and may actually be applied, to intimidate or to deter. In the other, pain and destruction *in* war are expected to serve little or no purpose but *prior threats* of sheer violence, even of automatic and uncontrolled violence, are coupled to military force. The difference is in the all-or-none character of deterrence and intimidation. Two acute dilemmas arise. One is the choice of making prospective violence as frightening as possible or hedging with some capacity for reciprocated restraint. The other is the choice of making retaliation as automatic as possible or keeping deliberate control over the fateful decisions. The choices are determined partly by governments, partly by technology. Both variants are characterized by the coercive role of pain and destruction—of threatened (not inflicted) pain and destruction. But in one the threat either succeeds or fails altogether, and any ensuing violence is gratuitous; in the other, progressive pain and damage may actually be used to threaten more. The present era, for countries possessing nuclear weapons, is a complex and uncertain blend of the two.

Coercive diplomacy, based on the power to hurt, was important even in those periods of history when military force was essentially the power to take and to hold, to fend off attack and to expel invaders, and to possess territory against opposition—that is, in the era in which military force tended to pit itself against opposing force. Even then, a critical question was how much cost and pain the other side would incur for the disputed territory. The judgment that the Mexicans would concede Texas, New Mexico, and California once Mexico City was a hostage in our hands was a diplomatic judgment, not a military one. If one could not readily take the particular territory he wanted or hold it against attack, he could take something else and trade it.[8] Judging what the enemy leaders would trade—be it a capital city or national survival—was a critical part of strategy even in the past. Now we are in an era in which the power to hurt—to inflict pain and shock and privation on a country itself, not just on its military

[8]Children, for example. The Athenian tyrant, Hippias, was besieged in the Acropolis by an army of Athenian exiles aided by Spartans; his position was strong and he had ample supplies of food and drink, and "but for an unexpected accident" says Herodotus, the besiegers would have persevered a while and then retired. But the children of the besieged were caught as they were being taken out of the country for their safety. "This disaster upset all their plans; in order to recover the children, they were forced to accept . . . terms, and agreed to leave Attica within five days." Herodotus, *The Histories*, p. 334. If children can be killed at long distance, by German buzz bombs or nuclear weapons, they do not need to be caught first. And if both can hurt each other's children the bargaining is more complex.

forces—is commensurate with the power to take and to hold, perhaps more than commensurate, perhaps decisive, and it is even more necessary to think of warfare as a process of violent bargaining. This is not the first era in which live captives have been worth more than dead enemies, and the power to hurt has been a bargaining advantage; but it is the first in American experience when that kind of power has been a dominant part of military relations.

The power to hurt is nothing new in warfare, but for the United States modern technology has drastically enhanced the strategic importance of pure, unconstructive, unacquisitive pain and damage, whether used against us or in our own defense. This in turn enhances the importance of war and threats of war as techniques of influence, not of destruction; of coercion and deterrence, not of conquest and defense; of bargaining and intimidation. . . .

War no longer looks like just a contest of strength. War and the brink of war are more a contest of nerve and risk-taking, of pain and endurance. Small wars embody the threat of a larger war; they are not just military engagements but "crisis diplomacy." The threat of war has always been somewhere underneath international diplomacy, but for Americans it is now much nearer the surface. Like the threat of a strike in industrial relations, the threat of divorce in a family dispute, or the threat of bolting the party at a political convention, the threat of violence continuously circumscribes international politics. Neither strength nor goodwill procures immunity.

Military strategy can no longer be thought of, as it could for some countries in some eras, as the science of military victory. It is now equally, if not more, the art of coercion, of intimidation and deterrence. The instruments of war are more punitive than acquisitive. Military strategy, whether we like it or not, has become the diplomacy of violence.

THE CLASH
OF CIVILIZATIONS?

Samuel P. Huntington

THE NEXT PATTERN OF CONFLICT

World politics is entering a new phase, and intellectuals have not hesitated to proliferate visions of what it will be—the end of history, the return of traditional rivalries between nation states, and the decline of the nation state from the conflicting pulls of tribalism and globalism, among others. Each of these visions catches aspects of the emerging reality. Yet they all miss a crucial, indeed a central, aspect of what global politics is likely to be in the coming years.

It is my hypothesis that the fundamental source of conflict in this new world will not be primarily ideological or primarily economic. The great divisions among humankind and the dominating source of conflict will be cultural. Nation states will remain the most powerful actors in world affairs, but the principal conflicts of global politics will occur between nations and groups of different civilizations. The clash of civilizations will dominate global politics. The fault lines between civilizations will be the battle lines of the future.

Conflict between civilizations will be the latest phase in the evolution of conflict in the modern world. For a century and a half after the emergence of the modern international system with the Peace of Westphalia, the conflicts of the Western world were largely among princes—emperors, absolute monarchs and constitutional monarchs attempting to expand their bureaucracies, their armies, their mercantilist economic strength and, most important, the territory they ruled. In the process they created nation states, and beginning with the French Revolution the principal lines of conflict were between nations rather than princes. In 1793, as R. R. Palmer put it, "The wars of kings were over; the wars of peoples had begun." This nineteenth-century pattern lasted until the end of World War I. Then, as a result of the Russian Revolution and the reaction against it, the conflict of nations yielded to the conflict of ideologies, first among communism, fascism-Nazism and liberal democracy, and then between communism and liberal democracy. During the Cold War, this latter conflict became embodied in the struggle between the two superpowers, neither of which was a nation state in the classical European sense and each of which defined its identity in terms of its ideology.

These conflicts between princes, nation states and ideologies were primarily conflicts within Western civilization, "Western civil wars," as William Lind has labeled them. This was as true of the Cold War as it was of the world wars and the earlier wars of the seventeenth, eighteenth and nineteenth centuries. With the end of the Cold War, international politics moves out of its Western phase, and its center-piece becomes the interaction between the West and non-Western civilizations and among non-Western civilizations. In the politics of civilizations, the peoples and governments of non-Western civilizations no longer remain the objects of history as targets of Western colonialism but join the West as movers and shapers of history.

The Nature of Civilizations

During the cold war the world was divided into the First, Second and Third Worlds. Those divisions are no longer relevant. It is far more meaningful now to group countries not in terms of their political or economic systems or in terms of their level of economic development but rather in terms of their culture and civilization.

What do we mean when we talk of a civilization? A civilization is a cultural entity. Villages, regions, ethnic groups, nationalities, religious groups, all have distinct cultures at different levels of cultural heterogeneity. The culture of a village in southern Italy may be different from that of a village in northern Italy, but both will share in a common Italian culture that distinguishes them from German villages. European communities, in turn, will share cultural features that distinguish them from Arab or Chinese communities. Arabs, Chinese and Westerners, however, are not part of any broader cultural entity. They constitute civilizations. A civilization is thus the highest cultural grouping of people and the broadest level of cultural identity people have short of that which distinguishes humans from other species. It is defined both by common objective elements, such as language, history, religion, customs, institutions, and by the subjective self-identification of people. People have levels of identity: a resident of Rome may define himself with varying degrees of intensity as a Roman, an Italian, a Catholic, a Christian, a European, a Westerner. The civilization to which he belongs is the broadest level of identification with which he intensely identifies. People can and do redefine their identities and, as a result, the composition and boundaries of civilizations change. . . .

Why Civilizations Will Clash

Civilization identity will be increasingly important in the future, and the world will be shaped in large measure by the interactions among seven or eight major civilizations. These include Western, Confucian, Japanese, Islamic, Hindu, Slavic-Orthodox, Latin American and possibly African civilization. The most important conflicts of the future will occur along the cultural fault lines separating these civilizations from one another.

Why will this be the case?

First, differences among civilizations are not only real; they are basic. Civilizations are differentiated from each other by history, language, culture, tradition and, most important, religion. The people of different civilizations have different views on the relations between God and man, the individual and the group, the citizen and the state, parents and children, husband and wife, as well as differing views of the relative importance of rights and responsibilities, liberty and authority, equality and hierarchy. These differences are the product of centuries. They will not soon disappear. They are far more fundamental than differences among political ideologies and political regimes. Differences do not necessarily mean conflict, and conflict does not necessarily mean violence. Over the centuries, however, differences among civilizations have generated the most prolonged and the most violent conflicts.

Second, the world is becoming a smaller place. The interactions between peoples of different civilizations are increasing; these increasing interactions intensify civilization consciousness and awareness of differences between civilizations and commonalities within civilizations. North African immigration to France generates hostility among Frenchmen and at the same time increased receptivity to immigration by "good" European Catholic Poles. Americans react far more negatively to Japanese investment than to larger investments from Canada and European countries. Similarly, as Donald Horowitz has pointed out, "An Ibo may be . . . an Owerri Ibo or an Onitsha Ibo in what was the Eastern region of Nigeria. In Lagos, he is simply an Ibo. In London, he is a Nigerian. In New York, he is an African." The interactions among peoples of different civilizations enhance the civilization-consciousness of people that, in turn, invigorates differences and animosities stretching or thought to stretch back deep into history.

Third, the processes of economic modernization and social change throughout the world are separating people from longstanding local identities. They also weaken the nation state as a source of identity. In much of the world religion has moved in to fill this gap, often in the form of movements that are labeled "fundamentalist." Such movements are found in Western Christianity, Judaism, Buddhism and Hinduism, as well as in Islam. In most countries and most religions the people active in fundamentalist movements are young, college-educated, middle-class technicians, professionals and business persons. The "unsecularization of the world," George Weigel has remarked, "is one of the dominant social facts of life in the late twentieth century." The revival of religion, "la revanche de Dieu," as Gilles Kepel labeled it, provides a basis for identity and commitment that transcends national boundaries and unites civilizations.

Fourth, the growth of civilization-consciousness is enhanced by the dual role of the West. On the one hand, the West is at a peak of power. At the same time, however, and perhaps as a result, a return to the roots phenomenon is occurring among non-Western civilizations. Increasingly one hears references to trends toward a turning inward and "Asianization" in Japan, the end of the Nehru legacy and the "Hinduization" of India, the failure of Western ideas of socialism and nationalism and hence "re-Islamization" of the Middle East, and now a debate over Westernization versus Russianization in Boris Yeltsin's country. A West at the peak of its power confronts non-Wests that increasingly have the desire, the will and the resources to shape the world in non-Western ways. . . .

Fifth, cultural characteristics and differences are less mutable and hence less easily compromised and resolved than political and economic ones. In the former Soviet Union, communists can become democrats, the rich can become poor and the poor rich, but Russians cannot become Estonians and Azeris cannot become Armenians. In class and ideological conflicts, the key question was "Which side are you on?" and people could and did choose sides and change sides. In conflicts between civilizations, the question is "What are you?" That is a given that cannot be changed. And as we know, from Bosnia to the Caucasus to the Sudan, the wrong answer to that question can mean a bullet in the head. Even more than ethnicity, religion discriminates sharply and exclusively among people. A person can be half-French and half-Arab and simultaneously even a citizen of two countries. It is more difficult to be half-Catholic and half-Muslim.

Finally, economic regionalism is increasing. The proportions of total trade that were intraregional rose between 1980 and 1989 from 51 percent to 59 percent in Europe, 33 percent to 37 percent in East Asia, and 32 percent to 36 percent in North America. The importance of regional economic blocs is likely to continue to increase in the future. On the one hand, successful economic regionalism will rein-force civilization-consciousness. On the other hand, economic regionalism may succeed only when it is rooted in a common civilization. The European Community rests on the shared foundation of European culture and Western Christianity. The success of the North American Free Trade Area depends on the convergence now underway of Mexican, Canadian and American cultures. Japan, in contrast, faces difficulties in creating a comparable economic entity in East Asia because Japan is a society and civilization unique to itself. However strong the trade and investment links Japan may develop with other East Asian countries, its cultural differences with those countries inhibit and perhaps preclude its promoting regional economic integration like that in Europe and North America. . . .

The clash of civilizations thus occurs at two levels. At the micro-level, adjacent groups along the fault lines between civilizations struggle, often violently, over the control of territory and each other. At the macro-level, states from different civilizations compete for relative military and economic power, struggle over the control of international institutions and third parties, and competitively promote their particular political and religious values.

The Fault Lines Between Civilizations

The fault lines between civilizations are replacing the political and ideological boundaries of the Cold War as the flash points for crisis and bloodshed. The Cold War began when the Iron Curtain divided Europe politically and ideologically. The Cold War ended with the end of the Iron Curtain. As the ideological division of Europe has disappeared, the cultural division of Europe between Western Christianity, on the one hand, and Orthodox Christianity and Islam, on the other, has reemerged. The most significant dividing line in Europe, as William Wallace has suggested, may well be the eastern boundary of Western Christianity in the year 1500. This line runs along what are now the boundaries between Finland and Russia and between the Baltic states and Russia, cuts through Belarus and Ukraine separating the more Catholic western Ukraine from Orthodox eastern Ukraine, swings westward separating Transylvania from the rest of Romania, and then goes through Yugoslavia almost exactly along the line now separating Croatia and Slovenia from the rest of Yugoslavia. In the Balkans this line, of course, coincides with the historic boundary between the Hapsburg and Ottoman empires. The peoples to the north and west of this line are Protestant or Catholic; they shared the common experiences of European history—feudalism, the

Renaissance, the Reformation, the Enlightenment, the French Revolution, the Industrial Revolution; they are generally economically better off than the peoples to the east; and they may now look forward to increasing involvement in a common European economy and to the consolidation of democratic political systems. The peoples to the east and south of this line are Orthodox or Muslim; they historically belonged to the Ottoman or Tsarist empires and were only lightly touched by the shaping events in the rest of Europe; they are generally less advanced economically; they seem much less likely to develop stable democratic political systems. The Velvet Curtain of culture has replaced the Iron Curtain of ideology as the most significant dividing line in Europe. As the events in Yugoslavia show, it is not only a line of difference; it is also at times a line of bloody conflict. . . .

After World War II, the West, began to retreat; the colonial empires disappeared; first Arab nationalism and then Islamic fundamentalism manifested themselves; the West became heavily dependent on the Persian Gulf countries for its energy; the oil-rich Muslim countries became money-rich and, when they wished to, weapons-rich. Several wars occurred between Arabs and Israel (created by the West). France fought a bloody and ruthless war in Algeria for most of the 1950s; British and French forces invaded Egypt in 1956; American forces went into Lebanon in 1958; subsequently American forces returned to Lebanon, attacked Libya, and engaged in various military encounters with Iran; Arab and Islamic terrorists, supported by at least three Middle Eastern governments, employed the weapon of the weak and bombed Western planes and installations and seized Western hostages. This warfare between Arabs and the West culminated in 1990, when the United States sent a massive army to the Persian Gulf to defend some Arab countries against aggression by another. In its aftermath nato planning is increasingly directed to potential threats and instability along its "southern tier."

This centuries-old military interaction between the West and Islam is unlikely to decline. It could become more virulent. The Gulf War left some Arabs feeling proud that Saddam Hussein had attacked Israel and stood up to the West. It also left many feeling humiliated and resentful of the West's military presence in the Persian Gulf, the West's overwhelming military dominance, and their apparent inability to shape their own destiny. Many Arab countries, in addition to the oil exporters, are reaching levels of economic and social development where autocratic forms of government become inappropriate and efforts to introduce democracy become stronger. Some openings in Arab political systems have already occurred. The principal beneficiaries of these openings have been Islamist movements. In the Arab world, in short, Western democracy strengthens anti-Western political forces. This may be a passing phenomenon, but it surely complicates relations between Islamic countries and the West. . . .

On both sides the interaction between Islam and the West is seen as a clash of civilizations. The West's "next confrontation," observes M. J. Akbar, an Indian Muslim author, "is definitely going to come from the Muslim world. It is in the sweep of the Islamic nations from the Maghreb to Pakistan that the struggle for a new world order will begin." Bernard Lewis comes to a similar conclusion:

> We are facing a mood and a movement far transcending the level of issues and policies and the governments that pursue them. This is no less than a clash of civilizations—the perhaps irrational but surely historic reaction of an ancient rival against our Judeo-Christian heritage, our secular present, and the worldwide expansion of both.[1]

. . .

On the northern border of Islam, conflict has increasingly erupted between Orthodox and Muslim peoples, including the carnage of Bosnia and Sarajevo, the simmering violence between Serb and Albanian, the tenuous relations between Bulgarians and their Turkish minority, the violence between Ossetians and Ingush, the unremitting slaughter of each other by Armenians and Azeris, the tense relations between Russians and Muslims in Central Asia, and the deployment of Russian troops to protect Russian interests in the Caucasus and Central Asia. Religion reinforces the revival of ethnic identities and restimulates Russian fears about the security of their southern borders. . . .

The conflict of civilizations is deeply rooted elsewhere in Asia. The historic clash between Muslim and Hindu in the subcontinent manifests itself now not only in the rivalry between Pakistan and India but also in intensifying religious strife within India between increasingly militant Hindu groups and India's substantial Muslim minority. The destruction of the Ayodhya mosque in December 1992 brought to the fore the issue of whether India will remain a secular democratic state or become a Hindu one. In East Asia, China has outstanding territorial disputes with most of its neighbors. It has pursued a ruthless policy toward the Buddhist people of Tibet, and it is pursuing an increasingly ruthless policy toward its Turkic-Muslim minority. With the Cold War over, the underlying differences between China and the United States have reasserted themselves in areas such as human rights, trade and weapons proliferation. These differences are unlikely to moderate. A "new cold war," Deng Xaioping reportedly asserted in 1991, is under way between China and America. . . .

The interactions between civilizations vary greatly in the extent to which they are likely to be characterized by violence. Economic competition clearly predominates between the American and European subcivilizations of the West and between both of them and Japan. On the Eurasian continent, however, the proliferation of ethnic conflict, epitomized at the extreme in "ethnic cleansing," has not been totally random.

---

[1]Bernard Lewis, "The Roots of Muslim Rage," *The Atlantic Monthly*, vol. 266, September 1990, p. 60; *Time*, June 15, 1992, pp. 24–28.

It has been most frequent and most violent between groups belonging to different civilizations. In Eurasia the great historic fault lines between civilizations are once more aflame. This is particularly true along the boundaries of the crescent-shaped Islamic bloc of nations from the bulge of Africa to central Asia. Violence also occurs between Muslims, on the one hand, and Orthodox Serbs in the Balkans, Jews in Israel, Hindus in India, Buddhists in Burma and Catholics in the Philippines. Islam has bloody borders.

Civilization Rallying: The Kin-Country Syndrome

Groups or states belonging to one civilization that become involved in war with people from a different civilization naturally try to rally support from other members of their own civilization. As the post-Cold War world evolves, civilization commonality, what H. D. S. Greenway has termed the "kin-country" syndrome, is replacing political ideology and traditional balance of power considerations as the principal basis for cooperation and coalitions. It can be seen gradually emerging in the post-Cold War conflicts in the Persian Gulf, the Caucasus and Bosnia. None of these was a full-scale war between civilizations, but each involved some elements of civilizational rallying, which seemed to become more important as the conflict continued and which may provide a foretaste of the future.

First, in the Gulf War one Arab state invaded another and then fought a coalition of Arab, Western and other states. While only a few Muslim governments overtly supported Saddam Hussein, many Arab elites privately cheered him on, and he was highly popular among large sections of the Arab publics. Islamic fundamentalist movements universally supported Iraq rather than the Western-backed governments of Kuwait and Saudi Arabia. Forswearing Arab nationalism, Saddam Hussein explicitly invoked an Islamic appeal. He and his supporters attempted to define the war as a war between civilizations. "It is not the world against Iraq," as Safar Al-Hawali, dean of Islamic Studies at the Umm Al-Qura University in Mecca, put it in a widely circulated tape. "It is the West against Islam." Ignoring the rivalry between Iran and Iraq, the chief Iranian religious leader, Ayatollah Ali Khamenei, called for a holy war against the West: "The struggle against American aggression, greed, plans and policies will be counted as a jihad, and anybody who is killed on that path is a martyr." "This is a war," King Hussein of Jordan argued, "against all Arabs and all Muslims and not against Iraq alone." . . .

Second, the kin-country syndrome also appeared in conflicts in the former Soviet Union. Armenian military successes in 1992 and 1993 stimulated Turkey to become increasingly supportive of its religious, ethnic and linguistic brethren in Azerbaijan. "We have a Turkish nation feeling the same sentiments as the Azerbaijanis," said one Turkish official in 1992. "We are under pressure. Our newspapers are full of the photos of atrocities and are asking us if we are still serious about pursuing our neutral policy. Maybe we should show Armenia that there's a big Turkey in the region." President Turgut Özal agreed, remarking that Turkey should at least "scare the Armenians a little bit." Turkey, Özal threatened again in 1993, would "show its fangs." Turkish Air Force jets flew reconnaissance flights along the Armenian border; Turkey suspended food shipments and air flights to Armenia; and Turkey and Iran announced they would not accept dismemberment of Azerbaijan. In the last years of its existence, the Soviet government supported Azerbaijan because its government was dominated by former communists. With the end of the Soviet Union, however, political considerations gave way to religious ones. Russian troops fought on the side of the Armenians, and Azerbaijan accused the "Russian government of turning 180 degrees" toward support for Christian Armenia.

Third, with respect to the fighting in the former Yugoslavia, Western publics manifested sympathy and support for the Bosnian Muslims and the horrors they suffered at the hands of the Serbs. Relatively little concern was expressed, however, over Croatian attacks on Muslims and participation in the dismemberment of Bosnia-Herzegovina. In the early stages of the Yugoslav breakup, Germany, in an unusual display of diplomatic initiative and muscle, induced the other 11 members of the European Community to follow its lead in recognizing Slovenia and Croatia. As a result of the pope's determination to provide strong backing to the two Catholic countries, the Vatican extended recognition even before the Community did. The United States followed the European lead. Thus the leading actors in Western civilization rallied behind their coreligionists. Subsequently Croatia was reported to be receiving substantial quantities of arms from Central European and other Western countries. Boris Yeltsin's government, on the other hand, attempted to pursue a middle course that would be sympathetic to the Orthodox Serbs but not alienate Russia from the West. Russian conservative and nationalist groups, however, including many legislators, attacked the government for not being more forthcoming in its support for the Serbs. By early 1993 several hundred Russians apparently were serving with the Serbian forces, and reports circulated of Russian arms being supplied to Serbia. . . .

Conflicts and violence will also occur between states and groups within the same civilization. Such conflicts, however, are likely to be less intense and less likely to expand than conflicts between civilizations. Common membership in a civilization reduces the probability of violence in situations where it might otherwise occur. In 1991 and 1992 many people were alarmed by the possibility of violent conflict between Russia and Ukraine over territory, particularly Crimea, the Black Sea fleet, nuclear weapons and economic issues. If civilization is what counts, however, the likelihood of violence between Ukrainians and Russians should be low. They are two Slavic, primarily Orthodox peoples who have had close relationships with each other for centuries. As of early 1993, despite all the reasons for conflict, the leaders of the two countries were effectively negotiating and defusing the issues between the two countries. While there has been serious fighting between Muslims and Christians elsewhere in the former Soviet Union and much tension and some fighting between Western and Orthodox Christians in the Baltic states, there has been virtually no violence between Russians and Ukrainians.

Civilization rallying to date has been limited, but it has been growing, and it clearly has the potential to spread much further. As the conflicts in the Persian Gulf, the Caucasus and Bosnia continued, the positions of nations and the cleavages between them increasingly were along civilizational lines. Populist politicians, religious leaders and the media have found it a potent means of arousing mass support and of pressuring hesitant governments. In the coming years, the local conflicts most likely to escalate into major wars will be those, as in Bosnia and the Caucasus, along the fault lines between civilizations. The next world war, if there is one, will be a war between civilizations.

The West Versus the Rest

The west is now at an extraordinary peak of power in relation to other civilizations. Its superpower opponent has disappeared from the map. Military conflict among Western states is unthinkable, and Western military power is unrivaled. Apart from Japan, the West faces no economic challenge. It dominates international political and security institutions and with Japan international economic institutions. Global political and security issues are effectively settled by a directorate of the United States, Britain and France, world economic issues by a directorate of the United States, Germany and Japan, all of which maintain extraordinarily close relations with each other to the exclusion of lesser and largely non-Western countries. Decisions made at the U.N. Security Council or in the International Monetary Fund that reflect the interests of the West are presented to the world as reflecting the desires of the world community. The very phrase "the world community" has become the euphemistic collective noun (replacing "the Free World") to give global legitimacy to actions reflecting the interests of the United States and other Western powers.[2] Through the imf and other international economic institutions, the West promotes its economic interests and imposes on

---

[2]Almost invariably Western leaders claim they are acting on behalf of "the world community." One minor lapse occurred during the run-up to the Gulf War. In an interview on "Good Morning America," Dec. 21, 1990, British Prime Minister John Major referred to the actions "the West" was taking against Saddam Hussein. He quickly corrected himself and subsequently referred to "the world community." He was, however, right when he erred.

other nations the economic policies it thinks appropriate. In any poll of non-Western peoples, the imf undoubtedly would win the support of finance ministers and a few others, but get an overwhelmingly unfavorable rating from just about everyone else, who would agree with Georgy Arbatov's characterization of imf officials as "neo-Bolsheviks who love expropriating other people's money, imposing undemocratic and alien rules of economic and political conduct and stifling economic freedom." Western domination of the U.N. Security Council and its decisions, tempered only by occasional abstention by China, produced U.N. legitimation of the West's use of force to drive Iraq out of Kuwait and its elimination of Iraq's sophisticated weapons and capacity to produce such weapons. It also produced the quite unprecedented action by the United States, Britain and France in getting the Security Council to demand that Libya hand over the Pan Am 103 bombing suspects and then to impose sanctions when Libya refused. After defeating the largest Arab army, the West did not hesitate to throw its weight around in the Arab world. The West in effect is using international institutions, military power and economic resources to run the world in ways that will maintain Western pre-dominance, protect Western interests and promote Western political and economic values.

That at least is the way in which non-Westerners see the new world, and there is a significant element of truth in their view. Differences in power and struggles for military, economic and institutional power are thus one source of conflict between the West and other civilizations. Differences in culture, that is basic values and beliefs, are a second source of conflict. V.S. Naipaul has argued that Western civilization is the "universal civilization" that "fits all men." At a superficial level much of Western culture has indeed permeated the rest of the world. At a more basic level, however, Western concepts differ fundamentally from those prevalent in other civilizations. Western ideas of individualism, liberalism, constitutionalism, human rights, equality, liberty, the rule of law, democracy, free markets, the separation of church and state, often have little resonance in Islamic, Confucian, Japanese, Hindu, Buddhist or Orthodox cultures. Western efforts to propagate such ideas produce instead a reaction against "human rights imperialism" and a reaffirmation of indigenous values, as can be seen in the support for religious fundamentalism by the younger generation in non-Western cultures. . . .

The central axis of world politics in the future is likely to be, in Kishore Mahbubani's phrase, the conflict between "the West and the Rest" and the responses of non-Western civilizations to Western power and values.[3] Those responses generally take one or a combination of three forms. At one extreme, non-Western states can, like Burma and North Korea, attempt to pursue a course of isolation, to insulate their

[3]Kishore Mahbubani, "The West and the Rest," *The National Interest*, Summer 1992, pp. 3–13.

societies from penetration or "corruption" by the West, and, in effect, to opt out of participation in the Western-dominated global community. The costs of this course, however, are high, and few states have pursued it exclusively. A second alternative, the equivalent of "band-wagoning" in international relations theory, is to attempt to join the West and accept its values and institutions. The third alternative is to attempt to "balance" the West by developing economic and military power and cooperating with other non-Western societies against the West, while preserving indigenous values and institutions; in short, to modernize but not to Westernize.

The Torn Countries

In the future, as people differentiate themselves by civilization, countries with large numbers of peoples of different civilizations, such as the Soviet Union and Yugoslavia, are candidates for dismemberment. Some other countries have a fair degree of cultural homogeneity but are divided over whether their society belongs to one civilization or another. These are torn countries. Their leaders typically wish to pursue a bandwagoning strategy and to make their countries members of the West, but the history, culture and traditions of their countries are non-Western. The most obvious and prototypical torn country is Turkey. The late twentieth-century leaders of Turkey have followed in the Attatürk tradition and defined Turkey as a modern, secular, Western nation state. They allied Turkey with the West in nato and in the Gulf War; they applied for membership in the European Community. At the same time, however, elements in Turkish society have supported an Islamic revival and have argued that Turkey is basically a Middle Eastern Muslim society. In addition, while the elite of Turkey has defined Turkey as a Western society, the elite of the West refuses to accept Turkey as such. Turkey will not become a member of the European Community, and the real reason, as President Özal said, "is that we are Muslim and they are Christian and they don't say that." Having rejected Mecca, and then being rejected by Brussels, where does Turkey look? Tashkent may be the answer. The end of the Soviet Union gives Turkey the opportunity to become the leader of a revived Turkic civilization involving seven countries from the borders of Greece to those of China. Encouraged by the West, Turkey is making strenuous efforts to carve out this new identity for itself. . . .

To redefine its civilization identity, a torn country must meet three requirements. First, its political and economic elite has to be generally supportive of and enthusiastic about this move. Second, its public has to be willing to acquiesce in the redefinition. Third, the dominant groups in the recipient civilization have to be willing to embrace the convert. All three requirements in large part exist with respect to Mexico. The first two in large part exist with respect to Turkey. It is not clear that any of them exist with respect to Russia's joining the West. The conflict between liberal democracy and

Marxism-Leninism was between ideologies which, despite their major differences, ostensibly shared ultimate goals of freedom, equality and prosperity. A traditional, authoritarian, nationalist Russia could have quite different goals. A Western democrat could carry on an intellectual debate with a Soviet Marxist. It would be virtually impossible for him to do that with a Russian traditionalist. If, as the Russians stop behaving like Marxists, they reject liberal democracy and begin behaving like Russians but not like Westerners, the relations between Russia and the West could again become distant and conflictual.[4]

The Confucian-Islamic Connection

The obstacles to non-Western countries joining the West vary considerably. They are least for Latin American and East European countries. They are greater for the Orthodox countries of the former Soviet Union. They are still greater for Muslim, Confucian, Hindu and Buddhist societies. Japan has established a unique position for itself as an associate member of the West: it is in the West in some respects but clearly not of the West in important dimensions. Those countries that for reason of culture and power do not wish to, or cannot, join the West compete with the West by developing their own economic, military and political power. They do this by promoting their internal development and by cooperating with other non-Western countries. The most prominent form of this cooperation is the Confucian-Islamic connection that has emerged to challenge Western interests, values and power.

Almost without exception, Western countries are reducing their military power; under Yeltsin's leadership so also is Russia. China, North Korea and several Middle Eastern states, however, are significantly expanding their military capabilities. They are doing this by the import of arms from Western and non-Western sources and by the development of indigenous arms industries. One result is the emergence of what Charles Krauthammer has called "Weapon States," and the Weapon States are not Western states. Another result is the redefinition of arms control, which is a Western concept and a Western goal. During the Cold War the primary purpose of arms control was to establish a stable military balance between the United States and its allies and the Soviet Union and its allies. In the post-Cold War world the primary objective

---

[4]Owen Harries has pointed out that Australia is trying (unwisely in his view) to become a torn country in reverse. Although it has been a full member not only of the West but also of the ABCA military and intelligence core of the West, its current leaders are in effect proposing that it defect from the West, redefine itself as an Asian country and cultivate close ties with its neighbors. Australia's future, they argue, is with the dynamic economies of East Asia. But, as I have suggested, close economic cooperation normally requires a common cultural base. In addition, none of the three conditions necessary for a torn country to join another civilization is likely to exist in Australia's case.

of arms control is to prevent the development by non-Western societies of military capabilities that could threaten Western interests. The West attempts to do this through international agreements, economic pressure and controls on the transfer of arms and weapons technologies.

The conflict between the West and the Confucian-Islamic states focuses largely, although not exclusively, on nuclear, chemical and biological weapons, ballistic missiles and other sophisticated means for delivering them, and the guidance, intelligence and other electronic capabilities for achieving that goal. The West promotes nonproliferation as a universal norm and nonproliferation treaties and inspections as means of realizing that norm. It also threatens a variety of sanctions against those who promote the spread of sophisticated weapons and proposes some benefits for those who do not. The attention of the West focuses, naturally, on nations that are actually or potentially hostile to the West.

The non-Western nations, on the other hand, assert their right to acquire and to deploy whatever weapons they think necessary for their security. They also have absorbed, to the full, the truth of the response of the Indian defense minister when asked what lesson he learned from the Gulf War: "Don't fight the United States unless you have nuclear weapons." Nuclear weapons, chemical weapons and missiles are viewed, probably erroneously, as the potential equalizer of superior Western conventional power. China, of course, already has nuclear weapons; Pakistan and India have the capability to deploy them. North Korea, Iran, Iraq, Libya and Algeria appear to be attempting to acquire them. A top Iranian official has declared that all Muslim states should acquire nuclear weapons, and in 1988 the president of Iran reportedly issued a directive calling for development of "offensive and defensive chemical, biological and radiological weapons."

Centrally important to the development of counter-West military capabilities is the sustained expansion of China's military power and its means to create military power. Buoyed by spectacular economic development, China is rapidly increasing its military spending and vigorously moving forward with the modernization of its armed forces. It is purchasing weapons from the former Soviet states; it is developing long-range missiles; in 1992 it tested a one-megaton nuclear device. It is developing power-projection capabilities, acquiring aerial refueling technology, and trying to purchase an aircraft carrier. Its military buildup and assertion of sovereignty over the South China Sea are provoking a multilateral regional arms race in East Asia. China is also a major exporter of arms and weapons technology. It has exported materials to Libya and Iraq that could be used to manufacture nuclear weapons and nerve gas. It has helped Algeria build a reactor suitable for nuclear weapons research and production. China has sold to Iran nuclear technology that American officials believe could only be used to create weapons and apparently has shipped components of 300-mile-range missiles to Pakistan. North Korea has had a nuclear weapons program under way for some while and has sold advanced missiles and missile technology to Syria and Iran. The flow of weapons and weapons technology is generally from East Asia to the Middle East. There is, however, some movement in the reverse direction; China has received Stinger missiles from Pakistan.

A Confucian-Islamic military connection has thus come into being, designed to promote acquisition by its members of the weapons and weapons technologies needed to counter the military power of the West. It may or may not last. At present, however, it is, as Dave McCurdy has said, "a renegades' mutual support pact, run by the proliferators and their backers." A new form of arms competition is thus occurring between Islamic-Confucian states and the West. In an old-fashioned arms race, each side developed its own arms to balance or to achieve superiority against the other side. In this new form of arms competition, one side is developing its arms and the other side is attempting not to balance but to limit and prevent that arms build-up while at the same time reducing its own military capabilities.

Implications for the West

This article does not argue that civilization identities will replace all other identities, that nation states will disappear, that each civilization will become a single coherent political entity, that groups within a civilization will not conflict with and even fight each other. This paper does set forth the hypotheses that differences between civilizations are real and important; civilization-consciousness is increasing; conflict between civilizations will supplant ideological and other forms of conflict as the dominant global form of conflict; international relations, historically a game played out within Western civilization, will increasingly be de-Westernized and become a game in which non-Western civilizations are actors and not simply objects; successful political, security and economic international institutions are more likely to develop within civilizations than across civilizations; conflicts between groups in different civilizations will be more frequent, more sustained and more violent than conflicts between groups in the same civilization; violent conflicts between groups in different civilizations are the most likely and most dangerous source of escalation that could lead to global wars; the paramount axis of world politics will be the relations between "the West and the Rest"; the elites in some torn non-Western countries will try to make their countries part of the West, but in most cases face major obstacles to accomplishing this; a central focus of conflict for the immediate future will be between the West and several Islamic-Confucian states.

This is not to advocate the desirability of conflicts between civilizations. It is to set forth descriptive hypotheses as to what the future may be like. If these are plausible hypotheses, however, it is necessary to consider their implications for Western policy. These implications should be divided between short-term advantage and long-term accommodation. In the short term it is clearly in the interest of the West to promote greater cooperation and unity within its own civilization, particularly between its European and North American components; to incorporate into the West societies in Eastern Europe and Latin America whose cultures are close to those of the West; to promote and maintain cooperative relations with Russia and Japan; to prevent escalation of local inter-civilization conflicts into major inter-civilization wars; to limit the expansion of the military strength of Confucian and Islamic states; to moderate the reduction of Western military capabilities and maintain military superiority in East and Southwest Asia; to exploit differences and conflicts among Confucian and Islamic states; to support in other civilizations groups sympathetic to Western values and interests; to strengthen international institutions that reflect and legitimate Western interests and values and to promote the involvement of non-Western states in those institutions.

In the longer term other measures would be called for. Western civilization is both Western and modern. Non-Western civilizations have attempted to become modern without becoming Western. To date only Japan has fully succeeded in this quest. Non-Western civilizations will continue to attempt to acquire the wealth, technology, skills, machines and weapons that are part of being modern. They will also attempt to reconcile this modernity with their traditional culture and values. Their economic and military strength relative to the West will increase. Hence the West will increasingly have to accommodate these non-Western modern civilizations whose power approaches that of the West but whose values and interests differ significantly from those of the West. This will require the West to maintain the economic and military power necessary to protect its interests in relation to these civilizations. It will also, however, require the West to develop a more profound understanding of the basic religious and philosophical assumptions underlying other civilizations and the ways in which people in those civilizations see their interests. It will require an effort to identify elements of commonality between Western and other civilizations. For the relevant future, there will be no universal civilization, but instead a world of different civilizations, each of which will have to learn to coexist with the others.

THE STRATEGIC LOGIC
OF SUICIDE TERRORISM

ROBERT A. PAPE

Terrorist organizations are increasingly relying on suicide attacks to achieve major political objectives. For example, spectacular suicide terrorist attacks have recently been employed by Palestinian groups in attempts to force Israel to abandon the West Bank and Gaza, by the Liberation Tigers of Tamil Eelam to compel the Sri Lankan government to accept an independent Tamil homeland, and by Al Qaeda to pressure the United States to withdraw from the Saudi Arabian Peninsula. Moreover, such attacks are increasing both in tempo and location. Before the early 1980s, suicide terrorism was rare but not unknown (Lewis 1968; O'Neill 1981; Rapoport 1984). However, since the attack on the U.S. embassy in Beirut in April 1983, there have

Robert A. Pape is Associate Professor, Department of Political Science, 5828 South University Avenue, The University of Chicago, Chicago, IL 60637 (r-pape@uchicago.edu).

From "The Strategic Logic of Suicide Terrorism" by Robert A. Pape from *The American Political Science Review*, Vol. 97, No. 3 (Aug 2003), pp. 343–352, 355–357. Copyright © 2003 American Political Science Association. Reprinted with the permission of Cambridge University Press.

been at least 188 separate suicide terrorist attacks worldwide, in Lebanon, Israel, Sri Lanka, India, Pakistan, Afghanistan, Yemen, Turkey, Russia and the United States. The rate has increased from 31 in the 1980s, to 104 in the 1990s, to 53 in 2000–2001 alone (Pape 2002). The rise of suicide terrorism is especially remarkable, given that the total number of terrorist incidents worldwide fell during the period, from a peak of 666 in 1987 to a low of 274 in 1998, with 348 in 2001 (Department of State 2001).

What accounts for the rise in suicide terrorism, especially, the sharp escalation from the 1990s onward? Although terrorism has long been part of international politics, we do not have good explanations for the growing phenomenon of suicide terrorism. Traditional studies of terrorism tend to treat suicide attack as one of many tactics that terrorists use and so do not shed much light on the recent rise of this type of attack (e.g., Hoffman 1998; Jenkins 1985; Laqueur 1987). The small number of studies addressed explicitly to suicide terrorism tend to focus on the irrationality of the act of suicide from the perspective of the individual attacker. As a result, they focus on individual motives—either religious indoctrination (especially Islamic Fundamentalism) or psychological predispositions that might drive individual suicide bombers (Kramer 1990; Merari 1990; Post 1990).

The first-wave explanations of suicide terrorism were developed during the 1980s and were consistent with the data from that period. However, as suicide attacks mounted from the 1990s onward, it has become increasingly evident that these initial explanations are insufficient to account for which individuals become suicide terrorists and, more importantly, why terrorist organizations are increasingly relying on this form of attack (Institute for Counter-Terrorism 2001). First, although religious motives may matter, modern suicide terrorism is not limited to Islamic Fundamentalism. Islamic groups receive the most attention in Western media, but the world's leader in suicide terrorism is actually the Liberation Tigers of Tamil Eelam (LTTE), a group who recruits from the predominantly Hindu Tamil population in northern and eastern Sri Lanka and whose ideology has Marxist/Leninist elements. The LTTE alone accounts for 75 of the 186 suicide terrorist attacks from 1980 to 2001. Even among Islamic suicide attacks, groups with secular orientations account for about a third of these attacks (Merari 1990; Sprinzak 2000).

Second, although study of the personal characteristics of suicide attackers may someday help identify individuals terrorist organizations are likely to recruit for this purpose, the vast spread of suicide terrorism over the last two decades suggests that there may not be a single profile. Until recently, the leading experts in psychological profiles of suicide terrorists characterized them as uneducated, unemployed, socially isolated, single men in their late teens and early 20s (Merari 1990; Post 1990). Now we know that suicide terrorists can be college educated or uneducated, married or single, men or women, socially isolated or integrated, from age 13 to age 47 (Sprinzak 2000). In other words, although only a tiny number of people become suicide terrorists, they come from a broad cross section of lifestyles, and it may be impossible to pick them out in advance.

In contrast to the first-wave explanations, this article shows that suicide terrorism follows a strategic logic. Even if many suicide attackers are irrational or fanatical, the leadership groups that recruit and direct them are not. Viewed from the perspective of the terrorist organization, suicide attacks are designed to achieve specific political purposes: to coerce a target government to change policy, to mobilize additional recruits and financial support, or both. Crenshaw (1981) has shown that terrorism is best understood in terms of its strategic function; the same is true for suicide terrorism. In essence, suicide terrorism is an extreme form of what Thomas Schelling (1966) calls "the rationality of irrationality," in which an act that is irrational for individual attackers is meant to demonstrate credibility to a democratic audience that still more and greater attacks are sure to come. As such, modern suicide terrorism is analogous to instances of international coercion. For states, air power and economic sanctions are often the preferred coercive tools (George et al. 1972; Pape 1996, 1997). For terrorist groups, suicide attacks are becoming the coercive instrument of choice.

To examine the strategic logic of suicide terrorism, this article collects the universe suicide terrorist attacks worldwide from 1980 to 2001, explains how terrorist organizations have assessed the effectiveness of these attacks, and evaluates the limits on their coercive utility.

Five principal findings follow. First, suicide terrorism is strategic. The vast majority of suicide terrorist attacks are not isolated or random acts by individual fanatics but, rather, occur in clusters as part of a larger campaign by an organized group to achieve a specific political goal. Groups using suicide terrorism consistently announce specific political goals and stop suicide attacks when those goals have been fully or partially achieved.

Second, the strategic logic of suicide terrorism is specifically designed to coerce modern democracies to make significant concessions to national self-determination. In general, suicide terrorist campaigns seek to achieve specific territorial goals, most often the withdrawal of the target state's military forces from what the terrorists see as national homeland. From Lebanon to Israel to Sri Lanka to Kashmir to Chechnya, every suicide terrorist campaign from 1980 to 2001 has been waged by terrorist groups whose main goal has been to establish or maintain self-determination for their community's homeland by compelling an enemy to withdraw. Further, every suicide terrorist campaign since 1980 has been targeted against a state that had a democratic form of government.

Third, during the past 20 years, suicide terrorism has been steadily rising because terrorists have learned that it pays. Suicide terrorists sought to compel American and French military forces to abandon Lebanon in 1983, Israeli forces to leave Lebanon in 1985,

Israeli forces to quit the Gaza Strip and the West Bank in 1994 and 1995, the Sri Lankan government to create an independent Tamil state from 1990 on, and the Turkish government to grant autonomy to the Kurds in the late 1990s. Terrorist groups did not achieve their full objectives in all these cases. However, in all but the case of Turkey, the terrorist political cause made more gains after the resort to suicide operations than it had before....

Fourth, although moderate suicide terrorism led to moderate concessions, these more ambitious suicide terrorist campaigns are not likely to achieve still greater gains and may well fail completely. In general, suicide terrorism relies on the threat to inflict low to medium levels of punishment on civilians. In other circumstances, this level of punishment has rarely caused modern nation states to surrender significant political goals, partly because modern nation states are often willing to countenance high costs for high interests and partly because modern nation states are often able to mitigate civilian costs by making economic and other adjustments. Suicide terrorism does not change a nation's willingness to trade high interests for high costs, but suicide attacks can overcome a country's efforts to mitigate civilian costs. Accordingly, suicide terrorism may marginally increase the punishment that is inflicted and so make target nations somewhat more likely to surrender modest goals, but it is unlikely to compel states to abandon important interests related to the physical security or national wealth of the state. National governments have in fact responded aggressively to ambitious suicide terrorist campaigns in recent years, events which confirm these expectations.

Finally, the most promising way to contain suicide terrorism is to reduce terrorists' confidence in their ability to carry out such attacks on the target society. States that face persistent suicide terrorism should recognize that neither offensive military action nor concessions alone are likely to do much good and should invest significant resources in border defenses and other means of homeland security.

THE LOGIC OF SUICIDE TERRORISM

Most suicide terrorism is undertaken as a strategic effort directed toward achieving particular political goals; it is not simply the product of irrational individuals or an expression of fanatical hatreds. The main purpose of suicide terrorism is to use the threat of punishment to coerce a target government to change policy, especially to cause democratic states to withdraw forces from territory terrorists view as their homeland. The record of suicide terrorism from 1980 to 2001 exhibits tendencies in the timing, goals, and targets of attack that are consistent with this strategic logic but not with irrational or fanatical behavior....

Defining Suicide Terrorism

…In general, terrorism has two purposes—to gain supporters and to coerce opponents. Most terrorism seeks both goals to some extent, often aiming to affect enemy calculations while simultaneously mobilizing support or the terrorists cause and, in some cases, even gaining an edge over rival groups in the same social movement (Bloom 2002). However, there are trade-offs between these objectives and terrorists can strike various balances between them. These choices represent different forms of terrorism, the most important of which are demonstrative, destructive, and suicide terrorism.

Demonstrative terrorism is directed mainly at gaining publicity, for any or all of three reasons: to recruit more activists, to gain attention to grievances from soft-liners on the other side, and to gain attention from third parties who might exert pressure on the other side. Groups that emphasize ordinary, demonstrative terrorism include the Orange Volunteers (Northern Ireland), National Liberation Army (Columbia), and Red Brigades (Italy) (Clutterbuck 1975; Edler Baumann 1973; St. John 1991). Hostage taking, airline hijacking, and explosions announced in advance are generally intended to use the possibility of harm to bring issues to the attention of the target audience. In these cases, terrorists often avoid doing serious harm so as not to undermine sympathy for the political cause. Brian Jenkins (1975, 4) captures the essence of demonstrative terrorism with his well-known remark, "Terrorists want a lot of people watching, not a lot of people dead."

Destructive terrorism is more aggressive, seeking to coerce opponents as well as mobilize support for the cause. Destructive terrorists seek to inflict real harm on members of the target audience at the risk of losing sympathy for their cause. Exactly how groups strike the balance between harm and sympathy depends on the nature of the political goal. For instance, the Baader-Meinhoft group selectively assassinated rich German industrialists, which alienated certain segments of German society but not others. Palestinian terrorists in the 1970s often sought to kill as many Israelis as possible, fully alienating Jewish society but still evoking sympathy from Muslim communities. Other groups that emphasize destructive terrorism include the Irish Republican Army, the Revolutionary Armed Forces of Colombia (FARC), and the nineteenth-century Anarchists (Elliott 1988; Rapoport 1971; Tuchman 1966).

Suicide terrorism is the most aggressive form of terrorism, pursuing coercion even at the expense of losing support among the terrorists' own community. What distinguishes a suicide terrorist is that the attacker does not expect to survive a mission and often employs a method of attack that requires the attacker's death in order to succeed (such as planting a car bomb, wearing a suicide vest, or ramming an airplane into a building). In essence, a suicide terrorist kills others at the same time that he kills himself.[1] In principle, suicide terrorists could be used for demonstrative purposes or could be limited to targeted assassinations.[2] In practice, however, suicide terrorists often seek simply to kill the largest number of people. Although this maximizes the coercive leverage that can be gained from terrorism, it does so at the greatest cost to the basis of support for the terrorist cause. Maximizing the number of enemy killed alienates those in the target audience who might be sympathetic to the terrorists cause, while the act of suicide creates a debate and often loss of support among moderate segments of the terrorists' community, even if also attracting support among radical elements. Thus, while coercion is an element in all terrorism, coercion is the paramount objective of suicide terrorism.

The Coercive Logic of Suicide Terrorism

…Suicide terrorism does not occur in the same circumstances as military coercion used by states, and these structural differences help to explain the logic of the strategy. In virtually all instances of international military coercion, the coercer is the stronger state and the target is the weaker state; otherwise, the coercer would likely be deterred or simply unable to execute the threatened military operations (Pape 1996). In these circumstances, coercers have a choice between two main coercive strategies, punishment and denial. Punishment seeks to coerce by raising the costs or risks to the target society to a level that overwhelms the value of the interests in dispute. Denial seeks to coerce by demonstrating to the target state that it simply cannot win the dispute regardless of its level of effort, and therefore fighting to a finish is pointless—for example, because the coercer has the ability to conquer the disputed territory. Hence, although coercers may initially rely on punishment, they often have the resources to create a formidable threat to deny the opponent victory in battle and, if necessary, to achieve a brute force military victory if the target government refuses to change its behavior. The Allied bombing of Germany in World War II, American

---

[1] A suicide attack can be defined in two ways, a narrow definition limited to situations in which an attacker kills himself and a broad definition that includes any instance when an attacker fully expects to be killed by others during an attack. An example that fits the broad definition is Baruch Goldstein, who continued killing Palestinians at the February 1994 Hebron Massacre until he himself was killed, who had no plan for escape, and who left a note for his family indicating that he did not expect to return. My research relies on the narrow definition, partly because this is the common practice in the literature and partly because there are so few instances in which it is clear that an attacker expected to be killed by others that adding this category of events would not change my findings.

[2] Hunger strikes and self-immolation are not ordinarily considered acts of terrorism, because their main purpose is to evoke understanding and sympathy from the target audience, and not to cause terror (Niebuhr 1960).

bombing of North Vietnam in 1972, and Coalition attacks against Iraq in 1991 all fit this pattern.

Suicide terrorism (and terrorism in general) occurs under the reverse structural conditions. In suicide terrorism, the coercer is the weaker actor and the target is the stronger. Although some elements of the situation remain the same, flipping the stronger and weaker sides in a coercive dispute has a dramatic change on the relative feasibility of punishment and denial. In these circumstances, denial is impossible, because military conquest is ruled out by relative weakness. Even though some groups using suicide terrorism have received important support from states and some have been strong enough to wage guerrilla military campaigns as well as terrorism, none have been strong enough to have serious prospects of achieving their political goals by conquest. The suicide terrorist group with the most significant military capacity has been the LTTE, but it has not had a real prospect of controlling the whole of the homeland that it claims, including Eastern and Northern Provinces of Sri Lanka.

As a result, the only coercive strategy available to suicide terrorists is punishment. Although the element of "suicide" is novel and the pain inflicted on civilians is often spectacular and gruesome, the heart of the strategy of suicide terrorism is the same as the coercive logic used by states when they employ air power or economic sanctions to punish an adversary: to cause mounting civilian costs to overwhelm the target state's interest in the issue in dispute and so to cause it to concede the terrorists' political demands. What creates the coercive leverage is not so much actual damage as the expectation of future damage. Targets may be economic or political, military or civilian, but in all cases the main task is less to destroy the specific targets than to convince the opposing society that they are vulnerable to more attacks in the future. These features also make suicide terrorism convenient for retaliation, a tit-for-tat interaction that generally occurs between terrorists and the defending government (Crenshaw 1981)....

Suicide terrorists' willingness to die magnifies the coercive effects of punishment in three ways. First, suicide attacks are generally more destructive than other terrorist attacks. An attacker who is willing to die is much more likely to accomplish the mission and to cause maximum damage to the target. Suicide attackers can conceal weapons on their own bodies and make last-minute adjustments more easily than ordinary terrorists. They are also better able to infiltrate heavily guarded targets because they do not need escape plans or rescue teams. Suicide attackers are also able to use certain especially destructive tactics such as wearing "suicide vests" and ramming vehicles into targets. The 188 suicide terrorist attacks from 1980 to 2001 killed an average of 13 people each, not counting the unusually large number of fatalities on September 11 and also not counting the attackers themselves. During the same period, there were about 4,155 total terrorist incidents worldwide, which killed 3,207 people (also excluding September 11), or less than one person per incident. Overall, from 1980 to 2001, suicide attacks amount to 3% of all terrorist attacks but account for 48% of total deaths due to terrorism, again excluding September 11 (Department of State 1983–2001).

Second, suicide attacks are an especially convincing way to signal the likelihood of more pain to come, because suicide itself is a costly signal, one that suggests that the attackers could not have been deterred by a threat of costly retaliation. Organizations that sponsor suicide attacks can also deliberately orchestrate the circumstances around the death of a suicide attacker to increase further expectations of future attacks. This can be called the "art of martyrdom" (Schalk 1997). The more suicide terrorists justify their actions on the basis of religious or ideological motives that match the beliefs of a broader national community, the more the status of terrorist martyrs is elevated, and the more plausible it becomes that others will follow in their footsteps. Suicide terrorist organizations commonly cultivate "sacrificial myths" that include elaborate sets of symbols and rituals to mark an individual attacker's death as a contribution to the nation. Suicide attackers' families also often receive material rewards both from the terrorist organizations and from other supporters. As a result, the art of martyrdom elicits popular support from the terrorists' community, reducing the moral backlash that suicide attacks might otherwise produce, and so establishes the foundation for credible signals of more attacks to come.

Third, suicide terrorist organizations are better positioned than other terrorists to increase expectations about escalating future costs by deliberately violating norms in the use of violence. They can do this by crossing thresholds of damage, by breaching taboos concerning legitimate targets, and by broadening recruitment to confound expectations about limits on the number of possible terrorists. The element of suicide itself helps increase the credibility of future attacks, because it suggests that attackers cannot be deterred. Although the capture and conviction of Timothy McVeigh gave reason for some confidence that others with similar political views might be deterred, the deaths of the September 11 hijackers did not, because Americans would have to expect that future Al Qaeda attackers would be equally willing to die.

The Record of Suicide Terrorism, 1980 to 2001

To characterize the nature of suicide terrorism, this study identified every suicide terrorist attack from 1980 to 2001 that could be found in Lexis Nexis's on-line database of world news media (Pape 2002).[3] Examination of the universe shows that

---

[3]This survey sought to include every instance of a suicide attack in which the attacker killed himself except those explicitly authorized by a state and carried out by the state government apparatus (e.g., Iranian human wave attacks in the Iran-Iraq war were not counted). The survey is probably

suicide terrorism has three properties that are consistent with the above strategic logic but not with irrational or fanatical behavior: (1) *timing*—nearly all suicide attacks occur in organized, coherent campaigns, not as isolated or randomly timed incidents; (2) *nationalist goals*—suicide terrorist campaigns are directed at gaining control of what the terrorists see as their national homeland territory, specifically at ejecting foreign forces from that territory; and (3) *target selection*—all suicide terrorist campaigns in the last two decades have been aimed at democracies, which make more suitable targets from the terrorists' point of view. Nationalist movements that face nondemocratic opponents have not resorted to suicide attack as a means of coercion.

Timing

As Table 1 indicates, there have been 188 separate suicide terrorist attacks between 1980 and 2001. Of these, 179, or 95%, were parts of organized, coherent campaigns, while only nine were isolated or random events. Seven separate disputes have led to suicide terrorist campaigns: the presence of American and French forces in Lebanon, Israeli occupation of West Bank and Gaza, the independence of the Tamil regions of Sri Lanka, the independence of the Kurdish region of Turkey, Russian occupation of Chechnya, Indian occupation of Kashmir, and the presence of American forces on the Saudi Arabian Peninsula. Overall, however, there have been 16 distinct campaigns, because in certain disputes the terrorists elected to suspend operations one or more times either in response to concessions or for other reasons. Eleven of the campaigns have ended and five were ongoing as of the end of 2001. The attacks comprising each campaign were organized by the same terrorist group (or, sometimes, a set of cooperating groups as in the ongoing "second *intifada*" in Israel/Palestine), clustered in time, publically justified in terms of a specified political goal, and directed against targets related to that goal.

The most important indicator of the strategic orientation of suicide terrorists is the timing of the suspension of campaigns, which most often occurs based on a strategic

quite reliable, because a majority of the incidents were openly claimed by the sponsoring terrorist organizations. Even those that were not were, in nearly all cases, reported multiple times in regional news media, even if not always in the U.S. media. To probe for additional cases, I interviewed experts and officials involved in what some might consider conflicts especially prone to suicide attacks, such as Afghanistan in the 1980s, but this did not yield more incidents. According to the CIA station chief for Pakistan from 1986 to 1988 (Bearden 2002), "I cannot recall a single incident where an Afghan launched himself against a Soviet target with the intention of dying in the process. I don't think these things ever happened, though some of their attacks were a little harebrained and could have been considered suicidal. I think it's important that Afghans never even took their war outside their borders—for example they never tried to blow up the Soviet Embassy in Pakistan."

decision by leaders of the terrorist organizations that further attacks would be counter-productive to their coercive purposes—for instance, in response to full or partial concessions by the target state to the terrorists' political goals. Such suspensions are often accompanied by public explanations that justify the decision to opt for a "cease-fire." Further, the terrorist organizations' discipline is usually fairly good; although there are exceptions, such announced ceasefires usually do stick for a period of months at least, normally until the terrorist leaders take a new strategic decision to resume in pursuit of goals not achieved in the earlier campaign. This pattern indicates that both terrorist leaders and their recruits are sensitive to the coercive value of the attacks....

If suicide terrorism were mainly irrational or even disorganized, we would expect a much different pattern in which either political goals were not articulated (e.g., references in news reports to "rogue" attacks) or the stated goals varied considerably even within the same conflict. We would also expect the timing to be either random or, perhaps, event-driven, in response to particularly provocative or infuriating actions by the other side, but little if at all related to the progress of negotiations over issues in dispute that the terrorists want to influence.

Nationalist Goals

Suicide terrorism is a high-cost strategy, one that would only make strategic sense for a group when high interests are at stake and, even then, as a last resort. The reason is that suicide terrorism maximizes coercive leverage at the expense of support among the terrorists' own community and so can be sustained over time only when there already exists a high degree of commitment among the potential pool of recruits. The most important goal that a community can have is the independence of its homeland (population, property, and way of life) from foreign influence or control. As a result, a strategy of suicide terrorism is most likely to be used to achieve nationalist goals, such as gaining control of what the terrorists see as their national homeland territory and expelling foreign military forces from that territory.

In fact, every suicide campaign from 1980 to 2001 has had as a major objective—or as its central objective—coercing a foreign government that has military forces in what they see as their homeland to take those forces out. Table 2 summarizes the disputes that have engendered suicide terrorist campaigns. Since 1980, there has not been a suicide terrorist campaign directed mainly against domestic opponents or against foreign opponents who did not have military forces in the terrorists homeland. Although attacks against civilians are often the most salient to Western observers, actually every suicide terrorist campaign in the past two decades has included attacks directly against the foreign military forces in the country, and most have been waged by guerrilla organizations that also use more conventional methods of attack against those forces....

Democracies as the Targets

Suicide terrorism is more likely to be employed against states with democratic political systems than authoritarian governments for several reasons. First, democracies are often thought to be especially vulnerable to coercive punishment. Domestic critics and international rivals, as well as terrorists, often view democracies as "soft," usually on the grounds that their publics have low thresholds of cost tolerance and high ability to affect state policy. Even if there is little evidence that democracies are easier to coerce than other regime types (Horowitz and Reiter 2001), this image of democracy matters. Since terrorists can inflict only moderate damage in comparison to even small interstate wars, terrorism can be expected to coerce only if the target state is viewed as especially vulnerable to punishment. Second, suicide terrorism is a tool of the weak, which means that, regardless of how much punishment the terrorists inflict, the target state almost always has the capacity to retaliate with far more extreme punishment or even by exterminating the terrorists' community. Accordingly, suicide terrorists must not only have high interests at stake, they must also be confident that their opponent will be at least somewhat restrained. While there are infamous exceptions, democracies have generally been more restrained in their use of force against civilians, at least since World War II. Finally, suicide attacks may also be harder to organize or publicize in authoritarian police states, although these possibilities are weakened by the fact that weak authoritarian states are also not targets.

In fact, the target state of every modern suicide campaign has been a democracy. The United States, France, Israel, India, Sri Lanka, Turkey, and Russia were all democracies when they were attacked by suicide terrorist campaigns, even though the last three became democracies more recently than the others. To be sure, these states vary in the degree to which they share "liberal" norms that respect minority rights; Freedom House rates Sri Lanka, Turkey, and Russia as "partly free" (3.5–4.5 on a seven-point scale) rather than "free" during the relevant years, partly for this reason and partly because terrorism and civil violence themselves lowers the freedom rating of these states. Still, all these states elect their chief executives and legislatures in multiparty elections and have seen at least one peaceful transfer of power, making them solidly democratic by standard criteria (Boix and Rosato 2001; Huntington 1991; Przeworski et al. 2000).

The Kurds, which straddle Turkey and Iraq, illustrate the point that suicide terrorist campaigns are more likely to be targeted against democracies than authoritarian regimes. Although Iraq has been far more brutal toward its Kurdish population than has Turkey, violent Kurdish groups have used suicide attacks exclusively against democratic Turkey and not against the authoritarian regime in Iraq. There are plenty of national groups living under authoritarian regimes with grievances that could possibly inspire suicide terrorism, but none have. Thus, the fact that rebels have resorted to this strategy only when they face the more suitable type of target counts against arguments that suicide terrorism is a nonstrategic response, motivated mainly by fanaticism or irrational hatreds.

TERRORISTS' ASSESSMENTS OF SUICIDE TERRORISM

Standards of Assessment

Terrorists, like other people, learn from experience. Since the main purpose of suicide terrorism is coercion, the learning that is likely to have the greatest impact on terrorists' future behavior is the lessons that they have drawn from past campaigns about the coercive effectiveness of suicide attack.

Most analyses of coercion focus on the decision making of target states, largely to determine their vulnerability to various coercive pressures (George 1972; Pape 1996). The analysis here, however, seeks to determine why terrorist coercers are increasingly attracted to a specific coercive strategy. For this purpose, we must develop a new set of standards, because assessing the value of coercive pressure for the coercer is not the same problem as assessing its impact on the target.

From the perspective of a target state, the key question is whether the value of the concession that the coercer is demanding is greater than the costs imposed by the coercive pressure, regardless of whether that pressure is in the form of lives at risk, economic hardship, or other types of costs. However, from the perspective of the coercer, the key question is whether a particular coercive strategy promises to be more effective than alternative methods of influence and, so, warrants continued (or increased) effort. This is especially true for terrorists who are highly committed to a particular goal and so willing to exhaust virtually any alternative rather than abandoning it. In this search for an effective strategy, coercers' assessments are likely to be largely a function of estimates of the success of past efforts; for suicide terrorists, this means assessments of whether past suicide campaigns produced significant concessions.

A glance at the behavior of suicide terrorists reveals that such trade-offs between alternative methods are important in their calculations. All of the organizations that have resorted to suicide terrorism began their coercive efforts with more conventional guerrilla operations, nonsuicide terrorism, or both. Hezbollah, Hamas, Islamic Jihad, the PKK, the LTTE, and Al Qaeda all used demonstrative and destructive means of violence long before resorting to suicide attack. Indeed, looking at the trajectory of terrorist groups over time, there is a distinct element of experimentation in the techniques and strategies used by these groups and distinct movement toward those techniques and strategies that produce the most effect. Al Qaeda actually prides itself for a commitment to even tactical learning over time—the infamous "terrorist manual" stresses at numerous points the importance of writing "lessons learned" memoranda that can be shared with other members to improve the effectiveness of future attacks. . . .

The Apparent Success of Suicide Terrorism

Perhaps the most striking aspect of recent suicide terrorist campaigns is that they are associated with gains for the terrorists' political cause about half the time. As Table 1 shows, of the 11 suicide terrorist campaigns that were completed during 1980–2001, six closely correlate with significant policy changes by the target state toward the terrorists' major political goals. In one case, the terrorists' territorial goals were fully achieved (Hezbollah v. US/F, 1983); in three cases, the terrorists territorial aims were partly achieved (Hezbollah v. Israel, 1983–85; Hamas v. Israel, 1994; and Hamas v. Israel, 1994–95); in one case, the target government to entered into sovereignty negotiations with the terrorists (LTTE v. Sri Lanka, 1993–94); and in one case, the terrorist organization's top leader was released from prison (Hamas v. Israel, 1997). Five campaigns did not lead to noticeable concessions (Hezbollah's second effort against Israel in Lebanon, 1985–86; a Hamas campaign in 1996 retaliating for an Israeli assassination; the LTTE v. Sri Lanka, 1995–2002; and both PKK campaigns). Coercive success is so rare that even a 50% success rate is significant, because international military and economic coercion, using the same standards as above, generally works less than a third of the time (Art and Cronin 2003).

There were limits to what suicide terrorism appeared to gain in the 1980s and 1990s. Most of the gains for the terrorists' cause were modest, not involving interests central to the target countries' security or wealth, and most were potential revocable. For the United States and France, Lebanon was a relatively minor foreign policy interest. Israel's apparent concessions to the Palestinians from 1994 to 1997 were more modest than they might appear. Although Israel withdrew its forces from parts of Gaza and the West Bank and released Sheikh Yassin, during the same period Israeli settlement in the occupied territories almost doubled, and recent events have shown that the Israel is not deterred from sending force back in when necessary. In two disputes, the terrorists achieved initial success but failed to reach greater goals. Although Israel withdrew from much of Lebanon in June 1985, it retained a six-mile security buffer zone along the southern edge of the country for another 15 years from which a second Hezbollah suicide terrorist campaign failed to dislodge it. The Sri Lankan government did conduct apparently serious negotiations with the LTTE from November 1994 to April 1995, but did not concede the Tamil's main demand, for independence, and since 1995, the government has preferred to prosecute the war rather than consider permitting Tamil secession.

Still, these six concessions, or at least apparent concessions, help to explain why suicide terrorism is on the rise. In three of the cases, the target government policy changes are clearly due to coercive pressure from the terrorist group. The American and French withdrawal was perhaps the most clear-cut coercive success for suicide terrorism. In his memoirs, President Ronald Reagan (1990, 465) explained the U.S. decision to withdraw from Lebanon:

> The price we had to pay in Beirut was so great, the tragedy at the barracks was so enormous.... We had to pull out.... We couldn't stay there and run the risk of another suicide attack on the Marines....

THE LIMITS OF SUICIDE TERRORISM

Despite suicide terrorists' reasons for confidence in the coercive effectiveness of this strategy, there are sharp limits to what suicide terrorism is likely to accomplish in the future. During the 1980s and 1990s, terrorist leaders learned that moderate punishment often leads to moderate concessions and so concluded that more ambitious suicide campaigns would lead to greater political gains. However, today's more ambitious suicide terrorist campaigns are likely to fail. Although suicide terrorism is somewhat more effective than ordinary coercive punishment using air power or economic sanctions, it is not drastically so.

Suicide Terrorism Is Unlikely to Achieve Ambitious Goals

In international military coercion, threats to inflict military defeat often generate more coercive leverage than punishment. Punishment, using anything short of nuclear weapons, is a relatively weak coercive strategy because modern nation states generally will accept high costs rather than abandon important national goals, while modern administrative techniques and economic adjustments over time often allow states to minimize civislian costs. The most punishing air attacks with conventional munitions in history were the American B-29 raids against Japan's 62 largest cities from March to August 1945. Although these raids killed nearly 800,000 Japanese civilians— almost 10% died on the first day, the March 9, 1945, fire-bombing of Tokyo, which killed over 85,000—the conventional bombing did not compel the Japanese to surrender.

Suicide terrorism makes adjustment to reduce damage more difficult than for states faced with military coercion or economic sanctions. However, it does not affect the target state's interests in the issues at stake. As a result, suicide terrorism can coerce states to abandon limited or modest goals, such as withdrawal from territory of low strategic importance or, as in Israel's case in 1994 and 1995, a temporary and partial withdrawal from a more important area. However, suicide terrorism is unlikely to cause targets to abandon goals central to their wealth or security, such as a loss of territory that would weaken the economic prospects of the state or strengthen the rivals of the state.

Suicide terrorism makes punishment more effective than in international military coercion. Targets remain willing to countenance high costs for important goals, but administrative, economic, or military adjustments to prevent suicide attack are harder, while suicide attackers themselves are unlikely to be deterred by the threat of retaliation. Accordingly, suicide attack is likely to present a threat of continuing limited civilian punishment that the target government cannot completely eliminate, and the upper bound on what punishment can gain for coercers is recognizably higher in suicidal terrorism than in international military coercion.

The data on suicide terrorism from 1980 to 2001 support this conclusion. While suicide terrorism has achieved modest or very limited goals, it has so far failed to compel target democracies to abandon goals central to national wealth or security. When the United States withdrew from Lebanon in 1984, it had no important security, economic, or even ideological interests at stake. Lebanon was largely a humanitarian mission and not viewed as central to the national welfare of the United States. Israel withdrew from most of Lebanon in June 1985 but remained in a security buffer on the edge of southern Lebanon for more than a decade afterward, despite the fact that 17 of 22 suicide attacks occurred in 1985 and 1986. Israel's withdrawals from Gaza and the West Bank in 1994 and 1995 occurred at the same time that settlements increased and did little to hinder the IDF's return, and so these concessions were more modest than they may appear. Sri Lanka has suffered more casualties from suicide attack than Israel but has not acceded to demands that it surrender part of its national territory. Thus, the logic of punishment and the record of suicide terrorism suggests that, unless suicide terrorists acquire far more destructive technologies, suicide attacks for more ambitious goals are likely to fail and will continue to provoke more aggressive military responses.

Policy Implications for Containing Suicide Terrorism

While the rise in suicide terrorism and the reasons behind it seem daunting, there are important policy lessons to learn. The current policy debate is misguided. Offensive military action or concessions alone rarely work for long. For over 20 years, the governments of Israel and other states targeted by suicide terrorism have engaged in extensive military efforts to kill, isolate, and jail suicide terrorist leaders and operatives, sometimes with the help of quite good surveillance of the terrorists' communities. Thus far, they have met with meager success. Although decapitation of suicide terrorist organizations can disrupt their operations temporarily, it rarely yields long-term gains. Of the 11 major suicide terrorist campaigns that had ended as of 2001, only one—the PKK versus Turkey—did so as a result of leadership decapitation, when the leader, in Turkish custody, asked his followers to stop. So far, leadership decapitation has also not ended Al Qaeda's campaign. Although the United States successfully toppled the Taliban in Afghanistan in December 2001, Al Qaeda launched seven successful suicide terrorist attacks from April to December 2002, killing some 250 Western civilians, more than in the three years before September 11, 2001, combined.

Concessions are also not a simple answer. Concessions to nationalist grievances that are widely held in the terrorists' community can reduce popular support for further terrorism, making it more difficult to recruit new suicide attackers and improving the standing of more moderate nationalist elites who are in competition with the terrorists. Such benefits can be realized, however, only if the concessions really do substantially satisfy the nationalist or self-determination aspirations of a large fraction of the community.

Partial, incremental, or deliberately staggered concessions that are dragged out over a substantial period of time are likely to become the worst of both worlds. Incremental compromise may appear—or easily be portrayed—to the terrorists' community as simply delaying tactics and, thus, may fail to reduce, or actually increase, their distrust that their main concerns will ever be met. Further, incrementalism provides time and opportunity for the terrorists to intentionally provoke the target state in hopes of derailing the smooth progress of negotiated compromise in the short term, so that they can reradicalize their own community and actually escalate their efforts toward even greater gains in the long term.[4] Thus, states that are willing to make concessions should do so in a single step if at all possible.

Advocates of concessions should also recognize that, even if they are successful in undermining the terrorist leaders' base of support, almost any concession at all will tend to encourage the terrorist leaders further about their own coercive effectiveness. Thus, even in the aftermath of a real settlement with the opposing community, some terrorists will remain motivated to continue attacks and, for the medium term, may be able to do so, which in term would put a premium on combining concessions with other solutions.

Given the limits of offense and of concessions, homeland security and defensive efforts generally must be a core part of any solution. Undermining the feasibility of suicide terrorism is a difficult task. After all, a major advantage of suicide attack is that it is more difficult to prevent than other types of attack. However, the difficulty of achieving perfect security should not keep us from taking serious measures

---

[4]The Bush administration's decision in May 2003 to withdraw most U.S. troops from Saudi Arabia is the kind of partial concession likely to backfire. Al Qaeda may well view this as evidence that the United States is vulnerable to coercive pressure, but the concession does not satisfy Al Qaeda's core demand to reduce American military control over the holy areas on the Arab peninsula. With the conquest and long term military occupation of Iraq, American military capabilities to control Saudi Arabia have substantially increased even if there are no American troops on Saudi soil itself.

to prevent would-be terrorists from easily entering their target society. As Chaim Kaufmann (1996) has shown, even intense ethnic civil wars can often be stopped by demographic separation because it greatly reduces both means and incentives for the sides to attack each other. This logic may apply with even more force to the related problem of suicide terrorism, since, for suicide attackers, gaining physical access to the general area of the target is the only genuinely demanding part of an operation, and as we have seen, resentment of foreign occupation of their national homeland is a key part of the motive for suicide terrorism.

The requirements for demographic separation depend on geographic and other circumstances that may not be attainable in all cases. For example, much of Israel's difficulty in containing suicide terrorism derives from the deeply intermixed settlement patterns of the West Bank and Gaza, which make the effective length of the border between Palestinian and Jewish settled areas practically infinite and have rendered even very intensive Israeli border control efforts ineffective (Kaufmann 1998). As a result, territorial concessions could well encourage terrorists leaders to strive for still greater gains while greater repression may only exacerbate the conditions of occupation that cultivate more recruits for terrorist organizations. Instead, the best course to improve Israel's security may well be a combined strategy: abandoning territory on the West Bank along with an actual wall that physically separates the populations.

Similarly, if Al Qaeda proves able to continue suicide attacks against the American homeland, the United States should emphasize improving its domestic security. In the short term, the United States should adopt stronger border controls to make it more difficult for suicide attackers to enter the United States. In the long term, the United States should work toward energy independence and, thus, reduce the need for American troops in the Persian Gulf countries where their presence has helped recruit suicide terrorists to attack America. These measures will not provide a perfect solution, but they may make it far more difficult for Al Qaeda to continue attacks in the United States, especially spectacular attacks that require elaborate coordination.

Perhaps most important, the close association between foreign military occupations and the growth of suicide terrorist movements in the occupied regions should give pause to those who favor solutions that involve conquering countries in order to transform their political systems. Conquering countries may disrupt terrorist operations in the short term, but it is important to recognize that occupation of more countries may well increase the number of terrorists coming at us.

WHAT IS ECONOMIC STATECRAFT?

ROBERT BALDWIN

. . .

In selecting a concept of economic statecraft for this study, two criteria are especially important. First, does the concept help with the identification and evaluation of policy options? And second, does it avoid unnecessary departures from common usage? "Ordinary language," however, does not necessarily mean the way most people would define the term, but rather the "set of rules they implicitly follow when applying it to a given situation."[1]

In the previous chapter economic techniques of statecraft were defined as governmental influence attempts relying primarily on resources that have a reasonable semblance of a market price in terms of money. Although the rationale for defining techniques of statecraft in terms of influence attempts was covered in the previous

---

[1]Oppenheim, "Language of Political Inquiry," p. 307.

chapter, the justification for defining "economic" in terms of money prices was postponed until now. . . .

Definition of the "economic" aspect of social life in terms of the production and consumption of wealth that is measurable in terms of money corresponds with long-standing usage by the classic textbooks[2] of economics and is descriptive of the interests of most contemporary economists. In addition, such usage captures the basic intuitive notion of economic activities used by laymen and policy makers.

There are, as always, borderline cases that are hard to classify. For example, should the sale or gift of military hardware be considered as economic or military statecraft? In general, the relevant distinction is between firing (or threatening to fire) weapons and selling (or promising to sell) them. Insofar as a market price for such items exists, these transactions could reasonably be labeled economic statecraft. A plausible case could also be made for classifying them as military since some items, e.g. nuclear bombs, may have no "going market price." Also, since providing weapons is so closely related to military statecraft, some might want to treat it as such. Depending on the particular research interest at hand, one might decide to classify them either way. The existence of such borderline cases, however, does not do serious harm to the value of this concept of economic statecraft for most purposes.

The concept of economic statecraft elucidated thus far has the following three basic components:

1. Type of policy instrument used in the influence attempt, i.e., economic.
2. Domain of the influence attempt, i.e., other international actor(s).
3. Scope of the influence attempt, i.e., some dimension(s) of the target(s') behavior (including beliefs, attitudes, opinions, expectations, emotions, and/or propensities to act).

. . .

It should be reemphasized that the scope of an influence attempt based on an economic technique may be *any dimension* of the target's behavior. The political quality of the act depends on the magnitude of the influence that the statesman is attempting to wield—not on the intrinsic qualities of any particular scope value. Thus an influence attempt intended to effect another state's tariff levels, economic growth rate, attitude toward private foreign investment, or economic welfare is a political act. To

[2]See, for example, John Stuart Mill, *Principles of Political Economy*, new ed. (London: Longmans, Green, 1923), pp. 1–3, 9; and Marshall, *Principles of Economics*, vol. 1, pp. 1, 14, 22, 27, 49, 57. See also Kindleberger, *Power and Money*, pp. 3, 14; and H. Van B. Cleveland, "Economics as Theory and Ideology," *World Politics* VI (April 1954):295–296. For a brilliant comparison of political and economic life that focuses on money as the distinctive feature of the latter, see G.E.G. Catlin, *The Science and Method of Politics* (New York: Alfred A. Knopf, 1927).

repeat, the political quality of the act is a function of the total (actual or potential) influence relationship; it is not a function of scope.[3]

ALTERNATIVE CONCEPTS

As with policy options, the value of a particular conceptualization is best measured by comparing it with available alternatives. Whereas economic statecraft is defined in terms of means, alternative concepts are usually defined in terms of actual or intended effects of a policy or in terms of the process by which the policy was made.

Foreign Economic Policy

The term "foreign economic policy" is sometimes used in much the same way as "economic statecraft" is used here. Other uses, however, should be noted. Benjamin Cohen and Robert Pastor define it in terms of governmental actions intended to affect the international economic environment.[4] An important drawback to this conception is that it makes it definitionally impossible to consider foreign economic policy as an option when a statesman wants to affect the *noneconomic* aspects of the international environment, say the international climate of opinion with respect to the legitimacy of the government of Rhodesia. Rational adaptation of means to ends in foreign policy making is not facilitated by defining some policy options in terms of particular ends. Still another objection to this definition is that it says nothing about the *means* to be used, thus leaving open the possibility that the use of noneconomic techniques, such as threats of violence, could be considered foreign economic policy. Such a possibility strays needlessly from common usage.

I. M. Destler offers a definition of "foreign economic policy" in terms of the actual impact of governmental actions on foreign and economic concerns.[5] This definition implies nothing whatever about either the means used or the effect intended; instead it focuses on the actual effects—intended or not. Thus, a nuclear war could be labeled as "foreign economic policy" if it had important side effects on foreign economic

---

[3]Although this point is continually misunderstood, it corresponds to the position of a wide variety of scholars. For examples, see the following: "The ends of politics may be anything" (Wright, *Study of International Relations*, p. 132); "The goals that might be pursued by nations in their foreign policy can run the whole gamut of objectives that any nation has ever pursued or might possibly pursue" (Morgenthau, *Politics Among Nations*, 3d ed., p. 9); "A's decisions may affect, say, . . . [B's] shaping and enjoyment of economic values" (Lasswell and Kaplan, *Power and Society*, p. 76).

[4]Benjamin J. Cohen, ed., *American Foreign Economic Policy: Essays and Comments* (New York: Harper and Row, 1968), p. 10; and Pastor, *Congress*, p. 12.

[5]*Making Foreign Economic Policy* (Washington, D.C.: Brookings Institution, 1980), p. 7.

matters. Any conception of foreign economic policy that cannot differentiate between nuclear attack and trade restrictions is hopelessly at odds with common usage. Any conception of "policy" that ignores both means and ends is unlikely to be of much use in assessing the rationality of a given policy.

International Economic Policy

Stephen D. Cohen argues that the term "international economic policy" is preferable to the more commonly used phrase, "foreign economic policy." He contends that "international economic policy must be viewed as being a separate phenomenon, not a tool for use by either foreign policy or domestic economic policy officials." The reasons underlying Cohen's position can be summarized as follows: (1) "International economic policy" is the "preferable term because . . . policy making in this area must take account of too many questions of domestic . . . policy to be considered 'foreign.' " (2) "The term 'foreign economic policy' usually connotes a subdivision of foreign policy as a whole and is therefore an oversimplification." And (3) acceptance of international economic policy as a distinct policy area is the "best and quickest way" to improve understanding of the "forces of economics in international economic policy" and of "the global political impact of U.S. international economic policy."[6] The following points, however, should be noted in response to Cohen's position: (1) Foreign policy has traditionally been defined in terms of attempts to influence foreigners, not in terms of the factors that should be taken into account in formulating the policy. The fact that making international economic policy requires consideration of foreign and domestic political and economic factors in no way distinguishes it from traditional conceptions of foreign economic policy. (2) It is not self-evident that treating foreign economic policy as a subdivision of foreign policy as a whole constitutes "oversimplification." Cohen provides little evidence or argument to support this contention. Indeed, from an *a priori* standpoint, it would seem simpler to consider international economic policy by itself than to treat it as part of a larger whole. Treating more variables may lead to overcomplexity, but it rarely leads to oversimplification. And (3) the question of whether Cohen's approach is the "best and quickest way" to enhance understanding is best answered after consideration of alternative approaches, a matter to which Cohen devotes scant attention. Indeed, Cohen's admissions that "economic relations with other countries have become a principal means of pursuing medium-to-longer-term U.S. foreign-policy goals" and that "instruments of

---

[6]*The Making of United States International Economic Policy: Principles, Problems, and Proposals for Reform* (New York: Praeger, 1977), p. xvii–xxiii.

economic warfare are being resorted to more frequently as a surrogate for military confrontation" raise serious doubts about the wisdom of treating foreign policy and international economic policy as separate and distinct topics.

Economic Diplomacy

The term "economic diplomacy" is sometimes used in much the same sense that "economic statecraft" is used here.[7] The primary disadvantage of such a definition is that it broadens the concept of "diplomacy" so much that it makes it difficult to think in terms of diplomatic alternatives to economic techniques.

Economic Leverage

Klaus Knorr uses the term "economic leverage" to discuss how economic factors can be used "*as means* to achieving state policy."[8] Such usage might appear similar to the concept of "economic statecraft."[9] There is a difference, however, between "levers" and "leverage"—a difference that is crucial to understanding the dynamics of influence attempts. "Lever" is a property concept, while "leverage" is a relational concept. Some levers permit the exercise of leverage; others do not. For reasons explained in chapter 2, policy instruments should be treated as property rather than relational concepts.

Economic Sanctions

At least three common meanings of the term "economic sanctions" may be identified. The first is a rather narrow concept referring to the use of economic measures to enforce international law. The second refers to the types of values that are intended to be reduced or augmented in the target state.[10] And the third usage corresponds to the concept of economic techniques of statecraft as used here.

The first is narrowly legalistic and therefore unsuitable for general foreign policy analysis. The second emphasizes intended effects rather than the means for achieving

---

[7]Pastor, *Congress*, p. 9; and John Pinder, "Economic Diplomacy," in *World Politics: An Introduction*, ed. James N. Rosenau, Kenneth W. Thompson, and Gavin Boyd (New York: Free Press, 1976), pp. 312–336.

[8]"International Economic Leverage and Its Uses," in *Economic Issues and National Security*, ed. Klaus Knorr and Frank N. Trager (Lawrence: Regents Press of Kansas, 1977), p. 99.

[9]One fundamental difference between Knorr's concept of "leverage" and the concept of "influence" used here stems from his insistence that pure exchange relationships do not involve either leverage or power (p. 101). This point will be discussed later.

[10]See, for example, Galtung, "International Economic Sanctions."

those effects. The difficulty is that any or all of the policy instruments discussed in the previous chapter can be used to affect the economic values in a target state. Diplomatic pressure on other states can be used to discourage trade with the target; propaganda can be used to undermine confidence in the target state's currency; and military attack can be used to destroy factories. Thus, conceiving of economic sanctions in terms of the intended effects on the receiving state is no help at all in distinguishing economic from noneconomic tools of statecraft.

The term "economic sanctions" is used in so many different ways that there is much to be said for avoiding it altogether. Unfortunately, the term is so deeply embedded in the literature of economic statecraft that ignoring it is impossible. Later chapters will therefore use this term, but only in its third sense.

Economic Warfare

Some conceptions of "economic warfare" emphasize means, while others emphasize effects. Thus, some writers portray the bombing of industrial targets during World War II as economic warfare.[11] This conception, which Knorr contends is "the standard one,"[12] would be classified as a form of military statecraft according to the taxonomy developed in the previous chapter. While military analysts may indeed consider an attack on industrial targets as economic warfare, the basic intuitive notion of most people is that firing weapons and dropping bombs are military undertakings.

Yuan-li Wu conceives of economic warfare in terms of "international economic measures" that enhance the "strength" of a country relative to an actual or potential "enemy."[13] The context of Wu's discussion makes it clear that he conceives of "strength" as war-making potential. War-making potential, of course, may take various forms, depending on the type of war to be fought. Wu seems to have World War II in mind, and the subtitle of his chapter on World War II reveals a tone that infuses the whole book—"The Test of Economic Power." Since the utility of any technique of statecraft varies from one policy-contingency framework to another, no overall assessment of the utility of a technique can be based on a single set of assumptions about who is trying to influence whom, when, where, and how. Although the "international economic measures" discussed by Wu are similar to the "economic techniques of statecraft" discussed here, Wu's

[11]Margaret P. Doxey, *Economic Sanctions and International Enforcement*, 2d ed. (New York: Oxford University Press, 1980), p. 13.

[12]*Power of Nations*, p. 139.

[13]*Economic Warfare* (New York: Prentice-Hall, 1952), pp. 1–2, 6, 366.

concentration on the utility of such techniques for promoting a particular kind of war-making ability severely restricts the applicability of his analysis to other kinds of situations.

Robert Loring Allen defines "economic warfare" as "state interference in international economic relations for the purpose of improving the relative economic, military, or political position of a country." By using the term "economic" in the definition, Allen, like Wu, leaves it undefined. By confining economic warfare to instances in which a state is trying to improve its relative position in the international "hierarchy of power," Allen, like Wu, makes it impossible to apply this concept to the full range of influence attempts based on economic statecraft. Sometimes policy makers use economic statecraft to improve (what they believe to be) their relative position in the "power hierarchy," and at other times they use such techniques to pursue other goals. Improving one's position in (what one perceives to be) the "power hierarchy" is not synonymous with the exercise of power in international relations. For analyzing the full range of influence attempts that might employ economic techniques, Allen's concept of "economic warfare," like Wu's, is too restrictive.

The concept of "economic warfare" most closely related to the concept of "economic statecraft" is Thomas Schelling's. He defines it in terms of the "*economic means by which damage is imposed on other countries or the threat of damage used to bring pressure on them*." He specifically rules out the use of military means to inflict economic damage, and he makes it clear that economic warfare can be used to pursue a wide variety of foreign policy goals, not merely economic ones. Although superior to most other concepts of "economic warfare," Schelling's concept includes only techniques intended to impose negative sanctions and is therefore too narrow to serve in place of "economic statecraft."

Economic Coercion

The concept of "economic coercion" is rarely defined by those who use it. Knorr's work stands as an admirable exception to this rule. The concept of "coercion" developed by Knorr, however, diverges substantially from conventional usage. The basic intuitive notion of coercion refers to a high degree of constraint on the alternative courses of action available to (i.e., perceived by) the target of an influence attempt. To be more precise, coercion usually refers to a situation in which one actor (A) is able to manipulate the cost/benefit ratios of the alternatives perceived by another actor (B) so that the latter would be foolish to choose any alternative other than X, where X represents either a single alternative or a category of alternatives. There are essentially five ways for A to do this: (1) by threats of punishment; (2) by promised rewards;

(3) by actual punishment; (4) by actual rewards; and (5) by conveying correct or incorrect information to B with respect to the cost/benefit ratios of his alternatives. Thus, the most common examples of coercion include the following: "Your money or your life!"; "Sink or swim!"; "Surrender or die!"; "An offer you can't refuse!"; and "Water for a person dying of thirst." The most often overlooked ways for A to coerce B are actual rewards and punishments.

Adding to or subtracting from B's capabilities to do X, however, can be effective means of coercion. Common parlance implicitly recognizes this with references to actors as "being so weak as to have no choice but to do X" or "being so strong that they cannot resist the temptation to do X." Knorr's conception of coercion refers only to situations in which B's choice is affected by A's threats and explicitly rules out the use of punishment to coerce. Thus, Knorr denies that destroying "part of a potential opponent's military capacity" is coercive.[14] For most people, however, bombing the enemy to the point at which it perceived itself as having to choose between surrender and total annihilation would be an example *par excellence* of coercion. The logic of this situation is directly analogous to that involved in throwing someone into a lake—one does not even have to say "sink or swim"; the person in the lake will immediately perceive these as his most important alternatives—and he is likely to feel coerced! Such a substantial departure from ordinary language might be justified if there were important advantages accruing to the definition that could not be attained by adhering more closely to conventional usage. Until such advantages have been demonstrated, however, the student of economic statecraft should be wary of Knorr's conception of "economic coercion."

In the study of techniques of statecraft the most important disadvantage of the concept of "economic coercion" is that it is a relational concept, not a property concept. Thus, attempts to treat it as an instrument of foreign policy are likely to blur the distinction between undertakings and outcomes. To describe an influence attempt as "coercive" says as much about B's perceptions and value system as it does about A's policy choice. A may choose to stop sending aid to B or to stop trading with B; but the coerciveness of such actions depends as much on B as on A. As a relational concept coercion is more useful in describing outcomes than in describing undertakings.

Choosing a concept of economic statecraft is not merely a matter of "semantic taste," at least not if that is meant to imply that "there is no disputing matters of taste." Some concepts are better suited for the analysis of governmental influence attempts than others. In comparison with available alternatives, the concept of "economic

---

[14]*Power of Nations*, p. 5.

statecraft" has several advantages. The most important of these can be summarized as follows:

1. "Economic statecraft" emphasizes means rather than ends. This usage is probably closer to ordinary language than definitions in terms of ends. Bombing a library is not called cultural warfare; bombing homes is not called residential warfare; bombing nuclear reactors (with conventional bombs) is not called nuclear warfare; and bombing factories should not be labeled economic warfare.
2. "Economic statecraft" does not restrict the range of goals that may be sought by economic means. It makes it conceptually possible to describe the empirically undeniable fact that policy makers sometimes use economic means to pursue a wide variety of noneconomic ends.
3. "Economic statecraft" treats policy instruments as property concepts, thus facilitating the maintenance of a clear distinction between undertakings and outcomes.
4. Unlike most alternative concepts, the definition of "economic statecraft" includes a definition of "economic." It thus provides criteria for distinguishing economic techniques of statecraft from noneconomic techniques.

FORMS OF ECONOMIC STATECRAFT

The concept of economic statecraft employed here is intentionally broad, as it must be if it is to subsume all of the economic means by which foreign policy makers might try to influence other international actors. some of the myriad specific forms of economic techniques of statecraft are listed in table 1. This table is intended to illustrate the wide variety of economic techniques and does not purport to be exhaustive. Table 1 provides examples of tools of statecraft normally associated with attempts to promise or provide rewards.

It should be noted that blacklisting and preclusive buying are especially instructive examples of the need to distinguish between the target of an influence attempt and the immediate recipient of a particular sanction. When describing the Arab blacklisting of Japanese firms that did business with Israel or the American purchase of wolfram from Spain in order to preclude its sale to Nazi Germany, it is more helpful to designate Israel and Germany as the targets than it is to focus on the intermediate targets of Japan and Spain.

Depending on the particular situation, any of the policy instruments listed in table 1 and 2 could be used for either positive or negative sanctions. The tables reflect only the typical use of such techniques. Such techniques have been or might be employed by statesmen to pursue a wide variety of foreign policy goals . . .

Table 1. Examples of Economic Statecraft: Negative Sancti

Trade	Capital
Embargo	Freezing assets
Boycott	Controls on import or export
Tariff increase	Aid suspension
Tariff discrimination (unfavorable)	Expropriation
Withdrawal of "most-favored-nation treatment"	Taxation (unfavorable)
Blacklist	Withholding dues to international organization
Quotas (import or export)	Threats of the above
License denial (import or export)	
Dumping	
Preclusive buying	
Threats of the above	

NOTE:

Embargo—prohibition on exports, sometimes used to refer to a ban on all trade.

Boycott—prohibition on imports.

Tariff increase—increase in taxes on imports from target state(s).

Tariff discrimination—imports from target countries may be treated less favorably than those from other countries.

Withdrawal of mfn—ceasing to treat imports from a country as favorably as similar imports from any other country are treated.

Blacklist—ban on doing business with firm that trade with the target country.

Quotas—quantitative restrictions on particular imports or exports.

License denial—refusing permission to import or export particular goods.

Dumping—deliberate sale of exports at prices below cost of production, e.g., to disrupt economy of target country by depressing world price of a key export or to gain foothold in a world market.

Preclusive buying—purchase of a commodity in order to deny it to the target country.

Freezing assets—impounding assets, denying access to bank accounts or other financial assets owned by the target country.

Controls on import or export of capital—restrictions on who can transfer how much capital for what purposes into or out of a country.

Aid suspension—the reduction, termination, or slow-down of aid transfers.

Expropriation—seizing ownership of property belonging to target state.

Taxation—assets of target state may be taxed in a discriminatory manner.

Withholding dues to international organization—nonpayment, late payment, or reduced payment of financial obligations agreed to in the past.

Threats of the above—making use of any of the above techniques conditional on certain kinds of behavior by the target.

Table 2. Examples of Economic Statecraft: Positive Sanctions

Trade	Capital
Tariff discrimination (favorable)	Providing aid
Granting "most-favored-nation" treatment	Investment guarantees
Tariff reduction	Encouragement of private capital exports or imports
Direct purchase	
Subsidies to exports or imports	Taxation (favorable)
Granting licenses (import or export)	Promises of the above
Promises of the above	

NOTE:

Tariff discrimination—import duties favoring imports from target state(s).

Granting mfn treatment—promising to treat imports from target state as favorably as imports of similar products from any other source.

Tariff reduction—lowering of tariffs in general or on particular products.

Direct purchase—payment for service or goods, e.g. purchase of Louisiana Territory by United States government.

Subsidies to exports or imports—exports to or imports from the target state may be subsidized, e.g., arms sales to Third World countries or above market prices paid for Cuban sugar by United States prior to 1960.

Granting licenses—permission to import or export particular goods.

Providing aid—extension or continuation of aid via bilateral or multilateral channels in the form of grants or loans.

Investment guarantees—governmental insurance against some of the risks of private foreign investors.

Encouragement of private capital exports or imports—variety of incentives to import or export capital.

Taxation—especially favorable taxation of foreign capital investment.

Promises of the above—making use of any of the above techniques conditional on certain kinds of behavior by the target.

SOME NOT-SO-OBVIOUS FORMS OF ECONOMIC STATECRAFT

Several of the forms of economic statecraft, such as trade embargoes and foreign aid, are obviously in conformity with conventional usage. Others, however, are less obvious and diverge from common usage. Closer scrutiny of some less obvious forms is therefore in order.

Purchase

Economic exchange may be viewed from three perspectives—the seller's, the buyer's, or the independent observer's. The independent observer is likely to describe the relationship as one in which each participant in the exchange voluntarily surrenders something of value for something he values even more. Each benefits, and neither is likely to feel coerced. This relationship is at odds with popular conceptions (or misconceptions) of power relations as zero-sum games, as involving a victim and a victor, as relations between unequal actors, as exploitative, coercive, and unpleasant from the standpoint of the actor being influenced. Some power relations, of course, do take this form and should be differentiated from normal economic exchange relationships. It does not follow, however, that all power relations take this form; nor does it follow that the basic intuitive notion of power elucidated by power theorists is necessarily incompatible with the common notion of economic exchange. Indeed, it can be shown that all exchange relationships can be described in terms of conventional power concepts without twisting the common-sense notions that underlie such concepts. Direct monetary payment is one of the most common ways for some people to get other people to do things they would not otherwise do. . . .

Free Trade

Is a policy of free trade a technique of economic statecraft, or is it the very antithesis of economic statecraft?[15] Some writers depict free trade as "a weapon" of economic warfare[16] or as a tool for promoting imperialist foreign policy goals.[17] Others, however, assert that "the free trade doctrine . . . denies the validity of the use of economic instruments for political ends" and compare a policy of free trade to disarmament.[18] Thus Knorr observes:

[15]A "policy of free trade," strictly speaking, implies the complete absence of trade barriers and nondiscrimination among foreign suppliers. Loosely speaking, the term refers to policies moving toward freer trade by lowering trade barriers and reducing discrimination. Although the latter usage is employed here, the comments on free trade as a technique of statecraft apply equally well to a policy of pure free trade.

[16]P.J.D. Wiles, *Communist International Economics* (Oxford: Basil Blackwell, 1968), p. 473.

[17]Bernard Semmel, *The Rise of Free Trade Imperialism: Classical Political Economy, the Empire of Free Trade, and Imperialism, 1750–1850* (Cambridge: Cambridge University Press, 1970); and John Gallagher and Ronald Robinson, "The Imperialism of Free Trade," *The Economic History Review* VI (1953):1–15.

[18]Pinder, "Economic Diplomacy," pp. 313–314. See also a similar comment by J. Henry Richardson: "As long as the Government maintained a *laissez-faire* policy it was not able to reinforce its political foreign policy by economic means. . . . " *British Economic Foreign Policy* (London: George Allen and Unwin, 1936), p. 11.

> It must be understood that after World War II the world's leading trading countries
> . . . agreed to disarm themselves regarding the power uses of trade . . . between
> themselves, especially in support of noneconomic objectives. They did so by
> establishing the GATT in 1947. Thereby, they created an international economic
> order characterized by the joint goal of freer trade on the basis of the most-favored-
> nation principle that precluded discrimination. And power uses of trade are essen-
> tially discriminatory.[19]

Disarmament, however, whether military or economic, does not necessarily
constitute the forswearing of statecraft. Military techniques of statecraft were defined
in chapter 2 as influence attempts relying primarily on violence, weapons, or force.
The essence of such techniques is the adoption of a policy stance vis-à-vis violence,
weapons, or force with the intention of thereby influencing other actors. Therefore,
a specific commitment not to shoot first, not to use certain kinds of weapons, or to
disarm completely *is* a military technique of statecraft if this commitment is undertaken for the purpose of influencing other actors. Military and economic disarmament
do not necessarily signal the renunciation of statecraft. As Thomas C. Schelling has
pointed out, sophisticated understanding of the relationship between arms and influence entails recognition that some influence attempts, e.g., nuclear deterrence, are
more likely to succeed if one forgoes certain kinds of arms, e.g., first-strike weapons.[20]
As Gene Sharp has shown, a commitment to nonviolence can be an instrument of
policy in the same sense as a commitment to violence.[21] One way to "use" violence
is to commit oneself not to use it. The apparent contradiction here is due solely to the
looseness of the term "use."

A policy of free trade, i.e., lower and less discriminatory trade barriers, was
employed by the United States after World War II in order to pursue a number of
foreign policy objectives, including strengthening military alliances, promoting economic recovery from the war in Western Europe and Japan, ensuring access to strategic raw materials, stimulating economic development in poor countries, creating
markets for American exports, and creating an international atmosphere conducive to
peace and security. Rather than disarming itself, the United States used its policy of
free trade to shape the postwar international political and economic order.

Although one can imagine a world economy based entirely on state trading with
neither trade barriers nor discrimination, the concept of free trade often connotes an
emphasis on private firms. Free trade in this sense is frequently depicted as "nonpolitical" or "depoliticized" trade. Thus, Kindleberger contends that "the glory of free

---

[19]*Power of Nations*, pp. 159–160.

[20]*Strategy of Conflict*, pp. 207–254.

[21]*The Politics of Nonviolent Action*, 3 vols. (Boston: Porter Sargent, 1973). See also Johan Galtung,
   "On the Meaning of Nonviolence," *Journal of Peace Research*, no. 3 (1965), pp. 228–257.

trade is that it decentralizes decisions about trade to non-political levels." Private international trade, however, is carried on within a framework of laws and policies created and maintained by governments of sovereign states. Attempts by statesmen to influence the pattern of international trade through manipulating this legal and political framework can be regarded as acts of economic statecraft. Policies of free trade may not be obvious economic techniques of statecraft, but they can be and have been important ones.

Tariffs

Are tariffs a form of economic statecraft? The answer is not obvious. Students of economic statecraft frequently go out of their way to deny that tariffs, at least certain kinds of tariffs, should be viewed as instruments for influencing the behavior of foreigners. Consider the following examples:

Immediately following a definition of economic warfare that includes "all those foreign economic policies that may have as their long-run objective the enlargement of a country's sphere of economic influence," Yuan-li Wu inserts a discussion of the "difference between economic warfare and a protective trade policy." Noting that among the most frequently advanced arguments in favor of trade barriers are protection of domestic wage levels, increased domestic employment, and enhanced self-sufficiency, he states that "obviously, only the last argument could be related to economic warfare."

Immediately after defining economic power in terms of the deliberate use of economic policy to modify the behavior or capabilities of other states, Klaus Knorr states his desire to

> exclude uses of foreign economic policy that, although instrumentally suited to the exercise of power, are adopted only to satisfy a domestic interest. Thus, protective import tariffs may be introduced to benefit the interests of politically influential domestic producers, to shape national production capacity in the interest of economic military potential, or to curtail domestic unemployment. Any effects on other states are purely incidental; there is no intent to wield power internationally.

Immediately after defining economic warfare as "state interference in international economic relations for the purpose of improving the relative economic, military, or political position of a country," Robert Allen exempts tariffs aimed primarily at "support of domestic industry to achieve purely domestic economic or political goals."

Immediately after describing a group of state actions having in common "the manipulation of economic relations for political objectives," Henry Bienen and Robert Gilpin exclude from this group tariffs intended to "protect domestic economic interests, to retaliate against foreign trade barriers, or to force economic concessions from other countries." The primary purpose of such actions, according to Bienen and Gilpin, is "economic rather than political."

The common theme of such authors is that tariffs imposed primarily for domestic purposes should not be viewed as techniques of statecraft, i.e., as attempts to influence foreigners. The effects on foreigners of such measures should be viewed as incidental, unintended, and perhaps even unwanted. The difficulty with this position stems mainly from two sources. The first is the hierarchy of ends inherent in the nature of means-ends analysis, and the second is the rhetorical smokescreen that usually enshrouds the imposition of a tariff for allegedly domestic purposes. . . .

Like other techniques of statecraft, the purposes of tariffs are many and varied. Like other techniques of statecraft, these purposes often include a significant concern for domestic implications. It is quite reasonable to emphasize these domestic matters and to depict tariffs as means for achieving domestic ends. It is not reasonable, however, to deny that tariffs almost always involve attempts to influence foreigners. Clear understanding of world affairs is more likely if tariffs are treated as techniques of statecraft than if they are conceived solely as domestic undertakings not involving any "intent to wield power internationally."

WAR

COOPERATION UNDER
THE SECURITY DILEMMA

Robert Jervis

...OFFENSE, DEFENSE, AND THE SECURITY DILEMMA

Another approach starts with the central point of the security dilemma—that an increase in one state's security decreases the security of others—and examines the conditions under which this proposition holds. Two crucial variables are involved: whether defensive weapons and policies can be distinguished from offensive ones, and whether the defense or the offense has the advantage. The definitions are not always clear, and many cases are difficult to judge, but these two variables shed a great deal of light on the question of whether status-quo powers will adopt compatible security policies. All the variables discussed so far leave the heart of the problem untouched. But when defensive weapons differ from offensive ones, it is possible for a state to make itself more secure without making others less secure. And when the defense has the advantage over the offense, a large increase in one state's security only slightly decreases the security of the others, and status-quo powers can all enjoy a high level of security and largely escape from the state of nature.

Offense-defense balance

When we say that the offense has the advantage, we simply mean that it is easier to destroy the other's army and take its territory than it is to defend one's own. When the defense has the advantage, it is easier to protect and to hold than it is to move forward, destroy, and take. If effective defenses can be erected quickly, an attacker may be able to keep territory he has taken in an initial victory. Thus, the dominance of the defense made it very hard for Britain and France to push Germany out of France in World War I. But when superior defenses are difficult for an aggressor to improvise on the battlefield and must be constructed during peacetime, they provide no direct assistance to him.

The security dilemma is at its most vicious when commitments, strategy, or technology dictate that the only route to security lies through expansion. Status-quo powers must then act like aggressors; the fact that they would gladly agree to forego the opportunity for expansion in return for guarantees for their security has no implications for their behavior. Even if expansion is not sought as a goal in itself, there will be quick and drastic changes in the distribution of territory and influence. Conversely, when the defense has the advantage, status-quo states can make themselves more secure without gravely endangering others.[1] Indeed, if the defense has enough of an advantage and if the states are of roughly equal size, not only will the security dilemma cease to inhibit status-quo states from cooperating, but aggression will be next to impossible, thus rendering international anarchy relatively unimportant. If states cannot conquer each other, then the lack of sovereignty, although it presents problems of collective goods in a number of areas, no longer forces states to devote their primary attention to self-preservation. Although, if force were not usable, there would be fewer restraints on the use of nonmilitary instruments, these are rarely powerful enough to threaten the vital interests of a major state.

Two questions of the offense-defense balance can be separated. First, does the state have to spend more or less than one dollar on defensive forces to offset each dollar spent by the other side on forces that could be used to attack? If the state has one dollar to spend on increasing its security, should it put it into offensive or defensive forces? Second, with a given inventory of forces, is it better to attack or to defend? Is there an incentive to strike first or to absorb the other's blow? These two aspects are often linked: if each dollar spent on offense can overcome each dollar spent on defense, and if both sides have the same defense budgets, then both are likely to build offensive forces and find it attractive to attack rather than to wait for the adversary to strike.

---

[1]Thus, when Wolfers (fn. 10), 126, argues that a status-quo state that settles for rough equality of power with its adversary, rather than seeking preponderance, may be able to convince the other to reciprocate by showing that it wants only to protect itself, not menace the other, he assumes that the defense has an advantage.

These aspects affect the security dilemma in different ways. The first has its greatest impact on arms races. If the defense has the advantage, and if the status-quo powers have reasonable subjective security requirements, they can probably avoid an arms race. Although an increase in one side's arms and security will still decrease the other's security, the former's increase will be larger than the latter's decrease. So if one side increases its arms, the other can bring its security back up to its previous level by adding a smaller amount to its forces. And if the first side reacts to this change, its increase will also be smaller than the stimulus that produced it. Thus a stable equilibrium will be reached. Shifting from dynamics to statics, each side can be quite secure with forces roughly equal to those of the other. Indeed, if the defense is much more potent than the offense, each side can be willing to have forces much smaller than the other's, and can be indifferent to a wide range of the other's defense policies.

The second aspect—whether it is better to attack or to defend—influences short-run stability. When the offense has the advantage, a state's reaction to international tension will increase the chances of war. The incentives for pre-emption and the "reciprocal fear of surprise attack" in this situation have been made clear by analyses of the dangers that exist when two countries have first-strike capabilities.[2] There is no way for the state to increase its security without menacing, or even attacking, the other. Even Bismarck, who once called preventive war "committing suicide from fear of death," said that "no government, if it regards war as inevitable even if it does not want it, would be so foolish as to leave to the enemy the choice of time and occasion and to wait for the moment which is most convenient for the enemy."[3] In another arena, the same dilemma applies to the policeman in a dark alley confronting a suspected criminal who appears to be holding a weapon. Though racism may indeed be present, the security dilemma can account for many of the tragic shootings of innocent people in the ghettos.

Beliefs about the course of a war in which the offense has the advantage further deepen the security dilemma. When there are incentives to strike first, a successful attack will usually so weaken the other side that victory will be relatively quick, bloodless, and decisive. It is in these periods when conquest is possible and attractive that states consolidate power internally—for instance, by destroying the feudal barons —and expand externally. There are several consequences that decrease the chance of cooperation among status-quo states. First, war will be profitable for the winner. The costs will be low and the benefits high. Of course, losers will suffer; the fear of losing could induce states to try to form stable cooperative arrangements, but the temptation of victory will make this particularly difficult. Second, because wars are expected to

[2]Schelling (fn. 20), chap. 9.

[3]Quoted in Fritz Fischer, War of Illusions (New York: Norton 1975), 377, 461.

be both frequent and short, there will be incentives for high levels of arms, and quick and strong reaction to the other's increases in arms. The state cannot afford to wait until there is unambiguous evidence that the other is building new weapons. Even large states that have faith in their economic strength cannot wait, because the war will be over before their products can reach the army. Third, when wars are quick, states will have to recruit allies in advance.[4] Without the opportunity for bargaining and re-alignments during the opening stages of hostilities, peacetime diplomacy loses a degree of the fluidity that facilitates balance-of-power policies. Because alliances must be secured during peacetime, the international system is more likely to become bipolar. It is hard to say whether war therefore becomes more or less likely, but this bipolarity increases tension between the two camps and makes it harder for status-quo states to gain the benefits of cooperation. Fourth, if wars are frequent, statesmen's perceptual thresholds will be adjusted accordingly and they will be quick to perceive ambiguous evidence as indicating that others are aggressive. Thus, there will be more cases of status-quo powers arming against each other in the incorrect belief that the other is hostile.

When the defense has the advantage, all the foregoing is reversed. The state that fears attack does not pre-empt—since that would be a wasteful use of its military resources—but rather prepares to receive an attack. Doing so does not decrease the security of others, and several states can do it simultaneously; the situation will therefore be stable, and status-quo powers will be able to cooperate. When Herman Kahn argues that ultimatums "are vastly too dangerous to give because . . . they are quite likely to touch off a pre-emptive strike,"[5] he incorrectly assumes that it is always advantageous to strike first.

More is involved than short-run dynamics. When the defense is dominant, wars are likely to become stalemates and can be won only at enormous cost. Relatively small and weak states can hold off larger and stronger ones, or can deter attack by raising the costs of conquest to an unacceptable level. States then approach equality in what they can do to each other. Like the .45-caliber pistol in the American West, fortifications were the "great equalizer" in some periods. Changes in the status quo are less frequent and cooperation is more common wherever the security dilemma is thereby reduced. . . .

The security dilemma was much less powerful after World War I than it had been before. In the later period, the expected power of the defense allowed status-quo states to pursue compatible security policies and avoid arms races. Furthermore, high tension

---

[4]George Quester, Offense and Defense in the International System (New York: John Wiley 1977), 105–06; Sontag (fn. 5), 4–5.

[5]Kahn (fn. 23), 211 (also see 144).

and fear of war did not set off short-run dynamics by which each state, trying to increase its security, inadvertently acted to make war more likely. The expected high costs of war, however, led the Allies to believe that no sane German leader would run the risks entailed in an attempt to dominate the Continent, and discouraged them from risking war themselves.

Technology and Geography

Technology and geography are the two main factors that determine whether the offense or the defense has the advantage. As Brodie notes, "On the tactical level, as a rule, few physical factors favor the attacker but many favor the defender. The defender usually has the advantage of cover. He characteristically fires from behind some form of shelter while his opponent crosses open ground."[6] Anything that increases the amount of ground the attacker has to cross, or impedes his progress across it, or makes him more vulnerable while crossing, increases the advantage accruing to the defense. When states are separated by barriers that produce these effects, the security dilemma is eased, since both can have forces adequate for defense without being able to attack. Impenetrable barriers would actually prevent war; in reality, decision makers have to settle for a good deal less. Buffer zones slow the attacker's progress; they thereby give the defender time to prepare, increase problems of logistics, and reduce the number of soldiers available for the final assault. At the end of the 19th century, Arthur Balfour noted Afghanistan's "non-conducting" qualities. "So long as it possesses few roads, and no railroads, it will be impossible for Russia to make effective use of her great numerical superiority at any point immediately vital to the Empire." The Russians valued buffers for the same reasons; it is not surprising that when Persia was being divided into Russian and British spheres of influence some years later, the Russians sought assurances that the British would refrain from building potentially menacing railroads in their sphere. Indeed, since railroad construction radically altered the abilities of countries to defend themselves and to attack others, many diplomatic notes and much intelligence activity in the late 19th century centered on this subject.[7]

Oceans, large rivers, and mountain ranges serve the same function as buffer zones. Being hard to cross, they allow defense against superior numbers. The defender has merely to stay on his side of the barrier and so can utilize all the men he can bring up to it. The attacker's men, however, can cross only a few at a time, and they are very vulnerable when doing so. If all states were self-sufficient islands, anarchy would

[6]Brodie (fn. 8), 179.

[7]Arthur Balfour, "Memorandum," Committee on Imperial Defence, April 30, 1903, pp. 2–3; see the telegrams by Sir Arthur Nicolson, in G. P. Gooch and Harold Temperley, eds., *British Documents on the Origins of the War,* Vol. 4 (London: H.M.S.O. 1929), 429, 524. These barriers do not prevent the passage of long-range aircraft; but even in the air, distance usually aids the defender.

be much less of a problem. A small investment in shore defenses and a small army would be sufficient to repel invasion. Only very weak states would be vulnerable, and only very large ones could menace others. As noted above, the United States, and to a lesser extent Great Britain, have partly been able to escape from the state of nature because their geographical positions approximated this ideal.

Although geography cannot be changed to conform to borders, borders can and do change to conform to geography. Borders across which an attack is easy tend to be unstable. States living within them are likely to expand or be absorbed. Frequent wars are almost inevitable since attacking will often seem the best way to protect what one has. This process will stop, or at least slow down, when the state's borders reach—by expansion or contraction—a line of natural obstacles. Security without attack will then be possible. Furthermore, these lines constitute salient solutions to bargaining problems and, to the extent that they are barriers to migration, are likely to divide ethnic groups, thereby raising the costs and lowering the incentives for conquest.

Attachment to one's state and its land reinforce one quasi-geographical aid to the defense. Conquest usually becomes more difficult the deeper the attacker pushes into the other's territory. Nationalism spurs the defenders to fight harder; advancing not only lengthens the attacker's supply lines, but takes him through unfamiliar and often devastated lands that require troops for garrison duty. These stabilizing dynamics will not operate, however, if the defender's war materiel is situated near its borders, or if the people do not care about their state, but only about being on the winning side. In such cases, positive feedback will be at work and initial defeats will be insurmountable.[8]

Imitating geography, men have tried to create barriers. Treaties may provide for demilitarized zones on both sides of the border, although such zones will rarely be deep enough to provide more than warning. Even this was not possible in Europe, but the Russians adopted a gauge for their railroads that was broader than that of the neighboring states, thereby complicating the logistics problems of any attacker—including Russia.

Perhaps the most ambitious and at least temporarily successful attempts to construct a system that would aid the defenses of both sides were the interwar naval treaties, as they affected Japanese-American relations. As mentioned earlier, the problem was that the United States could not defend the Philippines without denying Japan the ability to protect her home islands.[9] (In 1941 this dilemma became insoluble when

[8]See, for example, the discussion of warfare among Chinese warlords in Hsi-Sheng Chi, "The Chinese Warlord System as an International System," in Morton Kaplan, ed., *New Approaches to International Relations* (New York: St. Martin's 1968), 405–25.

[9]Some American decision makers, including military officers, thought that the best way out of the dilemma was to abandon the Philippines.

Japan sought to extend her control to Malaya and the Dutch East Indies. If the Philippines had been invulnerable, they could have provided a secure base from which the U.S. could interdict Japanese shipping between the homeland and the areas she was trying to conquer.) In the 1920's and early 1930's each side would have been willing to grant the other security for its possessions in return for a reciprocal grant, and the Washington Naval Conference agreements were designed to approach this goal. As a Japanese diplomat later put it, their country's "fundamental principle" was to have "a strength insufficient for attack and adequate for defense."[10] Thus, Japan agreed in 1922 to accept a navy only three-fifths as large as that of the United States, and the U.S. agreed not to fortify its Pacific islands.[11] (Japan had earlier been forced to agree not to fortify the islands she had taken from Germany in World War I.) Japan's navy would not be large enough to defeat America's anywhere other than close to the home islands. Although the Japanese could still take the Philippines, not only would they be unable to move farther, but they might be weakened enough by their efforts to be vulnerable to counterattack. Japan, however, gained security. An American attack was rendered more difficult because the American bases were unprotected and because, until 1930, Japan was allowed unlimited numbers of cruisers, destroyers, and submarines that could weaken the American fleet as it made its way across the ocean.[12]

The other major determinant of the offense-defense balance is technology. When weapons are highly vulnerable, they must be employed before they are attacked. Others can remain quite invulnerable in their bases. The former characteristics are embodied in unprotected missiles and many kinds of bombers. (It should be noted that it is not vulnerability *per se* that is crucial, but the location of the vulnerability. Bombers and missiles that are easy to destroy only after having been launched toward their targets do not create destabilizing dynamics.) Incentives to strike first are usually absent for naval forces that are threatened by a naval attack. Like missiles in hardened silos, they are usually well protected when in their bases. Both sides can then simultaneously be prepared to defend themselves successfully....

Concerning nuclear weapons, it is generally agreed that defense is impossible— a triumph not of the offense, but of deterrence. Attack makes no sense, not because it can be beaten off, but because the attacker will be destroyed in turn. In terms of the questions under consideration here, the result is the equivalent of the primacy of

---

[10]Quoted in Elting Morrison, *Turmoil and Tradition: A Study of the Life and Times of Henry L. Stimson* (Boston: Houghton Mifflin 1960), 326.

[11]The U.S. "refused to consider limitations on Hawaiian defenses, since these works posed no threat to Japan." Braisted (fn. 27), 612.

[12]That is part of the reason why the Japanese admirals strongly objected when the civilian leaders decided to accept a seven-to-ten ratio in lighter craft in 1930. Stephen Pelz, *Race to Pearl Harbor* (Cambridge: Harvard University Press 1974), 3.

the defense. First, security is relatively cheap. Less than one percent of the G.N.P. is devoted to deterring a direct attack on the United States; most of it is spent on acquiring redundant systems to provide a lot of insurance against the worst conceivable contingencies. Second, both sides can simultaneously gain security in the form of second-strike capability. Third, and related to the foregoing, second-strike capability can be maintained in the face of wide variations in the other side's military posture. There is no purely military reason why each side has to react quickly and strongly to the other's increases in arms. Any spending that the other devotes to trying to achieve first-strike capability can be neutralized by the state's spending much smaller sums on protecting its second-strike capability. Fourth, there are no incentives to strike first in a crisis.

Important problems remain, of course. Both sides have interests that go well beyond defense of the homeland. The protection of these interests creates conflicts even if neither side desires expansion. Furthermore, the shift from defense to deterrence has greatly increased the importance and perceptions of resolve. Security now rests on each side's belief that the other would prefer to run high risks of total destruction rather than sacrifice its vital interests. Aspects of the security dilemma thus appear in a new form. Are weapons procurements used as an index of resolve? Must they be so used? If one side fails to respond to the other's buildup, will it appear weak and thereby invite predation? Can both sides simultaneously have images of high resolve or is there a zero-sum element involved? Although these problems are real, they are not as severe as those in the prenuclear era: there are many indices of resolve, and states do not so much judge images of resolve in the abstract as ask how likely it is that the other will stand firm in a particular dispute. Since states are most likely to stand firm on matters which concern them most, it is quite possible for both to demonstrate their resolve to protect their own security simultaneously.

Offense-defense differentiation

The other major variable that affects how strongly the security dilemma operates is whether weapons and policies that protect the state also provide the capability for attack. If they do not, the basic postulate of the security dilemma no longer applies. A state can increase its own security without decreasing that of others. The advantage of the defense can only ameliorate the security dilemma. A differentiation between offensive and defensive stances comes close to abolishing it. Such differentiation does not mean, however, that all security problems will be abolished. If the offense has the advantage, conquest and aggression will still be possible. And if the offense's advantage is great enough, status-quo powers may find it too expensive to protect themselves by defensive forces and decide to procure offensive weapons even though this will menace others. Furthermore, states will still have to worry that even if the other's military posture shows that it is peaceful now, it may develop aggressive intentions in the future.

Assuming that the defense is at least as potent as the offense, the differentiation between them allows status-quo states to behave in ways that are clearly different from those of aggressors. Three beneficial consequences follow. First, status-quo powers can identify each other, thus laying the foundations for cooperation. Conflicts growing out of the mistaken belief that the other side is expansionist will be less frequent. Second, status-quo states will obtain advance warning when others plan aggression. Before a state can attack, it has to develop and deploy offensive weapons. If procurement of these weapons cannot be disguised and takes a fair amount of time, as it almost always does, a status-quo state will have the time to take countermeasures. It need not maintain a high level of defensive arms as long as its potential adversaries are adopting a peaceful posture. (Although being so armed should not, with the one important exception noted below, alarm other status-quo powers.) States do, in fact, pay special attention to actions that they believe would not be taken by a status-quo state because they feel that states exhibiting such behavior are aggressive. Thus the seizure or development of transportation facilities will alarm others more if these facilities have no commercial value, and therefore can only be wanted for military reasons. In 1906, the British rejected a Russian protest about their activities in a district of Persia by claiming that this area was "only of [strategic] importance [to the Russians] if they wished to attack the Indian frontier, or to put pressure upon us by making us think that they intend to attack it."[13] . . .

Of course these inferences can be wrong—as they are especially likely to be because states underestimate the degree to which they menace others.[14] And when they are wrong, the security dilemma is deepened. Because the state thinks it has received notice that the other is aggressive, its own arms building will be less restrained and the chances of cooperation will be decreased. But the dangers of incorrect inferences should not obscure the main point: when offensive and defensive postures are different, much of the uncertainty about the other's intentions that contributes to the security dilemma is removed.

The third beneficial consequence of a difference between offensive and defensive weapons is that if all states support the status quo, an obvious arms control agreement is a ban on weapons that are useful for attacking. As President Roosevelt put it in his message to the Geneva Disarmament Conference in 1933: "If all nations will agree wholly to eliminate from possession and use the weapons which make possible a successful attack, defenses automatically will become impregnable, and the frontiers and independence of every nation will become secure."[15] The fact that such treaties have been rare—the Washington naval agreements discussed above and the anti-ABM treaty can be cited as examples—shows either that states are not always

[13]Richard Challener, Admirals, Generals, and American Foreign Policy, 1898–1914 (Princeton: Princeton University Press 1973), 273; Grey to Nicolson, in Gooch and Temperley (fn. 47), 414.

[14]Jervis (fn. 5), 69–72, 352–55.

[15]Quoted in Merze Tate, The United States and Armaments (Cambridge: Harvard University Press 1948), 108.

willing to guarantee the security of others, or that it is hard to distinguish offensive from defensive weapons....

There are several problems. Even when a differentiation is possible, a status-quo power will want offensive arms under any of three conditions. (I) If the offense has a great advantage over the defense, protection through defensive forces will be too expensive. (2) Status-quo states may need offensive weapons to regain territory lost in the opening stages of a war. It might be possible, however, for a state to wait to procure these weapons until war seems likely, and they might be needed only in relatively small numbers, unless the aggressor was able to construct strong defenses quickly in the occupied areas. (3) The state may feel that it must be prepared to take the offensive either because the other side will make peace only if it loses territory or because the state has commitments to attack if the other makes war on a third party. As noted above, status-quo states with extensive commitments are often forced to behave like aggressors. Even when they lack such commitments, status-quo states must worry about the possibility that if they are able to hold off an attack, they will still not be able to end the war unless they move into the other's territory to damage its military forces and inflict pain. Many American naval officers after the Civil War, for example, believed that "only by destroying the commerce of the opponent could the United States bring him to terms."[16]

A further complication is introduced by the fact that aggressors as well as status-quo powers require defensive forces as a prelude to acquiring offensive ones, to protect one frontier while attacking another, or for insurance in case the war goes badly. Criminals as well as policemen can use bulletproof vests. Hitler as well as Maginot built a line of forts. Indeed, Churchill reports that in 1936 the German Foreign Minister said: "As soon as our fortifications are constructed [on our western borders] and the countries in Central Europe realize that France cannot enter German territory, all these countries will begin to feel very differently about their foreign policies, and a new constellation will develop."[17] So a state may not necessarily be reassured if its neighbor constructs strong defenses....

The essence of defense is keeping the other side out of your territory. A purely defensive weapon is one that can do this without being able to penetrate the enemy's land. Thus a committee of military experts in an interwar disarmament conference declared that armaments "incapable of mobility by means of self-contained power," or movable only after long delay, were "only capable of being used for the defense of a State's territory."[18] The most obvious examples are fortifications. They can shelter attacking forces, especially when they are built right along the

[16]Kenneth Hagan, *American Gunboat Diplomacy and the Old Navy, 1877–1889* (Westport, Conn.: Greenwood Press 1973), 20.
[17]Winston Churchill, *The Gathering Storm* (Boston: Houghton 1948), 206.
[18]Quoted in Boggs (fn. 28), 39.

frontier,[19] but they cannot occupy enemy territory. A state with only a strong line of forts, fixed guns, and a small army to man them would not be much of a menace. Anything else that can serve only as a barrier against attacking troops is similarly defensive. In this category are systems that provide warning of an attack, the Russian's adoption of a different railroad gauge, and nuclear land mines that can seal off invasion routes.

If total immobility clearly defines a system that is defensive only, limited mobility is unfortunately ambiguous. As noted above, short-range fighter aircraft and anti-aircraft missiles can be used to cover an attack. And, unlike forts, they can advance with the troops. Still, their inability to reach deep into enemy territory does make them more useful for the defense than for the offense. Thus, the United States and Israel would have been more alarmed in the early 1970's had the Russians provided the Egyptians with long-range instead of short-range aircraft. Naval forces are particularly difficult to classify in these terms, but those that are very short-legged can be used only for coastal defense.

Any forces that for various reasons fight well only when on their own soil in effect lack mobility and therefore are defensive. The most extreme example would be passive resistance. Noncooperation can thwart an aggressor, but it is very hard for large numbers of people to cross the border and stage a sit-in on another's territory....

Weapons that are particularly effective in reducing fortifications and barriers are of great value to the offense. This is not to deny that a defensive power will want some of those weapons if the other side has them: Brodie is certainly correct to argue that while their tanks allowed the Germans to conquer France, properly used French tanks could have halted the attack. But France would not have needed these weapons if Germany had not acquired them, whereas even if France had no tanks, Germany could not have foregone them since they provided the only chance of breaking through the French lines. Mobile heavy artillery is, similarly, especially useful in destroying fortifications. The defender, while needing artillery to fight off attacking troops or to counterattack, can usually use lighter guns since they do not need to penetrate such massive obstacles. So it is not surprising that one of the few things that most nations at the interwar disarmament conferences were able to agree on was that heavy tanks and mobile heavy guns were particularly valuable to a state planning an attack.[20]

Weapons and strategies that depend for their effectiveness on surprise are almost always offensive. That fact was recognized by some of the delegates to the interwar disarmament conferences and is the principle behind the common national ban on

[19]On these grounds, the Germans claimed in 1932 that the French forts were offensive (*ibid.*, 49). Similarly, fortified forward naval bases can be necessary for launching an attack; see Braisted (fn. 27), 643.
[20]Boggs (fn. 28), 14–15, 47–48, 60.

concealed weapons. An earlier representative of this widespread view was the mid-19th-century Philadelphia newspaper that argued: "As a measure of defense, knives, dirks, and sword canes are entirely useless. They are fit only for attack, and all such attacks are of murderous character. Whoever carries such a weapon has prepared himself for homicide."[21]

It is, of course, not always possible to distinguish between forces that are most effective for holding territory and forces optimally designed for taking it. Such a distinction could not have been made for the strategies and weapons in Europe during most of the period between the Franco-Prussian War and World War I. Neither naval forces nor tactical air forces can be readily classified in these terms. But the point here is that when such a distinction is possible, the central characteristic of the security dilemma no longer holds, and one of the most troublesome consequences of anarchy is removed....

FOUR WORLDS

The two variables we have been discussing—whether the offense or the defense has the advantage, and whether offensive postures can be distinguished from defensive ones—can be combined to yield four possible worlds.

	OFFENSE HAS THE ADVANTAGE	DEFENSE HAS THE ADVANTAGE
OFFENSIVE POSTURE NOT DISTINGUISHABLE FROM DEFENSIVE ONE	1 Doubly dangerous	2 Security dilemma, but security requirements may be compatible.
OFFENSIVE POSTURE DISTINGUISHABLE FROM DEFENSIVE ONE	3 No security dilemma, but aggression possible. Status-quo states can follow different policy than aggressors. Warning given.	4 Doubly stable

[21]Quoted in Philip Jordan, Frontier Law and Order (Lincoln: University of Nebraska Press 1970), 7; also see 16–17.

The first world is the worst for status-quo states. There is no way to get security without menacing others, and security through defense is terribly difficult to obtain. Because offensive and defensive postures are the same, status-quo states acquire the same kind of arms that are sought by aggressors. And because the offense has the advantage over the defense, attacking is the best route to protecting what you have; status-quo states will therefore behave like aggressors. The situation will be unstable. Arms races are likely. Incentives to strike first will turn crises into wars. Decisive victories and conquests will be common. States will grow and shrink rapidly, and it will be hard for any state to maintain its size and influence without trying to increase them. Cooperation among status-quo powers will be extremely hard to achieve.

There are no cases that totally fit this picture, but it bears more than a passing resemblance to Europe before World War I. Britain and Germany, although in many respects natural allies, ended up as enemies. Of course much of the explanation lies in Germany's ill-chosen policy. And from the perspective of our theory, the powers' ability to avoid war in a series of earlier crises cannot be easily explained. Nevertheless, much of the behavior in this period was the product of technology and beliefs that magnified the security dilemma. Decision makers thought that the offense had a big advantage and saw little difference between offensive and defensive military postures. The era was characterized by arms races. And once war seemed likely, mobilization races created powerful incentives to strike first.

In the nuclear era, the first world would be one in which each side relied on vulnerable weapons that were aimed at similar forces and each side understood the situation. In this case, the incentives to strike first would be very high—so high that status-quo powers as well as aggressors would be sorely tempted to pre-empt. And since the forces could be used to change the status quo as well as to preserve it, there would be no way for both sides to increase their security simultaneously. Now the familiar logic of deterrence leads both sides to see the dangers in this world. Indeed, the new understanding of this situation was one reason why vulnerable bombers and missiles were replaced. Ironically, the 1950's would have been more hazardous if the decision makers had been aware of the dangers of their posture and had therefore felt greater pressure to strike first. This situation could be recreated if both sides were to rely on MIRVed ICBM's.

In the second world, the security dilemma operates because offensive and defensive postures cannot be distinguished; but it does not operate as strongly as in the first world because the defense has the advantage, and so an increment in one side's strength increases its security more than it decreases the other's. So, if both sides have reasonable subjective security requirements, are of roughly equal power, and the variables discussed earlier are favorable, it is quite likely that status-quo states can adopt compatible security policies. Although a state will not be able to judge the other's intentions from the kinds of weapons it procures, the level of arms spending will give important evidence. Of course a state that seeks a high level of arms might be not an aggressor but merely an insecure state, which if conciliated will reduce its arms, and if confronted will reply in kind. To assume that the apparently excessive level of arms indicates aggressiveness could therefore lead to a response that would deepen the dilemma and create needless conflict. But empathy and skillful statesmanship can reduce this danger. Furthermore, the advantageous position of the defense means that a status-quo state can often maintain a high degree of security with a level of arms lower than that of its expected adversary. Such a state demonstrates that it lacks the ability or desire to alter the status quo, at least at the present time. The strength of the defense also allows states to react slowly and with restraint when they fear that others are menacing them. So, although status-quo powers will to some extent be threatening to others, that extent will be limited.

This world is the one that comes closest to matching most periods in history. Attacking is usually harder than defending because of the strength of fortifications and obstacles. But purely defensive postures are rarely possible because fortifications are usually supplemented by armies and mobile guns which can support an attack. In the nuclear era, this world would be one in which both sides relied on relatively invulnerable ICBM's and believed that limited nuclear war was impossible. Assuming no MIRV's, it would take more than one attacking missile to destroy one of the adversary's. Pre-emption is therefore unattractive. If both sides have large inventories, they can ignore all but drastic increases on the other side. A world of either ICBM's or SLBM's in which both sides adopted the "Schlesinger Doctrine" would probably fit in this category too. The means of preserving the status quo would also be the means of changing it, as we discussed earlier. And the defense usually would have the advantage, because compellence is more difficult than deterrence. Although a state might succeed in changing the status quo on issues that matter much more to it than to others, status-quo powers could deter major provocations under most circumstances.

In the third world there may be no security dilemma, but there are security problems. Because states can procure defensive systems that do not threaten others, the dilemma need not operate. But because the offense has the advantage, aggression is possible, and perhaps easy. If the offense has enough of an advantage, even a status-quo state may take the initiative rather than risk being attacked and defeated. If the offense has less of an advantage, stability and cooperation are likely. because the status-quo states will procure defensive forces. They need not react to others who are similarly armed, but can wait for the warning they would receive if others started to deploy offensive weapons. But each state will have to watch the others carefully, and there is room for false suspicions. The costliness of the defense and the allure of the offense can lead to unnecessary mistrust, hostility, and war, unless some of the variables discussed earlier are operating to restrain defection.

A hypothetical nuclear world that would fit this description would be one in which both sides relied on SLBM's, but in which ASW techniques were very effective. Offense and defense would be different, but the former would have the advantage. This situation is not likely to occur; but if it did, a status-quo state could show its lack of desire to exploit the other by refraining from threatening its submarines. The desire to have more protecting you than merely the other side's fear of retaliation is a strong one, however, and a state that knows that it would not expand even if its cities were safe is likely to believe that the other would not feel threatened by its ASW program. It is easy to see how such a world could become unstable, and how spirals of tensions and conflict could develop.

The fourth world is doubly safe. The differentiation between offensive and defensive systems permits a way out of the security dilemma; the advantage of the defense disposes of the problems discussed in the previous paragraphs. There is no reason for a status-quo power to be tempted to procure offensive forces, and aggressors give notice of their intentions by the posture they adopt. Indeed, if the advantage of the defense is great enough, there are no security problems. The loss of the ultimate form of the power to alter the status quo would allow greater scope for the exercise of non-military means and probably would tend to freeze the distribution of values.

This world would have existed in the first decade of the 20th century if the decision makers had understood the available technology. In that case, the European powers would have followed different policies both in the long run and in the summer of 1914. Even Germany, facing powerful enemies on both sides, could have made herself secure by developing strong defenses. France could also have made her frontier almost impregnable. Furthermore, when crises arose, no one would have had incentives to strike first. There would have been no competitive mobilization races reducing the time available for negotiations.

In the nuclear era, this world would be one in which the superpowers relied on SLBM's, ASW technology was not up to its task, and limited nuclear options were not taken seriously. We have discussed this situation earlier; here we need only add that, even if our analysis is correct and even if the policies and postures of both sides were to move in this direction, the problem of violence below the nuclear threshold would remain. On issues other than defense of the homeland, there would still be security dilemmas and security problems. But the world would nevertheless be safer than it has usually been.

PEACE, STABILITY, AND NUCLEAR WEAPONS

Kenneth N. Waltz

WHY COUNTRIES WANT NUCLEAR WEAPONS

In contemplating the likely future, we might first ask why countries want to have nuclear weapons. They want them for one or more of seven main reasons:

- First, great powers always counter the weapons of other great powers, usually by imitating those who have introduced new weapons. It was not surprising that the Soviet Union developed atomic and hydrogen bombs, but rather that we thought the Baruch-Lilienthal plan might persuade it not to.
- Second, a state may want nuclear weapons for fear that its great-power ally will not retaliate if another great power attacks. When it became a nuclear power, Britain thought of itself as being a great one, but its reasons for deciding to maintain a nuclear force arose from doubts that the United States could be counted on to retaliate in response to an attack by the Soviet Union on Europe and from Britain's

From "Peace, Stability and Nuclear Weapons" by Kenneth N. Waltz as appeared in *Policy Papers-Institute of Global Conflict and Cooperation*, No. 15 (Aug 1995), IGCC-University of California Berkeley. Reprinted by permission of Kenneth N. Waltz, Ford Professor Emeritus, University of California Berkeley.

consequent desire to place a finger on our nuclear trigger. As soon as the Soviet Union was capable of making nuclear strikes at American cities, West Europeans began to worry that America's nuclear umbrella no longer ensured that its allies would stay dry if it rained.

- Third, a country without nuclear allies will want nuclear weapons all the more if some of its adversaries have them. So China and then India became nuclear powers, and Pakistan naturally followed.
- Fourth, a country may want nuclear weapons because it lives in fear of its adversaries' present or future conventional strength. This was reason enough for Israel's nuclear weapons.
- Fifth, for some countries nuclear weapons are a cheaper and safer alternative to running economically ruinous and militarily dangerous conventional arms races. Nuclear weapons promise security and independence at an affordable price.
- Sixth, some countries are thought to want nuclear weapons for offensive purposes. This, however, is an unlikely motivation for reasons given below.
- Finally, by building nuclear weapons a country may hope to enhance its international standing. This is thought to be both a reason for and a consequence of developing nuclear weapons. One may enjoy the status that comes with nuclear weapons and even benefit from it. Thus, North Korea gained international attention by developing nuclear military capability. A yen for attention and prestige is, however, a minor motivation. Would-be nuclear states are not among the militarily most powerful ones. The security concerns of weaker states are too serious to permit them to accord much importance to the prestige that nuclear weapons may bring.

THE FEAR OF NUCLEAR WEAPONS

Fears of what the further spread of nuclear weapons will do to the world boil down to five. First, new nuclear states may put their weapons to offensive use. Second, as more countries get the weapons, the chances of accidental use increase. Third, with limited resources and know-how, new nuclear states may find it difficult to deploy invulnerable, deterrent forces. Fourth, American military intervention in the affairs of lesser states will be impeded by their possession of nuclear weapons. Fifth, as nuclear weapons spread, terrorists may more easily get hold of nuclear materials. (In this chapter, I leave the fifth fear aside, partly because the likelihood of nuclear terror is low and partly because terrorists can presumably steal nuclear weapons or buy them on the black market whether or not a few more states go nuclear.)[1]

---

[1]For a brief discussion, see Chapter 3 of Scott D. Sagan and Kenneth N. Waltz, *The Spread of Nuclear Weapons: A Debate* (New York: W. W. Norton, 1995).

Offensive use

Despite the variety of nuclear motivations, an American consensus has formed on why some states want their own weapons—to help them pursue expansionist ends. "The basic division in the world on the subject of nuclear proliferation," we are authoritatively told, "is not between those with and without nuclear weapons. It is between almost all nations and the very few who currently seek weapons to reinforce their expansive ambition."[2] Just as we first feared that the Soviet Union and China would use nuclear weapons to extend their sway, so we now fear that the likes of Iraq, Iran, and Libya will do so. The fear has grown despite the fact that nuclear capability added little to the Soviet Union's or China's ability to pursue their ends abroad, whether by launching military attacks or practicing blackmail.

The fear that new nuclear states will use their weapons for aggressive purposes is as odd as it is pervasive. Rogue states, as we now call them, must be up to no good, else we would not call them rogues. Why would states such as Iraq, Iran, and North Korea want nuclear weapons if not to enable them to conquer, or at least to intimidate, others? The answer can be given in one word: fear. The behavior of their rulers is often brazen, but does their bluster convey confidence or fear? Even though they may hope to extend their domination over others, they first have to maintain it at home.

What states do conveys more than what they say. Idi Amin and Muammar el-Qaddafi were favorite examples of the kinds of rulers who could not be trusted to manage nuclear weapons responsibly. Despite wild rhetoric aimed at foreigners, however, both of these "irrational" rulers became cautious and modest when punitive actions against them seemed to threaten their continued ability to rule. Even though Amin lustily slaughtered members of tribes he disliked, he quickly stopped goading Britain when it seemed that it might intervene militarily. Qaddafi showed similar restraint. He and Anwar Sadat were openly hostile. In July 1977, both launched commando attacks and air raids, including two large air strikes by Egypt on Libya's el-Adem airbase. Neither side let the attacks get out of hand. Qaddafi showed himself to be forbearing and amenable to mediation by other Arab leaders. Shai Feldman used these and other examples to argue that Arab leaders are deterred from taking inordinate risks, not because they engage in intricate rational calculations but simply because they, like other rulers, are "sensitive to costs." Saddam Hussein further illustrated the point during, and even prior to, the war of 1991. He invaded Kuwait only after the United States gave many indications that it would acquiesce in his actions. During the war, he launched missiles against Israel, but they were so lightly armed that little risk was run of prompting attacks more punishing than Iraq was already suffering. Deterrence worked once again.

[2]McGeorge Bundy, William J. Crowe, Jr. And Sidney D. Drell, *Reducing Nuclear Danger* (New York: Council on Foreign Relations, 1994), p. 81.

Many Westerners write fearfully about a future in which Third World countries have nuclear weapons. They seem to view Third World people in the old imperial manner as "lesser breeds without the law." As ever with ethnocentric views, speculation takes the place of evidence. How do we know that a nuclear-armed and newly-hostile Egypt, or a nuclear-armed and still-hostile Syria, would not strike to destroy Israel? Yet we have to ask whether either would do so at the risk of Israeli bombs falling on some of their cities? Almost a quarter of Egypt's people live in four cities: Cairo, Alexandria, El-Giza, and Shoubra el-Kheima. More than a quarter of Syria's live in three: Damascus, Aleppo, and Homs.[3] What government would risk sudden losses of such proportion, or indeed of much lesser proportion? Rulers want to have a country that they can continue to rule. Some Arab country may wish that some other Arab country would risk its own destruction for the sake of destroying Israel, but why would one think that any country would be willing to do so? Despite ample bitterness, Israelis and Arabs have limited their wars and accepted constraints placed on them by others. Arabs did not marshal their resources and make an all-out effort to destroy Israel in the years before Israel could strike back with nuclear war-heads. We cannot expect countries to risk more in the presence of nuclear weapons than they did in their absence.

Second, many fear that states that are radical at home will recklessly use their nuclear weapons in pursuit of revolutionary ends abroad. States that are radical at home, however, may not be radical abroad. Few states have been radical in the conduct of their foreign policy, and fewer have remained so for long. Think of the Soviet Union and the People's Republic of China. States coexist in a competitive arena. The pressures of competition cause them to behave in ways that make the threats they face manageable, in ways that enable them to get along. States can remain radical in foreign policy only if they are overwhelmingly strong—as none of the new nuclear states will be—or if their acts fall short of damaging vital interests of other nuclear powers. States that acquire nuclear weapons are not regarded with indifference. States that want to be freewheelers have to stay out of the nuclear business. A nuclear Libya, for example, would have to show caution, even in rhetoric, lest it suffer retaliation in response to someone else's anonymous attack on a third state. That state, ignorant of who attacked, might claim that its intelligence agents had identified Libya as the culprit and take the opportunity to silence it by striking a heavy conventional blow. Nuclear weapons induce caution in any state, especially in weak ones.

Would not nuclear weapons nevertheless provide a cheap and decisive offensive force when used against a conventionally armed enemy? Some people once thought that South Korea, and earlier, the Shah's Iran, wanted nuclear weapons for offensive

---

[3]*The Middle East and North Africa, 1994*, 40th ed. (London: Europa Publications, 1993), pp. 363, 810.

use. Yet one can neither say why South Korea would have used nuclear weapons against fellow Koreans while trying to reunite them nor how it could have used nuclear weapons against the North, knowing that China and the Soviet Union might have retaliated. And what goals might a conventionally strong Iran have entertained that would have tempted it to risk using nuclear weapons? A country that launches a strike has to fear a punishing blow from someone. Far from lowering the expected cost of aggression, a nuclear offense even against a non-nuclear state raises the possible costs of aggression to incalculable heights because the aggressor cannot be sure of the reaction of other states....

Nuclear weapons make states cautious, as the history of the nuclear age shows. "Rogue states," as the Soviet Union and China were once thought to be, have followed the pattern. The weaker and the more endangered a state is, the less likely it is to engage in reckless behavior. North Korea's external behavior has sometimes been ugly, but certainly not reckless. Its regime has shown no inclination to risk suicide. This is one good reason why surrounding states counseled patience.

Senator John McCain, a former naval officer, nevertheless believes that North Korea would be able to attack without fear of failure because a South Korean and American counterattack would have to stop at the present border for fear of North Korean nuclear retaliation.[4] Our vast nuclear forces would not deter an attack on the South, yet the dinky force that the North may have would deter us! A land-war game played by the American military in 1994 showed another side of American military thinking. The game pitted the United States against a Third World country similar to North Korea. Losing conventionally, it struck our forces with nuclear weapons. For unmentioned reasons, our superior military forces had no deterrent effect. Results were said to be devastating. With such possibilities in mind, Air Force General Lee Butler and his fellow planners called for a new strategy of deterrence, with "generic targeting" so we will be able to strike wherever "terrorist states or rogue leaders ... threaten to use their own nuclear, chemical or biological weapons." The strategy will supposedly deter states or terrorists from brandishing or using their weapons. Yet General Butler himself believes, as I do, that Saddam Hussein was deterred from using chemicals and biologicals in the Gulf War.[5]

During the 1993 American—South Korean "Team Spirit" military exercises, North Korea denied access to International Atomic Energy Agency inspectors and threatened to withdraw from the nuclear Non-Proliferation Treaty. The North's reaction suggests, as one would expect, that the more vulnerable North Korea feels, the

---

[4]John McCain, letter, *New York Times*, 28 March 1994, p. A10.
[5]Eric Schmitt, "U.S. is Redefining Nuclear Deterrence, Terrorist Nations Targeted," *International Herald Tribune*, 26 February 1993.

more strenuously it will pursue a nuclear program. The pattern has been a common one ever since the United States led the way into the nuclear age. Noticing this, we should be careful about conveying military threats to weak states.

The control of nuclear weapons

Will new nuclear states, many of them technologically backward and with weapons lacking effective safety devices, be able to prevent the accidental or unauthorized use of their weapons and maintain control of them despite possible domestic upheavals?

"War is like love," the chaplain says in Bertolt Brecht's *Mother Courage*, "it always finds a way."[6] For half a century, *nuclear* war has not found a way. The old saying, "accidents will happen," is translated as Murphy's Law holding that anything that can go wrong will go wrong. Enough has gone wrong, and Scott Sagan has recorded many of the nuclear accidents that have, or have nearly, taken place.[7] Yet none of them has caused anybody to blow anybody else up. In a speech given to American scientists in 1960, C.P. Snow said this: "We know, with the certainty of statistical truth, that if enough of these weapons are made—by enough different states—some of them are going to blow up. Through accident, or folly, or madness—but the motives don't matter. What does matter is the nature of the statistical fact." In 1960, statistical fact told Snow that within, "at the most, ten years some of these bombs are going off." Statistical fact now tells us that we are twenty-five years overdue.[8] But the novelist and scientist overlooked the fact that there are no "statistical facts."

Half a century of nuclear peace has to be explained since divergence from historical experience is dramatic. Never in modern history, conventionally dated from 1648, have the great and major powers of the world enjoyed such a long period of peace.

Large numbers of weapons increase the possibility of accidental use or loss of control, but new nuclear states will have only small numbers of weapons to care for. Lesser nuclear states may deploy, say, ten to fifty weapons and a number of dummies, while permitting other countries to infer that numbers of real weapons are larger. An adversary need only believe that some warheads may survive its attack and be visited on it. That belief is not hard to create without making command and control unreliable. All nuclear countries live through a time when their forces are crudely designed. All countries have so far been able to control them. Relations between the United

---

[6]Bertolt Brecht, *Mother Courage and her Children: a Chronicle of the Thirty Years' War*, trans. Eric Bentley (New York: Grove Press, 1966), p. 76.

[7]Scott D. Sagan, "More Will Be Worse," in Sagan and Waltz, *Spread of Nuclear Weapons*, pp. 47–91.

[8]C.P. Snow, "Excerpts from Snow's speech to American Scientists," *New York Times*, December 28, 1960, p. 14.

States and the Soviet Union, and later among the United States, the Soviet Union, and China, were at their bitterest just when their nuclear forces were in early stages of development and were unbalanced, crude, and presumably hard to control. Why should we expect new nuclear states to experience greater difficulties than the ones old nuclear states were able to cope with? Although some of the new nuclear states may be economically and technically backward, they will either have expert scientists and engineers or they will not be able to produce nuclear weapons. Even if they buy or steal the weapons, they will have to hire technicians to maintain and control them. We do not have to wonder whether they will take good care of their weapons. They have every incentive to do so. They will not want to risk retaliation because one or more of their warheads accidentally strike another country.

Deterrence is a considerable guarantee against accidents, since it causes countries to take good care of their weapons, and against anonymous use, since those firing the weapons can know neither that they will be undetected nor what punishment detection might bring. In life, uncertainties abound. In a conventional world, they more easily lead to war because less is at stake. Even so, it is difficult to think of conventional wars that were started by accident.[9] It is hard to believe that nuclear war may begin accidentally, when less frightening conventional wars have rarely done so.

Fear of accidents works against their occurring. This is illustrated by the Cuban Missile Crisis. Accidents happened during the crisis, and unplanned events took place. An American U-2 strayed over Siberia, and one flew over Cuba. The American Navy continued to play games at sea, such games as trying to force Soviet submarines to surface. In crises, political leaders want to control all relevant actions, while knowing that they cannot do so. Fear of losing control propelled Kennedy and Khrushchev to end the crisis quickly. In a conventional world, uncertainty may tempt a country to join battle. In a nuclear world, uncertainty has the opposite effect. What is not surely controllable is too dangerous to bear.

One must, however, consider the possibility that a nuclear state will one day experience uncertainty of succession, fierce struggles for power, and instability of regime. That such experiences led to the use of nuclear weapons neither during the Cultural Revolution in China nor during the dissolution of the Soviet Union is of some comfort. The possibility of one side in a civil war firing a nuclear warhead at its opponent's stronghold nevertheless remains. Such an act would produce a national tragedy, not an international one. This question then arises: Once the weapon is fired, what happens next? The domestic use of nuclear weapons is, of all the uses imaginable, least likely to lead to escalation and to regional or global tragedy.

---

[9]Scott Sagan has managed to find three, not all of which are unambiguous. *The Limits of Safety: Organizations, Accidents and Nuclear Weapons* (Princeton: Princeton University Press, 1993), p. 263.

Vulnerability of forces and problems of deterrence

The credibility of second strike forces has two faces. First, they have to be able to survive preemptive attacks. Second, they have to appear to be able to deliver a blow sufficient to deter.

The uneven development of the power of new nuclear states creates occasions that permit strikes and may invite them. Two stages of nuclear development should be distinguished. First, a country may be in an early stage of development and be obviously unable to make nuclear weapons. Second, a country may be in an advanced state of development and whether or not it has some nuclear weapons may not be surely known. All of the present nuclear countries went through both stages, yet until Israel struck Iraq's nuclear facility in June of 1981, no one had launched a preventive strike.

A number of causes combined may account for the reluctance of states to strike in order to prevent adversaries from developing nuclear forces. A preventive strike is most promising during the first stage of nuclear development. A state could strike without fearing that the country it attacked would be able to return a nuclear blow. But would one country strike so hard as to destroy another country's potential for future nuclear development? If it did not, the country struck could resume its nuclear career. If the blow struck is less than devastating, one must be prepared either to repeat it or to occupy and control the country. To do either would be forbiddingly difficult.

In striking Iraq, Israel showed that a preventive strike can be made, something that was not in doubt. Israel's act and its consequences, however, made clear that the likelihood of useful accomplishment is low. Israel's action increased the determination of Arabs to produce nuclear weapons. Israel's strike, far from foreclosing Iraq's nuclear career, gained Iraq support from some other Arab states to pursue it. Despite Prime Minister Menachem Begin's vow to strike as often as need be, the risks in doing so would have risen with each occasion.

A preemptive strike launched against a country that may have a small number of warheads is even less promising than a preventive strike during the first stage. If the country attacked has even a rudimentary nuclear capability, one's own severe punishment becomes possible. Nuclear forces are seldom delicate because no state wants delicate forces, and nuclear forces can easily be made sturdy. Nuclear warheads are fairly small and light; they are easy to hide and to move. Even the Model-T bombs dropped on Hiroshima and Nagasaki were small enough to be carried by a World War II bomber. Early in the nuclear age, people worried about atomic bombs being concealed in packing boxes and placed in the holds of ships to be exploded when a signal was given. Now more than ever, people worry about terrorists stealing nuclear warheads because various states have so many of them. Everybody seems to believe that terrorists are capable of hiding bombs.[10] Why should states be unable to do what terrorist gangs are thought to be capable of?

It was sometimes claimed that a small number of bombs in the hands of minor powers creates greater dangers than additional thousands in the hands of the United States or the Soviet Union. Such statements assume that preemption of a small force is easy. Acting on that assumption, someone may be tempted to strike; fearing this, the state with a small number of weapons may be tempted to use the few weapons it has rather than risk losing them. Such reasoning would confirm the thought that small nuclear forces create extreme dangers. But since protecting small forces by hiding and moving them is quite easy, the dangers evaporate.

Hiding nuclear weapons and being able to deliver them are tasks for which the ingenuity of numerous states is adequate. Means of delivery are neither difficult to devise nor hard to procure. Bombs can be driven in by trucks from neighboring countries. Ports can be torpedoed by small boats lying offshore. A thriving arms trade in ever more sophisticated military equipment provides ready access to what may be wanted, including planes and missiles suited to the delivery of nuclear warheads.

Lesser nuclear states can pursue deterrent strategies effectively. Deterrence requires the ability to inflict unacceptable damage on another country. "Unacceptable damage" to the Soviet Union was variously defined by former Secretary of Defense Robert S. McNamara as requiring the ability to destroy a fifth to a fourth of its population and a half to two-thirds of its industrial capacity. American estimates of what is required for deterrence were absurdly high. To deter, a country need not appear to be able to destroy a fourth or a half of another country, although in some cases that might be easily done. Would Libya try to destroy Israel's nuclear weapons at the risk of two bombs surviving to fall on Tripoli and Benghazi? And what would be left of Israel if Tel Aviv and Haifa were destroyed?

Survivable forces are seen to be readily deployed if one understands that the requirements of deterrence are low. Even the largest states recoil from taking adventurous steps if the price of failure is the possible loss of a city or two. An adversary is deterred if it cannot be sure that its preemptive strike will destroy all of another country's warheads. As Bernard Brodie put it, if a "small nation could threaten the Soviet Union with only a single thermonuclear bomb, which, however, it could and would certainly deliver on Moscow," the Soviet Union would be deterred.[11] I would change that sentence by substituting "might" for "would" and by adding that the threat of a fission bomb or two would also do the trick.

[10]E.g., David M. Rosenbaum, "Nuclear Terror," *International Security* Vol. 1 (Winter 1977), p. 145.

[11]Bernard Brodie, *Strategy in the Missile Age* (Princeton: Princeton University Press, 1959), p. 275.

Once a country has a small number of deliverable warheads of uncertain location, it has a second strike force. Belatedly, some Americans and Russians realized
this.[12] McNamara wrote in 1985 that the United States and the Soviet Union could get
along with 2,000 warheads between them instead of the 50,000 they may then have
had.[13] Talking at the University of California, Berkeley, in the spring of 1992, he
dropped the number the United States might need to sixty. Herbert York, speaking at
the Lawrence Livermore National Laboratory, which he once directed, guessed that
one hundred strategic warheads would be about the right number for us.[14] It does not
take much to deter. To have second-strike forces, states do not need large numbers of
weapons. Small numbers do quite nicely. Almost one-half of South Korea's population centers on Seoul. North Korea can deter South Korea by leading it to believe that
it has a few well-hidden and deliverable weapons. The requirements of second-strike
deterrence have been widely and wildly exaggerated.

The weak versus the strong

Nuclear weapons do not make lesser states into great powers. Nuclear weapons do
enable the weak to counter some of the measures that the strong may wish to take
against them.

Americans believe, rightly, that the possession of nuclear weapons has conferred
benefits on us. Our weapons place limits on what other countries can do. In similar
fashion, the possession of nuclear weapons by other countries places limits on our
freedom of action. It lessens our power. William C. Foster saw the point when he was
director of the Arms Control and Disarmament Agency. "When we consider the cost
to us of trying to stop the spread of nuclear weapons," he warned three decades ago,
"we should not lose sight of the fact that widespread nuclear proliferation would mean
a substantial erosion of the margin of power which our great wealth and industrial
base have long given us relative to much of the rest of the world."[15]

A strong country invading a weak nuclear country has to worry that it may use a
weapon or two against the invader's massed troops or retaliate against one of its cities
or a city of an ally. Thus in 1991, the United States could have put pressure on a nuclear
Iraq and exacted a price for its invasion of Kuwait, but it would have been deterred

[12]Kenneth N. Waltz, "Nuclear Myths and Political Realities," *American Political Science Review*, 84:3 (September 1990).

[13]Robert McNamara, "Reducing the Risk of Nuclear War: Is Star Wars the Answer?" *Millennium: Journal of International Studies* 15:2 (Summer 1986), p. 137.

[14]Cited in Robert L. Gallucci, "Limiting U.S. Policy Options to Prevent Nuclear Weapons Prolifera-
tion: The Relevance of Minimum Deterrence," Center for Technical Studies on Security, Energy and Arms Control, Lawrence Livermore National Laboratory, 28 February 1991.

[15]William C. Foster, Arms Control and Disarmament," *Foreign Affairs* Vol. 43 (July 1965), p. 591.

from leading a headlong invasion of the country. As Marc Dean Millot has said: "Small survivable arsenals of nuclear weapons in the hands of regional adversaries are likely to become an important obstacle to U.S. military operations in the post-cold war world."[16] The fourth reason for America's zeal in countering the spread of nuclear weapons is that, even in the hands of relatively weak states, they would cramp our style.

STABILITY

When he was Director of the CIA, James Woolsey said that he could "think of no example where the introduction of nuclear weapons into a region has enhanced that region's security or benefited the security interests of the United States."[17] But surely nuclear weapons helped to maintain stability during the Cold War and to preserve peace throughout the instability that came in its wake. Except for interventions by major powers in conflicts that for them are minor, peace has become the privilege of states having nuclear weapons, while wars are fought by those who lack them. Weak states cannot help noticing this. That is why states feeling threatened want their own nuclear weapons and why states that have them find it so hard to halt their spread.

At least some of the rulers of new and prospective nuclear states are thought to be ruthless, reckless, and war-prone. Ruthless, yes; war-prone, seldom; reckless, hardly. They have survived for many years, despite great internal and external dangers. They do not, as many seem to believe, have fixed images of the world and unbending aims within it. Instead they have to adjust constantly to a shifting configuration of forces around them. Our images of leaders of Third World states vary remarkably little, yet their agility is remarkable. Are hardy survivors in the Third World likely to run the greatest of all risks by drawing the wrath of the world down on them through aggressive use of their nuclear weapons?

Aside from the quality of national regimes and the identity of rulers, the behavior of nations is strongly conditioned by the world outside. With conventional weapons, a status-quo country must ask itself how much power it must harness to its policy in order to dissuade an aggressive state from striking. In conventional worlds, countries willing to run high risks are hard to dissuade. The characteristics of governments and the temperments of leaders have to be carefully weighed. With nuclear weapons, any state will be deterred by another state's second-strike forces. One need not be preoccupied with the qualities of the state that is to be deterred or scrutinize its leaders.

---

[16]Marc Dean Millot, "Facing the Emerging Reality of Regional Nuclear Adversaries," *The Washington Quarterly* 17:3 (Summer 1994), p. 66.

[17]"Proliferation Threats of the 1990's," Hearing before the Committee on Governmental Affairs, U.S. Senate, 103rd Congress, 1st Session, February 24, 1993 (Washington DC: GPO, 1993), p. 134.

America has long associated democracy with peace and authoritarianism with war, overlooking that weak authoritarian rulers often avoid war for fear of upsetting the balance of internal and external forces on which their power depends. Neither Italy nor Germany was able to persuade Franco's Spain to enter World War II. External pressures affect state behavior with a force that varies with conditions. Of all of the possible external forces, what could affect state behavior more strongly than nuclear weapons? Nobody but an idiot can fail to comprehend their destructive force. How can leaders miscalculate? For a country to strike first without certainty of success most of those who control a nation's nuclear weapons would have to go mad at the same time. Nuclear reality transcends political rhetoric. Did the Soviet Union's big words or our own prattling about nuclear war-fighting ever mean anything? Political, military, and academic hard-liners imagined conditions under which we would or should be willing to use nuclear weapons. None was of relevance. Nuclear weapons dominate strategy. Nothing can be done with them other than to use them for deterrence. The United States and the Soviet Union were both reluctant to accept the fact of deterrence. Weaker states find it easier to substitute deterrence for war-fighting, precisely because they are weak. The thought that a small number of nuclear weapons may tempt or enable weak countries to launch wars of conquest is the product of feverish imaginations.

States do what they can, to paraphrase Thucydides, and they suffer what they must. Nuclear weapons do not increase what states can do offensively; they do greatly increase what they may suffer should their actions prompt retaliation by others. Thus, far from contributing to instability in South Asia, Pakistan's nuclear military capability, along with India's, limits the provocative acts of both countries and provides a sense of security to them. Recalling Pakistan's recent history of military rule and the initiation of war, some have expected the opposite. For a more reasoned view we might listen to two of the participants. When asked recently why nuclear weapons are so popular in Pakistan, Prime Minister Benazir Bhutto answered: "It's our history. A history of three wars with a larger neighbor. India is five times larger than we are. Their military strength is five times larger. In 1971, our country was disintegrated. So the security issue for Pakistan is an issue of survival."[18] From the other side, Shankar Bajpai, former Indian Ambassador to Pakistan, China, and the United States, has said that "Pakistan's quest for a nuclear capability stems from its fear of its larger neighbor, removing that fear should open up immense possibilities"—possibilities for a less worried and more relaxed life.[19] Exactly.

[18]Claudia Dreyfus, "Benazir Bhutto," *New York Times Magazine*, 15 May 1994, p. 39.
[19]Shankar Bajpai, "Nuclear Exchange," *Far Eastern Economic Review*. 24 June 1993, p. 24.

CONCLUSION

Nuclear weapons continue to spread ever so slowly, and the world seems to fare better as they do so. Yet the rapid spread—that is, the proliferation—of nuclear weapons remains a frightening prospect; the mind boggles at the thought of all or most countries having them. Whatever the policies of the United States and other countries may be, that prospect is hardly even a distant one. Many more countries can make nuclear weapons than do. One can believe that American opposition to nuclear arming stays the deluge only by overlooking the complications of international life. Any state has to examine many conditions before deciding whether or not to develop nuclear weapons. Our opposition is only one factor and is not likely to dissuade a determined state from seeking the weapons. Many states feel fairly secure living with their neighbors. Why should they want nuclear weapons? The answer usually given is "for prestige." Yet it is hard to imagine a country entering the difficult and risky nuclear military business mainly for the sake of buoying its *amour propre* and gaining the attention that doing so may bring.

We can play King Canute if we wish to, but like him, we will be unable to hold the (nuclear) tides at bay.[20] What are the possible courses of action? I concentrate on six main ones:

1. Some fear that weakening opposition to the spread of nuclear weapons will lead numerous states to obtain them because it may seem that "everyone is doing it."[21] Why should we think that if we relax, numerous states will begin to make nuclear weapons? Both the United States and the Soviet Union were relaxed in the past, and those effects did not follow. The Soviet Union initially supported China's nuclear program. The United States helped both Britain and France to produce nuclear weapons. More recently, the United States Department of Energy gave technical assistance to Japan in the producing of weapons-grade plutonium.[22] Moreover, America's treatment of states that break into the nuclear military business

---

[20]Editor's note: During the early 11th century., Canute the Great ruled Denmark, Norway, and, after defeating Edmund Ironside at the Battle of Assandun, England. A 12th century historian, wishing to demonstrate the frailty of even the most comprehensive of earthly powers compared to the might of God, invented the legendary tale of Canute's unsuccessfully ordering the tide to recede to make way for his battle plans. Hence the aphorism, coined by William Shakespeare, "time and tide wait for no man."

[21]Joseph Nye, "Maintaining a Non-Proliferation Regime," *International Organization* Vol. 35 (Winter 1981).

[22]Arjun Makhijani, "What Non-Nuclear Japan Is Not Telling the World," *Outlook, Washington Post*, 10 April 1995, p. C2.

varies with our general attitude toward them. By 1968, the CIA had informed President Johnson of the existence of Israeli nuclear weapons, and in July of 1970 Richard Helms, director of the CIA, gave this information to the Senate Foreign Relations Committee. These and later disclosures were not followed by censure of Israel or by reductions of economic assistance.[23] In September of 1980, the executive branch, against the will of the House of Representatives but with the approval of the Senate, continued to do nuclear business with India despite its explosion of a nuclear device and despite its unwillingness to sign the NPT. North Korea's weapons program aroused our strong opposition while Pakistan's caused less excitement. On the nuclear question as on others, treating differently placed countries differently is appropriate. Doing so has not opened the floodgates and prompted the wild spread of nuclear weapons in the past, nor is it likely to do so in the future.

2. Chapter VI of the NPT calls on the original five nuclear powers to set a good example by reducing their nuclear arms and promising ultimately to eliminate them. Substantial reductions have been agreed upon in the past decade and more are easily possible in the arsenals of the United States and Russia without their reaching levels that would make the maintenance of second-strike forces difficult. Reductions may please non-nuclear adherents to the treaty, but one wonders whether many of them believe that nuclear states will reduce their arsenals below the level required to maintain deterrent forces. States paring their arsenals may claim to be on the road to nuclear disarmament, yet the elimination of nuclear weapons is well understood to be an impossible goal so long as anyone remembers how to make them or can figure out how to hide small numbers of them.

3. Various proposals have called upon nuclear states to help any non-nuclear state threatened by the nuclear weapons of others.[24] This is sometimes called "leveling the playing field." But for countries like Pakistan, it is the bumps in the conventional field that are hard to level. Promises of help against nuclear threats are easily offered since they are largely irrelevant. With the playing field unlevel, conventional attack is the fear.

4. The effective way to persuade states to forego nuclear weapons would seem to be to guarantee their security against conventional as well as nuclear threats. Few states, however, are able to guarantee other states' security or wish to do so. And guarantees, even if issued by the most powerful states, will not be found sufficiently reliable by states fearing for their security. Even at the height of the Cold

---

[23]Feldman, *Israeli Nuclear Deterrence*, ch. 5.

[24]Barbara Crossette, "UN Council Seeks Support to Renew Pact Curbing Spread of Nuclear Arms," *New York Times* 6 April 1995, p. A7.

War, America's promise to extend deterrence over Western Europe was thought to be of doubtful credibility. Since guarantees given by others can never be fully credited, each country is left to provide for its security as best it can. How then can one country tell another what measures to take for its own defense?

5. If some states want nuclear weapons to use in attacking other states, defenses against nuclear weapons appear to be an obvious remedy. Because of the great damage that nuclear warheads can do, however, a near perfect defense is at once required and unachievable. For this reason, those who advocate defense resort to the nugatory argument that it would complicate the enemy's attack and make it more expensive. No doubt, but improved defenses would, as ever, spur further offensive efforts and fuel arms races. If defenses did magically become absolutely reliable, they would simply make the world safe for conventional war. Perfect defenses would recreate the problem that nuclear weapons can solve. The notion of defending against absolute weapons is attractive mainly to the technologically mesmerized and the strategically naive.[25]

6. The one definitive way to stop the spread of nuclear weapons would seem to be to launch strikes to destroy other states' incipient nuclear-weapons programs or to fight preventive wars—now termed "wars of non-proliferation"—against them.[26] In truth, preventive wars promise only limited success at considerable cost. The trouble with preventive strikes is that one has to strike so hard that the country struck will be unable to resume its nuclear career for years to come. The trouble with preventive wars is that one has to fight them, win them, and impose effective controls over the indefinite future. The noblest wars may be those fought for the sake of establishing and maintaining peace, but I for one hope we won't take the lead in fighting them.

I end with two thoughts. Nuclear weapons continue to spread slowly, while conventional weapons proliferate and become ever more destructive. Nuclear weapons are relatively cheap, and they work against the fighting of major wars. For some countries, the alternative to nuclear weapons is to run ever-more expensive conventional arms races, with increased risk of fighting highly destructive wars. Not all choices are happy ones, and for some counties nuclear weapons may be the best choice available.

Nuclear weapons will long be with us. We should keep in perspective both the benefits they bring and the dangers they pose. States with huge nuclear arsenals may

---

[25]For a brief treatment of nuclear defense, see Kenneth N. Waltz, "Nuclear Myths and Political Realities," *American Political Science Review* 84:3 (September 1990), pp. 741–3.

[26]The term is used by Michael Mandelbaum, "Lessons of the Next Nuclear War," *Foreign Affairs* 74:2 (March/April 1995), pp. 35–6.

accidentally fire warheads in large numbers. One estimate has it that if Soviet missiles had accidentally gone off, 300 warheads might have hit the United States and that our missiles were set to shoot as many as 500 warheads in return. The accidents of small nuclear countries would be serious enough, but only large nuclear countries can do horrendous damage to themselves and the world. As ever in international politics, the biggest dangers come from the biggest powers; the smallest from the smallest. We should be more fearful of old nuclear countries and less fearful of recent and prospective ones. Efforts should concentrate more on making large arsenals safe and less on keeping weak states from obtaining the small number of warheads they may understandably believe they need for security.

POSSIBLE AND IMPOSSIBLE SOLUTIONS TO ETHNIC CIVIL WARS

Chaim Kaufmann

. . .

   This paper offers a theory of how ethnic wars end, and proposes an intervention strategy based on it.[1] The theory rests on two insights: First, in ethnic wars both hypernationalist mobilization rhetoric and real atrocities harden ethnic identities to

Chaim Kaufmann, "Possible and Impossible Solutions to Ethnic Civil Wars", *International Security*, 20:4 (Spring 1996), pp. 136–175. © 1996 by the President and Fellows of Harvard College and the Massachusetts Institute of Technology. Reprinted by permission of The MIT Press.

[1] Ethnic wars involve organized large-scale violence, whether by regular forces (Turkish or Iraqi operations against the Kurds) or highly mobilized civilian populations (the *interahamwe* in Rwanda or the Palestinian *intifada*). A frequent aspect is "ethnic cleansing": efforts by members of one ethnic group to eliminate the population of another from a certain area by means such as discrimination, expropriation, terror, expulsion, and massacre. For proposals on managing ethnic rivalries involving lower levels of ethnic mobilization and violence, see Stephen Van Evera, "Managing the Eastern Crisis: Preventing War in the Former Soviet Empire," *Security Studies*, Vol. 1, No. 3 (Spring 1992), pp. 361–382; Ted Hopf, "Managing Soviet Disintegration: A Demand for Behavioral Regimes," *International Security*, Vol. 17, No. 1 (Summer 1992), pp. 44–75.

the point that cross-ethnic political appeals are unlikely to be made and even less likely to be heard. Second, intermingled population settlement patterns create real security dilemmas that intensify violence, motivate ethnic "cleansing," and prevent de-escalation unless the groups are separated. As a result, restoring civil politics in multi-ethnic states shattered by war is impossible because the war itself destroys the possibilities for ethnic cooperation.

Stable resolutions of ethnic civil wars are possible, but only when the opposing groups are demographically separated into defensible enclaves. Separation reduces both incentives and opportunity for further combat, and largely eliminates both reasons and chances for ethnic cleansing of civilians. While ethnic fighting can be stopped by other means, such as peace enforcement by international forces or by a conquering empire, such peaces last only as long as the enforcers remain.

This means that to save lives threatened by genocide, the international community must abandon attempts to restore war-torn multi-ethnic states. Instead, it must facilitate and protect population movements to create true national homelands. Sovereignty is secondary: defensible ethnic enclaves reduce violence with or without independent sovereignty, while partition without separation does nothing to stop mass killing.[2] Once massacres have taken place, ethnic cleansing will occur. The alternative is to let the *interahamwe* and the Chetniks "cleanse" their enemies in their own way. . . .

How Ethnic Civil Wars End

Civil wars are not all alike.[3] Ethnic conflicts are disputes between communities which see themselves as having distinct heritages, over the power relationship between the communities, while ideological civil wars are contests between factions within the

---

[2]Although ethnic partitions have often been justified on grounds of self-determination, the argument for separation here is based purely on humanitarian grounds. The first to argue publicly for partition as a humanitarian solution was John J. Mearsheimer, "Shrink Bosnia to Save It," *New York Times*, March 31, 1993.

[3]To avoid discounting fundamentally similar conflicts because of differences in international legal status, "civil" wars are defined here as those among "geographically contiguous people concerned about possibly having to live with one another in the same political unit after the conflict." Roy Licklider, "How Civil Wars End," in Licklider, ed., *Stopping the Killing* (New York: New York University Press, 1993), p. 9. Thus the Abkhazian rebellion in Georgia and the war between Armenia and Azerbaijan are both properly considered ethnic civil wars.

same community over how that community should be governed.[4] The key difference is the flexibility of individual loyalties, which are quite fluid in ideological conflicts, but almost completely rigid in ethnic wars.

The possible and impossible solutions to ethnic civil wars follow from this fact. War hardens ethnic identities to the point that cross-ethnic political appeals become futile, which means that victory can be assured only by physical control over the territory in dispute. Ethnic wars also generate intense security dilemmas, both because the escalation of each side's mobilization rhetoric presents a real threat to the other, and even more because intermingled population settlement patterns create defensive vulnerabilities and offensive opportunities.

Once this occurs, the war cannot end until the security dilemma is reduced by physical separation of the rival groups. Solutions that aim at restoring multi-ethnic civil politics and at avoiding population transfers—such as power-sharing, state re-building, or identity reconstruction—cannot work because they do nothing to dampen the security dilemma, and because ethnic fears and hatreds hardened by war are extremely resistant to change.

The result is that ethnic wars can end in only three ways: with complete victory of one side; by temporary suppression of the conflict by third party military occupation; or by self-governance of separate communities. The record of the ethnic wars of the last half century bears this out.

THE DYNAMICS OF ETHNIC WAR

It is useful to compare characteristics of ethnic conflicts with those of ideological conflicts. The latter are competitions between the government and the rebels for the loyalties of the people. The critical features of these conflicts are that ideological loyalties are changeable and difficult to assess, and the same population serves as the shared mobilization base for both sides. As a result, winning the "hearts and minds" of the population is both possible and necessary for victory. The most important instruments are political, economic, and social reforms that redress popular grievances such as poverty, inequality, corruption, and physical insecurity. Control of access to population is also important, both to allow recruitment and implementation

---

[4]An ethnic group (or nation) is commonly defined as a body of individuals who purportedly share cultural or racial characteristics, especially common ancestry or territorial origin, which distinguish them from members of other groups. See Max Weber (Guenther Roth, and Claus Wittich, eds.), *Economy and Society: An Outline of Interpretive Sociology*, Vol. 1 (Berkeley, Calif.: University of California Press, 1968), pp. 389, 395; Anthony D. Smith, *National Identity* (Reno: University of Nevada Press, 1991), pp. 14, 21. . . .

of reform promises, and to block the enemy from these tasks.[5] Population control, however, cannot be guaranteed solely by physical control over territory, but depends on careful intelligence, persuasion, and coercion. Purely military successes are often indecisive as long as the enemy's base of political support is undamaged.[6]

Ethnic wars, however, have nearly the opposite properties. Individual loyalties are both rigid and transparent, while each side's mobilization base is limited to members of its own group in friendly-controlled territory. The result is that ethnic conflicts are primarily military struggles in which victory depends on physical control over the disputed territory, not on appeals to members of the other group.

Identity in Ethnic Wars.   Competition to sway individual loyalties does not play an important role in ethnic civil wars, because ethnic identities are fixed by birth. While not everyone may be mobilized as an active fighter for his or her own group, hardly anyone ever fights for the opposing ethnic group.

Different identity categories imply their own membership rules. Ideological identity is relatively soft, as it is a matter of individual belief, or sometimes of political behavior. Religious identities are harder, because while they also depend on belief, change generally requires formal acceptance by the new faith, which may be denied. Ethnic identities are hardest, since they depend on language, culture, and religion, which are hard to change, as well as parentage, which no one can change. . . .

Once the conflict reaches the level of large-scale violence, tales of atrocities—true or invented—perpetuated or planned against members of the group by the ethnic enemy provide hard-liners with an unanswerable argument. In March 1992 a Serb woman in foća in Eastern Bosnia was convinced that "there were lists of Serbs who were marked for death. My two sons were down on the list to be slaughtered like pigs. I was listed under rape." The fact that neither she nor other townspeople had seen any such lists did not prevent them from believing such tales without question.[7] The Croatian Ustasha in World War II went further, terrorizing Serbs in order to provoke a backlash that could then be used to mobilize Croats for defense against Serb retaliation.[8]

In this environment, cross-ethnic appeals are not likely to attract members of the other group. The Yugoslav Partisans in World War II are often credited with

---

[5]"Guerrillas are like fish, and the people are the water they swim in." Mao Zedong, quoted in Shafer, *Deadly Paradigms*, p. 21.

[6]"Winning a military war in Vietnam will be a hollow victory if the country remains politically and economically unstable, for it is under these conditions that a 'defeated' Viet Cong will be able to regroup and begin anew a 'war of national liberation'." Dow, *Nation Building*, p. viii.

[7]Reported by Andrej Gustinčić of *Reuters*, cited in Misha Glenny, *The Fall of Yugoslavia* (New York: Penguin, 1992), p. 166. . . .

[8]Aleksa Djilas, *The Contested Country* (Cambridge, Mass.: Harvard University Press, 1991), p. 122.

transcending the ethnic conflict between the Croatian Ustasha and the Serbian Chetniks with an anti-German, pan-Yugoslav program. In fact it did not work. Tito was a Croat, but Partisan officers as well as the rank and file were virtually all Serbs and Montenegrins.[9] Only in 1944, when German withdrawal made Partisan victory certain, did Croats begin to join the Partisans in numbers, not because they preferred a multi-ethnic Yugoslavia to a Greater Croatia, but because they preferred a multi-ethnic Yugoslavia to a Yugoslavia cleansed of Croatians. . . .

Ethnic war also shrinks scope for individual identity choice.[10] Even those who put little value on their ethnic identity are pressed towards ethnic mobilization for two reasons. First, extremists within each community are likely to impose sanctions on those who do not contribute to the cause. In 1992 the leader of the Croatian Democratic Union in Bosnia was dismissed on the ground that he "was too much Bosnian, too little Croat."[11] Conciliation is easy to denounce as dangerous to group security or as actually traitorous. Such arguments drove nationalist extremists to overthrow President Makarios of Cyprus in 1974, to assassinate Mahatma Gandhi in 1948, to massacre nearly the whole government of Rwanda in 1994, and to kill Yitzhak Rabin in 1995.[12]

Second and more important, identity is often imposed by the opposing group, specifically by its most murderous members. Assimilation or political passivity did no good for German Jews, Rwandan Tutsis, or Azerbaijanis in Nagorno-Karabakh. A Bosnian Muslim schoolteacher recently lamented:

[9]Partisan (as well as Chetnik) leaders were recruited mainly from among pre-war Army officers. Throughout most of 1942, the Partisans fielded two Montenegrin and four Serbian battalions, leavened with just a few fighters of other nationalities. A. Pavelic´, "How Many Non-Serbian Generals in 1941?" *East European Quarterly*, Vol. 16, No. 4 (January 1983), pp. 447–452; Anton Bebler, "Political Pluralism and the Yugoslav Professional Military," in Jim Seroka and Vukašin Petrović, eds., *The Tragedy of Yugoslavia: The Failure of Democratic Transformation* (Armonk, N.Y.: M.E. Sharpe, 1992), pp. 105–40, 106.

[10]The proportion of Yugoslav residents identifying themselves not by nationality but as "Yugoslavs" rose from 1.7 percent in the 1961 census to 5.4 percent in 1981, but fell to 3.0 percent in 1991. Ruža Petrović, "The National Structure of the Yugoslav Population," *Yugoslavia Survey*, Vol. 14, No. 1 (1973), pp. 1–22, 12; Petrović, "The National Composition of the Population," *Yugoslavia Survey*, Vol. 24, No. 3 (1983), pp. 21–34, 22; Petrović, "The National Composition of Yugoslavia's Population," *Yugoslavia Survey*, Vol. 33, No. 1 (1992), pp. 3–24, 12.

[11]*Balkan War Report*, February/March 1993, p. 14, quoted in Robert M. Hayden, "The Partition of Bosnia and Hercegovina, 1990–1993," *RFE/RL Research Reports*, Vol. 2, No. 22 (May 29, 1993), pp. 2–3. See also Blaine Harden, "In Bosnia 'Disloyal' Serbs Share Plight of Opposition," *Washington Post*, August 24, 1992. Hutu leaders in refugee camps in Zaire have murdered people suspected of wanting to return to Rwanda. "Telling Tales," *Economist*, August 13, 1994, p. 39.

[12]See Fred C. Iklé, *Every War Must End* (New York: Columbia University Press, 1981), on the problems of soft-liners in international wars.

> We never, until the war, thought of ourselves as Muslims. We were Yugoslavs.
> But when we began to be murdered, because we are Muslims, thing changed. The
> definition of who we are today has been determined by our killers.[13]

Choice contracts further the longer the conflict continues. Multi-ethnic towns as yet untouched by war are swamped by radicalized refugees, undermining moderate leaders who preach tolerance.[14] For example, while a portion of the pre-war Serb population remained in Bosnian government–controlled Sarajevo when the fighting started, their numbers have declined as the government has taken on a more narrowly Muslim religious character over years of war, and pressure on Serbs has increased. Where 80,000 remained in July 1993, only 30,000 were left in August 1995.[15] The Tutsi Rwandan Patriotic Front (RPF) showed remarkable restraint during the 1994 civil war, but since then the RPF has imprisoned tens of thousands of genocide suspects in appalling conditions, failed to prevent massacres of thousands of Hutu civilians in several incidents, and allowed Tutsi squatters to seize the property of many absent Hutus.[16] . . .

Identifying Loyalties.   A consequence of the hardness of ethnic identities is that in ethnic wars assessing individual loyalties is much easier than in ideological conflicts. Even if some members of both groups remain unmobilized, as long as virtually none actively support the other group, each side can treat all co-ethnics as friends without risk of coddling an enemy agent and can treat all members of the other group as enemies without risk of losing a recruit.

Although it often requires effort, each side can almost always identify members of its own and the other group in any territory it controls. Ethnicity can be identified by outward appearance, public or private records, and local social knowledge. In societies where ethnicity is important, it is often officially recorded in personal identity documents or in censuses. In 1994 Rwandan death squads used neighborhood target lists prepared in advance, as well as road-blocks that checked identity cards.[17] In 1983 riots in Sri Lanka, Sinhalese mobs went through mixed

---

[13]Mikica Babić, quoted in Chris Hedges, "War Turns Sarajevo Away from Europe," *New York Times*, July 28, 1995.

[14]Susan L. Woodward, *Balkan Tragedy: Chaos and Dissolution after the Cold War* (Washington, D.C.: Brookings, 1995), p. 363.

[15]Jonathan S. Landay, "Loyal Serbs and Croats in Sarajevo See Woe in Partition of Bosnia," *Christian Science Monitor*, July 30, 1993; Tracy Wilkinson, "Sarajevo's Serbs Face a Dual Hostility," *Los Angeles Times*, July 10, 1995; "Bosnia: The Coffee-cup State," *Economist*, August 26, 1995, p. 43.

[16]*Rwanda Human Rights Practices, 1994* (Washington, D.C.: U.S. Department of State, March 1995); Donatella Lorch, "As Many as 2,000 are Reported Dead in Rwanda," *New York Times*, April 24, 1995.

[17]Destexche, "Third Genocide," p. 8.

neighborhoods selecting Tamil dwellings for destruction with the help of Buddhist monks carrying electoral lists.[18] While it might not have been possible to predict the Yugoslav civil war thirty years in advance, one could have identified the members of each of the warring groups from the 1961 census, which identified the nationality of all but 1.8 percent of the population.[19] . . .

Finally, in unprepared encounters ethnicity can often be gauged by outward appearance: Tutsis are generally tall and thin, while Hutus are relatively short and stocky; Russians are generally fairer than Kazakhs.[20] When physiognomy is ambiguous, other signs such as language or accent, surname, dress, posture, ritual mutilation, diet, habits, occupation, region or neighborhood within urban areas, or certain possessions may give clues. Residents of Zagreb, for example, are marked as Serbs by certain names, attendance at an Orthodox church, or possession of books printed in Cyrillic.[21]

Perhaps the strongest evidence of intelligence reliability in ethnic conflicts is that—in dramatic contrast to ideological insurgencies—history records almost no instances of mistaken "cleansing" of co-ethnics.

The Decisiveness of Territory. Another consequence of the hardness of ethnic identities is that population control depends wholly on territorial control. Since each side can recruit only from its own community and only in friendly-controlled territory, incentives to seize areas populated by co-ethnics are strong, as is the pressure to cleanse friendly-controlled territory of enemy ethnics by relocation to *de facto* concentration camps, expulsion, or massacre.[22]

Because of the decisiveness of territorial control, military strategy in ethnic wars is very different than in ideological conflicts. Unlike ideological insurgents, who often evade rather than risk battle, or a counter-insurgent government, which might forbear

[18]Lakshmanan Sabaratnam, "The Boundaries of the State and the State of Ethnic Boundaries: Sinhala-Tamil Relations in Sri Lankan History," *Ethnic and Racial Studies*, Vol. 10, No. 3 (July 1987), pp. 291–316, 294.

[19]Petrović, "National Structure of the Yugoslav Population," p. 12.

[20]Despite claims that the Hutu-Tutsi ethnic division was invented by the Belgians, 1969 census data showed significant physical differences: Tutsi males averaged 5 feet 9 inches and 126 pounds, Hutus 5 feet 5 inches and 131 pounds. Richard F. Nyrop, et al., *Rwanda: A Country Study, 1985* (Washington, D.C.: Department of the Army, 1985), pp. 46–47, 63.

[21]Kit Roane, "Serbs in Croatia Live in World of Hate, Fear," *San Diego Union-Tribune*, August 19, 1995.

[22]Beginning in 1985, the Iraqi government destroyed all rural villages in Kurdistan, as well as animals and orchards, concentrating the Kurdish population in "victory cities" where they could be watched and kept dependent on the government for food. The Turkish government is currently doing the same, while the Burmese government has pursued this strategy against ethnic rebels at least since 1968. U.S. Senate Committee on Foreign Relations, *Civil War in Iraq* (Washington, D.C.: U.S. Government Printing Office [GPO], 1991), pp. 7–9; Michael Fredholm, *Burma: Ethnicity and Insurgency* (Westport, Conn.: Praeger, 1993), pp. 90–92.

to attack rather than risk bombarding civilians, ethnic combatants must fight for every piece of land. By contrast, combatants in ethnic wars are much less free to decline unfavorable battles because they cannot afford to abandon any settlement to an enemy who is likely to "cleanse" it by massacre, expulsion, destruction of homes, and possibly colonization. By the time a town can be retaken, its value will have been lost.[23]

In ethnic civil wars, military operations are decisive. Attrition matters because the side's mobilization pools are separate and can be depleted. Most important, since each side's mobilization base is limited to members of its own community in friendly-controlled territory, conquering the enemy's population centers reduces its mobilization base, while loss of friendly settlements reduces one's own. Military control of the entire territory at issue is tantamount to total victory.

SECURITY DILEMMAS IN ETHNIC WARS

The second problem that must be overcome by any remedy for severe ethnic conflict is the security dilemma. Regardless of the origins of ethnic strife, once violence (or abuse of state power by one group that controls it) reaches the point that ethnic communities cannot rely on the state to protect them, each community must mobilize to take responsibility for its own security.

Under conditions of anarchy, each group's mobilization constitutes a real threat to the security of others for two reasons. First, the nationalist rhetoric that accompanies mobilization often seems to and often does indicate offensive intent. Under these conditions, group identity itself can be seen by other groups as a threat to their safety.[24]

Second, military capability acquired for defense can usually also be used for offense. Further, offense often has an advantage over defense in inter-community conflict, especially when settlement patterns are inter-mingled, because isolated pockets are harder to hold than to take.

The reality of the mutual security threats means that solutions to ethnic conflicts must do more than undo the causes; until or unless the security dilemma can be reduced or eliminated, neither side can afford to demobilize.

Demography and Security Dilemmas. The severity of ethnic security dilemmas is greatest when demography is most intermixed, weakest when community settlements

[23]Serbs in Bosnia have destroyed and desecrated mosques, and raped tens of thousands of Muslim women, in part to eradicate the desire of any displaced Muslim to return to a former home. Gutman, *Witness to Genocide*, pp. 68, 70.

[24]Barry R. Posen, "The Security Dilemma and Ethnic Conflict," in Brown, *Ethnic Conflict and International Security*, pp. 103–124.

are most separate.[25] The more mixed the opposing groups, the stronger the offense in relation to the defense; the more separated they are, the stronger the defense in relation to offense. When settlement patterns are extremely mixed, both sides are vulnerable to attack not only by organized military forces but also by local militias or gangs from adjacent towns or neighborhoods. Since well-defined fronts are impossible, there is no effective means of defense against such raids. Accordingly, each side has a strong incentive—at both national and local levels—to kill or drive out enemy populations before the enemy does the same to it, as well as to create homogeneous enclaves more practical to defend.[26]

Better, but still bad, are well-defined enclaves with islands of one or both sides' populations behind the other's front. Each side then has an incentive to attack to rescue its surrounded co-ethnics before they are destroyed by the enemy, as well as incentives to wipe out enemy islands behind its own lines, both to pre-empt rescue attempts and to eliminate possible bases for fifth columnists or guerrillas.[27]

The safest pattern is a well-defined demographic front that separates nearly homogeneous regions. Such a front can be defended by organized military forces, so populations are not at risk unless defenses are breached. At the same time the strongest motive for attack disappears, since there are few or no endangered co-ethnics behind enemy lines.

Further, offensive and defensive mobilization measures are more distinguishable when populations are separated than when they are mixed. Although hypernationalist political rhetoric, as well as conventional military forces, have both offensive and defensive uses regardless of population settlement patterns, some other forms of ethnic mobilization do not. Local militias and ethnically based local self-governing authorities have both offensive and defensive capabilities when populations are mixed: ethnic militias can become death squads, while local governments dominated by one group can disenfranchise minorities. When populations are separated, however, such local organizations have defensive value only.

War and Ethnic Unmixing. Because of the security dilemma, ethnic war causes ethnic unmixing. The war between Greece and Turkey, the partition of India, the 1948–49 Arab-Israeli war, and the recent war between Armenia and Azerbaijan were all followed by emigration or expulsion of most of the minority populations on each

[25]Ibid., pp. 108–110.

[26]Stephen Van Evera, "Hypotheses on Nationalism," *International Security*, Vol. 18, No. 4 (Spring 1994), pp. 5–39.

[27]Although censuses from 1891 on show Greek and Turkish Cypriots gradually segregating themselves by village, violence between these still-intermingled settlements grew from 1955 onward. Tozun Bahcheli, *Greek-Turkish Relations since 1955* (Boulder, Colo.: Westview, 1990), p. 21.

side. More than one million Ibo left northern Nigeria during the Nigerian Civil
War. Following 1983 pogroms, three-fourths of the Tamil population of Colombo
fled to the predominantly Tamil north and east of the island. By the end of 1994,
only about 70,000 non-Serbs remained in Serb-controlled areas of Bosnia, with less
than 40,000 Serbs still in Muslim-and Croat-controlled regions. Of 600,000 Serbs in
pre-war Croatia, probably no more than 100,000 remain outside of Serb-controlled
eastern Slavonia.[28] . . .

Ethnic Separation and Peace.   Once ethnic groups are mobilized for war, the war
cannot end until the populations are separated into defensible, mostly homogeneous
regions. Even if an international force or an imperial conqueror were to impose peace,
the conflict would resume as soon as it left. Even if a national government were
somehow re-created despite mutual suspicions, neither group could safely entrust its
security to it. Continuing mutual threat also ensures perpetuation of hypernationalist
propaganda, both for mobilization and because the plausibility of the threat posed by
the enemy gives radical nationalists an unanswerable advantage over moderates in
intra-group debates.

      Ethnic separation does not guarantee peace, but it allows it. Once populations are
separated, both cleansing and rescue imperatives disappear; war is no longer manda-
tory. At the same time, any attempt to seize more territory requires a major conventional military offensive. Thus the conflict changes from one of mutual pre-emptive
ethnic cleansing to something approaching conventional interstate war in which normal deterrence dynamics apply. Mutual deterrence does not guarantee that there will
be no further violence, but it reduces the probability of outbreaks, as well as the likely
aims and intensity of those that do occur.

      There have been no wars among Bulgaria, Greece, and Turkey since their popu-
lation exchanges of the 1920s. Ethnic violence on Cyprus, which reached crisis on
several occasions between 1960 and 1974, has been zero since the partition and population exchange which followed Turkish invasion. The Armenian-Azeri ethnic conflict, sparked by independence demands of the mostly Armenian Nagorno-Karabakh
Autonomous Oblast, escalated to full-scale war by 1992. Armenian conquest of all of
Karabakh together with the land which formerly separated it from Armenia proper,
along with displacement of nearly all members of each group from enemy-controlled
territories, created a defensible separation with no minorities to fight over, leading to
a cease-fire in April 1994.

---

[28]*Fact Sheet: Azerbaijan* (Washington, D.C.: U.S. Department of State, May 2, 1994); Nelson,
      Nigeria, p. 54; Ravindran Casinader, "Sri Lanka: Minority Tamils Face an Uncertain Future,"
      Inter Press Service, May 15, 1984; *Balkan War Report*, December 1994–January 1995, p. 5; *World
      Refugee Survey 1995* (Washington, D.C.: U.S. Committee for Refugees, pp. 128–130).

Theories of Ethnic Peace

Those considering humanitarian intervention to end ethnic civil wars should set as their goal lasting safety, rather than perfect peace. Given the persistence of ethnic rivalries, "safety" is best defined as freedom from threats of ethnic murder, expropriation, or expulsion for the overwhelming majority of civilians of all groups. Absence of formal peace, even occasional terrorism or border skirmishes, would not undermine this, provided that the great majority of civilians are not at risk. "Lasting" must mean that the situation remains stable indefinitely after the intervention forces leave. Truces of weeks, months, or even years do not qualify as lasting safety if ethnic cleansing eventually resumes with full force.

Alternatives to Separation

Besides demographic separation, the literature on possible solutions to ethnic conflicts contains four main alternatives: suppression, reconstruction of ethnic identities, power-sharing, and state-building.[29]

Suppression.   Many ethnic civil wars lead to the complete victory of one side and the forcible suppression of the other. This may reduce violence in some cases, but will never be an aim of outsiders considering humanitarian intervention.[30] Further, remission of violence may be only temporary, as the defeated group usually rebels again at any opportunity. Even the fact that certain conquerors, such as the English in Scotland or the Dutch in Friesland, eventually permitted genuine political assimilation after decades of suppression, does not recommend this as a remedy for endangered peoples today.

Reconstruction of Ethnic Identities.   The most ambitious program to end ethnic violence would be to reconstruct ethnic identities according to the "Constructivist Model" of nationalism.[31] Constructivists argue that individual and group identities are fluid, continually being made and re-made in social discourse. Further, these identities are

---

[29]Sammy Smooha and Theodore Harf, "The Diverse Modes of Conflict Resolution in Deeply Divided Societies," *International Journal of Comparative Sociology*, Vol. 33, Nos. 1–2 (January–April 1992), pp. 26–47, briefly surveys most alternatives. See also Charles William Maynes, "Containing Ethnic Conflict," *Foreign Policy*, No. 90 (Spring 1993), pp. 3–21.

[30]On this solution, see Ian Lustick, "Stability in Deeply Divided Societies: Consociationalism versus Control," *World Politics*, Vol. 31, No. 3 (April 1979), pp. 325–344.

[31]Pfaff, "Invitation to War"; Hopf, "Managing Soviet Disintegration"; Jack Snyder, "Nationalism and the Crisis of the Post-Soviet State," in Brown, *Ethnic Conflict and International Security*, pp. 79–102; Gidon Gottlieb, *Nation Against State* (New York: Council on Foreign Relations Press, 1993); Stephen Ryan, *Ethnic Conflict and International Relations*, 2d ed. (Aldershot, England: Dartmouth, 1995).

manipulable by political entrepreneurs. Violent ethnic conflicts are the result of pernicious group identities created by hypernationalist myth-making; many inter-group
conflicts are quite recent, as are the ethnic identities themselves.

The key is elite rivalries within communities, in which aggressive leaders use hypernationalist propaganda to gain and hold power. History does not matter; whether past
inter-community relations have in fact been peaceful or conflictual, leaders can redefine, reinterpret, and invent facts to suit their arguments, including alleged atrocities and
exaggerated or imagined threats. This process can feed on itself, as nationalists use the
self-fulfilling nature of their arguments both to escalate the conflict and to justify their
own power, so that intra-community politics becomes a competition in hypernationalist
extremism, and inter-community relations enter a descending spiral of violence.[32]

It follows that ethnic conflicts generated by the promotion of pernicious, exclusive
identities should be reversible by encouraging individuals and groups to adopt more
benign, inclusive identities. Leaders can choose to mobilize support on the basis of
broader identities that transcend the ethnic division, such as ideology, class, or civic
loyalty to the nation-state. If members of the opposing groups can be persuaded to
adopt a larger identity, ethnic antagonisms should fade away. In 1993 David Owen
explained why reconciliation in Bosnia was still possible: "I think it's realistic because
these people are of the same ethnic stock¼. Many people there still see themselves as
European and even now don't think of themselves as Muslim, Croat, or Serb."[33]

However, even if ethnic hostility can be "constructed," there are strong reasons
to believe that violent conflicts cannot be "reconstructed" back to ethnic harmony.
Identity reconstruction under conditions of intense conflict is probably impossible
because once ethnic groups are mobilized for war, they will have already produced,
and will continue reproducing, social institutions and discourses that reinforce their
group identity and shut out or shout down competing identities. . . .

Even if constructivists are right that the ancient past does not matter, recent history does. Intense violence creates personal experiences of fear, misery, and loss
which lock people into their group identity and their enemy relationship with the
other group. Elite as well as mass opinions are affected; more than 5,000 deaths in the
1946 Calcutta riots convinced many previously optimistic Hindu and Muslim leaders
that the groups could not live together. The Tutsi-controlled government of Burundi,
which had witnessed the partial genocide against Tutsis in Rwanda in 1962–63 and

[32]Brass, *Language, Religion, and Politics in North India;* Stanley J. Tambiah, *Buddhism Betrayed?
Religion, Politics, and Violence in Sri Lanka* (Chicago: University of Chicago Press, 1992); V.P.
Gagnon, Jr., "Ethnic Nationalism and International Conflict: The Case of Serbia," *International Security,* Vol. 19, No. 3 (Winter 1994/95), pp. 130–166; Woodward, *Balkan Tragedy,* pp. 225–236.
[33]"Interview with David Owen on the Balkans," *Foreign Affairs,* Vol. 72, No. 2 (Spring 1993), pp.
1–9, at 6–7.

survived Hutu-led coup attempts in 1965 and 1969, regarded the 1972 rebellion as another attempt at genocide, and responded by murdering between 100,000 and 200,000 Hutus. Fresh rounds of violence in 1988 and 1993–94 have reinforced the apocalyptic fears of both sides.[34]

Finally, literacy preserves atrocity memories and enhances their use for political mobilization. The result is that atrocity histories cannot be reconstructed; victims can sometimes be persuaded to accept exaggerated atrocity tales, but cannot be talked out of real ones. The result is that the bounds of debate are permanently altered; the leaders who used World War II Croatian atrocities to whip up Serbian nationalism in the 1980s were making use of a resource which, since then, remains always available in Serbian political discourse.[35]

If direct action to transform exclusive ethnic identities into inclusive civic ones is infeasible, outside powers or international institutions could enforce peace temporarily in the hope that reduced security threats would permit moderate leaders within each group to promote the reconstruction of more benign identities. While persuading ethnic war survivors to adopt an overarching identity may be impossible, a sufficiently prolonged period of guaranteed safety might allow moderate leaders to temper some of the most extreme hypernationalism back towards more benign, albeit still separate nationalisms.[36] However, this still leaves both sides vulnerable to later revival of hypernationalism by radical political entrepreneurs, especially after the peace-keepers have left and security threats once again appear more realistic.

Power-Sharing. The best-developed blueprint for civic peace in multiethnic states is power-sharing or "consociational democracy," proposed by Arend Lijphart. This approach assumes that ethnicity is somewhat manipulable, but not so freely as constructivists say.[37] Ethnic division, however, need not result in conflict; even if political mobilization is organized on ethnic lines, civil politics can be maintained if ethnic elites adhere to a power-sharing bargain that equitably protects all groups. The key components are: 1) joint exercise of governmental power; 2) proportional distribution of government funds and jobs; 3) autonomy on ethnic issues (which, if groups are concentrated territorially, may be achieved by regional federation); and 4) a minority

---

[34]Thomas P. Melady, *Burundi: The Tragic Years* (Maryknoll, N.Y.: Orbis Books, 1974), pp. 12, 46–49; René Lemarchand, "Burundi in Comparative Perspective: Dimensions of Ethnic Strife," in John McGarry and Brendan O'Leary, eds., *The Politics of Ethnic Conflict Regulation: Case Studies of Protracted Conflicts* (New York: Routledge, 1993), pp. 151–171.

[35]Gagnon, "Ethnic Nationalism and International Conflict," p. 151.

[36]Van Evera, "Managing the Eastern Crisis," proposes not to dissolve ethnic identities but to remove their xenophobic content by encouraging honest histories of inter-group relations.

[37]Lijphart, "Consociational Democracy," *World Politics*, Vol. 21, No. 2 (January 1969).

veto on issues of vital importance to each group.[38] Even if power-sharing can avert potential ethnic conflicts or dampen mild ones, our concern here is whether it can bring peace under the conditions of intense violence and extreme ethnic mobilization that are likely to motivate intervention.

The answer is no. The indispensable component of any power-sharing deal is a plausible minority veto, one which the strongest side will accept and which the weaker side believes that the stronger will respect. Traditions of stronger loyalties to the state than to parochial groups and histories of inter-ethnic compromise could provide reason for confidence, but in a civil war these will have been destroyed, if they were ever present, by the fighting itself and accompanying ethnic mobilization.[39]

Only a balance of power among the competing groups can provide a "hard" veto—one which the majority must respect. Regional concentration of populations could partially substitute for balanced power if the minority group can credibly threaten to secede if its veto is overridden. In any situation where humanitarian intervention might be considered, however, these conditions too are unlikely to be met. Interventions are likely to be aimed at saving a weak group that cannot defend itself; balanced sides do not need defense. Demographic separation is also unlikely, because if the populations were already separated, the ethnic cleansing and related atrocities which are most likely to provoke intervention would not be occurring.

The core reason why power-sharing cannot resolve ethnic civil wars is that it is inherently voluntaristic; it requires conscious decisions by elites to cooperate to avoid ethnic strife. Under conditions of hypernationalist mobilization and real security threats, group leaders are unlikely to be receptive to compromise, and even if they are, they cannot act without being discredited and replaced by harder-line rivals.

Could outside intervention make power-sharing work? One approach would be to adjust the balance of power between the warring sides to a "hurting stalemate" by arming the weaker side, blockading the stronger, or partially disarming the stronger by direct military intervention. When both sides realize that further fighting will bring them costs but no profit, they will negotiate an agreement.[40] This can balance power, although if populations are still intermingled it may actually worsen security

---

[38]Lijphart cites Belgium as an archetypical example, as well as Malaysia, Canada, India, and Nigeria. "Power-Sharing Approach," pp. 492, 494–96.

[39]Indeed, Lijphart argues that the best way to avoid partition is not to resist it. If minorities, such as the Quebecois, know that they can secede if a satisfactory power-sharing agreement cannot be worked out, this exerts a moderating influence on bargaining. Lijphart, "Power Sharing Approach," p. 494. In short, partition is unnecessary when it is known to be feasible.

[40]I. William Zartman, *Ripe for Resolution: Conflict and Intervention in Africa* (New Haven: Yale University Press, 1989).

dilemmas and increase violence—especially against civilians—as both sides eliminate the threats posed by pockets of the opposing group in their midst.

Further, once there has been heavy fighting, the sides are likely to distrust each other far too much to entrust any authority to a central government that could potentially be used against them. The 1955–72 Sudanese Civil War was ended, under conditions of stalemate and limited outside pressure, by such an autonomy agreement, but the central government massively violated the agreement, leading to resumption of the war in 1983 and its continuation to the present.[41]

The final approach is international imposition of power-sharing, which requires occupying the country to coerce both sides into accepting the agreement and to prevent inter-ethnic violence until it can be implemented. The interveners, however, cannot bind the stronger side to uphold the agreement after the intervention forces leave. Lijphart argues that power-sharing could have prevented the troubles in Northern Ireland if the British had not guaranteed the Protestants that they would not be forced into union with Ireland, freeing them of the need to cooperate.[42] However, the union threat would have had to be maintained permanently; otherwise the Protestant majority could tear up the agreement later. The British did impose power-sharing as a condition for Cypriot independence, but it broke down almost immediately. The Greek Cypriots, incensed by what they saw as Turkish Cypriot abuse of their minority veto, simply overrode the veto and operated the government in violation of the constitution.[43] . . .

State-Building.   Gerald Helman and Steven Ratner argue that states in which government breakdown, economic failure, and internal violence imperil their own citizens and threaten neighboring states can be rescued by international "conservatorship" to administer critical government functions until the country can govern itself following a free and fair election.[44] Ideally, the failed state would voluntarily delegate specified functions to an international executor, although in extreme cases involving massive violations of human rights or the prospect of large-scale warfare, the international community could act even without an invitation.[45]

---

[41]The decisive acts were the division of the southern regional government specified in the agreement into three separate states, the imposition of Islamic law on non-Muslims, and—the trigger for violent resistance—an attempt to reduce regional self-defense capabilities by transferring Army units composed of southerners to the north. Ann Mosely Lesch, "External Involvement in the Sudanese Civil War," in Smock, ed., *Making War and Waging Peace*, pp. 79–106.

[42]Lijphart, "Power-Sharing Approach," pp. 496–497.

[43]Richard A. Patrick, *Political Geography and the Cyprus Conflict, 1963–1971* (Waterloo, Iowa: University of Waterloo, 1976).

[44]Helman and Ratner, "Saving Failed States."

[45]Helman and Ratner, "Saving Failed States," p. 13. "If the forces in a country cannot agree upon the basic components of a political settlement—such as free and fair elections—and accept administration by an impartial outside authority pending elections, then the UN Charter should provide a mechanism for direct international trusteeship." Ibid., p. 16.

As with imposing power-sharing, this requires occupying the country (and may require conquering it), coercing all sides to accept a democratic constitution, enforcing peace until elections can be held, and administering the economy and the elections. Conservatorship thus requires even more finesse than enforced power-sharing, and probably more military risks.

Helman and Ratner cite the UN intervention in Cambodia in 1992–93 to create a safe environment for free elections as conservatorship's best success.[46] However, this was an ideological war over the governance of Cambodia, not an ethnic conflict over disempowering minorities or dismembering the country. By contrast, the growth of the U.S.-UN mission in Somalia from famine relief to state-rebuilding was a failure, and no one has been so bold as to propose conservatorship for Bosnia or Rwanda.

Even if conservatorship could rapidly, effectively, and cheaply stop an ethnic civil war, rebuild institutions, and ensure free elections, nothing would be gained unless the electoral outcome protected all parties' interests and safety; that is, power-sharing would still be necessary. Thus, in serious ethnic conflicts, conservatorship would only be a more expensive way to reach the same impasse.

Ethnic Separation

Regardless of the causes of a particular conflict, once communities are mobilized for violence, the reality of mutual security threats prevents both demobilization and deescalation of hypernationalist discourse. Thus, lasting peace requires removal of the security dilemma. The most effective and in many cases the only way to do this is to separate the ethnic groups. The more intense the violence, the more likely it is that separation will be the only option.

The exact threshold remains an open question. The deductive logic of the problem suggests that the critical variable is fear for survival. Once a majority of either group comes to believe that the killing of noncombatants of their own group is not considered a crime by the other, they cannot accept any governing arrangement that could be captured by the enemy group and used against them.

The most persuasive source of such beliefs is the massacre of civilians, but it is not clear that there is a specific number of incidents or total deaths beyond which ethnic reconciliation becomes impossible. More important is the extent to which wide sections of the attacking group seem to condone the killings, and can be observed doing so by members of target group. In this situation the attacks are likely to be seen as reflecting not just the bloodthirstiness of a particular regime or terrorist faction, but the preference of the opposing group as a whole, which means that no promise of non-repetition can be believed.

[46]Ibid., pp. 14–17.

Testing this proposition directly requires better data on the attitudes of threatened populations during and after ethnic wars than we now have. Next best is aggregate analysis of the patterns of ends of ethnic wars, supplemented by investigation of individual cases as deeply as the data permits. I make a start at such an analysis below.

How Ethnic Wars Have Ended

The most comprehensive data set of recent and current violent ethnic conflicts has been compiled by Ted Robert Gurr.[47] This data set includes 27 ethnic civil wars that have ended. Of these, twelve were ended by complete victory of one side, five by *de jure* or *de facto* partition, and two have been suppressed by military occupation by a third party. Only eight ethnic civil wars have been ended by an agreement that did not partition the country. (See Table 1.)

The data supports the argument that separation of groups is the key to ending ethnic civil wars. Every case in which the state was preserved by agreement involved a regionally concentrated minority, and in every case the solution reinforced the ethnic role in politics by allowing the regional minority group to control its own destiny through regional autonomy for the areas where it forms a majority of the population. There is not a single case where non-ethnic civil politics were created or restored by reconstruction of ethnic identities, power-sharing coalitions, or state-building.

Further, deaths in these cases average an order of magnitude lower than in the wars which ended either in suppression or partition: less than 13,000, compared about 250,000. This lends support to the proposition that the more extreme the violence, the less the chances for any form of reconciliation. Finally, it should be noted that all eight of the cases resolved through autonomy involve groups that were largely demographically separated even at the beginning of the conflict, which may help explain why there were fewer deaths.

INTERVENTION TO RESOLVE ETHNIC CIVIL WARS

International interventions that seek to ensure lasting safety for populations endangered by ethnic war—whether by the United Nations, by major powers with global reach, or by regional powers—must be guided by two principles. First, settlements must aim at physically separating the warring communities and establishing a balance of relative strength that makes it unprofitable for either side to attempt to revise the territorial settlement. Second, although economic or military assistance may suffice in

[47]The data set surveyed here combines two overlapping sets presented by Gurr in *Minorities at Risk: A Global View of Ethnopolitical Conflicts* (Washington, D.C.: U.S. Institute of Peace, 1993), pp. 296–297; and Gurr, "Peoples Against States," pp. 369–375.

some cases, direct military intervention will be necessary when aid to the weaker side would create a window of opportunity for the stronger, or when there is an immediate need to stop ongoing genocide.

Designing Settlements

Unless outsiders are willing to provide permanent security guarantees, stable resolution of an ethnic civil war requires separation of the groups into defensible regions. The critical variable is demography, not sovereignty. Political partition without ethnic separation leaves incentives for ethnic cleansing unchanged; it actually increases them if it creates new minorities. Conversely, demographic separation dampens ethnic conflicts even without separate sovereignty, although the more intense the previous fighting, the smaller the prospects for preserving a single state, even if loosely federated.

Partition without ethnic separation increases conflict because, while boundaries of sovereign successor states may provide defensible fronts that reduce the vulnerability of the majority group in each state, stay-behind minorities are completely exposed. Significant irredenta are both a call to their ethnic homeland and a danger to their hosts. They create incentives to mount rescue or ethnic cleansing operations before the situation solidifies. Greece's 1920 invasion of Turkey was justified in this way, while the 1947 decision to partition Palestine generated a civil war in advance of implementation, and the inclusion of Muslim-majority Kashmir within India has helped cause three wars. International recognition of Croatian and Bosnian independence did more to cause than to stop Serbian invasion. The war between Armenia and Azerbaijan has the same source, as do concerns over the international security risks of the several Russian diasporas.[48]

Inter-ethnic security dilemmas can be nearly or wholly eliminated without partition if three conditions are met: First, there must be enough demographic separation that ethnic regions do not themselves contain militarily significant minorities. Second, there must be enough regional self-defense capability that abrogating the autonomy of any region would be more costly than any possible motive for doing so. Third, local autonomy must be so complete that minority groups can protect their key interests even lacking any influence at the national level. Even after an ethnic war, a single state could offer some advantages, not least of which are the economic benefits of a

---

[48]Dmitri A. Fadeyev and Vladimir Razuvayev, "Russia and the Western Post-Soviet Republics," in Robert D. Blackwill and Sergei A. Karaganov, eds., *Damage Limitation or Crisis? Russia and the Outside World* (Washington, D.C.: Brassey's, 1994), pp. 107–123, at 116–117; Vitaly V. Naumkin, "Russia and the States of Central Asia and the Caucasus," in ibid., pp. 199–216, 207.

common market. However, potential interveners should recognize that groups that control distinct territories can insist on the *de facto* partition, and often will.

While peace requires separation of groups into distinct regions, it does not require total ethnic purity. Rather, remaining minorities must be small enough that the host group does not fear them as either a potential military threat or a possible target for irredentist rescue operations. Before the Krajina offensive, for example, President Franjo Tudjman of Croatia is said to have thought that the 12 percent Serb minority in Croatia was too large, but that half as many would be tolerable.[49] The 173,000 Arabs remaining in Israel by 1951 were too few and too disorganized to be seen as a serious threat.[50]

Geographic distribution of minorities is also important; in particular, concentrations near disputed borders or astride strategic communications constitute both a military vulnerability and an irredentist opportunity, and so are likely to spark conflict. It is not surprising that India's portion of Kashmir, with its Muslim majority, has been at the center of three interstate wars and an ongoing insurgency which continues today, while there has been no international conflict over the hundred million Muslims who live dispersed throughout most of the rest of India, and relatively little violence.[51]

Where possible, inter-group boundaries should be drawn along the best defensive terrain, such as rivers and mountain ranges. Lines should also be as short as possible, to allow the heaviest possible manning of defensive fronts. (Croatian forces were able to overrun Krajina in part because its irregular crescent shape meant that 30,000 Krajina Serb forces had to cover a frontier of more than 725 miles.) Access to the sea or to a friendly neighbor is also important, both for trade and for possible military assistance. Successor state arsenals should be encouraged, by aid to the weaker or sanctions on the stronger, to focus on defensive armaments such as towed artillery and anti-aircraft missiles and rockets, while avoiding instruments that could make blitzkrieg attacks possible, such as tanks, fighter-bombers, and mobile artillery. These conditions would make subsequent offensives exceedingly expensive and likely to fail.

Intervention Strategy

The level of international action required to resolve an ethnic war will depend on the military situation on the ground. If there is an existing stalemate along defensible lines, the international community should simply recognize and strengthen it,

---

[49]"The Flight of the Krajina Serbs," *Economist*, August 12, 1995, p. 42.

[50]Dov Friedlander and Calvin Goldscheider, *The Population of Israel* (New York: Columbia University Press, 1979), p. 30.

[51]Hindu-Muslim violence has claimed approximately 25,000 lives in Kashmir since 1990, compared to about 3,000 in the rest of India. Gurr, "Peoples Against States," p. 371.

providing transportation, protection, and resettlement assistance for refugees. However, where one side has the capacity to go on the offensive against the other, intervention will be necessary.

Interventions should therefore almost always be on behalf of the weaker side; the
stronger needs no defense. Moreover, unless the international community can agree
on a clear aggressor and a clear victim, there is no moral or political case for intervention. If both sides have behaved so badly that there is little to choose between them,
intervention should not and probably will not be undertaken. Almost no one in the
West, for instance, has advocated assisting either side in the Croatian-Serb conflict.[52]
While the intervention itself could be carried out by any willing actors, UN sponsor-
ship is highly desirable, most of all to head off possible external aid to the group
identified as the aggressor.

The three available tools are sanctions, military aid, and direct military intervention. Economic sanctions have limited leverage against combatants in ethnic wars,
who often see their territorial security requirements as absolute. Whereas hyperin-
flation and economic collapse have apparently reduced Serbian government support for the Bosnian Serb rebels and thus limited the latter's material capabilities,
Armenians have already suffered five years of extreme privation rather than give up
Nagorno-Karabakh.

Whether military aid to the client can achieve an acceptable territorial outcome
depends on the population balance between the sides, the local geography, and the
organizational cohesion of the client group. Aid could not enable Chechen or Sikh
secession, but has been decisive in Abkhazia, and leaks in the embargo have significantly helped Bosnia.[53] The more serious problem with "arm's length" aid is that it
cannot prevent ethnic aggressors from killing members of the client group in territories from which they expect to have to retreat.[54] Aid also does not restrain possible
atrocities by the client group if their military fortunes improve.[55]

---

[52]Further, attempts at even-handed intervention rarely achieve their goals, leading either to nearly
complete passivity, as in the case of UNPROFOR in Bosnia, or eventually to open combat against
one or all sides. At worst, peace-keeping efforts may actually prolong fighting. See Richard K.
Betts, "The Delusion of Impartial Intervention," *Foreign Affairs*, Vol. 73, No. 6 (November/
December 1994), pp. 20–33.

[53]For an argument that weapons aid and air threats would have been sufficient to end the war in Bosnia, see John J. Mearsheimer and Robert A. Pape, "The Answer: A Three-Way Partition Plan for
Bosnia and How the U.S. Can Enforce It," *The New Republic*, June 14, 1993, pp. 22–28.

[54]Bosnian Serb forces evidently killed several thousand Muslims before retreating from several towns
in Northwest Bosnia in October 1995. Chris Hedges, "2 Officials Report New Mass Killings by
Bosnian Serbs," *New York Times*, October 20, 1995.

[55]Croatian forces attacked Serb refugees fleeing Krajina. Jane Perlez, "Thousands of Serbian Civilians
are Caught in Soldiers' Crossfire," *New York Times*, August 9, 1995.

If the client is too weak to achieve a viable separation with material aid alone, or if either or both sides cannot be trusted to abide by promises of non-retribution against enemy civilians, the international community must designate a separation line and deploy an intervention force to take physical control of the territory on the client's side of the line. We might call this approach "conquer and divide."

The separation campaign is waged as a conventional military operation. The larger the forces committed the better, both to minimize intervenors' casualties and to shorten the campaign by threatening the opponent with overwhelming defeat. Although some argue that any intervention force would become mired in a Vietnam-like quagmire,[56] the fundamentally different nature of ethnic conflict means that the main pitfalls to foreign military interventions in ideological insurgencies are either weaker or absent. Most important, the intervenors' intelligence problems are much simpler, since loyalty intelligence is both less important and easier: outsiders can safely assume that members of the allied group are friends and those of the other are enemies. Even if outsiders cannot tell the groups apart, locals can, and the loyalty of guides provided by the local ally can be counted on. As a result, the main intelligence task shifts from assessing loyalties to locating enemy forces, a task of which major power militaries are very capable.

On the ground, the intervenors would begin at one end of the target region and gradually advance to capture the entire target territory, maintaining a continuous front the entire time. It is not necessary to conquer the whole country; indeed, friendly ground forces need never cross the designated line. After enemy forces are driven out of each locality, civilians of the enemy ethnic group who remain behind are interned, to be exchanged after the war. This removes the enemy's local support base, preventing counterinsurgency problems from arising. Enemy civilians should be protected by close supervision of client troops in action, as well as by foreign control of internees.

The final concern is possible massacres of civilians of the client group in territory not yet captured or beyond the planned separation line. Some of this must be expected, since ongoing atrocities are the most likely impetus for outside intervention; the question is whether intervention actually increases the risk of attacks on civilians. A major advantage of a powerful ground presence is that opponent behavior can be coerced by threatening to advance the separation line in retaliation for any atrocities.

Once the military campaign is complete and refugees have been resettled, further reconstruction and military aid may be needed to help the client achieve a viable economy and self-defense capability before the intervenors can depart. The ease of exit will depend on the regional geography and balance of power. Bosnia has sufficient population and skills to be made economically and militarily viable, provided

---

[56]Henry Kissinger, "Bosnia Poses Another Vietnam-like Quagmire," *Houston Chronicle*, February 21, 1993; F. Charles Parker, "Vietnam, Bosnia, and the Historical Record," *In Depth*, Vol. 3, No. 2 (Spring 1993), p. 29.

Table 1.   Ethnic Civil Wars Resolved 1944–94.

Combatants	Dates	Deaths (000s)[1]	Outcome
Military victory (12):			
Karens vs. Myanmar	1945–	43[2]	Defeat imminent
Kurds vs. Iran	1945–80s	40	Suppressed
Tibetans vs. China	1959–89	100	Suppressed
Papuans vs. Indonesia	1964–86	19	Suppressed
Ibo vs. Nigeria	1967–70	2000[3]	Suppressed
Timorese vs. Indonesia	1974–80s	200	Suppressed
Aceh vs. Indonesia	1975–80s	15	Suppressed
Tigreans vs. Ethiopia	1975–91	350[4]	Rebels victorious
Uighurs etc. vs. China	1980	2	Suppressed
Bougainville vs. Papua	1988	1	Suppressed
Tutsis vs. Rwanda	1990–94	750[5]	Rebels victorious
Shiites vs. Iraq	1991	35	Suppressed
De facto or de jure partition (5):			
Ukrainians vs. USSR	1944–50s	150[6]	Suppressed, independent 1991
Lithuanians vs. USSR	1945–52	40[7]	Suppressed; independent 1991
Eritreans vs. Ethiopia	1961–91	350	Independent 1993
Armenians vs. Azerbaijan	1988–	15	De facto partition
Somali clans	1988–	350	De facto partition in N., ongoing in S.
Conflict suppressed by ongoing 3rd-party military occupation (2):			
Kurds vs. Iraq	1960–	215	De facto partition
Lebanese Civil War	1975–90	120[8]	Nominal power sharing, de facto partition
Settled by agreements other than partition (8):			
Nagas vs. India	1952–75	13[9]	Autonomy 1972
Basques vs. Spain	1959–80s	1	Autonomy 1980
Tripuras vs. India	1967–89	13	Autonomy 1972
Palestinians vs. Israel	1968–93	2	Autonomy 1993, partly implemented
Moros vs. Philippines	1972–87	50	Limited autonomy 1990

Table 1. *continued*

Chittagong hill peoples vs. Bangladesh	1975–89	24	Limited autonomy 1989
Miskitos vs. Nicaragua	1981–88	<1[10]	Autonomy 1990
Abkhazians vs. Georgia	1992–93	10	Autonomy 1993

NOTES:

[1] Figures are from Ted Robert Gurr, *Minorities at Risk: A Global View of Ethnopolitical Conflicts* (Washington, D.C.: U.S. Institute of Peace, 1993), and Gurr, "Peoples Against States: Ethnopolitical Conflict and the Changing World System," *International Studies Quarterly*, Vol. 38, No. 3 (September 1994), pp. 347–377.

[2] Gurr gives a combined total of 130,000 for three civil wars in Myanmar. Probably more than one-third of the total is attributable to the Karen.

[3] R. Ernest Dupuy and Trevor N. Dupuy, *Encyclopedia of Military History*, 4th ed. (New York: Harper and Row, 1993), p. 1447.

[4] 700,000 for Eritrean and Tigrean rebellions combined, including government forces and civilians, but not rebel combatants. Probably more than half the total attributable to Tigre. Alex de Waal, *Evil Days: Thirty Years of War and Famine in Ethiopia* (New York: Human Rights Watch, 1991), pp. 3, 5–6.

[5] Alex de Waal and Rakiya Omaar, "The Genocide in Rwanda and the International Response," *Current History*, Vol. 94, No. 591 (April 1995), pp. 156–161, at 156.

[6] Includes combatants on both sides, but not civilian losses. Thomas Remeikas, *Opposition to Soviet Rule in Lithuania, 1945–1980* (Chicago: Institute of Lithuanian Studies Press, 1980).

[7] Official Soviet estimate, not including losses by government forces. Heorhii Kasianov communication to author, November 27, 1995.

[8] Total for 1975–82. Richard A. Gabriel, *Operation Peace for Galilee: The Israeli-PLO War in Lebanon* (New York: Hill and Wang, 1984), pp. 45, 164–165.

[9] Gurr gives a combined total of 25,000 for the Naga and Tripura rebellions together.

[10] *The Reagan Administration's Record on Human Rights in 1986* (New York: The Watch Committees and Lawyers' Committee for Human Rights, 1987), pp. 93–94.

that access to the outside world through Croatia is maintained. Although the weakness of the Turkish Republic of Northern Cyprus has required a permanent Turkish garrison, the almost equal weakness of the Greek Cypriots allows the garrison to be small, cheap, and inactive. U.S. Operation Provide Comfort helps secure the Kurdish enclave in northern Iraq by prohibiting Iraqi air operations as well as by threatening air strikes against an Iraqi ground invasion of the region. This intervention has no easy exit, however, since the Iraqi Kurds are landlocked and threatened by Turkey, which is waging a war against its own Kurdish minority. Real security for the Kurds might require partitioning Turkey as well as Iraq, a task no outside actor is willing to contemplate. . . .

Objections to Ethnic Separation and Partition

There are five important objections to ethnic separation as policy for resolving ethnic conflicts: that it encourages splintering of states, that population exchanges cause human suffering, that it simply transforms civil wars into international ones, that rump states will not be viable, and that, in the end, it does nothing to resolve ethnic antagonisms.[57]

Among most international organizations, western leaders, and scholars, population exchanges and partition are anathema. They contradict cherished western values of social integration, trample on the international legal norm of state sovereignty, and suggest particular policies that have been condemned by most of the world (e.g., Turkey's unilateral partition of Cyprus). The integrity of states and their borders is usually seen as a paramount principle, while self-determination takes second place. In ethnic wars, however, saving lives may require ignoring state-centered legal norms. The legal costs of ethnic separation must be compared to the human consequences, both immediate and long term, if the warring groups are not separated. To paraphrase Winston Churchill: separation is the worst solution, except for all the others.

PARTITION ENCOURAGES SPLINTERING OF STATES

If international interventions for ethnic separation encourage secession attempts elsewhere, they could increase rather than decrease global ethnic violence. However, this is unlikely, because government use of force to suppress them makes almost all secession attempts extremely costly; only groups that see no viable alternative try. What intervention can do is reduce loss of life where states are breaking up anyway. An expectation that the international community will never intervene, however, encourages repression of minorities, as in Turkey or the Sudan, and wars of ethnic conquest, as by Serbia.

Population Transfers Cause Suffering

Separation of intermingled ethnic groups necessarily involves significant refugee flows, usually in both directions. Population transfers during ethnic conflicts have often led to much suffering, so an obvious question is whether foreign intervention to relocate populations would only increase suffering. In fact, however, the biggest cause of suffering in population exchanges is spontaneous refugee movement. Planned population transfers are much safer. When ethnic conflicts turn violent, they generate spontaneous refugee movements as people flee from intense fighting or are kicked out by neighbors, marauding gangs, or a conquering army. Spontaneous

---

[57]Robert Schaeffer, *Warpaths: The Politics of Partition* (New York: Hill and Wang, 1990), makes all these criticisms and several others.

refugees frequently suffer direct attack by hostile civilians or armed forces. They often leave precipitately, with inadequate money, transport, or food supplies, and before relief can be organized. They make vulnerable targets for banditry and plunder, and are often so needy as to be likely perpetrators also.[58] Planned population exchanges can address all of these risks by preparing refugee relief and security operations in advance.

In the 1947 India-Pakistan exchange, nearly the entire movement of between 12 and 16 million people took place in a few months. The British were surprised by the speed with which this movement took place, and were not ready to control, support, and protect the refugees. Estimates of deaths go as high one million. In the first stages of the population exchanges among Greece, Bulgaria, and Turkey in the 1920s, hundreds of thousands of refugees moved spontaneously and many died due to banditry and exposure. When after 1925 the League of Nations deployed capable relief services, the remaining transfers—one million, over 60 percent of the total—were carried out in an organized and planned way, with virtually no losses.[59]

A related criticism is that transfers require the intervenors to operate *de facto* concentration camps for civilians of the opposing ethnic groups until transfers can be carried out. However, this is safer than the alternatives of administration by the local ally or allowing the war to run its course. As with transfers, the risks to the internees depend on planning and resources.

Separation Merely Substitutes International for Civil Wars

Post-separation wars are possible, motivated either by revanchism or by security fears if one side suspects the other of revisionist plans. The frequency and human cost of such wars, however, must be compared to the likely consequences of not separating. When the alternative is intercommunal slaughter, separation is the only defensible choice.

In fact the record of twentieth-century ethnic partitions is fairly good. The partition of Ireland has produced no interstate violence, although intercommunal violence continues in demographically mixed Northern Ireland. India and Pakistan have fought two wars since partition, one in 1965 over ethnically mixed Kashmir, while the second in 1971 resulted not from Indo-Pakistani state rivalry or Hindu-Muslim religious conflict but from ethnic conflict between (West) Pakistanis and

[58]Frelick, *Faultlines of Nationality Conflict*, p. 11.

[59]Schaeffer, *Warpaths*, 155–56; Michael R. Marrus, *The Unwanted* (New York: Oxford University Press, 1985); Richard Ned Lebow, *Divided Nations in a Divided World*.

Bengalis. Indian intervention resolved the conflict by enabling the independence of Bangladesh. These wars have been much less dangerous, especially to civilians, than the political and possible physical extinction that Muslims feared if the subcontinent were not divided.[60] The worst post-partition history is probably that of the Arab-Israeli conflict. Even here, civilian deaths would almost certainly have been higher without partition. It is difficult even to imagine any alternative; the British could not and would not stay, and neither side would share power or submit to rule by the other.

Rump States will Not Be Viable

Many analysts of ethnic conflict question the economic and military viability of partitioned states.[61] History, however, records no examples of ethnic partitions which failed for economic reasons. In any case, intervenors have substantial influence over economic outcomes: they can determine partition lines, guarantee trade access and, if necessary, provide significant aid in relation to the economic sizes of likely candidates. Peace itself also enhances recovery prospects.

Thus the more important issue is military viability, particularly since interventions will most often be in favor of the weaker side. If the client has economic strength comparable to the opponent, it can provide for its own defense. If it does not, the intervenors will have to provide military aid and possibly a security guarantee.

Ensuring the client's security will be made easier by the opponent's scarcity of options for revision. First, any large-scale conventional attack is likely to fail because the intervenors will have drawn the borders for maximum defensibility and ensured that the client is better armed. If necessary, they can lend further assistance through air strikes. Breaking up conventional offensives is what high-technology air power does best.

Second, infiltration of small guerrilla parties, if successful over a period of time, could cause boundaries to become "fuzzy," and eventually to break down. This has been a major concern of some observers of Bosnia, but it should not be. Infiltration can only work where at least some civilians will support, house, feed, and hide

---

[60]Aside from physical security concerns, Muslims also feared that a Congress-dominated India would discriminate against them in public service jobs, education, and land tenure. Lance Brennan, "The Illusion of Security: The Background to Muslim Separatism in the United Provinces," in Hasan, ed., *India's Partition*, pp. 318–355.

[61]Schaeffer, *Warpaths*; Kamal S. Shehadi, *Ethnic Determination and the Break-up of States*, Adelphi Paper No. 283 (London: International Institute for Strategic Studies [IISS], 1993), p. 9. Amitai Etzioni, "The Evils of Self-Determination," *Foreign Policy*, No. 89 (Winter 1992–93), pp. 21–35, argues that secession states are likely to become both economic failures and undemocratic.

the guerrillas. After ethnic separation, however, any infiltrators would be entering a completely hostile region where no one will help them; instead, all will inform on them and cooperate fully with authorities against them. The worst case is probably Israel, where terrorist infiltration has cost lives, but never come close to threatening the state's territorial integrity. Retaliatory capabilities could also allow the client to dampen, even stop, such behavior.

Partition Does Not Resolve Ethnic Hatreds

It is not clear that it is in anyone's power to resolve ethnic hatreds once there has been large-scale violence, especially murders of civilians. In the long run, however, separation may help reduce inter-ethnic antagonism; once real security threats are reduced, the plausibility of hypernationalist appeals may eventually decline. Certainly ethnic hostility cannot be reduced without separation. As long as either side fears, even intermittently, that it will be attacked by the other, past atrocities and old hatreds can easily be aroused. If, however, it becomes and remains implausible that the other group could ever seriously endanger the nation, hypernationalist drum-beating may fall on deafer and deafer ears.

The only stronger measure would be to attempt a thorough re-engineering of the involved groups' political and social systems, comparable to the rehabilitation of Germany after World War II. The costs would be steep, since this would require conquering the country and occupying it for a long time, possibly for decades. The apparent benignification of Germany suggests that, if the international community is prepared to go this far, this approach could succeed.[62]

CONCLUSION

. . .

Ultimately we have a responsibility to be honest with ourselves as well as with the victims of ethnic wars all over the world. The world's major powers must decide whether they will be willing to spend any of their own soldiers' lives to save strangers, or whether they will continue to offer false hopes to endangered peoples.

---

[62]Elmer Pluschke, "Denazification in Germany," in Wolfe, ed., *Americans as Proconsuls: United States Military Governments in Germany and Japan, 1944–1952.* For a current proposal see Martin van Heuven, "Rehabilitating Serbia," *Foreign Policy*, No. 96 (Fall 1994), pp. 38–48.

Part IV

INTERNATIONAL POLITICAL ECONOMY

INTRODUCTION

The study of international political economy marries an economic focus on systems of producing, distributing, and using wealth with international relations' interest in power and the institutions and rules by which social and economic interactions are governed. Key topics of interest include the manner in which national and international economies constrain and enable political action, the tools and capabilities of policymakers to manipulate economics, and the international effects of interacting domestic policies designed to accomplish domestic economic goals. International political economy spans issues of trade, finance, economic distribution and justice, economic development, and globalization.

While the origins of International Political Economy (IPE) date back to the eighteenth and nineteenth centuries and classic studies by Adam Smith, David Ricardo, Friedrich List, and Karl Marx, many of the issues, ideas, and theoretical debates remain the same today. In general terms, International Political Economy concerns itself with the interaction between the two dominant forms of social interaction in the modern world, *"the state"* and *"the market."*[1] The former is a hierarchical, formal institution, while the latter is characterized by informal institutions and horizontal interactions between autonomous actors. Despite differences in their modes of operation, degree of organization, and formalization, markets and states often need each other. Even the free-est of markets depends upon the state to provide public goods, guarantees for property rights and contracts, and conventions like common units of weight and measurement. Without public goods like roads, telecommunications systems, and court systems, markets would be small and localized. Individual firms have no interest in producing these public goods themselves, as they cannot recoup sufficient profit to

---

[1]Susan Strange, *States and Markets* (London: Pinter, 1988).

cover the construction costs nor can they find a reliable way to share costs with other firms, and yet each firm benefits from the ability to ship its products to a greater number of markets and reliable enforcement of long term, arms-length contracts. A good or service for which the direct recuperation of the cost and the exclusivity of its use—that is, the two criteria for a private good—do not apply is by definition a public good. In this case, the costs for the road are not borne individually but jointly, through taxes. Once erected, there is also a jointness of demand; there can be no discrimination between different companies' trucks using the road. States in turn depend on markets to produce the best quality goods possible in the ideal quantities at the optimal prices, to distribute these goods in order to meet the demands and tastes of their citizens, to generate tax revenues, and to finance government projects (including war).

While in principle the need for the state to regulate the market and to provide public goods is undisputed, disagreement exists about the degree to which the state should attempt to control the market, the relations of power and interest between these two "actors," and proper bounds on the operations of both the state and the market. The three main strands of IPE theory, mercantilism, liberalism, and Marxism, each offer different prescriptions for the proper relationship between the state and the market. Each theoretical approach places different emphasis on the importance of power, interests, and class relations in explaining the current operation of the global economy and its historical evolution. While realism emphasizes the state as being in control the economy, liberalism and Marxism see economic groups as controlling the state for their own interests, although with different expectations for the resulting market and social welfare. Robert Gilpin expands upon each of these approaches to IPE more fully in "The Study of International Political Economy."

The dominant theoretical approaches to IPE can be placed on a continuum in two dimensions. Each approach addresses the relationship between the state (government institutions) and the market (economic entities within society) and the relative importance of each in determining the nature of economic policy and relations between groups. While realism emphasizes the state, liberalism and Marxism stress the role of the market and society. Each approach also needs to describe the relationship between domestic and international levels of analysis. In particular, do domestic economic groups and political institutions determine international economic outcomes, such as trade patterns and financial crises, or do international economic conditions, including the degree of openness in the international economy and global business cycles, determine the range of possible domestic economic policies? Realists (including hegemonic stability theorists discussed below) fall to the latter side—the international distribution of power (military and monetary) and prestige largely determine the policies available to individual states.

Realists argue similar states tend to respond similarly to economic opportunities and constraints. Liberals argue that domestic politics has an important role to play in determining economics at home and abroad. Different states will adopt different economic policies because of different preferences, needs, and resources. Michael J. Hiscox demonstrates in "The Domestic Sources of Foreign Economic Policies" that the interaction between domestic interest groups (society) and domestic political institutions (state) has a strong impact on the foreign economic policy of a given state (its trade and monetary policy). Furthermore, international economic trends and relations cannot be reduced to relative state power. While economic interest groups in each state take international economics into account in deciding upon their preferred policies, no group or state will fully accomplish its goals due to the effects of political institutions on actual policy outcomes.

International externalities from domestic economic policies—for instance, international financial crises resulting from a country's self-interested default on its debts or tightening global markets as each country increases its trade barriers—are becoming increasingly common and increasingly costly. Smooth economic exchange at the international level requires coordination and shared understandings and expectations, just as at the domestic level. But the public goods that enable markets are particularly scarce internationally due to the anarchic nature of the international system. There are no higher authorities to enforce contracts and maintain public safety and security (and worse yet a predisposition towards the view that might makes right), no agreement on who should provide public goods like roads, and states face a collective action problem in deciding on who should undertake how much of these tasks (and the associated costs).

The classic solution to international collective action problems is a hegemon. Hegemonic stability theorists argue that a dominant economic and political power is necessary to provide a liberal international economic order. Hegemons provide public goods, including financial stability, liquidity, and rules of exchange, because they expect the benefits of free flows of trade and finance to exceed the costs.[2] Hegemons then establish international economic regimes (such as the Bretton Woods regime and the International Monetary Fund and World Bank after World War II) to institutionalize their relative power, establish basic property rights and shared understandings of economic exchange, and provide a means to share information, resolve disputes, and monitor compliance with the rules. Marxists argue that hegemons need more than military and economic power to dominate the global economic order and such ideological hegemony rests upon the cooperation of other states in the international system. Gramscian ideas of intellectual hegemony also raise questions about whether a liberal international economic order is naturally in the best interests of all members

---

[2]On hegemonic stability theory, see David Lake, "Leadership, Hegemony, and the Naked Emperor," *International Studies Quarterly* 37 (1993): 459-489, and Joanne Gowa, *Allies, Adversaries, and International Trade* (Princeton: Princeton University Press, 1995).

of the international community. The implications of this line of reasoning have been taken up by anti-globalization thinkers and activists.

Increasing quantities of trade and money flowing increasingly rapidly between an ever larger number of states have raised questions about changes in the fundamental nature of the international economy and implications for state institutions, policies, and power. While dense networks of economic exchange bring material benefits to citizens and states, interdependence may have mixed effects. Realists remain concerned that unequal relations may be dangerous, as the oil crises in 1973 and 1979 made all too clear, exposing the dependence of "the West" on oil, and leading to the organization of the chief industrialized countries as the so-called G7 (the group of the seven largest economies in the 1970s). Kenneth Waltz contends in "Globalization and Governance" that states can and will limit trade and commerce, despite possible economic sacrifices, to protect state power. Liberals argue to the contrary that interdependence has fundamentally changed international relations for the better, by increasing exchanges between individuals, companies, and states; irreversibly linking markets, issues, and individuals' welfare; and making military action less likely because, as Richard Rosencrance argues in "Trade and Power," it makes little sense to kill your customers. Questions about the nature, extent, and implications of interdependence, now commonly known as globalization, lead Jeffrey Frankel to examine this phenomenon empirically in "The Globalization of the International Economy." Frankel examines both the extent to which markets are tied and the relative size of trade and financial flows compared to the size of the global economy and national economic profiles.

The very term *globalization* means different things to different people, and it is frequently employed with an ideological agenda in mind. Because different individuals use the term globalization differently, it poses analytical problems.[3] In public and academic debates, globalization can refer to market integration and international flows of factors of production, goods, services, and financial instruments. Globalization can also refer to the social and cultural effects of closer economic exchanges and greater awareness of other ways of life and standards of living as a result of greater flows of information. The term globalization can also refer to the effect of competition for investment and global market share in integrated markets on government policies for corporations' operations, labor standards, and environmental protection and so-called regulatory arbitrage. Thus globalization can be a noun describing the current state of the international political economy, a verb describing the process by which the international political economy arrived at this state, and as a pejorative adjective

---

[3]For a systematic analytical discussion of the phenomenon, see Axel Hülsemeyer, ed., *Globalization in the Twenty-First Century: Convergence or Divergence?* (Basingstoke, UK: Palgrave Macmillan, 2003).

insinuating exploitation and domination of countries in the "South," the Southern part of the globe. This degree of analytic confusion is both unhelpful and unnecessary.

Globalization has multiple aspects, including economic, political, social, cultural, and ideational. Disaggregating these aspects is useful to assess the actual extent of globalization and its implications for state power and policy, the growth of multinational corporations, economic development, the distribution of economic benefit and concerns for social welfare, and relations between the North and the South. Frankel argues that the hype and scare mongering around globalization needs to be reduced. The international economy is still far from fully integrated and the extent of globalization today is less than earlier eras of globalization (the end of the nineteenth century) in relative terms. While market integration and growing competition between states for investment by multinational corporations and banks may entice governments to lower regulations (reduce state, making more space for market), the ability of multinational corporations to evade national state regulations by relocating their operations to other countries is not absolute. Paul Krugman argues that views of globalization as a competitive power struggle between states are incorrect and potentially dangerous. While states may need to adjust their institutions and policies in order for their domestic populations to prosper in globalization, and this may mean increasing the size of the welfare state to protect against shifts in national economies production patterns as well as strengthening some aspects of the state to protect it from the downsides of globalization, the economic exchanges made possible by increasing globalization are beneficial to all.

The winners and losers of globalization are not neatly divided into the North and the South, but instead are spread within and across states. The problems of globalization come when the losers seek political power in order to maintain the status quo and protect themselves, thus reducing the potential economic gains of many within the state. Conservative forces within some states have a strong incentive to evoke powerful anti-globalization ideas and identities, including nationalism, as a means to strengthen their claims to political power and popular appeal in a process that might produce powerful backlashes to economic integration and violent political conflicts. Moises Naim examines the types of conflict which are likely to emerge as a result of globalization in "The Five Wars of Globalization."

THE STUDY OF INTERNATIONAL POLITICAL ECONOMY

ROBERT GILPIN

The study of international political economy (IPE) is of necessity highly dependent on the theories and insights of neoclassical economics. However, IPE and neoclassical economics ask different questions as they apply their own mode of analysis. Whereas economics is primarily concerned with efficiency and the mutual benefits of economic exchange, international political economy is interested not only in those subjects but also in a broader range of issues. IPE is particularly interested in the distribution of gains from market activities; neoclassical economics is not. Although, at least over the long term, every society gains absolutely from the efficient functioning of international markets, the gains are seldom distributed equally among all economic actors, and states generally are very much concerned over their own relative gains.

Whereas economists regard markets as self-regulating mechanisms isolated from political affairs, specialists in IPE are interested in the fact that the world economy has a considerable impact on the power, values, and political autonomy of national societies. States have a strong incentive to take actions that safeguard their own values and interests, especially their power and freedom of action, and they also attempt to manipulate market forces to increase their power and influence over rival states or to favor friendly states.[1]

Whereas economists and economic analysts are generally indifferent to the role of institutions in economic affairs (due to their focus on the market), the nature of the international institutions and those international regimes that govern international markets and economic activities constitute a central concern of international political economists. As regimes may significantly affect the distribution of gains from economic activities and the economic/political autonomy of individual states, states—especially powerful states—attempt to influence the design and functioning of institutions in order to advance their own political, economic, and other interests. Thus, the study of international political economy presumes that states, multinational corporations, and other powerful actors attempt to use their power to influence the nature of international regimes.[2]

DISTRIBUTION OF WEALTH AND ECONOMIC ACTIVITIES

Whereas the science of economics emphasizes the efficient allocation of scarce resources and the absolute gains enjoyed by everyone from economic activities, state-centric scholars of international political economy emphasize the distributive consequences of economic activities. According to economics, exchange takes place because of mutual gain; were it otherwise, the exchange would not occur. IPE's state-centric interpretation, on the other hand, argues that economic actors are attentive not only to absolute but also to relative gains from economic intercourse; that is, not merely to the absolute gain for themselves, but also to the size of their own gain relative to gains of other actors. Governments are concerned about the terms of trade, the distribution of economic returns from foreign investment, and, in particular, the relative rates of economic growth among national economies. Indeed, the issue of relative gains is seldom far from the minds of political leaders.

The significance of relative gains for economic behavior and in the calculations of nation-states was recognized at least as early as the economic writings of the eighteenth-century political philosopher David Hume (1711–1776). Hume's mercantilist

[1]Joanne Gowa, *Allies, Adversaries, and International Trade* (Princeton: Princeton University Press, 1994).

[2]Stephen D. Krasner, ed., *International Regimes* (Ithaca: Cornell University Press, 1983).

contemporaries argued that a nation should seek a trade and payments surplus, basing their arguments on the assumption that it was only relative gains that really mattered. In today's language of game theory, international commerce during the mercantilist era was considered to be a zero-sum game in which the gain to one party necessarily meant a loss to another. Hume himself demonstrated the folly and self-defeating nature of this mercantilist argument by introducing the "price-specie flow mechanism" into economic thought.[3] Subsequently, formulation by David Ricardo (1772–1823) of the law or principle of comparative advantage revealed that every nation could gain in absolute terms from free trade and from an international division of labor based on territorial specialization. Subsequent modifications of Ricardo's theory suggested that states were also interested in the relative gains from trade. Ricardo's demonstration that international economic exchange was not a zero-sum game but rather a positive-sum game from which everyone could gain led Paul Samuelson to call the law of comparative advantage "the most beautiful idea" in economic science. However, both absolute gains and the distribution of those gains are important in international economic affairs.

A number of political economists have addressed the issue of absolute versus relative gains in international affairs, and the ensuing debate has largely centered on Joseph Grieco's argument that states are more concerned about relative than absolute gains and that this creates difficulties in attaining international cooperation.[4] Although I know of no political economist who dismisses altogether the role of relative gains in international economic affairs, scholars of IPE do differ on the weight each gives to relative versus absolute gains. Whereas many scholars stress the importance of relative gains, liberals emphasize the importance of absolute gains and believe that Grieco has overstated the significance of relative gains. Absolute gains, they argue, are more important than Grieco's analysis suggests, and therefore international cooperation should be easier to attain than he postulates. While Grieco's emphasis on the importance of relative gains is, I believe, basically important, and states do, in general, prize relative gains, sometimes even at the expense of absolute gains, this argument cannot be elevated into a general law of state behavior. One can say about this generalization

---

[3]In oversimplified terms, the "price-specie flow mechanism" states that the flow of specie (gold or silver) into an economy as a consequence of a trade/payments surplus increases the domestic money supply and raises prices of a country's exports. This price rise in turn decreases the country's trade/payments surplus. In short, any attempt to have a permanent trade/payments surplus is self-defeating. See David Hume, in Eugene Rotwein, ed., *Writings on Economics* (London: Nelson, 1955).

[4]Joseph M. Grieco, *Cooperation Among Nations: Europe, America, and Non-Tariff Barriers to Trade* (Ithaca: Cornell University Press, 1990). An excellent volume on the debate over the importance of relative versus absolute gains is David A. Baldwin, ed., *Neorealism and Neoliberalsim: The Contemporary Debate* (New York: Columbia University Press, 1993).

in political economy no more than Kindleberger has said of most generalizations in economics: "It depends!"

The importance of absolute versus relative gains in state calculations is actually highly dependent upon the circumstances in which a specific trade-off occurs. While it may be true that states can never be totally unconcerned about the distributive consequences of economic activities for their relative wealth and power, they frequently do, largely for security reasons, ignore this concern in their dealings with others. During the height of the Cold War, for example, the United States fostered the economic unification of Western Europe for political reasons despite the costs to its own economic interests. Kenneth Waltz has noted that the conscious decision of the United States in the late 1940s to build the power of its European allies at a sacrifice to itself was a historically unprecedented action.[5]

States are particularly interested in the distribution of those gains affecting domestic welfare, national wealth, and military power. When a state weighs absolute versus relative gains, military power is by far the most important consideration; states are extraordinarily reluctant, for example, to trade military security for economic gains. Modern nation-states (like eighteenth-century mercantilists) are extremely concerned about the consequences of international economic activities for the distribution of economic gains. Over time, the unequal distribution of these gains will inevitably change the international balance of economic and military power, and will thus affect national security. For this reason, states have always been very sensitive to the effects of the international economy on relative rates of economic growth. At the beginning of the twenty-first century, concern is focused on the distribution of industrial power, especially in those high-tech industries vitally important to the relative power position of individual states. The territorial distribution of industry and of technological capabilities is a matter of great concern for every state and a major issue in international political economy.

NATIONAL AUTONOMY

One of the dominant themes in the study of international political economy (IPE) is the persistent clash between the increasing interdependence of the international economy and the desire of individual states to maintain their economic independence and political autonomy. At the same time that states want the benefits of free trade, foreign investment, and the like, they also desire to protect their political autonomy, cultural values, and social structures. However, the logic of the market system is to expand geographically and to incorporate more and more aspects of a society within the price mechanism, thus making domestic matters subject to forces external to the society. In

[5]Kenneth Waltz, *Theory of International Politics* (Reading, Mass.: Addison-Wesley, 1979).

time, if unchecked, the integration of an economy into the world economy, the intensifying pressures of foreign competition, and the necessity to be efficient in order to survive economically could undermine the independence of a society and force it to adopt new values and forms of social organization. Fear that economic globalization and the integration of national markets are destroying or could destroy the political, economic, and cultural autonomy of national societies has become widespread.

The clash between the evolving economic and technical interdependence of national societies and the continuing compartmentalization of the world political system into sovereign independent states is one of the dominant motifs of contemporary writings on IPE. Whereas powerful market forces (trade, finance, and investment) jump political boundaries and integrate societies, governments frequently restrict and channel their economic activities to serve the interests of their own societies and of powerful groups within those societies. Whereas the logic of the market is to locate economic activities wherever they will be most efficient and profitable, the logic of the state is to capture and control the process of economic growth and capital accumulation in order to increase the power and economic welfare of the nation. The inevitable clash between the logic of the market and the logic of the state is central to the study of international political economy.

Most economists and many political economists believe that the international economy has a positive impact on international political affairs. The international economy, many argue, creates webs of mutual interdependence and common interests that moderate the self-centered behavior of states. Underlying this benign interpretation is a particular definition of economic interdependence as dependence. However, as Albert Hirschman pointed out in *National Power and the Structure of Foreign Trade (1969)*, while economic interdependence may be characterized by mutual dependence, dependence is frequently not symmetrical.[6] Trade, investment, and markets establish dependencies among national societies that can be and are exploited. Integration of national markets creates power relations among states where, as Hirschman notes, economic power arises from the capacity to interrupt economic relations.[7] Economic ties among states almost always involve power relations.

Robert Keohane and Joseph Nye (1977) extended this analysis of economic power and the political aspects of economic interdependence by distinguishing "sensitivity" interdependence from "vulnerability" interdependence. Most economists really are referring to sensitivity interdependence exemplified by responsiveness among economic variables, such as changes in interest rates in one country that influence interest rates in another. Vulnerability interdependence, on the other hand, is what Hirschman

---

[6]Albert O. Hirschman, *National Power and the Structure of Foreign Trade* (Berkeley: University of California Press, 1969).

[7]Ibid., 16.

and political economists frequently have in mind when they speak of economic inter-dependence; this latter term refers to the possibilities of political exploitation of market interdependencies.[8] Individual states have a powerful incentive either to decrease their own dependence on other states through such policies as trade protection and industrial policies or to increase the dependence of other states upon them through such policies as foreign aid and trade concessions. International economic relations are never purely economic; they always have profound implications for the economic autonomy and political independence of national societies.

THE POLITICS OF INTERNATIONAL REGIMES

All economists and political economists acknowledge the need for some minimal rules or institutions to govern and regulate economic activities; even the most ardent public-choice economist would agree that laws are needed to enforce contracts and protect property rights. A liberal international economy—that is, an international economy characterized (at least in ideal terms) by such factors as open markets, freedom of capital movement, and nondiscrimination—certainly needs agreed-upon rules. A liberal economy can succeed only if it provides public goods like a stable monetary system, eliminates market failures, and prevents cheating and free-riding.[9] Although the primary purpose of rules or regimes is to resolve economic problems, many are actually enacted for political rather than for strictly economic reasons. For example, although economists may be correct that an economy benefits from opening itself to free trade whether or not other countries open their own markets to it, a liberal international economy could not politically tolerate too many free-riders who benefit from the opening of other economies but refuse to open their own markets.

In the past, the rules governing the international economy were quite simple and informal. Insofar as the implicit rules were enforced at all, they were enforced by the major powers whose interests were favored by those rules. For example, in the nineteenth century under the Pax Britannica, overseas property rights were frequently upheld by British "gunboat diplomacy,"[10] and the international gold standard, based

---

[8]Robert O. Keohane and Joseph S. Nye Jr., *Power and Interdependence: World Politics in Transition* (Boston: Little, Brown, 1977).

[9]In nontechnical language, a public or collective good is one that everyone can enjoy without having to pay for the use of the good. A frequently used example is a lighthouse. Because of this free use, no one usually has an incentive to provide them, and therefore public goods tend to be "underprovided." The literature on this subject and on proposed solutions to the underprovision problem is extensive.

[10]Charles Lipson, *Standing Guard: Protecting Foreign Capital in the Nineteenth and Twentieth Centuries* (Berkeley: University of California Press, 1985).

on a few generally accepted rules, was managed by the Bank of England. Now, formal international institutions have been created to manage today's extraordinarily complex international economy. The most important institutions are the Bretton Woods institutions such as the World Bank, the International Monetary Fund, and the World Trade Organization. The world economy would have difficulty functioning without these institutions. Therefore, understanding their functioning has become an extremely important concern of political economists.

The concept of international regimes, defined as "sets of implicit or explicit principles, norms, rules, and decision-making procedures around which actors' expectations converge in a given area of international relations," has been at the core of the research on international institutions.[11] Although a distinction can be made between an international regime as rules and understandings and an international institution as a formal organization, the word "regimes" and the word "institutions" are frequently used interchangeably in writings on international political economy. Moreover, what is really important for the functioning of the world economy are the rules themselves rather than the formal institutions in which they are usually embodied. To simplify the following discussion, I shall use "international regime" to encompass both rules and such formal international organizations as the International Monetary Fund or the General Agreement on Tariffs and Trade.

Robert Keohane has been the most influential scholar in the development of regime theory. In his book, After Hegemony (1984), Keohane set forth the definitive exposition and classic defense of regime theory.[12] He argues that international regimes are a necessary feature of the world economy and are required to facilitate efficient operation of the international economy. Among the tasks performed by regimes are reduction of uncertainty, minimization of transaction costs, and prevention of market failures. International regimes are created by self-centered states in order to further both individual and collective interests. Even though a particular regime might be created because of the pressures of a dominant power (or hegemon), Keohane argues that an effective international regime takes on a life of its own over time. Moreover, when states experience the success of an international regime, they "learn" to change their own behavior and even to redefine their national interests. Thus, according to Keohane's analysis, international regimes are necessary to preserve and stabilize the international economy.

From its beginning, regime theory has been surrounded by intense controversy. One major reason for the intensity of this debate is that regime theory arose as a

---

[11]Stephen Krasner, "Structural Causes and Regime Consequences: Regimes as Intervening Variables," *International Organization* 36, no. 2, (spring 1982): 186.

[12]Robert O. Keohane, *After Hegemony: Cooperation and Discord in the World Political Economy* (Princeton University Press, 1984).

response to what Keohane labeled "the theory of hegemonic stability."[13] Proponents of the latter theory had argued that the postwar liberal international economy was based on the economic and political leadership of the United States. Some theorists had argued that the hegemonic stability theory also suggested that the relative decline of American power due to the rise of new economic powers and the slowing of American productivity growth in the early 1970s placed the continued existence of a liberal world economy in jeopardy. As Steven Weber has pointed out, regime theory was largely a response to the perceived decline of American power, the 1973 energy price shock, and the global "stagflation" of the 1970s.[14] Keohane and others argued that international regimes and cooperation among the major economic powers would replace declining American leadership as the basis of the liberal international economic order. Thus, the political purpose of regime theory was, at least in part, to reassure Americans and others that a liberal international order would survive America's economic decline and the severe economic problems of the 1970s.

British scholar Susan Strange was the most outspoken critic of regime theory.[15] According to Strange, regime theory was at best a passing fad, and at worst a polemical device designed to legitimate America's continuing domination of the world economy. Strange and other critics alleged that such international regimes as those governing trade and monetary affairs had been economically, politically, and ideologically biased in America's favor, and that these regimes were put in place by American power, reflected American interests, and were not (as American regime theorists have argued) politically and economically neutral. Strange charged that many of the fundamental problems afflicting the world economy actually resulted from ill-conceived and predatory American economic policies rather than simply being symptoms of American economic decline.

Strange's foremost example of American culpability was the huge American demand in the 1980s and 1990s for international capital to finance America's federal

[13]Robert O. Keohane, "The Theory of Hegemonic Stability and Changes in International Economic Regimes, 1967–1977," in Ole Holsti et al., *Change in the International System* (Boulder, Colo.: Westview Press, 1980): 131–62.

[14]Steven Weber, "Institutions and Change" in Michael Doyle and John Ikenberry, eds., *New Thinking in International Relations* (Boulder, Colo.: Westview Press, 1997). The emphasis on regimes also grew out of the realization in the 1970s that international governance was not codeterminous with international organizations. Consult Friedrich Kratochwil and John Gerard Ruggie, "International Organization: A State of the Art on an Art of the State," *International Organization* 40, no. 4 (autumn 1986): 753–75.

[15]Susan Strange, "Cave! hic Dragones: A Critique of Regime Analysis," in Stephen D. Krasner, ed., *International Regimes*, 337–54. It is noteworthy that very few non-American scholars have been positively inclined toward regime theory or involved in its development. A major exception is Volker Rittberger, ed., *Regime Theory and International Relations* (New York: Oxford University Press, 1993).

budget and trade/payments deficit.[16] Through use of what she referred to as "structural power" (such as America's military, financial, and technological power), she alleged that the United States continued to run the world economy during that period and made a mess of it. Strange and other critics also alleged that the role of the dollar as the key international currency had permitted the United States to behave irresponsibly. More generally, Strange and other foreign critics charged that the American discipline of international political economy, and regime theory in particular, have been little more than efforts to defend America's continuing desire to reign economically and politically over the rest of the world. Whether or not we accept these criticisms, they should remind us that regimes and other social institutions are sometimes created to preserve inequalities as well as to improve coordination and overcome other obstacles to mutually beneficial cooperation.[17] It is desirable to study such important issues as the origins of international regimes, the content, rules, and norms of international regimes, and the history of compliance by affected states, particularly in situations when a regime is perceived as being counter to a state's interests.

Origins

International regimes have developed in a number of different ways. Some have arisen spontaneously and do not involve conscious design; many of the informal rules governing markets are of this type. Others have resulted from international negotiations among states; the post—World War II Bretton Woods system of trade and monetary regimes, for example, was the result of international negotiations, primarily between the United States and Great Britain. Still other regimes have been imposed by powerful states on less powerful ones; the colonial systems of the nineteenth century are a notorious example. This section will concentrate upon regimes created through international negotiations, especially the Bretton Woods regimes for trade and monetary affairs that were the result of American leadership.

In creating the post—World War II regimes, the most important task for American leadership was to promote international cooperation. The United States undertook the leadership role, and other economic powers (Canada, Japan, and Western Europe) cooperated for economic, political, and ideological reasons. These allies believed that a liberal world economy would meet their economic interests and also solidify their alliance against the Soviet threat. In addition, cooperation was greatly facilitated by the fact that these nations shared an ideological commitment to a liberal international

[16]Susan Strange, *Casino Capitalism* (New York: Basil Blackwell, 1986); and Susan Strange, *Mad Money* (Manchester, U.K.: Manchester University Press, 1998).

[17]Andrew Schotter, *The Economic Theory of Social Institutions* (New York: Cambridge University Press, 1981), 26.

economy based on free trade and open markets.[18] All three factors—leadership, coop-eration, and ideological consensus—were important to creation of the post—World War II liberal international economy.

Content

The content of an international regime—the precise rules and decision-making tech-niques embodied in a particular regime—is determined by technological, economic, and political factors. An international regime could not function well if its rules were counter to scientific and technological considerations. Regimes governing interna-tional economic affairs must be based on sound economic principles and must be able to solve complex economic matters. The postwar international monetary regime based on fixed exchange rates, for example, had to solve such difficult technical prob-lems as provision of international liquidity and creation of an adjustment mechanism for nations with balance of payments problems.

Economists, however, seldom agree on such complex issues; there are, for exam-ple, several competing theories on the determination of exchange rates. It is important to realize that the specific means chosen to solve a given economic problem may have significant consequences for individual states and/or may impinge on their national autonomy. In the early postwar monetary system, the central role of the U.S. dollar as a reserve and transaction currency greatly facilitated financing of American foreign policy. Thus, while the content of an international regime must be grounded on sound technical and economic considerations, it is important to recognize that regimes do produce political effects.

A number of regime theorists have a tendency to think of regimes as benign. Regime theory has emphasized the efficiency and efficacy of international cooperation and problem-solving and that regimes are instituted to achieve interstate cooperation and information sharing, to reduce transaction costs, and to solve common problems. While these goals do exist, it is also true, as some scholars of institutions point out, that institutions—and regimes—do create or preserve inequalities; regimes can also have a redistributive function. History is replete with such examples as the carving-up of Africa at the Congress of Berlin (1878) and the post—World War I mandate system. The purpose, content, and actual consequences of every international regime must be closely examined; there should be no assumption that regimes are ipso facto of equal or mutual benefit to every participant.

[18]The term "epistemic community," attributed to John Ruggie, has been given to the role of shared ideas or beliefs in promoting international cooperation.

Because international regimes frequently do have distributive consequences as well as implications for national autonomy, the rules, norms, and other factors embedded in regimes generally reflect the power and interests of the dominant power/s in the international system. Certainly, the liberal trade and monetary regimes following World War II promoted the economic and, I would emphasize, the political and security interests of the United States while also strengthening the anti-Soviet political alliance. Moreover, as American interests changed, the United States used its power to modify one or another of these regimes; the August 1971 Nixon decision to destroy the system of fixed exchange rates because he believed that it no longer suited American interests provided a particularly striking example of this type of behavior.

Nevertheless, it is unlikely that the regimes governing a liberal international economy do or will represent the interests of the dominant power/s alone and of no others. Liberal international regimes must satisfy the interests of all the major economic powers to at least some degree; if they do not, the regimes would neither function nor long survive. The major trading partners of the United States were satisfied with the postwar trade regime and, in fact, benefited economically from the regime more than did the United States. Although a liberal international economic order does reflect the interests of a dominant power, such a power cannot impose a liberal economic order on the rest of the world; ultimately, the regime must rest on international cooperation.

Compliance

Although some scholars deny, or at least minimize, the importance of the compliance issue, compliance with international regimes is a major problem, and it is important to understand the reasons for compliance or noncompliance. The compliance or enforcement problem arises because there is no authoritative international government, because states frequently value highly their relative gains and national autonomy, and because there is a collective action problem in which individual actors are tempted to cheat and free ride. While the compliance problem may be of minor significance in many or even the majority of international regimes, when the rules and principles of an international regime have significant distributive consequences for states and powerful domestic groups, or when they impinge significantly on the autonomy and security of states, the compliance problem becomes of overwhelming importance. Many of the international regimes governing the world economy, in fact, are of this latter type, because they do have important consequences for the distribution of global wealth and national autonomy.

Scholars of international political economy have devoted considerable attention to possible solutions to this problem. An important proposed solution is based on the theory of iterative (or repeated) games and, in particular, on what game theorists call the Prisoner's Dilemma. Another is based on insights from the new institutionalism or "new economics of organization."[19] These approaches fall within the larger category of "theories of international cooperation." Most scholars of international political economy would accept the definition made popular by Robert Keohane that cooperation occurs "when actors adjust their behavior to the actual or anticipated preferences of others, through a process of policy coordination."[20] Although theories of cooperation may be helpful in explicating the nature and difficulties of the compliance problem, they do not really solve the problem.

The Prisoner's Dilemma is undoubtedly familiar to most readers of this book. Nevertheless, I shall provide a brief reminder: Two prisoners are accused of a crime and held separately. If they both confess to the crime of which they are accused, they will both be punished. If neither confesses—that is, if in essence they cooperate with one another—they will both be punished, but less severely. However, if only one confesses (or defects) and the other does not confess, the latter will be punished more severely. Thus, although each has an incentive to cooperate with the other by not confessing, each also has an incentive to confess (defect). Uncertainty regarding what the other player will do could lead to a less than optimal outcome for both players.

This type of mixed motive game in which the players have a motive to cooperate and also a motive to defect is characteristic of almost every aspect of international politics and certainly of international economic affairs. Although the players would gain from cooperation, each might gain even more by defecting (cheating); yet both would lose if both cheat. For example, a nation might be able to increase its own relative gains in the international trading regime by exporting to other markets at the same time that it keeps its own markets closed; however, if others retaliate and close their markets, everyone would lose. In a monetary regime, a nation could increase its international competitiveness by unilaterally devaluing its own currency. However, if other countries simultaneously devalue their own currencies, everyone loses. Therefore, everyone is better off, at least in absolute terms, as a result of cooperation. Yet the possibility of increasing one's own relative gains by cheating or successfully "free-riding" always provides a powerful temptation in international affairs.

A number of attempts have been made by economists and other scholars to solve the Prisoner's Dilemma. Proposed solutions entail methods or techniques designed to increase the likelihood that players will cooperate and not cheat; they include creation

---

[19]The "new institutionalism" is based largely on the research of Oliver Williamson and on the concept of transaction costs; that is, the costs of doing business. For a discussion of the relevance of this literature for IPE, consult Beth V. Yarbrough and Robert M. Yarbrough, "International Institutions and the New Economics of Organization," *International Organization* 44, no. 2 (spring 1990): 235–59. These ideas have been elaborated in their book, *Cooperation and Governance in International Trade: The Strategic Organizational Approach* (Princeton: Princeton University Press, 1992).

[20]Keohane, *After Hegemony*, 51–52.

of norms of reciprocity, making each move in the game less distinct, and linking issues to one another. Such techniques attempt to lessen the incentive to cheat in a particular instance so that the players learn how to cooperate. The most noteworthy effort to solve the Prisoner's Dilemma has been the concept of iterative games developed by Robert Axelrod and others.[21] This concept leads to the conclusion that, if a game is repeated over and over again and a participant pursues a "tit-for-tat" strategy in which cooperative moves are rewarded and uncooperative moves are punished, the participants in the game will learn to trust and cooperate with one another.

The literature on the theory of repeated or iterative games has become extensive and has been subjected to intense theoretical criticism and defense. Although scrutiny of the theory has vastly increased our understanding of the compliance problem, this scholarly debate has not yet enabled us to predict when cooperation or defection from (cheating) a regime will in fact occur. The fundamental problem of uncertainty and hence of regime compliance has not yet been solved and probably never will be; a player can never be absolutely sure whether another player will cooperate or defect, and the costs of miscalculation could be extremely high. The absence of an adequate body of research on the actual functioning of specific regimes makes it impossible to be confident that regimes are of decisive important in the behavior of states. In addition, a fundamental methodological problem makes it difficult to determine whether or not regimes actually make a difference in the conduct of international affairs. As one strong supporter of regime theory has stated, "Investigating the consequences of international regimes requires a counterfactual argument," that is, knowledge of what would happen if the regime did not exist.[22]

The "new economics of organization," or what some scholars prefer to label "neo-institutionalism," has produced another important effort to solve the compliance problem. This theory of international cooperation has been described by George Downs and David Rocke as "a loose composite" of transaction-cost economics and noncooperative game theory.[23] According to new institutionalism, regimes can provide a solution to such problems as market inefficiencies, economic uncertainties, and market failures. However, as Downs and Rocke point out, this theory of international cooperation makes only a limited contribution to solution of the compliance problem, and compliance with international regimes ultimately rests on the domestic and, I would add, the foreign policy interests of individual states.

---

[21]Robert M. Axelrod, *The Evolution of Cooperation* (New York: Basic Books, 1984).

[22]Rittberger, ed., *Regime Theory and International Relations*.

[23]George W. Downs and David M. Rocke, *Optimal Imperfection? Domestic Uncertainty and Institutions in International Relations* (Princeton: Princeton University Press, 1995), 19.

Despite its important insights into the functioning of the world economy, regime theory frequently sidesteps problems of national autonomy and interests. For example, every nation joining an international regime reserves the right to withdraw from the regime if its interests change. In addition, concerns over national autonomy place severe limits on the types of international regimes that are created. Even in the North Atlantic Treaty Organization (NATO), each member reserves the right not to come to the aid of another alliance member if the other is attacked.[24]

The increasing importance of social welfare in state behavior has not substantially changed matters, although many scholars of international political economy have suggested that it has. As James Mayall points out, international regimes have resulted in few, if any, sacrifices of domestic social welfare.[25] Despite much talk of international distributive justice, for example, voluntary sharing by one society of a substantial portion of its wealth with other societies is rare indeed. Foreign aid, for example, has never absorbed more than a small percentage of a nation's GDP, and with a few notable exceptions such aid has been and is given for national security or economic (rather than humanitarian) reasons. The modern welfare system has actually made states even more attentive to their own economic interests. The nationalistic nature of the modern welfare state is well demonstrated by the singular fact that every state severely restricts immigration, at least in part to restrict access to its welfare system.

While international regimes are useful to provide solutions to technical, economic, and other problems associated with the world economy, they also invariably affect the economic welfare, national security, and political autonomy of individual states. For this reason, states frequently attempt to manipulate regimes for their own parochial economic and political advantage. This concept of international regimes as both technical solution and arena of political struggle diverges from that held by many economists and liberal scholars of political economy that regimes are economically and politically neutral. The realist interpretation maintains that international regimes are neither above nor outside the struggle for power and advantage among states. Regimes are both a part and an object of a political struggle. As a consequence, if a regime is to be effective and its rules are to be enforced, it must also rest on a strong political base. Due to the central importance of distribution and autonomy issues to most nations, the compliance problem is unlikely to be resolved, and regime rules are unlikely to be enforced unless there is strong international leadership.

[24]James Mayall, *Nationalism and International Society* (New York: Cambridge University Press, 1990). In the case of NATO, every member has reserved the right whether or not to declare war if another member of the alliance is attacked.

[25]Ibid., Chapter 6.

THEORY OF HEGEMONIC STABILITY

The theory of hegemonic stability, discussed below, in both its liberal and its realist versions, encountered a critical reception from a number of scholars.[26] The theory was attacked on theoretical, historical, and political grounds. The theoretical criticisms emphasized the possibility of a cooperative solution among nonhegemonic nations to the problems associated with creating and maintaining a liberal international economy. Although it may be possible to create a stable liberal international order through cooperation but without a hegemon, this has never happened, and with no counterfactual example neither the theory nor its critics can be proved wrong. This problem, of course, is endemic in many areas of the social sciences. Some critics of the theory have tested it against late-nineteenth-century experience and found weaknesses in the theory.[27] Political criticisms have ranged from denunciations of the theory as a defense of or rationale for American policies to the opposite idea that the theory predicted the absolute decline of the United States. No proponent of hegemonic stability theory, at least to my knowledge, has been motivated to justify American behavior; to the contrary, most were very critical of the self-centered and irresponsible American behavior that began in the 1960s, if not earlier.

A major reason for the criticisms of the theory by political scientists is that it was never adequately formulated. Indeed, the "theory" was more an intuitive idea based on a particular reading of history than a scientific theory. Because the theory was underdeveloped, it was open to both warranted and unwarranted criticisms. A number of critics, for example, interpreted the theory to mean that a dominant power is necessary to the emergence of a liberal international economy; they have gone on to make the point that Soviet hegemony did not create a liberal Soviet-dominated international economy. However, as I have emphasized in numerous writings, a liberal international economy requires a hegemon committed to liberal economic principles, as Great Britain was in the nineteenth century and the United States was in the twentieth century; the theory was never intended to suggest that a Soviet Union. Nazi Germany, or militaristic Japan would promote a liberal world economy. Moreover,

---

[26]Several of the most important criticisms of the theory are John A. C. Conybeare, "Public Goods, Prisoner's Dilemmas and the International Political Economy," *International Studies Quarterly* 28, no. 1 (March 1984): 5–22; David A. Lake, "Leadership, Hegemony, and the International Economy: Naked Emperor or Tattered Monarch with Potential?" *International Studies Quarterly* 37, no. 4 (December 1993): 459–89; Duncan Snidel, "The Limits of Hegemonic Stability Theory," *International Organization* 39, no. 4 (autumn 1985): 579–614; and Helen V. Milner, *Interests, Institutions, and Information: Domestic Politics and International Relations* (Princeton: Princeton University Press, 1997), 24–25.

[27]An example is Timothy J. McKeown, "Hegemonic Stability Theory and 19th Century Tariff Levels in Europe" *International Organization* 37, no. 1 (winter 1983): 73–91.

despite the implied criticisms of some authors, the theory, at least in my opinion, posited that a hegemon is a necessary but not a sufficient condition for establishment of a liberal international economy. It is possible, as some critics have argued, that a hegemon's interests would be best served by an optimum tariff; yet, such an aggressive tactic would be a highly unlikely course of action for a strong liberal power such as Great Britain or the United States. Instead, the theory rests on the idea of international cooperation. Hegemony makes cooperation more feasible and is not, as some have suggested, opposed to cooperation.

The strongest support for the theory, or at least for the idea that strong leadership is necessary, has come from economists. This endorsement is rather amazing, because economists (with the notable exception of Kindleberger) are likely to argue that markets by themselves will manage the world economy. The most detailed and systematic empirical critique of HST by an economist is that of economic historian Barry Eichengreen (1989).[28] However, support for the theory was not the purpose avowed by Eichengreen; in fact, he believed that he had refuted the theory. Through examination of the historical record, Eichengreen tried to discover whether or not a hegemon had played a determining role in the rise and maintenance of an open world economy. He inquired specifically into the roles of Great Britain in the late nineteenth century and of the United States in the post—World War II era, particularly regarding the genesis and functioning of the international monetary system. Although he concluded that the record gave only modest support to the theory, his analysis actually supports its validity.

Eichengreen's lukewarm assessment of the theory appears to rest on the erroneous assumption that the hegemon must be an imperialistic power that imposes its will on other countries. His language suggests that he identifies hegemony with coercion and imposition of the hegemon's will on other countries. Throughout his analysis, he uses such terms as "dictating," "force," and "coerced" to describe the actions of the British and American hegemons. Yet, no proponent of the theory has used such language, but instead each has emphasized the essential leadership role of the hegemon in promoting international cooperation. In fact, Eichengreen's analysis itself confirms that the British and American hegemons "significantly influenced" the nature of the international monetary system through promotion of international cooperation. Without a hegemon, international cooperation in trade, monetary, and most other matters in international affairs becomes exceptionally difficult, if not impossible, to achieve.

[28]Barry Eichengreen, "Hegemonic Stability Theories of the International Monetary System," in Richard N. Cooper et al., *Can Nations Agree?: Issues in International Economic Cooperation* (Washington, D.C.: Brookings Institution, 1989), 255–98.

Four years later (1993), Eichengreen again evaluated the theory of hegemonic stability from the perspective of historical experience.[29] Whereas his earlier analysis had focused on the international monetary system, this subsequent evaluation considered the international trading system. He stated that there was a positive association between hegemony and trade liberalization. Comparing the nineteenth century and post—World War II experiences, Eichengreen concluded that "the only example of successful multilateralism the historical record provides coincides with a period of exceptional economic dominance by a single power. And the growing difficulties of the GATT have coincided, of course, with US relative … economic decline." He then goes on to ask, "Why might this be?"

Eichengreen drew upon cartel theory to explain why a hegemon facilitates international cooperation: "Simple cartel theory suggests that it is possible to deter defection from a cartel containing many members only when there is a dominant firm capable of acting as enforcer. In its absence, duopolies of, say, neighboring firms may be the most that monitoring and enforcement capabilities can support. This suggests that the growing prevalence of bilateralism is a corollary of the increasingly multipolar nature of the world economy."[30] Thus, Eichengreen has set forth a plausible explanation of why the decline of American leadership has contributed to the increasing importance of bilateral negotiations and regional arrangements in the world economy.

Other leading economists have also supported the validity of the theory. For example, Nobel Laureate Robert Mundell, a distinguished expert on international monetary and financial affairs, has pointed out that the stability of the international monetary system is dependent upon a dominant power. Other international economists such as Robert Baldwin and Swiss economist Bruno Frey have also written in support of the idea that a hegemon is necessary. Baldwin writes, for example, that the hegemonic role played by the United States increased the economic welfare of most non-Communist countries.[31] According to Frey, public choice theory suggests that it is impossible for public goods to be provided if there is no hegemon.[32]

---

[29]Barry Eichengreen, in Jaime De Melo and Arvind Panagariya, eds., *New Dimensions in Regional Integration* (New York: Cambridge University Press, 1995), 120–21.

[30]Eichengreen, in ibid., 121.

[31]Robert E. Baldwin, "Adapting the GATT to a More Regionalized World: A Political Economy Perspective," in Kym Anderson and Richard Blackhurst, *Regional Integration and the Global Trading System* (New York: St. Martin's Press, 1993), Chapter 18; Bruno S. Frey, *International Political Economics*.

[32]Frey, *International Political Economics*. According to Frey, Arrow's "impossibility theorem" demonstrates that with three countries and three goals, common or coordinated policies cannot be reached when each country has a different ordering of priorities. Leadership is required to break the deadlock.

One of most the interesting arguments supporting the necessity of a hegemon was set forth by Mancur Olson. Olson's views are especially apposite because of his innovative work on provision of collective goods and the fact that many critics of the theory cite his work to support their own criticisms. Commenting on provision of the collective good of free trade, Olson presents an ingenious theory based on domestic politics to explain why it is so difficult for a country to reduce trade barriers unilaterally and in the absence of external pressures exerted by a powerful state.[33] He then concludes, "Thus the world works better when there is a 'hegemonic' power—one that finds it in its own self-interest to see that various international collective goods are provided." He continues, "Naturally, the incentive a hegemonic power has to provide international collective goods diminishes as it becomes relatively less important in the world economy. In the United States, there has been a conspicuous resurgence of protectionist thinking, and a diminishing willingness of the country to provide foreign aid, as the American economy has come to encompass relatively less of the world economy."[34] From this perspective, the emergence of new industrial powers and new exporters of manufactured goods has resulted in increased American protectionist policies, beginning with the New Protectionism in the mid-1970s and with the shift to a greater emphasis on economic regionalism made manifest in the 1994 formation of the North American Free Trade Agreement.

Lack of a counterfactual makes it impossible either to validate or refute the theory of hegemonic stability, but Eichengreen's empirical examination of the theory, the supportive commentary of other economists and political scientists, and the theoretical writings of Olson and others lend considerable support to its validity. For these reasons, even though the hegemonic stability theory (HST) does not provide a foolproof account of the eras of British and American leadership of the world economy, it does hold up quite well by the standards of the social sciences, including economics.

GOVERNANCE OF THE GLOBAL ECONOMY

Creation of effective international regimes and solutions to the compliance problem require both strong international leadership and an effective international governance structure. Regimes in themselves cannot provide governance structure because they lack the most critical component of governance—the power to enforce compliance. Regimes must rest instead on a political base established through leadership and cooperation. Although many liberal scholars consider the concepts of hegemony and

---

[33]Mancur Olson, in De Melo and Panagariya, eds., *New Dimensions in Regional Integration*, 122–27.
[34]Ibid, 125.

of regimes to be incompatible or even opposed to one another, regimes governing economic affairs cannot function without a strong leader or hegemon. The theory of hegemonic stability posits that the leader or hegemon facilitates international cooperation and prevents defection from the rules of the regime through use of side payments (bribes), sanctions, and/or other means but can seldom, if ever, coerce reluctant states to obey the rules of a liberal international economic order.

The American hegemon did indeed play a crucial role in establishing and managing the world economy following World War II; strong support and cooperation were provided by the Cold War allies of the United States. Moreover, as Downs and Rocke point out, regime compliance ultimately is dependent on domestic support. Post—World War II regimes rested on what John Ruggie called "the compromise of embedded liberalism," in which governments may and do intervene in their domestic economies to promote full employment but must also conform to internationally agreed-upon rules.[35] Postwar trade liberalization was politically acceptable because governments pursued policies to guarantee full employment and to compensate those harmed by the opening of national markets to international trade. Solution of the governance problem was, for decades, achieved through leadership, international cooperation, and domestic consensus.

The idea that a liberal international economy requires strong political leadership by the dominant economic power was initially set forth by Charles Kindleberger in *The World In Depression, 1929–1939* (1973).[36] According to Kindleberger, the scope, depth, and duration of the Great Depression were more severe because there was no leader to carry out several tasks necessary for the world economy to function properly. Some of these tasks must be performed even in normal times; others are needed in a crisis. In normal times a leader must (1) maintain the flow of capital to poor countries, (2) provide some order in foreign exchange rates, at least among the key currencies, and (3) arrange for at least moderate coordination of macroeconomic policies among the leading economies. In times of crisis, the leader, in Kindleberger's words, must provide "open markets for distressed goods in depression and be a source of extra-supply when goods are tight, as in the oil crises of 1973 and 1979. The economic leader must also be a 'lender of last resort' in the event of a serious international financial crisis. Lacking a leading country able and willing to discharge these functions, financial crises can be followed by prolonged depressions as happened in the 1930s. In short, the functions of the leader are capital lending, creation of a foreign-exchange regime,

---

[35]John Gerard Ruggie, "International Regimes, Transactions, and Change: Embedded Liberalism in the Postwar Economic Order," in Stephen D. Krasner, ed., *International Regimes*, 195–231.

[36]Charles P. Kindleberger, *The World In Depression, 1929–1939* (Berkeley: University of California Press, 1973).

macroeconomic coordination, maintaining open markets, and being the 'lender of last resort.'"[37]

Stephen Krasner and I each appropriated Kindleberger's basic idea that a political leader was needed to create and manage an international liberal economy. However, each of us made several modifications that placed Kindleberger's insight within a state-centric intellectual framework of political analysis and thus fashioned a state-centric version of the theory of hegemonic stability. Both of us used the Greek word "hege-mon" rather than "leader" to indicate that at times the leader had to exercise power to achieve its objective of establishing and managing a liberal world economy. A hegemon is defined as the leader of an alliance like that organized by Sparta to defeat the Per-sian invaders in ancient Greece or by the United States to defeat the Soviets. Whereas Kindleberger argued that the leader created a liberal international economy for both its own and cosmopolitan economic reasons, Krasner and I have both argued that the hegemon created a liberal international economy primarily to promote its own interests and its political/security interests in particular. Both of us have acknowledged that these security interests could also include the economic and military interests of allies.

When the United States played a central role in promoting an open and interdepen-dent international economy (composed mainly of the United States and its allies) in order to strengthen the anti-Soviet alliance, America's motives were hardly altruistic. Never-theless, despite the differences between Kindleberger's liberal version of the hegemonic stability theory and the Krasner/Gilpin state-centric version, both approaches maintain that provision of such international public goods as free trade and monetary stability requires a dominant power with an interest in a liberal world economy and a willingness to expend economic and political resources to achieve and maintain that goal.

The theory of hegemonic stability maintains that there can be no liberal interna-tional economy unless there is a leader that uses its resources and influence to estab-lish and manage an international economy based on free trade, monetary stability, and freedom of capital movement. The leader must also encourage other states to obey the rules and regimes governing international economic activities. The theory assumes that a liberal international economy requires that certain "public goods" will be pro-moted by the leader. A public good, as originally defined by Paul Samuelson, has the properties of "non-excludability" (inclusiveness) and nonrivalrous consumption. This rather obtuse jargon means that any individual's consumption of a public good does not affect (decrease) consumption of the good by others, and that no one can be prevented from consuming the good whether or not he or she has paid for it. A light-house, of benefit to every ship whether or not the ship has contributed to the upkeep of the lighthouse, fulfills such criteria. In such a situation, individuals (and individual

[37]Charles P. Kindleberger, *The World Economy and National Finance in Historical Perspective* (Ann Arbor: University of Michigan Press, 1995), 62.

nations) have an incentive to free ride—to take advantage of the public good without paying for it—since no one can be excluded from enjoying the good. This means that public goods will generally be undersupplied because few actors will have an incentive to pay the costs of providing such goods.

The public goods associated with a liberal international economy include an open trading system and a stable international monetary system. However, there are even greater tendencies toward free riding and for international public goods to be undersupplied within the international economy than in domestic affairs. This problem can, at least in theory, be overcome by a small group of cooperating states; however, I know of no example of this type of cooperation on such a large scale as the world economy. In practice, public goods have been and can be provided only by a leader (or hegemon) with an interest in supplying the good for all or in forcing others to share payment for the good.

A brief examination of the British and American eras of international leadership increases comprehension of the dynamics of the rise and erosion of a liberal world economy; both eras of economic liberalism required a hegemonic power. From the mid-nineteenth century to the outbreak of World War I, Great Britain led the efforts for trade liberalization and monetary stability; the United States has led the world economy since World War II. The liberal world economy in the late nineteenth century was truly global and was generally characterized by nondiscrimination in trade, unrestricted capital movements, and a stable monetary system based on the gold standard. For decades the American system was composed only of the Free World; during the Cold War it was characterized by trade discrimination, by capital controls until the 1970s, and by monetary instability after 1971. Whereas the British promoted and inspired free trade by example and through a series of bilateral agreements, the United States has championed trade liberalization through multilateral negotiations within the GATT. Although there is disagreement on this subject, according to Joanne Gowa, security concerns did influence British trade policy.[38] Certainly, international security considerations—forging the Western alliance against the Soviet Union—played an extremely important role in America's promotion of free trade. In the monetary realm, the Bank of England played a central role in management of the gold standard in the nineteenth-century system. However, even though the post—World War II international monetary system has been based on the dollar and subject to American influence, the Federal Reserve has had to share pride of place with the German Bundesbank and other powerful central banks.

British economic decline began in the late nineteenth century as other countries, especially Germany and the United States, industrialized; Britain responded with a gradual retrenchment of its global position and initiation of numerous measures

[38]Gowa, *Allies, Adversaries, and International Trade.*

to strengthen its security.[39] Although Great Britain modified a number of its economic policies, its huge dependence on trade forestalled a retreat into protectionism. Nevertheless, British leadership in trade liberalization did slacken, and by the 1930s Britain had retreated to a system of imperial preferences applied to the colonial empire and Commonwealth members. As early as the mid-1970s, American political leaders, business interests, and scholars expressed strong concerns over the relative decline and deindustrialization of the American economy caused by foreign competition, principally from the Japanese. Such worries produced the New Protectionism. As formal tariffs were reduced through trade negotiations, the United States erected such nontariff barriers as those embedded in the Multi-Fiber Agreement (1973), in which many nations were assigned quotas; the United States also imposed "voluntary" export restraints on Japanese products. Responding to the ballooning American trade deficit, intensifying fears of deindustrialization, and rising protectionist pressures, the Reagan Administration in the mid-1980s significantly modified America's commitment to multilateralism. It began to pursue a multitrack trade policy that has not only deemphasized multilateral negotiations but also increased unilateralism and bilateralism (especially "managed trade" with Japan) along with economic regionalism through the North American Free Trade Agreement with Canada and Mexico.

CONCLUSION

Although the science of economics is a necessary foundation for comprehension of international political economy, this book focuses attention on the interaction of markets and political actors. Economics alone is an inaccurate and insufficient tool for analysis of such vital issues as the international distribution of wealth and economic activities, the effects of the world economy on national interests, and the effectiveness of international regimes. This writer rejects the popular idea that universal economic laws and powerful economic forces now rule the global economy. Despite increasing economic globalization and integration among national economies, it is still necessary to distinguish between national and international economies. Political boundaries do and will divide the economies and economic policies of one nation from those of another; political considerations also significantly influence and distinguish economic activities in one country from the next. States, and other powerful actors as well, use their power to influence economic activities to maximize their own economic and political interests.

[39]Robert Gilpin, *War and Change in World Politics* (New York: Cambridge University Press, 1981).

THE DOMESTIC SOURCES
OF FOREIGN ECONOMIC
POLICIES

Michael J. Hiscox

INTRODUCTION

Each government must make choices about how best to manage the way its own economy is linked to the global economy. It must choose whether to open the national market to international trade, whether to liberalize trade with some nations more than with others, and whether to allow more trade in some sectors of the economy than in others. Each government must also decide whether to restrict international flows of investment in different sectors, and whether to regulate immigration and emigration by different types of workers. And it must either fix the exchange rate for the national currency or allow the rate to fluctuate to some degree, in response to supply and demand in international financial markets.

Of course, if every government always made the same choices in all these areas of policy, things would be very simple for us as scholars (and much more predictable for the citizens of the world). But governments in different countries, and at different moments in history, have often chosen radically different foreign economic policies. Some have closed off their national economies almost completely from the rest of the world, imposing strict limits on trade, immigration, and investment—an example is China in the 1960s, which kept itself isolated almost completely from the rest of the world's economies. In other situations, governments have adopted the opposite approach, allowing virtually unfettered economic exchange between their citizens and foreigners—ironically, Hong Kong in the 1960s may be the best example of this type of extreme openness. Most governments today adopt a mixture of policies that fall somewhere in the middle ground between these two extremes, imposing selective controls on activities that affect some sectors of their economy, and restricting exchanges with some foreign countries more than with others. Understanding why governments make the particular choices they do requires careful attention to the political pressures they face from different domestic groups and the political institutions that regulate the way collective decisions are made and implemented.

Politics, we know, is all about who gets what, when, and how. Different individuals and groups in every society typically have very different views about what their government should do when it comes to setting the policies that regulate international trade, immigration, investment, and exchange rates. These competing demands must be reconciled in some way by the political institutions that govern policy-making. To really understand the domestic origins of foreign economic policies we thus need to perform two critical tasks:

1. Identify or map the policy preferences of different groups in the domestic economy.
2. Specify how political institutions determine the way these preferences are aggregated or converted into actual government decisions.

The first step will require some *economic* analysis. How people are affected by their nation's ties with the global economy, and thus what types of policies they prefer to manage those ties, depends primarily on how they make their living. Steel-workers, for example, typically have very different views from wheat farmers about most foreign economic policies, because these policies rarely affect the steel and wheat industries in a similar fashion. Of critical importance here are the types of assets that individuals own, and how the income earned from these assets is affected by different policy choices.

The second step calls for *political* analysis. How political representatives are elected, how groups organize to lobby or otherwise influence politicians, and how policies are proposed, debated, amended, and passed in legislatures, and then implemented by government agencies, all depend on the structure of political institutions. Democratically elected leaders face very different institutional constraints from military dictators, of course, and even among democracies there is quite a wide range of institutional variation that can have a large impact on the behaviour of policy-makers.

These two analytical steps put together like this, combining both economic and political analysis in tandem, are generally referred to as the *political economy* approach to the study of policy outcomes. In the next two sections we shall consider each of the two analytical steps in some detail, examining the domestic sources of policies in the areas of trade, immigration, investment, and exchange rates. We shall then shift gears a little, and consider the ways in which ideas and information might affect policy-making. We shall also discuss linkages between the different policy dimensions and non-economic issues, focusing on environmental and human rights concerns, and how they feature in debates over foreign economic policies. Finally, in the conclusion, to link all this to the discussion of international collaboration and co-ordination in the previous chapter, we shall consider briefly the impact of domestic politics on bargaining over economic issues between governments at the international level.

POLICY PREFERENCES

The guiding assumption here is that, when it comes to taking positions on how to regulate ties with the global economy, individuals and groups are fundamentally concerned with how different policy choices affect their incomes. Of course, people may also have important non-material concerns that affect their attitudes toward foreign economic policies. Many people are concerned about the ways in which globalization affects national security, for example, and they worry about its impact on traditional cultures, on the world's environment, and on human rights; and these concerns may have a direct impact on their views about the regulation of international trade, immigration, and investment. We shall discuss some of these important considerations in more detail later in the chapter. But we begin here with the simplest possible framework in which economic policies are evaluated only in terms of their economic effects. Given that organized producer groups have almost always been the most vocal participants in domestic debates about foreign economic policies, and the debates themselves have been couched mainly in economic terms, this seems an appropriate way to begin.

Trade

The dramatic growth in international trade over the last few decades has intensified political debate over the costs and benefits of trade openness. In the United States, the controversy surrounding the creation of the North American Free Trade Agreement (NAFTA) in 1993 was especially intense, and similar arguments have arisen in Europe over the issue of enlargement of the European Union, and over attempts to reform the Common Agricultural Policy (CAP). Rapid trade policy reforms have also generated a significant political backlash in many developing nations, and recent years have witnessed violent protests and demonstrations by groups from a variety of countries that hope to disrupt meetings of the World Trade Organization (WTO). Political leaders around the world frequently voice concerns about the negative effects of trade, and the need to protect their firms and workers from foreign competition.

What is behind all this political fuss and bother? At first glance it may seem puzzling that there is so much conflict over trade. After all, the most famous insight from international economics is the proof that trade provides mutual gains; that is, when countries exchange goods and services they are all generally better off. Trade allows each country to specialize in producing those goods and services in which it has a comparative advantage, and in doing so world welfare is improved (see Appendix 4.1 on page 132).

While there are gains from trade for all countries *in the aggregate*, what makes trade so controversial is that, among individuals within each country, trade creates winners and losers. How trade affects different individuals depends on how they earn their living. To flesh out this story, economists have traditionally relied on a very simple theory of trade devised by two Swedish economists, Eli Heckscher and Bertil Ohlin. In the Heckscher–Ohlin model of trade, each nation's comparative advantage is traced to its particular endowments of different factors of production: that is, basic inputs such as land, labour, and capital that are used in different proportions in the production of different goods and services. Since the costs of these inputs in each country will depend on their availability, differences in factor endowments across countries will create differences in comparative advantage. Each country will tend to export items whose production requires intensive use of the factors with which it is abundantly endowed relative to other nations; conversely, each country will import goods whose production requires intensive use of factors that are relatively scarce. Countries well endowed with land, such as Australia and Canada, are expected to export agricultural products (for example, wheat and wool), while importing products that require the intensive use of labour (for example, textiles and footwear) from more labour-abundant economies like China and India. The advanced economies of Europe, Japan, and the United States, well endowed with capital relative to the rest of the world, should export capital-intensive products (for example, automobiles and pharmaceuticals), while importing labour-intensive goods from less developed trading partners where supplies of capital are scarce compared to supplies of labour.

Building on this simple model of trade, Wolfgang Stolper and Paul Samuelson (1941) derived a famous theorem in 1941 that outlined the likely effects of trade on the real incomes of different sets of individuals within any economy. According to the Stolper–Samuelson theorem, trade benefits those who own the factors of production with which the economy is relatively well endowed, but hurts owners of scarce factors. The reasoning is straight-forward: by encouraging specialization in each economy in export-orientated types of production, trade increases the demand for locally abundant factors (and bids up the earnings of those who own those factors), while reducing demand for locally scarce factors (and lowering the earnings of owners of such factors). In Australia and Canada, the theorem tells us, landowners should benefit most from trade, while workers can expect lower real wages as a consequence of increased imports of labour-intensive goods. In Europe, Japan, and the United States, the theorem predicts a fairly simple class division over trade: the trade issue should benefit owners of capital at the expense of workers. The converse should hold in relatively labour-abundant (and capital-scarce) developing economies such as China and India, where trade will raise the wages of workers relative to the profits earned by local owners of capital.

By revealing how trade benefits some people while making others worse off, the Stolper–Samuelson theorem thus accounts for why trade is such a divisive political issue. The theorem also provides a neat way to map the policy preferences of individuals in each economy. In each nation, owners of locally *abundant* factors should support greater trade openness, while owners of locally *scarce* factors should be protectionist.

There is a good deal of evidence in the histories of political conflict over trade in a variety of nations that fits with this simple prediction (see Rogowski 1989). In Australia, for example, the first national elections in 1901 were fought between a Free Trade party, representing predominantly rural voters, and a Protectionist party supported over-whelmingly by urban owners of capital and labour. A very similar kind of political division characterized most debates over trade policy in Canada in the late nineteenth century, with support for trade openness emanating mainly from farmers in the western provinces. In Europe and Japan, in contrast, much of the opposition to trade over the last century or so has come from agricultural interests, anxious to block cheap imports of farm products from abroad. In the United States and Europe, at least since the 1960s, labour unions have voiced some of the loudest opposition to trade openness and called for import restrictions aimed at protecting jobs in labour-intensive industries threatened by foreign competition.

On the other hand, political divisions and coalitions in trade politics often appear to contradict this simple model of preferences. It is quite common to see workers and owners in the same industry banding together to lobby for protective import barriers, for example, in contemporary debates about policy in Europe and the United States, even though the Stolper–Samuelson theorem tells us that capital and labour are supposed to have directly opposing views about trade in these economies. So what is going on here? The critical problem is that the theorem is derived by assuming that factors of production are highly mobile between different industries in each economy. An alternative approach to mapping the effects of trade on incomes, often referred to as the **specific factors model** allows instead that it can be quite costly to move factors of production between different sectors in the economy. That is, different types of land, labour skills, and capital equipment often have a very limited or specific use (or range of uses) to which they can be put when it comes to making products. The plant and machinery used in modern manufacturing industries is very specialized: the presses used to stamp out automobile bodies are designed only for that purpose, for example, and cannot be adapted easily or quickly to perform other tasks. Steel factories cannot easily be converted into pharmaceutical factories or software design houses. Nor can steelworkers quickly adapt their skills and become chemical engineers or computer programmers.

In the specific factors model, the real incomes of different individuals are tied very closely to the fortunes of the particular industries in which they make their living. Individuals employed or invested in export industries benefit from trade according to this model, while those who are attached to import-competing industries are harmed (see Jones 1971; Mussa 1974). In the advanced economies of Europe and the United States, the implication is that owners and employees in export-orientated industries such as aerospace, pharmaceuticals, computer software, construction equipment, and financial services, should be much more supportive of trade than their counterparts in, say, the steel, textiles, and footwear industries, which face intense pressure from import competition. There is much evidence supporting these predictions in the real world of trade politics, especially in the debates over trade in the most advanced economies, where technologies (and the skills that complement them) have become increasingly specialized in many different manufacturing and service industries, and even in various areas of agriculture and mining production (see Magee 1980; Hiscox 2002). In the recent debates over regional and multilateral trade agreements in the United States, for example, some of the most vociferous opposition to removing barriers to trade has come from owners and workers aligned together in the steel and textile industries....

FOREIGN INVESTMENT

Capital can also move from one country to another. These movements usually do not take the form of a physical relocation of some existing buildings and machinery from a site in one nation to another site abroad (the equivalent to worker migration). Instead, they take the form of financial transactions between citizens of different nations that transfer ownership rights over assets: a firm in one country buys facilities abroad that it can operate as a subsidiary, for example, or individuals in one country buy shares in foreign companies, or a bank in one country lends money to foreign firms. All such transactions increase the stock of capital available for productive use in one country, and decrease the stock of capital in another country.

The dramatic increase in the volume of international capital flows since the 1960s, outstripping the increase in trade, has had a profound impact on the international economy. Short-term flows of capital in the form of **portfolio investment** (purchases of company shares and other forms of securities, including government bonds), which can change direction quite rapidly in response to news and speculation about changing macroeconomic conditions and possible adjustments in exchange rates, have had a major impact on the choices governments can make when it comes to monetary and exchange-rate policies (see Pauly, Chapter 8 in this volume). Longer-term capital flows in the form of 'direct foreign investment' (where the purchase of foreign assets by a firm based in one country gives it ownership control of a firm located on foreign soil), have perhaps been even more politically controversial since the activities of these multinational firms have had major and highly visible effects in the host nations in which they manage affiliates (see Thun, Chapter 11 in this volume). Many critics of multinational corporations fear that the economic leverage enjoyed by these firms, especially in small, developing nations, can undermine national policies aimed at improving environment standards and human rights. The political debate over direct foreign investment is thus highly charged.

Tight restrictions on both short- and long-term investment by foreigners have been quite common historically, although the controls have been much less strict than those typically imposed on immigration. Clearly, these controls cannot be motivated by a desire for economic efficiency. If such controls are removed and capital is allowed to move freely to those locations in which it is used most productively (and where it will be rewarded, as a result, with higher earnings), it is easy to show that the total output of goods and services will be increased in both the country to which the capital is flowing and in the world economy as a whole. Again, this expansion in aggregate production makes it possible, in principle, to raise the standard of living for people everywhere. International investment, just like the migration of workers examined above, can serve the same economic purpose that is otherwise served by trade. International flows of capital substitute for the exports of capital-intensive goods and services in the benchmark Heckscher—Ohlin model. In general, then, we can expect that the advanced industrial economies of Europe and the United States, which have abundant local supplies of capital for investment, and in which rates of return on capital are thus quite low compared with earnings elsewhere, are the natural suppliers of capital (as well as capital-intensive goods) to poorer nations, in which capital is in relatively scarce supply....

Now, putting aside the aggregate welfare gains that international movements of capital make possible, which individuals are likely to benefit from such capital flows, and which individuals will lose out? Here we can simply apply the logic of the same 'factor proportions' approach we used above to outline the effects of immigration. We might distinguish between different types of capital, in the same way that we distinguished between low- and high-skilled labour above, and set apart lending and short-term or portfolio investment flows direct foreign investment. But to keep things simple here, we shall just consider them all as a single form of capital. What is critical here, of course, is the impact that inflows of any foreign capital have on relative supplies of factors of production in the local economy. Allowing more inflows of capital from abroad will increase the local supply of capital relative to other factors, and thus lower real returns for local owners of capital. At the same time, inflows of investment will raise the real earnings of local owners of land and labour by increasing demand for these other factors of production.

Again, even allowing for the fact that trade flows can partially offset the impact of international movements of factors of production—economies may adjust by importing lower quantities of some goods that are now less costly to produce at home—the direction of the effects on the incomes of different groups is always the same. Local owners of capital are disadvantaged by inflows of foreign capital; while local landowners and workers (in all categories) are better off. These effects may diminish in size in cases in which the local economy is small relative to others, as we noted above when discussing the income effects of immigration, but they are always working in the same direction. And again, in parallel with the analysis of immigration flows, these income effects are not affected drastically by allowing that capital can take forms that are highly 'specific' to particular industries—though the effects may be larger for owners of some types of capital than others. This is especially relevant when we think about direct foreign investment, which typically involves the relocation of particular set of manufacturing or marketing activities that require very specific types of technologies in a particular industry. An inflow of any type of specific capital will, of course, result in a decline in earnings for local owners of capital in the same industry; it will also hurt all others who own specific types of capital used in different industries—in a more marginal way, of course—as demand for their assets will fall in response to the expansion taking place in the industry favoured by foreign investment.

We can thus expect that policies allowing greater inflows of foreign capital will be strongly opposed by individuals who own capital in the local economy, but such policies will be supported by local landowners and workers. There is some evidence that does fit well with these basic predictions. Perhaps the best example involves the way European and American auto companies have supported restrictions on the operations of local affiliates of their Japanese rivals since the 1980s. In Europe, auto firms pushed hard for an agreement with Japan that included cars produced in Japanese affiliates within the limits set on the total Japanese market share of the European auto market. In the United States, after some initial hesitation (perhaps reflecting the fact that they had themselves set up numerous foreign transplant firms around the world) the US auto firms supported a variety of proposals for 'domestic content' laws that would have placed local affiliates of Japanese auto makers at a considerable disadvantage by disrupting their relationships with parts suppliers at home (Crystal 2003). The 'big three' American firms (Ford, General Motors, and Chrysler) also seized the opportunity to demand high local content requirements in the **rules of origin** for autos in the negotiations over the 1993 North American Free Trade Agreement, ensuring that they would have a major advantage over Japanese transplants producing cars in Mexico for the North American market. Interestingly, the workers we would expect to be strongly supportive of incoming Japanese investment in the auto industry, represented by the United Auto Workers union, were in fact quite lukewarm—perhaps because they had long advocated that tough domestic content rules be applied to American firms, to prevent them from transplanting their parts manufacturing facilities to Canada and Mexico, and perhaps also in response to concerns that the foreign transplants setting up in southern American states such as Tennessee (Nissan) and Kentucky (Toyota) were not employing union members.

Foreign investment tends to be even more politically controversial in developing nations, where the behaviour of large foreign corporations can have profound effects on the local economy and on local politics. One particular concern among critics of multinational firms has been the role that several large corporations have apparently played in supporting authoritarian governments that have restricted political organization among labour groups, limited growth in wage rates, and permitted firms to mistreat workers and pollute the environment (see Evans 1979; Klein 2002). While the evidence is not very clear, in some cases, local owners of capital may well have muted their opposition to investments by foreign firms in order to support authoritarian policies adopted by military regimes: in Nigeria, for example, where Shell (the European oil company) has long been the major foreign investor, or more recently in Myanmar, where Unocal (an American oil and gas firm) is the key foreign player. But the basic competitive tension between local capitalists and foreign firms (whose entry into the economy bids down local profits) is typically very obvious even in these unstable and non-democratic environments, as local firms have often encouraged their governments to impose severe restrictions on foreign investments, including onerous regulations stipulating that foreign firms use local rather than imported inputs, exclusion from key sectors of the economy, and even nationalization (seizure) of firms' assets (Jenkins 1987: 172). Newer evidence suggests that, as we might expect given the preferences of labour in capital-poor developing nations, left-wing governments backed by organized labour have made the strongest efforts to lure foreign firms to make investments (Pinto 2003).

EXCHANGE RATES

Of course, a critical difference between transactions that take place between individuals living in the same country and transactions between people in different countries is that the latter require that people can convert one national currency into another.

If a firm in Australia wants to import DVDs from a film studio in the United States, for example, it will need to exchange its Australian dollars for US dollars to pay the American company. The rate at which this conversion takes place will obviously affect the transaction: the more Australian dollars it takes to buy the number of US dollars required (the price of the DVDs), the more costly are the imports for movie-loving Australian buyers. All the trade and investment transactions taking place every day in the world economy are affected by the rates at which currencies are exchanged.

Before the First World War, almost all governments fixed the value of their 'currency in terms of gold, thereby creating an international monetary system in which all rates of conversion between individual currencies were held constant (for further discussion of this international **gold standard**, see Ravehnhill, Box 1.3, page 10 in this volume). Between the Second World War and 1973, most currencies were fixed in value to the US dollar, the most important currency in the post-war world economy. In this system, often referred to as the Bretton Woods system (see Ravehnhill, Box 1.4, page 14 in this volume), the United States agreed to guarantee the value of the dollar by committing to exchange dollars for gold at a set price of $35 per ounce. Since 1973, when the Nixon administration officially abandoned the fixed rate between the dollar and gold, all the major currencies have essentially been allowed to fluctuate freely in value in world financial markets (see Helleiner, Chapter 7 in this volume). Among developing nations, however, many governments continue to fix the value of their currency in terms of dollars or another of the major currencies (see Frieden *et al.* 2001). And groups of nations in different regions of the world, including the members of the European Union, have made separate efforts to stabilize exchange rates at the regional level, even progressing to the adoption of a common regional currency.

The fundamental choice each government must make involves decided whether to allow the value of the national currency to fluctuate freely in response to market demand and supply, or instead fix the value of the currency in terms of some other currency or external standard—typically, the currency of a major trading partner or, as was common in the past, gold (a precious metal valued highly in most societies throughout history). When a government chooses to fix the value of the national currency, it sets the official rate of exchange and commits itself to buy the currency at that fixed rate when requested to by private actors or foreign governments. Between a 'pure float' and a fixed exchange rate there are intermediate options: a government can choose a target value for the exchange rate and only allow the currency to fluctuate in value within some range around the target rate. The wider this range, of course, the more policy approximates floating the currency....

The crux of the choice between fixed and floating exchange rates is the choice between stability and policy control: a stable exchange rate will increase the economic benefits attainable from international trade and investment, but this requires giving up the ability to adjust monetary policy to suit domestic economic conditions.

Governments in the most advanced economies have generally decided that policy control is more important to them than exchange-rate stability, at least since the early 1970s. Governments in smaller, developing nations have mainly chosen exchange-rate stability over policy control. In part this is because these countries tend to rely more heavily on trade and foreign investment as sources of economic growth. This choice is also more attractive for governments in smaller countries trying to defeat chronic inflation. Government promises to deal with runaway inflation in these countries may not be regarded as credible by private actors if governments in the past have shown a tendency to act irresponsibly (for example, by printing and spending large amounts of money) when facing electoral challenges. Since the expectations that private actors have about government policy feed directly into the prices (and wages) set, inflationary expectations can have devastating effects. In such circumstances, fixing the nation's currency in terms of the currency of a major trading partner with a comparatively low rate of inflation can serve an important function, providing a way for the government to commit itself more credibly to a low-inflation monetary policy. In essence, by committing to keep the exchange rate fixed, the government is ceding control of monetary policy in a very clear and visible way, and anchoring inflation at home to the inflation rate in the partner country (see Giavazzi and Pagano 1988; Broz and Frieden 2001)....

Perhaps one major reason why it is difficult to find compelling evidence to support simple class-based interpretations of exchange-rate politics is that individuals tend to see things very differently depending on the industries in which they are employed and invested. If we allow, as in previous discussions above, that factors of production are typically very specific to particular industries, we get a very different picture of the alignment of individual preferences on the exchange-rate issue. And the picture is also much clearer. Individuals employed or invested in sectors that invest or sell in foreign markets are likely to favour exchange-rate stability, since fluctuations in rates impose costs on their international transactions and because they have a relatively small economic stake in domestic (versus foreign) macroeconomic conditions. Those individuals associated with firms and banks that invest heavily in foreign markets, for example, and export-orientated sectors that sell a large proportion of their output abroad, should thus tend to support fixed exchange rates. On the other hand, owners and employees in import-competing industries and those producing non-traded services (for example, building, transportation, sales) whose incomes depend overwhelmingly on domestic economic conditions, are likely to favour flexible exchange rates that allow the government more control over monetary policy. There is some compelling evidence supporting these predictions, especially in the debates over exchange-rate policy in the most advanced economies. In Europe in recent decades, for example, the strongest support for fixing exchange rates (and ultimately, for creating a common European currency) has come from the international banks, multinational firms in a diverse range of industries (including auto firms such as BMW and Mercedes), and from export-orientated sectors. The strongest opposition to fixed rates has tended to come from owners and labour unions associated with import-competing industries such as coal, steel, and textiles, especially in nations such as France and Italy that have battled relatively high rates of inflation (see Frieden 1994). In developing nations, recent studies have indicated that governments are more likely to float their currency when the import-competing manufacturing sector accounts for a large proportion of the local economy (Frieden *et al.* 2001)....

INSTITUTIONS

Once we have specified the preferences of different individuals and groups on any particular issue we need to think about how much influence they will have over policy outcomes. This is where political institutions come in to play. Political institutions establish the rules by which policy is made, and thus how the policy preferences of different groups are weighed in the process that determines the policy outcome. It is appropriate here to start with the broadest types of rules first, and consider the formal mechanisms by which governments and representatives in legislative bodies are elected (or otherwise come to power). These broad features of the institutional environment have large effects on all types of policies. But then we can move on to discuss more specific aspects of the legislative process and administrative agencies that have implications for the formulation and implementation of trade, immigration, investment, and exchange-rate policies.

Elections and representation

Perhaps it is best to start with the observation that the general relationship between democratization and foreign economic policy-making is a matter that is still open to considerable theoretical and empirical doubt. Part of the puzzle is that there is a great deal of variation in the levels of economic openness we have observed among autocratic nations. In autocratic regimes, the orientation of policy will depend on the particular desires and motivations of the (non-elected) leadership, and there are different theoretical approaches to this issue. Non-elected governments could pursue trade and investment liberalization, on the one hand, if they calculate that this will increase their own power or wealth (for example, through taxation) by increasing national economic output. Such policies may be easier to adopt because autocratic leaders are more insulated than their democratic counterparts from the political demands made by any organized domestic groups that favour trade protection and limits on foreign investment (Haggard 1990). Perhaps this is an apt description of the state of affairs in

China, as it has been opening its economy gradually to trade and investment since the 1980s, and non-democratic governments in Taiwan and South Korea pursued trade liberalization even more rapidly in the 1960s. On the other hand, autocratic governments may draw political support from small, powerful groups that favour trade protection. Many such governments appear to have used trade and investment barriers in ways that were aimed at consolidating their rule (Wintrobe 1998). The experience in Sub-Saharan African nations since the 1960s, and in Pakistan and Myanmar, seems to fit this mould. Without a detailed assessment of the particular groups upon which a particular authoritarian regime depends for political backing, it is quite difficult to make predictions about likely policy outcomes under non-democratic rule.

In formal democracies that hold real elections, the most fundamental set of political rules is the set that defines which individuals get to vote. If the franchise law gives more weight to one side in a policy contest compared to others, it can obviously have a large impact on policy outcomes. Where only those who own land can vote, for example, agricultural interests will be privileged in the policy-making process. If this landowning elite favours trade protection, as it did in Britain in the years before the Great Reform Act of 1832, then such a policy is almost certain to be held firmly in place. By shifting political power away from landowners and towards urban owners of capital and labour, extensions of the franchise had a major impact on all forms of economic policy during the late nineteenth and early twentieth centuries in Europe, America, and elsewhere. In England, the extension of voting power to the middle and working classes, achieved in the reforms of 1832 and 1867, had the effect of making free trade politically invincible—with a huge block of workers along with the urban business class supporting trade openness, and only a tiny fraction of the electorate (the traditional rural elites) against it, a government that endorsed tariffs or restrictions on investment would have been committing electoral suicide. In the United States and Australia, on the other hand, where labour and capital were in relatively scarce supply, the elimination of property qualifications for voting and the extension of suffrage had exactly the opposite effect, empowering a larger block of urban voters who favoured high tariffs. In general, extensions of the franchise to urban classes tend to produce more open policies toward trade, immigration, and investment in labour and capital-abundant countries, but more closed or protectionist policies in labour-and capital-scarce economies.

The precise rules by which representatives are elected to national legislatures are the next critical feature of the institutional environment. Scholars have suggested that, in parliamentary systems in which legislative seats are apportioned among parties according to the proportion of votes they receive ('proportional representation'), narrowly organized groups have far less impact on policy-making in general than they do in electoral systems in which individual seats are decided by the plurality rule (see Rogowski 1987). Parliamentary systems with proportional representation tend to encourage the formation of strong, cohesive political parties which appeal to a national constituency and have less to gain in electoral terms by responding to localized and particularistic demands in marginal or contested districts (McGillivray 1997). Other types of systems, in contrast, tend to encourage intra-party competition among individual politicians and the development of a 'personal vote' in particular electoral districts, and are thus more conducive to interest-group lobbying. The implications for foreign economic policies are usually spelt out in very clear terms: we expect that proportional representation systems with strong political parties (for example, Sweden) will typically produce lower levels of trade protection and other restrictions than alternative types of electoral systems (for example, Britain, the United States) in which particular local and regional interests have a greater influence.

These conclusions about the impact of particularistic groups in different types of electoral systems rest upon a critical insight derived from theoretical work on collective action in trade politics: that there is a fundamental asymmetry between the lobbying pressure generated from groups seeking protectionist policies, and the lobbying pressure that comes from groups who oppose such restrictions. The main reason for this is that restrictions on imports and other types of exchange, when imposed one at a time, tend to have very uneven effects. As we know from the analysis of the specific factors model above, the benefits of a tariff on a particular good are concentrated on the owners of capital and labour engaged in that particular industry. If the tariff is substantial, these benefits are likely to be quite large as a share of the incomes of those individuals, and thus they will typically be willing to spend a good deal of their time and energy (and savings) lobbying to ensure they get the tariff they want. The stakes are very high for them. In contrast, the costs of the tariff are shared among all the owners of other types of specific factors in the economy; they are dispersed so broadly, in fact, that they tend to be quite small as fraction of the incomes of these individuals. Thus it is unlikely that those hurt by the new tariff will be prepared to devote resources to lobbying against the policy proposal. Collective political action will always be much easier to organize in the relatively small groups that benefit from a particular trade restriction than in the much larger groups (the rest of the economy) that are hurt by the restriction (see Olson 1965). Perhaps the best example of this logic is the extraordinary political power that has been demonstrated by the small, highly organized agricultural groups in Europe, the United States, and Japan since the 1950s. These groups, which together represent a tiny fraction of the population in each political system, have been able to win extremely high (if not prohibitive) rates of protection from imports and lavish subsidies (see Tyers and Anderson 1992).

Other aspects of electoral institutions may also play a role in shaping policy outcomes. In general, smaller electoral districts in plurality systems may be expected to increase the influence of sectoral or particularistic groups over elected representatives, and thus lead to higher levels of protection (Rogoswki 1987; Alt and Gilligan 1994).

In larger districts, political representatives will be forced to balance the interests of a greater variety of industry groups when making decisions about policies, and will be less affected by the demands of any particular industry lobby, and a larger share of the costs of any tariff or restriction will be 'internalized' among voters within the district. From this perspective, upper chambers of parliaments, which typically allocate seats among representatives of much larger electoral districts than those in lower chambers, tend to be less inclined toward trade protection and other types of restrictive foreign economic policies. Meanwhile, in legislative chambers in which seats are defined along political—geographical lines without regard for population (for example, in the United States Senate, where each state receives two seats), agricultural, forestry, and mining interests in underpopulated areas typically gain a great deal more influence over policy-making than they can wield in chambers (for example, the United States House of Representatives) where legislative seats are defined based on the number of voters in each district.

We have generally been focusing on trade policies, since most of the past research on the effects of institutions has tended to concentrate on tariff levels. But recent studies also suggest that differences in electoral institutions can have a significant impact on exchange-rate policies. In particular, in plurality systems in which elections are all-or-nothing contests between the major parties, governments appear to be far less likely to fix exchange rates and give up control over monetary policy than governments in proportional representation systems (see Clark and Hallerberg 2000). It appears that the costs of having ceded control over monetary policy in plurality systems, should the government face an election contest during an economic slump, are much higher than elsewhere. This difference also appears to be more pronounced for governments in plurality systems, in which the timing of elections is predetermined by law (Bernhard and Leblang 1999).

Legislatures and policy-making rules

The rules that govern the way national legislatures go about making laws can have profound effects on the way the preferences of individuals and groups are aggregated into different types of foreign economic policies. These rules determine the way new policies are proposed, considered, amended, and voted upon. They structure the interactions among different legislative and executive bodies, and establish which branches have what types of agenda setting and veto power over policy.

Most of the recent research on the impact of legislative institutions on foreign economic policies has been focused on American trade policy. The point of departure for many studies is the infamous Smoot-Hawley Tariff Act of 1930, which was such a disaster that it helped to inspire a fairly radical change in the rules by which the Congress has dealt with trade policy ever since. The core of the legislative problem, as many see it, is the possibility for 'log rolling' or vote-trading between protection-ist interests. The benefits of a tariff or trade restriction can often go to an import-competing industry located almost entirely in one electoral district, with the costs borne generally by individuals across the rest of the economy. In such cases, lobbying pressure by these industries can generate a protectionist log roll when tariffs are being set by voting among members of a legislature: each member of the legislature will propose generous protective measures for industries in his or her own district without accounting for the costs they impose on individuals elsewhere. To gain support for these measures, each member will vote in favour of similar measures proposed by other legislators. If members can vote indefinitely on a sequence of such proposals, a policy that includes every new tariff can be the equilibrium outcome (supported by each legislator's belief that a vote against another's proposal would induce others to retaliate by offering an amendment to withdraw protection from the defector's dis-trict). The result of such unchecked log-rolling is a vast array of protective measures, such that all individuals are far worse off than they were before the bill was passed (see Weingast *et al.* 1981).

According to conventional wisdom, the Smoot—Hawley tariff was just such a log-rolling disaster, and Congress reacted to it in a remarkably sensible way by rede-signing the rules governing the way trade policy was made. Specifically, Congress delegated to the executive branch the authority to alter US trade policy by negotiating reciprocal trade agreements with other countries. This practice of delegating negotiat-ing authority to the president has been continued since 1934. By delegating authority over policy to the president, who would presumably set trade policy to benefit all individuals within the one, *national* electoral district, this innovation eliminated the spectre of protectionist log-rolling completely, and ensured that all the costs of trade protection were fully 'internalized' by a decision-maker accountable to all voters. In addition, by empowering the president to negotiate trade agreements that elicited reciprocal tariff reductions from other countries, the change helped to mobilize sup-port for trade liberalization among export interests who could now expect improved sales abroad as a result of tariff reductions at home....

THE TRADING WORLD

RICHARD ROSECRANCE

The Second World War initially strengthened both the military-political world and the trading world, but the second impetus was more enduring. After most major conflicts in Western history, peacetime brought a respite, a period of consolidation and agreement. This period did not last long after World War I when the victors concentrated on keeping Germany down, economically and militarily. After World War II, a peace of reconciliation was effected with the defeated powers, Germany and Japan, in part because the Cold War with the Soviet Union broke out at its close. As a new enemy emerged, the Western victors effected a rapprochement with the reformed ex-enemy states. The new trading system might have been undermined at the outset as political hostility and the threat of war overshadowed all other events. It was not, because despite the antagonism between Soviet and Western camps neither side wanted another round of war. Both Western Europe and the Soviet Union needed time to rebuild their economies and restore their devastated homelands. On the Western side there was a much greater understanding of the means by which liberal economies with convertible currencies could contribute to the rebuilding process. Part of the pressure for open economies came from the United States, no doubt desirous of extending her

From *The Rise of the Trading State: Commerce and Conquest in the Modern World* by Richard Rosecrance, 1986.

export markets. Part was based on conclusions reached in the 1930s that when financial collapse cuts the commercial links between societies, all nations will suffer, and some will move to seize what they cannot acquire through trade. Economic crisis and depression had been the fare that nourished domestic desperation and brought radical and nationalist leaders to power in more than one state. Prosperity, on the other hand, contributed to stable governments and to a more relaxed foreign policy stance.

The 1930s had also witnessed a transformation in domestic politics in a series of states. The Great Depression of 1929–37 convinced both peoples and governments that employment and social welfare were major national responsibilities: they were too important to be left to the private market and the workings of free enterprise. Henceforth governments in democratic countries—indeed in many others—would act to ensure basic levels of social and economic living. . . .

The creation of the International Monetary Fund at Bretton Woods in 1944 was a giant step toward a trading system of international relations. The new regime called for an open world economy with low tariffs and strictly limited depreciation of currencies. Tariff hikes and competitive devaluation of currencies were to be restricted by the General Agreement on Tariffs and Trade (GATT) and by the Fund. Unlike the situation after World War I, nations were to be persuaded not to institute controls by offering them liquid funds to float over any period of imbalance in international payments. They would then have a grace period to get their economies in order, after which they could repay the loans.

The plethora of small nations created after the war by the decolonization process in Africa, Asia, the Middle East, and Oceania were generally not large or strong enough to rely on domestic resources, industry, agriculture, and markets for all their needs. Unless they could trade, they could not live. This meant that the markets of the major Western and industrial economies had to take their exports and they in return would need manufacturing exports from the developed countries. The open international economy was critical to their growth and stability. This is not to say that there were no other factors which supported the independence of new nations in the post-World War II period. Military factors and superpower rivalries made the reconquest of colonial areas very costly; ethnic and cultural differences limited the success of attempts to subdue one country or another. But political and military viability were not enough. Small states could not continue to exist as independent entities unless they could earn an economic livelihood. To some degree economic assistance from developed nations or from multilateral agencies met this need. If tariffs and restrictions had inhibited the trade of new nations, however, they would not have been able to function as independent units.

But the open economy of the trading world did not benefit only small nations. The growth of world trade, which increased faster than gross national product until 1980, attracted larger states as well. As the cost of using force increased and its benefits declined, other means of gaining national welfare had to be found. The Federal Republic of Germany, following Hanseatic precedents, became more dependent on international trade than the old united Germany had been. The United Kingdom, France, Italy, Norway, Switzerland, Germany, Belgium, Holland, and Denmark had imports and exports which equalled 30 percent or more of their gross national product, nearly three times the proportion attained in the United States. Japan's huge economy was fueled by foreign trade, which amounted to 20 percent of her GNP total.

The role of Japan and Germany in the trading world is exceedingly interesting because it represents a reversal of past policies in both the nineteenth century and the 1930s. It is correct to say that the two countries experimented with foreign trade because they had been disabused of military expansion by World War II. For a time they were incapable of fighting war on a major scale; their endorsement of the trading system was merely an adoption of the remaining policy alternative. But that endorsement did not change even when the economic strength of the two nations might have sustained a much more nationalistic and militaristic policy. Given the choice between military expansion to achieve self-sufficiency (a choice made more difficult by modern conventional and nuclear weapons in the hands of other powers) and the procurement of necessary markets and raw materials through international commerce, Japan and Germany chose the latter. . . .

The increasing prevalence of the trading option since 1945 raises peaceful possibilities that were neglected during the late nineteenth century and the 1930s. It seems safe to say that an international system composed of more than 160 states cannot continue to exist unless trade remains the primary vocation of most of its members. Were military and territorial orientations to dominate the scene, the trend to greater numbers of smaller states would be reversed, and larger states would conquer small and weak nations.

The possibility of such amalgamations cannot be entirely ruled out. Industrialization had two possible impacts: it allowed a nation to develop its wealth peacefully through internal economic growth, but it also knit new sinews of strength that could coerce other states. Industrialization made territorial expansion easier but also less necessary. In the mid-nineteenth century the Continental states pursued the expansion of their territories while Britain expanded her industry. The industrialization of Prussia and the development of her rail network enabled her armies to defeat Denmark, Austria, and France. Russia also used her new industrial technology to strengthen her military. In the last quarter of the century, even Britain returned to a primarily military and imperialist policy. In his book on imperialism Lenin declared that the drive for colonies was an imminent tendency of the capitalist system. Raw materials would run short and investment capital would pile up at home. The remedy was imperialism with colonies providing new sources for the former and outlets for the latter. But Lenin did not fully understand that an open international economy and intensive economic development at home obviated the need for colonies even under a capitalist, trading system.

The basic effect of World War II was to create much higher world interdependence as the average size of countries declined. The reversal of past trends toward a consolidation of states created instead a multitude of states that could not depend on themselves alone. They needed ties with other nations to prosper and remain viable as small entities. The trading system, as a result, was visible in defense relations as well as international commerce. Nations that could not stand on their own sought alliances or assistance from other powers, and they offered special defense contributions in fighting contingents, regional experience, or particular types of defense hardware. Dutch electronics, French aircraft, German guns and tanks, and British ships all made their independent contribution to an alliance in which no single power might be able to meet its defense needs on a self-sufficient basis. Israel developed a powerful and efficient small arms industry, as well as a great fund of experience combating terrorism. Israeli intelligence added considerably to the information available from Western sources, partly because of its understanding of Soviet weapons systems accumulated in several Arab-Israeli wars.

Defense interdependencies, however, are only one means of sharing the burdens placed upon the modern state. Perhaps more important is economic interdependence among countries. One should not place too much emphasis upon the existence of interdependence per se. European nations in 1913 relied upon the trade and investment that flowed between them; that did not prevent the political crisis which led to a breakdown of the international system and to World War I. Interdependence only constrains national policy if leaders accept and agree to work within its limits. In 1914 Lloyds of London had insured the German merchant marine but that did not stop Germany attacking Belgium, a neutral nation, or England from joining the war against Berlin. The United States was Japan's best customer and source of raw materials in the 1930s, but that did not deter the Japanese attack on Pearl Harbor.

At least among the developed and liberal countries, interdependent ties since 1945 have come to be accepted as a fundamental and unchangeable feature of the situation. This recognition dawned gradually, and the United States may perhaps have been the last to acknowledge it, which was not surprising. The most powerful economy is ready to make fewer adjustments, and America tried initially to pursue its domestic economic policies without taking into account the effect on others, on itself, and on the international financial system as a whole. Presidents Kennedy and Lyndon B. Johnson tried to detach American domestic growth strategies from the deteriorating United States balance of payments, but they left a legacy of needed economic change to their successors. Finally, in the 1980s two American administrations accepted lower United States growth in order to control inflation and began to focus on the international impact of United States policies. The delay in fashioning a strategy of adjustment to international economic realities almost certainly made it more difficult. Smaller countries actively sought to find a niche in the structure of international comparative advantage and in the demand for their goods. Larger countries with large internal markets postponed that reckoning as long as they could. By the 1980s, however, such change could no longer be avoided, and United States leaders embarked upon new industrial and tax policies designed to increase economic growth and enable America to compete more effectively abroad.

The acceptance of new approaches was a reflection of the decline in economic sovereignty. As long as governments could control all the forces impinging upon their economies, welfare states would have no difficulty in implementing domestic planning for social ends. But as trade, investment, corporations, and to some degree labor moved from one national jurisdiction to another, no government could insulate and direct its economy without instituting the extreme protectionist and "beggar thy neighbor" policies of the 1930s. Rather than do this, the flow of goods and capital was allowed to proceed, and in recent years it has become a torrent. In some cases the flow of capital has increased to compensate for barriers or rigidities to the movement of goods.

In both cases the outcome is the result of modern developments in transportation and communications. Railway and high-speed highway networks now allow previously landlocked areas to participate in the international trading network that once depended on rivers and access to the sea. Modern communications and computers allow funds to be instantaneously transferred from one market to another, so that they may earn interest twenty-four hours a day. Transportation costs for a variety of goods have reached a new low, owing to container shipping and handling. For the major industrial countries, (member countries of the Organization for Economic Cooperation and Development, which include the European community, Austria, Finland, Iceland, Portugal, Norway, Spain, Sweden, Switzerland, Turkey, Australia, Canada, Japan, New Zealand, and the United States) exports have risen much faster than either industrial production or gross domestic product since 1965, with the growth of GDP (in constant prices) at 4 percent and that of exports at 7.7 percent. Only Japan's domestic growth has been able to keep pace with the increase in exports.

Foreign trade (the sum of exports and imports) percentages were roughly twice as large as these figures in each case. The explosion of foreign trade since 1945 has, if anything, been exceeded by the enormous movement of capital.

> In 1950 the value of the stock of direct foreign investment held by U.S. companies was $11.8 billions, compared with $7.2 billions in 1935, $7.6 billions in 1929 and $3.9 billions in 1914. In the following decade, these investments increased by $22.4 billions, and at the end of 1967 their total value stood at $59 billions.

In 1983, it had reached $226 billions. And direct investment (that portion of investment which buys a significant stake in a foreign firm) was only one part of total United States investment overseas. In 1983 United States private assets abroad totaled $774 billion, or about three times as much.

The amounts, although very large, were not significant in themselves. In 1913, England's foreign investments, equaled one and one-half times her GNP as compared to present American totals of one-quarter of United States GNP. England's foreign trade was more than 40 percent of her national income as compared with contemporary American totals of 15–17 percent. England's pre-World War I involvement in international economic activities was greater than America's today.

Part of what must be explained in the evolution of interdependence is not the high level reached post-1945, but how even higher levels in 1913 could have fallen in the interim. Here the role of industrialization is paramount. As Karl Deutsch, following the work of Werner Sombart, has shown, in the early stages of industrial growth nations must import much of their needed machinery: rail and transportation networks are constructed with equipment and materials from abroad. Once new industries have been created, in a variety of fields, ranging from textiles to heavy industry, the national economy can begin to provide the goods that previously were imported. The United States, the Scandinavian countries, and Japan reached this stage only after the turn of the century, and it was then that the gasoline-powered automobile industry and the manufacturing of electric motors and appliances began to develop rapidly and flourish. The further refinement of agricultural technology also rested on these innovations. Thus, even without restrictions and disruptions of trade, the 1920s would not have seen a rehabilitation of the old interdependent world economy of the 1890s. The further barriers erected in the 1930s confirmed and extended this outcome. If new industrial countries had less need for manufacturing imports, the growth and maintenance of general trade would then come to depend upon an increase in some other category of commerce than the traditional exchange of raw materials for finished goods. In the 1920s, as Albert Hirschman shows, the reciprocal exchange of industrial goods increased briefly, but fell again in the 1930s. That decrease was only made up after 1945 when there was a striking and continuing growth in the trade of manufactured goods among industrial countries. Some will say that this trade is distinctly expendable because countries could produce the goods they import on their own. None of the trade that the United States has today with Western Europe or Japan could really be dubbed "critical" in that the United States could not get along without it. American alternatives exist to almost all industrial products from other developed economies. Thus if interdependence means a trading link which "is costly to break," there is a sense that the sheer physical dependence of one country upon another, or upon international trade as a whole, has declined since the nineteenth century.

But to measure interdependence in this way misses the essence of the concept. Individuals in a state of nature can be quite independent if they are willing to live at a low standard of living and gather herbs, nuts, and fruits. They are not forced to depend on others but decide to do so to increase their total amount of food and security. Countries in an international state of nature (anarchy) can equally decide to depend only on themselves. They can limit what they consume to what they can produce at home, but they will thereby live less well than they might with specialization and extensive trade and interchange with other nations.

There is no shortage of energy in the world, for example, and all energy needs that previously have been satisfied by imported petroleum might be met by a great increase in coal and natural gas production, fission, and hydropower. But coal-generated electric power produces acid rain, and coal liquification (to produce fuel for automobiles) is expensive. Nuclear power leaves radioactive wastes which have to be contained. Importing oil is a cheaper and cleaner alternative. Thus even though a particular country, like the United States, might become energy self-sufficient if it wanted to, there is reason for dependence on the energy supplies of other nations. Does this mean creating a "tie that is costly to break"? Yes, in the sense that we live less well if we break the tie; but that doesn't mean that the tie could not be broken. Any tie can be broken. In this respect, all ties create "vulnerability interdependence" if they are in the interest of those who form them. One could get along without Japanese cars or European fashions, but eliminating them from the market restricts consumer choice and in fact raises opportunity costs. In this manner, trade between industrial countries may be equally important as trade linking industrial and raw material producing countries.

There are other ways in which interdependence has increased since the nineteenth century. Precisely because industrial countries imported agricultural commodities and sold their manufactured goods to less developed states, their dependence upon each other was much less in the nineteenth century and the 1920s than it is today. Toward the end of the nineteenth century Britain increasingly came to depend upon her empire for markets, food, and raw materials or upon countries in the early stages of industrialization. As Continental tariffs increased, Britain turned to her colonies, the United States, and Latin America to find markets for her exports. These markets provided

> ready receptacles for British goods when other areas became too competitive or unattractive; for example, Australia, India, Brazil and Argentina took the cotton, railways, steel and machinery that could not be sold in European markets. In the same way, whilst British capital exports to the latter dropped from 52 percent in the 1860s to 25 percent in the few years before 1914, those to the empire rose from 36 percent to 46 percent, and those to Latin America from 10.5 percent to 22 percent.

The British foreign trade which totalled 43.5 percent of GNP in 1913 went increasingly to the empire; thus, if one takes Britain and the colonies as a single economic unit, that unit was much less dependent upon the outside world than, say, Britain is today with a smaller (30.4 percent) ratio of trade to GNP. And Britain alone had much less stake in Germany, France, and the Continental countries' economies than she does today as a member of the European Common Market.

In the nineteenth century trade was primarily vertical in character, taking place between countries at different stages of industrial development, and involving an exchange of manufactured goods on the one hand for food and raw materials on the other. But trade was not the only element in vertical interdependence.

British investment was also vertical in that it proceeded from the developed center, London, to less developed capitals in the Western Hemisphere, Oceania, and the Far East. Such ties might contribute to community feeling in the British Empire, later the Commonwealth of Nations, but it would not restrain conflicts among the countries of Western Europe. Three-quarters of foreign investment of all European countries in 1914 was lodged outside of Europe. In 1913, in the British case 66 percent of her foreign investment went to North and South America and Australia, 28 percent to the Middle and Far East, and only 6 percent to Europe.

In addition, about 90 percent of foreign investment in 1913 was portfolio investment, that is, it represented small holdings of foreign shares that could easily be disposed of on the stock exchange. Direct investment, or investment which represented more than a 10 percent share of the total ownership of a foreign firm was only one-tenth of the total. Today the corresponding figure for the United States is nearly 30 percent. The growth of direct foreign investment since 1945 is a reflection of the greater stake that countries have in each other's well-being in the contemporary period.

In this respect international interdependence has been fostered by a growing interpenetration of economies, in the sense that one economy owns part of another, sends part of its population to live and work in it, and becomes increasingly dependent upon the progress of the latter. The multinational corporation which originates in one national jurisdiction, but operates in others as well, is the primary vehicle for such investment ownership. Stimulated by the demands and incentives of the product life cycle, the multinational corporation invests and produces abroad to make sure of retaining its market share. That market may be in the host country, or it may be in the home country, once the foreign production is imported back into the home economy. Foreign trade has grown enormously since 1945. But its necessary growth has been reduced by the operation of multinational companies in foreign jurisdictions: production abroad reduces the need for exports. In this way an interpenetrative stake has increased between developed economies even when tariffs and other restrictions might appear to have stunted the growth of exports. The application of a common external tariff to the European Economic Community in the 1960s greatly stimulated American foreign investment in Europe, which became such a massive tide that Europeans reacted against the "American challenge," worrying that their prized national economic assets might be preempted by the United States.

They need not have worried. The reverse flow of European and Japanese investment in the United States is reaching such enormous proportions that America has become a net debtor nation: a country that has fewer assets overseas than foreigners have in the United States. The threatened imposition of higher American tariffs and quotas on imports led foreign companies to invest in the United States in gigantic amounts, thereby obviating the need to send exports from their home nation. Such direct investment represents a much more permanent stake in the economic welfare of the host nation than exports to that market could ever be. Foreign production is a more permanent economic commitment than foreign sales, because large shares of a foreign company or subsidiary could not be sold on a stock exchange. The attempt to market such large holdings would only have the effect of depressing the value of the stock. Direct investment is thus illiquid, as opposed to the traditional portfolio investment of the nineteenth century.

After 1945 one country slowly developed a stake in another, but the process was not initially reciprocal. Until the beginning of the 1970s, the trend was largely for Americans to invest abroad, in Europe, Latin America, and East Asia. As the American dollar cheapened after 1973, however, a reverse flow began, with Europeans and Japanese placing large blocs of capital in American firms and acquiring international companies. Third World multinationals, from Hong Kong, the OPEC countries, and East Asia also began to invest in the United States. By the end of the 1970s world investment was much more balanced, with the European stake in the American economy nearly offsetting the American investment in Europe. Japan also moved to diversify her export offensive in the American market by starting to produce in the United States. But Japan did not benefit from a reciprocal stake in her own economy. Since foreign investors have either been kept out of the Japanese market or have been forced to accept cumbersome joint ventures with Japanese firms, few multinationals have a major commitment to the Japanese market. Japan imports the smallest percentage of manufactured goods of any leading industrial nation. Thus when economic policy makers in America and Europe formulate growth strategies, they are not forced to consider the Japanese economy on a par with their own because Americans and Europeans have little to lose if Japan does not prosper. In her own self-interest Japan will almost certainly have to open her capital market and economy to foreign penetration if she wishes to enjoy corresponding access to economies of other nations. Greater Japanese foreign direct investment will only partly mitigate the pressures on Tokyo in this respect.

It is nonetheless true that interpenetration of investment in industrial economies provides a mutual stake in each other's success that did not exist in the nineteenth century or before World War I. Then Germany cared little if France progressed and the only important loan or investment stake between major powers was that between France and Russia, a factor that could hardly restrain conflict in 1914. It is very important at the moment that the Arab oil countries have substantial investments in Europe and North America because their profitability will be influenced by changes in the oil price. Too high oil prices, throwing the industrial West into depression, would have the effect of cutting returns on Arab overseas investments. It would therefore restrain OPEC from precipitate price increases. American business interests with a large stake in Europe would hardly encourage their government to take steps to export American unemployment to other industrial economies for this would only depress their own holdings abroad. A recognition of the degree to which all industrial economies are in the same boat has led to a series of economic summit meetings of seven developed nations in hopes that policies of multilateral growth could be agreed upon to benefit all. These have not solved economic problems, but they have contributed to much greater understanding of the difficulties and policies of other states and perhaps to a greater tolerance for them. . . .

Yet the great dependence of industrial economies upon each other for markets and the need for Third World minerals and oil would not produce political interdependence between countries in all circumstances. If governments were committed to reducing or eliminating their interdependence with others, the network of economic ties could actually be a factor for conflict. One of the fundamental differences between the Western and democratic industrial countries in 1914 and today—was the lack of commitment to maintain the structure of international economic relations prior to World War I. War between such economies was accepted as a natural outcome of the balance of power system. No pre-1914 statesman or financier was fully aware of the damage that war would do to the European body economic because of the belief that it would be over very quickly. Few bankers or finance ministers interceded with their foreign office brethren to seek to reduce the probability of war.

But the economic interdependence of 1913 had little restraining effect in another respect. Depression and economic disturbances were believed to be natural events like earthquakes and floods; they were not expected to be mediated by governmental intercession or economic policy. It was not until the 1930s that one of the chief functions of the modern democratic state became the achievement of domestic welfare with full employment and an avoidance of inflation. Because it was not the business of government in 1914 to prevent economic disruption and dislocation, little effort was made to minimize the efffect of a prolonged war upon society, and no effort to prevent war altogether. Between Western industrial countries and Japan today, war is virtually unthinkable. Even if economic interdependence was lower after 1945 than it had been in 1913 (and this is not the case), the political significance of interdependence is still much greater today. Governments in the present era cannot achieve the objectives of high employment without inflation except by working together. . . .

THE GLOBALIZATION
OF THE ECONOMY

JEFFREY FRANKEL

Economic globalization is one of the most powerful forces to have shaped the postwar world. In particular, international trade in goods and services has become increasingly important over the past fifty years, and international financial flows over the past thirty years. This chapter documents quantitatively the process of globalization for trade and finance. It then briefly goes beyond the causes of international economic integration to consider its effects, concluding that globalization is overall a good thing, not just for economic growth but also when noneconomic goals are taken into account.

The two major drivers of economic globalization are reduced costs to transportation and communication in the private sector and reduced policy barriers to trade and investment on the part of the public sector. Technological progress and innovation have long been driving the costs of transportation and communication steadily lower. In the postwar period we have seen major further cost-saving advances, even within ocean shipping: supertankers, roll-on-roll-off ships, and containerized cargo. Between 1920 and 1990 the average ocean freight and port charges per short ton of U.S. import and export cargo fell from $95.00 to $29.00 (in 1990 dollars). An

Nye, Joseph S. Jr., and John D. Donahue, eds. *Governance in a Globalizing World*, pp 45-66, © 2000, Visions of Governance for the 21st Century. Reprinted with permission.

increasing share of cargo goes by air. Between 1930 and 1990, average air transport revenue per passenger mile fell from $0.68 to $0.11. Jet air shipping and refrigeration have changed the status of goods that had previously been classified altogether as not tradable internationally. Now fresh-cut flowers, perishable broccoli and strawberries, live lobsters, and even ice cream are sent between continents. Communications costs have fallen even more rapidly. Over this period the cost of a three-minute telephone call from New York to London fell from $244.65 to $3.32. Recent inventions such as faxes and the Internet require no touting.

It is easy to exaggerate the extent of globalization. Much excited discussion of the topic makes it sound as though the rapid increase in economic integration across national borders is unprecedented. Some commentators imply that it has now gone so far that it is complete; one hears that distance and national borders no longer matter, that the nation-state and geography are themselves no longer relevant for economic purposes, and that it is now as easy to do business with a customer across the globe as across town. After all, has not the World Wide Web reduced cross-border barriers to zero?

It would be a mistake for policymakers or private citizens to base decisions on the notion that globalization is so new that the experience of the past is not relevant, or that the phenomenon is now irreversible, or that national monetary authorities are now powerless in the face of the global marketplace, or that the quality of life of Americans—either economic or noneconomic aspects—is determined more by developments abroad than by American actions at home.

It is best to recognize that at any point in history many powerful forces are working to drive countries apart, at the same time as other powerful forces are working to shrink the world. In the 1990s, for example, at the same time that forces such as the Internet and dollarization have led some to proclaim the decline of the nation-state, more new nations have been created (out of the ruins of the former Soviet bloc) than in any decade other than the decolonizing 1960s, each with its own currencies and trade policies. The forces of shrinkage have dominated in recent decades, but the centrifugal forces are important as well.

TWO BENCHMARKS FOR MEASURING ECONOMIC INTEGRATION

The overall post—World War II record of economic integration across national borders, powerful as it has been, is, in two respects, not as striking as widely believed. The first perspective is to judge by the standard of 100 years ago. The second is to judge by the standard of what it would mean to have truly perfect global integration.

Judging Globalization 2000 by the Standard of 1900

The globalization that took place in the nineteenth century was at least as impressive as the current episode. The most revolutionary breakthroughs in transportation and communication had already happened by 1900—for example, the railroad, steamship, telegraph, and refrigeration. Freight rates had fallen sharply throughout the century. An environment of political stability was provided by the Pax Britannica, and an environment of monetary stability was provided by the gold standard. Kevin O'Rourke and Jeffrey Williamson show that, as a result of rapidly growing trade, international differences in commodity prices narrowed dramatically.

It is inescapable to invoke a particularly famous quote from John Maynard Keynes: "What an extraordinary episode in the progress of man that age was which came to an end in August 1914!… The inhabitant of London could order by telephone, sipping his morning tea in bed, the various products of the whole earth … he could at the same time and by the same means adventure his wealth in the natural resources and new enterprise of any quarter of the world."

The world took a giant step back from economic globalization during the period 1914–1944. Some of the causes of this retrogression were isolationist sentiments in the West that followed World War I, the monetary instability and economic depression that plagued the interwar period, increases in tariffs and other trade barriers including most saliently the adoption by the U.S. Congress of the Smoot-Hawley tariff of 1930, the rise of the fascist bloc in the 1930s, and the rise of the communist bloc in the 1940s. All of these factors pertain to barriers that were created by governments, in contrast to the forces of technology and the private marketplace, which tend to reduce barriers. As a result, the world that emerged in 1945 was far more fragmented economically than the world that had turned to war in 1914.

The victors, however, were determined not to repeat the mistakes they had made at the time of the first world war. This time, they would work to promote economic integration in large part to advance long-term political goals. To govern international money, investment, and trade, they established multilateral institutions—the International Monetary Fund, World Bank, and General Agreement on Tariffs and Trade. The United States initially led the way by reducing trade barriers and making available gold-convertible dollars.

By one basic measure of trade, exports or imports of merchandise as a fraction of total output, it took more than twenty-five years after the end of World War II before the United States around 1970 reached the same level of globalization that it had experienced on the eve of World War I. This fraction continued to increase rapidly between 1971 and 1997—reaching about 9 percent today, still far lower than that in Britain throughout the late and early twentieth centuries. By other measures, some pertaining to the freedom of factor movements, the world even by the turn of the millennium was no more integrated than that of the preceding turn of the century.

Most people find it surprising that trade did not reattain its pre–World War I importance until the early 1970s. The significance of the comparison with 100 years ago goes well beyond factoids that economic historians enjoy springing on the uninitiated. Because technological know-how is irreversible—or was irreversible over the second millennium, if not entirely over the first—there is a tendency to see globalization as irreversible. But the political forces that fragmented the world for thirty years (1914–44) were evidently far more powerful than the accretion of technological progress in transport that went on during that period. The lesson is that nothing is inevitable about the process of globalization. For it to continue, world leaders must make choices of the sort made in the aftermath of World War II, instead of those made in the aftermath of World War I.

Judging by the Globalization 2000 Standard of Perfect International Integration

Perhaps perfect economic integration across national borders is a straw man. (The reader is likely to think so by the end of this chapter, even if he or she did not at the beginning.) But straw men have their purposes, and in this case ample rhetoric exists to justify the interest. A good straw man needs to be substantial enough to impress the crows and yet not so substantial that he can't be knocked flat. On both scores the proposition of complete international integration qualifies admirably.

Consider again the basic statistics of trade integration—a country's total exports of goods and services, or total imports, as a fraction of GDP. With the rapid increase in services included, these ratios now average 12 percent for the United States. The current level of trade likely represents a doubling from 100 years ago. As remarkable as is this evidence of declining transportation costs, tariffs, and other barriers to trade, it is still very far from the condition that would prevail if these costs and barriers were zero. More sophisticated statistics below will document this claim. But a very simple calculation is sufficient to make the point. U.S. output is about one-fourth of gross world product. The output of producers in other countries is thus about three-fourths of gross world product. If Americans were prone to buy goods and services from foreign producers as easily as from domestic producers, then foreign products would constitute a share of U.S. spending equal to that of the spending of the average resident of the planet. The U.S. import-GDP ratio would equal .75. The same would be true of the U.S. export-GDP ratio. And yet these ratios are only about one-sixth of this hypothetical level (12 percent /75 percent = one-sixth). In other words, globalization would have to increase another sixfold, as measured by the trade ratio, before it would literally be true that Americans did business as easily across the globe as across the country.

Other countries are also a long way from perfect openness in this sense. The overall ratio of merchandise trade to output worldwide is about twice the U.S. ratio. This is to be expected, as other countries are smaller. For the other two large economies—Japan and the European Union considered as a whole—the ratio is closer to the U.S. level. In almost all cases, the ratio falls far short of the level that would prevail in a perfectly integrated world. . . .

Why is globalization still so far from complete? To get an idea of the combination of transportation costs, trade barriers, and other frictions that remains yet to be dismantled, we must delve more deeply into the statistics.

STATISTICAL MEASURES OF ECONOMIC INTEGRATION

It can be instructive to look at direct measures of how some of the barriers to transborder integration have changed during the twentieth century—the level of tariffs on manufactures as an illustration of trade policy, or the price of a trans-Atlantic telephone call as an illustration of technological change in communications and transportation. Nevertheless, the political and physical determinants are too numerous and varied to be aggregated into a few key statistics that are capable of measuring the overall extent of integration in trade or finance. Tariff rates, for example, differ tremendously across commodities, and there is no single sensible way to aggregate them. The situation is even worse for nontariff barriers. Alternative possible measures of the importance of tariffs and other trade barriers have very low correlation with each other. . . .

Measures of quantities might appear more direct: "just how big are international flows?" But economists often prefer to look at price measures. In the first place, the quality of the data is often higher for prices than quantities. (This is particularly true of data on international financial markets—the data on the prices of foreign securities are extremely good, the data on aggregate international trade in securities are extremely bad.) In the second place, even at a conceptual level, international differentials in the prices of specific goods or specific assets, which measure the ability of international arbitrage to hold these prices in line, are more useful indicators of the extent of integration in a causal sense. Consider the example of U.S. trade in petroleum products. It is not especially large as a percentage of total U.S. output or consumption of petroleum products. And yet arbitrage ties the price of oil within the United States closely to the price in the world market. Even a pair of countries that records no bilateral oil trade whatsoever will find that their prices move closely together. It is the absence of barriers and the *potential* for large-scale trade that keeps prices in line and makes the markets integrated in the most meaningful sense, not the magnitude of trade that takes place.

The Ability of Arbitrage to Eliminate International Differentials in Goods Prices

According to basic economic theory, arbitrage, defined as the activity of buying an item in a place where it is cheap and simultaneously selling the same item where it is expensive, should drive prices into equality. Its failure to do so perfectly is a source of repeated surprise to economists (though perhaps to nobody else). Often the explanation is that the commodities in question are not in fact identical. Brand names matter, if for no other reason than matters of retailing, warranty, and customer service. A BMW is certainly not the same automobile as a Lexus, and even a BMW sold in Germany is not the same as a BMW sold in the United States (different air pollution control equipment, for example). When the comparison across countries uses aggregate price indexes, as in standard tests of "purchasing power parity," it is no surprise to find only weak evidence of arbitrage. The finding of international price differentials is more surprising in the case of nondifferentiated non-brand-name commodities such as standardized ball bearings. Tests find that price differentials for specific goods are far larger across national borders than they are within countries. Exchange rate variability is a likely culprit.

Even more surprising is the paucity of evidence of a tendency for price differentials to diminish over the long sweep of history. Kenneth Froot, Michael Kim, and Kenneth Rogoff have obtained data on prices in England and Holland since the year 1273 for eight commodities (barley, butter, cheese, eggs, oats, peas, silver, and wheat). Deviations from the so-called Law of One Price across the English Channel are no smaller or less persistent now than they were in the past, even though technological progress has certainly reduced the cost of shipping these products dramatically. Evidently other forces have counteracted the fall in transport costs; candidates are trade barriers under Europe's Common Agricultural Policy and volatility in the exchange rate between the guilder and the pound.

Factors Contributing to Home-Country Bias in Trade

Geography in general—and distance in particular—remain far more important inhibitions to trade than widely believed.

Distance.   Distance is still an important barrier to trade and not solely because of physical shipping costs. The effects of informational barriers are observed to decrease with proximity and with linguistic, cultural, historical, and political links. We might call it social distance. Hans Linnemann called it "psychic distance," and Peter Drysdale and Ross Garnaut named it "subjective resistance."

Among many possible proofs that distance is still important, one of the simplest is the observed tendency toward geographical agglomeration of industries. The tendency for industry to concentrate regionally is evidence both of costs to transportation and communication and of increasing returns to scale in production.

The agglomeration occurs even in sectors where physical transport costs are negligible, as in financial services or computer software. Financial firms concentrate in Manhattan and information technology firms concentrate in Silicon Valley. The reason they choose to locate near each other is not because they are trading physical commodities with each other and wish to save on shipping costs. Rather, face-to-face contact is important for exchanging information and negotiating deals.

The importance of distance is also revealed by analysis of data on prices of goods in different locations. If transport costs and other costs of doing business at a distance are important, then arbitrage should do a better job of keeping prices of similar goods in line when they are sold at locations close together rather than far apart. Charles Engel and John Rogers study prices in fourteen consumption categories for twenty-three Canadian and U.S. cities. They find that the distance between two North American cities significantly affects the variability of their relative prices. . . .

Other geographical variables.   Other physical attributes of location also have statistically significant effects. Landlocked countries engage in less trade by a factor of about one-third, holding other factors equal. Two countries that are adjacent to each other trade about 80 percent more than two otherwise similar countries.

Linguistic and colonial factors.   Linguistic barriers remain an impediment to trade. Two countries that speak the same language trade about 50 percent more than two otherwise similar countries. The multitude of languages is one of the reasons why economic integration remains far from complete in the European Union.

Colonial links have also been important historically. In 1960, the year when the break-up of the largest colonial empires began in earnest, trade between colonies and the colonial power was on average two to four times greater than for otherwise similar pairs of countries. This effect, already reduced from an earlier peak in the colonial era, has continued to decline in the 1970s and 1980s. But it has not disappeared. Indeed, if small dependencies are included in the sample, then two units that share the same colonizer still trade on average an estimated 80 percent more with each other than two otherwise similar countries (as recently as 1990). In addition, if one of the pair is the colonial mother country, trade is five to nine times greater than it would otherwise be.

Military factors.   The effects on bilateral trade of politico-military alliances, wars, have also been examined. Theoretically and empirically (in the gravity framework) trade is generally higher among countries that are allies and lower among countries that are actual or potential adversaries. Understandably, if two countries are currently at war, there is usually a negative effect on trade. It runs as high as a 99 percent reduction in 1965. More typical is an 82 percent reduction in 1990.

Free trade areas.   Regional trading arrangements reduce tariffs and other trade barriers within a group of countries, though there is a range from mild preferential trading arrangements to full-fledged economic unions. Often the members of such groups are already tightly linked through proximity, common language, or other ties. But even holding constant for such factors, in the gravity model, the formation of a free trade area is estimated on average to raise trade by 70 to 170 percent. A serious common market, such as the European Union, can have a bigger effect. Nevertheless, in each of the EU member countries, a large bias toward trade within that country remains.

Political links.   A naive economist's view would be that once tariffs and other explicit trade barriers between countries are removed, and geographic determinants of transportation costs are held constant, trade should move as easily across national boundaries as within them. But this is far from the case in reality. If two geographic units belong to the same sovereign nation, such as France and its overseas departments, trade is roughly tripled. Thus political relationships among geographic units have larger effects on trade than such factors as explicit trade policies or linguistic barriers.

Common country.   Even after adjusting for distance (including non-contiguity) and linguistic barriers, all countries still exhibit a substantial bias toward buying domestic goods rather than foreign. Shang-Jin Wei estimates this bias for countries in the Organization for Economic Cooperation and Development; it has declined only very slowly over time and is still statistically significant (though the United States has the smallest bias of all).

There would be some great advantages of having data at the level of states or provinces within countries. We would be able to ascertain how trade between two geographical entities is affected by their common membership in a political union. We have learned that when two geographical units share such links as speaking a common language, their bilateral trade is clearly boosted. It stands to reason that when two units share a common cultural heritage or legal system, their trade will be enhanced by even more. Data are not generally available on trade among U.S. states, Japanese prefectures, German länder, British counties, or French departments. But there do exist data on trade undertaken by Canadian provinces, among one another and with major American states. They show a strong intranational bias to trade. Ontario exports three times as much to British Columbia as to California, even though the latter has ten times as many people. (The figures are for 1988.) . . .

Currencies.   There has long been reason to suspect that the existence of different currencies, and especially the large fluctuation in the exchange rates between currencies since the break-up of the Bretton Woods monetary system in 1971, has been a barrier to international trade and investment. Exchange rate fluctuations are clearly related to the failures of the law of one price observed in goods markets. When it is observed that, for example, Canadians and Americans trade far more with their countrymen than with each other, in a context where trade barriers, geography, and linguistic barriers have been eliminated, the currency difference is one of the prime suspects. Until recently, however, it has been difficult to find strong evidence that currency factors discourage trade and investment. The gravity model has now been used for this purpose. It turns out that eliminating one standard deviation in exchange rate variability—for example, from its mean of 7 percent to zero—raises trade between a pair of countries by an estimated 13 percent. Furthermore, Rose has found that going all the way and literally adopting a common currency has a much bigger effect; it multiplies trade by an additional 3.5 times.

Promoting trade and finance is one of several motivations for the recent adoption of common currencies or currency boards by roughly twenty countries over the past decade (including the eleven members of the European Economic and Monetary Union in 1999). At the same time, however, approximately the same number of new currencies have come into existence, as a result of the breakup of the former Soviet bloc.

Measures of Financial Market Integration

The delegates who met at Bretton Woods in 1944 had a design for the world monetary system that explicitly did not accord financial markets the presumption that was accorded trade in goods, the presumption that international integration was unambiguously good and that barriers should be liberalized as rapidly as possible. Although economic theory can make as elegant a case in favor of free trade in assets as for free trade in goods and services, the delegates had been persuaded by the experience of the 1930s that some degree of controls on international capital movements was desirable. It was not until the final 1973 breakdown of the system of fixed exchange rates that Germany and the United States removed their capital controls. Japan and the United Kingdom kept theirs until the end of the 1970s, and most other European countries did not liberalize until the end of the 1980s. Many emerging-market countries also opened up to large-scale international capital movements in the 1990s (though the subsequent crises have convinced some observers that those delegates at Bretton Woods might have had it right in the first place).

Tests regarding financial markets show international integration that has increased tremendously over the past thirty years but that is less complete than often supposed. This generalization applies to quantity-based tests as well as to price-based tests.

It is true that the gross volume of cross-border capital flows has grown very large. Perhaps the most impressive and widely cited statistic is the gross volume of turnover in foreign exchange markets: $1.5 trillion per day worldwide, by April 1998, which is on the order of a hundred times greater than the volume of trade in goods and services. *Net* capital flows are for most purposes more interesting than gross flows, however. Net capital flows today are far smaller as a share of GDP than were pre-World War I net flows out of Great Britain and into such land-abundant countries as Argentina, Australia, and Canada. Furthermore, Martin Feldstein and Charles Horioka argued in a very influential paper that net capital flows are far smaller than one would expect them to be in a world of perfect international capital mobility: a country that suffers a shortfall in national saving tends to experience an almost commensurate fall in investment, rather than making up the difference by borrowing from abroad. Similarly, investors in every country hold far lower proportions of their portfolios in the form of other countries' securities than they would in a well-diversified portfolio, a puzzle known as home country bias. Evidently, imperfect information and transactions costs are still important barriers to cross-country investment.

The ability of arbitrage to equate asset prices or rates of return across countries has been widely tested. One would expect that in the absence of barriers to cross-border financial flows, arbitrage would bring interest rates into equality. But the answer depends on the precise condition tested. Interest rates that have had the element of exchange risk removed by forward market cover are indeed virtually equated across national borders among industrialized countries, showing that they have few controls on international capital movements. But interest rates seem not to be equalized across countries when they are adjusted for expectations of exchange rate changes rather than for forward exchange rates, and interest rates are definitely not equalized when adjusted for expected inflation rates. Evidently, currency differences are important enough to drive a wedge between expected rates of return. Furthermore, residual transactions costs or imperfect information apparently affects cross-border investment in equities. They discourage investors altogether from investing in some information-intensive assets, such as mortgages, across national borders. Furthermore, country risk still adds a substantial penalty wedge to all investments in developing countries.

In short, though international financial markets, much like goods markets, have become far more integrated in recent decades, they have traversed less of the distance to perfect integration than is widely believed. Globalization is neither new, nor complete, nor irreversible.

The Impact of Economic Globalization

What are the effects of globalization and its merits? We must acknowledge a lower degree of certainty in our answers. It becomes harder to isolate cause and effect. Moreover, once we extend the list of objectives beyond maximizing national incomes, value judgments come into play. Nevertheless, economic theory and empirical research still have much to contribute.

The Effect of Trade on the Level and Growth of Real Income

Why do economists consider economic integration so important? What are the benefits of free trade for the economy?

The theoretical case for trade.   Classical economic theory tells us that there are national gains from trade, associated with the phrase "comparative advantage." Over the past two decades, scholars have developed a "new trade theory." It suggests the existence of additional benefits from trade, which are termed dynamic. We consider each theory in turn.

The classical theory goes back to Adam Smith and David Ricardo. Adam Smith argued that specialization—the division of labor—enhances productivity. David Ricardo extended this concept to trade between countries. The notion is that trade allows each country to specialize in what it does best, thus maximizing the value of its output. If a government restricts trade, resources are wasted in the production of goods that could be imported more cheaply than they can be produced domestically.

What if one country is better than anyone else at producing *every* good? The argument in favor of free trade still carries the day. All that is required is for a country to be *relatively* less skilled than another in the production of some good in order for it to benefit from trade. This is the doctrine of comparative advantage—the fundamental (if perhaps counterintuitive) principle that underlies the theory of international trade. It makes sense for Michael Jordan to pay someone else to mow his lawn, even if Jordan could do it better himself, because he has a comparative advantage at basketball over lawn mowing. Similarly, it makes sense for the United States to pay to import certain goods that can be produced more efficiently abroad (apparel, shoes, tropical agriculture, consumer electronics), because the United States has a comparative advantage in other goods (aircraft, financial services, wheat, and computer software).

This is the classical view of the benefits of free trade in a nutshell. Two key attributes of the classical theory are worth flagging. First, it assumes perfect competition, constant returns to scale, and fixed technology, assumptions that are not very realistic. Second, the gains from trade are primarily static in nature—that is, they affect the *level* of real income. The elimination of trade barriers raises income, but this is more along the lines of a one-time increase.

What of the "new trade theory"? It is more realistic than the classical theory, in that it takes into account imperfect competition, increasing returns to scale, and changing technology. It can be viewed as providing equally strong, or stronger, support for the sort of free trade policies that the United States has followed throughout the postwar period, that is, multilateral and bilateral negotiations to reduce trade barriers, than did the classical theory.

To be sure, these theories say that, under certain very special conditions, one country can get ahead by interventions (for example, subsidies to strategic sectors), provided the government gets it exactly right and provided the actions of other countries are taken as given. But these theories also tend to have the property that a world in which everyone is subsidizing at once is a world in which everyone is worse off, and that we are all better off if we can agree to limit subsidies or other interventions.

Bilateral or multilateral agreements where other sides make concessions to U.S. products, in return for whatever concessions the United States makes, are virtually the only sorts of trade agreements the United States has made. Indeed, most recent trade agreements (like the North American Free Trade Agreement and China's accession to the WTO) have required much larger reductions in import barriers by U.S. trading partners than by the United States. The reason is that their barriers were higher than those of the United States to start with. But the natural implication is that such agreements raise foreign demand for U.S. products by more than they raise U.S. demand for imports. Hence the United States is likely to benefit from a positive "terms of trade effect." This just adds to the usual benefits of increased efficiency of production and gains to consumers from international trade.

Furthermore, even when a government does not fear retaliation from abroad for trade barriers, intervention in practice is usually based on inadequate knowledge and is corrupted by interest groups. Seeking to rule out all sector-specific intervention is the most effective way of discouraging rent-seeking behavior. Globalization increases the number of competitors operating in the economy. Not only does this work to reduce distortionary monopoly power in the marketplace (which is otherwise exercised by raising prices), it can also reduce distortionary corporate power in the political arena (which is exercised by lobbying).

Most important, new trade theory offers reason to believe that openness can have a permanent effect on a country's rate of growth, not just the level of real GDP. A high rate of economic interaction with the rest of the world speeds the absorption of frontier technologies and global management best practices, spurs innovation and cost-cutting, and competes away monopoly.

These dynamic gains come from a number of sources. They include the benefits of greater market size and enhanced competition. Other sources include technological improvements through increased contact with foreigners and their alternative production styles. Such contact can come, for example, from direct investment by foreign firms with proprietary knowledge or by the exposure to imported goods that embody technologies developed abroad. Each of these elements of international trade and interactions has the effect of promoting growth in the domestic economy. When combined with the static effects, there is no question that the efforts to open markets, when successful, can yield significant dividends.

The empirical case for trade.   Citing theory is not a complete answer to the question, "how do we know that trade is good?" We need empirical evidence. Economists have undertaken statistical tests of the determinants of countries' growth rates. Investment in physical capital and investment in human capital are the two factors that emerge the most strongly. But other factors matter. Estimates of growth equations have found a role for openness, measured, for example, as the sum of exports and imports as a share of GDP. David Romer and I look at a cross-section of 100 countries during the period since 1960. The study sought to address a major concern about simultaneous causality between growth and trade: does openness lead to growth, or does growth lead to openness? We found that the effect of openness on growth is even stronger when we correct for the simultaneity compared with standard estimates.

The estimate of the effect of openness on income per capita ranges from 0.3 to 3.0. Consider a round middle number such as 1.0. The increase in U.S. openness since the 1950s is 0.12. Multiplying the two numbers together implies that the increased integration has had an effect of 12 percent on U.S. income. More dramatically, compare a stylized Burma, with a ratio close to zero, versus a stylized Singapore, with a ratio close to 100 percent. Our ballpark estimate, the coefficient of 1.0, implies that Singapore's income is 100 percent higher than Burma's as a result of its openness. The fact that trade can affect a country's growth rate—as opposed to affecting the level of its GDP in a "one-shot" fashion—makes the case for trade liberalization even more compelling.

One possible response is that this approach demonstrates only the growth benefits from geographically induced trade and need not necessarily extend to the effects of policy-induced trade. But popular critics of globalization seem to think that increased international trade and finance is the problem, regardless of whether it comes from technological progress or government liberalization. As the critics make their arguments against government dismantling of policy barriers, they seldom specify that cross-border interactions attributable to geography or to technological innovations in transport are economically beneficial.

Macroeconomic interdependence.   Trade and financial integration generally increase the transmission of business cycle fluctuations among countries. Floating exchange rates give countries some insulation against one another's fluctuations. When capital markets are highly integrated, floating rates do not give complete insulation, as the post-1973 correlation among major industrialized economies shows. But international transmission can be good for a country as easily as bad, as happens when adverse domestic developments are in part passed off to the rest of the world. The trade balance can act as an important automatic stabilizer for output and employment, improving in recessions and worsening in booms.

Contagion of financial crises is more worrying. The decade of the 1990s alone abounds with examples: the 1992–93 crises in the European exchange rate mechanism, the "tequila crisis" that began with the December 1994 devaluation of the

Mexican peso, and the crises in East Asia and emerging markets worldwide from July 1997 to January 1999. Evidently when one country has a crisis it affects others. There is now a greater consensus among economists than before that not all of the observed volatility, or its cross-country correlation, can be attributed to efficient capital markets punishing or rewarding countries based on a rational evaluation of the economic fundamentals. It is difficult to do justice in one paragraph to a discussion that is as voluminous and vigorous as the debate over the welfare implications of the swelling international capital flows. Still, the majority view remains that countries are overall better off with modern globalized financial markets than without them.

The Effect of Trade on Other Social Goals

Many who fear globalization concede that trade has a positive effect on aggregate national income but suspect that it has adverse effects on other highly valued goals such as labor rights, food safety, culture, and so forth. Here we consider only two major values—equality and the environment—and briefly at that.

Income distribution.   International trade and investment can be a powerful source of growth in poor countries, helping them catch up with those who are ahead in endowments of capital and technology. This was an important component of the spectacular growth of East Asian countries between the 1960s and the 1990s, which remains a miracle even in the aftermath of the 1997–98 currency crises. By promoting convergence, trade can help reduce the enormous worldwide inequality in income. Most of those who are concerned about income distribution, however, seem more motivated by within-country equality than global equality.

A standard textbook theory of international trade, the Heckscher-Ohlin-Samuelson model, has a striking prediction to make regarding within-country income distribution. It is that the scarce factors of production will lose from trade, and the abundant factors will benefit. This means that in rich countries, those who have capital and skills will benefit at the expense of unskilled labor, whereas in poor countries it will be the other way around. The same prediction holds for international capital mobility (or, for that matter, for international labor mobility). It has been very difficult, however, to find substantial direct evidence of the predictions of the model during the postwar period, including distribution effects within either rich or poor countries. Most likely the phenomena of changing technology, intraindustry trade, and worker ties to specific industries are more important today than the factor endowments at the heart of the Heckscher-Ohlin-Samuelson model.

In the United States, the gap between wages paid to skilled workers and wages paid to unskilled workers rose by 18 percentage points between 1973 and 1995 and then leveled off. The fear is that trade is responsible for some of the gap, by benefiting skilled workers more than unskilled workers. Common statistical estimates—which typically impose the theoretical framework rather than testing it—are that between 5 and 30 percent of the increase is attributable to trade. Technology, raising the demand for skilled workers faster than the supply, is the major factor responsible for the rest. One of the higher estimates is that trade contributes one-third of the net increase in the wage gap.

On a sample of seventy-three countries, Chakrabarti finds that trade actually reduces inequality, as measured by the Gini coefficient. This relationship also holds for each income class.

Clearly, income distribution is determined by many factors beyond trade. One is redistribution policies undertaken by the government. In some cases such policies are initiated in an effort to compensate or "buy off" groups thought to be adversely affected by trade. But a far more important phenomenon is the tendency for countries to implement greater redistribution as they grow richer.

A long-established empirical regularity is the tendency for income inequality to worsen at early stages of growth and then to improve at later stages. The original explanation for this phenomenon, known as the Kuznets curve, had to do with rural-urban migration. But a common modern interpretation is that income redistribution is a "superior good"—something that societies choose to purchase more of, even though at some cost to aggregate income, as they grow rich enough to be able to afford to do so. If this is right, then trade can be expected eventually to raise equality, by raising aggregate income.

Can Environment

. . .

The idea that trade can be good for environment is surprising to many. The pollution-haven hypothesis instead holds that trade encourages firms to locate production of highly polluting sectors in low-regulation countries in order to stay competitive. But economists' research suggests that environmental regulation is not a major determinant of firms' ability to compete internationally. Furthermore, running counter to fears of a "race to the bottom," is the Pareto-improvement point: trade allows countries to attain more of whatever their goals are, including higher market-measured income for a given level of environmental quality or a better environment for a given level of income. In a model that combines various effects of trade, including via the scale and composition of output, Werner Antweiler, Brian Copeland, and M. Scott Taylor estimate that if openness raises GDP by 1 percent, then it reduces sulphur dioxide concentrations by 1 percent. The implication is that, because trade is good for growth, it is also good for the environment.

The econometric studies of the effects of trade and growth on the environment get different results depending on what specific measures of pollution they use. There is a need to look at other environmental criteria as well. It is difficult to imagine, for example, that trade is anything but bad for the survival of tropical hardwood forests or endangered species, without substantial efforts by governments to protect them.

The argument that richer countries will take steps to clean up their environments holds only for issues when the effects are felt domestically—where the primary "bads," such as smog or water pollution, are external to the firm or household but internal to the country. Some environmental externalities that have received increased attention in recent decade, however, are global. Biodiversity, overfishing, ozone depletion, and greenhouse gas emissions are four good examples. A ton of carbon dioxide has the same global warming effect regardless of where in the world it is emitted. In these cases, individual nations can do little to improve the environment on their own, no matter how concerned their populations or how effective their governments. For each of the four examples, governments have negotiated international treaties in an attempt to deal with the problem. But only the attempt to address ozone depletion, the Montreal Protocol, can be said as yet to have met with much success.

Is the popular impression then correct, that international trade and finance exacerbates these global environmental externalities? Yes, but only in the sense that trade and finance promote economic growth. Clearly if mankind were still a population of a few million people living in pre-industrial poverty, greenhouse gas emissions would not be a big issue. Industrialization leads to environmental degradation, and trade is part of industrialization. But virtually everyone wants industrialization, at least for themselves. Deliberate self-impoverishment is not a promising option. Once this point is recognized, there is nothing special about trade compared with the other sources of economic growth: capital accumulation, rural-urban migration, and technological progress. . . .

SUMMARY OF CONCLUSIONS

This chapter gives confident answers to questions about the extent and sources of economic globalization and moderately confident answers to some questions about its effects.

The world has become increasingly integrated with respect to trade and finance since the end of World War II, owing to declining costs to transportation and communication and declining government barriers. The phenomenon is neither new nor complete, however. Globalization was more dramatic in the half-century preceding World War I, and much of the progress during the last half-century has merely reversed the closing off that came in between. In the second regard, globalization is far from complete. Contrary to popular impressions, national borders and geography still impede trade and investment substantially. A simple calculation suggests that the ratio of trade to output would have to increase at least another six-fold before it would be true that Americans trade across the globe as readily as across the country. Such barriers as differences in currencies, languages, and political systems each have their own statistically estimated trade-impeding influences, besides the remaining significant effects of distance, borders, and other geographical and trade policy variables.

The chapter's discussion of the impacts of economic globalization has necessarily been exceedingly brief. Both theory and evidence are read as clearly supportive of the proposition that trade has a positive effect on real incomes. This is why economists believe it is important that the process of international integration be allowed to continue, especially for the sake of those countries that are still poor.

Effects on social values other than aggregate incomes can be positive or negative, depending on the details, and the statistical evidence does not always give clear-cut answers about the bottom line. In the two most studied cases, income distribution and environmental pollution, there seems to be a pattern whereby things get worse in the early stages of industrialization but then start to get better at higher levels of income. Societies that become rich in terms of market-measured output choose to improve their quality of life in other ways as well. It is possible that the same principle extends to noneconomic values such as safety, human rights, and democracy. In short, there is reason to hope that, aside from the various more direct effects of trade on noneconomic values, there is a general indirect beneficial effect that comes through the positive effect of trade on income. . . .

GLOBALIZATION AND GOVERNANCE

KENNETH N. WALTZ

...THE STATE OF THE STATE

Globalization is the fad of the 1990s, and globalization is made in America. Thomas Friedman's *The Lexus and the Olive Tree* is a celebration of the American way, of market capitalism and liberal democracy. Free markets, transparency, and flexibility are the watchwords. The "electronic herd" moves vast amounts of capital in and out of countries according to their political and economic merits. Capital moves almost instantaneously into countries with stable governments, progressive economies, open accounting, and honest dealing, and out of countries lacking those qualities. States can defy the "herd," but they will pay a price, usually a steep one, as did Thailand, Malaysia, Indonesia, and South Korea in the 1990s. Some countries may defy the herd inadvertently (the countries just mentioned); others, out of ideological conviction

From "Globalization and Governance" by Kenneth N. Waltz from *PS: Political Science and Politics*, Vol. 32, No. 4 (Dec 1999), pp. 694–700. Copyright © 1999 by the American Political Science Association. Reprinted with the permission of Cambridge University Press.

(Cuba and North Korea); some, because they can afford to (oil-rich countries); others, because history has passed them by (many African countries).

Countries wishing to attract capital and to gain the benefits of today's and tomorrow's technology have to don the "golden straitjacket," a package of policies including balanced budgets, economic deregulation, openness to investment and trade, and a stable currency. The herd decides which countries to reward and which to punish, and nothing can be done about its decisions. In September 1997, at a World Bank meeting, Malaysia's prime minister, Dr. Mahathir Mohammad, complained bitterly that great powers and international speculators had forced Asian countries to open their markets and had manipulated their currencies in order to destroy them. Friedman (1999, 93) wonders what Robert Rubin, then-U.S. treasury secretary, might have said in response. He imagines it would have been something like this: "What planet are you living on? . . . Globalization isn't a choice, it's a reality, . . . and the only way you can grow at the speed that your people want to grow is by tapping into the global stock and bond markets, by seeking out multinationals to invest in your country, and by selling into the global trading system what your factories produce. And the most basic truth about globalization is this: *No one is in charge.*" . . .

The "end of the Cold War and the collapse of communism have discredited all models other than liberal democracy." The statement is by Larry Diamond, and Friedman repeats it with approval. There is one best way, and America has found it. "It's a post-industrial world, and America today is good at everything that is post-industrial" (145, 303). The herd does not care about forms of government as such, but it values and rewards "stability, predictability, transparency, and the ability to transfer and protect its private property." Liberal democracies represent the one best way. The message to all governments is clear: Conform or suffer.

There is much in what Friedman says, and he says it very well. But how much? And, specifically, what is the effect of closer interdependence on the conduct of the internal and external affairs of nations?

First, we should ask how far globalization has proceeded? As everyone knows, much of the world has been left aside: most of Africa and Latin America, Russia, all of the Middle East except Israel, and large parts of Asia. Moreover, for many countries, the degree of participation in the global economy varies by region. Northern Italy, for example, is in; southern Italy is out. In fact, globalization is not global but is mainly limited to northern latitudes. Linda Weiss points out that, as of 1991, 81% of the world stock of foreign direct investment was in high-wage countries of the north: mainly the United States, followed by the United Kingdom, Germany, and Canada. She adds that the extent of concentration has grown by 12 points since 1967 (Weiss 1998; cf., Hirst and Thompson 1996, 72).

Second, we should compare the interdependence of nations now with interdependence earlier. The first paragraph of this paper suggests that in most ways we have not exceeded levels reached in 1910. The rapid growth of international trade and investment from the middle 1850s into the 1910s preceded a prolonged period of war, internal revolution, and national insularity. After World War II, protectionist policies lingered as the United States opened it borders to trade while taking a relaxed attitude toward countries that protected their markets during the years of recovery from war's devastation. One might say that from 1914 into the 1960s an interdependence deficit developed, which helps to explain the steady growth of interdependence thereafter. Among the richest 24 industrial economies (the OECD countries), exports grew at about twice the rate of GDP after 1960. In 1960, exports were 9.5% of their GDPs; in 1900, 20.5% (Wade 1996, 62; cf., Weiss 1998, 171). Finding that 1999 approximately equals 1910 in extent of interdependence is hardly surprising. What is true of trade also holds for capital flows, again as a percentage of GDP (Hirst and Thompson 1996, 36). . . .

Obviously, the world is not one. Sadly, the disparities of the North and South remain wide. Perhaps surprisingly, among the countries that are thought of as being in the zone of globalization, differences are considerable and persistent. To take just one example, financial patterns differ markedly across countries. The United States depends on capital imports, Western Europe does not, and Japan is a major capital exporter. The more closely one looks, the more one finds variations. That is hardly surprising. What looks smooth, uniform, and simple from a distance, on closer inspection proves to be pock marked, variegated, and complex. Yet here, the variations are large enough to sustain the conclusion that globalization, even within its zone, is not a statement about the present, but a prediction about the future.

Many globalizers underestimate the extent to which the new looks like the old. In any competitive system the winners are imitated by the losers, or they continue to lose. In political as in economic development, latecomers imitate the practices and adopt the institution of the countries who have shown the way. Occasionally, someone finds a way to outflank, to invent a new way, or to ingeniously modify an old way to gain an advantage; and then the process of imitation begins anew. That competitors begin to look like one another if the competition is close and continuous is a familiar story. Competition among states has always led some of them to imitate others politically, militarily, and economically; but the apostles of globalization argue that the process has now sped up immensely and that the straitjacket allows little room to wiggle. In the old political era, the strong vanquished the weak; in the new economic era, "the fast eat the slow" (Klaus Schwab quoted in Friedman 1999, 171). No longer is it "Do what the strong party says or risk physical punishment'; but instead "Do what the electronic herd requires or remain impoverished." But then, in a competitive system there are always winners and losers. A few do exceptionally well, some get along, and many bring up the rear.

States have to conform to the ways of the more successful among them or pay a stiff price for not doing so. We then have to ask what is the state of the state? What becomes of politics within the coils of encompassing economic processes? The message of globalizers is that economic and technological forces impose near uniformity of political and economic forms and functions on states. They do so because the herd is attracted only to countries with reliable, stable, and open governments—that is, to liberal democratic ones.

Yet a glance at just the past 75 years reveals that a variety of political-economic systems have produced impressive results and were admired in their day for doing so. In the 1930s and again in the 1950s, the Soviet Union's economic growth rates were among the world's highest, so impressive in the '50s that America feared being overtaken and passed by. In the 1960s President Kennedy got "the country moving again," and America's radically different system gained world respect. In the '70s, Western European welfare states with managed and directed economics were highly regarded. In the late '70s and through much of the '80s, the Japanese brand of neomercantilism was thought to be the wave of the future; and Western Europe and the United States worried about being able to keep up. Imitate or perish was the counsel of some; pry the Japanese economy open and make it compete on our grounds was the message of others. America did not succeed in doing much of either. Yet in the 1990s, its economy has flourished. Globalizers offer it as the ultimate political-economic model—and so history again comes to an end. Yet it is odd to conclude from a decade's experience that the one best model has at last appeared. Globalization, if it were realized, would mean a near uniformity of conditions across countries. Even in the 1990s, one finds little evidence of globalization. The advanced countries of the world have enjoyed or suffered quite different fates. Major Western European countries were plagued by high and persistent unemployment; Northeast and Southeast Asian countries experienced economic stagnation or collapse while China continued to do quite well; and we know about the United States.

Variation in the fortunes of nations underlines the point: The country that has done best, at least lately, is the United States. Those who have fared poorly have supposedly done so because they have failed to conform to the American Way. Globalizers do not claim that globalization is complete, but only that it is in process and that the process is irreversible. Some evidence supports the conclusion; some does not. Looking at the big picture, one notices that nations whose economies have faltered or failed have been more fully controlled, directed, and supported governmentally than the American economy. Soviet-style economies failed miserably; in China, only the free-market sector flourishes; the once much-favored Swedish model has proved wanting. One can easily add more examples. From them it is tempting to leap to the conclusion that America has indeed found, or stumbled onto, the one best way.

Obviously, Thomas Friedman thinks so. Tip O'Neill, when he was a congressman from Massachusetts, declared that all politics are local. Wrong, Friedman says, all politics have become global. "The electronic herd," he writes, "turns the whole world into a parliamentary system, in which every government lives under the fear of a no-confidence vote from the herd" (1999, 62, 115).

I find it hard to believe that economic processes direct or determine a nation's policies, that spontaneously arrived at decisions about where to place resources reward or punish a national economy so strongly that a government either does what pleases the "herd" or its economy fails to prosper or even risks collapse. We all recall recent cases, some of them mentioned above, that seem to support Friedman's thesis. Mentioning them both makes a point and raises doubts.

First, within advanced countries at similar levels of development that are closely interrelated, one expects uniformities of form and function to be most fully displayed. Yet Stephen Woolcock, looking at forms of corporate governance within the European community, finds a "spectrum of approaches" and expects it to persist for the foreseeable future (1996, 196). Since the 1950s, the economies of Germany and France have grown more closely together as each became the principal trading partner of the other. Yet a study of the two countries concludes that France has copied German policies but has been unwilling or unable to copy institutions (Boltho 1996). GDP per work hour among seven of the most prosperous countries came close together between the 1950s and the 1980s (Boyer 1996, 37). Countries at a high level of development do tend to converge in productivity, but that is something of a tautology.

Second, even if all politics have become global, economies remain local perhaps to a surprising extent. Countries with large economies continue to do most of their business at home. Americans produce 88% of the goods they buy. Sectors that are scarcely involved in international trade, such as government, construction, nonprofit organizations, utilities, and wholesale and retail trade employ 82% of Americans (Lawrence 1997, 21). As Paul Krugman says, "The United States is still almost 90% an economy that produces goods and services for its own use" (1997, 166). For the world's three largest economies—the United States, Japan, and the European Union—taken as a unit, exports are 12% or less of GDP (Weiss 1998, 176). What I found to be true in 1970 remains true today: The world is less interdependent than is usually supposed (Waltz 1970). Moreover, developed countries, oil imports aside, do the bulk of their external business with one another, and that means that the extent of their dependence on commodities that they could not produce for themselves is further reduced.

Reinforcing the parochial pattern of productivity, the famous footloose corporations in fact turn out to be firmly anchored in their home bases. One study of the world's 100 largest corporations concludes that not one of them could be called truly "global" or "footloose." Another study found one multinational corporation that seemed to be leaving its home base: Britain's chemical company, ICI (Weiss 1998, 18, 22; cf., Hirst and Thompson 1996, 82–93, 90, 95ff.). On all the important counts—location of most assets, site of research and development, ownership, and management—the importance of a corporation's home base is marked. And the technological prowess of corporations corresponds closely to that of the countries in which they are located.

Third, the *"transformative capacity"* of states, as Linda Weiss emphasizes, is the key to their success in the world economy (Weiss 1998, xii). Because technological innovation is rapid, and because economic conditions at home and abroad change often, states that adapt easily have considerable advantages. International politics remains inter-national. As the title of a review by William H. McNeill (1997) puts it, "Territorial States Buried Too Soon." Global or world politics has not taken over from national politics. The twentieth century was the century of the nation-state. The twenty-first will be too. Trade and technology do not determine a single best way to organize a polity and its economy. National systems display a great deal of resilience. States still have a wide range of choice. Most states survive, and the units that survive in competitive systems are those with the ability to adapt. Some do it well, and they grow and prosper. Others just manage to get along. That's the way it is in competitive systems. In this spirit, Ezra Taft Benson, when he was President Eisenhower's secretary of agriculture, gave this kindly advice to America's small farmers: "Get big or get out." Success in competitive systems requires the units of the system to adopt ways they would prefer to avoid.

States adapt to their environment. Some are light afoot, and others are heavy. The United States looked to be heavy afoot in the 1980s when Japan's economy was booming. Sometimes it seemed that MITI (Ministry of International Trade and Industry) was manned by geniuses who guided Japan's economy effortlessly to its impressive accomplishments. Now it is the United States that appears light afoot, lighter than any other country. Its government is open: Accurate financial information flows freely, most economic decisions are made by private firms. These are the characteristics that make for flexibility and for quick adaptation to changing conditions.

Competitive systems select for success. Over time, the qualities that make for success vary. Students of American government point out that one of the advantages of a federal system is that the separate states can act as laboratories for social-economic experimentation. When some states succeed, others may imitate them. The same thought applies to nations. One must wonder who the next winner will be.

States adapt; they also protect themselves. Different nations, with distinct institutions and traditions, protect themselves in different ways. Japan fosters industries, defends them, and manages its trade. The United States uses its political, economic, and military leverage to protect itself and manipulate international events to promote its interests. Thus, as David E. Spiro elaborately shows, international markets and institutions did not recycle petrodollars after 1974. The United States did. Despite many statements to the contrary, the United States worked effectively through different administrations and under different cabinet secretaries to undermine markets and thwart international institutions. Its leverage enabled it to manipulate the oil crisis to serve its own interests (1999, chap. 6).

Many of the interdependers of the 1970s expected the state to wither and fade away. Charles Kindleberger wrote in 1969 that "the nation-state is just about through as an economic unit" (207). Globalizers of the 1990s believe that this time it really is happening. The state has lost its "monopoly over internal sovereignty," Wolfgang H. Reinecke writes, and as "an externally sovereign actor" it "will become a thing of the past" (1997, 137; cf., Thurow 1999). Internally, the state's monopoly has never been complete, but it seems more nearly so now than earlier, at least in well-established states. The range of governmental functions and the extent of state control over society and economy has seldom been fuller than it is now. In many parts of the world the concern has been not with the state's diminished internal powers but with their increase. And although state control has lessened somewhat recently, does anyone believe that the United States and Britain, for example, are back to a 1930s level, let alone to a nineteenth-century level of governmental regulation?

States perform essential political social-economic functions, and no other organization appears as a possible competitor to them. They foster the institutions that make internal peace and prosperity possible. In the state of nature, as Kant put it, there is "no mine and thine." States turn possession into property and thus make saving, production, and prosperity possible. The sovereign state with fixed borders has proved to be the best organization for keeping peace and fostering the conditions for economic well being.[1] We do not have to wonder what happens to society and economy when a state begins to fade away. We have all too many examples. A few obvious ones are China in the 1920s and '30s and again in the 1960s and '70s, post-Soviet Russia, and many African states since their independence. The less competent a state, the likelier it is to dissolve into component parts or to be unable to adapt to transnational developments. Challenges at home and abroad test the mettle of states. Some states fail, and other states pass the tests nicely. In modern times, enough states always make it to keep the international system going as a system of states. The challenges vary; states endure. They have proved to be hardy survivors.

Having asked how international conditions affect states, I now reverse the question and ask how states affect the conduct of international political affairs.

THE STATE IN INTERNATIONAL POLITICS

Economic globalization would mean tht the world economy, or at least the globalized portion of it, would be integrated and not merely interdependent. The difference between an interdependent and an integrated world is a qualitative one and

---

[1]The picture of the purpose and the performance of states is especially clear in Thomson and Krasner (1989).

not a mere matter of proportionately more trade and a greater and more rapid flow of capital. With integration, the world would look like one big state. Economic markets and economic interests cannot perform the functions of government. Integration requires or presumes a government to protect, direct, and control. Interdependence, in contrast to integration, is "the mere mutualism" of states, as Emile Durkheim put it. It is not only less close than usually thought but also politically less consequential. Interdependence did not produce the world-shaking events of 1989–91. A political event, the failure of one of the world's two great powers, did that. Had the configuration of international politics not fundamentally changed, neither the unification of Germany nor the war against Saddam Hussein would have been possible. The most important events in international politics are explained by differences in the capabilities of states, not by economic forces operating across states or transcending them. Interdependers, and globalizers even more so, argue that the international economic interests of states work against their going to war. True, they do. Yet if one asks whether economic interests or nuclear weapons inhibit war more strongly, the answer obviously is nuclear weapons. European great powers prior to World War I were tightly tied together economically. They nevertheless fought a long and bloody war. The United States and the Soviet Union were not even loosely connected economically. They coexisted peacefully through the four-and-a-half decades of the Cold War. The most important causes of peace, as of war, are found in international-political conditions, including the weaponry available to states. Events following the Cold War dramatically demonstrate the political weakness of economic forces. The integration (not just the interdependence) of the parts of the Soviet Union and of Yugoslavia, with all of their entangling economic interests, did not prevent their disintegration. Governments and people sacrifice welfare and even security to nationalism, ethnicity, and religion.

Political explanations weigh heavily in accounting for international-political events. National *politics*, not international markets, account for many international *economic* developments. A number of students of politics and of economics believe that blocs are becoming more common internationally. Economic interests and market forces do not create blocs; governments do. Without governmental decisions, the Coal and Steel Community, the European Economic Community, and the European Union would not have emerged. The representatives of states negotiate regulations in the European Commission. The Single-Market Act of 1985 provided that some types of directives would require less than a unanimous vote in the Council of Ministers. This political act cleared the way for passage of most of the harmonization standards for Europe (Dumez and Jeunemaître 1996, 229). American governments forged NAFTA; Japan fashioned an East and Southeast Asian producing and trading area. The decisions and acts of a country, or a set of countries arriving at political agreements, shape international political and economic institutions. Governments now intervene much more in international economic matters than they did in the earlier era of interdependence. Before World War I, foreign-ministry officials were famed for their lack of knowledge of, or interest in, economic affairs. Because governments have become much more active in economic affairs at home and abroad, interdependence has become less of an autonomous force in international politics.

The many commentators who exaggerate the closeness of interdependence, and even more so those who write of globalization, think in unit rather than in systemic terms. Many small states import and export large shares of their gross domestic products. States with large GDPs do not. They are little dependent on others, while a number of other states heavily depend on them. The terms of political, economic, and military competition are set by the larger units of the international-political system. Through centuries of multipolarity, with five or so great powers of comparable size competing with one another, the international system was quite closely interdependent. Under bi-and unipolarity the degree of interdependence declined markedly.

States are differentiated from one another not by function but primarily by capability. For two reasons, inequalities across states have greater political impact than inequalities across income groups within states. First, the inequalities of states are larger and have been growing more rapidly. Rich countries have become richer while poor countries have remained poor. Second, in a system without central governance, the influence of the units of greater capability is disproportionately large because there are no effective laws and institutions to direct and constrain them. They are able to work the system to their advantage, as the petrodollar example showed. I argued in 1970 that what counts are states' capacity to adjust to external conditions and their ability to use their economic leverage for political advantage. The United States was then and is still doubly blessed. It remains highly important in the international economy, serving as a principal market for a number of countries and as a major supplier of goods and services, yet its dependence on others is quite low. Precisely because the United States is relatively little dependent on others, it has a wide range of policy choices and the ability both to bring pressure on others and to assist them. The "herd" with its capital may flee from countries when it collectively decides that they are politically and economically unworthy, but some countries abroad, like some firms at home, are so important that they cannot be allowed to fail. National governments and international agencies then come to the rescue. The United States is the country that most often has the ability and the will to step in. The agency that most often acts is the IMF, and most countries think of the IMF as the enforcement arm of the U.S. Treasury (Strange 1996, 192). Thomas Friedman believes that when the "herd" makes its decisions, there is no appeal; but often there is an appeal, and it is for a bail out organized by the United States.

The international economy, like national economies, operates within a set of rules and institutions. Rules and institutions have to be made and sustained. Britain, to a large extent, provided this service prior to World War I; no one did between the wars, and the United States has done so since. More than any other state, the United States makes the rules and maintains the institutions that shape the international political economy.

Economically, the United States is the world's most important country; militarily, it is not only the most important country, it is the decisive one. Thomas Friedman puts the point simply: The world is sustained by "the presence of American power and America's willingness to use that power against those who would threaten the system of globalization. . . . The hidden hand of the market will never work without a hidden fist" (1999, 373). But the hidden fist is in full view. On its military forces, the United States outspends the next six or seven big spenders combined. When force is needed to keep or to restore the peace, either the United States leads the way or the peace is not kept. The Cold War militarized international politics. Relations between the United States and the Soviet Union, and among some other countries as well, came to be defined largely in a single dimension, the military one. As the German sociologist Erich Weede has remarked, "National security decision making in some . . . democracies (most notably in West Germany) is actually penetrated by the United States" (1989, 225). . . .

Many globalizers believe that the world is increasingly ruled by markets. Looking at the state among states leads to a different conclusion. The main difference between international politics now and earlier is not found in the increased interdependence of states but in their growing inequality. With the end of bipolarity, the distribution of capabilities across states has become extremely lopsided. Rather than elevating economic forces and depressing political ones, the inequalities of international politics enhance the political role of one country. Politics, as usual, prevails over economics.

COMPETITIVENESS:
A DANGEROUS OBSESSION

Paul Krugman

THE HYPOTHESIS IS WRONG

. . .

The rhetoric of competitiveness—the view that, in the words of President Clinton, each nation is "like a big corporation competing in the global marketplace"—has become pervasive among opinion leaders throughout the world. People who believe themselves to be sophisticated about the subject take it for granted that the economic problem facing any modern nation is essentially one of competing on world markets—that the United States and Japan are competitors in the same sense that Coca-Cola competes with Pepsi—and are unaware that anyone might seriously question that proposition. Every few months a new best-seller warns the American public of the

From "Competitiveness: A Dangerous Obsession" by Paul Krugman. Reprinted by permission of *Foreign Affairs*, Vol. 73, No. 2, March/April 1994. Copyright © 1994 by the Council on Foreign Relations, Inc. www.ForeignAffairs.com.

dire consequences of losing the "race" for the 21st century. A whole industry of councils on competitiveness, "geo-economists" and managed trade theorists has sprung up in Washington. Many of these people, having diagnosed America's economic problems in much the same terms as Delors did Europe's, are now in the highest reaches of the Clinton administration formulating economic and trade policy for the United States. So Delors was using a language that was not only convenient but comfortable for him and a wide audience on both sides of the Atlantic.

Unfortunately, his diagnosis was deeply misleading as a guide to what ails Europe, and similar diagnoses in the United States are equally misleading. The idea that a country's economic fortunes are largely determined by its success on world markets is a hypothesis, not a necessary truth; and as a practical, empirical matter, that hypothesis is flatly wrong. That is, it is simply not the case that the world's leading nations are to any important degree in economic competition with each other, or that any of their major economic problems can be attributed to failures to compete on world markets. The growing obsession in most advanced nations with international competitiveness should be seen, not as a well-founded concern, but as a view held in the face of overwhelming contrary evidence. And yet it is clearly a view that people very much want to hold—a desire to believe that is reflected in a remarkable tendency of those who preach the doctrine of competitiveness to support their case with careless, flawed arithmetic.

This article makes three points. First, it argues that concerns about competitiveness are, as an empirical matter, almost completely unfounded. Second, it tries to explain why defining the economic problem as one of international competition is nonetheless so attractive to so many people. Finally, it argues that the obsession with competitiveness is not only wrong but dangerous, skewing domestic policies and threatening the international economic system. This last issue is, of course, the most consequential from the standpoint of public policy. Thinking in terms of competitiveness leads, directly and indirectly, to bad economic policies on a wide range of issues, domestic and foreign, whether it be in health care or trade.

MINDLESS COMPETITION

Most people who use the term "competitiveness" do so without a second thought. It seems obvious to them that the analogy between a country and a corporation is reasonable and that to ask whether the United States is competitive in the world market is no different in principle from asking whether General Motors is competitive in the North American minivan market.

In fact, however, trying to define the competitiveness of a nation is much more problematic than defining that of a corporation. The bottom line for a corporation is literally its bottom line: if a corporation cannot afford to pay its workers, suppliers, and bondholders, it will go out of business. So when we say that a corporation is uncompetitive, we mean that its market position is unsustainable—that unless it improves its performance, it will cease to exist. Countries, on the other hand, do not go out of business. They may be happy or unhappy with their economic performance, but they have no well-defined bottom line. As a result, the concept of national competitiveness is elusive.

One might suppose, naively, that the bottom line of a national economy is simply its trade balance, that competitiveness can be measured by the ability of a country to sell more abroad than it buys. But in both theory and practice a trade surplus may be a sign of national weakness, a deficit a sign of strength. For example, Mexico was forced to run huge trade surpluses in the 1980s in order to pay the interest on its foreign debt since international investors refused to lend it any more money; it began to run large trade deficits after 1990 as foreign investors recovered confidence and began to pour in new funds. Would anyone want to describe Mexico as a highly competitive nation during the debt crisis era or describe what has happened since 1990 as a loss in competitiveness?

Most writers who worry about the issue at all have therefore tried to define competitiveness as the combination of favorable trade performance and something else. In particular, the most popular definition of competitiveness nowadays runs along the lines of the one given in Council of Economic Advisors Chairman Laura D'Andrea Tyson's *Who's Bashing Whom?:* competitiveness is "our ability to produce goods and services that meet the test of international competition while our citizens enjoy a standard of living that is both rising and sustainable." This sounds reasonable. If you think about it, however, and test your thoughts against the facts, you will find out that there is much less to this definition than meets the eye.

Consider, for a moment, what the definition would mean for an economy that conducted very little international trade, like the United States in the 1950s. For such an economy, the ability to balance its trade is mostly a matter of getting the exchange rate right. But because trade is such a small factor in the economy, the level of the exchange rate is a minor influence on the standard of living. So in an economy with very little international trade, the growth in living standards—and thus "competitiveness" according to Tyson's definition—would be determined almost entirely by domestic factors, primarily the rate of productivity growth. That's domestic productivity growth, period—not productivity growth relative to other countries. In other words, for an economy with very little international trade, "competitiveness" would turn out to be a funny way of saying "productivity" and would have nothing to do with international competition.

But surely this changes when trade becomes more important, as indeed it has for all major economies? It certainly could change. Suppose that a country finds that although its productivity is steadily rising, it can succeed in exporting only if it repeatedly devalues its currency, selling its exports ever more cheaply on world markets.

Then its standard of living, which depends on its purchasing power over imports as well as domestically produced goods, might actually decline. In the jargon of economists, domestic growth might be outweighed by deteriorating terms of trade.[1] So "competitiveness" could turn out really to be about international competition after all.

There is no reason, however, to leave this as a pure speculation; it can easily be checked against the data. Have deteriorating terms of trade in fact been a major drag on the U.S. standard of living? Or has the rate of growth of U.S. real income continued essentially to equal the rate of domestic productivity growth, even though trade is a larger share of income than it used to be?

To answer this question, one need only look at the national income accounts data the Commerce Department publishes regularly in the *Survey of Current Business*. The standard measure of economic growth in the United States is, of course, real GNP—a measure that divides the value of goods and services produced in the United States by appropriate price indexes to come up with an estimate of real national output. The Commerce Department also, however, publishes something called "command GNP." This is similar to real GNP except that it divides U.S. exports not by the export price index, but by the price index for U.S. imports. That is, exports are valued by what Americans can buy with the money exports bring. Command GNP therefore measures the volume of goods and services the U.S. economy can "command"—the nation's purchasing power—rather than the volume it produces. And as we have just seen, "competitiveness" means something different from "productivity" if and only if purchasing power grows significantly more slowly than output.

Well, here are the numbers. Over the period 1959–73, a period of vigorous growth in U.S. living standards and few concerns about international competition, real GNP per worker-hour grew 1.85 percent annually, while command GNP per hour grew a bit faster, 1.87 percent. From 1973 to 1990, a period of stagnating living standards, command GNP growth per hour slowed to 0.65 percent. Almost all (91 percent) of that slowdown, however, was explained by a decline in domestic productivity growth: real GNP per hour grew only 0.73 percent.

---

[1]An example may be helpful here. Suppose that a country spends 20 percent of its income on imports, and that the prices of its imports are set not in domestic but in foreign currency. Then if the country is forced to devalue its currency—reduce its value in foreign currency—by 10 percent, this will raise the price of 20 percent of the country's spending basket by 10 percent, thus raising the overall price index by 2 percent. Even if domestic *output* has not changed, the country's real *income* will therefore have fallen by 2 percent. If the country must repeatedly devalue in the face of competitive pressure, growth in real income will persistently lag behind growth in real output.

    It's important to notice, however, that the size of this lag depends not only on the amount of devaluation but on the share of imports in spending. A 10 percent devaluation of the dollar against the yen does not reduce U.S. real income by 10 percent—in fact, it reduces U.S. real income by only about 0.2 percent because only about 2 percent of U.S. income is spent on goods produced in Japan.

Similar calculations for the European Community and Japan yield similar results. In each case, the growth rate of living standards essentially equals the growth rate of domestic productivity—not productivity relative to competitors, but simply domestic productivity. Even though world trade is larger than ever before, national living standards are overwhelmingly determined by domestic factors rather than by some competition for world markets.

How can this be in our interdependent world? Part of the answer is that the world is not as interdependent as you might think: countries are nothing at all like corporations. Even today, U.S. exports are only 10 percent of the value-added in the economy (which is equal to GNP). That is, the United States is still almost 90 percent an economy that produces goods and services for its own use. By contrast, even the largest corporation sells hardly any of its output to its own workers; the "exports" of General Motors—its sales to people who do not work there—are virtually all of its sales, which are more than 2.5 times the corporation's value-added.

Moreover, countries do not compete with each other the way corporations do. Coke and Pepsi are almost purely rivals: only a negligible fraction of Coca-Cola's sales go to Pepsi workers, only a negligible fraction of the goods Coca-Cola workers buy are Pepsi products. So if Pepsi is successful, it tends to be at Coke's expense. But the major industrial countries, while they sell products that compete with each other, are also each other's main export markets and each other's main suppliers of useful imports. If the European economy does well, it need not be at U.S. expense; indeed, if anything a successful European economy is likely to help the U.S. economy by providing it with larger markets and selling it goods of superior quality at lower prices.

International trade, then, is not a zero-sum game. When productivity rises in Japan, the main result is a rise in Japanese real wages; American or European wages are in principle at least as likely to rise as to fall, and in practice seem to be virtually unaffected.

It would be possible to belabor the point, but the moral is clear: while competitive problems could arise in principle, as a practical, empirical matter the major nations of the world are not to any significant degree in economic competition with each other. Of course, there is always a rivalry for status and power—countries that grow faster will see their political rank rise. So it is always interesting to *compare* countries. But asserting that Japanese growth diminishes U.S. status is very different from saying that it reduces the U.S. standard of living—and it is the latter that the rhetoric of competitiveness asserts.

One can, of course, take the position that words mean what we want them to mean, that all are free, if they wish, to use the term "competitiveness" as a poetic way of saying productivity, without actually implying that international competition has anything to do with it. But few writers on competitiveness would accept this view. They believe that the facts tell a very different story, that we live, as Lester Thurow put it in his best-selling book, *Head to Head*, in a world of "win-lose" competition between the leading economies. How is this belief possible?

CARELESS ARITHMETIC

One of the remarkable, startling features of the vast literature on competitiveness is the repeated tendency of highly intelligent authors to engage in what may perhaps most tactfully be described as "careless arithmetic." Assertions are made that sound like quantifiable pronouncements about measurable magnitudes, but the writers do not actually present any data on these magnitudes and thus fail to notice that the actual numbers contradict their assertions. Or data are presented that are supposed to support an assertion, but the writer fails to notice that his own numbers imply that what he is saying cannot be true. Over and over again one finds books and articles on competitiveness that seem to the unwary reader to be full of convincing evidence but that strike anyone familiar with the data as strangely, almost eerily inept in their handling of the numbers. Some examples can best illustrate this point. Here are three cases of careless arithmetic, each of some interest in its own right.

Trade deficits and the loss of good jobs.   In a recent article published in Japan, Lester Thurow explained to his audience the importance of reducing the Japanese trade surplus with the United States. U.S. real wages, he pointed out, had fallen six percent during the Reagan and Bush years, and the reason was that trade deficits in manufactured goods had forced workers out of high-paying manufacturing jobs into much lower-paying service jobs.

This is not an original view; it is very widely held. But Thurow was more concrete than most people, giving actual numbers for the job and wage loss. A million manufacturing jobs have been lost because of the deficit, he asserted, and manufacturing jobs pay 30 percent more than service jobs.

Both numbers are dubious. The million-job number is too high, and the 30 percent wage differential between manufacturing and services is primarily due to a difference in the length of the workweek, not a difference in the hourly wage rate. But let's grant Thurow his numbers. Do they tell the story he suggests?

The key point is that total U.S. employment is well over 100 million workers. Suppose that a million workers were forced from manufacturing into services and as a result lost the 30 percent manufacturing wage premium. Since these workers are less than 1 percent of the U.S. labor force, this would reduce the average U.S. wage rate by less than 1/100 of 30 percent—that is, by less than 0.3 percent.

This is too small to explain the 6 percent real wage decline *by a factor of 20*. Or to look at it another way, the annual wage loss from deficit-induced deindustrialization, which Thurow clearly implies is at the heart of U.S. economic difficulties, is on the basis of his own numbers roughly equal to what the U.S. spends on health care every week.

Something puzzling is going on here. How could someone as intelligent as Thurow, in writing an article that purports to offer hard quantitative evidence of the importance of international competition to the U.S. economy, fail to realize that the evidence he offers clearly shows that the channel of harm that he identifies was *not* the culprit?

High value-added sectors.   Ira Magaziner and Robert Reich, both now influential figures in the Clinton Administration, first reached a broad audience with their 1982 book, *Minding America's Business*. The book advocated a U.S. industrial policy, and in the introduction the authors offered a seemingly concrete quantitative basis for such a policy: "Our standard of living can only rise if (i) capital and labor increasingly flow to industries with high value-added per worker and (ii) we maintain a position in those industries that is superior to that of our competitors."

Economists were skeptical of this idea on principle. If targeting the right industries was simply a matter of moving into sectors with high value-added, why weren't private markets already doing the job?[2] But one might dismiss this as simply the usual boundless faith of economists in the market; didn't Magaziner and Reich back their case with a great deal of real-world evidence?

Well, *Minding America's Business* contains a lot of facts. One thing it never does, however, is actually justify the criteria set out in the introduction. The choice of industries to cover clearly implied a belief among the authors that high value-added is more or less synonymous with high technology, but nowhere in the book do any numbers compare actual value-added per worker in different industries.

Such numbers are not hard to find. Indeed, every public library in America has a copy of the *Statistical Abstract of the United States*, which each year contains a table presenting value-added and employment by industry in U.S. manufacturing. All one needs to do, then, is spend a few minutes in the library with a calculator to come up with a table that ranks U.S. industries by value-added per worker.

The table on this page shows selected entries from pages 740–744 of the 1991 *Statistical Abstract*. It turns out that the U.S. industries with really high value-added per worker are in sectors with very high ratios of capital to labor, like cigarettes and petroleum refining. (This was predictable: because capital-intensive industries must earn a normal return on large investments, they must charge prices that are a larger markup over labor costs than labor-intensive industries, which means that

---

[2]"Value-added" has a precise, standard meaning in national income accounting: the value added of a firm is the dollar value of its sales, minus the dollar value of the inputs it purchases from other firms, and as such it is easily measured. Some people who use the term, however, may be unaware of this definition and simply use "high value-added" as a synonym for "desirable."

Value Added Per Worker, 1988
(*in thousands of dollars*)

CIGARETTES	488
PETROLEUM REFINING	283
AUTOS	99
STEEL	97
AIRCRAFT	68
ELECTRONICS	64
ALL MANUFACTURING	66

they have high value-added per worker). Among large industries, value-added per worker tends to be high in traditional heavy manufacturing sectors like steel and autos. High-technology sectors like aerospace and electronics turn out to be only roughly average.

This result does not surprise conventional economists. High value-added per worker occurs in sectors that are highly capital-intensive, that is, sectors in which an additional dollar of capital buys little extra value-added. In other words, there is no free lunch.

But let's leave on one side what the table says about the way the economy works, and simply note the strangeness of the lapse by Magaziner and Reich. Surely they were not calling for an industrial policy that would funnel capital and labor into the steel and auto industries in preference to high-tech. How, then, could they write a whole book dedicated to the proposition that we should target high value-added industries without ever checking to see which industries they meant?

Labor costs. In his own presentation at the Copenhagen summit, British Prime Minister John Major showed a chart indicating that European unit labor costs have risen more rapidly than those in the United States and Japan. Thus he argued that European workers have been pricing themselves out of world markets.

But a few weeks later Sam Brittan of the *Financial Times* pointed out a strange thing about Major's calculations: the labor costs were not adjusted for exchange rates. In international competition, of course, what matters for a U.S. firm are the costs of its overseas rivals measured in dollars, not marks or yen. So international comparisons of labor costs, like the tables the Bank of England routinely publishes, always convert them into a common currency. The numbers presented by Major, however, did not make this standard adjustment. And it was a good thing for his presentation that they didn't. As Brittan pointed out, European labor costs have not risen in relative terms when the exchange rate adjustment is made.

If anything, this lapse is even odder than those of Thurow or Magaziner and Reich. How could John Major, with the sophisticated statistical resources of the U.K. Treasury behind him, present an analysis that failed to make the most standard of adjustments?

These examples of strangely careless arithmetic, chosen from among dozens of similar cases, by people who surely had both the cleverness and the resources to get it right, cry out for an explanation. The best working hypothesis is that in each case the author or speaker wanted to believe in the competitive hypothesis so much that he felt no urge to question it; if data were used at all, it was only to lend credibility to a predetermined belief, not to test it. But why are people apparently so anxious to define economic problems as issues of international competition?

THE THRILL OF COMPETITION

The competitive metaphor—the image of countries competing with each other in world markets in the same way that corporations do—derives much of its attractiveness from its seeming comprehensibility. Tell a group of businessmen that a country is like a corporation writ large, and you give them the comfort of feeling that they already understand the basics. Try to tell them about economic concepts like comparative advantage, and you are asking them to learn something new. It should not be surprising if many prefer a doctrine that offers the gain of apparent sophistication without the pain of hard thinking. The rhetoric of competitiveness has become so wide-spread, however, for three deeper reasons.

First, competitive images are exciting, and thrills sell tickets. The subtitle of Lester Thurow's huge best-seller, *Head to Head*, is "The Coming Economic Battle among Japan, Europe, and America"; the jacket proclaims that "the decisive war of the century has begun ... and America may already have decided to lose." Suppose that the subtitle had described the real situation: "The coming struggle in which each big economy will succeed or fail based on its own efforts, pretty much independently of how well the others do." Would Thurow have sold a tenth as many books?

Second, the idea that U.S. economic difficulties hinge crucially on our failures in international competition somewhat paradoxically makes those difficulties seem easier to solve. The productivity of the average American worker is determined by a complex array of factors, most of them unreachable by any likely government policy. So if you accept the reality that our "competitive" problem is really a domestic productivity problem pure and simple, you are unlikely to be optimistic about any dramatic turnaround. But if you can convince yourself that the problem is really one of failures in international competition—that imports are pushing workers out of high-wage jobs, or subsidized foreign competition is driving the United States out of the high value-added sectors—then the answers to economic malaise may seem to you to involve simple things like subsidizing high technology and being tough on Japan.

Finally, many of the world's leaders have found the competitive metaphor extremely useful as a political device. The rhetoric of competitiveness turns out to provide a good way either to justify hard choices or to avoid them. The example of Delors in Copenhagen shows the usefulness of competitive metaphors as an evasion. Delors had to say something at the EC summit; yet to say anything that addressed the real roots of European unemployment would have involved huge political risks. By turning the discussion to essentially irrelevant but plausible-sounding questions of competitiveness, he bought himself some time to come up with a better answer (which to some extent he provided in December's white paper on the European economy—a paper that still, however, retained "competitiveness" in its title).

By contrast, the well-received presentation of Bill Clinton's initial economic program in February 1993 showed the usefulness of competitive rhetoric as a motivation for tough policies. Clinton proposed a set of painful spending cuts and tax increases to reduce the Federal deficit. Why? The real reasons for cutting the deficit are disappointingly undramatic: the deficit siphons off funds that might otherwise have been productively invested, and thereby exerts a steady if small drag on U.S. economic growth. But Clinton was able instead to offer a stirring patriotic appeal, calling on the nation to act now in order to make the economy competitive in the global market—with the implication that dire economic consequences would follow if the United States does not.

Many people who know that "competitiveness" is a largely meaningless concept have been willing to indulge competitive rhetoric precisely because they believe they can harness it in the service of good policies. An overblown fear of the Soviet Union was used in the 1950s to justify the building of the interstate highway system and the expansion of math and science education. Cannot the unjustified fears about foreign competition similarly be turned to good, used to justify serious efforts to reduce the budget deficit, rebuild infrastructure, and so on?

A few years ago this was a reasonable hope. At this point, however, the obsession with competitiveness has reached the point where it has already begun dangerously to distort economic policies.

THE DANGERS OF OBSESSION

Thinking and speaking in terms of competitiveness poses three real dangers. First, it could result in the wasteful spending of government money supposedly to enhance U.S.

competitiveness. Second, it could lead to protectionism and trade wars. Finally, and most important, it could result in bad public policy on a spectrum of important issues.

During the 1950s, fear of the Soviet Union induced the U.S. government to spend money on useful things like highways and science education. It also, however, led to considerable spending on more doubtful items like bomb shelters. The most obvious if least worrisome danger of the growing obsession with competitiveness is that it might lead to a similar misallocation of resources. To take an example, recent guidelines for government research funding have stressed the importance of supporting research that can improve U.S. international competitiveness. This exerts at least some bias toward inventions that can help manufacturing firms, which generally compete on international markets, rather than service producers, which generally do not. Yet most of our employment and value-added is now in services, and lagging productivity in services rather than manufactures has been the single most important factor in the stagnation of U.S. living standards.

A much more serious risk is that the obsession with competitiveness will lead to trade conflict, perhaps even to a world trade war. Most of those who have preached the doctrine of competitiveness have not been old-fashioned protectionists. They want their countries to win the global trade game, not drop out. But what if, despite its best efforts, a country does not seem to be winning, or lacks confidence that it can? Then the competitive diagnosis inevitably suggests that to close the borders is better than to risk having foreigners take away high-wage jobs and high-value sectors. At the very least, the focus on the supposedly competitive nature of international economic relations greases the rails for those who want confrontational if not frankly protectionist policies.

We can already see this process at work, in both the United States and Europe. In the United States, it was remarkable how quickly the sophisticated interventionist arguments advanced by Laura Tyson in her published work gave way to the simple-minded claim by U.S. Trade Representative Mickey Kantor that Japan's bilateral trade surplus was costing the United States millions of jobs. And the trade rhetoric of President Clinton, who stresses the supposed creation of high-wage jobs rather than the gains from specialization, left his administration in a weak position when it tried to argue with the claims of NAFTA foes that competition from cheap Mexican labor will destroy the U.S. manufacturing base.

Perhaps the most serious risk from the obsession with competitiveness, however, is its subtle indirect effect on the quality of economic discussion and policymaking. If top government officials are strongly committed to a particular economic doctrine, their commitment inevitably sets the tone for policy-making on all issues, even those which may seem to have nothing to do with that doctrine. And if an economic doctrine is flatly, completely and demonstrably wrong, the insistence that discussion adhere to that doctrine inevitably blurs the focus and diminishes the quality of policy discussion across a broad range of issues, including some that are very far from trade policy per se. . . .

ADVISERS WITH NO CLOTHES

If the obsession with competitiveness is as misguided and damaging as this article claims, why aren't more voices saying so? The answer is, a mixture of hope and fear.

On the side of hope, many sensible people have imagined that they can appropriate the rhetoric of competitiveness on behalf of desirable economic policies. Suppose that you believe that the United States needs to raise its savings rate and improve its educational system in order to raise its productivity. Even if you know that the benefits of higher productivity have nothing to do with international competition, why not describe this as a policy to enhance competitiveness if you think that it can widen your audience? It's tempting to pander to popular prejudices on behalf of a good cause, and I have myself succumbed to that temptation.

As for fear, it takes either a very courageous or very reckless economist to say publicly that a doctrine that many, perhaps most, of the world's opinion leaders have embraced is flatly wrong. The insult is all the greater when many of those men and women think that by using the rhetoric of competitiveness they are demonstrating their sophistication about economics. This article may influence people, but it will not make many friends.

Unfortunately, those economists who have hoped to appropriate the rhetoric of competitiveness for good economic policies have instead had their own credibility appropriated on behalf of bad ideas. And somebody has to point out when the emperor's intellectual wardrobe isn't all he thinks it is.

So let's start telling the truth: competitiveness is a meaningless word when applied to national economies. And the obsession with competitiveness is both wrong and dangerous.

THE FIVE WARS
OF GLOBALIZATION

Moisés Naím

The persistence of al Qaeda underscores how hard it is for governments to stamp out stateless, decentralized networks that move freely, quickly, and stealthily across national borders to engage in terror. The intense media coverage devoted to the war on terrorism, however, obscures five other similar global wars that pit governments against agile, well-financed networks of highly dedicated individuals. These are the fights against the illegal international trade in drugs, arms, intellectual property, people, and money. Religious zeal or political goals drive terrorists, but the promise of enormous financial gain motivates those who battle governments in these five wars. Tragically, profit is no less a motivator for murder, mayhem, and global insecurity than religious fanaticism.

Moisés Naím is editor of Foreign Policy *magazine.*

In one form or another, governments have been fighting these five wars for centuries. And losing them. Indeed, thanks to the changes spurred by globalization over the last decide, their losing streak has become even more pronounced. To be sure, nation-states have benefited from the information revolution, stronger political and economic linkages, and the shrinking importance of geographic distance. Unfortunately, criminal networks have benefited even more. Never fettered by the niceties of sovereignty, they are now increasingly free of geographic constraints. Moreover, globalization has not only expanded illegal markets and boosted the size and the resources of criminal networks, it has also imposed more burdens on governments: Tighter public budgets, decentralization, privatization, deregulation, and a more open environment for international trade and investment all make the task of fighting global criminals more difficult. Governments are made up of cumbersome bureaucracies that generally cooperate with difficulty, but drug traffickers, arms dealers, alien smugglers, counterfeiters, and money launderers have refined networking to a high science, entering into complex and improbable strategic alliances that span cultures and continents.

Defeating these foes may prove impossible. But the first steps to reversing their recent dramatic gains must be to recognize the fundamental similarities among the five wars and to treat these conflicts not as law enforcement problems but as a new global trend that shapes the world as much as confrontations between nation-states did in the past. Customs officials, police officers, lawyers, and judges alone will never win these wars. Governments must recruit and deploy more spies, soldiers, diplomats, and economists who understand how to use incentives and regulations to steer markets away from bad social outcomes. But changing the skill set of government combatants alone will not end these wars. Their doctrines and institutions also need a major overhaul.

THE FIVE WARS

Pick up any newspaper anywhere in the world, any day, and you will find news about illegal migrants, drug busts, smuggled weapons, laundered money, or counterfeit goods. The global nature of these five wars was unimaginable just a decade ago. The resources—financial, human, institutional, technological—deployed by the combatants have reached unfathomable orders of magnitude. So have the numbers of victims. The tactics and tricks of both sides boggle the mind. Yet if you cut through the fog of daily headlines and orchestrated photo ops, one inescapable truth emerges: The world's governments are fighting a qualitatively new phenomenon with obsolete tools, inadequate laws, inefficient bureaucratic arrangements, and ineffective strategies. Not surprisingly, the evidence shows that governments are losing.

Drugs

The best known of the five wars is, of course, the war on drugs. In 1999, the United Nations' "Human Development Report" calculated the annual trade in illicit drugs at $400 billion, roughly the size of the Spanish economy and about 8 percent of world trade. Many countries are reporting an increase in drug use. Feeding this habit is a global supply chain that uses everything from passenger jets that can carry shipments of cocaine worth $500 million in a single trip to custom-built submarines that ply the waters between Colombia and Puerto Rico. To foil eavesdroppers, drug smugglers use "cloned" cell phones and broadband radio receivers while also relying on complex financial structures that blend legitimate and illegitimate enterprises with elaborate fronts and structures of cross-ownership.

The United States spends between $35 billion and $40 billion each year on the war on drugs; most of this money is spent on interdiction and intelligence. But the creativity and boldness of drug cartels has routinely outstripped steady increases in government resources. Responding to tighter security at the U.S.-Mexican border, drug smugglers built a tunnel to move tons of drugs and billions of dollars in cash until authorities discovered it in March 2002. Over the last decade, the success of the Bolivian and Peruvian governments in eradicating coca plantations has shifted production to Colombia. Now, the U.S-supported Plan Colombia is displacing coca production and processing labs back to other Andean countries. Despite the heroic efforts of these Andean countries and the massive financial and technical support of the United States, the total acreage of coca plantations in Peru, Colombia, and Bolivia has increased in the last decade from 206,200 hectares in 1991 to 210,939 in 2001. Between 1990 and 2000, according to economist Jeff DeSimone, the median price of a gram of cocaine in the United States fell from $152 to $112.

Even when top leaders of drug cartels are captured or killed, former rivals take their place. Authorities have acknowledged, for example, that the recent arrest of Benjamin Arellano Felix, accused of running Mexico's most ruthless drug cartel, has done little to stop the flow of drugs to the United States. As Arellano said in a recent interview from jail, "They talk about a war against the Arellano brothers. They haven't won. I'm here, and nothing has changed."

Arms Trafficking

Drugs and arms often go together. In 1999, the Peruvian military parachuted 10,000 AK-47s to the Revolutionary Armed Forces of Colombia, a guerrilla group closely allied to drug growers and traffickers. The group purchased the weapons in Jordan. Most of the roughly 80 million AK-47s in circulation today are in the wrong hands. According to the United Nations, only 18 million (or about 3 percent) of the 550 million small arms and light weapons in circulation today are used by government, military, or police forces. Illict trade accounts for almost 20 percent of the total small arms trade and generates more than $1 billion a year. Small arms helped fuel 46 of the 49 largest conflicts of the last decade and in 2001 were estimated to be responsible for 1,000 deaths a day; more than 80 percent of those victims were women and children.

Small arms are just a small part of the problem. The illegal market for munitions encompasses top-of-the-line tanks, radar systems that detect Stealth aircraft, and the makings of the deadliest weapons of mass destruction. The International Atomic Energy Agency has confirmed more than a dozen cases of smuggled nuclear-weapons-usable material, and hundreds more cases have been reported and investigated over the last decade. The actual supply of stolen nuclear-, biological-, or chemical-weapons materials and technology may still be small. But the potential demand is strong and growing from both would-be nuclear powers and terrorists. Constrained supply and increasing demand cause prices to rise and create enormous incentives for illegal activities. More than one fifth of the 120,000 workers in Russia's former "nuclear cities"—where more than half of all employees earn less than $50 a month—say they would be willing to work in the military complex of another country.

Governments have been largely ineffective in curbing either supply or demand. In recent years, two countries, Pakistan and India, joined the declared nuclear power club. A U.N. arms embargo failed to prevent the reported sale to Iraq of jet fighter engine parts from Yugoslavia and the Kolchuga anti-Stealth radar system from Ukraine. Multilateral efforts to curb the manufacture and distribution of weapons are faltering, not least because some powers are unwilling to accept curbs on their own activities. In 2001, for example, the United States blocked a legally binding global treaty to control small arms in part because it worried about restrictions on its own citizens' rights to own guns. In the absence of effective international legislation and enforcement, the laws of economics dictate the sale of more weapons at cheaper prices: In 1986, an AK-47 in Kolowa, Kenya, cost 15 cows. Today, it costs just four.

Intellectual Property

In 2001, two days after recording the voice track of a movie in Hollywood, actor Dennis Hopper was in Shanghai where a street vendor sold him an excellent pirated copy of the movie with his voice already on it. "I don't know how they got my voice into the country before I got here," he wondered. Hopper's experience is one tiny slice of an illicit trade that cost the United States an estimated $9.4 billion in 2001. The piracy rate of business software in Japan and France is 40 percent, in Greece and South Korea it is about 60 percent, and in Germany and Britain it hovers around 30 percent. Forty percent of Procter & Gamble shampoos and 60 percent of Honda motorbikes sold in China in 2001 were pirated. Up to 50 percent of medical drugs in Nigeria and Thailand are bootleg copies. This problem is not limited to consumer products: Italian makers of industrial valves worry that their $2 billion a year export market is eroded by counterfeit Chinese valves sold in world markets at prices that are 40 percent cheaper.

The drivers of this bootlegging boom are complex. Technology is obviously boosting both the demand and the supply of illegally copied products. Users of Napster, the now defunct Internet company that allowed anyone, anywhere to download and reproduce copyrighted music for free, grew from zero to 20 million in just one year. Some 500,000 film files are traded daily through file-sharing services such as Kazaa and Morpheus; and in late 2002, some 900 million music files could be downloaded for free on the Internet—that is, almost two and a half times more files than those available when Napster reached its peak in February 2001.

Global marketing and branding are also playing a part, as more people are attracted to products bearing a well-known brand like Prada or Cartier. And thanks to the rapid growth and integration into the global economy of countries, such as China, with weak central governments and ineffective laws, producing and exporting near perfect knockoffs are both less expensive and less risky. In the words of the CEO of one of the best known Swiss watchmakers: "We now compete with a product manufactured by Chinese prisoners. The business is run by the Chinese military, their families and friends, using roughly the same machines we have, which they purchased at the same industrial fairs we go to. The way we have rationalized this problem is by assuming that their customers and ours are different. The person that buys a pirated copy of one of our $5,000 watches for less than $100 is not a client we are losing. Perhaps it is a future client that some day will want to own the real thing instead of a fake. We may be wrong and we do spend money to fight the piracy of our products. But given that our efforts do not seem to protect us much, we close our eyes and hope for the better." This posture stands in contrast to that of companies that sell cheaper products such as garments, music, or videos, whose revenues are directly affected by piracy.

Governments have attempted to protect intellectual property rights through various means, most notably the World Trade Organization's Agreement on Trade-Related Aspects of Intellectual Property Rights (TRIPS). Several other organizations such as the World Intellectual Property Organization, the World Customs Union, and Interpol are also involved. Yet the large and growing volume of this trade, or a simple stroll in the streets of Manhattan or Madrid, show that governments are far from winning this fight.

Alien Smuggling

The man or woman who sells a bogus Hermes scarf or a Rolex watch in the streets of Milan is likely to be an illegal alien. Just as likely, he or she was transported across several continents by a trafficking network allied with another network that specializes in the illegal copying, manufacturing, and distributing of high-end, brand-name products.

Alien smuggling is a $7 billion a year enterprise and according to the United Nations is the fastest growing business of organized crime. Roughly 500,000 people enter the United States illegally each year—about the same number as illegally enter the European Union, and part of the approximately 150 million who live outside their countries of origin. Many of these backdoor travelers are voluntary migrants who pay smugglers up to $35,000, the top-dollar fee for passage from China to New York. Others, instead, are trafficked—that is, bought and sold internationally—as commodities. The U.S. Congressional Research Service reckons that each year between 1 million and 2 million people are trafficked across borders, the majority of whom are women and children. A woman can be "bought" in Timisoara, Romania, for between $50 and $200 and "resold" in Western Europe for 10 times that price. The United Nations Children's Fund estimates that cross-border smugglers in Central and Western Africa enslave 200,000 children a year. Traffickers initially tempt victims with job offers or, in the case of children, with offers of adoption in wealthier countries, and then keep the victims in subservience through physical violence, debt bondage, passport confiscation, and threats of arrest, deportation, or violence against their families back home.

Governments everywhere are enacting tougher immigration laws and devoting more time, money, and technology to fight the flow of illegal aliens. But the plight of the United Kingdom's government illustrates how tough that fight is. The British government throws money at the problem, plans to use the Royal Navy and Royal Air Force to intercept illegal immigrants, and imposes large fines on truck drivers who (generally unwittingly) transport stowaways. Still, 42,000 of the 50,000 refugees who have passed through the Sangatte camp (a main entry point for illegal immigration to the United Kingdom) over the last three years have made it to Britain. At current rates, it will take 43 years for Britain to clear its asylum backlog. And that country is an island. Continental nations such as Spain, Italy, or the United States face an even greater challenge as immigration pressures overwhelm their ability to control the inflow of illegal aliens.

Money Laundering

The Cayman Islands has a population of 36,000. It also has more than 2,200 mutual funds, 500 insurance companies, 60,000 businesses, and 600 banks and trust companies with almost $800 billion in assets. Not surprisingly, it figures prominently in any discussion of money laundering. So does the United States, several of whose major banks have been caught up in investigations of money laundering, tax evasion, and fraud. Few, if any, countries can claim to be free of the practice of helping individuals and companies hide funds from governments, creditors, business partners, or even family members, including the proceeds of tax evasion, gambling, and other crimes. Estimates of the volume of global money laundering range between 2 and 5 percent of the world's annual gross national product, or between $800 billion and $2 trillion.

Smuggling money, gold coins, and other valuables is an ancient trade. Yet in the last two decades, new political and economic trends coincided with technological changes to make this ancient trade easier, cheaper, and less risky. Political changes led to the deregulation of financial markets that now facilitate cross-border money transfers, and technological changes made distance less of a factor and money less "physical." Suitcases full of banknotes are still a key tool for money launderers, but computers, the Internet, and complex financial schemes that combine legal and illegal practices and institutions are more common. The sophistication of technology, the complex web of financial institutions that crisscross the globe, and the ease with which "dirty" funds can be electronically morphed into legitimate assets make the regulation of international flows of money a daunting task. In Russia, for example, it is estimated that by the mid-1990s organized crime groups had set up 700 legal and financial institutions to launder their money.

Faced with this growing tide, governments have stepped up their efforts to clamp down on rogue international banking, tax havens, and money laundering. The imminent, large-scale introduction of e-money—cards with microchips that can store large amounts of money and thus can be easily transported outside regular channels or simply exchanged among individuals—will only magnify this challenge.

WHY GOVERNMENTS CAN'T WIN

The fundamental changes that have given the five wars new intensity over the last decade are likely to persist. Technology will continue to spread widely; criminal networks will be able to exploit these technologies more quickly than governments that must cope with tight budgets, bureaucracies, media scrutiny, and electorates. International trade will continue to grow, providing more cover for the expansion of illicit trade. International migration will likewise grow, with much the same effect, offering ethnically based gangs an ever growing supply of recruits and victims. The spread of democracy may also help criminal cartels, which can manipulate weak public institutions by corrupting police officers or tempting politicians with offers of cash for their increasingly expensive election campaigns. And ironically, even the spread of international law—with its growing web of embargoes, sanctions, and conventions—will offer criminals new opportunities for providing forbidden goods to those on the wrong side of the international community.

These changes may affect each of the five wars in different ways, but these conflicts will continue to share four common characteristics:

They are not Bound by Geography

Some forms of crime have always had an international component: The Mafia was born in Sicily and exported to the United States, and smuggling has always been by definition international. But the five wars are truly global. Where is the theater or front line of the war on drugs? Is it Colombia or Miami? Myanmar (Burma) or Milan? Where are the battles against money launderers being fought? In Nauru or in London? Is China the main theater in the war against the infringement of intellectual property, or are the trenches of that war on the Internet?

They Defy Traditional Notions of Sovereignty

Al Qaeda's members have passports and nationalities—and often more than one—but they are truly stateless. Their allegiance is to their cause, not to any nation. The same is also true of the criminal networks engaged in the five wars. The same, however, is patently *not* true of government employees—police officers, customs agents, and judges—who fight them. This asymmetry is a crippling disadvantage for governments waging these wars. Highly paid, hypermotivated, and resource-rich combatants on one side of the wars (the criminal gangs) can seek refuge in and take advantage of national borders, but combatants of the other side (the governments) have fewer resources and are hampered by traditional notions of sovereignty. A former senior CIA official reported that international criminal gangs are able to move people, money, and weapons globally faster than he can move resources inside his own agency, let alone worldwide. Coordination and information sharing among government agencies in different countries has certainly improved, especially after September 11. Yet these tactics fall short of what is needed to combat agile organizations that can exploit every nook and cranny of an evolving but imperfect body of international law and multilateral treaties.

They Pit Governments Against Market Forces

In each of the five wars, one or more government bureaucracies fight to contain the disparate, uncoordinated actions of thousands of independent, stateless organizations. These groups are motivated by large profits obtained by exploiting international price differentials, an unsatisfied demand, or the cost advantages produced by theft. Hourly wages for a Chinese cook are far higher in Manhattan than in Fujian. A gram of cocaine in Kansas City is 17,000 percent more expensive than in Bogotá. Fake Italian valves are 40 percent cheaper because counterfeiters don't have to cover the costs of developing the product. A wellfunded guerrilla group will pay anything to get the weapons it needs. In each of these five wars, the incentives to successfully overcome government-imposed limits to trade are simply enormous.

They Pit Bureaucracies Against Networks

The same network that smuggles East European women to Berlin may be involved in distributing opium there. The proceeds of the latter fund the purchase of counterfeit Bulgari watches made in China and often sold on the streets of Manhattan by illegal African immigrants. Colombian drug cartels make deals with Ukrainian arms traffickers, while Wall Street brokers controlled by the U.S.-based Mafia have been known to front for Russian money launderers. These highly decentralized groups and individuals are bound by strong ties of loyalty and common purpose and organized around semiautonomous clusters or "nodes" capable of operating swiftly and flexibly. John Arquilla and David Ronfeldt, two of the best known experts on these types of organizations, observe that networks often lack central leadership, command, or headquarters, thus "no precise heart or head that can be targeted. The network as a whole (but not necessarily each node) has little to no hierarchy; there may be multiple leaders. . . . Thus the [organization's] design may sometimes appear acephalous (headless), and at other times polycephalous (Hydra-headed)." Typically, governments respond to these challenges by forming interagency task forces or creating new bureaucracies. Consider the creation of the new Department of Homeland Security in the United States, which encompasses 22 former federal agencies and their 170,000 employees and is responsible for, among other things, fighting the war on drugs.

RETHINKING THE PROBLEM

Governments may never be able to completely eradicate the kind of international trade involved in the five wars. But they can and should do better. There are at least four areas where efforts can yield better ideas on how to tackle the problems posed by these wars:

Develop More Flexible Notions of Sovereignty

Governments need to recognize that restricting the scope of multilateral action for the sake of protecting their sovereignty is often a moot point. Their sovereignty is compromised daily, not by nation-states but by state-less networks that break laws and cross borders in pursuit of trade. In May 1999, for example, the Venezuelan government denied U.S. planes authorization to fly over Venezuelan territory to monitor air routes commonly used by narcotraffickers. Venezuelan authorities placed more importance on the symbolic value of asserting sovereignty over air space than on the fact that drug traffickers' planes regularly violate Venezuelan territory. Without new forms of codifying and "managing" sovereignty, governments will continue to face a large disadvantage while fighting the five wars.

Strengthen Existing Multilateral Institutions

The global nature of these wars means no government, regardless of its economic, political, or miltary power, will make much progress acting alone. If this seems obvious, then why does Interpol, the multilateral agency in charge of fighting international crime, have a staff of 384, only 112 of whom are police officers, and an annual budget of $28 million, less than the price of some boats or planes used by drug traffickers? Similarly, Europol, Europe's Interpol equivalent, has a staff of 240 and a budget of $51 million.

One reason Interpol is poorly funded and staffed is because its 181 member governments don't trust each other. Many assume, and perhaps rightly so, that the criminal networks they are fighting have penetrated the police departments of other countries and that sharing information with such compromised officials would not be prudent. Others fear today's allies will become tomorrow's enemies. Still others face legal impediments to sharing intelligence with fellow nation-states or have intelligence services and law enforcement agencies with organizational cultures that make effective collaboration almost impossible. Progress will only be made if the world's governments unite behind stronger, more effective multilateral organizations.

Devise New Mechanisms and Institutions

These five wars stretch and even render obsolete many of the existing institutions, legal frameworks, military doctrines, weapons systems, and law enforcement techniques on which governments have relied for years. Analysts need to rethink the concept of war "fronts" defined by geography and the definition of "combatants" according to the Geneva Convention. The functions of intelligence agents, soldiers, police officers, customs agents, or immigration officers need rethinking and adaptation to the new realities. Policymakers also need to reconsider the notion that ownership is essentially a physical reality and not a "virtual" one or that only sovereign nations can issue money when thinking about ways to fight the five wars.

Move From Repression to Regulation

Beating market forces is next to impossible. In some cases, this reality may force governments to move from repressing the market to regulating it. In others, creating market incentives may be better than using bureaucracies to curb the excesses of these markets. Technology can often accomplish more than government policies can. For example, powerful encryption techniques can better protect software or CDs from being copied in Ukraine than would making the country enforce patents and copyrights and trademarks.

In all of the five wars, government agencies fight against networks motivated by the enormous profit opportunities created by other government agencies. In all cases, these profits can be traced to some form of government intervention that creates a major imbalance between demand and supply and makes prices and profit margins skyrocket. In some cases, these government interventions are often justified and it would be imprudent to eliminate them—governments can't simply walk away from the fight against trafficking in heroin, human beings, or weapons of mass destruction. But society can better deal with other segments of these kinds of illegal trade through regulation, not prohibition. Policymakers must focus on opportunities where market regulation can ameliorate problems that have defied approaches based on prohibition and armed interdiction of international trade.

Ultimately, governments, politicians, and voters need to realize that the way in which the world is conducting these five wars is doomed to fail—not for lack of effort, resources, or political will but because the collective thinking that guides government strategies in the five wars is rooted in wrong ideas, false assumptions, and obsolete institutions. Recognizing that governments have no chance of winning unless they change the ways they wage these wars is an indispensable first step in the search for solutions.

Part V

NON-STATE ACTORS IN INTERNATIONAL RELATIONS

Non-state actors come in all sizes and descriptions with widely varying goals, resources bases, constituencies, and abilities. Generally grouped into two categories—non-governmental public interest organizations and multinational for-profit corporations—non-state actors are characterized as much by what they are not as by what they are. This category can also include sub-state actors, including interest groups, insurgency and rebel groups, and religious and cultural organizations. Realists argue that non-state actors are epiphenomenal in international relations—at most the temporary manifestations of state interests working to serve state goals in foreign affairs. Lacking traditional power resources—including military and economic resources—non-state actors were often dismissed or ignored by the dominant paradigms. Constructivists attention to ideational and normative power has opened the door for a larger role for non-state actors in determining foreign policy and the structure of the international system.

Non-governmental organizations (NGOs) are typically small, nonprofit groups who work on tight budgets to achieve principled, often philanthropic, goals. NGOs generally seek to change individual and government practices, usually the prevention or reversal of a negative effect or behavior such as environmental pollution, the loss of biodiversity, or starvation and disease as the result of a civil war. International NGOs can be categorized according to their issue of interest into relief and development (humanitarian), environmental, human rights, and peace and security organizations. Some, but by no means all, NGOs have a religious orientation or affiliation, such as World Vision or the American Friends Society. Generally speaking, NGOs' activities are geared toward either advocacy, public education, immediate intervention (service provision), or direct action (their word for public demonstrations and protests). Large NGOs, such as Friends of the Earth, Greenpeace, CARE, Amnesty International, or the International Committee of the Red Cross (ICRC) might do all of these things. While small NGOs can be located anywhere (and can be found everywhere), large NGOs tend to be headquartered in capital cities or near international organizations in order to have access to policymaking.

NGOs gain strength, including membership numbers and economic power, by networking with other organizations active in similar issues with common goals. Networks allow NGOs to share information, consolidate their resources, and cooperate to exert the most leverage possible. Keck and Sikkink in "Transnational Activist Networks" examine the benefits NGOs gain from networking and the resources they have at their disposal, including information, symbolic framing, and international norms, in order to challenge the common image of NGOs as weak or powerless in international relations. NGOs are not always pure of heart and motive, however. They must consider basic organizational imperatives for survival, which might contradict their stated normative goals. As Clifford Bob suggests in "Merchants of Morality," NGOs may need to undertake campaigns that increase their visibility, memberships, donations, and political leverage but produce questionable results. Public failures by NGOs have created concerns about their accountability, claims to speak for vulnerable populations, and whether they are truly democratic organizations.

While NGOs have not always accomplished their stated goals in terms of protecting the environment, fighting poverty and social injustice, and improving human rights, NGOs have made a significant impact on certain aspects of the international system. Most notably, NGOs have increased the prominence of, and attention paid to, the protection of basic human rights norms. While many states' behaviors fall short of their rhetorical commitments, there are basic human rights norms enshrined in a number of treaties, organizations, and declarations, as explained by Howard and Donnelly in "Human Rights and World Politics." Working with strong state advocates and international organizations, NGOs have helped to publicize, disseminate, and monitor increasingly stringent human rights obligations. Starting from a relatively vague statement of human rights norms in the "Universal Declaration of Human Rights," NGOs and their state partners have increased state compliance with norms via socialization and the institutionalization of norms in domestic law. The contentious practice of universal jurisdiction, in which a foreign actor, often a leader or corporation, is brought to trial in another country for violations of foreign human rights laws, has added teeth to international norms while raising concerns about state autonomy and sovereignty, as is discussed by Kenneth Roth.

NGOs and intergovernmental organizations (IGOs) have also made notable progress on environmental issues, slowly shifting debate on global warming toward the precautionary principle and thus adding impetus to states' efforts to combat greenhouse gas emissions and climate change. While there is much yet to be done to improve and enact the Kyoto Protocol, as David Victor explains in "International Cooperation on Climate Change," there is hope that states, IGOs, and NGOs can work together to overcome the collective action problem and Underdal's "law of the least ambitious program."

Although multinational corporations (MNCs) are usually addressed under the subheading international political economy, and most of the sustained attention given to MNCs in this volume is found in Part IV, MNCs are another form of non-state actors. Like NGOs, MNCs lack formal state recognition, legal personage in international relations, and access to the use of force. Unlike NGOs, however, MNCs do have access to greater economic resources and are generally considered to be more powerful actors (particularly by those who argue that states cater to MNCs by lowering regulations to attract their investment). NGOs and MNCs come face to face in many issues in international relations, including on labor standards (human rights), environmental protection, globalization, and even arms control. To the extent that NGOs such as Human Rights Watch, Greenpeace, and IANSA have failed to have accomplished their goals regarding climate change, labor protections, and the end to small weapons sales, this may be because there are powerful NGOs backed by MNCs on the other side of the table.[1]

While non-state actors have not made major in roads into changing the fundamental organizing principle of the international system, anarchy, nor have non-state actors usurped the power and primacy of states in the current state-based international system, non-state actors have increased the attention to, and resources devoted toward, issues once considered secondary to national security, including human rights, economic development, and environmental sustainability. Some would even go so far as to argue that non-state actors, working with international organizations, have redefined security as human security and thus fundamentally changed the priorities, interest, and tools of international politics.[2] In an increasingly interdependent world that may be approaching the ideal of complex interdependence, non-state actors are likely to become more numerous, more active, and more important, even if this does not mean the end of the state, but merely a change in the current international system.

---

[1]Susan Sell and Aseem Prakash, "Using Ideas Strategically: The Contest Between Business and NGO Networks in Intellectual Property Rights," *International Studies Quarterly* 48 (2004): 143–175.

[2]Peter Stoett, *Human and Global Security* (Toronto: University of Toronto Press, 2000).

WHAT IS A TRANSNATIONAL ADVOCACY NETWORK?

Margaret Keck and Kathryn Sikkink

. . . Networks are forms of organization characterized by voluntary, reciprocal, and horizontal patterns of communication and exchange. The organizational theorist Walter Powell calls them a third mode of economic organization, distinctly different from markets and hierarchy (the firm). "Networks are 'lighter on their feet' than hierarchy" and are "particularly apt for circumstances in which there is a need for efficient, reliable information," and "for the exchange of commodities whose value is not easily measured."[1] His insights about economic networks are extraordinarily suggestive for an understanding of political networks, which also form around issues where information plays a key role, and around issues where the value of the "commodity" is not easily measured.

In spite of the differences between domestic and international realms, the network concept travels well because it stresses fluid and open relations among committed and knowledgeable actors working in specialized issue areas. We call them advocacy

---

[1] Walter W. Powell, "Neither Market nor Hierarchy: Network Forms of Organization," *Research in Organizational Behavior* 12 (1990): 295–96, 303–4.

networks because advocates plead the causes of others or defend a cause or proposition. Advocacy captures what is unique about these transnational networks: they are organized to promote causes, principled ideas, and norms, and they often involve individuals advocating policy changes that cannot be easily linked to a rationalist understanding of their "interests."

Some issue areas reproduce transnationally the webs of personal relationships that are crucial in the formation of domestic networks.[2] Advocacy networks have been particularly important in value-laden debates over human rights, the environment, women, infant health, and indigenous peoples, where large numbers of differently situated individuals have become acquainted over a considerable period and developed similar world views. When the more visionary among them have proposed strategies for political action around apparently intractable problems, this potential has been transformed into an action network.

Major actors in advocacy networks may include the following: (1) international and domestic nongovernmental research and advocacy organizations; (2) local social movements; (3) foundations; (4) the media; (5) churches, trade unions, consumer organizations, and intellectuals; (6) parts of regional and international intergovernmental organizations; and (7) parts of the executive and/or parliamentary branches of governments. Not all these will be present in each advocacy network. Initial research suggests, however, that international and domestic NGOs play a central role in all advocacy networks, usually initiating actions and pressuring more powerful actors to take positions. NGOs introduce new ideas, provide information, and lobby for policy changes.

Groups in a network share values and frequently exchange information and services. The flow of information among actors in the network reveals a dense web of connections among these groups, both formal and informal. The movement of funds and services is especially notable between foundations and NGOs, and some NGOs provide services such as training for other NGOs in the same and sometimes other advocacy networks. Personnel also circulate within and among networks, as relevant players move from one to another in a version of the "revolving door."

Relationships among networks, both within and between issue areas, are similar to what scholars of social movements have found for domestic activism.[3] Individuals and foundation funding have moved back and forth among them. Environmentalists and women's groups have looked at the history of human rights campaigns for models of effective international institution building. Refugee resettlement and indigenous

---

[2]See Doug McAdam and Dieter Rucht, "The Cross-National Diffusion of Movement Ideas," *Annals of the American Academy of Political and Social Science* 528 (July 1993): 56–74.

[3]See McCarthy and Zald, "Resource Mobilization and Social Movements"; Myra Marx Feree and Frederick D. Miller, "Mobilization and Meaning: Toward an Integration of Social Psychological and Resource Perspectives on Social Movements," *Sociological Inquiry* 55 (1985): 49–50; and David S. Meyer and Nancy Whittier, "Social Movement Spillover," *Social Problems* 41:2 (May 1994): 277–98.

people's rights are increasingly central components of international environmental activity, and vice versa; mainstream human rights organizations have joined the campaign for women's rights. Some activists consider themselves part of an "NGO community."

Besides sharing information, groups in networks create categories or frames within which to generate and organize information on which to base their campaigns. Their ability to generate information quickly and accurately, and deploy it effectively, is their most valuable currency; it is also central to their identity. Core campaign organizers must ensure that individuals and organizations with access to necessary information are incorporated into the network; different ways of framing an issue may require quite different kinds of information. Thus frame disputes can be a significant source of change within networks. . . .

Transnational advocacy networks appear most likely to emerge around those issues where (1) channels between domestic groups and their governments are blocked or hampered or where such channels are ineffective for resolving a conflict, setting into motion the "boomerang" pattern of influence characteristic of these networks; (2) activists or "political entrepreneurs" believe that networking will further their missions and campaigns, and actively promote networks; and (3) conferences and other forms of international contact create arenas for forming and strengthening networks. Where channels of participation are blocked, the international arena may be the only means that domestic activists have to gain attention to their issues. Boomerang strategies are most common in campaigns where the target is a state's domestic policies or behavior; where a campaign seeks broad procedural change involving dispersed actors, strategies are more diffuse.

The Boomerang Pattern

It is no accident that so many advocacy networks address claims about rights in their campaigns. Governments are the primary "guarantors" of rights, but also their primary violators. When a government violates or refuses to recognize rights, individuals and domestic groups often have no recourse within domestic political or judicial arenas. They may seek international connections finally to express their concerns and even to protect their lives.

When channels between the state and its domestic actors are blocked, the boomerang pattern of influence characteristic of transnational networks may occur: domestic NGOs bypass their state and directly search out international allies to try to bring pressure on their states from outside. This is most obviously the case in human rights campaigns. Similarly, indigenous rights campaigns and environmental campaigns that support the demands of local peoples for participation in development projects that would affect them frequently involve this kind of triangulation. Linkages are important for both sides: for the less powerful third world actors, networks provide access, leverage, and information (and often money) they could not expect to have on their own; for northern groups, they make credible the assertion that they are struggling with, and not only for, their southern partners. Not surprisingly, such relationships can produce considerable tensions.

On other issues where governments are inaccessible or deaf to groups whose claims may nonetheless resonate elsewhere, international contacts can amplify the demands of domestic groups, pry open space for new issues, and then echo back these demands into the domestic arena. The cases of rubber tappers trying to stop encroachment by cattle ranchers in Brazil's western Amazon and of tribal populations threatened by the damming of the Narmada River in India are good examples of this.[4]

Political Entrepreneurs

Just as oppression and injustice do not themselves produce movements or revolutions, claims around issues amenable to international action do not produce transnational networks. Activists —"people who care enough about some issue that they are prepared to incur significant costs and act to achieve their goals"—do. They create them when they believe that transnational networking will further their organizational missions—by sharing information, attaining greater visibility, gaining access to wider publics, multiplying channels of institutional access, and so forth. For example, in the campaign to stop the promotion of infant formula to poor women in developing countries, organizers settled on a boycott of Nestlé, the largest producer, as its main tactic. Because Nestlé was a transnational actor, activists believed a transnational network was necessary to bring pressure on corporations and governments. Over time, in such issue areas, participation in transnational networks has become an essential component of the collective identities of the activists involved, and networking a part of their common repertoire. The political entrepreneurs who become the core networkers for a new campaign have often gained experience in earlier ones. . . .

HOW DO TRANSNATIONAL ADVOCACY NETWORKS WORK?

Transnational advocacy networks seek influence in many of the same ways that other political groups or social movements do. Since they are not powerful in a traditional sense of the word, they must use the power of their information, ideas, and strategies

---

[4]On the former, see Margaret E. Keck, "Social Equity and Environmental Politics in Brazil: Lessons from the Rubber Tappers of Acre," *Comparative Politics* 27 (July 1995): 409–24; on the latter, see William F. Fisher, ed., *Toward Sustainable Development? Struggling over India's Narmaaa River* (Armonk, N.Y.: M. E. Sharpe, 1995).

to alter the information and value contexts within which states make policies. The bulk of what networks do might be termed persuasion or socialization, but neither process is devoid of conflict. Persuasion and socialization often involve not just reasoning with opponents, but also bringing pressure, arm-twisting, encouraging sanctions, and shaming. Audie Klotz's work on norms and apartheid discusses coercion, incentive, and legitimation effects that are often part of a socialization process.[5]

Our typology of tactics that networks use in their efforts at persuasion, socialization, and pressure includes (1) *information politics*, or the ability to quickly and credibly generate politically usable information and move it to where it will have the most impact; (2) *symbolic politics*, or the ability to call upon symbols, actions, or stories that make sense of a situation for an audience that is frequently far away;[6] (3) *leverage politics*, or the ability to call upon powerful actors to affect a situation where weaker members of a network are unlikely to have influence; and (4) *accountability politics*, or the effort to hold powerful actors to their previously stated policies or principles.

A single campaign may contain many of these elements simultaneously. For example, the human rights network disseminated information about human rights abuses in Argentina in the period 1976–83. The Mothers of the Plaza de Mayo marched in circles in the central square in Buenos Aires wearing white handkerchiefs to draw symbolic attention to the plight of their missing children. The network also tried to use both material and moral leverage against the Argentine regime, by pressuring the United States and other governments to cut off military and economic aid, and by efforts to get the UN and the Inter-American Commission on Human Rights to condemn Argentina's human rights practices. Monitoring is a variation on information politics, in which activists use information strategically to ensure accountability with public statements, existing legislation and international standards.

The construction of cognitive frames is an essential component of networks' political strategies. David Snow has called this strategic activity "frame alignment": "by rendering events or occurrences meaningful, frames function to organize experience and guide action, whether individual or collective."[7] "Frame resonance" concerns the relationship between a movement organization's interpretive work and its ability to influence broader public understandings. The latter involve both the frame's internal

---

[5]Klotz, *Norms in International Relations*, pp. 152–64.

[6]Alison Brysk uses the categories "information politics" and "symbolic politics" to discuss strategies of transnational actors, especially networks around Indian rights. See "Acting Globally: Indian Rights and International Politics in Latin America," in *Indigenous Peoples and Democracy in Latin America*, ed. Donna Lee Van Cott (New York: St. Martin's Press/Inter-American Dialogue, 1994), pp. 29–51; and "Hearts and Minds: Bringing Symbolic Politics Back In," *Polity* 27 (Summer 1995): 559–85.

[7]David A. Snow et al., "Frame Alignment Processes, Micromobilization, and Movement. Participation," *American Sociologocial Review* 51 (1986): 464.

coherence and its experiential fit with a broader political culture.[8] In recent work, Snow and his colleagues and Sidney Tarrow, in turn, have given frame resonance a historical dimension by joining it to Tarrow's notion of protest cycles.[9] Struggles over meaning and the creation of new frames of meaning occur early in a protest cycle, but over time "a given collective action frame becomes part of the political culture—which is to say, part of the reservoir of symbols from which future movement entrepreneurs can choose."[10]

Network members actively seek ways to bring issues to the public agenda by framing them in innovative ways and by seeking hospitable venues. Sometimes they create issues by framing old problems in new ways; occasionally they help transform other actors' understandings of their identities and their interests. Land use rights in the Amazon, for example, took on an entirely different character and gained quite different allies viewed in a deforestation frame than they did in either social justice or regional development frames. In the 1970s and 1980s many states decided for the first time that promotion of human rights in other countries was a legitimate foreign policy goal and an authentic expression of national interest. This decision came in part from interaction with an emerging global human rights network. We argue that this represents not the victory of morality over self-interest, but a transformed understanding of national interest, possible in part because of structured interactions between state components and networks. This changed understanding cannot be derived solely from changing global and economic conditions, although these are relevant.

Transnational networks normally involve a small number of activists from the organizations and institutions involved in a given campaign or advocacy role. The kinds of pressure and agenda politics in which advocacy networks engage rarely involve mass mobilization, except at key moments, although the peoples whose cause they espouse may engage in mass protest (for example, those ousted from their land in the Narmada dam case).[11] Boycott strategies are a partial exception. Instead of

[8]David A. Snow and Robert D. Benford, "Ideology, Frame Resonance, and Participant Mobilization," in *From Structure to Action: Comparing Social Movement Research across Cultures*, ed. Bert Klandermans, Hanspeter Kriesi, and Sidney Tarrow (Greenwich, Conn.: JAI Press, 1988), pp. 197–217.

[9]David A. Snow and Robert D. Benford, "Master Frames and Cycles of Protest," in *Frontiers in Social Movement Theory*, pp. 133–55.

[10]Tarrow, "Mentalities," p. 197.

[11]Gerhards and Rucht, "Mesomobilization," details the organizational efforts to prepare demonstrations and parallel meetings to coincide with the 1988 meeting of the World Bank and International Monetary Fund in Berlin. This was by far the largest mass action in conjunction with the multilateral development bank campaign, which began holding meetings and demonstrations parallel to the banks' annual meetings in 1986. Interestingly, the authors seem not to have been aware of the existence of a transnational campaign of which this action was a part. On Narmada, see Medha Patkar, "The Struggle for Participation and Justice: A Historical Narrative," pp. 157–78; Anil Patel, "What Do the Narmada Tribals Want?," pp. 179–200; and Lori Udall, "The International Narmada Campaign: A Case of Sustained Advocacy," pp. 201–30, in *Toward Sustainable Development?* ed. Fisher.

mass mobilization, network activists engage in what Baumgartner and Jones, borrowing from law, call "venue shopping," which relies "more on the dual strategy of the presentation of an image and the search for a more receptive political venue."[12] The recent coupling of indigenous rights and environmental issues is a good example of a strategic venue shift by indigenous activists, who found the environmental arena more receptive to their claims than human rights venues had been.

Information Politics

Information binds network members together and is essential for network effectiveness. Many information exchanges are informal—telephone calls, E-mail and fax communications, and the circulation of newsletters, pamphlets and bulletins. They provide information that would not otherwise be available, from sources that might not otherwise be heard, and they must make this information comprehensible and useful to activists and publics who may be geographically and/or socially distant.[13]

Nonstate actors gain influence by serving as alternate sources of information. Information flows in advocacy networks provide not only facts but testimony—stories told by people whose lives have been affected. Moreover, activists interpret facts and testimony, usually framing issues simply, in terms of right and wrong, because their purpose is to persuade people and stimulate them to act. How does this process of persuasion occur? An effective frame must show that a given state of affairs is neither natural nor accidental, identify the responsible party or parties, and propose credible solutions. These aims require clear, powerful messages that appeal to shared principles, which often have more impact on state policy than advice of technical experts. An important part of the political struggle over information is precisely whether an issue is defined primarily as technical—and thus subject to consideration by "qualified" experts—or as something that concerns a broader global constituency.

Even as we highlight the importance of testimony, however, we have to recognize the mediations involved. The process by which testimony is discovered and presented normally involves several layers of prior translation. Transnational actors may identify what kinds of testimony would be valuable, then ask an NGO in the area to seek out people who could tell those stories. They may filter the testimony through expatriates, through traveling scholars like ourselves, or through the media. There is frequently a huge gap between the story's original telling and the retellings—in

---

[12]Baumgartner and Jones, "Agenda Dynamics," 1050.

[13]Rosenau, *Turbulence*, p. 199, argues that "as the adequacy of information and the very nature of knowledge have emerged as central issues, what were once regarded as the petty quarrels of scholars over the adequacy of evidence and the metaphysics of proof have become prominent activities in international relations."

its sociocultural context, its instrumental meaning, and even in its language. Local people, in other words, sometimes lose control over their stories in a transnational campaign. How this process of mediation/translation occurs is a particularly interesting facet of network politics.[14]

Networks strive to uncover and investigate problems, and alert the press and policymakers. One activist described this as the "human rights methodology"—"promoting change by reporting facts."[15] To be credible, the information produced by networks must be reliable and well documented. To gain attention, the information must be timely and dramatic. Sometimes these multiple goals of information politics conflict, but both credibility and drama seem to be essential components of a strategy aimed at persuading publics and policymakers to change their minds.

The notion of "reporting facts" does not fully express the way networks strategically use information to frame issues. Networks call attention to issues, or even create issues by using language that dramatizes and draws attention to their concerns. A good example is the recent campaign against the practice of female genital mutilation. Before 1976 the widespread practice of female circumcision in many African and a few Asian and Middle Eastern countries was known outside these regions mainly among medical experts and anthropologists.[16] A controversial campaign, initiated in 1974 by a network of women's and human rights organizations, began to draw wider attention to the issues by renaming the problem. Previously the practice was referred to by technically "neutral" terms such as female circumcision, clitoridectomy, or infibulation. The campaign around female genital "mutilation" raised its salience, literally creating the issue as a matter of public international concern. By renaming the practice the network broke the linkage with male circumcision (seen as a personal medical or cultural decision), implied a linkage with the more feared procedure of castration, and reframed the issue as one of violence against women. It thus resituated the practice as a human rights violation. The campaign generated action in many countries, including France and the United Kingdom, and the UN studied the problem and made a series of recommendations for eradicating certain traditional practices.[17]

[14]We are grateful to Anna Lowenhaupt Tsing for this point.

[15]Dorothy Q. Thomas, "Holding Governments Accountable by Public Pressure," in *Ours by Right: Women's Rights as Human Rights*, ed. Joanna Kerr (London: Zed Books, 1993), p. 83. This methodology is not new. See, for example, Lumsdaine, *Moral Vision*, pp. 187–88, 211–13.

[16]Female genital mutilation is most widely practiced in Africa, where it is reported to occur in at least twenty-six countries. Between 85 and 114 million women in the world today are estimated to have experienced genital mutilation. *World Bank Development Report* 1993 *Investing in Health* (New York: Oxford University Press, 1993), p. 50.

[17]See Leonard J. Kouba and Judith Muasher, "Female Circumcision in Africa: An Overview," *African Studies Review* 28:1 (March 1985): 95–110; Alison T. Slack, "Female Circumcision: A Critical Appraisal," *Human Rights Quarterly* 10:4 (November 1988): 437–86; and Elise A. Sochart, "Agenda Setting, The Role of Groups and the Legislative Process: The Prohibition of Female Circumcision in Britain," *Parliamentary Affairs* 41:4 (October 1988): 508–26. On France, see Marlise Simons,

Uncertainty is one of the most frequently cited dimensions of environmental issues. Not only is hard information scarce (although this is changing), but any given data may be open to a variety of interpretations. The tropical forest issue is fraught with scientific uncertainty about the role of forests in climate regulation, their regenerative capacity, and the value of undiscovered or untapped biological resources. Environmentalists are unlikely to resolve these questions, and what they have done in some recent campaigns is reframe the issue, calling attention to the impact of deforestation on particular human populations. By doing so, they called for action independent of the scientific data. Human rights activists, baby food campaigners, and women's groups play similar roles, dramatizing the situations of the victims and turning the cold facts into human stories, intended to move people to action. The baby food campaign, for example, relied heavily on public health studies that proved that improper bottle feeding contributed to infant malnutrition and mortality, and that corporate sales promotion was leading to a decline in breast feeding.[18] Network activists repackaged and interpreted this information in dramatic ways designed to promote action: the British development organization War on Want published a pamphlet entitled "The Baby Killers," which the Swiss Third World Action Group translated into German and retitled "Nestlé Kills Babies." Nestlé inadvertently gave activists a prominent public forum when it sued the Third World Action Group for defamation and libel.

Nongovernmental networks have helped legitimize the use of testimonial information along with technical and statistical information. Linkage of the two is crucial, for without the individual cases activists cannot motivate people to seek changed policies. Increasingly, international campaigns by networks take this two-level approach to information. In the 1980s even Greenpeace, which initially had eschewed rigorous research in favor of splashy media events, began to pay more attention to getting the facts right. Both technical information and dramatic testimony help to make the need for action more real for ordinary citizens.

A dense web of north-south exchange, aided by computer and fax communication, means that governments can no longer monopolize information flows as they could a mere half-decade ago. These technologies have had an enormous impact on moving information to and from third world countries, where mail service has often been slow and precarious; they also give special advantages of course, to organizations that have access to them. A good example of the new informational role of networks occurred when U.S. environmentalists pressured President George Bush to raise the issue of

---

"Mutilation of Girls' Genitals: Ethnic Gulf in French Court," *New York Times*, 23 November 1993, p. 13. For UN recommendations, see the "Report of the Working Group on Traditional Practices Affecting the Health of Women and Children," UN Document E/CN.4/1986/42 at 26 (1986).

[18]See D. B. Jellife and E. F. P. Jellife, *Human Milk in the Modern World* (Oxford: Oxford University Press, 1978).

gold miners' ongoing invasions of the Yanomami indigenous reserve when Brazilian president Fernando Collor de Mello was in Washington in 1991. Collor believed that he had squelched protest over the Yanomami question by creating major media events out of the dynamiting of airstrips used by gold miners, but network members had current information faxed from Brazil, and they countered his claims with evidence that miners had rebuilt the airstrips and were still invading the Yanomami area.

The central role of information in these issues helps explain the drive to create networks. Information in these issue areas is both essential and dispersed. Nongovernmental actors depend on their access to information to help make them legitimate players. Contact with like-minded groups at home and abroad provides access to information necessary to their work, broadens their legitimacy, and helps to mobilize information around particular policy targets. Most nongovernmental organizations cannot afford to maintain staff people in a variety of countries. In exceptional cases they send staff members on investigation missions, but this is not practical for keeping informed on routine developments. Forging links with local organizations allows groups to receive and monitor information from many countries at a low cost. Local groups, in turn, depend on international contacts to get their information out and to help protect them in their work.

The media is an essential partner in network information politics. To reach a broader audience, networks strive to attract press attention. Sympathetic journalists may become part of the network, but more often network activists cultivate a reputation for credibility with the press, and package their information in a timely and dramatic way to draw press attention.[19]

Symbolic Politics

Activists frame issues by identifying and providing convincing explanations for powerful symbolic events, which in turn become catalysts for the growth of networks. Symbolic interpretation is part of the process of persuasion by which networks create awareness and expand their constituencies. Awarding the 1992 Nobel Peace Prize to Maya activist Rigoberta Menchú and the UN's designation of 1993 as the Year of Indigenous Peoples heightened public awareness of the situation of indigenous peoples in the Americas. Indigenous people's use of 1992, the 500th anniversary of the voyage of Columbus to the Americas, to raise a host of issues well illustrates the use of symbolic events to reshape understandings.[20]

---

[19]See on social movements and media, see Todd Gitlin, *The Whole World Is Watching* (Berkeley: University of California Press, 1980). For a report on recent research, see William A. Gamson and Gadi Wolfsfeld, "Movements and Media As Interacting Systems," *Annals of the American Association of Political and Social Science* 528 (July 1993): 114–25.

[20]Brysk, "Acting Globally."

The 1973 coup in Chile played this kind of catalytic role for the human rights community. Because Chile was the symbol of democracy in Latin America, the fact that such a brutal coup could happen there suggested that it could happen anywhere. For activists in the United States, the role of their government in undermining the Allende government intensified the need to take action. Often it is not one event but the juxtaposition of disparate events that makes people change their minds and act. For many people in the United States it was the juxtaposition of the coup in Chile, the war in Vietnam, Watergate, and the Civil Rights Movement that gave birth to the human rights movement. Likewise, dramatic footage of the Brazilian rainforest burning during the hot summer of 1988 in the United States may have convinced many people that global warming and tropical deforestation were serious and linked issues. The assassination of Brazilian rubber tapper leader Chico Mendes at the end of that year crystallized the belief that something was profoundly wrong in the Amazon.

Leverage Politics

Activists in advocacy networks are concerned with political effectiveness. Their definition of effectiveness often includes some policy change by "target actors" such as governments, international financial institutions like the World Bank, or private actors like transnational corporations. In order to bring about policy change, networks need to pressure and persuade more powerful actors. To gain influence the networks seek leverage (the word appears often in the discourse of advocacy organizations) over more powerful actors. By leveraging more powerful institutions, weak groups gain influence far beyond their ability to influence state practices directly. The identification of material or moral leverage is a crucial strategic step in network campaigns.

Material leverage usually links the issue to money or goods (but potentially also to votes in international organizations, prestigious offices, or other benefits). The human rights issue became negotiable because governments or financial institutions connected human rights practices to military and economic aid, or to bilateral diplomatic relations. In the United States, human rights groups got leverage by providing policy-makers with information that convinced them to cut off military and economic aid. To make the issue negotiable, NGOs first had to raise its profile or salience, using information and symbolic politics. Then more powerful members of the network had to link cooperation to something else of value: money, trade, or prestige. Similarly, in the environmentalists' multilateral development bank campaign, linkage of environmental protection with access to loans was very powerful.

Although NGO influence often depends on securing powerful allies, their credibility still depends in part on their ability to mobilize their own members and affect public opinion via the media. In democracies the potential to influence votes gives large membership organizations an advantage over nonmembership organizations in lobbying for policy change; environmental organizations, several of whose memberships number in the millions, are more likely to have this added clout than are human rights organizations.

Moral leverage involves what some commentators have called the "mobilization of shame," where the behavior of target actors is held up to the light of international scrutiny. Network activists exert moral leverage on the assumption that governments value the good opinion of others; insofar as networks can demonstrate that a state is violating international obligations or is not living up to its own claims, they hope to jeopardize its credit enough to motivate a change in policy or behavior. The degree to which states are vulnerable to this kind of pressure varies, and will be discussed further below.

Accountability Politics

Networks devote considerable energy to convincing governments and other actors to publicly change their positions on issues. This is often dismissed as inconsequential change, since talk is cheap and governments sometimes change discursive positions hoping to divert network and public attention. Network activists, however, try to make such statements into opportunities for accountability politics. Once a government has publicly committed itself to a principle—for example, in favor of human rights or democracy—networks can use those positions, and their command of information, to expose the distance between discourse and practice. This is embarrassing to many governments, which may try to save face by closing that distance.

Perhaps the best example of network accountability politics was the ability of the human rights network to use the human rights provisions of the 1975 Helsinki Accords to pressure the Soviet Union and the governments of Eastern Europe for change. The Helsinki Accords helped revive the human rights movement in the Soviet Union, spawned new organizations like the Moscow Helsinki Group and the Helsinki Watch Committee in the United States, and helped protect activists from repression.[21] The human rights network referred to Moscow's obligations under the Helsinki Final Act and juxtaposed these with examples of abuses. In an illustration of the boomerang effect, human rights activist Yuri Orlov said, "We do not have the means to reach our government. My appeal to Brezhnev probably got as far as the regional KGB office. ... The crucial question is what means are there for a Soviet citizen to approach his own government, other than indirectly through the governments of other countries."[22]

[21]Discussion of the Helsinki Accords is based on Daniel Thomas, "Norms and Change in World Politics: Human Rights, the Helsinki Accords, and the Demise of Communism, 1975–1990," Ph.D. diss., Cornell University, 1997.

[22]Walter Parchomenko, *Soviet Images of Dissidents and Nonconformists* (New York: Praeger, 1986), p. 156, as cited in Thomas, p. 219.

Domestic structures through which states and private actors can be held account-able to their pronouncements, to the law, or to contracts vary considerably from one nation to another, even among democracies. The centrality of the courts in U.S. poli-tics creates a venue for the representation of diffuse interests that is not available in most European democracies.[23] It also explains the large number of U.S. advocacy organizations that specialize in litigation. The existence of legal mechanisms does not necessarily make them feasible instruments, however; Brazil has had a diffuse inter-ests law granting standing to environmental and consumer advocacy organizations since 1985, but the sluggishness of Brazil's judiciary makes it largely ineffective.

UNDER WHAT CONDITIONS DO ADVOCACY NETWORKS HAVE INFLUENCE?

To assess the influence of advocacy networks we must look at goal achievement at several different levels. We identify the following types or stages of network influ-ence: (1) issue creation and agenda setting; (2) influence on discursive positions of states and international organizations; (3) influence on institutional procedures; (4) influence on policy change in "target actors" which may be states, international orga-nizations like the World Bank, or private actors like the Nestlé Corporation; and (5) influence on state behavior.

Networks generate attention to new issues and help set agendas when they pro-voke media attention, debates, hearings, and meetings on issues that previously had not been a matter of public debate. Because values are the essence of advocacy net-works, this stage of influence may require a modification of the "value context" in which policy debates takes place. The UN's theme years and decades, such as Inter-national Women's Decade and the Year of Indigenous Peoples, were international events promoted by networks that heightened awareness of issues.

Networks influence discursive positions when they help persuade states and international organizations to support international declarations or to change stated domestic policy positions. The role environmental networks played in shaping state positions and conference declarations at the 1992 "Earth Summit" in Rio de Janeiro is an example of this kind of impact. They may also pressure states to make more bind-ing commitments by signing conventions and codes of conduct.

The targets of network campaigns frequently respond to demands for policy change with changes in procedures (which may affect policies in the future). The multilateral

[23]On access to the courts and citizen oversight of environmental policy in the U.S. and Germany, see Susan Rose Ackerman, *Controlling Environmental Policy: The Limits of Public Law in Germany and the United States* (New Haven: Yale University Press, 1995).

bank campaign, discussed in Chapter 4, is largely responsible for a number of changes in internal bank directives mandating greater NGO and local participation in discussions of projects. It also opened access to formerly restricted information, and led to the establishment of an independent inspection panel for World Bank projects. Procedural changes can greatly increase the opportunity for advocacy organizations to develop regular contact with other key players on an issue, and they sometimes offer the opportunity to move from outside to inside pressure strategies.

A network's activities may produce changes in policies, not only of the target states, but also of other states and/or international institutions. Explicit policy shifts seem to denote success, but even here both their causes and meanings may be elusive. We can point with some confidence to network impact where human rights network pressures have achieved cutoffs of military aid to repressive regimes, or a curtailment of repressive practices. Sometimes human rights activity even affects regime stability. But we must take care to distinguish between policy change and change in behavior; official policies regarding timber extraction in Sarawak, Malaysia, for example, may say little about how timber companies behave on the ground in the absence of enforcement.

We speak of stages of impact, and not merely types of impact, because we believe that increased attention, followed by changes in discursive positions, make governments more vulnerable to the claims that networks raise. (Discursive changes can also have a powerfully divisive effect on networks themselves, splitting insiders from outsiders, reformers from radicals.[24]) A government that claims to be protecting indigenous areas or ecological reserves is potentially more vulnerable to charges that such areas are endangered than one that makes no such claim. At that point the effort is not to make governments change their position but to hold them to their word. Meaningful policy change is thus more likely when the first three types or stages of impact have occurred.

Both issue characteristics and actor characteristics are important parts of our explanation of how networks affect political outcomes and the conditions under which networks can be effective. Issue characteristics such as salience and resonance within existing national or institutional agendas can tell us something about where networks are likely to be able to insert new ideas and discourses into policy debates. Success in influencing policy also depends on the strength and density of the network and its ability to achieve leverage. Although many issue and actor characteristics are relevant here, we stress issue resonance, network density, and target vulnerability.

Issue Characteristics

Issues that involve ideas about right and wrong are amenable to advocacy networking because they arouse strong feelings, allow networks to recruit volunteers and activists,

---

[24]We thank Jonathan Fox for reminding us of this point.

and infuse meaning into these volunteer activities. However, not all principled ideas lead to network formation, and some issues can be framed more easily than others so as to resonate with policymakers and publics. In particular, problems whose causes can be assigned to the deliberate (intentional) actions of identifiable individuals are amenable to advocacy network strategies in ways that problems whose causes are irredeemably structural are not. The real creativity of advocacy networks has been in finding intentionalist frames within which to address some elements of structural problems. Though the frame of violence against women does not exhaust the structural issue of patriarchy, it may transform some of patriarchy's effects into problems amenable to solution. Reframing land use and tenure conflict as environmental issues does not exhaust the problems of poverty and inequality, but it may improve the odds against solving part of them. Network actors argue that in such reframing they are weakening the structural apparatus of patriarchy, poverty, and inequality and empowering new actors to address these problems better in the future. Whether or not they are right, with the decline almost everywhere of mass parties of the left, few alternative agendas remain on the table within which these issues can be addressed.

As we look at the issues around which transnational advocacy networks have organized most effectively, we find two issue characteristics that appear most frequently: (1) issues involving bodily harm to vulnerable individuals, especially when there is a short and clear causal chain (or story) assigning responsibility; and (2) issues involving legal equality of opportunity. The first respond to a normative logic, and the second to a juridical and institutional one.

Issues involving physical harm to vulnerable or innocent individuals appear particularly compelling. Of course, what constitutes bodily harm and who is vulnerable or innocent may be highly contested. As the early failed campaign against female circumcision shows, one person's harm is another's rite of passage. Still, campaigns against practices involving bodily harm to populations perceived as vulnerable or innocent are most likely to be effective transnationally. Torture and disappearance have been more tractable than some other human rights issues, and protesting torture of political prisoners more effective than protesting torture of common criminals or capital punishment. Environmental campaigns that have had the greatest transnational effect have stressed the connection between protecting environments and protecting the often vulnerable people who live in them.

We also argue that in order to campaign on an issue it must be converted into a "causal story" that establishes who bears responsibility or guilt.[25] But the causal chain needs to be sufficiently short and clear to make the case convincing. The responsibility of a torturer who places an electric prod to a prisoner's genitals is quite clear.

---

[25]Deborah A. Stone, "Causal Stories and the Formation of Policy Agendas," *Political Science Quarterly* 104:2 (1989): 281–300.

Assigning blame to state leaders for the actions of soldiers or prison guards involves a longer causal chain, but accords with common notions of the principle of strict chain of command in military regimes.

Activists have been able to convince people that the World Bank bears responsibility for the human and environmental impact of projects it directly funds, but have had a harder time convincingly making the International Monetary Fund (IMF) responsible for hunger or food riots in the developing world. In the latter case the causal chain is longer, more complex, and much less visible, since neither the IMF nor governments reveal the exact content of negotiations.

An example from the Nestlé Boycott helps to illustrate the point about causal chains. The boycott was successful in ending direct advertising and promotion of infant formula to mothers because activists could establish that the corporation directly influenced decisions about infant feeding, with negative effects on infant health. But the boycott failed to prevent corporations from donating infant formula supplies to hospitals. Although this was the single most successful marketing tool of the corporation, the campaign's longer and more complex story about responsibility failed here because publics believe that doctors and hospitals buffer patients from corporate influence.

The second issue around which transnational campaigns appear to be effective is increased legal equality of opportunity (as distinguished from outcome). Our discussions of slavery and woman suffrage in Chapter 2 address this issue characteristic, as does one of the most successful transnational campaigns we don't discuss—the antiapartheid campaign. What made apartheid such a clear target was the legal denial of the most basic aspects of equality of opportunity. Places where racial stratification is almost as severe as it is in South Africa, but where such stratification is not legally mandated, such as Brazil and some U.S. cities, have not generated the same concern.[26]

Actor Characteristics

However amenable particular issues may be to strong transnational and transcultural messages, there must be actors capable of transmitting those messages and targets who are vulnerable to persuasion or leverage. Networks operate best when they are dense, with many actors, strong connections among groups in the network, and reliable information flows. (Density refers both to regularity and diffusion of information exchange within networks and to coverage of key areas.) Effective networks must involve reciprocal information exchanges, and include activists from target countries as well as those able to get institutional leverage. Measuring network density

[26]See Douglas S. Massey and Nancy A. Denton, *American Apartheid: Segregation and the Making of the Underclass* (Cambridge: Harvard University Press, 1993).

is problematic; sufficient densities are likely to be campaign-specific, and not only numbers of "nodes" in the network but also their quality—access to and ability to disseminate information, credibility with targets, ability to speak to and for other social networks—are all important aspects of density as well.

Target actors must be vulnerable either to material incentives or to sanctions from outside actors, or they must be sensitive to pressure because of gaps between stated commitments and practice. Vulnerability arises both from the availability of leverage and the target's sensitivity to leverage; if either is missing, a campaign may fail. Countries that are most suceptible to network pressures are those that aspire to belong to a normative community of nations. This desire implies a view of state preferences that recognizes states' interactions as a social—and socializing—process. Thus moral leverage may be especially relevant where states are actively trying to raise their status in the international system. Brazilian governments since 1988, for example, have been very concerned about the impact of the Amazon issue on Brazil's international image. President José Sarney's invitation to hold the 1992 United Nations Conference on Environment and Development in Brazil was an attempt to improve that image. Similarly, the concern of recent Mexican administrations with Mexico's international prestige has made it more vulnerable to pressure from the human rights network. In the baby food campaign, network activists used moral leverage to convince states to vote in favor of the WHO/UNICEF codes of conduct. As a result, even the Netherlands and Switzerland, both major exporters of infant formula, voted in favor of the code. . . .

TOWARD EFFECTIVE INTERNATIONAL COOPERATION ON CLIMATE CHANGE: NUMBERS, INTERESTS AND INSTITUTIONS

DAVID G. VICTOR

. . .

In this essay I'd like to revisit Underdal's law, along with some findings from the IIASA project it helped to inspire, to suggest ways to improve international cooperation on climate change. The time for new thinking is opportune. The Kyoto Protocol

David G. Victor, "Toward Effective International Cooperation on Climate Change: Numbers, Interests and Institutions", *Global Environmental Politics*, 6:3 (August, 2006), pp. 90–103. © 2006 by the Massachusetts Institute of Technology. Reprinted by permission of The MIT Press.

is set to run through 2012, yet negotiations on the form and substance of international commitments for 2013 and beyond have just begun. Although the diplomatic community is talented at painting stiff smiles on their client instruments, the situation with Kyoto does not portend well for the planet. The world's largest emitter, the US, is not a member of the treaty. The second largest emitter, the EU, has joined Kyoto and is making some significant efforts toward compliance, but these barely alter the global trajectory of CO2 emissions. The third largest emitter, China, is a member but faces no limit on its emissions (which will soon surpass those of the EU). The fourth largest emitter, Russia, is a member only because the treaty condones inaction and offers the prospect of profit from selling surplus emission credits. The fifth largest emitter is Japan, whose interests are similar to those of the EU, but who is struggling to find ways to adjust greenhouse gas emissions. The sixth is India which, like China, has vehemently protested limits on its emissions.

According to Underdal's law, a treaty negotiated by these emitters (and a host of other countries whose interests are not dissimilar to those of the "big six") will be nearly devoid of substance. That's because the interests of these different countries diverge—some, such as China and Russia have little ambition for effective cooperation. This prediction accurately describes Kyoto's fate; the "commitments" being implemented under Kyoto are, in effect, a non-cooperative outcome.[1] Governments have promised to do what they would have done anyway. The European Union's efforts reflect that some European governments (especially in the Northern countries with active Green parties and publics who are animated by the dangers of a changing climate) are under intense pressure to address the issue even as other Europeans (notably the ten new entrants as well as most of the poorer nations in the south) are not. The developing countries and Russia are focused on development, not controlling emissions, and thus they have consented to participate in an agreement that requires no efforts whose cost is not compensated. And in a few cases (notably Australia and the US), governments misunderstood or misrepresented what they could deliver and made erroneous promises in Kyoto. Those nations realized their false promises in painful ways and have since withdrawn. The United States, under the Bush administration, has withdrawn in a particularly aggressive and unconstructive fashion.

Crafting a more effective climate change response requires returning to fundamentals, and here I briefly address three: the demand for international cooperation; the numbers of countries participating and their interests; and the design of the institutions that aim to promote cooperation. For each a wooly conventional wisdom has arisen, but a closer analysis suggests policy choices that vary considerably. And for

---

[1]Barrett 1994.

each we can look to Arild Underdal in part, to chart a path toward more effective international institutions.

1. THE DEMAND FOR COOPERATION

Every analysis of international cooperation must begin with the question: who wants to cooperate, and why? The conventional wisdom is that global cooperation arises out of the interests shared by all countries, to varying degrees to address the problem of changing climate. Failures to cooperate, therefore, are the result of some "market failure"—for example, the failure of countries to understand their interests, or the transactional difficulties associated with assembling many nations into a cooperative solution. International institutions—such as treaties, organizations, and behavioral norms—aid cooperation by reducing those transaction costs, focusing efforts on particular solutions, creating reputational risks for failure and the like.[2]

The demand for cooperative climate policy, like any matter for international collaboration, should not be conceived in general terms but through the eyes of particular societies and the governments who serve as their agents. This is the standard rationalist assumption that usually holds.[3] The following four aspects of climate damages will affect whether and how nations are likely to mobilize to address the dangers of changing climate.

One aspect of this issue is the increasing capacity of societies to "climate proof" themselves. An ever-smaller fraction of economic activity depends directly on the weather and climate; human capacity to adapt to changing weather, such as by building dikes and irrigation systems, has risen sharply in the last century and shows no sign of exhaustion.[4] The countries that have the greatest capabilities to respond to changing climate and which are also, in general, the largest emitters (at least on a percapita basis) are also those most proofed against vagaries in the climate.

A second important aspect of what is known about climate effects is that their time horizons are long. Thus the calculation of reluctant developing countries is, perhaps, entirely rational. Combating global warming would require them to incur possibly a substantial cost in controlling emissions today for quite uncertain benefits in the future. By contrast, they could invest the same resources today in development, which automatically will improve their future capacity to adapt if climate should change (while also achieving many other benefits from development). This line of logic is rooted in Wildavsky's famous dictum that "richer is safer."[5]

[2]Keohane 1984; and Young 1989.
[3]Sprinz and Vaahtoranta 1994.
[4]Ausubel 1991.
[5]Wildavsky 1988; and Schelling 1992.

A third aspect of climate science is that in fact some societies might welcome a dose of new climate—up to a point. The most famous of these is Russia (and more generally the former Soviet Union), where agriculture and forestry—which are the most climate-sensitive of economic activities—probably stand to gain from the longer growing seasons that accompany warmer weather.

The fourth aspect of climate damages is that there is one scenario for changing climate that all countries have an unequivocal interest in avoiding: abrupt (or so-called "catastrophic") climate change, such as would be caused if any of the following were to occur: the sea level were to rise a meter or more over just a few decades; the world's climate were to "flip" to a different regime; warming destabilized large amounts of methane currently locked in the permafrost (which would trigger still more warming, as methane is a strong green-house gas); or the ecological integrity of the Amazon or some other huge swath of the world's ecosystems were undermined. Even the most "climate proofed" societies will have a hard time responding to such abrupt change. Natural ecosystems, which societies tend to value even more as they become wealthier, will be particularly vulnerable to extinctions and other catastrophic consequences if the climate changes abruptly. Paleoclimatologists have uncovered evidence for incidents of abrupt climate changes in the past[6] and some models point to such dangers over the next century.[7] This is one of the few ways that risks of climate change could become evaluated in ways that are akin to traditional security threats, and nearly every society has shown that it is willing to spend something (often much) to avert even low probability threats that could have large catastrophic consequences.

These four attributes of the climate problem make it possible to venture some predictions. It seems likely that all societies will be willing to contribute at least marginally to the effort to avoid extreme dangers. However, nobody knows how to chart the thresholds, and societies are likely to vary in their tolerance of risk. For example, as with Russia, Canadian agriculture stands to benefit from a longer growing season. But some Canadians are much more concerned about the risks of unchecked climate change—such as on the country's permafrost region—and thus the country as a whole is now making some effort to control emissions. Political entrepreneurs are discovering that extreme events make for a more compelling political logic for controlling the emissions that cause climate change, and with time and learning an ever-larger amount of political activity on climate change will focus on these scenarios.

For the same reasons, efforts to build an international regime to control climate change on a shared "objective" are likely to fail because countries, in fact, do not have shared assessments of the danger and opportunity. Article 2 of the UNFCCC lays out

[6]Lourens et al. 2005.
[7]Broecker 1987; Oppenheimer 1998; and National Research Council 2003.

exactly that objective (it calls for avoiding "dangerous anthropogenic interference in the climate system"), and considerable diplomatic and scientific effort have focused on putting Article 2 into practice. Those efforts are built on an unrealistic vision of politics. In fact, there is a whole range of interests and objectives; the only area where they are likely to coincide is in avoiding obviously extreme scenarios. But those obvious extremes are so distinct in time that they have no meaningful impact on the debate today.

Underdal's pessimistic logic is particularly applicable here because the dispersion of interests partly explains the difficulty of collective action. If some key emitters are unconcerned with all but an extreme change in climate then even those who are more risk-averse will be reluctant to invest in emission controls that could be undone by others whose efforts lag.

2. THE SUPPLY OF COOPERATION: NUMBERS

A second area of misrule by conventional wisdom concerns the architecture of cooperation. Analysts and diplomats have arrived at the conclusion that climate change is best addressed through cooperative processes that are broad in membership. Part of this conventional wisdom rests on the observation that climate change is a global problem and thus requires a global solution. Part rests on the notion that cooperative regimes are best established in broad, nondiscriminatory terms and then deepened with experience.[8] Here, too, the conventional wisdom is incomplete or wrong.

All else equal, cooperative regimes with broad membership are better for global problems than are narrow systems. But the choice of a broad regime carries costs that are so severe that "all else" is never equal. These costs include, notably, the complexity of negotiating package deals among countries whose interests are highly diverse. Complexity probably rises exponentially with membership because each new member creates new nodes in a network of relationships (and thus complications). And leverage over the problem—measured by emissions—saturates quickly as numbers rise. The top six emitters (counting the EU as a single emitter) account for 64% of world emissions of CO_2 from burning fossil fuels; the top dozen are responsible for about 74%. Gaining another ten percent of emissions requires adding another 10 countries. Political scientists haven't worked out a tight, empirically grounded theory to suggest the optimal number of countries to engage. But we do have some theoretical tools that point to the minimum number of countries (or units) that must participate to make collective action rational—the so-called "k group."[9] My hunch is that it is about

[8]Schmalensee 1990; and Sand 1990.
[9]Hardin 1982; Schelling 1978; and Snidal 1985.

a dozen—the top ten emitters from burning fossil fuels, plus Brazil and Indonesia (two of the top emitters of CO2 from changes in land use). At numbers greater than a dozen negotiating complexity will overwhelm the advantages of additional leverage. If engaging fewer than a dozen members, the club will be too exclusive to gain leverage and too exclusive to allow concerns about the disadvantages to competitors. Even with a relatively small group it will be extremely difficult to negotiate a viable package deal—interests vary enormously and so do the starting points. (China's per-capita emissions, for example, are one-tenth that of the US.)

Advocates for broad membership claim that larger numbers are needed, nonetheless, to confer legitimacy on the enterprise, promote shared understanding, and set standards. The legitimacy claim is hardest to test, but the accumulated evidence in other areas of international cooperation suggests it is wrong. The World Trade Organization, notably, has emerged to be the most effective example of global cooperation by focusing, through the original General Agreement on Tariffs and Trade (GATT), on a limited number of countries whose interests (and capabilities) were sufficiently aligned to allow cooperation. Over time, experience and success have allowed deeper and wider cooperation (and also led to negotiations that extend over much longer time periods because they are more complex). Widening and deepening occurred at the same time, rather than in sequential order. The GATT round that ended in the early 1990s with the creation of the WTO has included much more than simply the tariff bindings that were the core of the first GATT agreement. Similarly, the EU emerged from a more focused cooperation (on infrastructures and key commodities such as coal and steel) among a limited number of countries. With experience and the confidence of success the EU has expanded and deepened. The recent expansion to include 10 new countries, and the agenda for talks with Turkey, may test the limits of EU expansion. . . .

3. ORGANIZING COOPERATION: THE ROLE OF INSTITUTIONS

A third area of erroneous conventional wisdom concerns the design of institutions. Here, the common assumption is that legally binding instruments, negotiated within the universal framework of the United Nations, are the best keystones for international cooperation. Much of that conventional wisdom is based on practice: every high profile global environmental problem has been the subject of a global binding treaty and thus, by assumption, treaty instruments must be best.

The evidence for this proposition is scant. . . . Nonbinding agreements are more flexible and less prone to raise concerns about noncompliance, and thus they allow governments to adopt ambitious targets and far-ranging commitments. In contrast, binding agreements are usually crafted through processes dominated by lawyers who are particularly focused on assuring compliance. A binding commitment might be useful for codifying an effort that is already in hand (or which requires actions that are easy for governments to deliver). But uncertain, strenuous efforts at cooperation are easier to organize when the commitments are not formally binding. Non-binding commitments, alone, can be as ineffective as much binding law (or even more so). However, the nonbinding instrument allows for a process through which governments commit to (and implement) more ambitious courses of action. This liberating role for nonbinding instruments usually requires high-level political engagement and special institutions that review and focus on national performance.[10] . . .

The propensity to use binding instruments despite growing evident that nonbinding agreements can play an important complementary role may help to explain the extremely large supply of shallow environmental cooperation (Downs et al. 1996). In Europe, the first targets for cutting the emissions that led to acid rain were signed in 1985 and required only a 30% cut (below 1980 levels) in SO2 emissions. Such commitments typify shallow cooperation—they didn't affect competitiveness, cost little to implement, and for most countries had little effect on behavior. Eight years were allowed for compliance; several countries had complied by the time the ink on the 1985 Sulphur Protocol was dry. Many countries made deep cuts in emissions but the most dramatic reductions were mainly achieved by countries that would have made those cuts anyway.[11] Similarly, the 1972 London Dumping Convention, which is famous for banning ocean dumping of high-level (and now also low-level) radioactive materials, was spearheaded by the United States because by the early 1970s the US had already passed national legislation to halt such dumping.[12] For the US, and scores of other countries that had no waste to dump, the treaty yielded symbolic benefits while requiring no marginal change in behavior. (The treaty also put into place a backstop against future dumping, although it remains unclear whether that is a benefit or a cost. It has forced land-based solutions to radioactive waste disposal although under the ocean floor, if not for the London Convention, might actually be an environmentally superior sequestration.) Treaty registers are littered with similar examples. No doubt that part of this phenomenon is the consequence of environmentalism as a mass movement. Especially in liberal democracies, where public opinion is both fickle and relevant to political survival, governments are constantly on the prowl for actions that have low short-term costs and high symbolic value.

[10]Victor 2000.

[11]Levy 1993.

[12]Personal communication with Gordon MacDonald, member of US Delegation to the negotiations for a London Dumping Convention.

Environmental cooperation has been focused on problems that are easy to solve—games of harmony or simple coordination. Environmental cooperation has rarely tackled problems of real collaboration, where self-interested parties defect from the solution that is best for their collective interest, unless they face strong penalties (enforcement) or inducements (compensation) to implement costly measures and sustain the collective effort. Every environmental issue has within it a universe of cooperation games—from harmony cases where interests align, to coordination games where there is a self-enforcing agreement but initial dispute over the best design, to collaboration games where each member cooperates only if it thinks others will as well, to instances of deadlock where no meaningful agreement is possible. For example, the effort to protect wetlands spans from a game of harmony (e.g., governments agree to declare their intention to protect wetlands) to coordination (e.g., governments agree to focus wetland protection efforts on wetlands along bird migration corridors) to deep collaboration (e.g., every government to specific costly measures that, collectively, ensure protection of bird migration routes) to deadlock (e.g., governments agree not to alter wetlands from their natural state and to forfeit one billion dollars in escrow if they don't comply). The global 1971 Ramsar Convention, which is the focus of international legal efforts to protect wetlands, is at the harmony end of the scale. Other regional agreements that affect wetlands, notably in Europe, are examples a bit further along the scale to coordination. Thus for the purposes of political analysis, there isn't a "wetlands" problem but rather many different wetlands problems.

The multiplicity of problem types may explain why treaty registers are filled with so many environmental treaties. As soon as an issue appears on the international agenda, almost immediately an effort is launched to negotiate an agreement. If the treaty-making process were focused on reaching agreements to *solve* the environmental problem at hand then treaty registers would be practically empty. Instead, the negotiation process is a diplomatic effort to identify the problem type that can earn agreement. Since the willingness to pay is often low when negotiations begin and failure to reach agreement yields symbolic costs, the negotiation process usually discovers a way to frame the issue at hand so that the agreement is marked by harmony or simple coordination. Most issues that arrive on the environmental agenda can quickly yield a stable, shallow agreement. My sense is that over the last three decades—from the 1972 Stockholm Conference to the present—the efficiency of this search for shallowness has increased as participants and institutions have learned how to play the game. It has become easier to agree on formats and language because models can be adopted from the scores of precedents. Extant organizations can serve new agreements. Institutionalization has facilitated further institutionalization. This process may also explain why nearly every effort at environmental cooperation now begins with a "framework convention" that is long on vision and procedure but short on commitments. No other area of international cooperation has adopted this kind of process because, perhaps, no other area of cooperation is so focused on ensuring the delivery of symbolic benefits.

It is no surprise, therefore, that many agreements result, participation in those agreements is high, and compliance is nearly perfect. That outcome is a reflection of binding design.

Binding instruments still play an important role—not so much as leaders of action but as codifiers. That, indeed, is one of the ways that binding instruments contributed to the overall effectiveness of the North Sea, Baltic Sea and European acid rain regimes. By this theory, international cooperation emerges through ambitious commitments, efforts, and experiments that are undertaken more readily when agreements are nonbinding. Through those experiments governments gain confidence in what they can deliver and then become more willing to embrace binding commitments. Applied to the case of climate change, the strictest elements of cooperation will emerge from the "bottom up," rooted in experience, rather than being imposed "top down" through commitments whose ambition is realized through binding enforcement.[13] That's what we learned from Arild Underdal's skepticism about international cooperation, although I suspect that even Arild would be surprised (perhaps alarmed) by the direction this research has taken.

4. TOWARD A NEW SYNTHESIS

On each of these three fronts—the demand for international cooperation, the numbers of essential countries, and the choice of instruments—conventional wisdom is not well rooted in the actual practice of effective international cooperation. With an eye to conventional wisdom, the advocates who care most about devising effective solutions to the climate problem have, ironically, sent policy astray into schemes and institutions that are neither sustainable nor likely to exert much leverage. . . .

In the area of international cooperation the solutions lie in efforts to create a club of a small number of important countries and craft the elements of serious cooperation. Those efforts probably can't emerge within the UNFCCC process because it is too large and inclusive. Nor can it easily arise from other available forums, such as the G8, because their membership is too skewed to include the core dozen or so countries that must be part of an effective solution. The most interesting idea for a new institution is outgoing Canadian Prime Minister Paul Martin's concept for a forum of

---

[13]Victor et al. 2005.

leaders from the twenty key countries (L20). Martin has offered a general vision; a series of meetings have applied the concept to major issues in world affairs, including climate change and energy (www.l20.org). Whether by creation of a new institution such as the L20 or reform of an existing forum such as the G8, such a standing body would offer a way to craft deals among the smaller number of countries that matters most. (Even then, 20 may be too large.) . . .

HUMANITARIAN INTERVENTION AND HUMAN RIGHTS

WHAT ARE HUMAN RIGHTS?

RHODA E. HOWARD AND JACK DONNELLY

The International Human Rights Covenants[1] note that human rights "derive from the inherent dignity of the human person." But while the struggle to assure a life of dignity is probably as old as human society itself, reliance on human rights as a mechanism to realize that dignity is a relatively recent development.

Human rights are, by definition, the rights one has simply because one is a human being. This simple and relatively uncontroversial definition, though, is more complicated than it may appear on the surface. It identifies human rights as *rights*, in the strict and strong sense of that term, and it establishes that they are held simply by virtue of being human. . . .

WHAT RIGHTS DO WE HAVE?

What is it in human nature that gives rise to human rights? There are two basic answers to this question. On the one hand, many people argue that human rights arise from

[1]The international Bill of Human Rights includes the Universal Declaration of Human Rights (1948; reprinted below as appendix 1), the International Covenant on Economic, Social and Cultural Rights (1996), the International Covenant on civil and Political Rights (1966), and the Optional Protocol to the latter Covenant.

human needs, from the naturally given requisites for physical and mental health and well-being. On the other hand, many argue that human rights reflect the minimum requirements for human dignity or *moral* personality. These latter arguments derive from essentially philosophical theories of human "nature," dignity, or moral personality.

Needs theories of human rights run into the problem of empirical confirmation; the simple fact is that there is sound scientific evidence only for a very narrow list of human needs. But if we use "needs" in a broader, in part nonscientific, sense, then the two theories overlap. We can thus say that people have human rights to those things "needed" for a life of dignity, for the full development of their moral personality. The "nature" that gives rise to human rights is thus *moral* nature.

This moral nature is, in part, a social creation. Human nature, in the relevant sense, is an amalgam consisting both of psycho-biological facts (constraints and possibilities) and of the social structures and experiences that are no less a part of the essential nature of men and women. Human beings are not isolated individuals, but rather individuals who are essentially social creatures, in part even social creations. Therefore, a theory of human rights must recognize both the essential universality of human nature and the no less essential particularity arising from cultural and socioeconomic traditions and institutions.

Human rights are, by their nature, universal; it is not coincidental that we have a *Universal* Declaration of Human Rights, for human rights are the rights of all men and women. Therefore, in its basic outlines a list of human rights must apply at least more or less "across the board." But the nature of human beings is also shaped by the particular societies in which they live. Thus the universality of human rights must be qualified in at least two important ways.

First, the forms in which universal human rights are institutionalized are subject to some legitimate cultural and political variation. For example, what counts as popular participation in government may vary, within a certain range, from society to society. Both multiparty and single-party regimes may reflect legitimate notions of political participation. Although the ruling party cannot be removed from power, in some one-party states individual representatives can be changed and electoral pressure may result in significant policy changes.

Second, and no less important, the universality (in principle) of human rights is qualified by the obvious fact that any particular list, no matter how broad its cross-cultural and international acceptance, reflects the necessarily contingent understandings of a particular era. For example, in the seventeenth and eighteenth centuries, the rights of man were indeed the rights of men, not women, and social and economic rights (other than the right to private property) were unheard of. Thus we must expect a gradual evolution of even a consensual list of human rights, as collective understandings of the essential elements of human dignity, the conditions of moral personality, evolve in response to changing ideas and material circumstances.

In other words, human rights are by their essential nature universal in form. They are, by definition, the rights held by each (and every) person simply as a human being. But any universal list of human rights is subject to a variety of justifiable implementations.

In our time, the Universal Declaration of Human Rights (1948) is a minimum list that is nearly universally accepted, although additional rights have been added (e.g., self-determination) and further new rights (e.g., the right to nondiscrimination on the grounds of sexual orientation or the right to peace) may be added in the future. We are in no position to offer a philosophical defense of the list of rights in the Universal Declaration. To do so would require an account of the source of human rights—human nature—that would certainly exceed the space available to us. Nonetheless, the Universal Declaration is nearly universally accepted by states. For practical political purposes we can treat it as authoritative. . . .

INTERNATIONAL HUMAN RIGHTS INSTITUTIONS

In the literature on international relations it has recently become fashionable to talk of "international regimes," that is, norms and decision-making procedures accepted by states in a given issue area. National human rights practices do take place within the broader context of an international human rights regime centered on the United Nations.

We have already sketched the principal norms of this regime—the list of rights in the Universal Declaration. These norms/rights are further elaborated in two major treaties, the International Covenant on Economic, Social and Cultural Rights and the International Covenant on Civil and Political Rights, which were opened for signature and ratification in 1966 and came into force in 1976. Almost all of the countries studied in this volume have ratified (become a party to) both the Covenant on Civil and Political Rights and the Covenant on Economic, Social and Cultural Rights.) Even those countries that are not parties to the Covenants often accept the principles of the Universal Declaration. In addition, there are a variety of single-issue treaties that have been formulated under UN auspices on topics such as racial discrimination, the rights of women, and torture. These later Covenants and Conventions go into much greater detail than the Universal Declaration and include a few important changes. For example, the Covenants prominently include a right to national self-determination, which is absent in the Universal Declaration, but do not include a right to private property. Nevertheless, for the most part they can be seen simply as elaborations on the Universal Declaration, which remains the central normative document in the international human rights regime.

What is the legal and political force of these norms? The Universal Declaration of Human Rights was proclaimed in 1948 by the United Nations General Assembly.

As such, it has no force of law. Resolutions of the General Assembly, even solemn declarations, are merely recommendations to states; the General Assembly has no international legislative powers. Over the years, however, the Universal Declaration has come to be something more than a mere recommendation.

There are two principal sources of international law, namely, treaty and custom. Although today we tend to think first of treaty, historically custom is at least as important. A rule or principle attains the force of customary international law when it can meet two tests. First, the principle or rule must reflect the general practice of the overwhelming majority of states. Second, what lawyers call *opinio juris*, the sense of obligation, must be taken into account. Is the customary practice seen by states as an obligation, rather than a mere convenience or courtesy? Today it is a common view of international lawyers that the Universal Declaration has attained something of the status of customary international law, so that the rights it contains are in some important sense binding on states.

Furthermore, the International Human Rights Covenants are treaties and as such do have the force of international law, but only for the parties to the treaties, that is, those states that have (voluntarily) ratified or acceded to the treaties. The same is true of the single-issue treaties that round out the regime's norms. It is perhaps possible that the norms of the Covenants are coming to acquire the force of customary international law even for states that are not parties. But in either case, the fundamental weakness of international law is underscored: virtually all international legal obligations are voluntarily accepted.

This is obviously the case for treaties; states are free to become parties or not entirely as they choose. It is no less true, though, of custom, where the tests of state practice and *opinio juris* likewise assure that international legal obligation is only voluntarily acquired. In fact, a state that explicitly rejects a practice during the process of custom formation is exempt even from customary international legal obligations. For example, Saudi Arabia's objection to the provisions on the equal rights of women during the drafting of the Universal Declaration might be held to exempt it from such a norm, even if the norm is accepted internationally as customarily binding. Such considerations are particularly important when we ask what force there is to international law and what mechanisms exist to implement and enforce the rights specified in the Universal Declaration and the Covenants.

Acceptance of an obligation by states does not carry with it acceptance of any method of international enforcement. Quite the contrary. Unless there is an explicit enforcement mechanism attached to the obligation, its enforcement rests simply on the good faith of the parties. The Universal Declaration contains no enforcement mechanisms of any sort. Even if we accept it as having the force of international law, its implementation is left entirely in the hands of individual states. The Covenants do have some implementation machinery, but the machinery's practical weakness is perhaps its most striking feature. . . .

The one other major locus of activity in the international human rights regime is the UN Commission on Human Rights. In addition to being the body that played the principal role in the formulation of the Universal Declaration, the Covenants, and most of the major single-issue human rights treaties, it has some weak implementation powers. Its public discussion of human rights situations in various countries can help to mobilize international public opinion, which is not always utterly useless in helping to reform national practice. For example, in the 1970s the Commission played a major role in publicizing the human rights conditions in Chile, Israel, and South Africa. Furthermore, it is empowered by ECOSOC resolution 1503 (1970) to investigate communications (complaints) from individuals and groups that "appear to reveal a consistent pattern of gross and reliably attested violations of human rights."

The 1503 procedure, however, is at least as thoroughly hemmed in by constraints as are the other enforcement mechanisms that we have considered. Although individuals may communicate grievances, the 1503 procedure deals only with "*situations*" of gross and systematic violations, not the particular cases of individuals. Individuals cannot even obtain an international judgment in their particular case, let alone international enforcement of the human rights obligations of their government. Furthermore, the entire procedure remains confidential until a case is concluded, although the Commission does publicly announce a "blacklist" of countries being studied. In only four cases (Equatorial Guinea, Haiti, Malawi, and Uruguay) has the Commission gone public with a 1503 case. Its most forceful conclusion was a 1980 resolution provoked by the plight of Jehovah's Witnesses in Malawi, which merely expressed the hope that all human rights were being respected in Malawi.

In addition to this global human rights regime, there are regional regimes. The 1981 African Charter of Human and Peoples' Rights, drawn up by the Organization of African Unity, provides for a Human Rights Commission, but it is not yet functioning. In Europe and the Americas there are highly developed systems involving both commissions with very strong investigatory powers and regional human rights courts with the authority to make legally binding decisions on complaints by individuals (although only eight states have accepted the jurisdiction of the Inter-American Court of Human Rights).

Even in Europe and the Americas, however, implementation and enforcement remain primarily national. In nearly thirty years the European Commission of Human Rights has considered only about 350 cases, while the European Court of Human Rights has handled only one-fifth that number. Such regional powers certainly should not be ignored or denigrated. They provide authoritative interpretations in cases of genuine disagreements and a powerful check on backsliding and occasional deviations by states. But the real force of even the European regime lies in the voluntary acceptance of human rights by the states in question, which has infinitely more to do with domestic politics than with international procedures.

In sum, at the international level there are comprehensive, authoritative human rights norms that are widely accepted as binding on all states. Implementation and enforcement of these norms, however, both in theory and in practice, are left to states. The international context of national human rights practices certainly cannot be ignored. Furthermore, international norms may have an important socializing effect on national leaders and be useful to national advocates of improved domestic human rights practices. But the real work of implementing and enforcing human rights takes place at the national level. Therefore, the case studies that make up this volume focus on individual nation-states, the central arena in which the struggle for human rights today takes place. Before the level of the nation-state is discussed, however, one final element of the international context needs to be considered, namely, human rights as an issue in national foreign policies.

HUMAN RIGHTS AND FOREIGN POLICY

Beyond the human rights related activities of states in international institutions such as those discussed in the preceding section, many states have chosen to make human rights a concern in their bilateral foreign relations. In fact, much of the surge of interest in human rights in the last decade can be traced to the catalyzing effect of President Jimmy Carter's (1977–1981) efforts to make international human rights an objective of U.S. foreign policy.

In a discussion of human rights as an issue in national foreign policy, at least three problems need to be considered. First, a nation must select a particular set of rights to pursue. Second, the legal and moral issues raised by intervention on behalf of human rights abroad need to be explored. Third, human rights concerns must be integrated into the nation's broader foreign policy, since human rights are at best only one of several foreign policy objectives.

The international normative consensus on human rights noted above largely solves the problem of the choice of a set of rights to pursue, for unless a state chooses a list very similar to that of the Universal Declaration, its efforts are almost certain to be dismissed as fatally flawed by partisan or ideological bias. Thus, for example, claims by officials of the Reagan administration that economic and social rights are not really true human rights are almost universally denounced. By the same token, the Carter administration's serious attention to economic and social rights, even if it was ultimately subordinate to a concern for civil and political rights, greatly contributed to the international perception of its policy as genuinely concerned with human rights, not just a new rhetoric for the Cold War or neo-colonialism. Such an international perception is almost a necessary condition—although by no means a sufficient condition—for an effective international human rights policy.

A state is, of course, free to pursue any objectives it wishes in its foreign policy. If it wishes its human rights policy to be taken seriously, however, the policy must at least be enunciated in terms consistent with the international consensus that has been forged around the Universal Declaration. In practice, some rights must be given particular prominence in a nation's foreign policy, given the limited material resources and international political capital of even the most powerful state, but the basic contours of policy must be set by the Universal Declaration.

After the rights to be pursued have been selected, the second problem, that of intervention on behalf of human rights, arises. When state A pursues human rights in its relations with state B, A usually will be seeking to alter the way that B treats its own citizens. This is, by definition, a matter essentially within the domestic jurisdiction of B and thus outside the legitimate jurisdiction of A. A's action, therefore, is vulnerable to the charge of intervention, a charge that carries considerable legal, moral, and political force in a world, such as ours, that is structured at the international level around sovereign nation-states.

The legal problems raised by foreign policy action on behalf of human rights abroad are probably the most troubling. Sovereignty entails the principle of nonintervention; to say that A has sovereign jurisdiction over x is essentially equivalent to saying that no one else may intervene in A with respect to x. Because sovereignty is the foundation of international law, any foreign policy action that amounts to intervention is prohibited by international law. On the face of it at least, this prohibition applies to action on behalf of human rights as much as any other activity.

It might be suggested that we can circumvent the legal proscription of intervention in the case of human rights by reference to particular treaties or even the general international normative consensus discussed above. International norms per se, however, do not authorize even international organizations, let alone individual states acting independently, to enforce those norms. Even if all states are legally bound to implement the rights enumerated in the Universal Declaration, it simply does not follow, in logic or in law, that any particular state or group of states is entitled to enforce that obligation. States are perfectly free to accept international legal obligations that have no enforcement mechanisms attached.

This does not imply, though, that for a state to comply with international law it must stand by idly in the face of human rights violations abroad. International law prohibits intervention. It does, however, leave considerable room for *action*—perhaps even interference—on behalf of human rights.

Intervention is most often defined as coercive interference (especially by the threat or use of force) in the internal affairs of another country. But there are many kinds of noncoercive "interference," which is the stuff of foreign policy. For example, barring explicit treaty commitments to the contrary, no state is under an international legal obligation to deal with any other state. Should state A choose to deny B the benefits of its friendly relations, A is perfectly free, as a matter of international law, to reduce or eliminate its relations with B. And should A decide to do so on the basis of B's human rights performance, A is legally within its rights.

Scrupulously avoiding intervention (coercive interference) thus still leaves considerable room for international action aimed at improving the human rights performance of a foreign country. Quiet diplomacy, public protests or condemnations, downgrading or breaking diplomatic relations, reducing or halting foreign aid, and selective or comprehensive restrictions of trade and other forms of interaction are all actions that fall far short of intervention. Thus in most circumstances they will be legally permissible actions on behalf of human rights abroad.

An international legal perspective on humanitarian intervention, however, does not exhaust the subject. Recently, several authors have argued, strongly and we believe convincingly, that moral considerations in at least some circumstances justify humanitarian intervention on behalf of human rights. Michael Walzer, whose book *Just and Unjust Wars* has provoked much of the recent moral discussion of humanitarian intervention, can be taken as illustrative of such arguments.

Walzer presents a strong defense of the morality of the general international principle of nonintervention, arguing that it gives force to the basic right of peoples to self-determination, which in turn rests on the rights of individuals, acting in concert as a community, to choose their own government. Walzer has been criticized for interpreting this principle in a way that is excessively favorable to states by arguing that the presumption of legitimacy (and thus against intervention) should hold in all but the most extreme circumstances. Nonetheless, even Walzer allows that intervention must be permitted "when the violation of human rights is so terrible that it makes talk of community or self-determination … seem cynical and irrelevant,"when gross, persistent, and systematic violations of human rights shock the moral conscience of mankind.

The idea underlying such arguments is that human rights are of such paramount moral importance that gross and systematic violations present a moral justification for remedial international action. If the international community as a whole cannot or will not act—and above we have shown that an effective collective international response will usually be impossible—then one or more states may be morally justified in acting ad hoc on behalf of the international community.

International law and morality thus lead to different and conflicting conclusions in at least some cases. One of the functions of international politics is to help to resolve such a conflict; political considerations will play a substantial role in determining how a state will respond in its foreign policy to the competing moral and legal demands placed on it. But the political dimensions of such decisions point to the practical dangers posed by moral arguments in favor of humanitarian intervention. . . .

Reasonable people may disagree on whether the danger of abuse outweighs the benefits of openly acknowledging and advocating a right to coercive humanitarian intervention. At the very least it should be noted that such a right is at best a very dangerous double-edged sword. Our preference would be to keep that particular sword sheathed and focus the pursuit of human rights in national foreign policy instead on actions short of military intervention. Such nonmilitary actions are legally and morally relatively unproblematic, and far less subject to catastrophic political abuse. . . .

Sometimes a country can afford to act on its human rights concerns; other times it cannot. Politics involves compromise, as a result of multiple and not always compatible goals that are pursued and the resistance of a world that more often than not is unsupportive of the particular objectives being sought. Human rights, like other goals of foreign policy, must at times be compromised. In some instances there is little that a country can afford to do even in the face of major human rights violations. For example, because of other interests in the relationship between the United States and the USSR, such as arms control and the avoidance of war, not much can be done about Soviet human rights violations—either in a period of détente or one of cold war. . . .

Standards will be undeniably difficult to formulate, and their application will raise no less severe problems. Hard cases and exceptions are unavoidable. So are gray areas and fuzzy boundaries. Unless such efforts are seriously undertaken, however, the resulting policy is likely to appear baseless or inconsistent, and probably will be so in fact as well. . . .

Culture and Human Rights

This view of the creation of the individual, with individual needs for human rights, is criticized by many advocates of the "cultural relativist" school of human rights. They present the argument that human rights are a "Western construct with limited [universal] applicability." But cultural relativism, as applied to human rights, fails to grasp the nature of culture. A number of erroneous assumptions underlie this viewpoint.

Criticism of the universality of human rights often stems from erroneous perceptions of the persistence of traditional societies, societies in which principles of social justice are based not on rights but on status and on the intermixture of privilege and responsibility. Often anthropologically anachronistic pictures are presented of premodern societies, taking no account whatsoever of the social changes we have described above. It is assumed that culture is a static entity. But culture—like the individual—is adaptive. One can accept the principle that customs, values, and norms do indeed glue society together, and that they will endure, without assuming cultural stasis. Even though elements of culture have a strong hold on people's individual psyches, cultures can and do change. Individuals are actors who can influence their own fate, even if their range of choice is circumscribed by the prevalent social structure, culture, or ideology.

Cultural relativist arguments also often assume that culture is a unitary and unique whole; that is, that one is born into, and will always be, a part of a distinctive, comprehensive, and integrated set of cultural values and institutions that cannot be changed incrementally or only in part. Since in each culture the social norms and roles vary, so, it is argued, human rights must vary. The norms of each society are held to be both valuable in and of their own right, and so firmly rooted as to be impervious to challenge. Therefore, such arguments run, the universal standards embodied in the main UN instruments are applicable only to certain Western societies; to impose them on other societies from which they did not originally arise would do serious and irreparable damage to those cultures. In fact, though, people are quite adept cultural accommodationists; they are able to choose which aspects of a "new" culture they wish to adopt and which aspects of the "old" they wish to retain. For example, the marabouts (priests), who lead Senegal's traditional Muslim brotherhoods, have become leading political figures and have acquired considerable wealth and power through the peanut trade.

Still another assumption of the cultural relativism school is that culture is unaffected by social structure. But structure does affect culture. To a significant extent cultures and values reflect the basic economic and political organization of a society. For example, a society such as Tokugawa Japan, that moves from a feudal structure to an organized bureaucratic state is bound to experience changes in values. Or the amalgamation of many different ethnic groups into one nation-state inevitably changes the way that individuals view themselves: for example, state-sponsored retention of ethnic customs, as under Canada's multicultural policy of preserving ethnic communities, cannot mask the fact that most of those communities are merging into the larger Canadian society.

A final assumption of the cultural relativist view of human rights is that cultural practices are neutral in their impact on different individuals and groups. Yet very few social practices, whether cultural or otherwise, distribute the same benefits to each member of a group. In considering any cultural practice it is useful to ask, who benefits from its retention? Those who speak for the group are usually those most capable of articulating the group's values to the outside world. But such spokesmen are likely to stress, in their articulation of "group", values, those particular values that are most to their own advantage. Both those who choose to adopt "new" ideals, such as political democracy or atheism, and those who choose to retain "old" ideals, such as a God-fearing political consensus, may be doing so in their own interests. Culture is both influenced by, and an instrument of, conflict among individuals or social groups. Just as those who attempt to modify or change customs may have personal interests in so doing, so also do those who attempt to preserve them. Quite often, relativist arguments are adopted principally to protect the interests of those in power.

Thus the notion that human rights cannot be applied across cultures violates both the principle of human rights and its practice. Human rights mean precisely that: rights held by virtue of being human. Human rights do not mean human dignity, nor do they represent the sum total of personal resources (material, moral, or spiritual) that an individual might hold. Cultural variances that do not violate basic human rights undoubtedly enrich the world. But to permit the interests of the powerful to masquerade behind spurious defenses of cultural relativity is merely to lessen the chance that the victims of their policies will be able to complain. In the modern world, concepts such as cultural relativity which deny to individuals the moral right to make comparisons and to insist on universal standards of right and wrong, are happily adopted by those who control the state. . . .

THIRD WORLD CRITICISMS

In recent years a number of commentators from the Third World have criticized the concept of universal human rights. Frequently, the intention of the criticisms appears to be to exempt some Third World governments from the standard of judgment generated by the concept of universal human rights. Much of the criticism in fact serves to cover abuses of human rights by state corporatist, developmental dictatorship, or allegedly "socialist" regimes.

A common criticism of the concept of universal human rights is that since it is Western in origin, it must be limited in its applicability to the Western world. Both logically and empirically, this criticism is invalid. Knowledge is not limited in its applicability to its place or people of origin—one does not assume, for example, that medicines discovered in the developed Western world will cure only people of European origin. Nor is it reasonable to state that knowledge or thought of a certain kind—about social arrangements instead of about human biology or natural science—is limited to its place of origin. Those same Third World critics who reject universal concepts of human rights often happily accept Marxist socialism, which also originated in the Western world, in the mind of a German Jew.

The fact that human rights is originally a liberal notion, rooted in the rise of a class of bourgeois citizens in Europe who demanded individual rights against the power of kings and nobility, does not make human rights inapplicable to the rest of the world. As we argue above, all over the world there are now formal states, whose citizens are increasingly individualized. All over the world, therefore, there are people who need protections against the depradations of class-ruled governments.

Moreover, whatever the liberal origins of human rights, the list now accepted as universal includes a wide range of economic and social rights that were first advocated by socialist and social-democratic critics of liberalism. Although eighteenth-century liberals stressed the right to private property, the 1966 International Human Rights Covenants do not mention it, substituting instead the right to sovereignty over national resources. Indeed, much liberal thinking also now restricts property rights; for example, Henry Shue argues that property rights must always be subsidiary to subsistence rights. To attribute the idea of universal human rights to an outdated liberalism, unaffected by later notions of welfare democracy and uninfluenced by socialist concerns with economic rights, is simply incorrect.

The absence of a right to private property in the Covenants indicates a sensitivity to the legitimate preoccupations of socialist and postcolonial Third World governments. Conservative critics of recent trends in international human rights in fact deplore the right to national sovereignty over resources, as some of them also deplore any attention to the economic rights of the individual. We certainly do not share this view of rights; we believe that the economic rights of the individual are as important as civil and political rights. But it is the individual we are concerned with. We would like to see a world in which every *individual* has enough to eat, not merely a world in which every *state* has the right to economic sovereignty.

We are skeptical, therefore, of the radical Third Worldist assertion that "group" rights ought to be more important than individual rights. Too often, the "group" in question proves to be the state. Why allocate rights to a social institution that is already the chief violator of individuals' rights? Similarly, we fear the expression "peoples' rights." The communal rights of individuals to practice their own religion, speak their own language, and indulge in their own ancestral customs are protected in the Covenant on Civil and Political Rights. Individuals are free to come together in groups to engage in those cultural practices which are meaningful to them. On the other hand, often a "group" right can simply mean that the individual is subordinate to the group—for example, that the individual Christian fundamentalist in the Soviet Union risks arrest because of the desire of the larger "group" to enforce official atheism.

The one compelling use that we can envisage for the term "group rights" is in protection of native peoples, usually hunter-gatherers, pastoralists, or subsistence agriculturalists, whose property rights as collectivities are being violated by the larger state societies that encroach upon them. Such groups are fighting a battle against the forces of modernization and the state's accumulative tendencies. For example, native peoples in Canada began in the 1970s to object to state development projects, such as the James Bay Hydroelectric project in Quebec, which deprived them of their traditional lands. At the moment, there is no international human rights protection for such groups or their "way of life."

One way to protect such group rights would be to incorporate the group as a legal entity in order to preserve their land claims. However, even if the law protects such group rights, individual members of the group may prefer to move into the larger society in response to the processes of modernization discussed above. Both options must be protected.

If the purpose of group rights is to protect large, established groups of people who share the same territory, customs, language, religion, and ancestry, then such protection could only occur at the expense of states' rights. These groups, under international human rights law, do not have the right to withdraw from the states that enfold them. Moreover, it is clearly not the intention of Third World defenders of group rights to allow such a right to secession. A first principle of the Organization of African Unity, for example, is to preserve the sovereignty of all its member states not only against outside attack but also against internal attempts at secession. Group rights appear to mean, in practice, states' rights. But the rights of states are the rights of the individuals and classes who control the state.

Many Third World and socialist regimes also argue that rights ought to be tied to duties. A citizen's rights, it is argued, ought to be contingent upon his duties toward the society at large—privilege is contingent on responsibility. Such a view of rights made sense in nonstate societies in which each "person" fulfilled his roles along with others, all of the roles together creating a close-knit, tradition-bound group. But in modern state societies, to tie rights to duties is to risk the former's complete disappearance. All duties will be aimed toward the preservation of the state and of the interests of those who control it.

It is true that no human rights are absolute; even in societies that adhere in principle to the liberal ethos, individuals are frequently deprived of rights, especially in wartime or if they are convicted of criminal acts. However, such deprivations can legitimately be made only after the most scrupulous protection of civil and political rights under the rule of law. The difficulty with tying rights to duties without the intermediate step of scrutiny by a genuinely independent judiciary is the likelihood of wholesale cancellation of rights by the ruling class. But if one has rights merely because one is human, and for no other reason, then it is much more difficult, in principle, for the state to cancel them. It cannot legitimate the denial of rights by saying that only certain types of human beings, exhibiting certain kinds of behavior, are entitled to them.

One final criticism of the view of universal human rights embedded in the International Covenants is that an undue stress is laid on civil and political rights, whereas the overriding rights priority in the Third World is economic rights. In this view, the state as the agent of economic development—and hence, presumably, of eventual distribution of economic goods or "rights" to the masses—should not be bothered with problems of guaranteeing political participation in decision making, or of protecting people's basic civil rights. These rights, it is argued, come "after" development is completed. The empirical basis for this argument is weak, as for example

Rhoda Rabkin indicates in her chapter on Cuba. A number of other studies indicate that both in what is now the developed Western world and in the Third World civil and political rights are essential to obtaining economic rights from the state. Economic development per se will not guarantee future human rights, whether of an economic or any other kind. Often, development means economic growth, but without equitable distributive measures. Moreover, development strategies often fail because of insufficient attention to citizens' needs and views. Finally, development plans are often a cover for the continued violations of citizens' rights by the ruling class.

Thus we return to where we started: the rights of all men and women against all governments to treatment as free, equal, materially and physically secure persons. This is what human dignity means and requires in our era. And the individual human rights of the Universal Declaration and the Covenants are the means by which individuals today carry out the struggle to achieve their dignity.

UNIVERSAL DECLARATION
OF HUMAN RIGHTS

PREAMBLE

Whereas recognition of the inherent dignity and of the equal and inalienable rights of all members of the human family is the foundation of freedom, justice and peace in the world,

Whereas disregard and contempt for human rights have resulted in barbarous acts which have outraged the conscience of mankind, and the advent of a world in which human beings shall enjoy freedom of speech and belief and freedom from fear and want has been proclaimed as the highest aspiration of the common people,

Whereas it is essential, if man is not to be compelled to have recourse, as a last resort, to rebellion against tyranny and oppression, that human rights should be protected by the rule of law,

Whereas it is essential to promote the development of friendly relations between nations,

---

Universal Declaration of Human Rights, adopted and proclaimed by General Assembly resolution 217 A (III) of 10 December 1948. Reprinted by permission of United Nations.

Whereas the peoples of the United Nations have in the Charter reaffirmed their faith in fundamental human rights, in the dignity and worth of the human person and in the equal rights of men and women and have determined to promote social progress and better standards of life in larger freedom,

Whereas Member States have pledged themselves to achieve, in cooperation with the United Nations, the promotion of universal respect for and observance of human rights and fundamental freedoms,

Whereas a common understanding of these rights and freedoms is of the greatest importance for the full realization of this pledge,

Now, therefore,

The General Assembly

Proclaims this Universal Declaration of Human Rights as a common standard of achievement for all peoples and all nations, to the end that every individual and every organ of society, keeping this Declaration constantly in mind, shall strive by teaching and education to promote respect for these rights and freedoms and by progressive measures, national and international, to secure their universal and effective recognition and observance, both among the peoples of Member States themselves and among the peoples of territories under their jurisdiction.

ARTICLE 1

All human beings are born free and equal in dignity and rights. They are endowed with reason and conscience and should act towards one another in a spirit of brotherhood.

ARTICLE 2

Everyone is entitled to all the rights and freedoms set forth in this Declaration, without distinction of any kind, such as race, colour, sex, language, religion, political or other opinion, national or social origin, property, birth or other status. Furthermore, no distinction shall be made on the basis of the political, jurisdictional or international status of the country or territory to which a person belongs, whether it be independent, trust, non-self-governing or under any other limitation of sovereignty.

ARTICLE 3

Everyone has the right to life, liberty and security of person.

ARTICLE 4

No one shall be held in slavery or servitude; slavery and the slave trade shall be prohibited in all their forms.

ARTICLE 5

No one shall be subjected to torture or to cruel, in human or degrading treatment or punishment.

ARTICLE 6

Everyone has the right to recognition everywhere as a person before the law.

ARTICLE 7

All are equal before the law and are entitled without any discrimination to equal protection of the law. All are entitled to equal protection against any discrimination in violation of this Declaration and against any incitement to such discrimination.

ARTICLE 8

Everyone has the right to an effective remedy by the competent national tribunals for acts violating the fundamental rights granted him by the constitution or by law.

ARTICLE 9

No one shall be subjected to arbitrary arrest, detention or exile.

ARTICLE 10

Everyone is entitled in full equality to a fair and public hearing by an independent and impartial tribunal, in the determination of his rights and obligations and of any criminal charge against him.

ARTICLE 11

(1) Everyone charged with a penal offence has the right to be presumed innocent until proved guilty according to law in a public trial at which he has had all the guarantees necessary for his defence.
(2) No one shall be held guilty of any penal offence on account of any act or omission which did not constitute a penal offence, under national or international law, at the time when it was committed. Nor shall a heavier penalty be imposed than the one that was applicable at the time the penal offence was committed.

ARTICLE 12

No one shall be subjected to arbitrary interference with his privacy, family, home or correspondence, nor to attacks upon his honour and reputation. Everyone has the right to the protection of the law against such interference or attacks.

ARTICLE 13

(1) Everyone has the right to freedom of movement and residence within the borders of each State.

(2) Everyone has the right to leave any country, including his own, and to return to his country.

ARTICLE 14

(1) Everyone has the right to seek and to enjoy in other countries asylum from persecution.

(2) This right may not be invoked in the case of prosecutions genuinely arising from non-political crimes or from acts contrary to the purposes and principles of the United Nations.

ARTICLE 15

(1) Everyone has the right to a nationality.

(2) No one shall be arbitrarily deprived of his nationality nor denied the right to change his nationality.

ARTICLE 16

(1) Men and women of full age, without any limitation due to race, nationality or religion, have the right to marry and to found a family. They are entitled to equal rights as to marriage, during marriage and at its dissolution.

(2) Marriage shall be entered into only with the free and full consent of the intending spouses.

(3) The family is the natural and fundamental group unit of society and is entitled to protection by society and the State.

ARTICLE 17

(1) Everyone has the right to own property alone as well as in association with others.

(2) No one shall be arbitrarily deprived of his property.

ARTICLE 18

Everyone has the right to freedom of thought, conscience and religion; this right includes freedom to change his religion or belief, and freedom, either alone or in community with others and in public or private, to manifest his religion or belief in teaching, practice, worship and observance.

ARTICLE 19

Everyone has the right to freedom of opinion and expression; this right includes freedom to hold opinions without interference and to seek, receive and impart information and ideas through any media and regardless of frontiers.

ARTICLE 20

(1) Everyone has the right to freedom of peaceful assembly and association.
(2) No one may be compelled to belong to an association.

ARTICLE 21

(1) Everyone has the right to take part in the government of his country, directly or through freely chosen representatives.
(2) Everyone has the right to equal access to public service in his country.
(3) The will of the people shall be the basis of the authority of government; this will shall be expressed in periodic and genuine elections which shall be by universal and equal suffrage and shall be held by secret vote or by equivalent free voting procedures.

ARTICLE 22

Everyone, as a member of society, has the right to social security and is entitled to realization, through national effort and international cooperation and in accordance with the organization and resources of each State, of the economic, social and cultural rights indispensable for his dignity and the free development of his personality.

ARTICLE 23

(1) Everyone has the right to work, to free choice of employment, to just and favourable conditions of work and to protection against unemployment.
(2) Everyone, without any discrimination, has the right to equal pay for equal work.
(3) Everyone who works has the right to just and favourable remuneration ensuring for himself and his family an existence worthy of human dignity, and supplemented, if necessary, by other means of social protection.
(4) Everyone has the right to form and to join trade unions for the protection of his interests.

ARTICLE 24

Everyone has the right to rest and leisure, including reasonable limitation of working hours and periodic holidays with pay.

ARTICLE 25

(1) Everyone has the right to a standard of living adequate for the health and well-being of himself and of his family, including food, clothing, housing and medical care and necessary social services, and the right to security in the event of unemployment, sickness, disability, widowhood, old age or other lack of livelihood in circumstances beyond his control.

(2) Motherhood and childhood are entitled to special care and assistance. All children, whether born in or out of wedlock, shall enjoy the same social protection.

ARTICLE 26

(1) Everyone has the right to education. Education shall be free, at least in the elementary and fundamental stages. Elementary education shall be compulsory. Technical and professional education shall be made generally available and higher education shall be equally accessible to all on the basis of merit.

(2) Education shall be directed to the full development of the human personality and to the strengthening of respect for human rights and fundamental freedoms. It shall promote understanding, tolerance and friendship among all nations, racial or religious groups, and shall further the activities of the United Nations for the maintenance of peace.

(3) Parents have a prior right to choose the kind of education that shall be given to their children.

ARTICLE 27

(1) Everyone has the right freely to participate in the cultural life of the community, to enjoy the arts and to share in scientific advancement and its benefits.

(2) Everyone has the right to the protection of the moral and material interests resulting from any scientific, literary or artistic production of which he is the author.

ARTICLE 28

Everyone is entitled to a social and international order in which the rights and freedoms set forth in this Declaration can be fully realized.

ARTICLE 29

(1) Everyone has duties to the community in which alone the free and full development of his personality is possible.

(2) In the exercise of his rights and freedoms, everyone shall be subject only to such limitations as are determined by law solely for the purpose of securing due recognition and respect for the rights and freedoms of others and of meeting the just

requirements of morality, public order and the general welfare in a democratic society.

(3) These rights and freedoms may in no case be exercised contrary to the purposes and principles of the United Nations.

ARTICLE 30

Nothing in this Declaration may be interpreted as implying for any State, group or person any right to engage in any activity or to perform any act aimed at the destruction of any of the rights and freedoms set forth herein.

MERCHANTS OF MORALITY

CLIFFORD BOB

For decades, Tibet's quest for self-determination has roused people around the world. Inspired by appeals to human rights, cultural preservation, and spiritual awakening, tens of thousands of individuals and organizations lend moral, material, and financial support to the Tibetan cause. As a result, greater autonomy for Tibet's 5.2 million inhabitants remains a popular international campaign despite the Chinese government's 50-year effort to suppress it.

However, while Tibet's light shines brightly abroad, few outsiders know that China's borders hold other restive minorities: Mongols, Zhuang, Yi, and Hui, to name only a few. Notable are the Uighurs, a group of more than 7 million located northwest of Tibet. Like the Tibetans, the Uighurs have fought Chinese domination for centuries. Like the Tibetans, the Uighurs face threats from Han Chinese in-migration, communist development policies, and newly strengthened antiterror measures. And like the Tibetans, the Uighurs resist Chinese domination with domestic and international protest that, in Beijing's eyes, makes them dangerous separatists. Yet the Uighurs have failed to inspire the broad-based foreign networks that generously support and bankroll the Tibetans. International celebrities—including actors Richard Gere and

Goldie Hawn, as well as British rock star Annie Lennox—speak out on Tibet's behalf. But no one is planning an Uighur Freedom Concert in Washington, D.C. Why?

Optimistic observers posit a global meritocracy of suffering in which all deserving causes attract international support. Howard H. Frederick, founder of the online activist network Peacenet, has argued that new communications technologies help create global movements in which individuals "rise above personal, even national self-interest and aspire to common good solutions to problems that plague the entire planet." And Allen L. Hammond of the World Resources Institute recently wrote that the combination of global media, new technologies, and altruistic nongovernmental organizations (NGOS) may soon empower the have-nots of the world, bringing them "simple justice" by creating a "radical transparency" in which "no contentious action would go unnoticed and unpublicized."

But even while a handful of groups such as the Tibetans have capitalized on the globalization of NGOS and media to promote their causes, thousands of equally deserving challengers, such as the Uighurs, have not found their place in the sun. While the world now knows about East Timor, similar insurrections in Indonesian Aceh and Irian Jaya remain largely off the international radar screen. Among environmental conflicts, a small number of cases such as the Brazilian rubber tappers' struggle to "save" the Amazon, the conflict over China's Three Gorges Dam, and the recent fight over the Chad-Cameroon pipeline have gained global acclaim. But many similar environmental battles, like the construction of India's Tehri Dam, the destruction of the Guyanese rain forests, and the construction of the Trans Thai-Malaysia gas pipeline are waged in anonymity. Whole categories of other conflicts—such as landlessness in Latin America and caste discrimination in South Asia—go likewise little noticed. To groups challenging powerful opponents in these conflicts, global civil society is not an open forum marked by altruism, but a harsh, Darwinian marketplace where legions of desperate groups vie for scarce attention, sympathy, and money.

In a context where marketing trumps justice, local challengers—whether environmental groups, labor rights activists, or independence-minded separatists—face long odds. Not only do they jostle for attention among dozens of equally worthy competitors, but they also confront the pervasive indifference of international audiences. In addition, they contend against well-heeled opponents (including repressive governments, multinational corporations, and international financial institutions) backed by the world's top public relations machines. Under pressure to sell their causes to the rest of the world, local leaders may end up undermining their original goals or alienating the domestic constituencies they ostensibly represent. Moreover, the most democratic and participatory local movements may garner the least assistance, since Western NGOS are less likely to support groups showing internal strife and more inclined to help a group led by a strong, charismatic leader. Perhaps most troubling of all, the perpetuation of the myth of an equitable and beneficent global civil society breeds apathy and self-satisfaction among the industrialized nations, resulting in the neglect of worthy causes around the globe.

PITCHING THE PRODUCT

The ubiquity of conflict worldwide creates fierce competition for international support. In a 2001 survey, researchers at Leiden University in the Netherlands and the Institute for International Mediation and Conflict Resolution in Washington, D.C., identified 126 high-intensity conflicts worldwide (defined as large-scale armed conflicts causing more than 1,000 deaths from mid-1999 to mid-2000), 78 low-intensity conflicts (100 to 1,000 deaths from mid-1999 to mid-2000), and 178 violent political conflicts (less than 100 deaths from mid-1999 to mid-2000). In these and many other simmering disputes, weak challengers hope to improve their prospects by attracting international assistance.

Local movements usually follow two broad marketing strategies: First, they pitch their causes internationally to raise awareness about their conflicts, their opponents, and sometimes their very existence. Second, challengers universalize their narrow demands and particularistic identities to enhance their appeal to global audiences.

Critical to the success of local challengers is access to major Western NGOs. Many groups from low-profile countries are ignored in the developed world's key media centers and therefore have difficulty gaining visibility among even the most transnational of NGOs. Moreover, despite the Internet and the much-ballyhooed "CNN effect," repressive regimes can still obstruct international media coverage of local conflicts. In the 1990s, for example, the government of Papua New Guinea did just that on Bougainville island, site of a bloody separatist struggle that cost 15,000 lives, or roughly 10 percent of the island's population. During an eight-year blockade (1989–97), foreign journalists could enter the island only under government guard, while the rebels could dispatch emissaries abroad only at great risk. India has used similar tactics in Kashmir, prohibiting independent human rights monitors from entering the territory and seizing passports of activists seeking to plead the Kashmiri case before the U.N. General Assembly and other bodies. Less effectively, Sudan has tried to keep foreigners from entering the country's vast southern region to report on the country's 19-year civil war.

Even for causes from "important" countries, media access—and therefore global attention—remains highly uneven. Money makes a major difference, allowing wealthier movements to pay for media events, foreign lobbying trips, and overseas offices, while others can barely afford places to meet. For example, long-term support from Portugal helped the East Timorese eventually catch the world's attention; other Indonesian separatist movements have not had such steady friends. And international prizes such as the Goldman Environmental Prize, the Robert F. Kennedy Human Rights Award, and the Nobel Peace Prize have become important vehicles of internationalization. In addition to augmenting a leader's resources, these awards raise a cause's visibility, facilitate invaluable contacts with key transnational NGOs and media, and result in wider support. For instance, Mexican "farmer ecologist" Rodolfo Montiel Flores's receipt of the $125,000 Goldman Prize in 2000 boosted the campaign to release him from prison on false charges stemming from his opposition to local logging practices. Not surprisingly, such prizes have become the object of intense salesmanship by local groups and their international champions.

Local challengers who have knowledge of global NGOs also have clear advantages. Today's transnational NGO community displays clear hierarchies of influence and reputation. Large and powerful organizations such as Human Rights Watch, Amnesty International, Greenpeace, and Friends of the Earth have the resources and expertise to investigate claims of local groups from distant places and grant them legitimacy. Knowledge of these key "gatekeeper" NGOs—their identities, goals, evidentiary standards, and openness to particular pitches—is crucial for a local movement struggling to gain support [see sidebar on opposite page]. If homegrown knowledge is scarce, local movements may try to link themselves to a sympathetic and savvy outsider, such as a visiting journalist, missionary, or academic. Some Latin American indigenous groups, including Ecuador's Huaoroni and Cofán, Brazil's Kayapó, and others, have benefited from the kindness of such strangers, who open doors and guide their way among international networks.

Small local groups with few connections or resources have more limited options for raising international awareness and thus may turn to protest. Yet domestic demonstrations often go unseen abroad. Only spectacular episodes—usually violent ones—draw international media coverage. And since violence is anathema to powerful international NGOs, local groups who use force as an attention-grabbing tactic must carefully limit, justify, and frame it. For example, the poverty and oppression that underlay the 1994 uprising by Mexico's Zapatista National Liberation Army went largely unnoticed at home and abroad for decades. In the face of such indifference, the previously unknown Zapatistas resorted to arms and briefly seized the city of San Cristóbal on January 1, 1994. Immediately tarred by the Mexican government as "terrorists," the Zapatistas in fact carefully calibrated their use of force, avoiding civilian casualties and courting the press. Other tactics also contributed to the Zapatistas' international support, but without these initial dramatic attacks, few people beyond Mexico's borders would now know or care about the struggles of Mexico's indigenous populations.

THE NGO IS ALWAYS RIGHT

To improve their chances of gaining support, local movements also conform themselves to the needs and expectations of potential backers in Western nations. They simplify and universalize their claims, making them relevant to the broader missions and interests of key global players. In particular, local groups try to match themselves to the substantive concerns and organizational imperatives of large transnational NGOs.

Consider Nigeria's Ogoni ethnic group, numbering perhaps 300,000 to 500,000 people. Like other minorities in the country's southeastern Niger delta, the Ogoni have long been at odds with colonial authorities and national governments over political representation. In the late 1950s, as Royal Dutch/Shell and other multinationals began producing petroleum in the region, the Ogoni claimed that the Nigerian federal government was siphoning off vast oil revenues yet returning little to the minorities who bore the brunt of the drilling's impact. In the early 1990s, an Ogoni movement previously unknown outside Nigeria sought support from Greenpeace, Amnesty International, and other major international NGOs. Initially, these appeals were rejected as unsubstantiated, overly complex, and too political. Ogoni leaders responded by downplaying their contentious claims about minority rights in a poor, multiethnic developing state and instead highlighting their environmental grievances, particularly Shell's "ecological warfare" against the indigenous Ogoni. Critical to this new emphasis was Ogoni leader Ken Saro-Wiwa's recognition of "what could be done by an environment group [in the developed world] to press demands on government and companies."

The Ogoni's strategic shift quickly led to support from Greenpeace, Friends of the Earth, and the Sierra Club. These and other organizations provided funds and equipment, confirmed and legitimated Ogoni claims, denounced the Nigerian dictatorship, boycotted Shell, and eased Ogoni access to governments and media in Europe and North America. In the summer of 1993, as the Ogoni's domestic mobilizations brought harsh government repression, human rights NGOs also took notice. The 1994 arrest and 1995 execution of Saro-Wiwa ultimately made the Ogoni an international symbol of multinational depredation in the developing world, but it was their initial repositioning as an environmental movement that first put them on the global radar screen. (For its part, Shell countered with its own spin, attacking Saro-Wiwa's credibility as a spokesman for his people and denying his allegations against the company.)

Similar transformations have helped other local causes male global headway. In drumming up worldwide support for Guatemala's Marxist insurgency in the 1980s, activist Rigoberta Menchú projected an indigenous identity that resonated strongly with left-leaning audiences in Western Europe and North America. Her book *I. Rigoberta Menchú* made her an international symbol of indigenous oppression, helping her win the Nobel Peace Prize in 1992, year of the Columbus quincentenary, despite her association with a violent rebel movement. As anthropologist David Stoll later showed, however, Menchú and the guerrillas may have enjoyed more backing among international solidarity organizations than among their country's poor and indigenous peoples. According to Stoll, external support may have actually delayed the guerrillas' entry into domestic negotiations by several years, prolonging the war and costing lives.

Mexico's Zapatistas have also benefited abroad from their indigenous identity. At the beginning of their 1994 rebellion, the Zapatistas issued a hodgepodge of demands. Their initial call for socialism was quickly jettisoned when it failed to catch on with domestic or international audiences, and their ongoing demands for Mexican democratization had mainly domestic rather than international appeal. But it was the Zapatistas' "Indianness" and their attacks first on the North American Free Trade Agreement (NAFTA) and then on globalization that found pay dirt in the international arena. (Little coincidence that the day they chose to launch the movement—January 1, 1994—was also the day NAFTA went into effect.) Once the appeal of these issues had become clear, they took center stage in the Zapatistas' contacts with external supporters. Indeed, the Zapatistas and their masked (non-Indian) leader Subcomandante Marcos became potent symbols for antiglobalization activists worldwide. In February and March 2001, when a Zapatista bus caravan traversed southern Mexico and culminated in a triumphant reception in the capital's central square, dozens of Italian *tute bianche* ("White Overalls"), activists prominent in antiglobalization protests in Europe, accompanied the Zapatistas as bodyguards. Even the French farmer and anti-McDonald's campaigner José Bové was present to greet Marcos.

Focusing on an internationally known and notorious enemy (such as globalization or NAFTA) is a particularly effective way of garnering support. In recent years, multinational corporations and international financial institutions have repeatedly served as standins for obscure or recalcitrant local enemies. Even when a movement itself is little known, it can project an effective (if sometimes misleading) snapshot of its claims by identifying itself as the anti-McDonald's movement, the anti-Nike movement, or the anti-Unocal movement. Blaming a villain accessible in the developed world also forges strong links between distant social movements and the "service station on the block," thus inspiring international solidarity.

Such strategies are not aimed only at potential supporters on the political left. The recent growth of a well-funded Christian human rights movement in the United States and Europe has helped many local groups around the world. One major beneficiary is John Garang's Sudan People's Liberation Army, made up mostly of Christians from southern Sudan fighting against the country's Muslim-dominated north. Rooted in ethnic, cultural, and religious differences, the conflict has been aggravated by disputes over control of natural resources. Since fighting broke out in 1983, the war has attracted little attention, despite the deaths of an estimated 2 million people. As late as September 1999, then Secretary of State Madeleine Albright reportedly stated that "the human rights situation in Sudan is not marketable to the American people." However, in the mid-1990s, "slave redemptions" (in which organizations like Christian Solidarity International buy back Christians from their Muslim captors) as well as international activism by Christian human rights organizations began to raise the conflict's profile. The start of oil extraction by multinationals provided another hook to attract concern from mainstream human rights and environmental organizations. Joined by powerful African-American politicians in the United States angered over the slave trade, conservative NGOs have thrown their support behind Garang's group, thereby feeding perceptions of the conflict as a simple Christian-versus-Muslim clash. These NGOs have also found a receptive audience in the administration of U.S. President George W. Bush, thus boosting Garang's chances of reaching a favorable settlement.

By contrast, failure to reframe obscure local issues (or reframing them around an issue whose time has passed) can produce international isolation for a struggling insurgent group. Two years after the Zapatista attacks, another movement sprang from the poverty and oppression of southern Mexico, this time in the state of Guerrero. The Popular Revolutionary Army attacked several Mexican cities and demanded an old-style communist revolution. But these rebels drew little support or attention, particularly in contrast to the Zapatistas and their fashionable antiglobalization rhetoric. Meanwhile, Brazil's Landless Peasants Movement and smaller movements of the rural poor in Paraguay and Venezuela have suffered similar fates both because their goals seem out of step with the times and because their key tactic—land invasions—is too controversial for many mainstream international NGOs. In the Niger delta, radical movements that have resorted to threats, sabotage, and kidnappings have also scared off international support despite the similarity of their grievances to those of the Ogoni.

LEADERS FOR SALE

If marketing is central to a local movement's gaining international support, a gifted salesman, one who identifies himself completely with his "product," is especially valuable. Many individual leaders have come to embody their movements: Myanmar's (Burma) Aung San Suu Kyi, South Africa's Nelson Mandela, as well as the Dalai Lama, Menchú, and Marcos. Even when known abroad only through media images, such leaders can make a host of abstract issues seem personal and concrete, thus multiplying a movement's potential support. For this reason, international tours have long been a central strategy for domestic activists. In the late-19th and early-20th centuries, for example, Sun Yat-sen crisscrossed the world seeking support for a nationalist revolution in China. Attracting international notice when he was briefly kidnapped by the Manchus in London, Sun found himself in Denver, Colorado, on another lobbying trip when the revolution finally came in 1911. Today, for well-supported insurgents, such roadshows are highly choreographed, with hard-charging promoters; tight schedules in government, media, and NGO offices; and a string of appearances in churches, college lecture halls, and community centers. In November 2001, for example, Oronto Douglas, a leader of Nigeria's Ijaw minority, embarked on a six-city, seven-day tour throughout Canada, where he promoted the Ijaw cause along with his new Sierra Club book *Where Vultures Feast: Shell, Human Rights, and Oil in the Niger Delta.*

What transforms insurgent leaders into international icons? Eloquence, energy, courage, and single-mindedness can undeniably create a charismatic mystique. But transnational charisma also hinges on a host of pedestrian factors that are nonetheless unusual among oppressed groups. Fluency in a key foreign language, especially English; an understanding of Western protest traditions; familiarity with the international political vogue; and expertise in media and NGO relations—all these factors are essential to giving leaders the chance to display their more ineffable qualities. Would the Dalai Lama appear as charismatic through a translator? For his part, Subcomandante Marcos has long insisted that he is but an ordinary man, whose way with words just happened to strike a responsive chord at an opportune moment.

Most of these prosaic characteristics are learned, not innate. Indeed, many NGOs now offer training programs to build advocacy capacity, establish contacts, and develop media smarts. The Unrepresented Nations and Peoples Organization in the Hague regularly holds intensive, week-long media and diplomacy training sessions for its member "nations," replete with role plays and mock interviews, helping them put their best foot forward in crucial venues. (Among others, Ken Saro-Wiwa praised the program for teaching him nonviolent direct action skills.) One of the most elaborate programs is the Washington, D.C.-based International Human Rights Law Group's two-year Advocacy Bridge Program, which aims to "increase the skills of local activists to amplify their issues of concern globally" and to "facilitate their access to international agenda-setting venues." Under the program, dozens of participants from around the world, chosen to ensure equal participation by women, travel to Washington for one week of initial training and then to Geneva for three weeks of on-site work at the U.N. Human Rights Commission. In their second year, "graduates" help train a new crop of participants.

Successful insurgent leaders therefore often look surprisingly like the audiences they seek to capture, and quite different from their downtrodden domestic constituencies. Major international NGOs often look for a figure who neatly embodies their own ideals, meets the pragmatic requirements of a "test case," or fulfills romantic Western notions of rebellion—in short, a leader who seems to mirror their own central values. Other leaders, deaf to the international zeitgeist or simply unwilling to adapt, remain friendless and underfunded.

THE HIGH PRICE OF SUCCESS

Many observers have trumpeted global civil society as the great last hope of the world's have-nots. Yet from the standpoint of local challengers seeking international support, the reality is bleak. The international media is often myopic: Conflicts attract meager reporting unless they have clear relevance, major importance, or huge death tolls. Technology's promise also remains unfulfilled. Video cameras, Web access, and cellular phones are still beyond the reach of impoverished local challengers. Even if the vision of "radical transparency" were realized—and if contenders involved in messy political wrangles in fact desired complete openness—international audiences, flooded with images and appeals, would have to make painful choices. Which groups deserve support? Which causes are more "worthy" than others?

Powerful transnational NGOs, emblematic of global civil society, also display serious limitations. While altruism plays some role in their decision making, NGOs are strategic actors who seek first and foremost their own organizational survival. At times this priority jibes nicely with the interests of local clients in far-flung locations, but often it does not. When selecting clients from a multitude of deserving applicants, NGOs must be hard-nosed, avoiding commitments that will harm their reputations or absorb excessive resources. Their own goals, tactics constituencies, and bottom lines constantly shape their approaches. Inevitably, many deserving causes go unsupported.

Unfortunately, the least participatory local movements may experience the greatest ease in winning foreign backing. Charismatic leadership is not necessarily democratic, for instance, yet external support will often strengthen a local leader's position, reshaping the movement's internal dynamics as well as its relations with opponents. Among some Tibetan communities today, there are rumblings of discontent over the Dalai Lama's religiously legitimated leadership, but his stature has been so bolstered by international support hat dissident elements are effectively powerless. Indeed, any internal dissent—if visible to outsiders—will often reduce international interest. NGOs want their scarce resources to be used effectively. If they see discord instead of unity, they may take their money and clout elsewhere rather than risk wasting them on internal disputes.

The Internet sometimes exacerbates this problem: Internecine feuds played out on public listservs and chat rooms may alienate foreign supporters, as has happened with some members of the pro-Ogoni networks. And although much has been made about how deftly the Zapatistas used the Internet to get their message out, dozens of other insurgents, from Ethiopia's Oromo Liberation Front to the Western Sahara's Polisario Front have Web sites and use e-mail. Yet they have failed to spark widespread international enthusiasm. As the Web site for Indonesia's Papua Freedom Organization laments, "We have struggled for more than 30 years, and the world has ignored our cause." Crucial in the Zapatistas' case was the appeal of their message (and masked messenger) to international solidarity activists, who used new technologies to promote the cause to broader audiences. In fact, for most of their conflict with the Mexican government, the Zapatistas have not had direct access to the Internet. Instead, they have sent communiqués by hand to sympathetic journalists and activists who then publish them and put them on the Web. Thus the Zapatistas' seemingly sophisticated use of the Internet has been more a result of their appeal to a core group of supporters than a cause of their international backing.

Perhaps most worrisome, the pressure of conform to the needs of international NGOs can undermine the original goals of local movements. By the time the Ogoni had gained worldwide exposure, some of their backers in the indigenous rights community were shaking their heads at how the movement's original demands for political autonomy had gone understated abroad compared to environmental and human rights issues. The need for local groups to click with trendy international issues fosters a homogeneity of humanitarianism: Unfashionable, complex, or intractable conflicts fester in isolation, while those that match or—thanks to savvy marketing—appear to match international issues of the moment attract disproportionate support. Moreover, the effort to please international patrons can estrange a movement's jet-setting elite from its mass base or leave it unprepared for domestic responsibilities. As one East Timorese leader stated after international pressure moved the territory close to independence, "We have been so focused on raising public awareness about our cause that we didn't seriously think about the structure of a government."

The quest for international support may also be dangerous domestically. To gain attention may require risky confrontations with opponents. Yet few international NGOs can guarantee a local movement's security, leaving it vulnerable to the attacks of enraged authorities. If a movement's opponent is receptive to rhetorical pressure, the group may be saved, as the Zapatistas were. If not, it will likely face its enemies alone. The NATO intervention in Kosovo provides a rare exception. But few challengers have opponents as notorious and strategically inconvenient as Slobodan Milosevic. Even in that case, Albanian leader Ibrahim Rugova's nonviolent strategies met years of international inaction and neglect; only when the Kosovo Liberation Army brought the wrath of Yugoslavia down on Kosovo and after Milosevic thumbed his nose at NATO did the intervention begin.

Historically, desperate local groups have often sought support from allies abroad. Given geographical distance as well as political and cultural divides, they have been forced to market themselves. This was true not only in the Chinese Revolution but also in the Spanish Civil War, the Indian nationalist movement, and countless Cold War struggles. But the much-vaunted emergence of a global civil society was supposed to change all that, as the power of technologies meshed seamlessly with the good intentions of NGOs to offset the callous self-interest of states and the blithe indifference of faraway publics.

But for all the progress in this direction, an open and democratic global civil society remains a myth, and a potentially deadly one. Lost in a self-congratulatory haze, international audiences in the developed world all too readily believe in this myth and in the power and infallibility of their own good intentions. Meanwhile, the grim realities of the global morality market leave many local aspirants helpless and neglected, painfully aware of international opportunities but lacking the resources, connections, or know-how needed to tap them.

THE CASE FOR UNIVERSAL
JURISDICTION

KENNETH ROTH

Behind much of the savagery of modern history lies impunity. Tyrants commit atrocities, including genocide, when they calculate they can get away with them. Too often, dictators use violence and intimidation to shut down any prospect of domestic prosecution. Over the past decade, however, a slowly emerging system of international justice has begun to break this pattern of impunity in national courts.

The United Nations Security Council established international war crimes tribunals for the former Yugoslavia in 1993 and Rwanda in 1994 and is now negotiating the creation of mixed national-international tribunals for Cambodia and Sierra Leone. In 1998, the world's governments gathered in Rome to adopt a treaty for an International Criminal Court (ICC) with potentially global jurisdiction over genocide, war crimes, and crimes against humanity.

With growing frequency, national courts operating under the doctrine of universal jurisdiction are prosecuting despots in their custody for atrocities committed abroad. Impunity may still be the norm in many domestic courts, but international justice is an increasingly viable option, promising a measure of solace to victims and their families and raising the possibility that would-be tyrants will begin to think twice before embarking on a barbarous path.

In "The Pitfalls of Universal Jurisdiction" (July/August 2001), former Secretary of State Henry Kissinger catalogues a list of grievances against the juridical concept that people who commit the most severe human rights crimes can be tried wherever they are found. But his objections are misplaced, and the alternative he proposes is little better than a return to impunity.

Kissinger begins by suggesting that universal jurisdiction is a new idea, at least as applied to heads of state and senior public officials. However, the exercise by U.S. courts of jurisdiction over certain heinous crimes committed overseas is an accepted part of American jurisprudence, reflected in treaties on terrorism and aircraft hijacking dating from 1970. Universal jurisdiction was also the concept that allowed Israel to try Adolf Eichmann in Jerusalem in 1961.

Kissinger says that the drafters of the Helsinki Accords—the basic human rights principles adopted by the Conference on Security and Cooperation in Europe in 1975—and the U.N.'s 1948 Universal Declaration of Human Rights never intended to authorize universal jurisdiction. But this argument is irrelevant, because these hortatory declarations are not legally binding treaties of the sort that could grant such powers.

As for the many formal treaties on human rights, Kissinger believes it "unlikely" that their signatories "thought it possible that national judges would use them as a basis for extradition requests regarding alleged crimes committed outside their jurisdictions." To the contrary, the Torture Convention of 1984, ratified by 124 governments including the United States, requires states either to prosecute any suspected torturer found on their territory, regardless of where the torture took place, or to extradite the suspect to a country that will do so. Similarly, the Geneva Conventions of 1949 on the conduct of war, ratified by 189 countries including the United States, require each participating state to "search for" persons who have committed grave breaches of the conventions and to "bring such persons, regardless of nationality, before its own courts." What is new is not the concept of extraterritorial jurisdiction but the willingness of some governments to fulfill this duty against those in high places.

ORDER AND THE COURT

Kissinger's critique of universal jurisdiction has two principal targets: the soon-to-be-formed International Criminal Court and the exercise of universal jurisdiction by national courts. (Strictly speaking, the ICC will use not universal jurisdiction but, rather, a delegation of states' traditional power to try crimes committed on their own territory.) Kissinger claims that the crimes detailed in the ICC treaty are "vague and highly susceptible to politicized application." But the treaty's definition of war crimes closely resembles that found in the Pentagon's own military manuals and is derived from the widely ratified Geneva Conventions and their Additional Protocols adopted in 1977. Similarly, the ICC treaty's definition of genocide is borrowed directly from the Genocide Convention of 1948, which the United States and 131 other governments have ratified and pledged to uphold, including by prosecuting offenders. The definition of crimes against humanity is derived from the Nuremberg Charter, which, as Kissinger acknowledges, proscribes conduct that is "self-evident[ly]" wrong.

Kissinger further asserts that the ICC prosecutor will have "discretion without accountability," going so far as to raise the specter of Independent Counsel Kenneth Starr and to decry "the tyranny of judges." In fact, the prosecutor can be removed for misconduct by a simple majority of the governments that ratify the ICC treaty, and a two-thirds vote can remove a judge. Because joining the court means giving it jurisdiction over crimes committed on the signatory's territory, the vast majority of member states will be democracies, not the abusive governments that self-protectively flock to U.N. human rights bodies, where membership bears no cost.

Kissinger criticizes the "extraordinary attempt of the ICC to assert jurisdiction over Americans even in the absence of U.S. accession to the treaty." But the United States itself asserts such jurisdiction over others' citizens when it prosecutes terrorists or drug traffickers, such as Panamanian dictator Manuel Noriega, without the consent of the suspect's government. Moreover, the ICC will assert such power only if an American commits a specified atrocity on the territory of a government that has joined the ICC and has thus delegated its prosecutorial authority to the court.

Kissinger claims that ICC defendants "will not enjoy due process as understood in the United States"—an apparent allusion to the lack of a jury trial in a court that will blend civil and common law traditions. But U.S. courts martial also do not provide trials by jury. Moreover, U.S. civilian courts routinely approve the constitutionality of extradition to countries that lack jury trials, so long as their courts otherwise observe basic due process. The ICC clearly will provide such due process, since its treaty requires adherence to the full complement of international fair-trial standards.

Of course, any court's regard for due process is only as good as the quality and temperament of its judges. The ICC's judges will be chosen by the governments that join the court, most of which, as noted, will be democracies. Even without ratifying the ICC treaty, the U.S. government could help shape a culture of respect for due process by quietly working with the court, as it has done successfully with the international war crimes tribunals for Rwanda and the former Yugoslavia. Regrettably, ICC opponents in Washington are pushing legislation—the misnamed American Servicemembers Protection Act—that would preclude such cooperation.

The experience of the Yugoslav and Rwandan tribunals, of which Kissinger speaks favorably, suggests that international jurists, when forced to decide the fate of a particular criminal suspect, do so with scrupulous regard for fair trial standards. Kissinger's only stated objection to these tribunals concerns the decision of the prosecutor of the tribunal for the former Yugoslavia to pursue a brief inquiry into how nato conducted its air war against the new Yugoslavia—an inquiry that led her to exonerate nato.

It should be noted, in addition, that the jurisdiction of the Yugoslav tribunal was set not by the prosecutor but by the U.N. Security Council, with U.S. consent. The council chose to grant jurisdiction without prospective time limit, over serious human rights crimes within the territory of the former Yugoslavia committed by anyone— not just Serbs, Croats, and Bosnian Muslims. In light of that mandate, the prosecutor would have been derelict in her duties not to consider nato's conduct; according to an extensive field investigation by Human Rights Watch, roughly half of the approximately 500 civilian deaths caused by nato's bombs could be attributed to nato's failure, albeit not criminal, to abide by international humanitarian law.

Kissinger claims that the ICC would violate the U.S. Constitution if it asserted jurisdiction over an American. But the court is unlikely to prosecute an American because the Rome treaty deprives the ICC of jurisdiction if, after the court gives required notice of its intention to examine a suspect, the suspect's government conducts its own good-faith investigation and, if appropriate, prosecution. It is the stated policy of the U.S. government to investigate and prosecute its own war criminals.

Moreover, the ICC's assertion of jurisdiction over an American for a crime committed abroad poses no greater constitutional problem than the routine practice under status-of-forces agreements of allowing foreign prosecution of American military personnel for crimes committed overseas, such as Japan's arrest in July of a U.S. Air Force sergeant for an alleged rape on Okinawa. An unconstitutional delegation of U.S. judicial power would arguably take place only if the United States ratified the ICC treaty; then an American committed genocide, war crimes, or crimes against humanity on U.S. soil; and then U.S. authorities did not prosecute the offender. Yet that remote possibility would signal a constitutional crisis far graver than one spawned by an ICC prosecution.

NO PLACE TO HIDE

National courts come under Kissinger's fire for selectively applying universal jurisdiction. He characterizes the extradition request by a Spanish judge seeking to try former Chilean President Augusto Pinochet for crimes against Spanish citizens on Chilean soil as singling out a "fashionably reviled man of the right." But Pinochet was sought not, as Kissinger writes, "because he led a coup d'état against an elected leader" who was a favorite of the left. Rather, Pinochet was targeted because security forces under his command murdered and forcibly "disappeared" some 3,000 people and tortured thousands more.

Furthermore, in recent years national courts have exercised universal jurisdiction against a wide range of suspects: Bosnian war criminals, Rwandan *génocidaires*, Argentine torturers, and Chad's former dictator. It has come to the point where the main limit on national courts empowered to exercise universal jurisdiction is the availability of the defendant, not questions of ideology.

Kissinger also cites the Pinochet case to argue that international justice interferes with the choice by democratic governments to forgive rather than prosecute past offenders. In fact, Pinochet's imposition of a self-amnesty at the height of his dictatorship limited Chile's democratic options. Only after 16 months of detention in the United Kingdom diminished his power was Chilean democracy able to begin prosecution. Such imposed impunity is far more common than democratically chosen impunity.

Kissinger would have had a better case had prosecutors sought, for example, to overturn the compromise negotiated by South Africa's Nelson Mandela, widely recognized at the time as the legitimate representative of the victims of apartheid. Mandela agreed to grant abusers immunity from prosecution if they gave detailed testimony about their crimes. In an appropriate exercise of prosecutorial discretion, no prosecutor has challenged this arrangement, and no government would likely countenance such a challenge.

Kissinger legitimately worries that the nations exercising universal jurisdiction could include governments with less-entrenched traditions of due process than the United Kingdom's. But his fear of governments robotically extraditing suspects for sham or counterproductive trials is overblown. Governments regularly deny extradition to courts that are unable to ensure high standards of due process. And foreign ministries, including the U.S. State Department, routinely deny extradition requests for reasons of public policy.

If an American faced prosecution by an untrustworthy foreign court, the United States undoubtedly would apply pressure for his or her release. If that failed, however, it might prove useful to offer the prosecuting government the face-saving alternative of transferring the suspect to the ICC, with its extensive procedural protections, including deference to good-faith investigations and prosecutions by a suspect's own government. Unfortunately, the legislation being pushed by ICC opponents in Washington would preclude that option.

Until the ICC treaty is renegotiated to avoid what Kissinger sees as its "short-comings and dangers," he recommends that the U.N. Security Council determine which cases warrant an international tribunal. That option was rejected during the Rome negotiations on the ICC because it would allow the council's five permanent members, including Russia and China as well as the United States, to exempt their nationals and those of their allies by exercising their vetoes.

As a nation committed to human rights and the rule of law, the United States should be embracing an international system of justice, even if it means that Americans, like everyone else, might sometimes be scrutinized.